Frommer's®

South Florida

POSTCARDS FROM

Biscayne National Park and the Florida Keys offer some of the best snorkeling and scuba diving in South Florida. See chapters 10 and 11. © Stephen Frink/Waterhouse Stock Photography.

Stop in at Sloppy Joe's, the quintessential Key West watering hole. See chapter 11 for more on Key West's nightlife. © Darrell Ray Jones/The Stock Market.

Every winter, millions of sunbathers head for the warm, pristine beaches of South Florida. See chapter 1 for a list of the best beaches in the region. © Trevor Wood/Tony Stone Worldwide.

See the house where "Papa" Hemingway wrote some of his most famous works and check out other Hemingway haunts while in Key West. See chapter 11. © Michael Ventura Photography.

Built alongside the ruins of oil magnate Henry Flagler's incredible Overseas Railroad, the Seven Mile Bridge is an excellent vantage point from which to view the stunning waters of the Keys. See chapter 11. © Michael Ventura Photography.

Take a boat tour through the wilds of Everglades National Park—you're almost guaranteed to glimpse a gator. See chapter 10. © D.E. Cox/Tony Stone Images.

With each cigar he rolls, this South Beach gentleman creates a work of art. See chapters 8 and 11.
© Michael Ventura Photography.

Sip cocktails at a hotel bar, see a show, or dance the night away at a South Beach club; when the sun goes down, Miami just begins to heat up. See chapter 9 for more on Miami's nightlife.
© Catherine Karnow Photography.

Miami Beach—home to a multitude of hotels, clubs, and crowded beaches— offers a great nightlife, but if you're looking for peace and quiet, look elsewhere. See chapters 4 through 9 for all Miami has to offer. © Alan Schein/The Stock Market.

The oldest hotel in Coral Gables, the stately Biltmore is a National Historic Landmark—one of only two operating hotels in Florida so designated. See chapter 5. © *Darrell Jones Photography.*

South Florida has the largest concentration of Art Deco architecture in the United States, and it's hard to walk anywhere in Miami's South Beach without encountering magnificent examples of it. See chapter 7 for information on walking tours of South Beach's Art Deco District. © *Gail Mooney/Kelly/Mooney Photography.*

Every year, eager baseball fans from across the country flock to Florida for spring training. See chapter 13.
© M. Timothy O'Keefe Photography.

You'll have no trouble renting a boat or hopping on a water taxi when you visit Fort Lauderdale's Isle of Venice, the "yachting capital of the world." See chapter 12.
© Jeff Greenberg/Silver Images.

Known as the "Taj Mahal of North America," The Flagler Museum features a 55-room Edwardian-style mansion and stunning grounds. See chapter 12. © M. Timothy O'Keefe Photography.

Taking a kayak trip down the Loxahatchee River is a great way to see the abundance of plant and animal life found on South Florida's Treasure Coast. See chapter 13. © Murry H. Sill/Silver Images.

A New Star-Rating System & Other Exciting News from Frommer's!

In our continuing effort to publish the savviest, most up-to-date, and most appealing travel guides available, we've added some great new features.

Frommer's guides now include a new **star-rating system.** Every hotel, restaurant, and attraction is rated from 0 to 3 stars to help you set priorities and organize your time.

We've also added **seven brand-new features** that point you to the great deals, in-the-know advice, and unique experiences that separate travelers from tourists. Throughout the guide, look for:

Finds	Special finds—those places only insiders know about
Fun Fact	Fun facts—details that make travelers more informed and their trips more fun
Kids	Best bets for kids—advice for the whole family
Moments	Special moments—those experiences that memories are made of
Overrated	Places or experiences not worth your time or money
Tips	Insider tips—some great ways to save time and money
Value	Great values—where to get the best deals

We've also added a **"What's New"** section in every guide—a timely crash course in what's hot and what's not in every destination we cover.

Blue Door @ Delano
Tanh
Wish

Here's what the critics say about Frommer's:

Other Great Guides for Your Trip:

Frommer's Florida

Frommer's Florida from $70 a Day

Frommer's Caribbean Cruises & Ports of Call

Frommer's Walt Disney World® & Orlando

Frommer's Portable Miami

Frommer's Portable Tampa & St. Petersburg

Frommer's Florida's Best-Loved Driving Tours

The Unofficial Guide to Walt Disney World®

The Unofficial Guide to Florida with Kids

Frommer's®

South Florida
including Miami & the Keys

3rd Edition

by Lesley Abravanel

Wiley Publishing, Inc.

About the Author

Lesley Abravanel is a freelance journalist and a graduate of the University of Miami School of Communication. When she isn't combing South Florida for the latest hotels, restaurants, and attractions, she is on the lookout for vacationing celebrities, about whom she writes in her weekly nightlife and gossip column, "Velvet Underground," for both the *Miami Herald* and its weekly entertainment newspaper, *Street*. She is also a contributor to *Star Magazine* and is the Miami correspondent for *Black Book Magazine*.

Published by:

Wiley Publishing, Inc.

909 Third Ave.
New York, NY 10022

ISBN 0-7645-6664-4
ISSN 1530-8758

Editor: Kendra L. Falkenstein
Production Editor: Donna Wright
Cartographer: Elizabeth Puhl
Photo Editor: Richard Fox
Production by Wiley Indianapolis Composition Services

Front cover photo: People relaxing at Little Palm Island resort.
Back cover photo: Hemingway look-alike contest.

For information on our other products and services or to obtain technical support, please contact our Customer Care Department within the U.S. at 800-762-2974, outside the U.S. at 317-572-3993 or fax 317-572-4002.

Wiley also publishes its books in a variety of electronic formats. Some content that appears in print may not be available in electronic formats.

Manufactured in the United States of America

5 4 3 2

Contents

11 The Keys & the Dry Tortugas   251

12 The Gold Coast: Hallandale to the Palm Beaches   308

13 The Treasure Coast: Stuart to Sebastian   368

Index   392

List of Maps

Acknowledgments

To my mother and father, without whose influence, encouragement, and support I would never have ended up in Miami doing what I'm doing.

To all the publicists and proprietors for putting up with the endless e-mails, inquiries, and spur-of-the-moment visits, I thank you for your cooperation and eagerness to answer pressing questions about hair dryers, irons, hours, and credit cards.

Thanks to Kendra Falkenstein, my fabulous editor, for being on the same page as me and "getting it."

To Married Brett, with whom I commiserated and rejoiced over the birth of her baby Daelyn and my baby Frommer's, thanks for an inspiring 9 months and your votes of confidence.

To my best-friend-turned-mapmaker extraordinaire, Tricia—the Patsy to my Edina—for your tireless efforts and for listening intently to my useless knowledge, rough drafts, and incessant complaints, proving that there are no limits to fun and friendship when it comes to life and all its amazing journeys.

Last but not least, thank you, Mrs. Ritchie, for inspiring me to express myself and aspire to greatness.

—Lesley Abravanel

An Invitation to the Reader

In researching this book, we discovered many wonderful places—hotels, restaurants, shops, and more. We're sure you'll find others. Please tell us about them, so we can share the information with your fellow travelers in upcoming editions. If you were disappointed with a recommendation, we'd love to know that, too. Please write to:

Frommer's South Florida including Miami & the Keys, 3rd Edition
Wiley Publishing, Inc. • 909 Third Ave. • New York, NY 10022

An Additional Note

Please be advised that travel information is subject to change at any time—and this is especially true of prices. We therefore suggest that you write or call ahead for confirmation when making your travel plans. The authors, editors, and publisher cannot be held responsible for the experiences of readers while traveling. Your safety is important to us, however, so we encourage you to stay alert and be aware of your surroundings. Keep a close eye on cameras, purses, and wallets, all favorite targets of thieves and pickpockets.

New! Frommer's Star Ratings & Icons

Every hotel, restaurant, and attraction listing in this guide has been ranked for quality, value, service, amenities, and special features using a star-rating scale. In country, state, and regional guides, we also rate towns and regions to help you narrow down your choices and budget your time accordingly. Hotels and restaurants in the Very Expensive and Expensive categories are rated on a scale of one (highly recommended) to three stars (exceptional). Those in the Moderate and Inexpensive categories rate from zero (recommended) to two stars (very highly recommended). Attractions, towns, and regions are rated according to the following scale: zero stars (recommended), one star (highly recommended), two stars (very highly recommended), and three stars (must-see).

In addition to the rating system, we also use seven icons to highlight insider information, useful tips, special bargains, hidden gems, memorable experiences, kid-friendly venues, places to avoid, and other useful information:

(Finds   (Fun Fact   (Kids   (Moments   (Overrated   (Tips   (Value

The following abbreviations are used for credit cards:

AE	American Express	DISC Discover	V Visa
DC	Diners Club	MC MasterCard	

FROMMERS.COM

Now that you have the guidebook to a great trip, visit our website at **www.frommers.com** for travel information on nearly 2,500 destinations. With features updated regularly, we give you instant access to the most current trip-planning information available. At Frommers.com, you'll also find the best prices on airfares, accommodations, and car rentals—and you can even book travel online through our travel booking partners. At Frommers.com, you'll also find the following:

- Online updates to our most popular guidebooks
- Vacation sweepstakes and contest giveaways
- Newsletter highlighting the hottest travel trends
- Online travel message boards with featured travel discussions

What's New in South Florida

At last, South Florida has broken free from its tired stereotypes. No longer equated with sleepy retirement communities and rowdy Spring Break beaches, South Florida's varied regions, from the Palm Beaches down to the Keys, offer something for everyone. Here's a rundown of what's new.

MIAMI A cash crop of luxury hotels, restaurants, and nightclubs has sprouted throughout Miami, though there are still deals to be found. And while the city remains a mostly seasonal destination, what used to be a completely somber summer in the city has been resurrected as a lively, cheaper, albeit much hotter, time to visit.

Accommodations The **Ritz-Carlton Key Biscayne,** 455 Grand Bay Dr. (*C* 800/241-3333) is the first of three Ritz-Carltons to open in Miami. Two more locations, on South Beach (1 Lincoln Rd.) and in Coconut Grove (2700 Tigertail Ave.), were scheduled to open in mid-2002. To compete with the hauter-than-thou Delano Hotel on South Beach, the hyper-hip **Shore Club,** 1901 Collins Ave., (*C* 877/640-9500), has officially opened, practically next door. The **Ritz Plaza,** 1701 Collins Ave., (*C* 305/534-3500), taken over by W Hotels, has been resuscitated from its decrepit state into a revitalized stylish boutique hotel. **W South Beach** (*C* 877-W-HOTELS) and its wing of oceanfront rooms is set to open in the fall of 2002. Miami's first **Four Seasons Hotel and Tower** on Brickell Avenue was set to open in the spring of 2002, with 63 stories, 1.5 million square feet, shops, and a spa.

Dining Proving its affection for things in the raw, Miami boasts two hot new sushi options. **Nobu,** a New York sushi import, opened (with Madonna's presence) at Shore Club, 1901 Collins Ave., South Beach (*C* 305/695-3100), as did **Sushi Samba Dromo,** 600 Lincoln Rd., at the corner of Pennsylvania Avenue (*C* 305/673-5337). A slew of trendy restaurant/lounge combos has also opened. **Kiss,** 301 Lincoln Rd. (*C* 305/695-4445), a steakhouse-cum-cabaret attached to the Albion Hotel, puts the strip show in strip steak, while **Rumi,** 330 Lincoln Rd. (*C* 305/672-4353), serves haute cuisine in the early hours before giving way to the A-list scenesters.

Sightseeing Even after Elián González was returned to his father's custody in Cuba, his relatives' Little Havana house remained a shrine. As a result, the house (United in Elián House, at 2319 NW 2nd Street, Little Havana; no phone) is now a museum dedicated to the plight of Cubans in the United States. Also about to open as a museum dedicated to Cuban Americans is downtown Miami's Freedom Tower, 600 Biscayne Blvd. (*C* 305/592-7768) purchased by the Cuban American National Foundation. Work still continues on the **Miami Beach Cultural Park** in South Beach, which includes the new Arquitectonica-designed home of the **Miami City Ballet,** the Miami Beach Regional Library, the **Bass Museum of Art,** and a sculpture garden. The Bass (*C* 305/673-7530) has expanded and received a dramatically new look by world-renowned Japanese architect Arata Isozaki. Additions include triple the amount of exhibition space, an outdoor sculpture terrace, and a museum cafe. **The Vizcaya Museum & Gardens** has a new permanent orchid display garden.

After Dark   At press time, the hottest nightspots are located on the still-sizzling South Beach. However, over the causeway, a burgeoning nocturnal buzz is emanating from the once-desolate area of **downtown Miami,** off of Biscayne Boulevard, thanks to cheaper rents and 24-hour liquor licenses. Among them, the former South Beach hotspot, the Living Room, has opened on NE 11th Street as the **Living Room Downtown.** South Beach's **Mynt,** 1921 Collins Ave. (© **786/276-6132**) and **Rain,** 323 23rd St. (© **786/295-9540**), have opened for the luxe and lithe lounge lizards, while an old hot spot, **Liquid,** 1532 Washington Ave. (© **305/531-9411**) has reopened under different ownership in a space formerly known as Shadow Lounge. The cavernous **Billboard Live** music and dance club debuted, featuring several bars, restaurants, and a recording studio at 1501 Collins Ave.

THE GOLD COAST   While the Gold Coast's beaches remain less congested than those in Miami, the area isn't impervious to development—especially when it comes to resorts, restaurants, and nightlife. Whereas the Gold Coast used to be a sleepy beachfront, today it's en route to rivaling the liveliness of a big city like Miami.

Accommodations   Fort Lauderdale broke ground for the posh 132-suite **Atlantic** hotel/condo, managed by Starwood's Luxury Collection and said to debut in early to mid-2003. The Boca Raton Resort and Club, 501 E. Camino Real (© **800/327-0101**),

unveiled its **Spa Palazzo,** a brand-new Mediterranean-style spa with 22 treatment rooms as well as lap pools and indoor and outdoor lounges. West Palm Beach gets hip to the idea of the boutique hotel with **Hotel Biba,** 320 Belvedere Rd. (© **561/832-0094**), a very mod revamped motel turned hipster hangout. **The Boca Raton Resort & Club** opened its 112-unit Yacht Club wing in February 2002. The guest rooms overlook the Intracoastal Waterway, and personal butler service and a concierge lounge are provided for guests.

Dining   Boca Raton's new American restaurant, **Zemi,** 5050 Town Center Circle (© **561/391-7177**), is drawing rave reviews for its chili-crusted shrimp. For the West Palm Beach wine-and-cheese set, the Hotel Biba's **Biba Bar,** 320 Belvedere Rd. (© **561/832-0094**), serves sleek portions of cheese and various *charcuterie.* And over at the ever-expanding City Place, star chef Mark Militello opened a branch of his successful New World chain, **Mark's City Place,** 700 S. Rosemary Ave., West Palm Beach (© **561/514-0770**).

Shopping   Fort Lauderdale's **Beach Place,** 17 S. Fort Lauderdale Beach Blvd., is receiving a face-lift, transforming itself from a Spring Break-y hangout into something more upscale. West Palm Beach's **City Place,** 222 Lakeview Ave. (© **561/835-0862**), is a $550 million outdoor Mediterranean-style complex featuring 78 stores (including Macy's and FAO Schwarz), a multiplex movie theater, and several restaurants such as Legal Seafoods and the Cheesecake Factory. It seems that something new is always opening here. The most recent places to sign on are New York City's NV Lounge and Tsunami, the Pan Asian haute spot.

1

The Best of South Florida

There's much more to South Florida than the neon-hued nostalgia of *Miami Vice* and pink flamingos. In fact, what used to be a relatively sleepy beach-vacation destination has awoken from its humid slumber, upped its tempo, and finally earned its place in the Palm Pilots of cutting-edge jet-setters worldwide. But don't be fooled by the hipper-than-thou celebrity-drenched playground known as South Beach. While the chic elite do, indeed, flock to Miami's coolest enclave, it is surprisingly accessible to the average Joe, Jane, or José. For every Phillippe Starck–designed, bank-account-busting boutique hotel on South Beach, there's a kitschy, candy-coated Art Deco one that's much less taxing on the pockets. For each Pan-MediterAsian haute cuisinerie, there's always the down-home, no-nonsense Cuban *bodega* (a small corner grocery store, usually with a walk-up window for ordering) offering hearty food at ridiculously cheap prices.

Beyond the whole glitzy, *Access Hollywood*–meets-beach-blanket-bacchanalia as seen on TV, Miami has an endless number of sporting, cultural, and recreational activities to keep you entertained. Our sparkling beaches are beyond compare. Plus, there's excellent shopping and other nightlife activities that include ballet, theater, and opera.

Leave Miami, be it for the Keys, the Gold Coast, or the Treasure Coast, and you'll expose yourself not only to more UV rays, but to a world of cultural, historical, and sybaritic surprises where you can take in a spring baseball game, walk in the footsteps of Hemingway, get up close and personal with the area's sea life, soak up the serenity of unspoiled landscapes, and much more.

Forget what you've heard about South Florida being Heaven's Waiting Room. That slogan is as passé as the concept of "early bird" dinners (which you can still get—they just no longer define the region). In fact, according to some people, South Florida *is* heaven. So what are *you* waiting for?

1 Frommer's Favorite South Florida Experiences

- **Driving Along Florida A1A:** This oceanfront route, which runs north up Miami Beach, through Sunny Isles and Hollywood, and into Fort Lauderdale (starting at Ocean Dr. and First St. in Miami and merging onto Collins Ave. before running north), embodies the essence that is South Florida. From time-warped hotels steeped in Art Deco kitsch to multimillion-dollar modern high-rises, A1A is one of the most scenic, albeit heavily trafficked, roads in all of Florida.

- **South Beach Nightlife:** If you can handle it, you can boogie down until the sun comes up in cavernous, pulsating dance clubs, which are considered amongst the best in the world. If dancing isn't your thing, consider the restaurant-as-nightclub concept defined by places such as **Tantra,**

Florida

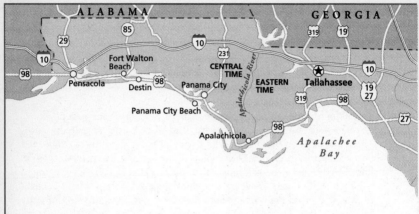

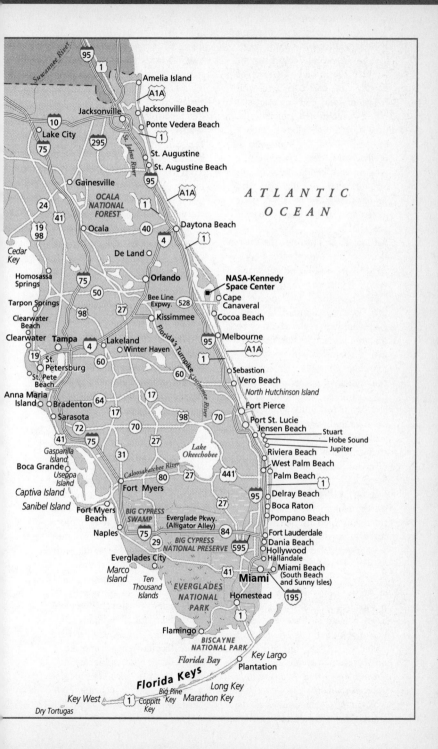

a grass-floored restaurant/lounge in which Marrakesh meets Miami Beach, or **Rumi,** a swank resto-lounge in which the likes of Jennifer Lopez and members of Mötley Crüe mix with a colorful crowd of local and international hipsters. Where else can us ordinary folk brush elbows with—or spill Cosmopolitans on—Hollywood starlets, entertainment moguls, and living legends but in South Beach's hot clubs, bars, and restaurants, many of which don't get going until the crack of dawn? See p. 213.

- **Airboat Ride Through the Outskirts of the Everglades:** Unfettered by jet skis, cruise ships, and neon bikinis, the Everglades are Florida's outback, resplendent in their swampy nature. The Everglades are best explored either by slow-moving canoes that really get you acquainted with your surroundings or via an airboat that can quickly navigate its way through the most stubborn of saw grass while providing you with an up-close and personal (as well as fun) view of the land's inhabitants, from alligators and manatees to raccoons and Florida panthers. See p. 240.

- **Dining at Big Fish Restaurant on the Miami River:** Some consider dining on the Miami River to be industrial chic; others consider it seedy in a *Miami Vice* sort of way. However you choose to look at it, by all means *do* look at it; the sleepy Miami River is nestled below the sweeping downtown Miami skyline, reminding you that even though you're in a major metropolis, things in this often-frenetic city are capable of slowing down to a more soothing pace. See p. 146.

- **Vizcaya Museum and Gardens:** Built in 1916, this Italian Renaissance–style manse on Biscayne Bay in Miami features 34 rooms of antiques, art, and tapestries; 10 acres of Italian gardens, statues, and fountains; a new orchid display; and a picture-perfect view of the skyline and Key Biscayne. See p. 179.

- **Wolfie Cohen's Rascal House:** You *will* wait on line at Miami Beach's landmark diner, but it's never dull, as the cacophony of mostly Northeastern U.S. accents will keep you entertained until you are seated in what seems to be an ancient vinyl booth. The octogenarian waitress will serve you corned-beef sandwiches, brisket, or potato pancakes, and, if you're lucky, she may tell you about the time Sinatra and his Rat Pack came in way back when. See p. 141.

- **Moonlight Concerts at the Barnacle State Historic Site:** Once a month, on or near the full moon (except during July and August), the Barnacle State Historic Site hosts a concert in the backyard of their charming 1908 Coconut Grove bungalow built on 5 acres of waterfront property. Listeners are welcome to picnic and bask in this sublime setting for a mere $5. See p. 176.

- **Midnight Snacking at Versailles:** This iconoclastic, gaudy Cuban diner in the heart of Miami's Little Havana is humming with the buzz of old-timers reminiscing about pre-Castro Cuba, local politicos trying to appease them, and a slew of detached people only there for the fantastically cheap and authentic Cuban fare. Much like its French namesake in whose image it's been literally mirrored, Miami's Versailles provides a palatial view of Miami's ever-changing Cuban landscape. See p. 152.

Impressions

What could be better than to sit on the beach playing cards in my shirt-sleeves in January?

—Anonymous Miami Beach resident

- **Lunch at News Café on Ocean Drive:** The quintessential South Beach experience, lunching at News Café is more of a spectator sport than a dining experience. What the Big Mac is to McDonald's, people-watching is to News Café, whose Ocean Drive location is one of the best sidewalk spots from which to observe the wacky, colorful mix of pedestrians on parade. See p. 134.

- **Relishing the View from Bill Baggs Cape Florida State Recreation Area:** You haven't truly seen South Florida until you've checked out the view from the southern point of Key Biscayne. Whether it's the turquoise water or the sight of Stiltsville—seven still-inhabited aquatic cabins dating back to the 1930s, perched smack in the middle of the Biscayne Channel—it may take a little coercing to get you to leave. See p. 179.

- **Scuba Diving off Jupiter Beach:** In 1988, Jupiter Beach lifeguard Peter Leo spotted an anchor and a cannon while on his routine morning swim. Turns out, they belonged to what is believed to be the shipwreck of a Spanish galleon dating back to the 16th or 17th century. Giving literal meaning to South Florida's Treasure and Gold coasts, this wreck is worth holding your breath for. See p. 316.

- **Happy Hour at Mai Kai:** Polynesia meets Fort Lauderdale at Mai Kai, the trippiest tiki hut this side of Tahiti, with its sarong-clad bartenders, a fiery hula show, and an exhaustive menu of frozen concoctions. See p. 332.

- **Discovering Your Inner Flipper at the Dolphin Research Center:** Learn to communicate with and touch, swim, or play with the mammals at the nonprofit Dolphin Research Center in Marathon Key, home to a school of approximately 15 dolphins. See p. 258.

- **Eyeing the Estates on Palm Beach:** The winter playground for the *Lifestyles of the Rich and Famous* set, Palm Beach is lined with jaw-dropping palatial estates. While many of them are hidden behind towering shrubbery, head south on South County Road, from Brazilian Avenue, where you will see some of the most opulent homes ever built. Make sure someone holds the steering wheel if you're driving, because you *will* do a double take. See p. 344.

- **Lounging Poolside at the Delano:** In addition to tanning, the scene here is about striking a pose and pretending not to notice the others doing so. If you're staying at Miami's Delano, and if you're savvy enough to score one of the luxe lounges, prepare to overhear some interesting conversations between the movers and shakers who bake here. Though the hotel itself is overrated, the pool is worth every bit of its splash and flash. See p. 74.

- **Boating Through the Intracoastal Waterway:** The waterway that connects the natural bays, lagoons, and rivers along Florida's East Coast snakes around from the Florida-Georgia border all the way to the port of Miami. A ride through the Fort Lauderdale Intracoastal provides a sublime view of million-dollar waterfront houses. See p. 314.

- **Having a Postbeach Beer at Jimbo's on Key Biscayne:** Who knew that a dive housed in a wooden shack in the mangroves of Virginia Key, serving beer from a cooler, would become one of Miami's best-kept local secrets? That is, until now. See p. 154.

- **Salsa Lessons at Bongo's Cuban Cafe:** If the only salsa you're familiar with is the kind you put on your tacos, get over to Bongo's, the hottest salsa club north of Havana, where Miami's most talented salsa dancers will teach you how to move your two left feet in the right direction. See p. 219.

2 The Best Beaches

- **For Tranquility: Matheson Hammock Park Beach** (℗ 305/665-5475) in South Miami features an enclosed man-made lagoon that is flushed naturally by the tidal action of the adjacent Biscayne Bay. The serene beach is surrounded by the bay's warm, calm waters and a backdrop of tropical hardwood forest. See p. 166.

  The beach at **Bahia Honda State Park** (℗ 305/872-2353) in Bahia Honda Key is one of the nicest and most peaceful in Florida, located amidst 635 acres of nature trails and even a portion of Henry Flagler's railroad. See p. 274.

- **For Watersports: Hobie Beach** (℗ 305/361-2833), located on the south side of Key Biscayne's Rickenbacker Causeway, is one of the most popular beaches for watersport enthusiasts, featuring jet-ski, sailboat, windsurfing, and sailboard rentals; shade, if necessary, from the Australian pine; and a sublime view of the picturesque downtown Miami skyline. See p. 166.

- **For People-Watching: Lummus Park Beach** (℗ 305/673-7714) is world renowned, not necessarily for its pristine sands, but for its more common name of **South Beach**. Here, seeing, being seen, and, at times, the obscene, go hand in hand with the sunscreen and beach towels. See p. 166.

Not nearly as scenic, but still heavily populated, **Fort Lauderdale Beach** (℗ 954/468-1597) is the site of many a bacchanalian Spring Break, Frankie and Annette, and now, an eclectic—albeit calmer—mix of young, buff beach bums. See p. 312.

- **For Nature Lovers: MacArthur Beach** (℗ 561/624-6950), in West Palm Beach, is considered by many nature enthusiasts to be the most beautiful nature park in South Florida, with a nice stretch of beach set against a lush and diverse background of foliage, plus a state-of-the-art nature center and renowned sea turtle awareness program. See p. 361.

- **For Nude Sunbathing:** For that all-over tan, the place to be is the north end of **Haulover Beach** (℗ 305/944-3040), nestled between the Intracoastal Waterway and the ocean. A gay, nude beach is also there, as is an area for nude volleyball. See p. 166.

- **For Seclusion:** The producers of *Survivor* could feasibly shoot their show on the ultra-secluded, picturesque, and deserted **Virginia Key** (℗ 305/361-2749), on Key Biscayne, where people go purposely not to be found. See p. 166.

  John U. Lloyd State Park (℗ 954/923-6711) in Dania Beach is unfettered by high-rise condos, T-shirt shops, and hotels, and remains intact with an untouched shoreline surrounded by a canopy of Australian pine to ensure that your seclusion is, indeed, highly guarded. See p. 313.

- **For Gay Beachgoers:** South Beach's **12th Street Beach** (© **305/673-7714**) is the beach of choice for gay residents and travelers who come to show off just how much time they've spent in the gym, and, of course, catch up on the latest gossip and upcoming must-attend parties

and events. Oftentimes, this beach is the venue for some of the liveliest parties South Beach has ever seen.

- **For Kids:** Miami's **Crandon Beach** (© **305/361-5421**) is extremely popular for families with kids because of the shallow water created by a neighboring sandbar. Convenient parking, picnic areas, a winding boardwalk, and a multi-ethnic mix of families grilling, dancing, and relaxing are the benchmarks of this beach. See p. 164.

3 Best Hotel Bets

- **Best Historic Hotel:** With a guest registry that reads like a who's who of history crossed with an engrossing whodunit, Miami's monumental, Mediterranean revivalist–style **Biltmore Hotel** (© **800/727-1926** or 305/445-1926) opened its doors in 1926. Guests ranging from Al Capone to the duke and duchess of Windsor loved the stately hotel so much that they never left, so say those who claim the hotel is haunted. Ghosts aside, this national landmark boasts the largest hotel pool in the continental United States as well as a 300-foot bell tower modeled after the Cathedral of Seville. See p. 106.

- **Best Cheap-Chic Hotel:** West Palm Beach's **Hotel Biba** (© **561/832-0094**) is a funky, single-story, converted 1940s motor-lodge-turned-boutique hotel featuring an oversized swimming pool, Asian gardens with sitting areas, a reflection pond, and the ultrahip Biba Bar. Rooms start at $79. See p. 356.

- **Best Celebrity-Saturated Hotel:** The **Delano** (© **800/555-5001** or 305/672-2000) still reigns as Miami's number one celebrity

magnet, attracting stars and starlets who you'd find at A-list Hollywood parties. The hotel's star power makes up for its sterile rooms. See p. 74.

- **Best Role-Playing Hotel:** With rooms such as "Me Tarzan, You Vain," or "Best Whorehouse," South Beach's **Pelican Hotel** (© **800/7-PELICAN** or 305/673-3373) takes the concept of escapism to an entirely new level. See p. 88.

- **Best Out-of-Place Bed-and-Breakfast:** Located on the outskirts of gritty, bustling downtown Miami is the historic **Miami River Inn** (© **800/468-3589** or 305/325-0045), housed in five restored clapboard buildings dating back to 1906. By the looks of this place, you could swear you were somewhere in New England—until you step out for a breath of the balmy air. See p. 105.

- **Best Hotel in a League of Its Own:** Jules' Undersea Lodge (© **305/451-2353**) in Key Largo really gives you the low-down on the full Keys experience by requiring all guests to scuba 30 feet underwater to get to their rooms, which are literally located under the sea, in the mangrove habitat of Emerald Lagoon. See p. 265.

- **Best Art Deco Hotel:** The **Raleigh Hotel** (© 800/848-1775 or 305/534-6300) in Miami is the reigning diva of Deco, dating back to 1940. It features one of the most photographed palm-lined swimming pools, reminiscent of the days of Esther Williams. See p. 82.

- **Best Gatsby-esque Hotel:** As you drive up to the **Breakers** (© 800/833-3141) in posh Palm Beach, you can't help but feel the spirit of Jay Gatsby beckoning you into this mammoth Italian Renaissance–style hotel. See p. 352.

- **Best Beach Hotel:** Miami's **Beach House Bal Harbour** (© 877/782-3557 or 305/865-3551) was inspired by the great beach homes of the Hamptons, Nantucket, and coastal Maine, and when you stay here, you will feel like someone's houseguest rather than an anonymous hotel guest. See p. 94.

- **Best Inexpensive Hotel:** It's hard to find a hotel on South Beach with both good value and excellent service, but the **Crest Hotel Suites** (© 800/531-3880 or 305/531-0321) delivers and peaks as one of Miami's best bargains and coolest hotels. See p. 85.

  In Key West, the **Grand** (© 888/947-2630), despite its name, will not leave you with a huge tab at the end of your stay. The rooms in this hotel are bright and airy and the proprietor works hard to keep you happy. See p. 298.

  The **Blue Seas Courtyard** (© 877/225-8373) in Lauderdale-by-the-Sea is a terrific deal that's just 1 block from the beach. It features rooms drenched in Haitian and Peruvian art, as well as a garden pool. See p. 326.

- **Best for Families:** In Miami, the **Sonesta Beach Resort Key Biscayne** (© 800/SONESTA or 305/361-2021) is known for its complimentary children's programs led by trained counselors who supervise kids, grouped by age, in pool and beach activities and on field trips including dinner, movie, and museum excursions. Fees apply for meals/certain excursions. See p. 102.

  In Fort Lauderdale, **Marriott's Harbor Beach** (© 800/222-6543) has a Beachside Buddies program for children ages 5 to 12, offering half-day and all-day children's activities that range from seashell collecting to hula-hoop contests. The 8,000-square-foot, free-form swimming pool, expansive sand beach, and instant access to water toys also keep kids entertained. See p. 322.

  The **Boca Raton Resort and Club** (© 800/327-0101) has activity programs designed for distinct age groups: Boca Tots (ages 3–5), Boca Bunch (ages 6–11), and Boca Sport (ages 12–17). Upon registering children in the program, each parent is given a beeper with a 60-mile radius so that they may be contacted by their children at any time. See p. 338.

- **Best for Romance:** In Miami, the **Hotel Place St. Michel** (© 800/848-HOTEL or 305/444-1666) is a cozy European-style hotel whose wood-floored dark-paneled rooms are adorned in antiques, transporting you from sunny Florida to gay Paris. See p. 107.

  Imagine an intimate haven on your own private island and you've got **Little Palm Island** (© 800/343-8567), located just 3 miles offshore in the Florida Keys, accessible only by boat or seaplane, and quite possibly the closest thing to paradise, with only one telephone on the entire island. See p. 277.

In Palm Beach, modeled after a quaint English inn, the **Chesterfield Hotel** (© 800/243-7871) is absolutely seductive, thanks in part to its sexy, sultry Leopard Lounge, its cozy fireside library, and Churchill's Cigar Room. See p. 354.

- **Best Guesthouses/B&Bs:** The **Villa Paradiso Guest House** (© 305/532-0616) may be smack in the heart of frenetic South Beach, but once you're inside you're worlds away, with rooms facing a sun-drenched courtyard and a host who is genuinely glad to see you, unlike some of the more attitudinal staff found in other nearby hotels. See p. 92.

In Fort Lauderdale, **La Casa Del Mar** (© 954/467-2037) is located right on the beach and offers cozily appointed rooms. The owners bend over backward to make sure your stay is a fantastic one. See p. 352.

4 Best Dining Bets

- **Best for Celebrating a Big Deal:** The **Forge Restaurant** on Miami Beach (© 305/538-8533) is a multichambered, ornately decorated (and priced) monument known for its decadent wines, steak, and fish. See p. 136.
- **Best Romantic Restaurant: La Vieille Maison,** in Boca Raton (© 561/391-6701), is housed in a 1920s-era structure, with a stunning courtyard, superlative haute French cuisine, and intimate, private dining rooms. See p. 341.
- **Best Waterfront Dining:** It's a tossup between Biscayne Bay and the Atlantic Ocean, but whichever you prefer, there are two restaurants that provide front-row seats to both. The Mandarin Oriental Hotel's global fusion restaurant, **Azul** (© 305/913-8258), faces the Miami skyline and beautiful, tranquil Biscayne Bay, while the Ritz Carlton Key Biscayne's **Aria** (© 305/365-4500) faces the Atlantic, but its Mediterranean cuisine could have you thinking you're floating off the coast of, say, Spain. Tough decisions, but both are winners. See p. 144 and p. 100. **Louie's Backyard** in Key West (© 305/294-1061) offers Caribbean cuisine and one of the best views of the gulf you'll ever have. See p. 300.
- **Best Restaurant Worth the Wait for a Table:** The legendary South Florida institution known as **Joe's Stone Crab Restaurant,** in Miami Beach (© 305/673-0365), refuses to take reservations, but that doesn't stop people from clawing their way into the restaurant for a table—despite a wait that's often in excess of 3 hours. See p. 121.
- **Best Cuban Restaurant:** There's always a debate on who has the best, most authentic Cuban cuisine, but for those of you who have never been to Havana, Miami's **Versailles,** in Little Havana (© 305/444-0240), is *the* quintessential Cuban diner, featuring enormous portions at paltry prices. See p. 152.
- **Best Steak House:** Boca Raton's **New York Prime** (© 561/998-3881) may be part of a South Carolina–based chain, but its steaks are a cut above the rest. The only problem may be scoring a reservation. See p. 341.

In addition to the **Forge Restaurant** (see above), **Christy's,**

Impressions

I come to Miami to relax, so I've never had a power lunch or dinner there.

—Madonna

in Coral Gables (© 305/446-1400), is the Miami carnivore's choice, with superb steaks and famous Caesar salads. See p. 156.

- **Best New World Cuisine:** It's a tossup between the restaurants of the original founders of the palate-pleasing fusion of Florida and Caribbean (Floribbean) ingredients: **Norman's,** in Coral Gables (© 305/446-6767), owned by James Beard chef Norman van Aken, and **Chef Allen's,** in Aventura (© 305/935-2900), owned by chef Allen Susser. Whichever chef's cuisine you choose, they both do wonders with mangoes. See p. 157 and p. 142.
- **Sexiest Restaurant: Tantra,** in Miami Beach (© 305/672-4765), brings a bit of exotic Marrakesh to South Beach with an aphrodisiac-inspired menu, grass-lined floors, and an equally sultry crowd that isn't afraid of getting in touch with its sensual side. See p. 124.
- **Best Scene: Rumi,** in Miami Beach (© 305/672-4353), is a sexy, cacophonous global-fusion restaurant/lounge whose gorgeously prepared dishes are enough to rival the beautiful and sometimes famous people who convene here. See p. 221. **Joia,** also in Miami Beach (© 305/674-8871), exemplifies South Beach's spin on *La Dolce Vita* with its fine Italian cuisine, celebrity clientele, and requisite paparazzi hiding nearby in the bushes. See p. 126.
- **Best Sunday Brunch: Nemo,** on Miami Beach (© 305/532-4550), turns its open kitchen into a help-yourself-to-anything, calorie-busting Sunday brunch of gourmet fare and insanely good desserts. See p. 123. Boca Raton's **Mizner Park** (© 561/ 395-0770) features a gourmet all-you-can-eat $19 brunch—an unheard-of value in swanky Mizner Park. See p. 338.
- **Best View: Big Fish,** in Miami (© 305/373-1770), is all about gritty-chic, located on the Miami River, where tugboats and cargo ships slink by as you indulge in fresh fish and sip good Italian wine under the glow of the brilliant downtown skyline hovering above. See p. 146. **Red Fish Grill** (© 305/668-8788) is ensconced in Coral Gables' Matheson Hammock Park and located on the edge of a saltwater lagoon, a setting so blissfully distracting, you may forget to pay attention to what's on your plate. See p. 159.
- **Best Haute Cuisine: Mark's Las Olas,** in Fort Lauderdale (© 954/ 463-1000), and Miami Beach's **Mark's South Beach** (© 305/ 604-9050) are both owned by celebrity chef Mark Militello, whose New American cuisine restores the faith of gourmands whose palates once belonged to the Pan-Asian Fusion movement. See p. 327 and p. 122.
- **Best People-Watching:** The **News Café,** in South Beach (© 305/538-6397), practically invented the sport of people-watching, encouraging its customers to sit at an outdoor table all day if they want, lingering over the passing parades of people

while sipping a cappuccino. The Delano Hotel's pricey **Blue Door** restaurant (© **305/674-6400**), in Miami Beach, provides a front-row seat to the hordes of hipsters who flock there. See p. 134 and p. 120.

- **Best Comfort Food: Big Pink,** in Miami Beach (© **305/532-4700**), serves kitsch in large doses, featuring TV dinners served in trays. Fun and funky, and the food's pretty good, too. See p. 128.

- **Best Italian Food:** Miami Beach's **Macaluso's** (© **305/604-1811**) would make Tony Soprano very proud of his Italian heritage, thanks to Chef Michael's expertly prepared Staten Island–meets-SoHo cuisine. See p. 131. **Tuscan Today Trattoria,** in Fort Lauderdale (© **954/566-1716**), churns out primo Tuscan fare in its imported-from-Italy wood-burning brick oven. See p. 330.

- **Best Mexican:** The fresh, authentic Mexican fare at **El Rancho Grande,** in Miami Beach (© **305/673-0480**), will have you swearing off Taco Bell forever. See p. 129.

- **Best Star-Studded Sushi Restaurant: Nobu,** at the Shore Club Hotel in Miami Beach (© **305/695-3100**), is known for its star sushi chef and owner, the legendary Nobu Matsuhisa, but the raw facts about this restaurant are as simple as its stellar clientele (which includes Madonna, among others): It's unquestionably the best sushi in town. For fabulous

sushi minus the Hollywood vibe, Miami Beach's **Shoji Sushi** (© **305/532-4245**) is at the top of the A-list. See p. 123 and p. 127.

- **Best Seafood: Grillfish,** in South Beach (© **305/538-9908**), is simple, unpretentious, and consistently serves the freshest fish in town—any which way you desire. See p. 129.

- **Best Late-Night Dining:** In addition to the 24-hour **News Café** (see above and p. 134) and **Big Pink** (see above and p. 128), Ft. Lauderdale's **Lester's Diner** (© **954/525-5641**) is a 24-hour institution, serving classic greasy-spoon fare at ridiculously cheap prices. The **Floridian,** also in Fort Lauderdale (© **954/463-4041**), serves everything from eggs to steaks, 24 hours a day, but the vantage point for people-watching rates higher than the food. See p. 330.

- **Kitschiest Dining: Wolfie Cohen's Rascal House** (© **305/947-4581**) is a must for those looking for a retro-fabulous North Miami Beach experience, with a wait staff as old as the vinyl booths and the best corned beef on rye south of the Lower East Side. See p. 141. **Green Turtle Inn,** on Islamorada (© **305/664-9031**), is an old-fashioned Florida Keys institution since 1947, featuring moderately priced steaks, stone crabs, and, yes, turtle, to the tune of campy pianist Tina Martin. See p. 270.

5 The Rest of the Best

- **Best Museum:** A collector's dream come true, Miami's **Wolfsonian** is a treasure trove of miscellany (a matchbook that once belonged to the King of Egypt) and artifacts hailing from the

propaganda age of World War II. See p. 173.

- **Best Cultural Experience:** A walk through **Little Havana** is a fascinating study in the juxtaposition and fusion of two very vibrant cultures in which pre-Castro Cuba is as alive and well as the McDonald's right next door. See p. 61.

- **Best Cheap Thrill:** Riding the **Metrorail** in Miami. Originally created to relieve traffic congestion, the city's billion-dollar transportation network is hardly used by commuters and is little more than Miami's own version of Disney's Monorail. Nonetheless, for little more than a dollar, you can tour many of Miami's neighborhoods and see much of its skyline without having to stop, look at a map, or ask for directions. See p. 63.

- **Best Snorkeling Spot: Looe Key National Marine Sanctuary,** Bahia Honda State Park. With 5.3 square miles of gorgeous coral reef, rock ledges up to 35 feet tall, and a colorful and motley marine community, you may never want to come up for air. See p. 276.

- **Best Public Golf Course:** Miami's **Biltmore Golf Course,** Biltmore Hotel. If it's good enough for former President Clinton, it's good enough for those of you who don't travel with a bevy of Secret Service agents. But the real question is: Are *you* good enough for the course? The sixth hole is notoriously difficult, with distracting water hazards among other difficulties. Nonetheless, it's an excellent course with picture-postcard setting. See p. 190.

- **Best Dive Bar: Jose Cuervo's Underwater Bar.** In May 2000, the legendary tequila company celebrated Cinco de Mayo by submerging an actual, $45,000 full-size bar and six stools about 200 yards off South Beach's First Street beach. For expert divers, this bar is more than your average watering hole. See p. 186.

- **Best Place to Satisfy Your Morbid Curiosity: The Mystery, Murder, and Mayhem Bus Tour.** Not that we're implying anything here, but Miami is a haven for people like O.J. Simpson and, at one time, Al Capone. It's a place where shady characters come to reinvent themselves. However, at times, they also tend to reincriminate themselves. See the spots where some of these criminals fell off the wagon—it's morbidly delicious. See p. 184.

- **Best Latin Club:** Although the predominant language spoken at Miami's **La Covacha** is Spanish, the only word you really need to know here is *agua,* because you will certainly need it after working up a sweat on the dance floor. Music—the best Latin music in town—is, in fact, the common language at this rustic, open-aired Latin dance club that features salsa, merengue, and Latin rock. See p. 225.

- **Best Dance Club: Club Space.** South Beach devotees said that downtown Miami would never make it as a club hub, but they were wrong. A 24-hour liquor license, stellar DJs, and a dance room the size of four converted warehouses make Club Space Miami's best dance club. Sorry, South Beach. See p. 219.

- **Best Offbeat Experience:** Although it's little more than a tropical shantytown, **Jimbo's,** located at the tip of Virginia Key, is consistently fantastic, with no-frills smoked fish, beer out of the bucket, and colorful locals, all of which make it the best offbeat and off-the-beaten-track experience in South Florida. See p. 154.

2

Planning Your Trip to South Florida

Peak season in South Florida runs from October to March. And while peak season is the most popular time to visit, pre- and postseason offer you a less congested, less expensive travel experience. Regardless of when you choose to travel, a little advanced planning will help you make the most of your trip.

1 Visitor Information

The **Greater Miami Convention and Visitor's Bureau,** 701 Brickell Ave., Miami, FL 33131 (© 800/933-8448; www.miamiandbeaches.com), is the best source for specialized information about the city and its beaches. Even if you don't have a specific question, you should request a free copy of *Tropicool,* the bureau's vacation planner for greater Miami and the beaches. And remember that just because information on a particular establishment you're inquiring about is not available, that doesn't mean the place doesn't exist: The GMCVB only endorses member businesses.

The **Greater Miami and Beaches Hotel Association,** 407 Lincoln Rd., Miami Beach, FL 33139 (© 800/531-3553; www.gmbha.org), provides information on accommodations and tours.

Because Miami is such a vast city, some of the more popular neighborhoods have their own chambers of commerce that will provide you with specific information on events, accommodations, and attractions in their areas. Here's a partial list:

- **Miami Beach Chamber of Commerce,** 420 Lincoln Rd., Miami Beach, FL 33139 (© 305/672-1270; www.miamibeachchamber.com)

- **Coral Gables Chamber of Commerce,** 2333 Ponce de León Blvd., Suite 650, Coral Gables, FL 33134 (© 305/446-1657; www.gableschamber.org)
- **Coconut Grove Chamber of Commerce,** 2820 McFarlane Rd., Coconut Grove, FL 33133 (© 305/444-7270; www.coconutgrove.com)
- **Florida Gold Coast Chamber of Commerce** (representing Bal Harbour, Sunny Isles, and Surfside), 1100 Kane Concourse, Bay Harbor Islands, FL 33154 (© 561/866-6020; www.flgoldcc.org)

For information on visiting the Fort Lauderdale area, the **Greater Fort Lauderdale Convention & Visitor's Bureau,** 1850 Eller Dr., Suite 303, Fort Lauderdale, FL 33316 (© 954/765-4466; www.sunny.org), offers a 71-page vacation planner, as well as maps and other helpful information on the area and its beaches.

The **Palm Beach County Convention and Visitors Bureau,** 1555 Palm Beach Lakes Blvd., Suite 204, West Palm Beach, FL 33401 (© 561/471-3995; www.palmbeachfl.com), offers maps, brochures, and, if you request it, a coupon book of over $500 in savings in the Palm Beach area. Ask for it!

Because there are so many islands in the Florida Keys, the best place for information is at www.florida-keys.fl. us/chamber.htm, where you can send e-mail requests to each individual Florida Keys chamber of commerce. To call, contact the chambers of commerce at the following numbers: **Key Largo** ℂ 800/822-1088 or 305/451-1414; **Islamorada** ℂ 800/332-5397 or 305/664-4503; **Marathon** ℂ 800/262-7284 or 305/743-5417; **Lower Keys** ℂ 800/872-3722 or 305/872-2411; and **Key West** ℂ 800/527-8539 or 305/294-2587.

For the Everglades, the **Tropical Everglades Visitor's Center,** 160 U.S. Hwy. 1, Florida City, FL 33034 (ℂ **305/245-9180**), will provide you with information on tours, sites, and parks in the area.

For information on traveling throughout Florida, including a calendar of events, a guide to accommodations, and a list of useful websites, contact **Visit Florida,** P.O. Box 1100, 66 E. Jefferson St., Tallahassee, FL 32302 (ℂ **888/7-FLA-USA;** www.fla usa.com).

Florida State Parks have a new website at www.floridastateparks.org.

2 Money

ATMS

For as many palm trees as there are in South Florida, there are just as many, if not more, ATM machines linked to a major national network that will likely include your bank at home. Using common sense at ATM machines is first and foremost. Avoid withdrawing money at those machines located on sparsely populated streets; machines are available in many hotels, at most major tourist attractions, shopping malls, and even restaurants and nightclubs.

Check the back of your ATM card to see which network your bank belongs to and use the toll-free numbers on the card to locate ATMs in your destination. Be sure you know your four-digit PIN access number before you leave home, and be sure to find out your daily withdrawal limit before you depart. You can also get cash advances on your credit card at an ATM. Keep in mind that credit card companies try to protect themselves from theft by limiting the funds someone can withdraw away from home. It's therefore best to call your credit card company before you leave and let them know where you're going

and how much you plan to spend. You'll get the best exchange rate if you withdraw money from an ATM, but keep in mind that many banks impose a fee every time a card is used at an ATM in a different city or bank. Additionally, the bank from which you withdraw cash may charge its own fee.

TRAVELER'S CHECKS

Traveler's checks are something of an anachronism from the days before the ATM made cash accessible at any time. The only sound alternative to traveling with dangerously large amounts of cash, traveler's checks were as reliable as currency, unlike personal checks, but could be replaced if lost or stolen, unlike cash.

These days, traveler's checks seem less necessary because most cities have 24-hour ATMs that allow you to withdraw small amounts of cash as needed. However, you're likely to be charged an ATM withdrawal fee if the bank is not your own, so if you're withdrawing money every day, you might be better off with traveler's checks—provided that you don't mind showing identification every time you want to cash one.

You can get traveler's checks at almost any bank. You can also get American Express traveler's checks over the phone by calling ☎ 800/221-7282; AAA members can obtain checks without a fee at most AAA offices.

Visa offers traveler's checks at Citibank locations nationwide, as well as at several other banks. Call ☎ 800/732-1322 for information. **Master-Card** also offers traveler's checks. Call ☎ 800/223-9920 for a location near you.

CREDIT CARDS

Credit cards are invaluable when traveling. They are a safe way to carry money and provide a convenient record of all your expenses. You can also withdraw cash advances from your credit cards at any bank (though you'll start paying hefty interest on the advance the moment you receive the cash). At most banks, you don't even need to go to a teller; you can get a cash advance at the ATM if you know your PIN access number. If you've forgotten yours, or didn't even know you had one, call the number on the back of your credit card and ask the bank to send it to you. It usually takes 5 to 7 business days, though some banks will provide the number over the phone if you tell them your mother's maiden name or pass some other security clearance.

WHAT TO DO IF YOUR WALLET GETS STOLEN

Be sure to block charges against your account the minute you discover a card has been lost or stolen. Then be sure to file a police report.

Almost every credit card company has an emergency toll-free number to call if your card is stolen. It may be able to wire you a cash advance off your credit card immediately, and in many places, it can deliver an emergency credit card in a day or two. The issuing bank's 800 number is usually on the back of your credit card—though, of course, if your card has been stolen, that won't help you unless you recorded the number elsewhere.

Citicorp Visa's U.S. emergency number is ☎ 800/336-8472. American Express cardholders and traveler's check holders should call ☎ 800/221-7282. MasterCard holders should call ☎ 800/307-7309. Otherwise, call the toll-free number directory at ☎ 800/555-1212.

Odds are that if your wallet is gone, the police won't be able to recover it. However, it's still worth informing the authorities. Your credit card company or insurer may require a police report number or record of the theft.

If you choose to carry traveler's checks, be sure to keep a record of their serial numbers separate from your checks. You'll get a refund faster if you know the numbers.

If you need emergency cash over the weekend when all banks and American Express offices are closed, you can have money wired to you from **Western Union** (☎ 800/325-6000; www.westernunion.com). You must present valid ID to pick up the cash at the Western Union office. However, in most countries, you can pick up a money transfer even if you don't have valid identification, as long as you can answer a test question provided by the sender. Be sure to let the sender know in advance that you don't have ID. If you need to use a test question instead of ID, the sender must take cash to his or her local Western Union office, rather than transferring the money over the phone or online.

3 When to Go

Contrary to popular belief, the notion of sunny Florida isn't always 100%

correct. While the term is hardly an oxymoron, when it comes to weather, sunny Florida undergoes major mood swings. While it may be pouring on the ocean side of Miami Beach, on the bay side, the only thing pouring down may be UV rays.

Rain showers aside, the most pressing concern for every South Florida visitor is the dreaded "H" word—the unpredictable, unstoppable hurricane. Official hurricane season is from June to November, and while the hurricane's actual pattern is unpredictable, for the most part, the meteorologists at the National Hurricane Center in Coral Gables are able to give fair enough warning so that people can take proper precautions. One of the safest places during a hurricane happens to be in a hotel, because most hotels are sturdy enough to withstand high winds and have generators in case of power failures.

For many people, the worst time to come to South Florida is during the summer, when temperatures are usually scorching, humidity is oppressive, and rain at 4pm is a daily

occurrence. Wintertime in South Florida is spectacular—not too hot, not too cool. Temperatures can, however, dip down into the low 50s during a cold front.

Weather aside, peak season in South Florida means more tourists, snowbirds, and models—and the influx of celebrities, who also call South Florida their winter home.

In the summer, South Florida practically comes to a standstill as far as special events, cultural activities, and overall pace is concerned. Locals love it; it is their time to reclaim their cities. Tourists may want to take advantage of the summers down here as long as they can stand the heat. If you can brave the temperature, you will not have to face the long lines in restaurants and at attractions that you will encounter during peak season. For some people, however, the lines and the waiting are all part of the allure of South Florida, as they provide an opportunity to see and be seen.

Miami's Average Monthly High/Low Temperatures & Rainfall

	Jan	Feb	Mar	Apr	May	June	July	Aug	Sept	Oct	Nov	Dec
Avg. High (°F)	76	77	80	83	86	88	89	90	88	85	80	77
Avg. Low (°F)	60	61	64	68	72	75	76	76	76	72	66	61
Avg. High (°C)	24.4	25	26.7	28.3	30	31.1	31.7	32.2	31.1	29.4	26.7	25
Avg. Low (°C)	15.6	16.1	17.8	20	22.2	23.9	24.4	24.4	24.4	22.2	18.9	16.1
Avg. Rain (in.)	2.0	2.1	2.4	3.0	5.9	8.8	6.0	7.8	8.5	7.0	3.1	1.8

SOUTH FLORIDA CALENDAR OF EVENTS

January

FedEx Orange Bowl Classic, Miami. Football fanatics flock down to the big Orange Bowl game (oddly taking place not at the Orange Bowl in seedy downtown, but at the much more savory Pro Player Stadium) on New Year's Day, featuring two of the year's best college football teams. Tickets are available from March 1 of the previous year through the Orange

Bowl Committee (© **305/371-4600**), but call early as they sell out quickly.

Polo Season, Palm Beach. Join the crisp and clean Ralph Lauren–clad polo fanatics (including stars and socialites) at the Palm Beach Polo and Country Club for polo season. Call © **561/793-1440** for details. Begins in early January.

Three Kings Parade, Miami. Miami's Cuban community makes up for the fact that Castro banned this religious celebration over 25

years ago by throwing a no-holds-barred parade throughout the streets of Little Havana's Calle Ocho neighborhood, usually the first Sunday of January. Call *C* **305/447-1140.**

Art Deco Weekend, South Beach. Gain a newfound appreciation for the Necco-wafered Art Deco buildings, Deco furniture, history, and fashion at this weekend-long festival of street fairs, films, lectures, and other events. Call *C* **305/672-2014.** Mid- to late January.

Martin Luther King Jr. Day Parade, Miami. The culmination of the week's celebration of Dr. King's birthday, this parade occurs in the not-so-great neighborhood of Liberty City, along NW 54th Street, between NW 12th and 32nd avenues. For information, call *C* **305/636-1924.** Mid-January.

Taste of the Grove Food and Music Festival, Coconut Grove. Brave massive crowds of hungry folk at this fund-raising festival featuring booths from various neighborhood eateries hawking their goods for the price of a few prepurchased tickets. Call *C* **305/444-7270.** Dates vary from mid-November to mid-January.

Royal Caribbean Golf Classic, Key Biscayne. Watch as pro golfers tee off for over $1 million at this tournament played on the scenic Crandon Park Golf Course. Call *C* **305/374-6180.** Late January.

Palm Beach International Art and Antiques Fair, West Palm Beach. With antiques and art older than some of Palm Beach's very own residents, this fair has become a premier stomping ground for domestic artifacts. Call *C* **561/220-2690.** Late January or early February.

Key West Literary Seminar, Key West. Literary types get a good reason to put down the books and head to Key West. This annual 3-day event features a different theme every year, such as "the Memoir" or "Science Fiction," and a roster of incredible authors, writers, and other literary types such as Joyce Carol Oates, Barbara Ehrenreich, and Jamaica Kincaid. The event is so popular it sells out well in advance, so call early for tickets (available for individual lectures or events, or the entire conference). For information, call *C* **888/293-9291** or visit www.keywestliterary seminar.org. January 9 to 13, 2003.

February

Miami Film Festival. Though not exactly Cannes, the Miami Film Festival, sponsored by the Film Society of America, is an impressive 10-day celluloid celebration, featuring world premiers of Latin American, domestic, and other foreign and independent films. Actors, producers, and directors show up to plug their films and participate in Q&A sessions with the audiences. Call *C* **305/377-FILM.** Early to mid-February.

Everglades Seafood Festival, Florida City. What seems like schools of fish-loving people flock down to Florida City for a 2-day feeding frenzy, in which Florida delicacies from stone crab to gator tails are served from shacks and booths on the outskirts of this quaint old Florida town. Free admission, but you pay for the food you eat, booth by booth. Call *C* **941/695-4100.** First full weekend in February.

Homestead Rodeo, Homestead. One of South Florida's only rodeo shows, this one features clowns, competitions, and bucking broncos. Call *C* **305/247-3515.** Early February.

Coconut Grove Arts Festival, Coconut Grove. Florida's largest art festival features over 300 artists who are selected from thousands of entries. Possibly one of the most crowded street fairs in South Florida, the festival attracts art lovers, artists, and lots of college students who seem to think this event is the Mardi Gras of art fairs. Call ⓒ **305/447-0401** for information. Presidents' Day weekend.

Miami International Boat Show, Miami Beach. Agoraphobics beware, as this show draws a quarter of a million boat enthusiasts to the Miami Beach Convention Center. Some of the world's priciest megayachts, speedboats, sailboats, and schooners are displayed for purchase or for gawking. Call ⓒ **305/531-8410.** Mid-February.

Winter Equestrian Festival, West Palm Beach. With over 1,000 horses and three grand-prix equestrian events, the Palm Beach Polo Club's winter festival is an equestrian's dream. For information, call ⓒ **561/798-7000.** Late February.

Doral Ryder Golf Open, West Miami. This prestigious annual golf tournament swings into Miami at the legendary courses at the Doral Resort and Club. Call ⓒ **305/477-GOLF.** Late February.

Hatsume Fair, Delray Beach. A 2-day fair celebrating the first buds of spring in a state that barely has seasons may seem like an odd notion, but the Hatsume Fair takes place at the Morikami Japanese Museum and Gardens—a place where visitors can appreciate truly exotic flora and fauna. Call ⓒ **561/495-0233.** Last weekend in February.

March

Winter Party, Miami Beach. Gays and lesbians from around the world book trips to Miami as far as a year in advance to attend this weekend-long series of parties and events benefiting the Dade Human Rights Foundation. Travel arrangements can be made through Different Roads Travel, the event's official travel company, by calling ⓒ **888/ROADS-55,** ext. 510. For information on the specific events and prices, call ⓒ **305/538-5908** or visit www.winterparty.com. Early March.

Italian Renaissance Festival, Miami. Villa Vizcaya gets in touch with its Renaissance roots at this festival, which features strolling musicians, stage plays, and a cast of period-costumed characters who do their best to convince you that you're in a time warp. Call ⓒ **305/250-9133.** Mid-March.

Miami Gay & Lesbian Film Festival, Miami Beach. This 10-day event is the Sundance of festivals for gay and lesbian films and filmmakers. It features an impressive roster of independent and commercial films, plus appearances by some of the films' directors, actors, and writers. Call ⓒ **305/532-7256.** Mid-March.

Calle Ocho Festival, Little Havana. What Carnavale is to Rio, the Calle Ocho Festival is to Miami. This 10-day extravaganza, also called Carnival Miami, features a lengthy block party spanning 23 blocks, live salsa music, parades, and, of course, tons of savory Cuban delicacies. Those afraid of mob scenes should avoid this party at all costs. Call ⓒ **305/644-8888.** Mid-March.

Grand Prix of Miami, Homestead. A little bit of Daytona in Miami, the Grand Prix is a premier racing event, attracting celebrities, Indy car drivers, and curious spectators who get a buzz off the smell of gasoline. Get tickets early, as this event sells out quickly. Call ℂ **305/250-5200.** Late March.

NASDAQ 100 Open, Key Biscayne. Sampras, Agassi, Kournikova, and the Williams sisters are only a few of the Grand Slammers who appear at this, one of the world's foremost tennis tournaments. Tickets for the semifinals and finals are hard to come by, so order early. Call ℂ **305/446-2200.** End of the month.

April

World Cup Polo Tournament, Palm Beach. The last tournament of the polo season, this event draws the diamond-studded mallet set who gather one more time in the name of scene and sport. Call ℂ **561/793-1440.** Mid-April.

PGA Seniors Golf Championship, Palm Beach Gardens. This is the oldest and most prestigious of the senior golf tournaments in which aging swingers prove they've still got spunk in their swing. Call ℂ **561/624-8400.** Mid-April.

Little Acorns International Kite Festival, South Beach. A great event for the kids and kids at heart, this kite festival is a true spectacular in the sky, attracting thousands of expert flyers and their flying works of art from 5th to 15th streets. Kids can build their own kites and scrounge for candy, which is dropped piñata style along the beach. Call ℂ **888/298-9815.** Free. Third weekend in April.

Sunfest, West Palm Beach. Sleepy downtown West Palm comes alive at the end of April for this street fair and concert, featuring big-name entertainment, food stands, a youth fair, and hordes of people. Admission charges are reasonable, but, unless there's someone performing whom you must see, not always worth the price. Stick to the free

nontented area on Clematis Street for excellent people-watching. For information, call ℂ **561/659-5992.** Late April.

Texaco Key West Classic, Key West. This catch-and-release fishing competition offers $50,000 in prizes to be divided among the top anglers in three divisions: sailfish, marlin, and light tackle. You won't believe the size of some of these catches. Call ℂ **305/294-4042.** Late April.

May

McDonald's Air & Sea Show, Fort Lauderdale. It's a tough call as far as what's more crowded—the air, the sea, or the ground, which attracts over 2 million onlookers craning their necks for a view of big-name airwolves such as the Blue Angels and the Thunderbirds. In addition to the various planes doing tricks in the sky, you'll also see battleships pull into port. Remember: It's an *air* and *sea* show, not a car show, so consider leaving yours at the hotel. Call ℂ **954/467-3555.** Early May.

Cajun Zydeco Crawfish Festival, Fort Lauderdale. A little bit of Nawlins in South Florida. Enjoy the crawfish delicacies at this 3-day festival paying homage to all things hot, spicy, and, er, crunchy. Call ℂ **954/761-5934.** Early May.

Arabian Nights Festival, Hialeah. A colorful celebration of Hialeah's Moorish architecture, this festival features a mix of entertainment, food, and fantasy inspired by Arabian culture. Call ℂ **305/758-4166.** Mid-May.

June

Coconut Grove Goombay Festival, Coconut Grove. They may say it's better in the Bahamas, but that's questionable after you've attended Miami's own Bahamian bash, featuring lots of dancing in the streets, marching bands, scorching Caribbean temperatures, and the ever buzz-worthy and refreshing Goombay punch. For information, call ℂ **305/372-9966.** Early June.

July

Independence Day, Miami. Watch as one of the nation's most spectacular skylines is further illuminated with the masterful display of professional fireworks throughout the entire city. Best views are from Key Biscayne and Bayfront Park. For specific information on July 4 events, check the local newspapers.

Lower Keys Underwater Music Fest, Looe Key. When you hear the phrase "the music and the madness," you may want to think of this amusing aural aquatic event in which boaters head out to the underwater reef at the Looe Key Marine Sanctuary, drop speakers into the water, and pipe in all sorts of music, creating a disco-diving spectacular. Considering the heat at this time of year, underwater is probably the coolest place for a concert. Call ℂ **800/872-3722.** Early July.

Miccosukee Everglades Festival, West Miami (close to the Everglades). South Florida's Native American community celebrates its own unique heritage with music, food, and fanfare including shriek-inducing alligator wrestling. Call ℂ **305/223-8380** for prices and information. Early and late July.

Hemingway Days Festival, Key West. The legendary author is alive and well—many times over—at this celebration of the literary world's most famous papa, to which eerily accurate Hemingway clones flock in the hopes of winning the big look-alike contest. Call ℂ **305/ 294-4440.** Mid- to late July.

Wine and All That Jazz, Boca Raton. Though the experts may recommend water as the ideal summer thirst quencher, the organizers of this event prefer the fruits of the vine. Sip over 100 vintages to the tune of jazz at this swank wine-tasting party. Call ℂ **561/278-0424.** Late July.

Beethoven by the Beach, Fort Lauderdale. The Florida Philharmonic takes Beethoven to the beach with its summer music festival, featuring symphonies, chamber pieces, and piano concertos. Call ℂ **954/ 561-2997.**

August

This month is possibly the most scorching, which is why event planners try to avoid it altogether. Your best bet? The beach, the pool, or anywhere with air-conditioning.

September

Festival Miami, Miami. The University of Miami School of Music presents a 4-week program of performing arts, classical, jazz, and world music. For a schedule of performances, call ℂ **305/284-4940.** Mid-September.

October

Caribbean Carnival, Miami. If you've never been to the Caribbean, then this can be your introduction to the colorful, multicultural island nations of Trinidad, Jamaica, Haiti, St. Vincent, Barbados, and St. Croix, as natives from the islands participate in a masquerade parade in their traditional costumes. Call ℂ **305/653-1877.** Early October.

Columbus Day Regatta, Miami. On the day that Columbus discovered America, the party-hearty of today's Florida discover their fellow Americans' birthday suits—this bacchanalia in the middle of Biscayne Bay encourages participants in this so-called regatta (there is a boat race at some point during the day, but most people are too preoccupied to notice) to strip down to their bare necessities and party at the sandbar in the middle of the bay. You may not need a bathing suit, but you will need a boat to get out to where all the action is. Consider renting one on Key Biscayne, which is the closest to the sandbar.

Fort Lauderdale International Boat Show, Fort Lauderdale. The world's largest boat show, this one's got boats of every size, shape, and status symbol displayed at the scenic Bahia Mar marina and four other locations in the area. Traffic-phobes beware. Call ✆ **954/764-7642.** Mid-October.

Fantasy Fest, Key West. Mardi Gras takes a Floridian holiday as the streets of Key West are overtaken by wildly costumed revelers who have no shame and no parental guidance. This weeklong, hedonistic, X-rated Halloween party is not for children under 18. Make reservations in Key West early, as hotels tend to book up quickly during this event. Call ✆ **305/296-1817.** Last week of October.

November

Blues Festival at Riverwalk, Fort Lauderdale. The scenic landscape of downtown Fort Lauderdale's Riverwalk will make your own personal blues go away, but you'll want to immerse yourself in the music of big-name performers who sing and play the blues here at various venues. Call ✆ **954/761-5934.** Early November.

South Florida International Auto Show, Miami Beach. Cars are everywhere—literally—at this massive auto show, displaying the latest and most futuristic modes of transportation on the market. Try to take public transportation or call a cab to get to this gridlocked event. Call ✆ **305/947-5950.** Early November.

Jiffy Lube Miami 300 Weekend of NASCAR, Homestead. World-class racing takes place on Miami's world-class 344-acre motor sports complex. Rev your engines early for tickets to this event. Call ✆ **305/230-5200.** Mid-November.

Miami Book Fair International, downtown Miami. Bibliophiles, literati, and some of the world's most prestigious and prolific authors descend upon downtown Miami for a week-long homage to the written word, which also happens to be the largest book fair in the United States. The weekend street fair is the most well attended of the entire event, in which regular folk mix with wordsmiths such as Tom Wolfe and Jane Smiley while indulging in snacks, antiquarian books, and literary gossip. All lectures are free, but they fill up quickly, so get there early. Call ✆ 305/237-3258 for lecture schedules. Mid-November.

White Party Week, Miami and Fort Lauderdale. This week-long series of parties to benefit AIDS research is built around the main event, the White Party, which takes place at Villa Vizcaya and sells out as early as a year in advance. Philanthropists and celebrities such as Calvin Klein and David Geffen join thousands of white-clad, mostly gay men (and some women) in what has become one of the world's hottest and hardest-to-score party tickets. Call ✆ **305/667-9296** or visit www.whitepartyweek.com for a schedule of parties and events. Thanksgiving week.

Santa's Enchanted Forest, Miami. Billing itself as the world's largest Christmas theme park, Santa's Enchanted Forest is an assault on the eyes, with thousands of lights lining Tropical Park plus rides, games, and lots of food. This is a great place to bring younger kids. Call ✆ **305/893-0090.** Early November to mid-January.

December

Winterfest Boat Parade, Fort Lauderdale. People who complain that the holiday season just isn't as festive in South Florida as it is in colder parts of the world haven't been to this spectacular boat parade along the Intracoastal Waterways. Forget decking the halls. At this parade, the decks are decked out in magnificent holiday regalia as they gracefully—and boastfully—glide up and down the water. If you're not on a boat, the best views are from waterfront restaurants or anywhere you can squeeze in along the water. Call ✆ **954/767-0686.** Mid-December.

4 Health, Insurance & Safety

STAYING HEALTHY

Paramount to staying well in South Florida (and maintaining a sunny disposition) is sunscreen. Even on the cloudiest of days, you *will* feel the effects of the powerful UV rays, so it's best to take precautions at all times. Limit your exposure to the sun, especially during the first few days of your trip and thereafter from 11am to 2pm. Use a sunscreen with a high sun protection factor (SPF) and apply it liberally. Remember that children need more protection than do adults. Mosquito repellent, especially if you travel to the Everglades or other swampy areas and parks, is a good idea.

WHAT TO DO IF YOU GET SICK AWAY FROM HOME

If you worry about getting sick away from home, consider purchasing **medical travel insurance** and carry your ID card in your purse or wallet. In most cases, your existing health plan will provide the coverage you need.

If you suffer from a chronic illness, consult your doctor before your departure. For conditions like epilepsy, diabetes, or heart problems, wear a **Medic Alert Identification Tag** (✆ **800/825-3785;** www.medicalert. org), which will immediately alert doctors to your condition and give them access to your records through Medic Alert's 24-hour hot line.

Pack **prescription medications** in your carry-on luggage, and carry them in their original containers. Also bring along copies of your prescriptions in case you lose your pills or run out.

If you get sick, consider asking your hotel concierge to recommend a local doctor—even his or her own. You can also try the emergency room at a local hospital; many have walk-in clinics for emergency cases that are not life-threatening. You may not get immediate attention, but you won't pay the high price of an emergency room visit (usually a minimum of $300 just for signing your name). For any medical concerns or emergencies, Doctor's Hospital, 5000 University Dr., Coral Gables (✆ **305/666-2111**), has a 24-hour physician-staffed emergency department.

TRAVEL INSURANCE AT A GLANCE

Check your existing insurance policies before you buy travel insurance to cover trip cancellation, lost luggage, medical expenses, or car rental insurance. You're likely to have partial or complete coverage. But if you need some, ask your travel agent about a comprehensive package. The cost of travel insurance varies widely, depending on the cost and length of your trip, your age and overall health, and the type of trip you're taking.

And keep in mind that in the aftermath of the World Trade Center attacks, a number of airlines, cruise lines, and tour operators are no longer covered by insurers. *The bottom line:* Always, always check the fine print before you sign on; more and more policies have built-in exclusions and restrictions that may leave you out in the cold if something does go awry.

For information, contact one of the following popular insurers:

- **Access America** (© 800/284-8300; www.accessamerica.com)
- **Travel Guard International** (© 800/826-1300; www.travel guard. com)
- **Travel Insured International** (© 800/243-3174; www.travel insured.com)
- **Travelex Insurance Services** (© 800/228-9792; www.travelex-insurance.com)

TRIP-CANCELLATION INSURANCE (TCI)

There are three major types of trip-cancellation insurance—one, in the event that you prepay a cruise or tour that gets canceled, and you can't get your money back; a second, when you or someone in your family gets sick or dies, and you can't travel (but be aware that you may not be covered for a pre-existing condition); and a third, when bad weather makes travel impossible. Some insurers provide coverage for events like jury duty; natural disasters close to home, floods, or fire; or even the loss of a job. A few have added provisions for cancellations due to terrorist activities. Always check the fine print before signing on, and don't buy

trip-cancellation insurance from the tour operator that may be responsible for the cancellation; buy it only from a reputable travel insurance agency. Don't overbuy: You won't be reimbursed for more than the cost of your trip.

MEDICAL INSURANCE

Most health insurance policies cover you if you get sick away from home—but check, particularly if you're insured by an HMO.

If you require additional insurance, try one of the following companies:

- **MEDEX International**, 9515 Deereco Rd., Timonium, MD 21093-5375 (© 888/MEDEX-00 or 410/453-6300; fax 410/453-6301; www.medexassist.com)
- **Travel Assistance International** (© 800/821-2828; www.travel assistance.com), 9200 Keystone Crossing, Suite 300, Indianapolis, IN 46240 (for general information on services, call the company's Worldwide Assistance Services, Inc., at © 800/777-8710)

The cost of travel medical insurance varies widely. Check your existing policies before you buy additional coverage. Also, check to see if your medical insurance covers you for emergency medical evacuation; if you have to buy a one-way same-day ticket home and forfeit your nonrefundable roundtrip ticket, you may be out big bucks.

5 Tips for Travelers with Special Needs

TRAVELERS WITH DISABILITIES

Most disabilities shouldn't stop anyone from traveling. There are more options and resources out there than ever before. Because South Florida is an outdoor destination, disabled accessible ramps and areas are found at every park, attraction, and marina.

The U.S. National Park Service offers a **Golden Access Passport** that

gives free lifetime entrance to U.S. national parks for persons who are blind or permanently disabled, regardless of age. You may pick up a Golden Access Passport at any NPS entrance fee area by showing proof of medically determined disability and eligibility for receiving benefits under federal law. Besides free entry, the Golden Access Passport also offers a 50% discount on federal-use fees charged for such facilities as camping, swimming, parking, boat launching, and tours. For more information, click onto www. nps.gov/fees_passes.htm or call ℭ **888-go-parks.**

AGENCIES/OPERATORS

- **Flying Wheels Travel** (ℭ **800/ 535-6790;** www.flyingwheels travel.com) offers escorted tours and cruises that emphasize sports and private tours in minivans with lifts.
- **Access Adventures** (ℭ **716/ 889-9096**), a Rochester, N.Y.–based agency, offers customized itineraries for a variety of travelers with disabilities.
- **Accessible Journeys** (ℭ **800/ TINGLES** or 610/521-0339; www.disabilitytravel.com) caters specifically to slow walkers and wheelchair travelers and their families and friends.

ORGANIZATIONS

- **The Moss Rehab Hospital** (ℭ **215/456-9603;** www.moss resourcenet.org) provides friendly, helpful phone assistance through its **Travel Information Service.**
- **The Society for Accessible Travel and Hospitality** (ℭ **212/447-7284;** fax 212/725-8253; www. sath.org) offers a wealth of travel resources for all types of disabilities and informed recommendations on destinations, access guides, travel agents, tour operators, vehicle rentals, and companion services. Annual membership costs $45 for adults; $30 for seniors and students.

PUBLICATIONS

- **Mobility International USA** (ℭ **541/343-1284;** www.miusa. org) publishes *A World of Options,* a 658-page book of resources, covering everything from biking trips to scuba outfitters, and a biannual newsletter, *Over the Rainbow.* Annual membership is $35.

- **Twin Peaks Press** (ℭ **360/694-2462**) publishes travel-related books for travelers with special needs.
- *Open World for Disability and Mature Travel* magazine, published by the Society for Accessible Travel and Hospitality (see above), is full of good resources and information. A year's subscription is $13 ($21 outside the U.S.).

GAY & LESBIAN TRAVELERS

South Florida, particularly Key West, South Beach, and Fort Lauderdale, has a thriving gay community, supported by a wide range of services and establishments. There are several local gay-oriented publications full of information on gay and gay-friendly events, businesses, and services. *TWN, Wire, Hot Spots,* and *Miamigo* are among the free publications available in boxes on street corners, in stores, and on newsstands.

For a map and directory of gay businesses or a copy or the gay and lesbian community calendar sponsored by the **Dade Human Rights Foundation,** call ℭ **305/572-1841.** For a copy of the calendar and other information, you can also visit www.dhrf. com. Two organizations that are extremely helpful for gay and lesbian travelers are the **Miami Dade and South Beach Business Guild** (better known as the Gay Chamber of Commerce; ℭ 305/751-8855), and the **Gay and Lesbian Community Center of Fort Lauderdale** (ℭ 954/563-9500).

The **International Gay & Lesbian Travel Association** (IGLTA) (ℭ **800/ 448-8550** or 954/776-2626; fax 954/ 776-3303; www.iglta.org) links travelers up with gay-friendly hoteliers, tour operators, and airline and cruise-line representatives. It offers monthly newsletters, marketing mailings, and a membership directory that's updated once a year. Membership is $150 yearly, plus a $100 administration fee for new members.

AGENCIES/OPERATORS

- **Above and Beyond Tours** (✆ **800/397-2681;** www.above beyondtours.com) offers gay and lesbian tours worldwide and is the exclusive gay and lesbian tour operator for United Airlines.
- **Olivia Cruises & Resorts** (✆ **800/631-6277** or 510/655-0364; http://oliviatravel.com) charters entire resorts and ships for exclusive lesbian vacations all over the world.

PUBLICATIONS

- *Out and About* (✆ **800/929-2268** or 415/644-8044; www.out andabout.com) offers guidebooks and a newsletter 10 times a year packed with solid information on the global gay and lesbian scene.
- *Spartacus International Gay Guide* and *Odysseus* are good, annual English-language guidebooks focused on gay men, with some information for lesbians. You can get them from most gay and lesbian bookstores, or order them from **Giovanni's Room** bookstore, 1145 Pine St., Philadelphia, PA 19107 (✆ **215/923-2960;** www.giovannisroom.com).
- *Gay Travel A to Z: The World of Gay & Lesbian Travel Options at Your Fingertips,* by Marianne Ferrari (Ferrari Publications; www. ferrariguides.com), is a very good gay and lesbian guidebook series.

WEBSITES

Ferrariguides.com (www.ferrari guides.com) is a comprehensive gay travel website that grew out of the Ferrari Guides, one of the world's oldest gay publishing companies. Buy books, find planning and booking information on a variety of tours, and learn of upcoming gay events.

SENIOR TRAVEL

Mention the fact that you're a senior citizen when you first make your travel reservations. All major airlines and many hotels offer discounts for seniors. Major airlines also offer coupons for domestic travel for seniors over 60. Typically, a book of four coupons costs less than $700, which means you can fly anywhere in the continental U.S. for under $350 round trip. In most cities, people over the age of 60 qualify for reduced admission to theaters, museums, and other attractions, as well as discounted fares on public transportation.

"Early bird" specials at restaurants are no longer as common as they used to be, but it doesn't hurt to ask for any "twilight" specials or something similar. Many restaurants do honor AARP and senior discounts, as do all the area's parks and attractions.

Members of **AARP** (formerly known as the American Association of Retired Persons), 601 E St. NW, Washington, DC 20049 (✆ **800/424-3410** or 202/434-2277; www. aarp.org), get discounts on hotels, airfares, and car rentals. AARP offers members a wide range of benefits, including *Modern Maturity* magazine and a monthly newsletter. Anyone over 50 can join.

The Alliance for Retired Americans, 8403 Colesville Rd., Suite 1200, Silver Spring, MD 20910 (✆ **301/578-8422;** www.retiredamericans.org), offers a newsletter six times a year and discounts on hotel and auto rentals; annual dues are $13 per person or couple. *Note:* Members of the former National Council of Senior Citizens receive automatic membership in the alliance.

AGENCIES/OPERATORS

- **Grand Circle Travel** (✆ **800/221-2610** or 617/350-7500; www. gct.com) offers package deals for the 50-plus market, mostly of the tour-bus variety, with free trips thrown in for those who organize groups of 10 or more.
- **Elderhostel** (✆ **877/426-8056;** www.elderhostel.org) arranges

study programs for those aged 55 and over (and a spouse or companion of any age) in the U.S. and in more than 80 countries around the world. Most courses last 5 to 7 days in the U.S. (2 to 4 weeks abroad), and many include airfare, accommodations in university dormitories or modest inns, meals, and tuition.

- **Interhostel** (© **800/733-9753;** www.learn.unh.edu/interhostel), organized by the University of New Hampshire, also offers educational travel for seniors. On these escorted tours, the days are packed with seminars, lectures, and field trips, with sightseeing led by academic experts. **Interhostel** takes travelers 50 and over (with companions over 40), and offers one- and two-week trips, mostly international.

PUBLICATIONS

- *The Book of Deals* is a collection of more than 1,000 senior discounts on airlines, lodging, tours, and attractions around the country; it's available for $9.95 by calling © **800/460-6676.**
- *101 Tips for the Mature Traveler* is available from Grand Circle Travel (© **800/221-2610** or 617/350-7500; fax 617/346-6700).
- *The 50+ Traveler's Guidebook* (St. Martin's Press).
- *Unbelievably Good Deals and Great Adventures That You Absolutely Can't Get Unless You're Over 50* (Contemporary Publishing Co.).

FAMILY TRAVEL

South Florida is chock-full of kid-friendly hotels, attractions, and restaurants. When visiting the Keys, be sure to check that the hotel or inn allows children, as many do not. Look for the icon throughout this book.

If your family would like to travel with Fido, call ahead to find out if a hotel will accept pets. An excellent resource is www.petswelcome.com, which dispenses medical tips, names of animal-friendly lodgings and campgrounds, and lists of kennels and veterinarians.

Make sure your pet is wearing a name tag with the name and phone number of a contact person who can take the call if your pet gets lost while you're away from home. Also, don't forget a leash, as many places allow pets, but only if they're on a leash.

AGENCIES/OPERATORS

Familyhostel (© **800/733-9753;** www.learn.unh.edu/familyhostel) takes the whole family on moderately priced domestic and international learning vacations. The program is for kids ages 8 to 15, accompanied by their parents and/or grandparents.

PUBLICATIONS

- *The Unofficial Guide to Florida with Kids*
- *The Unofficial Guide to Walt Disney World*
- *How to Take Great Trips with Your Kids* is full of good general advice that can apply to travel anywhere.

WEBSITES

- **Family Travel Network** (www.familytravelnetwork.com) offers travel tips and reviews of family-friendly destinations, vacation deals, as well as thoughtful features.
- **Travel with Your Children** (www.travelwithyourkids.com) is a comprehensive site offering sound advice for traveling with children.
- **The Busy Person's Guide to Travel with Children** (http://wz.com/travel/TravelingWithChildren.html) offers a "45-second newsletter" where experts weigh in on the best websites and resources for tips for traveling with children.

STUDENT TRAVEL

The **Council on International Educational Exchange**, or CIEE (www.ciee.org), has a travel branch, **Council**

Travel Service (② 800/226-8624; www.counciltravel.com), which is the biggest student travel agency in the world. **STA Travel** (② **800/781-4040;** www.statravel.com) is another travel agency catering especially to young travelers, although their bargain-basement prices are available to people of all ages.

In Canada, **Travel CUTS** (② **800/ 667-2887** or 416/614-2887; www. travelcuts.com) offers similar services. In London, **Campus Travel** (② **0171/ 730-3402**), opposite Victoria Station, is Britain's leading specialist in student and youth travel.

PUBLICATIONS
The Hanging Out Guides (www. frommers.com/hangingout/), published by Frommer's, are the top student-travel series for today's youth, covering everything from adrenaline sports to the hottest club and music scenes.

WOMEN TRAVELERS
Women are generally safe traveling alone in South Florida. However, when going out to the nightclubs and bars in South Beach, Fort Lauderdale, Key West, and other nightlife-heavy areas, it's best that you don't go alone. If you do, always keep an eye on your drink and avoid side streets and alleys at all costs.

AGENCIES/OPERATORS
- **Women Welcome Women World Wide (5W)** (② **203/259-7832** in the U.S.; www.womenwelcome women.org.uk) works to foster international friendships by enabling women of different countries to visit one another (men can come along on the trips; they just can't join the club). It's a big, active organization, with more than 3,000 members from all walks of life in some 70 countries.
- **The Women's Travel Club** (② **800/480-4448;** www.womens travelclub.com) was designed by a woman in search of female travel companions because her husband preferred work to travel. Now the group organizes 25 to 30 tours a year, with an emphasis on foreign culture, scenery, and safety.

PUBLICATIONS
- *Safety and Security for Women Who Travel,* by Sheila Swan Laufer and Peter Laufer (Travelers' Tales, Inc.), offers commonsense advice and tips on safe travel.

WEBSITES
- **Journeywoman** (www.journey woman.com) is a lively travel resource just for women.

6 Getting There

BY PLANE
Miami is one of **American Airlines'** (② 800/433-7300; www.aa.com) biggest hubs, and most major domestic airlines fly to and from many Florida cities, including **Continental** (② 800/ 525-0280; www.continental.com), **Delta** (② 800/221-1212; www.delta. com), **Northwest/KLM** (② 800/ 241-6522; www.nwa.com), **United** (② 800/241-6522; www.united.com), and **US Airways** (② 800/ 428-4322; www.usairways.com).

Several budget airlines also fly to South Florida, including **Southwest Airlines** (② 800/435-9792; www. southwest.com), **Air Tran** (② 800/ AIR-TRAN; www.airtran.com), **Spirit** (② 800/772-7117; www.spiritair. com), and **Jet Blue** (② 800/538-2583; www.jetblue.com).

If you're planning to visit Florida from another country, see chapter 3, "For International Visitors," for information on which international carriers serve the Miami area.

Tips   Fly for Less

When booking airfare to Miami, consider flying into the Fort Lauderdale Hollywood International Airport for considerably cheaper fares. The airport is only a half hour from downtown Miami.

NEW AIR TRAVEL SECURITY MEASURES

In the wake of the terrorist attacks of September 11, 2001, the airline industry began implementing sweeping security measures in airports. Expect a lengthy check-in process and extensive delays. Although regulations vary from airline to airline, you can expedite the process by taking the following steps:

- **Arrive early.** Arrive at the airport at least 2 hours before your scheduled flight.

- **Be sure to carry plenty of documentation.** A government-issued photo ID (federal, state, or local) is now required. You may need to show this at various checkpoints. With an E-ticket, you may be required to have with you printed confirmation of purchase, and perhaps even the credit card with which you bought your ticket. This varies from airline to airline, so call ahead to make sure you have the proper documentation. And be sure that your ID is **up-to-date:** An expired driver's license, for example, may keep you from boarding the plane altogether.

- **Know what you can carry on— and what you can't.** See the Tips box below.

- **Prepare to be searched.** Expect spot checks. Electronic items, such as a laptop or cell phone, should be readied for additional screening. Limit the metal items you wear on your person.

- **No ticket, no gate access.** Only ticketed passengers will be allowed beyond the screener checkpoints, except for those people with specific medical or parental needs.

FLYING FOR LESS: TIPS FOR GETTING THE BEST AIRFARE

Passengers within the same airplane cabin are rarely paying the same fare. Business travelers who need to purchase tickets at the last minute, change their itinerary at a moment's notice, or get home for the weekend pay the premium rate. Passengers who can book their ticket long in advance, who can stay over Saturday night, or who are willing to travel on a Tuesday, Wednesday, or Thursday after 7pm will pay a fraction of the full fare. Here are a few other easy ways to save:

- Airlines periodically lower prices on their most popular routes. Check the travel section of your Sunday newspaper for advertised discounts or call the airlines directly and ask if any **promotional rates** or special fares are available. If your schedule is flexible, say so, and ask if you can secure a cheaper fare by staying an extra day, by flying midweek, or by flying at less trafficked hours. If you already hold a ticket when a sale breaks, it may even pay to exchange your ticket, which usually incurs a charge.

  Note: The lowest-priced fares are often nonrefundable, require advance purchase of 1 to 3 weeks and a certain length of stay, and carry penalties for changing dates of travel.

- **Consolidators**, also known as bucket shops, are a good place to find low fares. Consolidators buy seats in bulk from the airlines and then sell them back to the public at prices usually below even the

> **Tips   What You Can Carry On—And What You Can't**
>
> The Transportation Security Administration (TSA), the government agency that now handles all aspects of airport security, has devised new restrictions for carry-on baggage, not only to expedite the screening process but also to prevent potential weapons from passing through airport security. Passengers are now limited to bringing just one carry-on bag and one personal item onto the aircraft (previous regulations allowed two carry-on bags and one personal item, like a briefcase or a purse). For more information, go to the TSA's website, www.tsa.gov. The agency has released an updated list of items passengers are not allowed to carry onto an aircraft:
>
> **Not permitted:** knives and box cutters, corkscrews, straight razors, metal scissors, golf clubs, baseball bats, pool cues, hockey sticks, ski poles, ice picks.
>
> **Permitted:** nail clippers, tweezers, eyelash curlers, safety razors (including disposable razors), syringes (with documented proof of medical need), walking canes, and umbrellas (must be inspected first).

airlines' discounted rates. Their small ads usually run in Sunday newspaper travel sections. And before you pay, request a confirmation number from the consolidator and then call the airline to confirm your seat. Be aware that bucket-shop tickets are usually nonrefundable or rigged with stiff cancellation penalties, often as high as 50% to 75% of the ticket price. Protect yourself by paying with a credit card rather than cash. Keep in mind that if there's an airline sale going on, or if it's high season, you can often get the same or better rates by contacting the airlines directly, so do some comparison shopping before you buy. Also, check out the name of the airline; you may not want to fly on some obscure Third World airline. And check whether you're flying on a charter or a scheduled airline; the latter is more expensive but more reliable.

Council Travel (© 800/226-8624; www.counciltravel.com)

and **STA Travel** (© 800/781-4040; www.statravel.com) cater especially to young travelers, but their bargain-basement prices are available to people of all ages. **The TravelHub** (© 888/AIR-FARE; www.travelhub.com) represents nearly 1,000 travel agencies, many of whom offer consolidator and discount fares. Other reliable consolidators include **1-800-FLY-CHEAP** (www.1800flycheap. com); **TFI Tours International** (© 800-745-8000 or 212/736-1140; www.lowestprice.com), which serves as a clearinghouse for unused seats; or "rebators" such as **Travel Avenue** (© 800/333-3335; www.travelavenue.com) and the **Smart Traveller** (© 800/448-3338 in the U.S. or 305/448-3338), which rebate part of their commissions to you.

• Search **the Internet** for cheap fares. Great last-minute deals are available through free weekly e-mail services provided directly by the airlines. See "Planning Your

---

⟨Tips⟩ Canceled Plans

If your flight is canceled, don't book a new fare at the ticket counter. Find the nearest phone and call the airline directly to reschedule. You'll be relaxing while other passengers are still standing.

Trip Online," below, for more information.

- Join a travel club such as **Moment's Notice** (① 718/234-6295; www.moments-notice.com) or **Sears Discount Travel Club** (① 800/433-9383, or 800/255-1487 to join; www.travelers advantage.com), which supply unsold tickets at discounted prices. You pay an annual membership fee to get the club's hotline number. Of course, you're limited to what's available, so you have to be flexible.

- Join **frequent-flier clubs.** It's best to accrue miles on one program, so you can rack up free flights and achieve elite status faster. But it makes sense to open as many accounts as possible, no matter how seldom you fly a particular airline. It's free, and you'll get the best choice of seats, faster response to phone inquiries, and prompter service if your luggage is stolen, your flight is canceled or delayed, or if you want to change your seat.

BY CAR

Although four major roads run to and through Miami—I-95, S.R. 826, S.R. 836, and U.S. 1—chances are you'll reach Miami and the rest of South Florida by way of I-95. This north-south interstate is South Florida's lifeline and an integral part of the region. The highway connects all of Miami's different neighborhoods, the airport, the beaches, and all of South Florida to the rest of the country. Miami's road signs are notoriously confusing and notably absent when you most need them. Think twice before you exit from the highway if you aren't

sure where you're going: Some exits lead to unsavory neighborhoods.

Other highways that will get you to Florida include I-10, which originates in Los Angeles and terminates at the tip of Florida in Jacksonville, and I-75, which begins in North Michigan and runs through the center of the state to Florida's west coast.

Florida law allows drivers to make a right turn on a red light after a complete stop, unless otherwise indicated. In addition, all passengers are required to wear seat belts, and children under 3 must be securely fastened in government-approved car seats.

If you plan to be in your car quite a bit during your visit, you may want to join the **American Automobile Association (AAA)** (① 800/596-2227; www.aaa.com), which has hundreds of offices nationwide. Members receive excellent maps, emergency road service, and, upon request, planned, detailed itineraries.

For information on car-rental companies with offices in South Florida, see "Getting Around" in chapter 4, "Getting to Know Miami."

Saving Money on a Rental Car Car-rental rates vary even more than airline fares. The price you pay will depend on the size of the car, where and when you pick it up and drop it off, the length of the rental period, where and how far you drive it, whether you purchase insurance, and a host of other factors. A few key questions could save you hundreds of dollars:

- Are weekend rates lower than weekday rates? Ask if the rate is the same for pickup Friday morning, for instance, as it is for Thursday night.

- Is a weekly rate cheaper than the daily rate? Even if you only need the car for 4 days, it may be cheaper to keep it for 5.
- Does the agency assess a drop-off charge if you don't return the car to the same location where you picked it up? Is it cheaper to pick up the car at the airport compared to a downtown location?
- Are special promotional rates available? If you see an advertised price in your local newspaper, be sure to ask for that specific rate; otherwise you may be charged the standard cost.
- Are discounts available for members of AARP, AAA, frequent-flier programs, or trade unions?
- How much tax will be added to the rental bill? Local tax? State tax?
- What is the cost of adding an additional driver's name to the contract?
- How many free miles are included in the price? Free mileage is often negotiable, depending on the length of your rental.
- How much does the rental company charge to refill your gas tank if you return with the tank less

than full? Fuel is almost always cheaper in town; try to allow enough time to refuel the car yourself before returning it.

For information on car renter's insurance, please see section 4, earlier in this chapter.

Many packages are available that include airfare, accommodations, and a rental car with unlimited mileage. Compare these prices with the cost of booking airline tickets and renting a car separately to see if these offers are good deals.

Arranging Car Rentals on the Web
Internet resources can make comparison shopping easier. **Expedia.com** (www.expedia.com) and **Travelocity** (www.travelocity.com) help you compare prices and locate car-rental bargains from various companies nationwide. They will even make your reservation for you once you've found the best deal.

BY TRAIN

Amtrak (© **800/USA-RAIL;** www.amtrak.com) is an option if you don't want to fly or drive down to South Florida. Two trains leave daily from New York. They both take from 26½ to 29 hours to complete the entire journey to Miami.

7 Packaged Deals

Before you start your search for the lowest airfare, you may want to consider booking your flight as part of a package tour. What you lose in adventure, you'll gain in time and money saved when you book accommodations, and maybe even food and entertainment, along with your flight.

PACKAGE TOURS FOR INDEPENDENT TRAVELERS

Package tours are not the same thing as escorted tours. With a package tour, you travel independently but pay a group rate. Packages usually include airfare, a choice of hotels, and car

rental. In many cases, a package that includes airfare, hotel, and transportation to and from the airport will cost you less than just the hotel alone would have, had you booked it yourself. That's because packages are sold in bulk to tour operators—who resell them to the public at a cost that drastically undercuts standard rates.

RECOMMENDED PACKAGE TOUR OPERATORS

One good source of package deals is the airlines themselves. Most major airlines offer air/land packages, including **American Airlines Vacations**

(✆ 800/321-2121; http://aav1.aavacations.com), **Delta Vacations** (✆ 800/221-6666; www.deltavacations.com), **US Airways Vacations** (✆ 800/455-0123 or 800/422-3861; www.usairwaysvacations.com), **Continental Airlines Vacations** (✆ 800/301-3800; www.coolvacations.com), and **United Vacations** (✆ 888/854-3899; www.unitedvacations.com/)

Online Vacation Mall (✆ **800/839-9851;** www.onlinevacationmall.com) allows you to search for and book packages offered by a number of tour operators and airlines. The **United States Tour Operators Association's** website (www.ustoa.com) has a search engine that allows you to look for operators that offer packages to a specific destination. Travel packages are also listed in the travel section of your local Sunday newspaper. **Liberty Travel** (✆ **888/271-1584**; www.libertytravel.com), one of the biggest packagers in the Northeast, often runs full-page ads in Sunday papers. Or check ads in the national travel magazines such as *Arthur Frommer's Budget Travel Magazine, Travel & Leisure, National Geographic Traveler,* and *Condé Nast Traveler.*

For information on package tours to South Florida, consult the following companies: **CWS Tours & Transportation** (✆ **407/448-3969;** www.cwstours.com/sfltour.htm), **Eyre Tour and Travel** (✆ **800/321-EYRE;** www.eyre.com), **Miami City Web** (✆ **888/MIAMI-MALL** or 305/715-9080; www.miamicity.net).

THE PROS & CONS OF PACKAGE TOURS

Packages can save you money by offering group prices for independent travelers. The disadvantages are that you're usually required to make a large payment upfront; you may end up on a charter flight; and you have to deal with your own luggage and with transfers between your hotel and the airport, if transfers are not included in the package price. Packages often don't allow for complete flexibility or a wide range of choices. For instance, you may prefer a quiet inn but have to settle for a popular chain hotel instead. Your choice of travel days may be limited as well.

QUESTIONS TO ASK IF YOU BOOK A PACKAGE TOUR

- What are the **accommodation choices** available and are there price differences?
- What **type of room** will you be staying in? Request whatever you fancy.
- Look for **hidden expenses.** Ask whether airport departure fees and taxes are included in the total cost.

8 Planning Your Trip Online

Researching and booking your trip online can save time and money. Then again, it may not. It is simply not true that you always get the best deal online. Most booking engines do not include schedules and prices for budget airlines, and from time to time you'll get a better last-minute price by calling the airline directly, so it's best to call the airline to see if you can do better before booking online.

On the plus side, Internet users today can tap into the same travel-planning databases that were once accessible only to travel agents—and do it at the same speed. Sites such as **Frommers.com, Travelocity, Expedia.com,** and **Orbitz** allow consumers to comparison shop for airfares, access special bargains, book flights, and reserve hotel rooms and rental cars.

Although online booking sites offer tips and hard data to help you bargain shop, they cannot endow you with the hard-earned experience that makes a seasoned, reliable travel agent an invaluable resource, even in the Internet age. And for consumers with a complex itinerary, a trusty travel agent is still the best way to arrange the most direct flights to and from the best airports.

Still, there's no denying the Internet's emergence as a powerful tool in researching and plotting travel time. The benefits of researching your trip online can be well worth the effort.

Last-minute specials, such as weekend deals or Internet-only fares, are offered by airlines to fill empty seats. Most of these are announced on Tuesday or Wednesday and must be purchased online. They are only valid for travel that weekend, but some can be booked weeks or months in advance. Sign up for weekly e-mail alerts at airline websites or check megasites that compile comprehensive lists of last-minute specials, such as **Smarter Living** (smarterliving.com) or **WebFlyer** (www.webflyer.com).

Some sites, such as Expedia.com, will send you **e-mail notification** when a cheap fare becomes available to your favorite destination. Some will also tell you when fares to a particular destination are lowest.

TRAVEL PLANNING & BOOKING SITES

Keep in mind that because several airlines are no longer willing to pay commissions on tickets sold by online travel agencies, these agencies may either add a $10 surcharge to your bill if you book on that carrier—or neglect to offer those carriers' schedules.

The list of sites below is selective, not comprehensive. Some sites will have evolved or disappeared by the time you read this.

- **Travelocity** (www.travelocity.com or www.frommers.travelocity.com) and **Expedia** (www.expedia.com) are among the most popular sites, each offering an excellent range of options. Travelers search by destination, dates, and cost.
- **Orbitz** (www.orbitz.com) is a popular site launched by United, Delta, Northwest, American, and Continental airlines. (Stay tuned: At press time, travel-agency associations were waging an antitrust battle against this site.)
- **Qixo** (www.qixo.com) is another powerful search engine that allows you to search for flights and accommodations from some 20 airline and travel-planning sites (such as Travelocity) at once. Qixo sorts results by price.
- **Priceline** (www.priceline.com) lets you "name your price" for airline tickets, hotel rooms, and rental cars. For airline tickets, you can't say what time you want to fly—you have to accept any flight between 6am and 10pm on the dates you've selected, and you may have to make one or more stopovers. Tickets are nonrefundable, and no frequent-flyer miles are awarded.

SMART E-SHOPPING

The savvy traveler is armed with insider information. Here are a few tips to help you navigate the Internet successfully and safely.

- **Know when sales start.** Last-minute deals may vanish in minutes. If you have a favorite booking site or airline, find out when last-minute deals are released to the public.
- **Shop around.** If you're looking for bargains, compare prices on different sites and airlines—and against a travel agent's best fare. Try a range of times and alternative airports before you make a purchase.

- **Avoid online auctions.** Sites that auction airline tickets and frequent-flier miles are the number one perpetrators of Internet fraud, according to the National Consumers League.
- **Maintain a paper trail.** If you book an E-ticket, print out a confirmation, or write down your confirmation number, and keep it safe and accessible—or your trip could be a virtual one!

ONLINE TRAVELER'S TOOLBOX

Following are some online tools to bookmark and use.

- **Visa ATM Locator** (www.visa.com), for locations of Plus ATMs worldwide, or **MasterCard ATM Locator** (www.mastercard.com), for locations of Cirrus ATMs worldwide.
- **Mapquest** (www.mapquest.com). This best of the mapping sites lets you choose a specific address or destination, and in seconds it will return a map and detailed directions.
- **Cybercafes.com** (www.cybercafes.com) or **Net Café Guide** (www.netcafeguide.com/map index.htm). Locate Internet cafes at hundreds of locations around the globe. Catch up on your e-mail and log onto the Web for a few dollars per hour.

9 Tips on Accommodations

Although South Florida is a resort destination, the focus as far as accommodations are concerned ironically has moved away from resort hotels and toward smaller boutique hotels. This applies especially on South Beach, where the hip factor plays as much a role as beach access. Dilapidated Art Deco hotels are now hot spots that can be seen in the pages of magazines such as *In Style*. If boutique hotels don't appeal to you, fret not, as there are several resorts—you just have to look a bit harder these days. The major chains—Loew's, Marriott, Sheraton, Ritz-Carlton, Wyndham, and Hyatt, among others—appeal more to those with families or couples looking for a resort vacation. They can be found everywhere from the Keys to Hutchinson Island.

TIPS FOR SAVING ON YOUR HOTEL ROOM

The **rack rate** is the maximum rate that a hotel charges for a room. It's the rate you'd get if you walked in off the street and asked for a room for the night. Hardly anybody pays these prices, however, and there are many ways around them.

- **Don't be afraid to bargain.** Most rack rates include commissions of 10% to 25% for travel agents, which some hotels may be willing to reduce if you make your own reservations and haggle a bit. Always ask whether a room less expensive than the first one quoted is available, or whether any special rates apply to you. You may qualify for corporate, student, military, senior, or other discounts. Be sure to mention membership in AAA, AARP, frequent-flier programs, or trade unions, which may entitle you to special deals as well. Find out the hotel policy on children—do kids stay free in the room, or is there a special rate?
- **Rely on a qualified professional.** Certain hotels give travel agents discounts in exchange for steering business their way, so if you're shy about bargaining, an agent may be better equipped to negotiate discounts for you.

- **Dial direct.** When booking a room in a chain hotel, compare the rates offered by the hotel's local line with that of the toll-free number. Also check with an agent and online. A hotel makes nothing on a room that stays empty, so the local hotel reservation desk may be willing to offer a special rate unavailable elsewhere.

- **Remember the law of supply and demand.** Resort hotels are most crowded and therefore most expensive on weekends, so discounts are usually available for midweek stays. Business hotels in downtown locations are busiest during the week, so you can expect big discounts over the weekend. Avoid high-season stays whenever you can: Planning your vacation just a week before or after official peak season can mean big savings.

- **Look into long-stay discounts**. If you're planning a long stay (at least five days), you might qualify for a discount. As a general rule, expect 1 night free after a 7-night stay.

- **Avoid excess charges.** When you book a room, ask whether the hotel charges for parking. Find out whether your hotel imposes a surcharge on local and long-distance calls. Ask about local taxes and service charges, which could increase the cost of a room by 25% or more. Always ask what's included in the price of a room— a so-called moderate hotel that charges for beach towels and chairs may cost a lot more than a so-called expensive hotel that includes extras in the price. And finally, be sure to ask if your hotel gives free transfers from the airport and if kids stay free.

- **Watch for coupons and advertised discounts.** Scan ads in your local Sunday newspaper travel section, an excellent source for up-to-the-minute hotel deals.

- **Consider a suite or efficiency.** If you are traveling with your family or another couple, you can pack more people into a suite (which usually comes with a sofa bed), and thereby reduce your per-person rate. Remember that some places charge for extra guests. A room with a kitchenette allows you to shop for groceries and cook your own meals. This is a big moneysaver, especially for families on long stays.

- Join hotel **frequent-visitor clubs,** even if you don't use them much. You'll be more likely to get upgrades and other perks.

- **Investigate reservations services.** These outfits usually work as consolidators, buying up or reserving rooms in bulk, and then dealing them out to customers at a profit. You can get 10% to 50% off; but remember, these discounts apply to inflated rack rates that savvy travelers rarely end up paying. You may get a decent rate, but always call the hotel as well to see if you can do better.

Among the more reputable reservations services, offering both telephone and online bookings, are **Accommodations Express** (© 800/950-4685; www.accommodationsexpress.com); **Hotel Reservations Network** (© 800/715-7666; www.hoteldiscounts.com or www.180096HOTEL.com); **Quikbook** (© 800/789-9887, includes fax on demand service; www.quikbook.com). For bed-and-breakfast information throughout the state, contact **Florida Bed and Breakfast Inns** (© 800/524-1880; www.florida-inns.com). Online, try booking your hotel through **Frommers.com** (www.frommers.com). **Microsoft Expedia** (www.expedia.com) features a "Travel Agent" that will also direct you to affordable lodgings.

For short-term condo and vacation house rentals, www.A1vacations.com, cyberrentals.com, and www.leisure-linkintl.com are websites that will provide you with a selection of condos and resorts throughout South Florida.

LANDING THE BEST ROOM

Somebody has to get the best room in the house. It might as well be you.

Always ask about a corner room. They're often larger and quieter, with more windows and light, and they often cost the same as standard rooms.

When you make your reservation, ask if the hotel is renovating; if it is, request a room away from the construction. Ask about nonsmoking rooms, rooms with views, rooms with twin, queen- or king-size beds. If you're a light sleeper, request a quiet room away from vending machines, elevators, restaurants, bars, and discos. Ask for one of the rooms that have been most recently renovated or redecorated. If you aren't happy with your room when you arrive, talk to the front desk.

In resort areas, particularly in warm climates, there are some other questions to ask before you book a room:

- What's the view like? Cost-conscious travelers may be willing to pay less for a back room facing the parking lot, especially if they don't plan to spend much time in their room.
- Does the room have air conditioning or just ceiling fans?
- Do the windows open?
- What is the noise level outside the room? If the climate is warm and nighttime entertainment takes place alfresco, you may want to find out when show time is over.
- Is the hotel pool fresh or saltwater? Is it heated?
- Are airport transfers included in the price?
- If it's off-season, will any facilities be shut down while you're there?
- What programs are available for kids?
- How far is the room from the beach?
- What is the dining plan? You don't want to pay for three meals if you plan to eat out a lot.
- What is the cancellation policy?

10 Tips on Dining

In many restaurants and cafes on South Beach, in particular, a 15% gratuity is automatically added to your bill. This tip can be raised *or lowered* at your discretion. Always be sure to look carefully at your bill to make sure you don't overtip.

Dining in South Florida is no longer just an early bird's paradise. Thanks to Latin and European influences, there are now restaurants in which you can have your dinner at, say, 2am, if that's what appeals to you. Still hot in South Florida is fusion, eclectic, and the South Florida–born New World cuisine.

As far as dress is concerned, it all depends on where you eat. Even in fancy restaurants in the Keys, for instance, shorts and T-shirts are usually acceptable and commonplace. On South Beach, things tend to get a bit dressier, though jackets are never required and black is always the safest bet. Up in Fort Lauderdale, dress code ranges from beachy casual to South Beach hip. If you have a hankering for jacket-required restaurants, head to Palm Beach. The Treasure Coast is pretty casual, as well.

11 Suggested Itineraries

Key West to Miami (or Vice Versa)
Despite the fact that the only way to get to Key West via car is a one-lane road, it's a beautiful 3½ hour drive that's typically only marred by traffic on weekends and holidays. Depending on your level of interest, 3 days in Key West is more than enough. The combo of the laid-back Conch Republic and cosmopolitan-chic Miami is best described as a little bit country and a little bit rock 'n' roll.

Miami & the Everglades From high-tech, high-style, and high-energy Miami back to the basics of the natural resources of the Florida Everglades, this combo is a reality check, one that many people find necessary to fully appreciate the fact that Florida is not all prefab pink flamingoes and neon.

South Beach & Fort Lauderdale If beachcombing and club hopping are on your list of things to do, the best cocktail that's guaranteed to both shake and stir is 2 days on South Beach—day and night—and 2 more in Fort Lauderdale. While South Beach is the kind of place where you can stay up all night and sleep it off on the beach the next day, Fort Lauderdale exudes a calmer, yet no less lively, kind of beached excitement.

Boca Raton & Palm Beach The country-club lifestyle is alive and well in these parts of South Florida, where days are spent on the golf course or shopping at Mizner Park or Worth Avenue, and evenings are spent in an elegant restaurant, all before the clock strikes midnight.

Jupiter & Hutchinson Island After you pass Palm Beach's stately mansions and Bentleys, you will enter a no-flash zone, one in which Old Florida is alive and well, regardless of whether the money's new, old, or barely there. Here you'll find relaxing waterfront restaurants, boating, and friendly folks who don't take the term "gone fishin'" lightly.

12 Recommended Reading

FICTION

- *The Perez Family* by Christine Bell—Cuban immigrants from the Mariel Boat Lift exchange their talents for an immigration deal in Miami.
- *Miami, It's Murder* by Edna Buchannan—Miami's Agatha Christie keeps you in suspense with her reporter protagonist and her life as an investigative crime solver in Miami.
- *To Have and Have Not* by Ernest Hemingway—One of the many must-reads by Key West's most famous resident.
- *Naked Came the Manatee* by Carl Hiassen—Thirteen *Miami Herald* writers contributed to this hilarious story about the discovery of Castro's head.
- *Killing Mister Watson* by Peter Matthiessen—A fascinating story about the settlement of the Everglades and the problems that ensued.

NONFICTION

- *Miami* by Joan Didion—An intriguing compilation of impressions of the Magic City.
- *Miami, the Magic City* by Arva Moore Parks—An authoritative history of the city.
- *The Everglades: River of Grass* by Marjory Stoneman Douglas—Eco-maniacs will love this personal account of the treasures of Florida's most famous natural resource.

13 The Top Websites for Miami & South Florida

GENERAL SOUTH FLORIDA SITES

- For entertainment, dining, sports, and festival information produced in cooperation with the *Sun-Sentinel:* **southflorida.digital city.com**.
- The site of Florida's official tourism bureau, this extensive website includes information on attractions, beaches, golfing, and water sports, as well as airport information, weather, and maps: **www.flausa.com**.
- This site links to more than a dozen convention bureaus throughout the state. Most of the sites include information on attractions, dining, lodging, and shopping: **www.facvb.org**.
- Detailed information on state parks, right down to what kind of wildlife hangs out where, and the lowdown on fees, attractions, and facilities: **www.dep.state.fl.us/ parks**.
- A nicely organized guide to theme parks, marine attractions, museums, boating, fishing, and much more, as well as advice for first-time visitors to the Sunshine State: **www.see-florida.com**.

CITY GUIDES, DINING & ENTERTAINMENT SITES

- A collection of websites regarding Miami, all with links to other relevant websites: **gomiami. about.com**.
- For listings and reviews for Miami arts and entertainment events, restaurants, shopping, and attractions: **miami.citysearch.com**.
- A well-rounded guide to Key West, including an events calendar and extensive listings for attractions, sightseeing and eco-tours, theater, art galleries, dining, lodging, fishing, and shopping: **key-west.com**.
- A guide to gay-friendly Key West: **www.gaykeywestfl.com**.
- Featuring local news and up-to-date information on events and entertainment options from the *Miami Herald:* **www.miami.com**.
- This site offers reviews and listings for attractions, entertainment, restaurants, hotels, and shopping, and includes categories for kids, and gays and lesbians. Unlike some other city guides, Time Out: Miami makes a concerted effort to cater to tourists as well as locals: **www.timeout.com/miami**.
- Miami's leading alternative weekly includes features and listings for music, theater, film, and more: **www.miaminewtimes.com**.
- Here's a nice roundup of music, theater, sports, and dining choices in South Florida: **www.sun-sentinel.com/showtime**.
- Listings and reviews for Miami. Each restaurant has a capsule review and ratings based on surveys received from site users. For many restaurants, only two or three people have bothered to submit ratings, so they may not be statistically significant. However, comments can be instructive, as CuisineNet's readers discuss service, parking, free birthday desserts, and a host of other insightful topics: **www.cuisine net.com**.
- Reviewing top restaurants, Zagat has made a name for itself as the people's choice, as its listings are based on extensive surveys: **www. zagat.com**.

FAST FACTS: South Florida

American Express You'll find American Express offices in downtown Miami at 330 Biscayne Blvd. (℃ **305/358-7350**); 9700 Collins Ave., Bal Harbour (℃ **305/865-5959**); and 32 Miracle Mile, Coral Gables (℃ **305/446-3381**). Offices are open weekdays from 9am to 5pm and Saturday from 10am to 4pm. The Bal Harbour office is also open on Sunday from noon to 6pm. To report lost or stolen traveler's checks, call ℃ **800/221-7282.** Other South Florida American Express offices include 2451 E. Atlantic Blvd., Pompano Beach, (℃ **954/952-2300**) and 3312 NE 32nd St., Fort Lauderdale, (℃ **954/565-9481**).

Area Codes The original area code for Miami and all of Dade County was 305. That is still the code for older phone numbers, but all phone numbers assigned since July 1998 have the area code 786 (SUN). For all local calls, even if you're calling across the street, you must dial the area code (305 or 786) first. Even though the Keys still share the Dade County area code of 305, calls to there from Miami are considered long distance and must be preceded by 1-305. (Within the Keys, simply dial the seven-digit number.) The area code for Fort Lauderdale is 954; for Palm Beach, Boca Raton, Vero Beach, and Port St. Lucie, it's 561.

ATM Networks ATMs are as ubiquitous in South Florida as the palm trees. Machines are found on nearly every street corner, main shopping area and, in most cases, supermarkets and even in convenience stores.

Business Hours Banking hours vary, but most banks are open weekdays from 9am to 3pm. Several stay open until 5pm or so at least 1 day during the week, and many banks feature ATMs for 24-hour banking. Most stores are open daily from 10am to 6pm; however, there are many exceptions. In Miami, shops in the Bayside Marketplace are usually open until 9 or 10pm, as are the boutiques in Coconut Grove. Boutiques on South Beach operate on their own time zone and range from 11 am-midnight, sometimes earlier, sometimes later. Stores in Bal Harbour and other malls are usually open an extra hour 1 night during the week (usually Thursday). As far as business offices are concerned, Miami is generally a 9-to-5 town. In the Keys, hours are much more leisurely, and often left at the discretion of the proprietors. Call ahead before you go. In Key West, however, hours are similar to those in South Beach. Things are open rather late there. In Fort Lauderdale, hours are typically 9-to-5 for businesses, but on the "Strip" (Las Olas Boulevard and downtown Fort Lauderdale), shops, restaurants, and clubs tend to stay open into the wee hours, or at least after midnight. Boca Raton, Palm Beach, and the Treasure Coast are entirely different and tend to keep earlier hours, with stores closing between 5 and 6pm and restaurants closing around 11pm, with the exception of those stores and restaurants on Clematis Street.

Car Rentals See "Getting There," section 6 in this chapter.

Climate See "When to Go," section 3 in this chapter.

Emergencies To reach the police, ambulance, or fire department, dial ℃ **911** from any phone. No coins are needed. Emergency hotlines include **Crisis Intervention** (℃ **305/358-HELP** or 305/358-4357) and the **Poison**

Information Center ((C) 800/282-3171). For crisis emergencies in Broward County, call First Call for Help ((C) 954/467-6333), and in Palm Beach, call Crisis Line ((C) 561/930-1234).

Liquor Laws Only adults 21 or older may legally purchase or consume alcohol in the state of Florida. Minors are usually permitted in bars that also serve food. Liquor laws are strictly enforced; if you look young, carry identification. Beer and wine are sold in most supermarkets and convenience stores. Most liquor stores throughout South Florida are closed on Sundays, but liquor stores in the city of Miami Beach are open all week.

Newspapers & Magazines The *Miami Herald* is Miami's only English-language daily. It is especially known for its extensive Latin American coverage and has a decent Friday "Weekend" entertainment guide. It also publishes a Broward County edition for the Fort Lauderdale area. Fort Lauderdale's major daily is the *Sun-Sentinel,* while Palm Beach has the *Post*. The most respected alternative weekly in South Florida is the give-away tabloid called *New Times,* which contains up-to-date listings and reviews of food, films, theater, music, and whatever else is happening in town. There are Miami as well as Broward/Palm Beach editions. Also free, if you can find it, is *Ocean Drive,* an oversized glossy magazine that's limited on text and heavy on ads and society photos; it's available at a number of chic South Beach, Fort Lauderdale, and Palm Beach boutiques, hotels, and restaurants. It is also available on newsstands.

Police For emergencies, dial (C) 911 from any phone. No coins are needed. For other matters, call (C) 305/595-6263. The Broward County Sheriff's Office number is ((C) 954/831-8900); the Palm Beach County Sheriff's Office number is ((C) 561/470-5257).

Taxes A 6% state sales tax (plus 0.5% local tax, for a total of 6.5% in Miami) is added on at the register for all goods and services purchased in Florida. In addition, most municipalities levy special taxes on restaurants and hotels. In Surfside, hotel taxes total 10.5%; in Bal Harbour, 9.5%; in Miami Beach (including South Beach), 11.5%; and in the rest of Dade County, a whopping 12.5%. In Miami Beach, Surfside, and Bal Harbour, the resort (hotel) tax also applies to hotel restaurants and restaurants with liquor licenses. Broward and Palm Beach County sales tax is 6.5%. Resort taxes in Palm Beach are 4%, while Broward County only charges a 5% tax for conventions, not tourists.

Time Zone Florida, like New York, is in the Eastern Standard Time zone. Between April and October, daylight saving time is adopted, and clocks are set 1 hour ahead. America's eastern seaboard is 5 hours behind Greenwich Mean Time. To find out what time it is, call (C) 305/324-8811.

Weather Hurricane season runs from August through November. For an up-to-date recording of current weather conditions and forecast reports, call (C) 305/229-4522.

3

For International Visitors

Whether it's your first visit or your tenth, a trip to the United States may require an additional degree of planning. This chapter will provide you with essential information, helpful tips, and advice for the more common problems that some visitors encounter.

1 Preparing for Your Trip

ENTRY REQUIREMENTS

Immigration laws are a hot political issue in the United States these days, and the following requirements may have changed somewhat by the time you plan your trip. Check at any U.S. embassy or consulate for current information and requirements. You can also plug into the **U.S. State Department's** Internet site at **http://state.gov**.

VISAS The U.S. State Department has a **Visa Waiver Program** allowing citizens of certain countries to enter the United States without a visa for stays of up to 90 days. At press time these included Andorra, Australia, Austria, Belgium, Brunei, Denmark, Finland, France, Germany, Iceland, Ireland, Italy, Japan, Liechtenstein, Luxembourg, Monaco, the Netherlands, New Zealand, Norway, Portugal, San Marino, Singapore, Slovenia, Spain, Sweden, Switzerland, the United Kingdom, and Uruguay. Citizens of these countries need only a valid passport and a round-trip air or cruise ticket in their possession upon arrival. If they first enter the United States, they may also visit Mexico, Canada, Bermuda, and/or the Caribbean islands and return to the United States without a visa. Canadian citizens may enter the United States without visas; they need only proof of residence.

Citizens of all other countries must have (1) a valid passport that expires at least 6 months later than the scheduled end of their visit to the United States, and (2) a tourist visa, which may be obtained from any U.S. consulate.

To obtain a visa, the traveler must submit a completed application form (either in person or by mail) with a 1½-inch-square photo, and must demonstrate binding ties to a residence abroad. If you cannot go in person, contact the nearest U.S. embassy or consulate for directions on applying by mail. Your travel agent or airline office may also be able to provide you with visa applications and instructions. The U.S. consulate or embassy that issues your visa will determine whether you will be issued a multiple- or single-entry visa and any restrictions regarding the length of your stay.

British subjects can obtain up-to-date passport and visa information by calling the **U.S. Embassy Visa Information Line** (© 0891/200-290) or the **London Passport Office** (© 0990/210-410 for recorded information), or they can find the visa information on the U.S. Embassy Great Britain website (**www.usembassy.org.uk/cons_web/visa/visaindex.htm**).

Irish citizens can obtain up-to-date passport and visa information through the **Embassy of USA Dublin,** 42 Elgin Rd., Dublin 4, Ireland (℅ **353/1-668-8777;** or checking the visa website at **www.usembassy.ie/consulate/applications.html**).

Australian citizens can obtain up-to-date passport and visa information by calling the **U.S. Embassy Canberra,** Moonah Place, Yarralumla, ACT 2600 (℅ **02/6214-5600**) or check the website's visa page (**www.usis-australia.gov/consular/niv.html**).

Citizens of **New Zealand** can obtain up-to-date passport and visa information by calling the **U.S. Embassy New Zealand,** 29 Fitzherbert Terr., Thorndon, Wellington, New Zealand (℅ **644/472-2068**) or get the information directly from the website (**http://usembassy.org.nz**).

MEDICAL   REQUIREMENTS

Unless you're arriving from an area known to be suffering from an **epidemic** (particularly cholera or yellow fever), inoculations or vaccinations are not required for entry into the United States. If you have a medical condition that requires **syringe-administered medications,** carry a valid signed prescription from your physician—the Federal Aviation Administration (FAA) no longer allows airline passengers to pack syringes in their carry-on baggage without documented proof of medical need. If you have a disease that requires treatment with **narcotics,** you should also carry documented proof with you—smuggling narcotics aboard a plane is a serious offense that carries severe penalties in the U.S.

For **HIV-positive visitors,** requirements for entering the United States are somewhat vague and change frequently. According to the latest publication of *HIV and Immigrants: A Manual for AIDS Service Providers,* the Immigration and Naturalization Service (INS) doesn't require a medical exam for entry into the United States, but INS officials may stop individuals because they look sick or because they are carrying AIDS/HIV medicine.

DRIVER'S   LICENSES Foreign driver's licenses are mostly recognized in the U.S., although you may want to get an international driver's license if your home license is not written in English.

PASSPORT INFORMATION

Safeguard your passport in an inconspicuous, inaccessible place like a money belt. Make a copy of the critical pages, including the passport number, and store it in a safe place, separate from the passport itself. If you lose your passport, visit the nearest consulate of your native country as soon as possible for a replacement. Passport applications are downloadable from the Internet sites listed below.

FOR RESIDENTS OF CANADA

You can pick up a passport application at one of 28 regional passport offices or most travel agencies. As of December 11, 2001, Canadian children who travel will need their own passport. However, if you hold a valid Canadian passport issued before December 11, 2001, that bears the name of your child, the passport remains valid for you and your child until it expires. Passports cost C$85 for those 16 years and older (valid 5 years), C$35 children 3 to 15 (valid 5 years), and C$20, children under 3 (valid for 3 years). Applications, which must be accompanied by two identical passport-sized photographs and proof of Canadian citizenship, are available at travel agencies throughout Canada or from the central **Passport Office, Department of Foreign Affairs and International Trade**, Ottawa, ON K1A 0G3 (℅ **800/567-6868;**

www.dfait-maeci.gc.ca/passport). Processing takes 5 to 10 days if you apply in person, or about 3 weeks by mail.

FOR RESIDENTS OF THE UNITED KINGDOM

To pick up an application for a regular 10-year passport (the Visitor's Passport has been abolished), visit your nearest passport office, major post office, or travel agency. You can also contact the **London Passport Office** at ℂ **0171/ 271-3000** or search its website at **www.ukpa.gov.uk.** Passports are £21 for adults and £11 for children under 16.

FOR RESIDENTS OF IRELAND

You can apply for a 10-year passport, costing 57€, at the **Passport Office,** Setanta Centre, Molesworth Street, Dublin 2 (ℂ **01/671-1633;** www.irl gov.ie/iveagh). Those under age 18 and over 65 must apply for a 12€ 3-year passport. You can also apply at 1A South Mall, Cork (ℂ **021/272- 525**) or over the counter at most main post offices.

FOR RESIDENTS OF AUSTRALIA

Apply at your local post office or passport office, or search the government website at **www.dfat.gov.au/ passports/.** Passports for adults are A$126 and for those under 18 are A$63.

FOR RESIDENTS OF NEW ZEALAND

You can pick up a passport application at any travel agency or Link Centre. For more info, contact the **Passport Office,** P.O. Box 805, Wellington (ℂ **0800/225-050**). Passports for adults are NZ$80 and for those under 16, they're NZ$40.

CUSTOMS
WHAT YOU CAN BRING IN

Every visitor more than 21 years of age may bring in, free of duty, the following: (1) 1 liter of wine or hard liquor; (2) 200 cigarettes, 100 cigars (but not from Cuba), or 3 pounds of smoking tobacco; and (3) $100 worth of gifts. These exemptions are offered to travelers who spend at least 72 hours in the United States and who have not claimed them within the preceding 6 months. It is altogether forbidden to bring into the country foodstuffs (particularly fruit, cooked meats, and canned goods) and plants (vegetables, seeds, tropical plants, and the like). For more specific information regarding U.S. Customs, call your nearest U.S. embassy or consulate, or the **U.S. Customs** office at ℂ **202/ 927-1770** or look up www.customs. ustreas.gov on the Internet.

WHAT YOU CAN TAKE HOME

U.K. citizens returning from a non- EC country have a customs allowance of: 200 cigarettes; 50 cigars; 250 grams of smoking tobacco; 2 liters of still table wine; 1 liter of spirits or strong liqueurs (over 22% volume); 2 liters of fortified wine, sparkling wine or other liqueurs; 60cc (ml) perfume; 250cc (ml) of toilet water; and £145 worth of all other goods, including gifts and souvenirs. People under 17 cannot have the tobacco or alcohol allowance. For more information, contact HM Customs & Excise, Passenger Enquiry Point, 2nd Floor Wayfarer House, Great South West Road, Feltham, Middlesex, TW14 8NP (ℂ **0181/910-3744;** from outside the U.K. 44/181-910-3744), or consult their website at www.open.gov.uk.

For a clear summary of **Canadian** rules, write for the booklet *I Declare,* issued by **Revenue Canada**, 2265 St. Laurent Blvd., Ottawa, ON K1G 4K3 (ℂ **506/636-5064**). Canada allows its citizens a C$750 exemption, and you're allowed to bring back duty-free 1 carton of cigarettes, 1 can of tobacco, 40 imperial ounces of liquor, and 50 cigars. In addition, you're allowed to mail gifts to Canada valued at less than C$60 a day, provided they're unsolicited and don't contain alcohol or tobacco (write on the package "Unsolicited gift, under C$60 value"). All valuables should be declared on the Y-38 form before departure from Canada, including serial numbers of valuables you already own, such as expensive foreign cameras. *Note:* The $750 exemption can be used once a year and only after an absence of 7 days.

The duty-free allowance in **Australia** is A$400 or, for those under 18, A$200. Upon returning to Australia, citizens can bring in 250 cigarettes or 250 grams of loose tobacco, and 1,125ml of alcohol. If you're returning with valuable goods you already own, such as foreign-made cameras, file form B263. A helpful brochure, available from Australian consulates or Customs offices, is *Know Before You Go*. For more information, contact **Australian Customs Services,** GPO Box 8, Sydney NSW 2001 (© **02/ 9213-2000**).

The duty-free allowance for **New Zealand** is NZ$700. Citizens over 17 can bring in 200 cigarettes, or 50 cigars, or 250 grams of tobacco (or a mixture of all three if their combined weight doesn't exceed 250 grams); plus 4.5 liters of wine and beer, or 1.125 liters of liquor. New Zealand currency does not carry import or export restrictions. Fill out a certificate of export, listing the valuables you are taking out of the country; that way, you can bring them back without paying duty. Most questions are answered in a free pamphlet available at New Zealand consulates and Customs offices: *New Zealand Customs Guide for Travellers, Notice no. 4.* For more information, contact New Zealand Customs, 50 Anzac Ave., P.O. Box 29, Auckland (© **09/359-6655**).

HEALTH INSURANCE

Although it's not required of travelers, health insurance is highly recommended. Unlike many European countries, the United States does not usually offer free or low-cost medical care to its citizens or visitors. Doctors and hospitals are expensive, and in most cases will require advance payment or proof of coverage before they render their services. Policies can cover everything from the loss or theft of your baggage and trip cancellation to the guarantee of bail in case you're arrested. Good policies will also cover the costs of an accident, repatriation, or death. See "Health & Insurance" in chapter 2, "Planning Your Trip to South Florida," for more information. Packages such as **Europ Assistance's "Worldwide Healthcare Plan"** are sold by European automobile clubs and travel agencies at attractive rates. **Worldwide Assistance Services,** Inc. (© **800/821-2828;** www.worldwide assistance.com) is the agent for Europ Assistance in the United States.

Though lack of health insurance may prevent you from being admitted to a hospital in nonemergencies, don't worry about being left on a street corner to die; the American way is to fix you now and bill the living daylights out of you later.

INSURANCE FOR BRITISH TRAVELERS   Most big travel agents offer their own insurance, and will probably try to sell you their package when you book a holiday. Think before you sign. **Britain's Consumers' Association** recommends that you insist on seeing the policy and reading the fine print before buying travel insurance. **The Association of British Insurers** (© **0171/600- 3333;** www.abi.org.uk/) gives advice by phone and publishes *Holiday Insurance,* a free guide to policy provisions and prices. You might also shop around for better deals: Try **Columbus Direct** (© **0171/375-0011;** www.columbusdirect.net/) or, for students, **Campus Travel** (© **0171/730-2101;** www.campustravel.co.uk).

INSURANCE FOR CANADIAN TRAVELERS Canadians should check with their provincial health plan offices or call **Health Canada** (© **613/957-2991;** www.hc-sc.gc.ca/) to find out the extent of their coverage and what documentation and receipts they must take home in case they are treated in the United States.

MONEY

CURRENCY The U.S. monetary system is very simple: The most common **bills** are the $1 (colloquially, a "buck"), $5, $10, and $20 denominations. There are also $2 bills (seldom encountered), $50 bills, and $100 bills (the last two are usually not welcome as payment for small purchases). All the paper money was recently redesigned, making the famous faces adorning them disproportionately large. The old-style bills are still legal tender.

There are seven denominations of **coins:** 1¢ (1 cent, or a penny); 5¢ (5 cents, or a nickel); 10¢ (10 cents, or a dime); 25¢ (25 cents, or a quarter); 50¢ (50 cents, or a half dollar); the new gold "Sacagawea" coin worth $1; and, prized by collectors, the rare, older silver dollar.

Note: The "foreign-exchange bureaus" so common in Europe are rare even at airports in the United States, and nonexistent outside major cities. It's best not to change foreign money (or traveler's checks denominated in a currency other than U.S. dollars) at a small-town bank, or even a branch in a big city; in fact, leave any currency other than U.S. dollars at home—it may prove a greater nuisance to you than it's worth.

TRAVELER'S CHECKS Though traveler's checks are widely accepted, make sure that they're denominated in U.S. dollars, as foreign-currency checks are often difficult to exchange. The three traveler's checks that are most widely recognized—and least likely to be denied—are **Visa, American Express,** and **Thomas Cook.** Be sure to record the numbers of the checks, and keep that information in a separate place in case they get lost or stolen. Most businesses are pretty good about taking traveler's checks, but you're better off cashing them in at a bank (in small amounts, of course) and paying in cash. *Remember:* You'll need identification, such as a driver's license or passport, to change a traveler's check.

CREDIT CARDS & ATMS Credit cards are the most widely used form of payment in the United States: **Visa** (BarclayCard in Britain), **MasterCard** (EuroCard in Europe, Access in Britain, Chargex in Canada), **American Express, Diners Club,** and **Discover.** There are, however, a handful of stores and restaurants that do not take credit cards, so be sure to ask in advance. Most businesses display a sticker near their entrance to let you know which cards they accept. (Note: Businesses may require a minimum purchase, usually around $10, to use a credit card.)

It is strongly recommended that you bring at least one major credit card. You must have a credit or charge card to rent a car. Hotels and airlines usually require a credit-card imprint as a deposit against expenses, and in an emergency a credit card can be priceless.

You'll find **automated teller machines (ATMs)** on just about every block—at least in almost every town—across the country. In South Florida, there are ATMs in malls, grocery stores, convenience stores, bars, nightclubs, and in every major, highly trafficked neighborhood, from Key West to Lake Okeechobee. Some

Travel Tip

Be sure to keep a copy of all your travel papers separate from your wallet or purse, and leave a copy with someone at home should you need it faxed in an emergency.

ATMs will allow you to draw U.S. currency against your bank and credit cards. Check with your bank before leaving home, and remember that you will need your personal identification number (PIN) to do so. Most accept Visa, MasterCard, and American Express, as well as ATM cards from other U.S. banks. Expect to be charged up to $3 per transaction, however, if you're not using your own bank's ATM.

One way around these fees is to ask for cash back at grocery stores that accept ATM cards and don't charge usage fees. Of course, you'll have to purchase something first.

ATM cards with major credit card backing, known as "debit cards," are now a commonly acceptable form of payment in most stores and restaurants. Debit cards draw money directly from your checking account. Some stores enable you to receive cash back on your debit-card purchases as well.

SAFETY

GENERAL SAFETY SUGGESTIONS Although tourist areas are generally safe, U.S. urban areas tend to be less safe than those in Europe or Japan. You should always stay alert. This is particularly true of large American cities. If you're in doubt about which neighborhoods are safe, don't hesitate to make inquiries with the hotel front desk staff or the local tourist office.

Avoid deserted areas, especially at night, and don't go into public parks after dark unless there's a concert or similar occasion that will attract a crowd.

Avoid carrying valuables with you on the street, and keep expensive cameras or electronic equipment bagged up or covered when not in use. If you're using a map, try to consult it inconspicuously—or better yet, study it before you leave your room. Hold onto your pocketbook, and place your billfold in an inside pocket. In theaters, restaurants, and other public places, keep your possessions in sight.

Always lock your room door—don't assume that once you're inside the hotel you are automatically safe and no longer need to be aware of your surroundings. Hotels are open to the public, and in a large hotel, security may not be able to screen everyone who enters.

DRIVING SAFETY Driving safety is important too, especially given the highly publicized carjackings of foreign tourists in Florida. Question your rental agency about personal safety and ask for a traveler-safety brochure when you pick up your car. Obtain written directions—or a map with the route clearly marked—from the agency showing how to get to your destination. (Many agencies now offer the option of renting a cellular phone for the duration of your car rental; check with the rental agent when you pick up the car.) And, if possible, arrive and depart during daylight hours.

If you drive off a highway and end up in a dodgy-looking neighborhood, leave the area as quickly as possible. If you have an accident, even on the highway, stay in your car with the doors locked until you assess the situation or until the police arrive. If you're bumped from behind on the street or are involved in a minor accident with no injuries, and the situation appears to be suspicious, motion to the other driver to follow you. Never get out of your car in such situations. Go directly to the nearest police precinct, well-lit service station, or 24-hour store. You may want to look into renting a cell phone on a short-term basis. One recommended wireless rental company is **InTouch USA** (© **800/872-7626;** www.intouchusa.com).

Park in well-lit and well-traveled areas whenever possible. Always keep your car doors locked, whether the vehicle is attended or unattended. Never leave any packages or valuables in sight. If someone attempts to rob you or steal your car, don't try to resist the thief/carjacker. Report the incident to the police department immediately by calling © **911.**

2 Getting to the United States

British Airways (© **081/897-4000** from within the UK) offers direct flights from London to Miami (and Orlando), as does **Virgin Atlantic** (© **012/937-47747** from within the UK). Canadian readers might book flights with **Air Canada** (© **800/776-3000**), which offers service from Toronto and Montreal to Miami and Tampa.

Miami International Airport is a hub for flights to and from Latin America. Carriers include **Aerolinas Argentinas** (© 800/333-0276), **Aeromexico** (© 800/245-8585), **American Airlines** (© 800/433-7300), **Avianca** (© 800/284-2622), **Lan Chile Airlines** (© 800/735-5526), and **Varig Brazilian Airlines** (© 800/468-2744).

AIRLINE DISCOUNTS The smart traveler can find numerable ways to reduce the price of a plane ticket simply by taking time to shop around. For example, overseas visitors can take advantage of the APEX (Advance Purchase Excursion) reductions offered by all major U.S. and European carriers. For more money-saving airline advice, see "Getting There" in chapter 2. For the best rates, compare fares and be flexible with the dates and times of travel.

IMMIGRATION & CUSTOMS CLEARANCE Visitors arriving by air, no matter what the port of entry, should cultivate patience and resignation before setting foot on U.S. soil. Getting through immigration control can take as long as 2 hours on some days, especially on summer weekends, so be sure to carry this guidebook or something else to read. This is especially true in the aftermath of the World Trade Center attacks, when security clearances have been considerably beefed up at U.S. airports.

3 Getting Around the United States

BY PLANE Some large airlines (for example, Northwest and Delta) offer travelers on their transatlantic or transpacific flights special discount tickets under the name **Visit USA,** allowing mostly one-way travel from one U.S. destination to another at very low prices. These discount tickets are not on sale in the United States and must be purchased abroad in conjunction with your international ticket. This system is the best, easiest, and fastest way to see the United States at low cost. You should obtain information well in advance from your travel agent or the office of the airline concerned, since the conditions attached to these discount tickets can be changed without advance notice.

BY TRAIN International visitors (excluding Canada) can also buy a **USA Railpass,** good for 15 or 30 days of unlimited travel on Amtrak (© **800/USA-RAIL;** www.amtrak. com). The pass is available through many foreign travel agents. Prices in 2002 for a 15-day pass were $295 off-peak, $440 peak; a 30-day pass costs $385 off-peak, $550 peak. With a foreign passport, you can also buy passes at some Amtrak offices in the United States, including locations in San Francisco, Los Angeles, Chicago, New York, Miami, Boston, and Washington, D.C. Reservations are generally required and should be made for each part of your trip as early as possible. Regional rail passes are also available.

BY BUS Although bus travel is often the most economical form of public transit for short hops between U.S. cities, it can also be slow and uncomfortable—certainly not an option for everyone (particularly when Amtrak, which is far more luxurious, offers similar rates). **Greyhound/Trailways** (© **800/231-2222**), the sole nationwide bus line, offers an **International Ameripass** that must be purchased before coming to the United States, or by phone through the Greyhound International Office at the Port Authority Bus Terminal in New York City (© **212/971-0492**). The pass can be obtained from foreign travel agents and costs less than the domestic version. 2002 passes cost as follows: 4 days ($135), 7 days ($184), 10 days ($234), 15 days ($274), 21 days ($324), 30 days ($364), 45 days ($404), or 60 days ($494). You can get more info on the

pass at www.greyhound.com, or by calling © **212/971-0492** (14:00–21:00 GMT) and © **402/330-8552** (all other times). In addition, special rates are available for seniors and students.

BY CAR Unless you plan to spend the bulk of your vacation time in a city where walking is the best and easiest way to get around (read: New York City or New Orleans), the most cost-effective, convenient, and comfortable way to travel around the United States is by car. The interstate highway system connects cities and towns all over the country; in addition to these high-speed, limited-access roadways, there's an extensive network of federal, state, and local highways and roads. Some of the national car-rental companies include **Alamo** (© 800/327-9633; www.goalamo. com), **Avis** (© 800/331-1212; www. avis.com), **Budget** (© 800/527-0700; https://rent.drivebudget.com), **Dollar** (© 800/800-4000; www.dollar.com), **Hertz** (© 800/654-3131; www.hertz. com), **National** (© 800/227-7368; www.nationalcar.com), and **Thrifty** (© 800/367-2277; www.thrifty.com).

If you plan to rent a car in the United States, you probably won't need the services of an additional automobile organization. If you're planning to buy or borrow a car, automobile-association membership is recommended. **The American Automobile Association** (© 800/222-4357) is the country's largest auto club and supplies its members with maps, insurance, and, most important, emergency road service. The cost of joining runs from $63 for singles to $87 for two members, but if you're a member of a foreign auto club with reciprocal arrangements, you can enjoy free AAA service in America (see below).

FAST FACTS: For the International Traveler

Automobile Organizations Auto clubs will supply maps, suggested routes, guidebooks, accident and bail-bond insurance, and emergency road service. The **American Automobile Association (AAA)** is the major auto club in the United States. If you belong to an auto club in your home country, inquire about AAA reciprocity before you leave. You may be able to join AAA even if you're not a member of a reciprocal club; to inquire, call AAA (© **800/222-4357**). AAA is actually an organization of regional auto clubs; so look under "AAA Automobile Club" in the White Pages of the telephone directory. AAA has a free nationwide emergency road service telephone number (© **800/AAA-HELP**).

Business Hours Offices are usually open weekdays from 9am to 5pm. Banks are open weekdays from 9am to 3pm or later, and sometimes Saturday mornings. Stores, especially those in shopping complexes on South Beach, in Coconut Grove, and in Key West, tend to stay open late: until about 9pm on weekdays and as late as 11pm on weekends.

Currency See "Entry Requirements" and "Money," under "Preparing for Your Trip," earlier in this chapter.

Currency Exchange Foreign exchange bureaus in South Florida are, unfortunately, foreign to the area. There are currency exchanges at the Miami International Airport, such as **Miami Currency Exchanges** (© 305/876-0040). **Abbot Foreign Exchange,** 230 NE First St. (© 305/374-2336), is located in downtown Miami and is open on weekdays from 8am to 5pm and on Saturday from 8am to 2pm.

Drinking Laws The legal age for purchase and consumption of alcoholic beverages is 21; proof of age is required and often requested at bars, nightclubs, and restaurants, so it's always a good idea to bring ID when you go out. On South Beach, in particular, the clubs and bars have become stricter since they raised the minimum age of entry from 18 to 21. Beer and wine can often be purchased in supermarkets, but liquor laws vary throughout the state.

Do not carry open containers of alcohol in your car or any public area that isn't zoned for alcohol consumption. The police can, and probably will, fine you on the spot. And nothing will ruin your trip faster than getting a citation for DUI ("driving under the influence"), so don't even think about driving while intoxicated.

Electricity Like Canada, the United States uses 110 to 120 volts AC (60 cycles), compared to 220 to 240 volts AC (50 cycles) in most of Europe, Australia, and New Zealand. If your small appliances use 220 to 240 volts, you'll need a 110-volt transformer and a plug adapter with two flat parallel pins to operate them here. Downward converters that change 220–240 volts to 110–120 volts are difficult to find in the United States, so bring one with you.

Embassies & Consulates All embassies are located in the nation's capital, Washington, D.C. Some consulates are located in Miami and are listed below. Travelers from other countries can get telephone numbers for their embassies and consulates by calling directory information in Washington, D.C. (© **202/555-1212**).

In South Florida, the **Canadian Consulate** is located at 200 S. Bayshore Dr., Miami, FL 33131 (© 305/579-1600). The **British Consulate** is located at the Brickell Bay Tower, Suite 2110, 1001 S. Bayshore Dr., Coconut Grove, FL 33131 (© 305/374-1522). The **French Consulate** is located at 1 Biscayne Tower, Suite 1710, Miami, FL 33131(© 305/372-9799), the **Italian Consulate** is located at 1200 Brickell Ave., Miami, FL 33131(© 305/374-6322), the **Israeli Consulate** is located at 100 N. Biscayne Blvd., Miami, FL 33132 (© 305/925-9400), the **German Consulate** is located at 100 N. Biscayne Blvd., Suite 2200, Miami, FL 33132 (© 305/358-0290), the **Australian Consulate** is located at 2525 SW Third Ave., Suite 208, Miami, FL 33129 (© 305/858-7633), and **Brazil's Consulate General** is located at 2601 S. Bayshore Dr., Suite 800, Coconut Grove, FL 33133 (© 305/285-6200).

Emergencies Call © **911** to report a fire, call the police, or get an ambulance anywhere in the United States. This is a toll-free call (no coins are required at public telephones).

If you encounter serious problems, contact the **Traveler's Aid Society International** (© **202/546-1127**; www.travelersaid.org) to help direct you to a local branch. This nationwide, nonprofit, social-service organization, geared to helping travelers in difficult straits, offers services that might include reuniting families separated while traveling, providing food and/ or shelter to people stranded without cash, or even emotional counseling. If you're in trouble, seek them out.

Gasoline (Petrol) Petrol is known as gasoline (or simply "gas") in the United States, and petrol stations are known as both gas stations and service stations. Gasoline costs about half as much here as it does in Europe (about $1.55 or more per gallon at press time), and taxes are already included in the printed price. One U.S. gallon equals 3.8 liters or .85 Imperial gallons.

Holidays Banks, government offices, post offices, and many stores, restaurants, and museums are closed on the following legal national holidays: January 1 (New Year's Day), the third Monday in January (Martin Luther King, Jr. Day), the third Monday in February (Presidents' Day, Washington's Birthday), the last Monday in May (Memorial Day), July 4 (Independence Day), the first Monday in September (Labor Day), the second Monday in October (Columbus Day), November 11 (Veterans' Day/Armistice Day), the fourth Thursday in November (Thanksgiving Day), and December 25 (Christmas). Also, the Tuesday following the first Monday in November is Election Day and is a federal government holiday in presidential-election years (held every four years, and next in 2004).

Legal Aid If you are "pulled over" for a minor infraction (such as speeding), never attempt to pay the fine directly to a police officer; this could be construed as attempted bribery, a much more serious crime. Pay fines by mail, or directly into the hands of the clerk of the court. If accused of a more serious offense, say and do nothing before consulting a lawyer. In the United States, the burden is on the state to prove a person's guilt beyond a reasonable doubt, and everyone has the right to remain silent, whether he or she is suspected of a crime or actually arrested. Once arrested, a person can make one telephone call to a party of his or her choice. Call your embassy or consulate.

Mail If you aren't sure what your address will be in the United States, mail can be sent to you, in your name, c/o General Delivery at **Miami's Main Post Office,** 2200 Milam Dairy Rd., Miami, FL 33152 (© 305/639-4280); in **Broward County,** 1801 Polk St., Hollywood, FL 33020 (© 954/923-0201); and in **Palm Beach County,** 14280 Military Trail, Delray Beach, FL 33484 (© 561/498-8504). The addressee must pick mail up in person and must produce proof of identity (driver's license, passport, etc.). Most post offices will hold your mail for up to 1 month and are open Monday to Friday from 8am to 6pm, and Saturday from 9am to 3pm.

Generally found at intersections, mailboxes are blue with a red-and-white stripe and carry the inscription U.S. Mail. If your mail is addressed to a U.S. destination, don't forget to add the five-digit postal code (or ZIP code), after the two-letter abbreviation of the state to which the mail is addressed. This is essential for prompt delivery.

At press time, domestic postage rates were 23¢ for a postcard and 37¢ for a letter. For international mail, a first-class letter of up to one-half ounce costs 80¢ (60¢ to Canada and Mexico); a first-class postcard costs 70¢ (50¢ to Canada and Mexico); and a preprinted postal aerogramme costs 70¢.

Measurements See the chart on the inside front cover of this book for details on converting metric measurements to U.S. equivalents.

Newspapers The *Miami Herald* is the premier daily newspaper in South Florida, particularly in Miami–Dade County. The *Sun-Sentinel* is Broward County's daily newspaper, and the *Palm Beach Post* and *Key West Citizen* cover local and national news. The *Miami New Times* and *Broward/Palm Beach New Times* are free weekly alternative newspapers with comprehensive calendars and event listings, as well as local items of interest.

Taxes In the United States there is no value-added tax (VAT) or other indirect tax at the national level. Every state, county, and city has the right to levy its own local tax on all purchases, including hotel and restaurant checks, airline tickets, and so on. A 6% state sales tax (plus 0.5% local tax, for a total of 6.5% in Miami) is added on at the register for all goods and services purchased in Florida. In addition, most municipalities levy special taxes on restaurants and hotels. In Surfside, hotel taxes total 10.5%; in Bal Harbour, Miami Beach (including South Beach), and the rest of Miami–Dade County, a whopping 12.5%. In Miami Beach, Surfside, and Bal Harbour, the resort (hotel) tax also applies to hotel restaurants and restaurants with liquor licenses.

Telephone, Telegraph, Telex & Fax The telephone in the United States is run by private corporations, so rates, especially for long-distance service and operator-assisted calls, can vary widely. Generally, hotel surcharges on long-distance and local calls are astronomical, so you're usually better off using a **public pay telephone,** which you'll find clearly marked in most public buildings and private establishments as well as on the street. Convenience grocery stores and gas stations always have them. Many convenience groceries and packaging services sell **prepaid calling cards** in denominations up to $50; these can be the least expensive way to call home. Many public phones at airports now accept American Express, MasterCard, and Visa credit cards. **Local calls** made from public pay phones in most locales cost either 25¢ or 35¢. Pay phones do not accept pennies, and few will take anything larger than a quarter.

You may want to look into leasing a cell phone for the duration of your trip.

Most long-distance and international calls can be dialed directly from any phone. **For calls within the United States and to Canada,** dial 1 followed by the area code and the seven-digit number. **For other international calls,** dial 011 followed by the country code, city code, and telephone number of the person you are calling.

Calls to area codes **800, 888,** and **877** are toll-free. However, calls to numbers in area codes **700** and **900** (chat lines, bulletin boards, "dating" services, and so on) can be very expensive—usually a charge of 95¢ to $3 or more per minute, and they sometimes have minimum charges that can run as high as $15 or more.

For **reversed-charge or collect calls** and for person-to-person calls, dial 0 (zero, not the letter O), followed by the area code and number you want; an operator will then come on the line, and you should specify that you are calling collect, or person-to-person, or both. If your operator-assisted call is international, ask for the overseas operator.

For **local directory assistance** ("information"), dial 411; for long-distance information, dial 1, then the appropriate area code and 555-1212.

Telegraph and telex services are provided primarily by Western Union. You can bring your telegram into the nearest Western Union office (there are hundreds across the country) or dictate it over the phone (✆ 800/325-6000). You can also telegraph money or have it telegraphed to you very quickly over the Western Union system, but this service can cost as much as 15% to 20% of the amount sent.

Most hotels have **fax machines** available for guest use (be sure to ask about the charge to use it), and many hotel rooms are even wired for guests' fax machines. A less expensive way to send and receive faxes may be at stores such as Mail Boxes Etc., a national chain of packing service shops (look in the Yellow Pages directory under "Packing Services").

There are two kinds of telephone directories in the United States. The so-called **White Pages** list private households and business subscribers in alphabetical order. The inside front cover lists emergency numbers for police, fire, ambulance, the Coast Guard, poison-control center, crime victims hotline, and so on. The first few pages will tell you how to make long-distance and international calls, complete with country codes and area codes. Government numbers are usually printed on blue paper within the White Pages. Printed on yellow paper, the so-called **Yellow Pages** list local services, businesses, industries, and houses of worship according to activity with an index at the front or back. (Drugstores/pharmacies and restaurants are also listed by geographic location.) The Yellow Pages also include city plans or detailed area maps, postal ZIP codes, and public transportation routes.

Time   The continental United States is divided into **four time zones:** eastern standard time (EST), central standard time (CST), mountain standard time (MST), and Pacific standard time (PST). Alaska and Hawaii have their own zones. For example, noon in Miami (EST) is 11am in Chicago (CST),

10am in Denver (MST), 9am in Los Angeles (PST), 8am in Anchorage (AST), and 7am in Honolulu (HST).

Daylight saving time is in effect from 1am on the first Sunday in April through 1am on the last Sunday in October, except in Arizona, Hawaii, part of Indiana, and Puerto Rico. Daylight saving time moves the clock 1 hour ahead of standard time.

Tipping Tipping is so ingrained in the American way of life that the annual income tax of tip-earning service personnel is based on how much they should have received in light of their employers' gross revenues. Accordingly, they may have to pay tax on a tip you didn't actually give them.

Here are some rules of thumb:

In hotels, tip **bellhops** at least $1 per bag ($2 to $3 if you have a lot of luggage) and tip the **chamber staff** $1 to $3 per day (more if you've left a disaster area for him or her to clean up, or if you're traveling with kids and/or pets). Tip the **doorman** or **concierge** only if he or she has provided you with some specific service (for example, calling a cab for you or obtaining difficult-to-get theater tickets). Tip the **valet parking attendant** $1 every time you get your car.

In restaurants, bars, and nightclubs, tip **service staff** 15% to 20% of the check, tip **bartenders** 10% to 15%, and tip **valet parking attendants** $1 per vehicle. Tip the **doorman** only if he has provided you with some specific service (such as calling a cab for you). Tipping is not expected in cafeterias and fast-food restaurants. Many restaurants on South Beach include a 15% tip in the check due to the enormous influx of European tourists who are not accustomed to tipping. Keep in mind that this amount is the *suggested* amount and can be adjusted, either higher or lower, depending on your assessment of the service provided. Because of this tipping-included policy, South Beach wait staff are best known for their lax or inattentive service. Make sure to always read the bottom of your check to see if tipping is included. People tend to get ripped off because they assume the tip is not included.

Tip **cab drivers** 15% of the fare.

As for other service personnel, tip **skycaps** at airports at least $1 per bag and tip **hairdressers** and **barbers** 15% to 20%.

Tipping ushers at movies and theaters and tipping gas station attendants is not expected.

Toilets You won't find public toilets or "rest rooms" on the streets in most U.S. cities, but they can be found in hotel lobbies, bars, restaurants, museums, libraries, department stores, railway and bus stations, or service stations. Note, however, that restaurants and bars in resorts or heavily visited areas may reserve their rest rooms for the use of their patrons. Some establishments display a notice that toilets are for the use of patrons only. You can ignore this sign, or, better yet, avoid arguments by paying for a cup of coffee or a soft drink, which will qualify you as a patron. Large hotels and fast-food restaurants are probably the best bet for good, clean facilities. If possible, avoid the toilets at parks and beaches, which tend to be dirty.

4

Getting to Know Miami

Apropos jokes about bad drivers, Grandma forgetting to shut off her turn signal, and traffic nightmares aside, Miami is a fascinating city to explore, be it by foot, bike, scooter, boat, or car. Because of its larger-than-life persona, Miami may seem a lot bigger than it really is, but although the city comprises many different neighborhoods, it's really not that difficult to learn the lay of the land. Much like the body beautifuls on Ocean Drive, the Magic City is a tidy package that's a little less than 2,000 square miles.

1 Orientation

ARRIVING

Originally carved out of scrubland in 1928 by Pan American Airlines, **Miami International Airport (MIA)** has become second in the United States for international passenger traffic and 10th in the world for total passengers. Despite the heavy traffic, the airport is quite user-friendly and not as much of a hassle as you'd think. You can change money or use your ATM card at Nation's Bank of South Florida, located near the exit. Visitor information is available 24 hours a day at the **Miami International Airport Main Visitor Counter,** Concourse E, second level (© **305/876-7000**). Information is also available at **www.miami-airport.com**. Because MIA is the busiest airport in South Florida, travelers may want to consider flying into the less crowded, but expanding, **Fort Lauderdale Hollywood International Airport (FLL)** (© **954/359-1200**), which is closer to north Miami than MIA, or the **Palm Beach International Airport (PBI)** (© **561/471-7420**), about 90 minutes away.

GETTING INTO TOWN

Miami International Airport is located about 6 miles west of downtown and about 10 miles from the beaches, so it's likely you can get from the plane to your hotel room in less than half an hour. Of course, if you're arriving from an international destination, it will take more time to go through Customs and Immigration.

BY CAR All the major car-rental firms operate off-site branches reached via shuttles from the terminals. See "Getting Around," later in this chapter, for a list of major rental companies. Signs at the airport's exit clearly point the way to various parts of the city, but the car-rental firm should also give you directions to

---

Words to Live By

I figure marriage is kind of like Miami; it's hot and stormy, and occasionally a little dangerous . . . but if it's really so awful, why is there still so much traffic?

—Sarah Jessica Parker's character, Gwen Marcus, in *Miami Rhapsody*

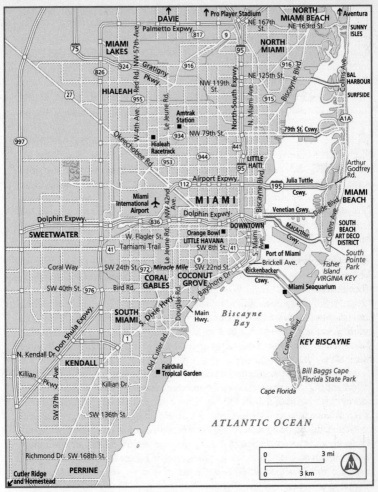

your destination. If you're arriving late at night, you might want to take a taxi to your hotel and have the car delivered to you the next day.

BY TAXI Taxis line up in front of a dispatcher's desk outside the airport's arrivals terminals. Most cabs are metered, though some have flat rates to popular destinations. The fare should be about $20 to Coral Gables, $18 to downtown, and $24 to South Beach, plus tip, which should be at least 10% (add more for each bag the driver handles). Depending on traffic, the ride to Coral Gables or downtown takes about 15 to 20 minutes and 20 to 25 minutes to South Beach.

BY LIMO OR VAN Group limousines (multipassenger vans) circle the arrivals area looking for fares. Destinations are posted on the front of each van, and a flat rate is charged for door-to-door service to the area marked.

SuperShuttle (✆ **305/871-2000;** www.supershuttle.com) is one of the largest airport operators, charging between $10 and $20 per person for a ride within the county. Its vans operate 24 hours a day and accept American Express,

MasterCard, and Visa. This is a cheaper alternative to a cab (if you are traveling alone or with one other person), but be prepared to be in the van for quite a while, as you may have to make several stops to drop passengers off before you reach your own destination. SuperShuttle also began service from Palm Beach International Airport to the surrounding communities. The door-to-door, shared-ride service operates from the airport to Stuart, Fort Pierce, Palm Beach, and Broward counties.

Private limousine arrangements can be made in advance through your local travel agent. A one-way meet-and-greet service should cost about $50. Limo services include **City Limousine (℗ 800/819-LIMO)** and **DLS Limousine Service (℗ 888/988-9567)**.

BY PUBLIC TRANSPORTATION   Public transportation in South Florida is a major hassle bordering on a nightmare. Painfully slow and unreliable, buses heading downtown leave the airport only once per hour (from the arrivals level), and connections are spotty at best. It could take about an hour and a half to get to South Beach. Journeys to downtown and Coral Gables are more direct. The fare is $1.25, plus an additional 25¢ for a transfer.

VISITOR INFORMATION

The most up-to-date information is provided by the **Greater Miami Convention and Visitor's Bureau,** 701 Brickell Ave., Suite 700, Miami, FL 33131 (℗ **800/933-8448** or 305/539-3000; fax 305/530-3113; www.miamiand beaches.com). Several chambers of commerce in Greater Miami will send out information on their particular neighborhoods; for addresses and numbers, please see "Visitor Information" in chapter 2, "Planning Your Trip to South Florida."

If you arrive at the Miami International Airport, you can pick up visitor information at the airport's main visitor counter on the second floor of Concourse E. It's open 24 hours a day.

Always check local newspapers for special events during your visit. The city's only daily, the *Miami Herald,* is a good source for current events listings, particularly the "Weekend" section in Friday's edition and the paper's entertainment weekly offshoot, *The Street,* available free every Friday in freestanding boxes anchored to city streets. Even better is the free weekly alternative paper, the *Miami New Times,* found in bright red boxes throughout the city.

Information on everything from dining to entertainment in Miami is available on the Internet at www.miami.citysearch.com.

CITY LAYOUT

Miami may seem confusing at first, but it quickly becomes easy to negotiate. The small cluster of buildings that make up the downtown area is at the geographical heart of the city. In relation to downtown, the airport is northwest, the beaches are east, Coconut Grove is south, Coral Gables is west, and the rest of the city is north.

FINDING AN ADDRESS   Miami is divided into dozens of areas with official and unofficial boundaries. Street numbering in the city of Miami is fairly straightforward, but you must first be familiar with the numbering system. The mainland is divided into four sections (NE, NW, SE, and SW) by the intersection of Flagler Street and Miami Avenue. Flagler divides Miami from north to south and Miami Avenue divides the city from east to west. It's helpful to remember that avenues generally run north-south, while streets go east-west.

Street numbers (First Street, Second Street, and so forth) start from here and increase as you go further out from this intersection, as do numbers of avenues, places, courts, terraces, and lanes. Streets in Hialeah are the exceptions to this pattern; they are listed separately in map indexes.

Getting around the barrier islands that make up Miami Beach is somewhat easier than moving around the mainland. Street numbering starts with First Street, near Miami Beach's southern tip, and increases to 192nd Street, in the northern part of Sunny Isles. Collins Avenue makes the entire journey, from head to toe of the island. As in the city of Miami, some streets in Miami Beach have numbers as well as names. When they are part of listings in this book, both name and number are given.

The numbered streets in Miami Beach are not the geographical equivalents of those on the mainland, but they are close. For example, the 79th Street Causeway runs into 71st Street on Miami Beach.

STREET MAPS   It's easy to get lost in sprawling Miami, so a reliable map is essential. The Trakker Map of Miami is a four-color accordion map that encompasses all of Dade County. The map is available at newsstands and shops throughout South Florida or online at www.trakkermaps.com.

Some maps of Miami list streets according to area, so you'll have to know which part of the city you are looking for before the street can be found. All the listings in this book include area information for this reason.

THE NEIGHBORHOODS IN BRIEF

South Beach—The Art Deco District   Though there are many monikers used to describe Miami's publicity darling—Glitter Beach, SoBe, America's Riviera, Hollywood South, Manhattan South—South Beach is a uniquely surreal, Dalí-esque cocktail of cosmopolitan influences with a splash of saltwater thrown in to remind you that you're not in a concrete jungle anymore. South Beach's 10 miles of beach are alive with a frenetic, circus-like atmosphere and are center stage for a motley crew of characters, from eccentric locals, seniors, snowbirds, and college students to gender-benders, celebrities, club kids, and curiosity seekers: individuality is as widely accepted on South Beach as Visa and MasterCard.

Bolstered by a Caribbean-chic cafe society and a sexually charged, tragically hip nightlife, people-watching on South Beach (from 1st to 23rd streets) is almost as good as a front-row seat at a Milan fashion show. Sure, the beautiful people do flock here, but the models aren't the only sights worth drooling over. The thriving Art Deco District within South Beach contains the largest concentration of Art Deco architecture in the world. In 1979, much of South Beach was listed in the National Register of Historic Places. The pastel-hued structures are supermodels in their own right—only these models improve with age.

Miami Beach   In the fabulous '40s and '50s, Miami Beach was America's true Riviera. The stomping ground of choice for the Rat Pack and notorious mobsters such as Al Capone, its huge self-contained resort hotels were vacations unto themselves, providing a full day's worth of meals, activities, and entertainment. Then, in the 1960s and 1970s, people who fell in love with Miami began to buy apartments rather than rent hotel rooms. Tourism declined, Capone disappeared, the Rat Pack fled to Vegas, and many area hotels fell into disrepair.

However, since the late 1980s and South Beach's renaissance, Miami

Beach (24th Street and up) has experienced a tide of revitalization. Huge beach hotels are finding their niche with new international tourist markets and are attracting large convention crowds. New generations of Americans are discovering the qualities that originally made Miami Beach so popular, and they are finding out that the sand and surf now come with a thriving international city.

Surfside, Bal Harbour, and **Sunny Isles** make up the north part of the beach (island). Hotels, motels, restaurants, and beaches line Collins Avenue and, with some outstanding exceptions, the farther north one goes, the cheaper lodging becomes. All told, excellent prices, location, and facilities make Surfside and Sunny Isles attractive places to stay, although they are still a little rough around the edges. However, a revitalization is in the works for these areas, and, while it's highly unlikely they will ever become as chic as South Beach, there is potential, especially as South Beach falls prey to the inevitable spoiler: commercialism. Keep in mind that beachfront properties are at a premium, so many of the area's moderately priced hotels have been converted to condominiums, leaving fewer and fewer affordable places to stay.

In exclusive and ritzy Bal Harbour, where well-paid police officers are instructed to ticket drivers who go above the 30 mph speed limit, few hotels remain amid the many beachfront condominium towers. Instead, fancy homes, tucked away on the bay, hide behind gated communities, and the Rodeo Drive of Miami (known as the Bal Harbour Shops) attracts shoppers who don't flinch at four-, five-, and six-figure price tags.

Note that **North Miami Beach,** a residential area near the Dade–Broward County line (north of 163rd Street; part of North Dade County), is a misnomer. It is actually northwest of Miami Beach, on the mainland, and has no beaches, though it does have some of Miami's better restaurants and shops. Located within North Miami Beach is the posh residential community of **Aventura,** best known for its high-priced condos, the Turnberry Isle Resort, and the Aventura Mall.

Note: South Beach, the historic Art Deco District, is treated as a separate neighborhood from Miami Beach.

Key Biscayne Miami's forested and secluded Key Biscayne is technically one of the first islands in the Florida Keys. However, this island is nothing like its southern neighbors. Located south of Miami Beach, off the shores of Coconut Grove, Key Biscayne is protected from the troubles of the mainland by the long Rickenbacker Causeway and its $1 toll.

Largely an exclusive residential community, with million-dollar homes and sweeping water views, Key Biscayne also offers visitors great public beaches, some top (read: pricey) resort hotels, and several good restaurants. Hobie Beach, adjacent to the causeway, is the city's premier spot for sailboarding and jet-skiing (see "Watersports," in chapter 7, "What to See and Do in Miami"). On the island's southern tip, Bill Baggs State Park has great beaches, bike paths, and dense forests for picnicking and partying.

Downtown Miami's downtown boasts one of the world's most beautiful cityscapes. Unfortunately, that's about all it offers. During the day, a vibrant community of students, businesspeople, and merchants make their way through the bustling streets. Vendors sell fresh-cut pineapples and mangos while young consumers on shopping sprees lug bags and boxes. However, at night, downtown is desolate (except for NE 11th St, where there is a burgeoning nightlife scene) and not a place in which you'd want to get lost. The downtown area does have a mall (Bayside Marketplace, where many cruise passengers come to browse), some culture (Metro-Dade Cultural Center), and a few decent restaurants (see chapter 6, "Where to Dine in Miami"), as well as the new American Airlines Arena. Additionally, a downtown revitalization project is in the works, in which a cultural arts center, among other things, is expected to bring downtown back to life.

Design District With restaurants springing up between galleries and furniture stores galore, the Design District is, as locals say, the new South Beach, adding a touch of New York's SoHo to an area formerly known as downtown Miami's "Don't Go." The district, which is a hotbed for furniture import companies, interior designers, architects, and more, has also become a player in Miami's ever-changing nightlife, with a cavernous nightclub/restaurant/production studio/recording studio/live music venue that has become hipster central for South Beach expatriates and artsy bohemian types. In anticipation of its growing popularity, the district has also banded together to create an up-to-date website, www.designmiami.com, which includes a calendar of events and is chock-full of information. The district is loosely defined as the area bounded by NE 2nd Avenue, NE 5th Avenue east and west, and NW 36th Street to the south.

Biscayne Corridor From downtown near Bayside to the 70s, where trendy curio shops and upscale restaurants are slowly opening, Biscayne Boulevard is aspiring to reclaim itself as a safe thoroughfare where tourists can wine, dine, and shop. Previously known for sketchy, dilapidated 1950s- and '60s-era hotels that had fallen on hard times, residents fleeing the high prices of the beaches in search of affordable housing are renovating Biscayne block by block, trying to make this once-again famous boulevard worthy of a Sunday drive. With the trendy Design District immediately west of 36th and Biscayne by two blocks, there is hope for the area.

Little Havana If you've never been to Cuba, just visit this small section of Miami and you'll come pretty close. The sounds, tastes, and rhythms are very reminiscent of Cuba's capital city. Some even jokingly say you don't have to speak a word of English to live an independent life here—even street signs are in Spanish and English.

Cuban coffee shops, tailor and furniture stores, and inexpensive restaurants line *Calle Ocho* (pronounced *Ka-*yey O-choh), SW 8th Street, the region's main thoroughfare. Salsa and merengue beats ring loudly from old record stores while old men in *guayaberas* (loose fitting cotton or gauzy shirts, short sleeved, used to keep cool in Cuba and now a fashion statement in Miami) smoke cigars over their daily game of dominoes. The spotlight focused on the neighborhood during the Elián González situation in 2000, but the area was previously noted for the groups of artists and nocturnal types who have moved their galleries and performance spaces here, sparking a culturally charged neo-bohemian nightlife.

Fun Fact **The Mistress of Miami**

From 10,000 B.C. to about 1875, much of Miami was a swamp until an unsuspecting woman named Julia Tuttle arrived to collect her inheritance—a large swath of swamp in the Miami area. Over the next 20 years, Tuttle acquired much more property throughout the Miami area and prepared it for the major development that exists today. Following Tuttle, Henry Morrison Flagler arrived in Miami circa 1895. A developer and Standard Oil cohort of J. D. Rockefeller, Flagler had no intention of traveling down to Miami's swampland and instead focused on building a railroad that began at the northern tip of Florida and ended in Palm Beach. A hopeful Tuttle contacted Flagler with a proposal asking him to extend his railroad down to Miami in exchange for half of her property. Flagler declined the offer until a cold front froze out most of northern Florida, and, ultimately, all the tourists. It was then that Flagler decided to see Miami for himself. What he found was a warm tropical paradise, and, ultimately, a partner in Tuttle. Train service to Miami began in April 1896 and the swampy city has never been the same.

Coral Gables "The City Beautiful," created by George Merrick in the early 1920s, is one of Miami's first planned developments. This is not Levittown: The houses here were built in a Mediterranean style along lush tree-lined streets that open onto beautifully carved plazas, many with centerpiece fountains. The best architectural examples of the era have Spanish-style tiled roofs and are built from Miami oolite, native limestone commonly called "coral rock."

The Gables' European-flaired shopping and commerce center is home to many thriving corporations. Coral Gables also has landmark hotels, great golfing, upscale shopping, and some of the city's best restaurants, headed by world-renowned chefs.

Coconut Grove An arty, hippie hangout in the psychedelic '60s, Coconut Grove has given way from swirls of tie-dyes to the uniform color schemes of the Gap. Chain stores, theme restaurants, a megaplex, and bars galore make Coconut Grove a commercial success, but this gentrification has pushed most alternative types out.

The intersection of Grand Avenue, Main Highway, and McFarlane Road pierces the area's heart. Right in the center of it all is CocoWalk and the Shops at Mayfair, filled with boutiques, eateries, and bars. Sidewalks here are often crowded, especially at night, when University of Miami students who frequent this adopted college town come out to play.

Southern Miami–Dade County To locals, South Miami is both a specific area, southwest of Coral Gables, and a general region that encompasses all of southern Dade County and includes Kendall, Perrine, Cutler Ridge, and Homestead. For the purposes of clarity, this book has grouped all these southern suburbs under the rubric "Southern Miami–Dade County." Similar attributes unite the communities: They are heavily residential and packed with strip malls amidst a few remaining plots of farmland. Tourists don't usually stay in these parts, unless they are on their way to the Everglades or the Keys. However, Southern Miami–Dade County contains many of the city's top attractions (see chapter 7), meaning that you're likely to spend some time here.

2 Getting Around

Officially, Dade County has opted for a "unified, multimodal transportation network," which basically means you can get around the city by train, bus, and taxi. However, in practice, the network doesn't work very well. Things may improve when the city completes its transportation center in 2005, but until then, unless you are going from downtown Miami to a not-too-distant spot, you are better off in a rental car or taxi.

With the exception of downtown Coconut Grove and South Beach, Miami is not a walker's city. Because it is so spread out, most attractions are too far apart to make walking between them feasible. In fact, most Miamians are so used to driving that they do so even when going just a few blocks.

BY PUBLIC TRANSPORTATION

BY RAIL Two rail lines, operated by the **Metro-Dade Transit Agency** (© **305/770-3131;** www.co.miami-dade.fl.us/mdta/), run in concert with each other:

Metrorail, the city's modern high-speed commuter train, is a 21-mile elevated line that travels north-south, between downtown Miami and the southern suburbs. Locals like to refer to this semi-useless rail system as Metro*fail*. If you are staying in Coral Gables or Coconut Grove, you can park your car at a nearby station and ride the rails downtown. However, that's about it. There are plans to extend the system to service Miami International Airport, but until those tracks are built, these trains don't go most places tourists go, with the exception of the Vizcaya Museum in Coconut Grove. Metrorail operates daily from about 6am to midnight. The fare is $1.25.

> **Joy Ride**
> Metromover offers a panoramic view of the city and skyline, which you might want to take to complement your downtown tour.

Metromover, a 4½-mile elevated line, circles the downtown area and connects with Metrorail at the Government Center stop. This is a good way to get to Bayside (a waterfront marketplace, see p. 209) if you don't have a car. Riding on rubber tires, the single-car train winds past many of the area's most important attractions and shopping and business districts. You may not go very far, but you will get a beautiful perspective from the towering height of the suspended rails. System hours are daily from about 6am to midnight. The fare is 25¢.

BY BUS Miami's suburban layout is not conducive to getting around by bus. Lines operate and maps are available, but instead of getting to know the city, you'll find that relying on bus transportation will acquaint you only with how it feels to wait at bus stops. In short, a bus ride in Miami is grueling. You can get a bus map by mail, either from the Greater Miami Convention and Visitor's Bureau (see "Visitor Information," earlier in this chapter) or by writing the Metro-Dade Transit System, 3300 NW 32nd Ave., Miami, FL 33142. In Miami, call © **305/770-3131** for public-transit information. The fare is $1.25.

BY CAR

Tales circulate about vacationers who have visited Miami without a car, but they are very few indeed. If you are counting on exploring the city, even to a modest degree, a car is essential. Miami's restaurants, hotels, and attractions are far from one another, so any other form of transportation is relatively impractical. You won't need a car, however, if you are spending your entire vacation at a resort, are traveling directly to the Port of Miami for a cruise, or are here for a short stay centered in one area of the city, such as South Beach, where everything is within walking distance and parking is a costly nightmare.

When driving across a causeway or through downtown, allow extra time to reach your destination because of frequent drawbridge openings and slow boat crossings. Some bridges open about every half hour for large sailing vessels to make their way through the wide bays and canals that crisscross the city, stalling traffic for several minutes.

RENTALS   It seems as though every car-rental company, big and small, has at least one office in Miami. Consequently, the city is one of the cheapest places in the world to rent a car. Many firms regularly advertise prices in the neighborhood of $140 per week for their economy cars. You should also check with the airline you have chosen to get to Miami; there are often special discounts when you book a flight and reserve your rental car simultaneously. A minimum age, generally 25, is usually required of renters, while some rental agencies have also set maximum ages. A national car-rental broker, **Car Rental Referral Service** (© **800/404-4482**), can often find companies willing to rent to drivers between the ages of 21 and 24 and can also get discounts from major companies as well as some regional ones.

National car-rental companies with toll-free numbers include **Alamo** (© 800/327-9633), **Avis** (© 800/331-1212), **Budget** (© 800/527-0700), **Dollar** (© 800/800-4000 or 800/327-7607), **Hertz** (© 800/654-3131), **National** (© 800/328-4567), and **Thrifty** (© 800/367-2277). One excellent company that has offices in every conceivable part of town and offers extremely competitive rates is **Enterprise** (© 800/325-8007). Call around and comparison shop— car-rental prices can fluctuate more than airfares. For information on car-rental insurance, see "Getting There" in chapter 2.

Many car-rental companies also offer cellular phones or electronic map rentals. It might be wise to opt for these additional safety features (the phone will definitely come in handy if you get lost), although the cost can be exorbitant.

Finally, think about splurging on a convertible (at most companies, the price for convertibles is approximately 20% more). Not only are convertibles one of the best ways to see the beautiful surroundings, but they're also an ideal way to perfect a tan!

PARKING   Always keep plenty of quarters on hand to feed hungry meters. Or, on Miami Beach, stop by the Chamber of Commerce at 1920 Meridian Ave. or any Publix grocery store to buy a magnetic **parking card** in denominations of $10, $20, or $25. Parking is usually plentiful (except on South Beach and Coconut Grove), but when it's not, be careful: Fines for illegal parking can be stiff, starting at a hefty $18.

In addition to parking garages, valet services are commonplace and often used. Expect to pay from $5 to $15 for parking in Coconut Grove and on South Beach's busy weekend nights.

LOCAL DRIVING RULES   Florida law allows drivers to make a right turn on a red light after a complete stop, unless otherwise indicated. In addition, all passengers are required to wear seat belts, and children under 3 must be securely fastened in government-approved car seats.

BY TAXI

If you're not planning on traveling much within the city, an occasional taxi is a good alternative to renting a car. If you plan on spending your vacation within the confines of South Beach's Art Deco District, you might also want to avoid the parking hassles that come with renting your own car. Taxi meters start at $1.50 for the first ¼ mile and 25¢ for each additional ⅛ mile. There are standard flat-rate charges for frequently traveled routes—for example, Miami Beach's Convention Center to Coconut Grove will cost about $16.

Major cab companies include **Metro** (© 305/888-8888), **Yellow** (© 305/444-4444), and, on Miami Beach, **Central** (© 305/532-5555).

BY BIKE

Miami is a biker's paradise, especially on Miami Beach, where the hard-packed sand and boardwalks make it an easy and scenic route. However, unless you are a former New York City bike messenger, you won't want to use a bicycle as your main means of transportation.

For more information on bicycles, including where to rent the best ones, see "More Ways to Play, Indoors & Out" in chapter 7.

FAST FACTS: Miami

Airport See "Orientation," earlier in this chapter.

American Express You'll find American Express offices in downtown Miami at 100 North Biscayne Blvd. (© 305/358-7350); 9700 Collins Ave., Bal Harbour (© 305/865-5959); and 32 Miracle Mile, Coral Gables (© 305/446-3381). Offices are open weekdays from 9am to 5:30pm and Saturday from 9am to 5pm. To report lost or stolen traveler's checks, call © 800/221-7282.

Area Code The original area code for Miami and all of Dade County was 305. That is still the code for older phone numbers, but all phone numbers assigned since July 1998 have the area code 786 (SUN). For all local calls, even if you're just calling across the street, you must dial the area code (305 or 786) first. Even though the Keys still share the Dade County area code of 305, calls to there from Miami are considered long distance and must be preceded by 1-305. (Within the Keys, simply dial the seven-digit number.) The area code for Fort Lauderdale is 954; for Palm Beach, Boca Raton, Vero Beach, and Port St. Lucie, it's 561.

Business Hours Banking hours vary, but most banks are open weekdays from 9am to 3pm. Several stay open until 5pm or so at least 1 day during the week, and many banks feature automated teller machines (ATMs) for 24-hour banking. Most stores are open daily from 10am to 6pm; however, there are many exceptions. Shops in the Bayside Marketplace are usually open until 9 or 10pm, as are the boutiques in Coconut Grove. Boutiques on South Beach operate on their own time zone and range from 11 am to midnight, sometimes earlier, sometimes later. Stores in Bal Harbour and other malls are usually open an extra hour 1 night during the week (usually Thursday). As far as business offices are concerned, Miami is generally a 9-to-5 town.

Car Rentals See "Getting Around," earlier in this chapter.

Climate See "When to Go," in chapter 2.

Curfew Although not strictly enforced, there is an alleged curfew in effect for minors after 11pm on weeknights and midnight on weekends in all of Miami–Dade County. After those hours, children under 17 cannot be out on the streets or driving unless accompanied by a parent or on their way to work. Somehow, however, they still manage to sneak out and congregate in popular areas such as Coconut Grove and South Beach.

Dentists **A&E Dental,** 11400 N. Kendall Dr., Mega Bank Building (© **305/ 271-7777**), offers round-the-clock care and accepts MasterCard and Visa.

Doctors In an emergency, call an ambulance by dialing © **911** from any phone. The Dade County Medical Association sponsors a **Physician Referral Service** (© **305/324-8717**), weekdays from 9am to 5pm. **Health South Doctors' Hospital,** 5000 University Dr., Coral Gables (© **305/666-2111**), is a 285-bed acute-care hospital with a 24-hour physician-staffed emergency department.

Driving Rules See "Getting Around," earlier in this chapter.

Drugstores See "Pharmacies," later in this section.

Embassies/Consulates See "Fast Facts" section in chapter 3, "For International Visitors."

Emergencies To reach the police, ambulance, or fire department, dial © **911** from any phone. No coins are needed. Emergency hotlines include **Crisis Intervention** (© **305/358-HELP** or 305/358-4357) and the **Poison Information Center** (© **800/282-3171**).

Eyeglasses **Pearle Vision Center,** 7901 Biscayne Blvd. (© **305/754-5144**) can usually fill prescriptions in about an hour.

Hospitals See "Doctors," earlier in this section.

Information See "Visitor Information," earlier in this chapter.

Laundry/Dry Cleaning For dry cleaning, self-service machines, and a wash-and-fold service by the pound, call **All Laundry Service,** 5701 NW 7th St. (© **305/261-8175**); it's open daily from 7am to 10pm. **Clean Machine Laundry,** 226 12th St., South Beach (© **305/534-9429**), is convenient to South Beach's Art Deco hotels and is open 24 hours a day. **Coral Gables Laundry & Dry Cleaning,** 250 Minorca Ave., Coral Gables (© **305/446-6458**), has been dry cleaning, altering, and laundering since 1930. It offers a life-saving same-day service and is open weekdays from 7am to 7pm and Saturday from 8am to 3pm.

Liquor Laws Only adults 21 or older may legally purchase or consume alcohol in the state of Florida. Minors are usually permitted in bars, as long as they also serve food. Liquor laws are strictly enforced; if you look young, carry identification. Beer and wine are sold in most supermarkets and convenience stores. The city of Miami's liquor stores are closed on Sundays. Liquor stores in the city of Miami Beach are open all week.

Lost Property If you lost something at the airport, call the **Airport Lost and Found** office (© **305/876-7377**). If you lost something on the bus, Metrorail, or Metromover, call **Metro-Dade Transit Agency** (© **305/770-3131**). If you lost something anywhere else, phone the **Dade County Police**

Lost and Found (© 305/375-3366). You may also want to fill out a police report for insurance purposes.

Luggage Storage/Lockers In addition to the baggage check at Miami International Airport, most hotels offer luggage storage facilities. If you are taking a cruise from the Port of Miami (see "Cruises & Other Caribbean Getaways" in chapter 7), bags can be stored in your ship's departure terminal.

Newspapers/Magazines The **Miami Herald** is the city's only English-language daily. It is especially known for its extensive Latin American coverage and has a decent Friday "Weekend" entertainment guide. The most respected alternative weekly is the give-away tabloid called **New Times,** which contains up-to-date listings and reviews of food, films, theater, music, and whatever else is happening in town. Also free, if you can find it, is **Ocean Drive,** an oversize glossy magazine that's limited on text (no literary value) and heavy on ads and society photos. It's what you should read if you want to know who's who and where to go for fun; it's available at a number of chic South Beach boutiques and restaurants. It is also available on newsstands.

For a large selection of foreign-language newspapers and magazines, check with any of the large bookstores (see chapter 8, "Miami Shopping") or try **News Café** at 800 Ocean Dr., South Beach (© 305/538-6397), or in Coconut Grove at 2901 Florida Ave. (© 305/774-6397). Adjacent to the **Van Dyke Cafe,** 846 Lincoln Rd., South Beach (© 305/534-3600) is a fantastic newsstand with magazines and newspapers from all over the world. Also check out **Eddie's Normandy,** 1096 Normandy Dr., Miami Beach (© 305/866-2026), and **Worldwide News,** 1629 NE 163rd St., North Miami Beach (© 305/940-4090).

Pharmacies **Walgreens Pharmacy** has dozens of locations all over town, including 8550 Coral Way (© 305/221-9271) in Coral Gables; 1845 Alton Rd. (© 305/531-8868) in South Beach; and 6700 Collins Ave. (© 305/861-6742) in Miami Beach. The branch at 5731 Bird Rd. at SW 40th St. (© 305/666-0757) is open 24 hours, as is **Eckerd Drugs,** 1825 Miami Gardens Dr. NE, at 185th Street, North Miami Beach (© 305/932-5740).

Photographic Needs **One Hour Photo,** in the Bayside Marketplace (© 305/377-FOTO), is pricey (about $17 to develop and print a roll of 36 pictures), but they're open Monday to Saturday from 10am to 10pm and Sunday from noon to 8pm. Walgreens or Eckerd (see above, under "Pharmacies") will develop film for the next day for about $6 or $7.

Police For emergencies, dial © **911** from any phone. No coins are needed. For other matters, call © 305/595-6263.

Post Office The **Main Post Office,** 2200 Milam Dairy Rd., Miami, FL 33152 (© 305/639-4280), is located west of Miami International Airport. Conveniently located post offices include 1300 Washington Ave. in South Beach and 3191 Grand Ave. in Coconut Grove. There is one central number for all post offices: © **800/275-8777.**

Radio On the AM dial, 610 (WIOD), 790 (WNWS), 1230 (WJNO), and 1340 (WPBR) are all talk. There is no all-news station in town, although 940 (WINZ) gives traffic updates and headline news in between its talk shows.

WDBF (1420) is a good big-band station and WPBG (1290) features golden oldies. Switching to the FM dial, the two most popular R&B stations are WEDR/99 Jams (99.1) and Hot 105 (105.1). The best rock stations on the FM dial are WZTA (94.9), WBGG/Big 106 (105.9), and the progressive college station WVUM (90.5). WKIS (99.9) is the top country station. Top-40 music can be heard on WHYI (100.3) and classic disco on Mega 103 (103.5). WGTR (97.3) plays easy listening, WDNA (88.9) has the best Latin jazz and multiethnic sounds, and public radio can be heard either on WXEL (90.7) or WLRN (91.3).

Religious Services Miami houses of worship are as varied as the city's population and include St. Patrick Catholic Church, 3716 Garden Ave., Miami Beach (© 305/531-1124); Coral Gables Baptist Church, 5501 Granada Blvd. (© 305/665-4072); Temple Judea, 5500 Granada Blvd., Coral Gables (© 305/667-5657); Coconut Grove United Methodist, 2850 SW 27th Ave. (© 305/443-0880); Christ Episcopal Church, 3481 Hibiscus St. (© 305/442-8542); Plymouth Congregational Church, 3400 Devon Rd., at Main Highway (© 305/444-6521); Hindu Temple of South Florida, 12511 SW 112th Ave. (© 305/792-2494); Masjid Al-Ansar (Muslim), 5245 NW 7th Ave. (© 305/757-8741); and Buddhist Temple of Miami, 15200 SW 240th St. (© 305/245-2702).

Restrooms Stores rarely let customers use their rest rooms, and many restaurants offer their facilities only for their patrons. However, most malls have bathrooms, as do many fast-food restaurants. Public beaches and large parks often provide toilets, though in some places you have to pay or tip an attendant. Most large hotels have clean rest rooms in their lobbies.

Safety As always, use your common sense and be aware of your surroundings at all times. Don't walk alone at night, and be extra wary when walking or driving though downtown Miami and surrounding areas.

Reacting to several highly publicized crimes against tourists several years ago, both local and state governments have taken steps to help protect visitors. These measures include special highly visible police units patrolling the airport and surrounding neighborhoods and better signs on the state's most tourist-traveled routes.

Spas & Massage There are a number of great spa packages at some of the ritzier hotels (see "The Best Hotel Spas," in chapter 5, "Where to Stay in Miami"), but those without spas often have relationships with on-call massage therapists, which can be arranged by asking the concierge to make an appointment for an in-room session. Popular day spas include the **Russian Turkish Baths**, 5445 Collins Ave. at the Castle Hotel (© 305/867-8316), otherwise known as "The Schvitz," where the old guard meets the new in eucalyptus-scented Turkish steam rooms and aroma baths bolstered by marble columns. **Some Like It Hot**, 841 Lincoln Rd., Miami Beach (© 305/532-8703), has expanded from a small second-floor salon into a full-service, 5,250-square-foot spa, offering massages, waxing, manicures, and a sublime signature hot-rock massage. **Le Spa Miami**, 150 8th St., Miami Beach (© 305/674-6744), is the newest day spa to hit the shores, exclusively using Lancôme products and featuring a laundry list of facials, body treatments, make-up applications, waxing, manicure, pedicures, and even photo shoots.

Taxes A 6% state sales tax (plus 0.5% local tax, for a total of 6.5% in Miami–Dade County [from Homestead to North Miami Beach]) is added on at the register for all goods and services purchased in Florida. In addition, most municipalities levy special taxes on restaurants and hotels. In Surfside, hotel taxes total 10.5%; in Bal Harbour, 9.5%; in Miami Beach (including South Beach), 11.5%; and in the rest of Dade County, a whopping 12.5%. In Miami Beach, Surfside, and Bal Harbour, the resort (hotel) tax also applies to hotel restaurants and restaurants with liquor licenses.

Taxis See "Getting Around," earlier in this chapter.

Television The local stations are Channel 6, WTVJ (NBC); Channel 4, WCIX (CBS); Channel 7, WSVN (Fox); Channel 10, WPLG (ABC); Channel 17, WLRN (PBS); Channel 23, WLTV (independent); and Channel 33, WBFS (independent). Channel 39 is the WB (WBZL) and channel 33 is UPN (WBFS).

Time Zone Miami, like New York, is in the Eastern Standard Time zone. Between April and October, daylight saving time is adopted, and clocks are set 1 hour ahead. America's eastern seaboard is 5 hours behind Greenwich Mean Time. To find out what time it is, call © 305/324-8811.

Transit Information For Metrorail or Metromover schedule information, phone © 305/770-3131 or surf over to www.co.miami-dade.fl.us/mdta/.

Weather Hurricane season runs from August through November. For an up-to-date recording of current weather conditions and forecast reports, call © 305/229-4522. Also see the "When to Go" section in chapter 2.

5

Where to Stay in Miami

As much a part of the landscape as the palm trees, many of Miami's hotels are on display as if they were contestants in a beauty pageant. The city's long-lasting status on the destination A-list has given rise to an ever-increasing number of upscale hotels, and no place in Miami has seen a greater increase in construction than Miami Beach. Since the area's renaissance, which began in the late 1980s, the beach has turned what used to be a beachfront retirement home into a sand-swept hot spot for the Gucci and Prada set. Contrary to popular belief, however, the beach does not discriminate, and it's the juxtaposition of the chic elite and the hoi polloi that contributes to its allure.

While the increasing demand for rooms on South Beach means increasing costs, you can still find a decent room at a fair price. In fact, most hotels in the Art Deco District are less Ritz-Carlton than they are Holiday Inn, unless, of course, they've been renovated (many hotels in this area were built in the 1930s for the middle class). Unless you plan to center your vacation entirely in and around your hotel, most of the cheaper Deco hotels are adequate and a wise choice for those who plan to use the room only to sleep. Smart vacationers can almost name their price if they're willing to live without a few luxuries, such as an oceanfront view.

Many of the old hotels from the 1930s, 1940s, and 1950s have been totally renovated, giving way to dozens of "boutique" (small, swanky, and independently owned) hotels. Keep in mind that when a hotel claims that it was just renovated, it can mean that they've completely gutted the building—or just applied a coat of fresh paint. Always ask what specific changes were made during a renovation, and be sure to ask if a hotel will be undergoing construction while you're there. You should also find out how near your room will be to the center of the nightlife crowd; trying to sleep directly on Ocean Drive or Collins and Washington avenues, especially during the weekend, is next to impossible, unless your lullaby of choice happens to include throbbing salsa and bass beats.

The best hotel options in each price category and those that have been fully upgraded recently are listed below. You should also know that along South Beach's Collins Avenue, there are dozens of hotels and motels—in all price categories—so there's bound to be a vacancy somewhere. If you do try the walk-in routine, don't forget to ask to see a room first. A few dollars extra could mean all the difference between flea and fabu.

While South Beach may be the nucleus of all things hyped and hip, it's not the only place with hotels. The advantage to staying on South Beach as opposed to, say, Coral Gables or Coconut Grove, is that the beaches are within walking distance, the nightlife and restaurant options are aplenty, and, basically, everything you would need is right there. However, staying there is definitely not for everyone. If you're wary, don't worry: South Beach is centrally located and only about a 15- to 30-minute drive from most other parts of Miami.

For a less expensive stay that's only a 10-minute cab ride from South Beach, Miami Beach proper (the area north of 23rd Street and Collins Avenue all the way up to 163rd Street and Collins Avenue) offers a slew of reasonable stays, right on the beach, that won't cost you your kids' college education fund.

For a less frenetic, more relaxed, and more tropical experience, the resorts on Key Biscayne exude an island feel, even though, if you look across the water, a cosmopolitan vibe beckons, thanks to the shimmering, spectacular Miami skyline.

Those who'd rather bag the beach in favor of shopping bags will enjoy North Miami Beach's proximity to the Aventura Mall as much as tan-o-holics are drawn to the sand on South Beach. And for Miami with an Old World European flair, Coral Gables and its charming hotels and exquisite restaurants provide a more prim and proper, well-heeled perspective of Miami than the trendy boutique hotels on South Beach.

SEASONS & RATES South Florida's tourist season is well defined, beginning in mid-November and lasting until Easter. Hotel prices escalate until about March, after which they begin to decline. During the off-season, hotel rates are typically 30% to 50% lower than their winter highs.

But timing isn't everything. In many cases, rates also depend on your hotel's proximity to the beach and how much ocean you can see from your window. Small motels a block or two from the water can be up to 40% cheaper than similar properties right on the sand.

Rates below have been broken down into two broad categories:

winter (generally, Thanksgiving through Easter) and off-season (about mid-May through August). The months in between, the shoulder season, should fall somewhere in between the highs and lows, while rates always go up on holidays. Remember, too, that state and city taxes can add as much as 12.5% to your bill in some parts of Miami. Some hotels, especially those in South Beach, also tack on additional service charges, and don't forget that parking is a pricey endeavor.

PRICE CATEGORIES The hotels below are divided first by area and then by price (**very expensive, expensive, moderate,** or **inexpensive**). Prices are based on published rates (or rack rates) for a standard double room during the high season. You should also check with the reservations agent, since many rooms are available above and below the category ranges listed below, and ask about packages, since it's often possible to get a better deal than these "official" rates. Most importantly, always call the hotel to confirm rates, which may be subject to change without notice because of special events, holidays, or blackout dates.

LONG-TERM STAYS If you plan to visit Miami for a month, a season, or more, think about renting a condominium apartment or a room in a long-term hotel. Long-term accommodations exist in every price category, from budget to deluxe, and in general are extremely reasonable, especially during the off-season. Check with the reservation services below, or write a short note to the chamber of commerce in the area where you plan to stay. In addition, many local real estate agents also handle short-term rentals (meaning less than a year).

RESERVATION SERVICES Central Reservation Service (© 800/950-0232 or 305/274-6832; www.reservation-services.com) works with many of Miami's hotels and can often secure discounts of up to 40%. It also gives advice on specific locales, especially in Miami Beach and downtown. During holiday time, there may be a minimum of a 3- to 5-day stay to use their services. Call for more information.

For bed-and-breakfast information throughout the state, contact **Florida Bed and Breakfast Inns** (© 800/524-1880; www.florida-inns.com).

1 South Beach

Choosing a hotel on South Beach is similar to deciding whether you'd rather pay $1.50 for french fries at Denny's or $8.50 for the same fries—but let's call them *pomme frites*—in a pricey haute cuisinerie. It's all about atmosphere. The rooms of some hotels may *look* ultrachic, but they can be as comfortable as sleeping on a concrete slab. Once you decide how much atmosphere you want, the choice will be easier. Fortunately, for every chichi hotel in South Beach—and there are many—there are just as many moderately priced, more casual options.

Prices mentioned here are rack rates—that is, the price you would be quoted if you walked up to the front desk and inquired about rates. The actual price you will end up paying will usually be less than this—especially if a travel agent makes the reservations for you. Many hotels on South Beach have stopped quoting seasonal and off-season rates and have, instead, chosen to go with a low-to-high rate representing the hotel's complete pricing range. It pays to try to negotiate the price of a room. In some of the trendier hotels, however, negotiating is highly unfashionable and not well regarded. In other words, your attempt at negotiation will either be met with a blank stare or a snippy refusal. It never hurts to try, though.

If status is important to you, as it is to many South Beach visitors, then you will be quite pleased with the number of haute hotels in the area, which are as popular as nightclubs and restaurants are on South Beach.

Art Deco hotels, while pleasing to the eye, may be a bit run-down inside. Par for the course on South Beach, appearances are at times deceiving.

VERY EXPENSIVE

Bentley Hotel 🕏🕏   The biggest coup the Bentley Hotel pulls off is its ability to remain immune to the throngs of pedestrians on the well-traveled Ocean Drive. Guests enjoy a private front entrance that leads, via elevator, to the main lobby. Inside this enclave of Old World luxury you will find a charming ambience and an overly accommodating, professional staff. The hotel's 53 suites are both hotel rooms and condos; some of them can be rented year-round. Rooms come complete with marble floors, well-stocked kitchens, and roomy bathrooms with steam showers. Try not to get a corner room, though, or you will learn more about your neighbors than you'd ever want to. Because it is located on South Beach's bustling strip of neon and nightlife, the Bentley, despite its efforts to stand apart from the rest of its neighbors, isn't impervious to noise. However, if you want luxe in the midst of all the action, the Bentley is a great choice.

510 Ocean Dr., South Beach, FL 33139. © 800/236-8510 or 305/538-1700. Fax 305/532-4865. www.thebentleyhotel.com. 53 units. Winter $295–$1,250 double. Off-season $220–$900 double. AE, DC, DISC, MC, V. **Amenities:** Rooftop pool; concierge; 24-hr. room service; dry-cleaning service. *In room:* A/C, TV/DVD player, fax, dataport, kitchen, minibar, coffeemaker, hair dryer.

Casa Grande Suite Hotel 🕏🕏   A touch of prim Europe clashes with the exotic at this all-suite hotel favored by the jet set and located on the busy, noisy

Abbey Hotel **2**
Albion Hotel **12**
Aqua **15**
Banana Bungalow **1**
Bayliss Guest House **20**
Beachcomber Hotel **23**
Bentley Hotel **47**
Brigham Gardens **21**
Casa Grande Suite Hotel **43**
Casa Tua **7**
Cavalier **24**
Chesterfield **38**
Clay Hotel & International Hostel **17**
Clevelander **22**
Crest Hotel Suites **9**
The Delano **8**
Essex House Hotel and Suites **33**
Fisher Island Club **50**
Greenview **11**
The Hotel **45**
Hotel Astor **34**
Hotel Chelsea **35**
Hotel Impala **26**
Hotel Leon **42**
Hotel Nash **31**
Hotel Ocean **27**
The Kent **30**
La Flora Hotel **25**
Lily Guest House **39**
Loew's Hotel **14**
The Loft Hotel **36**
Marlin **28**
Mercury **49**
Mermaid Guest House **37**
Miami Beach Marriott
   at South Beach **48**
Nassau Suite Hotel **19**
National Hotel **10**
Park Washington Hotel **32**
Pelican Hotel **44**
Raleigh Hotel **5**
The Ritz-Carlton **13**
Royal Hotel **46**
Royal Palm Crown Plaza Resort **16**
The Shore Club **3**
The Tides **29**
Townhouse **4**
Villa Paradiso **18**
Villas at Caffé Milano **41**
W South Beach **6**
Whitelaw Hotel **40**

thoroughfare of Ocean Drive. No matter how well insulated the windows may be, you're nevertheless likely to hear, or feel, the thunderous bass coming from cars cruising by. Fortunately, however, you will have privacy, thanks to the impeccable service of the hotel's accommodating staff.

This hotel is a tasteful visual extravaganza, with towering antique columns from Rajasthan lining the lobby, and French and Italian Tagina tiles adorning the floors. Rooms are decorated in exotic fabrics and furnished with carved Balinese teak and mahogany antiques. Making up for the lack of a pool are the hotel's unrivaled in-room amenities such as a state-of-the-art sound system, plush beds, full kitchens with custom stocked refrigerators, and enormous baths.

834 Ocean Dr., South Beach, FL 33139. ℭ **800/OUTPOST** or 305/672-7003. Fax 305/673-3669. www.casagrandehotel.com. 34 units. Winter $310 junior suite; $340 1-bedroom suite; $525 2-bedroom suite; $1,500 3-bedroom suite. Off-season $195 junior suite; $230 1-bedroom suite; $350 2-bedroom suite; $750 3-bedroom suite. Additional person $15. AE, DC, DISC, MC, V. Limited street parking; valet parking $14. **Amenities:** Discount access to nearby health club; activities desk; room service; babysitting; overnight dry-cleaning and laundry services. *In room:* A/C, TV/VCR, stereo with CD and cassette players, kitchen, minibar, coffeemaker, hair dryer, iron.

Casa Tua ⚑   This outrageous boutique offers custom-tailored amenities (from toiletries to snacks) for each of its guests, who fill out a detailed profile when booking one of Casa Tua's five suites. Styled like a glorious Mediterranean beach house, Casa Tua also has a posh restaurant with an Italian-accented menu and a second-floor lounge for afternoon tea and evening cocktails. At press time, the hotel's management was very cagey as far as hotel details were concerned, expressing a deep concern for "keeping its clientele extremely exclusive" and, essentially, by word of mouth. Enough said, I suppose.

1700 James Ave., Miami Beach, FL 33139. ℭ **305/673-1010.** 5 suites. $750 and up. Call for details.

The Delano ⚑ *Overrated*   Unless your name's Madonna or the equivalent, you will definitely feel like you are paying for the privilege of staying here. The Delano may not be the friendliest place, but it certainly is amusing to look at—with 40-foot sheer white billowing curtains hanging outside, mirrors everywhere, Adirondack chairs, and faux-fur-covered beds. The rooms are done up sanitarium style: sterile, yet toxically trendy, in pure white save for a perfectly crisp green Granny Smith apple in each room—the only freebie you're going to get here. A bathroom renovation recently took place in all of the rooms—but they remain small and Spartan.

Checking into Hotel Bars

While South Beach is known for its trendy club scene, hotel bars are also very much a part of the nightlife. Among the hottest hotel bars are the **Rose Bar** at the Delano, the **lobby bar at the Hotel Astor,** the **Bond St. Lounge** at the Townhouse, the **Tower Bar** at the Shore Club (scheduled to open at press time), the **lobby bar at the Whitelaw Hotel,** and the **Marlin Bar** at the Marlin Hotel. A South Beach outpost of the boutique chain of W Hotels, featuring hot watering hole Whiskey Blue and owned by Cindy Crawford's husband, Rande Gerber, is scheduled to open in fall 2002 at 1701 Collins Ave. (ℭ **305/534-3500**). See chapter 9, "Miami After Dark," for more details.

An attractive, white-clad staff looks as if they were handpicked from last month's *Vogue*. While they may sigh if you ask for something, eventually they'll get it for you. The gym here is great, but is costs $15 a day, even if you are a guest. The fantastic wading pool, thankfully, is free, but get out early to snag a chair. The Blue Door restaurant, formerly part-owned by Madonna, serves lots of attitude with its pricey haute cuisine; the lobby's Rose Bar is command central for the chic elite who don't flinch at paying in excess of $10 for a martini. The hotel's major saving grace is Agua, the rooftop spa, where, if you can afford it, an hour massage while overlooking the ocean is blissful.

1685 Collins Ave., South Beach, FL 33139. ℂ 800/555-5001 or 305/672-2000. Fax 305/532-0099. 209 units, 1 penthouse. Winter $325–$810 standard; $750–$2,000 suite; $2,000–$3,000 bungalow or 2-bedroom; $2,800–$3,000 penthouse. Off-season $245–$660 standard; $600–$2,000 suite; $940–$3,000 bungalow or 2-bedroom; $2,400–$3,000 penthouse. Additional person $35. AE, DC, DISC, MC, V. Valet parking $20. **Amenities:** 3 restaurants, bar; large outdoor pool; 24-hr. state-of-the-art David Barton gym; extensive watersports equipment; children's programs; concierge; business center; room service; in-room massage; same-day dry-cleaning and laundry services. *In room:* A/C, TV/VCR, CD player, minibar, hair dryer.

Fisher Island Club ★★★ *Finds*   Located on an exclusive island just off Miami Beach, this hotel is a luxurious cross between *Fantasy Island, Lifestyles of the Rich and Famous,* and *Survivor.* But you will not be roughing it on this island, which serves as a retreat for those with enough money to afford it, including the likes of Luciano Pavarotti and Oprah Winfrey, who sold her multimillion-dollar condo here in favor of a multi-, multimillion manse in Santa Barbara.

To get to the resort, visitors and residents take a private ferry, which shuttles guests to and from the mainland every 15 to 20 minutes. It can be somewhat of a hassle—especially if you need to make a quick return to the island—but it does run on a very regular schedule. Be forewarned that the ferry lets residents on first, so if there's no room after all the Rolls Royces and Ferraris roll on, you're outta luck and will have to wait for the next one. Don't worry if you are carless— on this exclusive island, golf carts will get you anywhere you need to go.

As for location, you're only minutes from the airport, South Beach, Coral Gables, and Coconut Grove (not counting ferry time). Still, considering the pampering you'll receive in this former Vanderbilt mansion turned resort extraordinaire, you probably won't want to leave the seclusion of the island for the frenetic city. Rooms vary in size and shape, and cottages come with hot tubs. A world-class spa and club offer all the amenities you could imagine. And you definitely won't go hungry: The elegant Vanderbilt Club offers continental cuisine; the Beach Club and Golfer's Grill serve basic but expensive sandwiches and salads; an Italian cafe prepares good pizza and pastas; and a gourmet general store sells everything else.

1 Fisher Island Dr., Fisher Island, FL 33190. ℂ 800/537-3708 or 305/535-6020. Fax 305/535-6003. www.fisherisland-florida.com. 60 units. Winter $385–$840 double; $795–$1,900 suite or cottage. Off-season $330–$435 double; $550–$1,140 suite or cottage. Golf, tennis, and spa packages available seasonally. 20% gratuity added to all food and beverages. AE, DC, MC, V. **Amenities:** 3 restaurants, 3 bars; P. B. Dye Golf Course; 18 tennis courts; 2 marinas; world-class spa; concierge; airport transportation; secretarial service; limited room service; babysitting; dry-cleaning and laundry services. *In room:* A/C, TV/VCR, minibar, coffeemaker, hair dryer.

Loews Hotel ★ *Kids*   The Loews Hotel is one of the largest beach hotels to arrive in South Beach in almost 30 years, consuming an unprecedented 900 feet of oceanfront. This 800-room behemoth is considered an eyesore by many, an architectural triumph by others. However you perceive it, you can't miss the hotel's multitiered cone-shaped 18-story tower perched high above the rest of South Beach. Rooms are a bit boxy and bland: nothing to rave about, but are clean and have new carpets and bedspreads to erase signs of early wear and tear from the hotel's heavy traffic.

The best rooms are those that do not face the very congested Collins Avenue, since those tend to be quite noisy. Though Loews attempts to maintain the intimacy of an Art Deco hotel while trying to accommodate business travelers, it is so large that it tends to feel like a convention hall. You're not going to get personal doting service here, but the staff does try, even if it takes them awhile. If you can steer your way through all the name-tagged business people in the lobby, you can escape to the pool (with an undisputedly gorgeous, landscaped entrance that's more Maui than Miami), which is large enough to accommodate families and conventioneers alike. In addition to children's fare such as the Loews Loves Kids program—featuring special menus, tours, welcome gifts for children under 10, supervised programs, free accommodations for children under 18, and the Generation G program for grandparents and grandkids traveling together—the hotel hosts fun activities for adults, too, such as Dive in Movies at the pool, salsa lessons, and bingo. The hotel's Argentine steak house, Gaucho Room, is superb.

1601 Collins Ave., South Beach, FL 33139. ℂ **800/23-LOEWS** or 305/604-1601. www.loewshotels.com. 800 units. Winter from $229 double. Off-season from $189 double. AE, DC, DISC, MC, V. Valet parking $19. Pets accepted. **Amenities:** 3 restaurants, 3 bars; coffee bar; sprawling outdoor pool; health club; Jacuzzi; sauna; watersports rentals; children's programs; concierge; business center; 24-hr. room service; babysitting; dry cleaning. *In room:* A/C, TV, dataport, minibar, coffeemaker, hair dryer.

National Hotel 🎯   With its towering ceilings, sultry furnishings, and massive gilded mirrors, the elegant 1940s-style National ought to be the backdrop for a gangster flick. At 11 stories, the main building stands taller than most of its neighbors and offers grand views of the beach and ocean below. Rooms in the garden wing are slightly larger and have balconies, but all are comfortable and pretty spacious with sleek and modern bathrooms. Poolside rooms have slightly larger bathrooms, but beyond that, are really just a step above motel rooms.

However, the National's pool is a winner. It's Miami's longest pool (205 ft.) and can be considered the supermodel of hotel pools, lithe and graceful and almost too sleek (rivaling even the Delano's pool) for splashing. The hotel's Café Mosaic is an elegant and formal dining room offering tropical Floridian fare with a Latin twist. The nicest aspects of the hotel are the ultra-Deco lobby bar and Press Room cigar bar, which look like 1940s movie sets. Live entertainment on weekends and happy hours during the week add to the ambiance.

1677 Collins Ave., South Beach, FL. 33139. ℂ **800/327-8370** or 305/532-2311. Fax 305/534-1426. www.nationalhotel.com. 152 units. Winter $325–$450 double. Off-season $265–$345 double. AE, DC, DISC, MC, V. Valet parking $17. **Amenities:** Restaurant, 3 bars; large outdoor pool; exercise room; watersports equipment rental; concierge; limited room service; babysitting; dry-cleaning and laundry services. *In room:* A/C, TV/VCR, minibar, hair dryer, stereo.

The Ritz-Carlton 🎯🎯🎯   The luxe life comes to a congested and somewhat seedy corner of South Beach in the form of this beachfront, lushly landscaped Ritz-Carlton, slated to open in the fall of 2002, which has restored a landmark 1950s building to its original Art Moderne style and filled it with the hotel's signature five-star service. Far from ostentatious, the Ritz-Carlton's South Beach property moves away from gilded opulence in favor of the more soothing pastel-washed touches of Deco. Though South Beach is better known for its trendy boutique hotels, the Ritz-Carlton offers comfort to those who might pre-fer 100% cotton sheets and goose-down pillows to high-style minimalism.

With impeccable service, an impressive stretch of sand, and a world-class 13,000-square-foot spa and wellness center, the Ritz-Carlton kicks sand in the faces of some of the smaller hotels that think they're doing *you* a favor by allowing you to sleep there.

1 Lincoln Rd., South Beach, FL 33139. (©) **800/241-3333** or 786/276-4000. Fax 786/276-4100. www.ritz carlton.com. 375 units. Winter $450–$690 double. Off-season $245–$425 double. AE, DISC, MC, V. Valet park-ing $30. **Amenities:** 3 restaurants; outdoor heated pool; health club; spa; extensive watersports rentals; children's program; 24-hr. business center; salon; 24-hr. room service; babysitting; overnight laundry service. *In room:* A/C, TV, dataport, minibar, coffeemaker, hair dryer, iron, safe.

The Shore Club ✿
Despite the fact that this newly opened, hyper-hip hotel is little more than a concrete canyon, a mod version of the eerily deserted house in *The Shining,* it has been slowly making waves within the jet set and fabulatti thanks to one thing in particular: Florida's first-ever Nobu sushi restaurant and cocktail lounge (a major hit in New York, Las Vegas, Paris, and London). The hotel's other restaurant, Sirena, also makes up for the hotel's somewhat trying-too-hard-to-be-hip lackluster vibe.

The Shore Club also boasts that 80% of its 325 rooms have an ocean view. Contrary to the cold, cavernous lobby, exquisite gardens draw guests toward the beach through courtyards and reflecting pools. Rooms are loaded with state-of-the-art amenities, not to mention 400-thread linen bedding, Mexican sandstone flooring in the bathroom with custom-designed glass, and an enclosed "wet area" with bathtub, shower, and teak bench. (Molton Brown bathroom amenities are worth bringing an extra bag for.) If you can't afford the penthouse or a poolside cabana, consider an Ocean View room, which is stellar in its own right, with its massive, two-nozzled shower-tub combo that's almost better than a day at the beach. If you are wondering whether to choose the always-hip mainstay, the Delano, over this hotel, consider that the Shore Club is hardly as crowded, has little or no scene, and its rooms boast a bit more personality than the Delano's.

1901 Collins Ave., Miami Beach, FL 33139. (©) **877/640-9500** or 305/695-3100. Fax 305/695-3299. www.shoreclubsouthbeach.com. 325 units; 8 cabanas. Winter $525–$775 double; $1,125 suite; $2,500 cabana. Off-season $425–$675 double; $1,025 suite; $1,500 cabana. AE, DC, MC, V. Valet parking $20. **Amenities:** 3 restaurants, 4 bars; outdoor reflecting pools with poolside dataports; health club with steam room and outdoor equipment; spa; concierge; 24-hr. room service. *In room:* A/C, TV, Intrigue System with digitally downloaded movies and high-speed Internet access, CD player, stereo, fax, minibar.

The Tides ✿✿✿
This 12-story Art Deco masterpiece is reminiscent of a gleaming ocean liner, with porthole windows and lots of stainless steel and frosted glass. Rooms are starkly white but much more luxurious and comfortable than those at the Delano. Also, all rooms are at least twice the size of a typical South Beach hotel room and have a view of the ocean. They feature king beds, spacious closets, large bathrooms, and even a telescope from which to view the vast ocean. The penthouses on the 9th and 10th floors are situated at the high-est point on Ocean Drive, allowing for a priceless panoramic view of the ocean, the skyline, and the beach. Even if you can't afford it, you must ask for a tour of the Goldeneye Suite, a room suited for James Bond and his Bond girls, with hot tub in the middle, private deck, and high-tech toys. Although small, the fresh-water pool is a welcome plus for those who aren't in the mood to feel the sand between their toes; but it really doesn't fit with the rest of the hotel, lacking in ambience and view (it overlooks an alley). The hotel's restaurant, Twelve Twenty,

is an elegant, excellent, and pricey eatery with seating in the lobby. The Terrace is a less expensive outdoor cafe. The Tides is a place where celebrities like Ben Affleck, Jennifer Lopez, and Bono come to stay for some R&R, but you won't find gawkers or paparazzi lurking in the lobby, just an elegant clientele and staff who are respectful of people's privacy and desire for peace and quiet.

1220 Ocean Dr., South Beach, FL 33139. ℂ 800/OUTPOST or 305/604-5000. Fax 305/672-6288. www.islandoutpost.com. 45 units. Winter $525 suite; $3,000 penthouse. Off-season $375 suite; $2,000 penthouse. Additional person $15. AE, DC, DISC, MC, V. Valet parking $18. **Amenities:** 2 restaurants, lounge, bar; outdoor heated pool; small health club and discount at large nearby health club or yoga studio; concierge; secretarial services; 24-hr. room service; beach lounge service; in-room massage; babysitting; laundry and dry-cleaning service. *In room:* A/C, TV/VCR, stereo/CD player with selection of music, video rentals, minibar, hair dryer, iron, safe.

Villas at Caffé Milano 🏆🏆 *Finds* With prices like these, you could've actually gone to Milan, but nonetheless, this 11-room boutique hotel boasts enormous, luxurious oceanfront rooms with state-of-the-art industrial-style kitchen appliances, flat- or big-screen televisions, and DVD players. In addition to the fantastic in-room amenities, the service here is particularly attentive, as well it should be for these prices. The one drawback, for some, is its location on a busy stretch of Ocean Drive—the noise level is rather high here and there's nothing the hotel can do about it. But they will try to fulfill any other requests you might have.

850 Ocean Dr., South Beach, FL 33139. ℂ 888/535-5135 or 305/ 535-8879. Fax: 305/695-2942. 11 units. Year-round $500–$1,500 double. AE, DISC, MC, V. Valet parking $18. **Amenities:** Restaurant, lounge; dry-cleaning service. *In room:* A/C, TV/VCR, DVD, kitchen, coffeemaker, hair dryer, washer and dryer; Jacuzzi in one unit.

EXPENSIVE

Albion Hotel 🏆🏆 An architectural masterpiece, originally designed in 1939 by internationally acclaimed architect Igor Polevitzky (of Havana's legendary Hotel Nacional fame), this sleek, modern, nautical-style hotel was once the local headquarters for Abbie Hoffman and the Students for a Democratic Society during the 1972 Democratic National Convention in Miami. Though it was totally renovated under the guidance of the hip hotel family, the Rubells, the hotel still maintains a neo-hippie democratic feeling of peace, love, togetherness—albeit with a hipster twist. Despite its location 2 blocks from the beach, a large portholed pool and artificial beach are enough to keep you at the property and off the real beach. Rooms are industrial chic, and, for some people, not very warm; recent renovations have taken a little of the edge off. Penthouse 9 is the hotel's most popular—especially for private, in-room parties. The staff is wonderful and cookies at the registration desk make you feel as if you're a guest in someone's home and not a hotel. Kiss, a pricey, sceney steakhouse/cabaret opened in the hotel in October 2001; for lighter fare, the mezzanine-level Pantry provides snacks and continental breakfast items.

1650 James Ave. (at Lincoln Rd.), South Beach, FL 33139. ℂ 877/RUBELLS or 305/913-1000. Fax 305/674-0507. www.rubellhotels.com. 94 units. Winter $255–$375 double. Off-season $165–$265 double. AE, DC, DISC, MC, V. Valet parking $17. Pets accepted. **Amenities:** Restaurant, bar; large outdoor heated pool with adjacent artificial sand beach; small exercise room; concierge; airport limo service; business and secretarial services; 24-hr. room service; in-room massage; babysitting; dry cleaning. *In room:* A/C, TV/VCR, stereo with CD and cassette player, dataport, minibar, hair dryer, iron.

The Hotel 🏆🏆🏆 Kitschy fashion designer Todd Oldham whimsically restored this 1939 gem (formerly the Tiffany Hotel) as he would have a vintage

Hotel Dining

While travelers don't necessarily choose a hotel by their dining options, a number of Miami's best restaurants can be found inside hotels. Some of the city's most hailed cuisine can be had at the Delano's **Blue Door,** the Hotel Nash's **Mark's South Beach,** The Hotel's **Wish,** and the Mandarin Oriental's **Azul. Nobu,** a New York import at the Shore Club, is the primary reason why people go to that cavernous hotel. *Warning:* In some cases, your tab at these restaurants may be almost as high as the price of a room. See chapter 6, "Where to Dine in Miami," for reviews of these and other hotel restaurants.

piece of couture. He laced it with lush, cool colors, hand-cut mirrors, and glass mosaics from his ready-to-wear factory, then added artisan detailing, terrazzo floors, and porthole windows. The small, soundproof rooms are very comfortable and incredibly stylish, though the bathrooms are a bit cramped. There's no need to pay more for an oceanfront view—go up to the rooftop, where the pool is located, and you'll see an amazing view of the Atlantic. The hotel's restaurant, Wish (see p. 126), is one of South Beach's best.

801 Collins Ave., South Beach, FL 33139. ⓒ 877/843-4683 or 305/531-2222. Fax 305/531-2222. www.the hotelofsouthbeach.com. 52 units. Winter $275–$405 double. Off-season $215–$355 double. AE, DC, DISC, MC, V. Valet parking $18. **Amenities:** Restaurant, bar; pool bar; small pool; health club; concierge; business center; room service. *In room:* A/C, TV/VCR, stereo system with CD and cassette players, Kiehl's products, video library, dataport, minibar, coffeemaker, hair dryer.

Hotel Astor 🐾🐾🐾   Cozy-chic best describes this diminutive Deco hotel built in 1936. A 1995 renovation greatly improved on the original design of this simple three-story property, which has hosted the likes of Cameron Diaz and Madonna and continues to attract a lively local crowd to the small but sleek lobby bar. Though the hotel isn't as sceney (a la the Delano) as it once was, it's still a favorite spot for repeat visitors who wouldn't think of staying anywhere else.

There is a small lap pool and a beautiful waterfall outside the bar area, but if you're looking to catch some sun, you may want to consider walking the 2 blocks to the beach, because there are very few lounge chairs at the pool. The rooms are small but soothing, featuring plush and luxurious details—Belgian linens and towels, funky custom mood lighting with dimmer switches, and incredibly plush mattresses that are difficult to leave. I especially recommend the rooms overlooking the courtyard, for their views and for a bit more serenity than that which is afforded in rooms overlooking the street. Views are probably the worst thing about this hotel, as most rooms face the street or a neighboring seedy hotel. The hotel staff is known for its extreme attentiveness—especially Arturo, the hotel's *Cheers*-y bartender who actually knows everybody's names and their drinks of choice. Astor Place Bar and Grill in the hotel's basement is one of the city's finest—and most expensive.

956 Washington Ave., South Beach, FL 33139. ⓒ 800/270-4981 or 305/531-8081. Fax 305/531-3193. www.hotelastor.com. 40 units. Winter $155–$420 double. Off-season $110–$250 double. Additional person $30. AE, DC, MC, V. Valet parking $20. **Amenities:** Restaurant, 2 bars; small outdoor pool; access to nearby health club; 24-hr. concierge service; secretarial services; limited room service; in-room massage; babysitting; laundry and dry-cleaning service. *In room:* A/C, TV, dataport, minibar, fridge, hair dryer.

Hotel Impala ⭐⭐⭐ *(Finds)*   This renovated Mediterranean inn is one of the area's best, and it's just beautiful, from the Greco-Roman frescos and friezes to an intimate garden that is perfumed with the scents from carefully hanging lilies and gardenias. Rooms are extremely comfortable, with super-cushy sleigh beds, sisal floors, wrought-iron fixtures, imported Belgian cotton linens, wood furniture, and fabulous roomy bathrooms done up in stainless steel and coral rock. Adjacent to the hotel is Spiga, an intimate, excellent Italian restaurant that is reasonably priced. Enclaves like this one are rare on South Beach.

1228 Collins Ave., South Beach, FL 33139. ✆ **800/646-7252** or 305/673-2021. Fax 305/673-5984. hotel impala1@aol.com. 17 units. Winter $200–$400 double. Off-season $169–$279 double. AE, DC, MC, V. Valet parking $18. No children under 16 permitted. **Amenities:** Restaurant; concierge; room service. *In room:* A/C, TV/VCR, stereo, CD player, complimentary videos, dataport, hair dryer.

Hotel Nash ⭐⭐⭐   Bridging the gap between the hypertrendy and schlocky hotels often found on South Beach, the Hotel Nash is a rarity in that it boasts both style and substance. Located a block from the beach and behind the infamous Versace mansion, the Nash is housed in a 1930s Deco structure, which received an $11 million renovation. The result is a soothing, almost therapeutic hotel in which the scents of aromatherapy seep into every room and public space on the property. An aromatic indoor garden of jasmine, bougainvillea, star anise, and cypress, three tiny yet intimate pools—freshwater, saltwater, and mineral water—and possibly the best restaurant on the beach—Mark's South Beach—are permanent fixtures in this beautiful hotel. Rooms overlook either the city or the Versace mansion observatory. Ricky Martin chose the Nash's penthouse as the site to host a private dinner party. The best room in the house (that's not a penthouse) is the duplex suite, a tri-level room with sitting area downstairs, second-floor bedroom, and third-floor terrace.

1120 Collins Ave., Miami Beach, FL 33139. ✆ **305/674-7800.** Fax 305/538-8288. www.hotelnash.com. 55 units. Winter $210–$255 double; $275–$625 suite; $775 duplex; $625–$1,600 penthouse. Off-season $180 double; $250–$480 suite; $780 duplex; $580–$1,100 penthouse. Rates change frequently. AE, DC, DISC, MC, V. Valet parking $16. **Amenities:** Restaurant, bar; 3 outdoor pools; watersports equipment rental; car service. *In room:* A/C, TV/VCR or DVD, CD player, dataport, minibar, hair dryer, iron, safe.

Hotel Ocean ⭐⭐   This Mediterranean enclave, located smack in the middle of crazy Ocean Drive, remains somehow protected from the disarray, perhaps due to the lovely French-style courtyard, on which live jazz is often performed. The European-style hotel's 27 suites are fabulous, with authentic Art Deco furniture, soundproof windows, terraces facing the ocean, massive bathrooms with French toiletries, and original fireplaces that add to the coziness, even if you're not likely to use them. Room 504 is the hotel's best-kept secret, with ocean view and private balcony for a reasonable $250 to $270. Insiders who stay at this hotel know to request the Deep Sleep experience upon checking in. This complimentary, by-request-only amenity includes a magnetic mattress (not recommended for pregnant women or patients with a pacemaker), known to create balance and rest the body, as well as an orthopedic pillow. The hotel's restaurant, Les Deux Fontaines, is known for its superb service, excellent seafood, and intimate Speakeasy Bar. The only drawback to this hotel is its lack of a pool, but since the beach is directly across the street, it really shouldn't stop you from staying at this excellent spot.

1230 Ocean Dr., Miami Beach, FL 33139. ✆ **800/783-1725** or 305/672-2579. Fax 305/672-7665. www.hotel ocean.com. 27 units. Winter $200–$280 double; $300–$450 suite; $600 penthouse. Off-season $179–$275 double; $325–$345 suite; $515 penthouse. Rates include continental breakfast. AE, DC, DISC, MC, V.

Valet parking $16. Pets accepted for $15 per day. **Amenities:** Half-price admission to nearby health club; concierge; secretarial services; limited room service; babysitting; laundry and dry-cleaning service. *In room:* A/C, TV/VCR, CD player, dataport, minibar (stocked with guests' personalized order), fridge, hair dryer.

Marlin ✿✿ Don't be surprised if you hear guitar riffs upon entering the Marlin. This rock-and-roll hotel, owned by Chris Blackwell, founder of Island Records, also houses South Beach Studios, a recording and mixing facility, which has been put to use by Aerosmith and U2 among others. And don't be taken aback if you see beautiful models strolling by—the Elite Modeling Agency also calls the Marlin home.

The rooms here sport a sleek, industrial Caribbean decor, with soft earth tones, custom furniture, and hardwood floors; each suite feels like a private bungalow. No two rooms are alike, and each one is distinctive enough that even Martha Stewart approved by staying here. The very hip and whimsical but relaxed Marlin Bar and restaurant attracts a sleek crowd trying to escape the overblown South Beach bar scene and features what only music industry people could describe as Hi Fidelity cuisine. The major drawbacks of this hotel are its location on a busy, highly trafficked corner of Collins Avenue and its lack of a pool. However, the rooftop garden/bar area provides a fantastic view of the beach and the city.

1200 Collins Ave., Miami Beach, FL 33139. © **800/OUTPOST** or 305/672-5254. Fax 305/672-6288. www.islandoutpost.com. 11 units. Winter $325–$395 double. Off-season $195–$275 double. AE, DC, DISC, MC, V. Valet parking $16. **Amenities:** Restaurant; bar; reduced rates at Crunch Fitness and VIP access to local clubs; concierge; secretarial services; room service provided by the Tides (see above); babysitting; laundry service. *In room:* A/C, TV/VCR, CD player, dataport, kitchenette, minibar, fridge, microwave, coffeemaker, hair dryer.

Mercury ✿ *(Finds)* This small boutique hotel is located in the fast-rising area known as SoFi, or South of Fifth Street, South Beach's latest recipient of a hipster takeover. The Mercury is an upscale, modern all-suite resort that combines Mediterranean charm with trendy South Beach flair. A member of Design Hotels, a worldwide collection of notable boutique hotels, the Mercury is actually a well-kept secret that's attached to two of the beach's best restaurants, Nemo and Shoji Sushi, which also provides the hotel's room service. A small outdoor heated pool and Jacuzzi are located in a courtyard that's shared with the restaurant (yes, diners can see you swim). Accommodations are ultrastylish, with sleek light-wood furnishings, Belgian cotton bedding, European kitchens, and spacious bathrooms with spa tubs. If you're able to splurge, the penthouse here is hypercool, with wraparound terrace, and massive living and bedroom areas and kitchen. If you're looking to stay in style without the hassle of the South Beach hustle and bustle, this is the place.

100 Collins Ave., Miami Beach, FL 33139. © **877/786-2732** or 305/398-3000. Fax 305/398-3001. www. mercuryresort.com. 44 units. Seasonal rates $165–$995. AE, DC, DISC, MC, V. Valet parking $18. **Amenities:** Heated pool; access to local fitness center (Crunch); full-service spa; Jacuzzi; concierge; room service; in-room massage; laundry service; free airport pickup. *In room:* TV/VCR, entertainment center with CD player and stereo, video and music library, fax, dataport, kitchen, minibar, coffeemaker, hair dryer.

Miami Beach Marriott at South Beach ✿ This is not your father's Marriott. Located in the throbbing heart of South Beach, this mammoth oceanfront property works hard to leave its mass-market image behind, with a rain forest aviary and waterfall in the lobby, funky flower arrangements on every floor, and a punchy blue-and-lime room decor (a bit tacky, but a world apart from standard Marriott interiors). A fantastic beachfront pool, cabanas, and watersports rentals

---

Fun Fact Desi Was Here

During the Raleigh Hotel's opening night white-tie ball in 1940, a sick band member was replaced by a then-unknown local drummer. You may have heard of him: Desi Arnaz.

---

are an added plus, and a rarity on Ocean Drive. Some rooms have balconies with ocean and city views. I suggest the ones with the ocean views, as the city views will provide you with little more than views and noises of cranes and construction.

161 Ocean Dr., Miami Beach, FL 33139. ℂ 305/536-7700. Fax 305/536-9900. www. marriott.com. 236 units. $219 general view; $239 city view; $279 ocean view; $299 direct oceanfront; $309 concierge level. Rates change frequently. AE, DC, DISC, MC, V. Valet parking $18. **Amenities:** Restaurant, coffee shop, lounge; pool; health club; extensive watersports rentals; bike rental; concierge; business center; 24-hr. room service; laundry service. *In room:* A/C, TV, dataport, high-speed Internet access, minibar, coffeemaker, hair dryer.

Raleigh Hotel 🏵🏵 Upon entering the lobby of this oceanfront Art Deco hotel, you will feel like you've stepped back into the 1940s. Polished wood, original terrazzo floors, and an intimate martini bar add to the fabulous atmosphere that's favored by fashion photographers and production crews, for whom the hotel's fleur-de-lis pool is the favorite subject. In fact, one look at the pool and you'll expect Esther Williams to splash up in a dramatic, aquatic plié. Should you glance quickly inside the dimly lit lobby restaurant, the constantly changing Tiger Oak Room (last we checked, it was Mediterranean), you could swear Dorothy Parker and her fellow round-tablers took a detour from New York's Algonquin Hotel and landed here. Rooms are tidy and efficient (those overlooking the resplendent pool and ocean are the most peaceful)—nothing too elaborate, but that's not why people stay here. It's the Raleigh's romantic Deco lure that has people skipping over from the chilly, antiseptic Delano a few blocks up for much-needed warmth.

1775 Collins Ave., Miami Beach, FL 33139. ℂ 800/848-1775 or 305/534-6300. Fax 305/538-8140. www.raleighhotel.com. 111 units. Winter $339–$769 double. Off-season $209–$609 double. Rates are cheaper if booked on the hotel's website. AE, DC, DISC, MV, V. Valet parking $20. **Amenities:** Restaurant, bar, coffee bar; large outdoor pool; small open-air fitness center; concierge; business services; room service (24 hr. in winter; limited off-season), massage; overnight laundry service. *In room:* A/C, TV/VCR, CD player, dataport, minibar, fridge, safe.

Royal Palm Crowne Plaza Resort 🏵 This conveniently located 422-room resort stands apart from other area resorts in that it's the nation's first and largest African-American owned and developed beachfront resort. The hotel is massive, too, composed of five buildings located adjacent to Ocean Drive. Three of the five buildings are restored, the two towers are brand new, and, despite the fact that this resort is a small city, it miraculously maintains a sense of intimacy not typical with many large resorts thanks to the renowned design team Arquitectonica. While the rooms aren't as appealing as the building itself, they are comfortable and modern. The outdoor areas of the hotel are spectacular, with one pool on a mezzanine level and the other beachside. As to be expected, the hotel is decidedly Deco, albeit with a modern twist.

1545 Collins Ave., Miami Beach, FL 33139. ℂ 800/2-CROWNE or 305/604-5700. Fax 305/604-2059. www.sixcontinentshotels.com. 422 units. Winter $189–$599 double. Off-season $159–$559 double. AE, DC, DISC, MC, V. Valet parking $20. Pets under 20 lb. welcome with $50 deposit. **Amenities:** 2 restaurants, lounge; 2 large outdoor pools; state-of-the-art fitness center; concierge; babysitting; business services; room service; overnight laundry service; watersports rental. *In room:* A/C, TV, dataport, minibar, hair dryer, iron, safe.

W South Beach   The Ritz Plaza, located at 17th Street and Collins Avenue, has been resuscitated from its decrepit state into a revitalized stylish boutique hotel with a new wing of oceanview rooms. Located next door to the super-chic Delano Hotel and scheduled to open in 2002, we expect this W to approximate its sister properties that cater to business travelers (and others who don't spend too much time in their rooms) with stylish yet functional guest rooms, super-comfortable beds, attentive service, and a fabulous scene at its restaurant and bar. The hotel's Away Spa and Gym is the mind and body equivalent of a haute nightspot, featuring all the in treatments and classes, from antioxidant facials to Pilates and yoga.

1701 Collins Avenue, Miami Beach ✆ **877/WHOTELS.** Call for details.

MODERATE

Abbey Hotel ✭✭ *(Finds)*   This charming, off-the-beaten-path, '40s-revival boutique hotel is possibly the best deal on the entire beach. A haven for artists looking for quiet inspiration, the Abbey has recently undergone a $2.5 million renovation that restored its original Deco glory. Soft, white-covered chairs and candles grace the lobby, which doubles as a chic Mediterranean-style restaurant, the Abbey Dining Room, and the rooftop sundeck has been restored to its 1940s glamour as a bar and grill. Rooms are furnished with oversized earth-toned chairs and chrome beds that are surprisingly comfortable. It's extremely quiet at this hotel, as it is located in the midst of a sleepy residential neighborhood, but it's only 1 block from the beach and within walking distance of the Jackie Gleason Theater, the Convention Center, the Bass Museum of Art, and the Miami City Ballet.

300 21st St., Miami Beach, FL 33139. ✆ **305/531-0031.** Fax 305/672-1663. www.abbeyhotel.com. 50 units. Winter $165–$210 double; $225 studio. Off-season $80–$165 double; $195 studio. AE, DC, DISC, MC, V. Off-site parking $17. Pets accepted with $500 deposit. **Amenities:** Restaurant, bar; exercise room; concierge; business center; room service; laundry and dry-cleaning service. *In room:* A/C, TV/VCR, dataport, hair dryer, iron, safe. Studios also have stereo with CD player, minibar, safe.

Aqua ✭ *(Value)*   It's been described as the Jetsons meets Jaws, but the Aqua isn't all Hollywood. Animated, yes, but with little emphasis on special effects and more on a friendly staff, Aqua is a good catch for those looking to stay in style without compromising their budget. Rooms are ultra-modern in an Ikea sort of way; in other words, cheap chic. There are apartment-like junior suites, suites, and a really fabulous penthouse, but the standard deluxe rooms aren't too shabby either, with decent-sized bathrooms and high-tech amenities. It's a favorite amongst Europeans and young hipsters on a budget. This '50s-style motel has definitely been spruced up and its sundeck, courtyard garden, and small pool are popular hangouts for those who prefer to stay off the nearby sand. A small yet sleek lounge inside is a good place for a quick cocktail, breakfast, or a snack.

1530 Collins Ave., Miami Beach, FL 33139. ✆ **305/538-4361.** Fax 305/673-8109. www.aquamiami.com. 50 units. Winter $125–$395; off-season $95–$295. Rates include European-style breakfast buffet. AE, DC, DISC, MC, V. Valet parking $18. **Amenities:** Cafe, bar; small pool; sundeck. *In room:* A/C, TV, CD player, minibar, Web TV.

Cavalier ✭   The name of this hotel is quite ironic, as there is nothing cavalier about this reasonably priced Chris Blackwell–owned Island Outpost property. It's warm and welcoming and you can't beat its oceanfront location, which is adjacent to shops and restaurants. Palm trees brush the ceiling of the modest

The Best Hotel Spas

- **Agua Spa at the Delano,** 1685 Collins Ave., Miami Beach (© 305/673-2900), is sublimely situated on the rooftop of the hotel, overlooking the Atlantic, and features stellar treatments such as the milk-and-honey massage that make it popular with celebs and laywomen alike. Lose yourself in a tub of fragrant oils, algae, or minerals for a 20-minute revitalization, or try the collagen, mud, and hydrating masks.

- **The Ritz-Carlton Spa, Key Biscayne,** 415 Grand Bay Dr., Key Biscayne (© 305/648-5900), is a sublime 20,000-square-foot West Indies–colonial style Eden in which you can treat yourself to over 60 treatments, including the Key Lime Coconut Body Scrub and the Everglades Grass Body Wrap. For a real splurge, the Fountain of Youth treatment is a 6-hour indulgence featuring a facial, massage, manicure, pedicure, shampoo, styling, and lunch served on the ocean terrace.

- **Turnberry Isle Resort & Club,** 19999 W. Country Club Dr., Aventura (© 305/932-6200), offers a sprawling 25,000-square-foot spa with a massive menu of treatments, Finnish saunas, Turkish steam rooms, turbulent whirlpools, and bracing cold plunge tubs that are sure to give you an uplifting jolt.

- **Spa Internazionale at Fisher Island,** 1 Fisher Island Dr., Fisher Island (© 800/537-3708), is the city's poshest spa, known for its picturesque setting and the Guinot Paris Hydradermie facial—a 75-minute moisturizing and cleansing facial that leaves the skin silky smooth.

- **Spa of Eden at the Eden Roc Resort,** 4525 Collins Ave., Miami Beach (© 304/531-0000), offers salt glows, chamomile polishes, seaweed wraps, and Swedish and shiatsu massages in a spectacular setting overlooking the ocean.

- **Away Spa at the W South Beach,** 1701 Collins Ave., Miami Beach, (© 877-WHOTELS). At press time, we were still awaiting the grand opening of Away, but it will no doubt offer stiff competition to South Beach neighbor Agua. The spa will offer eight different facials, numerous styles of massage (including Hot Stone), and three body scrubs and wraps. There are also alternative healing services like Reiki and craniosacral therapy, herbal mineral baths, and exotic body treatments such as the Star of India (a 90-min. facial-massage-wrap combo), and, for the truly indulgent, the nearly 2-hour Javanese Lulur, which originated as a prewedding service for the princesses of Java.

lobby. Funky prints, the colors of a tequila sunrise, cover the walls, and African fabrics cover cozy couches. A young, competent staff waits on guests and offers lots of good advice about local clubs, restaurants, and shopping. While there is no pool here, guests have access to the pool at the hotel's swankier sister property, the Tides. Bathrooms here are small, tiled, and no frills, with a small window, tub, and shower.

1320 Ocean Dr., South Beach, FL 33139. © **800/OUTPOST** or 305/604-5064. Fax 305/531-5543. www.islandoutpost.com. 45 units. Winter $185–$395 double. Off-season $130–]$295 double. Additional person $15. AE, DC, DISC, MC, V. Valet parking $16; self-parking $6. **Amenities:** Concierge; massage; room service; babysitting; dry cleaning. *In room:* A/C, TV/VCR, CD player, minibar, fridge, hair dryer, iron, safe.

Chesterfield Hotel ★★
The Chesterfield Hotel is an oft-overlooked kitschy place, located in the heart of South Beach's Deco District, just a skip away from all the restaurants on Ocean Drive or the nightclubs on Washington Avenue. Its Zimbabwe-meets-baroque lobby is a far cry from its original 1930s Art Deco beginnings, but it remains an attractive place for funk-loving hipsters. A recent renovation to the 50 rooms added a luxe touch, with Frette linens and robes, down feather pillows, Judith Jackson spa amenities, and wood, chrome, and glass accents. Bathrooms are industrial, with free-floating showers with rainmaker showerheads, concrete sinks on aluminum stands, and mirrored walls. A new full-service spa features yoga and Pilates. The hotel's Safari Bar/Café is now a full-service restaurant and caters to both a European and an alternative crowd and turns into a spot for a quaint Euro continental breakfast in the morning. There's also a happy hour each evening from 4 to 8pm, with two-for-one cocktails. The hotel's proximity to area clubs and modeling agencies, and its ability to create its own eclectic nightlife, make the Chesterfield an award-worthy locale for people-watching.

855 Collins Ave., South Beach, FL 33139. © **800/244-6023** or 305/531-5831. Fax 305/672-4900. www.southbeachgroup.com. Winter $175–$250 double. Off-season $135–$175 double. Rates include complimentary continental breakfast and complimentary cocktails from 8–9pm nightly. AE, MC, DC, V. Valet parking $18. **Amenities:** Restaurant, bar; full-service spa; in-room massage; rooftop sundeck; concierge; access to VIP lists at area clubs; free airport transportation; dry-cleaning services; free Internet connection. *In room:* A/C, TV, CD player, fax, minibar, coffeemaker, hair dryer, iron, safe.

Crest Hotel Suites ★★ *Finds*
One of South Beach's best-kept secrets, the Crest Hotel is located next to the pricier, trendier Albion Hotel, in the heart of the Art Deco Historic District near all the major attractions, and features a quietly fashionable, contemporary, relaxed atmosphere with fantastic service. Built in 1939, the Crest was restored to preserve its Art Deco architecture, but the interior of the hotel is thoroughly modern, with rooms resembling cosmopolitan apartments. All suites have a living room/dining room area, kitchenette, and executive workspace. An indoor/outdoor cafe with terrace and poolside dining isn't besieged with trendy locals, but does attract a younger crowd. Around the corner from the hotel is Lincoln Road, with its sidewalk cafes, gourmet restaurants, theaters, and galleries. At press time, the Crest was about to open its second hotel, the South Beach Hotel, at 236 21st St.

1670 James Ave., Miami Beach, FL 33139. © **800/531-3880** or 305/531-0321. Fax 305/531-8180. www.cresthotel.com. Winter $155–$235 double. Off-season $115–$175 double. Packages available and 10% discount offered if booked on website. AE, MC, V. **Amenities:** Restaurant, cafe; pool; laundry and dry-cleaning service. *In room:* A/C, TV, dataport, kitchenette, fridge, coffeemaker.

Essex House Hotel and Suites ★★
The Essex House Hotel was created by Deco pioneer Henry Hohauser in 1938 and has received numerous awards for its authentic restoration. The hotel's whimsically created ship-like architecture rises from the shore with decks that are designed to take in succulent ocean breezes. The sleek Bauhaus interiors add to the distinct charm of the place. All

suites feature solid-oak furnishings and have a fridge, wet bar, and Jacuzzi. Although the hotel is right on the pulse of South Beach's constant activity, the new double-glazed, sound-absorbing windows provide an acoustical barrier to the street noise. A spa pool graces the south patio and gardens. In an area where the infamous Al Capone used to play cards, there is now an intimate dining area where complimentary breakfast is served and evening cocktails can be enjoyed.

1001 Collins Ave., Miami Beach, FL 33139. © **800/553-7739** or 305/534-2700. Winter $169–$379 double. Off-season $119–$300 double. Rates include breakfast. AE, DC, DISC, MC, V. **Amenities:** Bar; outdoor pool; concierge. *In room:* A/C, TV, dataport, minibar in deluxe suites, fridge, coffeemaker, hair dryer, iron.

Greenview ✦
Art Deco takes a decidedly Parisian turn in this 1939 Hohauser hotel completely renovated in 1994 by Parisian designer Chahan Minassian. A member of the family-run Rubell Hotels, the Greenview is located just 2 blocks from the ocean on a quiet corner that's close enough to the action, but far enough away that you'll actually feel secluded from the nearby hyperactivity. Recordings of Edith Piaf and Marlene Dietrich provide background to this elegantly understated hotel, whose jewel-box, living-room-like lobby opens to a serene courtyard. Rooms feature handcrafted furnishings, original Modernist artwork, hardwood floors, and sisal area rugs. Typical at Rubell Hotels is the feel-at-home factor, bolstered by the complimentary baker's breakfast and iced tea and chocolate-chip cookies in the afternoon.

1671 Washington Ave. (at Lincoln Rd.), Miami Beach, FL 33139. © **877/RUBELLS** or 305/531-6588. Fax 305/531-4580. www.rubellhotels.com. 45 units. Winter $150–$230 double. Off-season $95–$175 double. Rates include complimentary baker's breakfast. AE, DC, DISC, MC, V. **Amenities:** Small business center; same-day laundry service. *In room:* A/C, TV.

Hotel Chelsea ✦✦
This recently restored Art Deco property is a boutique hotel with a bit of a twist, with accents and decor based on the Japanese art of Feng Shui. Soft amber lighting, bamboo floors, full-slate baths, and Japanese-style furniture arranged in a way that's meant to refresh and relax you are what separate the Chelsea from just about any other so-called boutique hotel on South Beach. Complimentary breakfast, beach yoga classes, free sake at happy hour, and, in case you've had enough relaxation, free passes to South Beach's hottest nightclubs are added bonuses.

944 Washington Ave. (at 9th St.), Miami Beach, FL 33139. © **305/534-4069.** Fax 305/672-6712. www.the hotelchelsea.com. 42 units. $95–$225 double. Rates include complimentary continental breakfast and complimentary cocktails 8–9pm daily. AE, MC, DC, V. Valet parking $18. **Amenities:** Bar; concierge; access to local gym; full-service spa; beach yoga; in-room massage; laundry services; free pickup from the airport. *In room:* A/C, TV, CD player, dataport, hair dryer, iron, minibar, safe.

Hotel Leon ✦✦ *Finds*
A fabulous hotel without the fabulous attitude, the Hotel Leon is like a reasonably priced high-fashion garment found hidden on a rack full of overpriced threads. This charismatic sliver of a property has won the loyalty of fashion industrialists and romantics alike. Built in 1929 and restored in 1996, the hotel still retains many original details such as facades, woodwork, and even fireplaces (every room has one, not that you'll need to use it). The very central location 1 block from the ocean is a plus, especially since the Leon lacks a pool. Most of the spacious and stylish rooms are immaculate and reminiscent of a loft apartment; spacious bathrooms with large, deep tubs are especially enticing.

Wood floors and simple pale furnishings are appreciated in a neighborhood where many others overdo the Art Deco motif. However, some rooms are dark and have not seen such upgrades (we have gotten complaints) and are to be avoided; do not hesitate to ask to change rooms. Service is warm, friendly, and accommodating. The lobby has an informal bar and restaurant, not to mention a large communal table at which guests—production crews, fashion photographers, Europeans, and young hipsters—tend to mix and mingle. Because its entrance is not directly on pedestrian-heavy Collins Avenue, the Hotel Leon remains one of South Beach's best-kept secrets.

841 Collins Ave., South Beach, FL 33139. © **305/673-3767.** Fax 305/673-5866. www.hotelleon.com. 18 units. Winter $145–$245 suite; $395 penthouse. Off-season $100–$195 suite; $335 penthouse. Additional person $10. AE, DC, MC, V. Valet parking $18. "Well-behaved" pets accepted for $20 per night. **Amenities:** Restaurant, lobby bar; reduced rates at local gym; concierge, business services; room service (breakfast); massage; babysitting; laundry and dry-cleaning service. *In room:* A/C, TV, CD player, hair dryer.

The Kent ☆☆ *Value*   This is an excellent value, right in South Beach's active center. All rooms were recently made over and feature wood floors and ultra modern steel furnishings and accessories, which surprisingly aren't cold, but rather inviting and whimsical. The staff is eager to please and the clientele comes largely from the fashion industry. Frequent photo shoots are coordinated in the lobby and conference room, where full office services are available. Thanks to a vacant lot in the backyard (for now), some rooms in the rear offer nice views of the ocean. The decor is high on the kitsch factor, heavy on multicolored Lucite with toys and other assorted articles of whimsy, and even if you can't afford to stay in it, the very James Bond-esque Lucite Suite is a must-see. There's no pool or sundeck, but you're only 1 block from the beach.

1131 Collins Ave., South Beach, FL 33139. © **800/OUTPOST** or 305/604-5000. Fax 305/531-0720. www.islandlife.com. 54 units. Winter $145–$250 suite. Off-season $125–$250 suite. Additional person $15. Rates include continental breakfast bar. AE, DC, DISC, MC, V. Valet parking $16; self-parking $6. **Amenities:** Access to concierge at the Tides and massage service at the Marlin (see listings earlier in this chapter). *In room:* A/C, TV/VCR, CD player, minibar, hairdryer, iron, safe.

La Flora Hotel ☆   It's hard to keep up with the number of Art Deco, streamlined hotels turned boutique hotels these days, but attention should be paid to La Flora, one of the newer members of the club. A minimalist 28-room hotel located 1 block from the ocean, La Flora is a very peaceful alternative to the sceney boutique hotels that surround it. Rooms are extremely comfortable and stylish, with damask linens, soothing beige tones, and fabulous black-out curtains that come in handy when you've come in at the crack of dawn. As with many hotels on Collins Avenue, there's no pool, but La Flora's lobby bar, with frequent happy hours and sometimes karaoke nights, is swimming with interesting people.

1238 Collins Ave., South Beach, FL 33139. © **877/LAFLORA** or 305/531-3406. Fax 305/538-0850. www.hotellaflora.com. 28 units. Winter $179–$399 suite. Off-season $149–$329 suite. Rates include complementary continental breakfast. AE, DC, DISC, MC, V. Valet parking $20; self-parking $8. **Amenities:** Concierge; access to full-service fitness center within walking distance; massage spa. *In room:* A/C, TV, dataport, hairdryer, minibar, safe.

Lily Guest House ☆☆   The Lily was built in 1936 and completely remodeled in 1999 by local interior designers who gave the place a modern look without stripping its laid-back atmosphere. The decor can best be described as eclectic, mixing Art Deco walls with European cabinetry and furniture. The all-suite property has just 19 guest rooms, all featuring wrought-iron and wood furnishings, hardwood floors, and marble bathrooms. While not all rooms are decorated exactly alike, all have plush oversized furniture and gauzy white curtains; the marble bathrooms are fantastic and surprisingly large for a guesthouse. The ambience is very relaxing and homey. It's also immaculate. All guests have access to a private sundeck.

835 Collins Ave., South Beach, FL 33139. © **888/742-6600** or 305/535-9900. Fax 305/535-0077. www.lilyguesthouse.com. 19 units. Winter $159–$259 double. Off-season $99–$209 double. Rates include complimentary continental breakfast and complimentary cocktails 6–10pm every night. AE, DC, MC, V. Valet parking $18; self-parking $6; parking garage $10. Pets accepted for $10 a day. **Amenities:** Lounge; sundeck, access to nearby gym; concierge; free airport transportation; secretarial services; limited room service; laundry service; passes to nearby nightclubs. *In room:* A/C, TV, CD player, dataport, kitchenette, minibar, coffeemaker, hair dryer.

Mermaid Guesthouse 👬👬

There's something magical about this little hideaway tucked behind tropical gardens in the very heart of South Beach and less than 2 blocks from the ocean. You won't find the amenities of the larger hotels here, but the charm and hospitality at this one-story guesthouse keep people coming back. Owners Ana and Gonzalo Torres did a thorough cleanup, adding new brightly colored fretwork around the doors and windows and installing phones in each room. Also, the wood floors have been stripped or covered in straw matting, one of the many Caribbean touches that make this place so cheery. Rooms have four-poster beds with mosquito nets. There are no TVs, so guests tend to congregate in the lush garden in the evenings. The owners sometimes host free impromptu dinners for their guests and friends. Ask if they've scheduled any live Latin music during your stay; you won't want to miss it. What you also don't want to miss is a preview of your room before you put down a deposit, as some rooms tend not to be as tidy as the quaint garden.

909 Collins Ave., Miami Beach, FL 33140. © **305/538-5324.** Fax 305/538-2822. 8 units. Winter $115–$280 single or double. Off-season $95–$215 single or double. Additional person $10. Discounts available for longer stays. AE, MC, V. **Amenities:** Bar. *In room:* A/C, TV upon request, radio.

Nassau Suite Hotel 👬👬

Stylish and reasonably priced, this 1937 hotel feels more like a modern apartment building with its 22 suites (studios or one-bedrooms), featuring wood floors, rattan furniture, and fully equipped open kitchens. Beds are all king-size and rather plush, but the bed isn't the room's only place to rest: Each room also has a sitting area that's quite comfortable. Registered as a National Historic Landmark, the Nassau Suite Hotel may exist in an old building, but both rooms and lobby are fully modernized. The Nassau Suite caters to a young, hip crowd of both gay and straight guests. Continental breakfast is available for $5 per person.

1414 Collins Ave., South Beach, FL 33139. © **866/859-4177** or 305/532-0043. Fax 305/534-3133. www.nassausuite.com. 22 units. Winter $150 studio; $190 1-bedroom. Off-season $120 studio; $160 1-bedroom. AE, DC, DISC, MC, V. Parking $12. **Amenities:** Access to nearby health club; bike rental; concierge; secretarial services. *In room:* A/C, TV, fax, DSL connection, coffeemaker, hair dryer.

Pelican Hotel 👬👬

Owned by the same creative folks behind the Diesel Jeans company, the Pelican is South Beach's only self-professed "toy-hotel," in which each of its 30 rooms and suites is decorated as outrageously as some of the area's more colorful drag queens. Each room has been designed daringly and rather wittily by Swedish interior decorator Magnus Ehrland, whose countless trips to antiques markets, combined with his wild imagination, have turned Room 309, for instance, into the "Psychedelic(ate) Girl," Room 201 into the "Executive Fifties" suite, and Room 313 into the "Jesus Christ Megastar" room. But the most popular room is the tough-to-score Room 215, or the "Best Whorehouse," which is said to have made even former Hollywood madam Heidi Fleiss red with envy. As South Beach is known for poseurs of all types, this hotel fits right in.

826 Ocean Dr., Miami Beach, FL 33139. ✆ **800/7-PELICAN** or 305/673-3373. Fax 305/673-3255. www. pelicanhotel.com. Winter $170–$220 double; $240 oceanfront suite. Off-season $135–$155 double; $225 oceanfront suite. AE, DC, MC, V. Valet parking $16. **Amenities:** Restaurant, bar; access to area gyms; concierge; business services; same-day laundry and dry cleaning. *In room:* A/C, TV/VCR, stereo/CD player, dataport, fridge, hair dryer, iron, safe.

Royal Hotel 🏨🏨 *(Finds)*   There are several words to describe this mod, hipster hotel located in the heart of South Beach. Jetsonian, funkadelic, and, as the hotel proudly and aptly declares, "Barbarella at bedtime." What it really is, however, is truly different, in that the rooms' curvy, white plastic beds (less comfortable than chic) have headboards that double as bars! Designer Jordan Mozer of Barneys New York fame has managed to transform this historic Art Deco hotel into a trippy, 21st-century, state-of-the-art facility. Chaise lounges are "digital," with attached computer and television. Italian marble, pastel colors, and large, newly tiled baths manage to successfully thwart a sterility that's all too common with many chic boutique hotels.

758 Washington Ave., Miami Beach, FL 33139. ✆ **888/394-6835** or 305/673-9009. Fax 305/673-9244. www.royalhotelsouthbeach.com. Winter $130–$240 double. Off-season $120–$230 double. AE, DC, MC, V. Valet parking $20. **Amenities:** Bar; small swimming pool; rooftop sundeck; concierge. *In room:* A/C, TV/VCR, stereo/CD player, dataport, fridge, hair dryer, iron, safe.

Townhouse 🏨🏨   New York hipster Jonathan Morr felt that Miami Beach had lost touch with the bon vivants who gave the city its original cache, so he decided to take matters into his own hands. His solution: this 67-room, five-story hotel in which standard rooms started at just $99 during its opening in the fall of 2000. The $99 rate proved too good to be true, but even the revised starting rates of $195 during season and $125 off-season are still a great deal. The charm of this hotel is found in its clean and simple yet chic design with quirky details: exercise equipment that stands alone in the hallways, free laundry machines in the lobby, a water-bed-lined rooftop. Comfortable, shabby-chic rooms boast L-shaped couches for extra guests (for whom you aren't charged). Though the rooms are all pretty much the same, consider the ones with the partial ocean view. The hotel's basement features the hot New York import, Bond St. Lounge.

150 20th St., South Beach, FL 33139. ✆ **877/534-3800** or 305/534-3800. Fax 305/534-3811. www. townhousehotel.com. Winter $195–$225 double; $395 penthouse. Off-season $125–$155 double; $395 penthouse. Rates include Parisian-style breakfast. AE, MC, V. Valet parking $18. **Amenities:** Restaurant, bar; workout stations; bike rental; free laundry; rooftop terrace with water beds. *In room:* A/C, TV/VCR, CD player, dataport, fridge, hair dryer, safe.

Whitelaw Hotel 🏨🏨   With a slogan that reads "clean sheets, hot water, and stiff drinks," the Whitelaw Hotel stands apart from the other boutique hotels with a fierce sense of humor, but never compromises on its fabulous amenities. Only half a block from Ocean Drive, this hotel, like its clientele, is full of distinct personalities, pairing such disparate elements as luxurious Belgian sheets with shag carpeting to create a completely innovative setting. All-white rooms manage to be homey and plush and not at all antiseptic. Bathrooms are large and well stocked with just about everything you may have forgotten at home. Complimentary cocktails in the lobby every night from 8 to 10pm contribute to a very social atmosphere.

808 Collins Ave., Miami Beach, FL 33139. ✆ **305/398-7000.** Fax 305/398-7010. www.whitelawhotel.com. Winter $175 double; $195 suite. Off-season $125 double; $145 suite. Rates include complimentary continental breakfast and free cocktails in the lobby 8–10pm every night. AE, MC, DC, V. Parking $18. **Amenities:** Lounge; concierge; business services; laundry service; free airport pickup; complimentary passes to area nightclubs. *In room:* A/C, TV, CD player, dataport, minibar, hair dryer, safe.

INEXPENSIVE

Banana Bungalow   This hostel-like hotel is cheap, campy, and quintessentially Miami Beach. Popular with the MTV set, this is a redone 1950s two-story motel where it's always Spring Break. The hotel surrounds a pool and deck complete with shuffleboard, a small alfresco cafe serving cheap meals, and a tiki bar where young European travelers hang out. The best rooms face a narrow canal where motorboats and kayaks are available for a small charge. In general, rooms are clean and well kept, despite a few rusty faucets and chipped Formica furnishings. Guests in shared rooms need to bring their own towels. This is one of the only hotels in this price range with a private pool.

2360 Collins Ave., Miami Beach, FL 33139. © 800/746-7835 or 305/538-1951. Fax 305/531-3217. www.bananabungalow.com. 90 units. Winter $18–$20 per person in shared units; $95–$104 double. Off-season $16–$18 per person in shared units; $50–$60 double. MC, V. Free parking. **Amenities:** Cafe, bar; large pool; access to nearby health club; game room; theater; coin-op laundry. *In room:* A/C, TV, fridge.

Bayliss Guest House ♠   The Bayliss Guest House is the antibudget budget hotel, with enormous, sparkling clean rooms, complete with sitting rooms and baths. Built in 1939 in the tropical Art Deco style, rounded corners, glass blocks, neon, and a lobby floor of fancy terrazzo give the Bayliss a definite '40s feel. The property (offering hotel rooms, large efficiencies, and one-bedroom apartments) is a bit off the beaten path, but this quiet residential spot offers a break from the racket that defines Collins and Washington avenues.

504 14th St., South Beach, FL 33139. © 888/305-4863 or 305/538-5620. Fax 305/531-4440. Riviere1@aol.com. 20 units. Winter $75 double; $95 efficiency. Off-season $45 double; $60 efficiency. AE, DC, DISC, MC, V. **Amenities:** Room service 9am–7pm. *In room:* A/C, TV, kitchenette, coffeemaker, hair dryer.

Beachcomber Hotel ♠   The Beachcomber Hotel was built in 1937 and renovated in 1997. The rooms are decorated in a colorful Art Deco style and all have a private bathroom and shower, but they are a bit lackluster—blasé, in fact. Though nothing to rave about, they are clean and functional, serving the purpose of a place to crash after a day—or night—on South Beach. A Deco terrace on Collins Avenue provides a great place for sipping a cocktail. The hotel's restaurant serves breakfast, lunch, and dinner, but dine there only as a last resort. Check if a continental breakfast is included in your rate. The property's location couldn't be better, since it's away from the noise but near the action.

1340 Collins Ave., South Beach, FL 33139. © 888/305-4683 or 305/531-3755. Fax 305/673-8609. www.beachcombermiami.com. 29 units. Winter $90–$145 double. Off-season $70–$125 double. Continental breakfast included. AE, DC, DISC, MC, V. Municipal parking $7. **Amenities:** Restaurant, bar. *In room:* A/C, TV, fridge, hair dryer.

Brigham Gardens ♠♠   In a prime location, this funky place, consisting of two buildings (Art Deco and Mediterranean) is a homey and affordable oasis run by a mother-daughter team that will make sure you feel like a member of the family. Because most rooms have full kitchens—you can also barbecue in the garden—you'll find many people staying for longer than a weekend. Room 12, in particular, is extremely charming and quiet, with cathedral ceilings, Art Deco

---

Impressions

I think South Beach targets vacationers who, if not affluent, would like to feel that way for a little while.

—Rachel Ponce on PBS's *Going Places*

decor, and views of the garden. When you enter the tropically landscaped garden, you'll hear macaws and parrots and see cats and lizards running through the bougainvillea. The tiny but lush grounds are framed by quaint Mediterranean buildings, which are pleasant, though in need of some improvements. A rooftop sundeck, with a view of the ocean, is the hotel's newest attraction, though the rooms are constantly being spruced up with funky artwork, furniture, and a colorful array of fresh paint.

1411 Collins Ave., South Beach, FL 33139. ✆ **305/531-1331.** Fax 305/538-9898. www.brigham gardens.com. 23 units. Winter $100–$145 1-bedroom. Off-season $70–$110 1-bedroom. Additional person $10. 10% discount on stays of 7 days or longer. Pets accepted for $6 a night. AE, MC, V. **Amenities:** Concierge; coin-op washers and dryers. *In room:* A/C, TV, dataport, kitchen, microwave, coffeemaker.

Clay Hotel & International Hostel 🦋
A member of the International Youth Hostel Federation (IYHF), the Clay occupies a beautiful 1920s-style Spanish Mediterranean building at the corner of historic Española Way. Like other IYHF members, this hostel is open to all ages and is a great place to meet people. The usual smattering of Australians, Europeans, and other budget travelers makes it Miami's best clearinghouse of "insider" travel information. Even if you don't stay here, you might want to check out the ride board or mingle with fellow travelers over a beer at the sidewalk cafe.

Although a thorough renovation in 1996 made this hostel an incredible value and a step above any others in town, don't expect nightly turndown service or chocolates. But, for a hostel, it's full of extras. Ninety rooms have private baths and 12 VIP rooms have balconies overlooking quaint Española Way. You will find occasional movie nights, an outdoor weekend market, and a tour desk with car rental available. Reservations for private rooms are essential in season and recommended year-round. Don't bother with a car in this congested area.

1438 Washington Ave. (at Española Way), South Beach, FL 33139. ✆ **800/379-2529** or 305/534-2988. Fax 305/673-0346. www.theclayhotel.com. 350 units. $45–75 double; $15–$17 dorm beds. During the off-season, pay for 6 nights in advance and get 7th night free. MC, V. Parking $10. **Amenities:** Cafe; access to nearby health club; bike rental; concierge; computer center; coin-op washers and dryers; lockers; kitchen. *In room:* A/C, TV, dataport, fridge, hair dryer.

Clevelander
A South Beach institution favored by the beer-swilling set, the Clevelander is best known for its neon- and glass-blocked poolside and bar used in countless photo shoots and Budweiser commercials. As far as its reputation as a hotel, well, it's conveniently located on Ocean Drive and it's dirt cheap considering its location. Unfortunately, the dirt doesn't stop there. It seems that the hotel is more concerned with polishing its poolside glass than its rooms. And the noise level can be deafening. Party animals don't mind at all. But if your idea of a party doesn't involve drinking challenges and wet T-shirt contests, visit the Clevelander for a cocktail and stay elsewhere.

1020 Ocean Dr., Miami Beach, FL 33139. ✆ **305/531-3485.** Fax 305/534-4707. 57 units. Winter $140–$250 double. Off-season $95–$190 double. AE, DC, MC, V. Valet parking $6. **Amenities:** Outdoor cafe; bar; outdoor pool; health club. *In room:* A/C, TV.

The Loft Hotel
A boutique hotel along the lines of the Aqua Hotel (though less whimsical, enticing, and airy-feeling), this renovated apartment building (which really gives you the feeling of staying in an apartment rather than a hotel) offers 20 suites, all surrounding a tidy, tropically landscaped garden. Rooms are especially spacious, with queen-sized beds, breakfast room, conversation area, and hardwood or tile floors. Bathrooms are brand new and, for an old Art Deco building, pretty spacious. This hotel is popular with young, hip European types,

just as the Aqua Hotel is, but there isn't that much difference between the two hotels other than the fact that the Loft's rooms have fully equipped kitchens while Aqua's rooms don't, and Aqua has a bar/restaurant while the Loft does not. Prices at the Loft are very reasonable and the owners, who hail from Villa Paradiso, are extremely accommodating.

952 Collins Ave., Miami Beach, FL 33139. ✆ **305/534-2244.** Fax 305/538-1509. 57 units. Winter $149–$179 double. Off-season $89–$129 double. AE, DC, MC, V. Valet parking $20. **Amenities:** On-site laundry; VIP passes to local nightclubs. *In room:* A/C, TV/VCR, kitchen, hair dryer.

Park Washington Hotel 🌴🌴 *Value*   The Park Washington, designed in the 1930s by Henry Hohauser, is a large, refurbished hotel just 2 blocks from the ocean that offers some of the best values in South Beach. Most of the rooms have original furnishings and well-kept interiors, and some have kitchenettes. Bathrooms are small but clean. Guests also enjoy a decent-sized outdoor heated pool with a sundeck, bikes for rent, and access to a nearby health club, as well as privacy, lush landscaping, consistent quality, and a value-oriented philosophy. This hotel attracts a large gay clientele.

1020 Washington Ave., South Beach, FL 33139. ✆ **305/532-1930.** Fax 305/672-6706. www.parkwashington resort.com. 36 units. Winter $129–$159 double. Off-season $79–$109 double. Rates include self-serve coffee and Danish. Additional person $20. AE, MC, V. Off-site parking $6. **Amenities:** Pool. *In room:* A/C, TV, kitchenettes in some rooms, fridge.

Villa Paradiso 🌴🌴 *Finds*   This guesthouse, like Brigham Gardens, is more like a cozy apartment house than a hotel. There's no elegant lobby or restaurant, but the amicable hosts, Lisa and Pascal Nicolle, are happy to give you a room key and advice on what to do. The recently renovated spacious apartments are simple but elegant—hardwood floors, French doors, and stylish wrought-iron furniture—and are remarkably quiet considering their location, a few blocks from Lincoln Road and all of South Beach's best clubs. Most have full kitchens or at least a fridge, and Murphy beds or foldout couches for extra friends. Bathrooms have recently been renovated with marble tile. All rooms overlook the hotel's pretty courtyard garden.

1415 Collins Ave., Miami Beach, FL 33139. ✆ **305/532-0616.** Fax 305/673-5874. www.villaparadiso hotel.com. 17 units. Winter $100–$165 apartment. Off-season $75–$129 apartment. Weekly rates are 10% cheaper. Additional person $10. AE, DC, MC, V. Parking nearby $12. Pets (including small "nonbarking" dogs) accepted for $10 with a $100 deposit. **Amenities:** Coin-op washers and dryers. *In room:* A/C, TV, kitchen, fridge, coffeemaker.

2 Miami Beach: Surfside, Bal Harbour & Sunny Isles

The area just north of South Beach, known as Miami Beach, encompasses Surfside, Bal Harbour, and Sunny Isles. Unrestricted by zoning codes throughout the 1950s, 1960s, and especially the 1970s, area developers went crazy, building ever-bigger and more brazen structures, especially north of 41st Street, which is now known as Condo Canyon. Consequently, there's now a glut of medium-quality condos, with a few scattered holdouts of older hotels and motels casting shadows over the beach by afternoon.

The western section of the neighborhood used to be inundated with Brooklyn's elderly Jewish population during the season. Though the area still maintains a religious preference, visiting tourists from Argentina to Germany, replete with Speedos and thong bikinis, are clearly taking over.

Miami Beach, as described here, runs from 24th Street to 192nd Street, a long strip that varies slightly from end to end. Staying in the southern section, from

Where to Stay in Miami Beach, Surfside, Bal Harbour & Sunny Isles

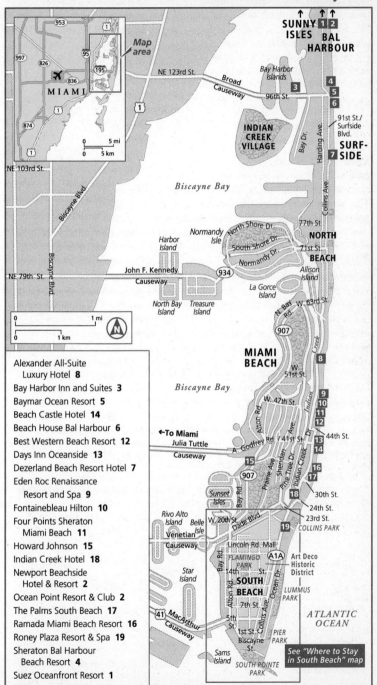

Alexander All-Suite
  Luxury Hotel **8**
Bay Harbor Inn and Suites **3**
Baymar Ocean Resort **5**
Beach Castle Hotel **14**
Beach House Bal Harbour **6**
Best Western Beach Resort **12**
Days Inn Oceanside **13**
Dezerland Beach Resort Hotel **7**
Eden Roc Renaissance
  Resort and Spa **9**
Fontainebleau Hilton **10**
Four Points Sheraton
  Miami Beach **11**
Howard Johnson **15**
Indian Creek Hotel **18**
Newport Beachside
  Hotel & Resort **2**
Ocean Point Resort & Club **2**
The Palms South Beach **17**
Ramada Miami Beach Resort **16**
Roney Plaza Resort & Spa **19**
Sheraton Bal Harbour
  Beach Resort **4**
Suez Oceanfront Resort **1**

24th to 42nd streets, can be a good deal—it's still close to the South Beach scene, but the rates are more affordable. The North Beach area begins at 63rd Street and extends north to the city limit at 87th Terrace and west to Biscayne Bay (at Bay Drive West). Bal Harbour and Bay Harbor are at the center of Miami Beach and retain their exclusivity and character. The neighborhoods north and south of here, like Surfside and Sunny Isles, have nice beaches and some shops, but are a little worn around the edges.

The **Howard Johnson** (© **800/446-4656** or 305/532-4411) at 4000 Alton Rd., just off the Julia Tuttle Causeway (I-95), is a generic eight-story building, near a busy road, that is convenient to the beach by car or bike. Rooms, renovated in 1995, are clean and spacious, and some have pretty views of the city and the Intracoastal Waterway. Winter rates start at $100.

VERY EXPENSIVE

Alexander All-Suite Luxury Hotel ★★★

This luxury hotel is a place Robin Leach would give his "champagne wishes and caviar dreams" approval rating. Just a few miles from either happening South Beach or ritzy Bal Harbour, the Alexander is pricey, but worth it for the size of the suites and the doting attention. The Alexander features spacious one- and two-bedroom miniapartments with private balconies overlooking the Atlantic Ocean and Miami's Intracoastal Waterway. Each contains a living room, a fully equipped kitchen, *two* bathrooms (one with just a shower and the other with a shower/tub combo), and a balcony. The rooms are elegant without being pretentious and have every convenience you could want. The hotel itself is well decorated, with sculptures, paintings, antiques, and tapestries, most of which were garnered from the Cornelius Vanderbilt mansion. An ongoing renovation to upgrade the suites promises to keep the Alexander on the forefront of modern luxury. Two oceanfront pools are surrounded by lush vegetation; one of these "lagoons" is fed by a cascading waterfall. Shula's Steakhouse, owned by former Dolphins football coach Don Shula, is open for lunch and dinner daily, and is a favorite of both meat eaters and Dolphins fans.

5225 Collins Ave., Miami Beach, FL 33140. © **800/327-6121** or 305/865-6500. Fax 305/341-6553. www.alexanderhotel.com. 150 units. Winter $325 1-bedroom suite; $470 2-bedroom suite. Off-season $250 1-bedroom suite; $370 2-bedroom suite. Additional person $35. Packages available. AE, MC, V. Valet parking $18. Very small pets accepted for a $250 nonrefundable deposit for cleaning the suite. **Amenities:** 2 restaurants, 2 bars; 2 large outdoor pools; small fitness center; Jacuzzis, sauna; watersports equipment; concierge; car rental through concierge; business center and secretarial services; salon; limited room service; in-room massage; dry-cleaning and laundry services. *In room:* A/C, TV, VCR upon request, fax, dataport, kitchen, coffeemaker, hair dryer, radio.

Beach House Bal Harbour ★★★ (Finds)

The Beach House Bal Harbour is the closest thing the city has to a summer beach home—comfortable, unpretentious, and luxurious, yet decidedly low-key. In place of an elaborate hotel lobby, the public spaces of the Rubell-owned Beach House are divided into a series of intimate homey environments, from the wicker-furnished screened-in porch to the Asian-inspired Bamboo Room, with overstuffed Ralph Lauren leather couches and Japanese bric-a-brac. The 24-hour Pantry, inspired by Long Island's Sagaponack General Store, is packed with all the needs of the hotel's "unplugged" urban clientele.

The ultraspacious rooms (those ending in 04 are the most spacious) are literally brimming with the comforts of home. The Atlantic Restaurant offers a little of Nantucket in Miami from Sheila Lukins, author of the best-selling Silver Palate cookbooks, who creates some delicious feasts (such as buttermilk fried chicken with Austin baked beans and homemade cornbread). The Seahorse Bar features a giant tank of—you guessed it—seahorses. The 200-foot private beach, hammock grove, and topiary garden are so lush, they're said to have caused several New York hipsters to renege on their summer shares in the Hamptons in favor of the Beach House.

9449 Collins Ave., Surfside, FL 33154. © **877/RUBELLS** or 305/535-8606. Fax 305/535-8602. www.rubell hotels.com. 170 units. Winter $215–$315 double; $245–$305 junior suite. Off-season $180–$210 double; $230–$270 junior suite. Year-round $800 1-bedroom suite. AE, DC, DISC, MC, V. Valet parking $15. **Amenities:** Restaurant, 24-hr. pantry bar; heated pool, health club & spa; watersports equipment; children's playground; business center. *In room:* A/C, TV, stereo/CD player, dataport, fridge, hair dryer, iron, wireless TV Web access.

Eden Roc Renaissance Resort and Spa ★★

Just next door to the mammoth Fontainebleau Hilton, this large Morris Lapidus–designed flamboyant hotel, which opened in 1956, seems almost intimate by comparison. The hotel completed a top-to-bottom $24 million renovation in late 1999 and an $11 million renovation of the beachfront in 2001. The nautical deco decor is a bit gaudy, but nonetheless reminiscent of Miami Beach's Rat-Packed glory days of the '50s. The 55,000-square-foot modern Spa of Eden has excellent facilities and exercise classes, including yoga. The big, open, and airy lobby is often full of name-tagged conventioneers and tourists looking for a taste of Miami Beach kitsch. The rooms, uniformly outfitted with purple- and aquatic-colored interiors and retouched 1930s furnishings, are unusually spacious, and the bathrooms boast Italian marble baths. Because of the hotel's size, you should be able to negotiate a good rate unless there's a big event going on. Harry's Grille specializes in seafood and steaks. From Jimmy Johnson's, the poolside sports bar, patrons can watch swimmers through an underwater "porthole" window.

4525 Collins Ave., Miami Beach, FL 33140. © **800/327-8337** or 305/531-0000. Fax 305/674-5568. www.edenrocresort.com. 349 units. Winter $299–$359 double; $369 suite; $2,500 penthouse. Off-season $159–$224 double; $310 suite; $1,500 penthouse. Additional person $15. Packages available. AE, DC, DISC, MC, V. Valet parking $20–$25. Pets under 20 lb. accepted for a $75 fee. **Amenities:** 2 restaurants, lounge, bar; 2 outdoor pools; squash courts; racquetball courts; basketball courts; rock-climbing arena; health club & spa; watersports equipment; concierge; tour desk; car-rental desk; business center; salon; limited room service; in-room massage; babysitting; laundry and dry-cleaning service. *In room:* A/C, TV, VCRs for rent, dataport, kitchenettes in suites and penthouse, minibar, hair dryer.

Fontainebleau Hilton ★★ *Overrated* *Kids*

In many ways, this is the quintessential Miami Beach hotel. Also designed by Morris Lapidus, who oversaw an expansion in 2000, this grand monolith symbolizes Miami decadence. Since its opening in 1954, the Fontainebleau has hosted presidents, pageants, and movie productions, including the James Bond thriller *Goldfinger*. This is where all the greats, including Sinatra and his pals, performed in their prime. Club Tropigala is reminiscent of Ricky Ricardo's Tropicana and features a Las Vegas–style floor show with dozens of performers and two orchestras. Rooms are luxurious and decorated in various styles from 1950s to ultramodern; bathrooms are done up in Italian marble a la Caesar's Palace. In 2001, the hotel underwent a $10 million food and beverage renovation, introducing the massive, cruise-ship-esque 150-seat Bleu View Mediterranean restaurant and cocktail lounge. Adding to the Fontainebleau's opulence is the 7,000-square-foot Cookie's World water park; the water slide and river-raft ride bring a bit of Disney to Deco-land, which, along with supervised children's activities, is catered toward (though not reserved for) the little ones.

4441 Collins Ave., Miami Beach, FL 33140. ℂ 800/HILTONS or 305/538-2000. Fax 305/674-4607. www.
fontainebleau.hilton.com. 1,206 units. Winter $289–$459 double. Off-season $209–$329 double. Year-round
$525–$1300 suite. Additional person $30. Packages available. AE, DC, DISC, MC, V. Overnight valet parking
$13. Pets accepted at no extra cost. **Amenities:** 7 restaurants (including 2 by the pool), 5 cocktail lounges;
2 large outdoor pools; 7 lighted tennis courts; state-of-the-art health club; 3 whirlpool baths; watersports
rentals; children's programs; game rooms; concierge; tour desk; car-rental desk; business center; shopping
arcade; salon; room service; in-room massage; babysitting; laundry and dry-cleaning service. *In room:* A/C, TV,
fax, dataport, minibar, coffeemaker, hair dryer, iron, safe.

Roney Palace Resort & Spa ✪

In its heyday, this luxury hotel and apart-
ment building hosted such celebrities as Rita Hayworth, Orson Welles, and the
duke and duchess of Windsor. Fortunately, a recent $25 million renovation has
restored much of its luster. The outdated pink-and-green-flamingo furnishings
have been replaced with an ultramodern decor and natural woods. Located
directly on the ocean, the hotel offers its guests a private beach club and an
indoor-outdoor cafe. Because of its prerenovation reputation as a run-down
apartment building, most people don't consider the Roney Palace to be a luxe
resort, but it is once more. The location on a trafficky, tacky Collins Avenue
corner doesn't help the hotel's new image, but once you're inside, you'll forget
about the unsightly Lums restaurant across the street. One of the hotel's greatest
attractions is the Larry North Fitness Center of South Beach, a 10,000-square-
foot fitness center and spa.

2399 Collins Ave., Miami Beach, FL 33139. ℂ 305/604-1000. Fax 305/538-7141. www.roney-palace.com.
585 units. Year-round $300–$450 executive suite; $400–$750 1-bedroom suite; $600–$800 2-bedroom suite;
$1,275–$2,950 penthouse suite. AE, DC, MC, V. Valet parking $10. **Amenities:** 24-hr. restaurant, poolside bar
and grill; in-suite spa services; game room; concierge; airport pickup and delivery service; business center;
room service; babysitting; child-care center; laundry and dry-cleaning service. *In room:* A/C, TV/VCR, dataport,
minibar, microwave, coffeemaker, hair dryer, safe.

Sheraton Bal Harbour Beach Resort ✪✪✪ *Kids*

This hotel has the best
location in Bal Harbour, on the ocean and just across from the swanky Bal Harbour Shops. Bill and Hillary Clinton have stayed here, and Bill even jogged
along the beach with local fitness enthusiasts. It's one of the nicest Sheratons I've
seen, with a glass-enclosed two-story atrium lobby that's especially welcoming.
A spectacular staircase wraps itself around a cascading fountain full of wished-
on pennies. A lushly landscaped pool area reminds you of an island resort, and
a waterslide will keep the kids occupied while you work on your tan. Speaking
of kids, a maximum of four children through the age of 17 stay free in existing
bedding with a least one adult. Rooms are large and fairly standard as far as
Sheratons are concerned, with the exception of oceanview rooms, which have
balconies. Make sure to ask for a free coupon book with over $800 in savings at
the Bal Harbour Shops.

9701 Collins Ave., Bal Harbour, FL 33154. ℂ 800/999-9898 or 305/865-7511. Fax 305/864-2601. 659 units.
Winter $289–$589 double. Off-season $129–$449 double. Year-round $650–$2,000 suite or villa. Additional
person $25. Packages and senior discounts available. Lowest rates reflect bookings made at least 14 days in
advance for rooms without ocean views. AE, DC, DISC, MC, V. Valet parking $17. **Amenities:** 4 restaurants,
lounges; 2 outdoor heated pools (1 kids' pool); nearby golf course; 2 outdoor tennis courts; large state-of-
the-art health club & spa; watersports equipment; children's programs; game room; concierge; tour desk;
business center; shopping arcade; 24-hr. room service; in-room massage; babysitting; laundry and dry-
cleaning service. *In room:* A/C, TV, VCRs in some rooms, minibar, coffeemaker, hair dryer, iron, safe.

EXPENSIVE

Ocean Point Resort & Club ✪✪ *Kids*

If you drive too quickly past this sleek
building, you may wrongly assume it's yet another condo, adding to the growing

area's canyon of high-priced residences. Luckily for you, it's not, but the 166 all-suite luxury resort is so nice, you may just want to move in! The first resort to open in the Sunny Isles area of Miami Beach in 30 years, Ocean Point loses a star only because of its Sunny Isles location (not exactly a hotbed of activity). However, it is a short drive from Aventura shopping and South Beach nightlife, if, in fact, you feel the need to go elsewhere for entertainment. With Ocean Point, you may not. Rooms are all done up a la condos—with studio, one-, two-, and three-bedroom floor plans. The rooms are quite luxurious, with 220-thread-count linens, a huge bathroom (with Jacuzzi tub), and kitchenettes. The European Health Spa has the usual menu of services as well as informative lectures. Tai chi on the beach and poolside treatments will have you wondering if working out is such a chore. Kids' programs are impressive as well, as are the well-heeled, savvy staff, the landscaped gardens, beach club, and pool with waterfalls.

17375 Collins Ave., Sunny Isles, FL 33160. ⓒ **866/623-2678** or 305/940-5422. Fax 786/528-2519. www.oceanpointresort.com. 585 units. Winter $199–$868. Off-season $159–$865. AE, DC, MC, V. Valet parking $16. **Amenities:** 2 restaurants, poolside bar and grill; in-suite spa services; game room; concierge; airport pickup and delivery service; business center; room service; babysitting; child-care center; laundry and dry-cleaning service. *In room:* A/C, TV/ VCR, CD player, high-speed Internet dataport, fully equipped kitchen, washer and dryer, minibar, microwave, coffeemaker, hair dryer, safe.

The Palms South Beach ✿ A $5 million renovation has transformed this formerly shabby, uninspired oceanfront tourist trap into an antebellum tropical oasis in which Art Deco meets *Gone With the Wind.* Lush tropical landscaping, both indoors and out, is a welcome respite from the hustle and bustle on congested Collins Avenue. In fact, the landscaping renovations of the hotel were so impressive, Fairchild Tropical Garden (see p. 180) opened a gift shop at the hotel, The Palm Collection by Fairchild Tropical Garden, which offers an impressive collection of items for the home and garden. Rooms have been spruced up beautifully, bordering on boutiquey, with high-tech amenities. A huge outdoor area is landscaped with palms and hibiscus and has a large freshwater pool as its centerpiece. It faces a popular boardwalk for runners and strollers as well as a large beach where watersports equipment is available. To sway you from leaving the premises, the Palms has an excellent beach service, in which umbrellas, towels, lounges, and, of course, that tropical drink with a paper umbrella are just a short order away. *Note:* This hotel is not in South Beach, as the name would have you believe. However, it is in the heart of Miami Beach and only a short ride to South Beach.

3025 Collins Ave., Miami Beach, FL 33140. ⓒ **800/550-0505** or 305/534-0505. Fax 305/534-0515. www.thepalmshotel.com. 243 units. Winter $245–$295 double; $365–$700 suite. Off-season $220–$265 double; $325–$650 suite. AE, DC, MC, V. Valet parking $8. **Amenities:** Restaurant, garden cafe, poolside bar, lounge; outdoor freshwater pool; bike rental; game room; concierge; tour desk; car-rental desk; salon; room service; babysitting; coin-op washers and dryers; laundry and dry-cleaning services. *In room:* A/C, TV, CD player, dataport, minibar, coffeemaker, hair dryer, iron, safe.

MODERATE

Bay Harbor Inn and Suites ✿✿ This thoroughly renovated inn is just moments from the beach, fine restaurants, and the Bal Harbour Shops. The inn comes in two parts: The more modern section overlooks a swampy river, a heated outdoor pool, and a yacht named *Celeste,* where guests eat a complimentary breakfast buffet. On the other side of the street, "townside," is the cozier, antiques-filled portion, where glass-covered bookshelves hold good beach reading. The rooms have a hodgepodge of wood furnishings (mostly Victorian replicas), while suites boast an extra half-bathroom. You can often smell the aroma of cooking from the restaurant below, which is operated by students at Johnson & Wales Culinary Institute.

9660 E. Bay Harbor Dr., Bay Harbor Island, FL 33154. ℂ **305/868-4141.** Fax 305/867-9094. www.bay harborinn.com. 45 units. Winter $149–$239 double; $159–$279 suite. Off-season $80–$159 double; $95–$179 suite. Additional person $35. Rates include continental breakfast. AE, MC, V. Free parking and dockage space. **Amenities:** Restaurant, brunch room, bar; exercise room; concierge; business center; limited room service. *In room:* A/C, TV, dataport, minibar, hair dryer.

Baymar Ocean Resort (Value)
Depending on what you're looking for, this hotel could be one of the beach's best buys. It's just south of Bal Harbour, in sleepy Surfside, right on the ocean, with a low-key beach that attracts few other tourists. In 2001, efficiencies were transformed into junior suites and all carpets were removed and replaced with terra-cotta tile. The location is close enough to walk to tennis courts and some shopping and dining; it's just a few minutes' drive to larger attractions. It may not be worth it to pay more for the oceanfront rooms, since they tend to be smaller than the others. Rooms overlooking the large pool and sundeck area can get loud on busy days. The first-floor oceanview rooms have a nice shared balcony space.

9401 Collins Ave., Miami Beach, FL 33154. ℂ **800/8-BAYMAR** or 305/866-5446. Fax 305/866-8053. 96 units. Winter $115–$125 double; $125–$235 suite. Off-season $75–$95 double; $95–$185 suite. Additional person $10. AE, DC, DISC, MC, V. Parking $5. **Amenities:** Restaurant, lounge, Tiki bar; Olympic-size pool. *In room:* A/C, TV, kitchen.

Dezerland Beach Resort Hotel
Designed by car enthusiast Michael Dezer, the Dezerland is where *Happy Days* meets Miami Beach, with its visible homage to hot rods and antique cars. Visitors, many of them German tourists, are welcomed by a 1959 Cadillac stationed by the front door, one of a dozen mint-condition classics around the grounds and lobby. This kitschy beachfront hotel recently underwent a $2 million renovation of its guest rooms, lobby, and public areas. The rooms are still somewhat lackluster, despite the fact that the renovation added new drapes, bedspreads, furniture, and wall coverings. Though named for various fabulous cars, these, alas, are the Pintos of hotel rooms—nothing more than a typical motel room. The lovely pool, however, has its requisite Cadillac—a mosaic pink one, located at the bottom. For '50s kitsch and car fanatics, this is a fun place to stay; otherwise, you may think you were taken for a ride.

8701 Collins Ave., Miami Beach, FL 33154. ℂ **800/331-9346** in the U.S., 800/331-9347 in Canada, or 305/865-6661. Fax 305/866-2630. www.dezerhotels.com. 227 units. Winter $99–$139 double. Off-season $69–$99 double. Additional person $10. Special packages and group rates available. AE, DC, DISC, MC, V. **Amenities:** Restaurant, pool; nearby tennis courts; small spa; Jacuzzi; watersports rentals; game room; car-rental desk, tour desk; shuttle service to Aventura Mall and nearby antiques shop; coin-op washers and dryers. *In room:* A/C, TV, kitchen in some rooms, fridge on request, hair dryer, iron, safe.

Four Points Sheraton Miami Beach 𝕽
Right on the Miami Beach boardwalk, this chain hotel aspires to elegance with gaudy interiors inspired by the grandeur of ancient Greece. *Yikes!* A lobby of marble and rich mahogany goes against the grain of a typical South Beach hotel and only adds to this contrived, out-of-place decor. However, its location right on the beach is obviously a perk, as are its spacious rooms and good Sheraton-quality service. This hotel is not luxury, but it's not a bad choice if you're looking to be right on the beach and near the trendier, less ancient side of town.

4343 Collins Ave., Miami Beach, FL 33140. © **800/525-6994** or 305/531-7494. Fax 305/532-2490. www.sheratonfourpoints.com. 216 units. Winter $199–$299 double. Off-season $119–$199 double. AE, DC, DISC, MC, V. Valet parking $12.50. **Amenities:** Restaurant, bar; pool; exercise room; Jacuzzi; concierge; car-rental desk; business center; room service; same-day dry cleaning. *In room:* A/C, TV, dataport, coffeemaker.

Indian Creek Hotel *(Finds)*   Located off the beaten path, the Indian Creek Hotel is a meticulously restored 1936 building featuring one of the beach's first operating elevators. It's also the most charming hotel in the area, with impeccable service, too. Because of its location facing the Indian Creek waterway and its lush landscaping, this place feels more like an old-fashioned Key West bed-and-breakfast than your typical Miami Beach Art Deco hotel. The rooms are outfitted in Art Deco furnishings, such as an antique writing desk, pretty tropical prints, and small but spotless bathrooms. All the rooms have been completely renovated. Just 1 short block from a good stretch of sand, the hotel is also within walking distance of shops and restaurants and has a landscaped pool area that is a great place to lounge in the sun. If you're looking for charm, friendly service, and peace and quiet, stay away from the South Beach hype and come here instead.

2727 Indian Creek Dr. (1 block west of Collins Ave. and the Ocean), Miami Beach, FL 33140. © **800/ 491-2772** or 305/531-2727. Fax 305/531-5651. www.indiancreekhotel.com. 61 units. Winter $140–$240 double. Off-season $90–$150 double. Additional person $10. Group packages and summer specials available. AE, DC, DISC, MC, V. **Amenities:** Restaurant, bar; pool; concierge; car-rental desk; limited room service; laundry and dry-cleaning service. *In room:* A/C, TV/VCR, CD player, dataport, fridge in suites, hair dryer.

Newport Beachside Hotel & Resort *(Value) (Kids)*   This hotel is a great budget option, especially for young families who don't mind being away from the hustle and bustle of South Beach. The continental Newport Pub restaurant is very good and reasonably priced. The pool area is massive, which makes it great for kids. The hotel is situated directly on the beach, and for the aspiring angler, there is also a fishing pier out back. At night, by the poolside bar, a calypso band plays. Another plus is its location directly across the street from the R. K. Centres, a destination for both tourists and residents, with shopping and restaurants from fine dining to fast food. Guest rooms are comfortable and spacious, and most have ocean views and balconies.

16701 Collins Ave., Sunny Isles, FL 33160. © **800/327-5476** or 305/949-1300. Fax 305/947-5873. www.newportbeachsideresort.com. 300 units. Winter $129–$299 double. Off-season $95–$250 double. AE, DC, MC, V. Valet parking $5. **Amenities:** Restaurant, sports bar, massive outdoor pool; concierge; business center; babysitting. *In room:* A/C, TV, minibar, fridge, microwave, coffeemaker, hair dryer, iron, safe.

Ramada Miami Beach Resort   Situated in the heart of Miami Beach—within minutes of the 41st Street shopping area, the Convention Center, the Art Deco District, and the Bal Harbour Shops—the Ramada is located on a strip known as Millionaire's Row. Fortunately, this hotel was not created for millionaires. Formerly the kosher Crowne Hotel, Ramada has revamped this lush property, making it less a tawdry chain hotel and more of a pretty nice beach resort. The rooms have been refurbished and a complimentary fitness center has been added. The outdoor pool and tiki bars are relaxing; the inside bar and cafe are quaint and intimate. This is one property that is no secret—even in the off-season it operates at 85% capacity.

4041 Collins Ave., Miami Beach, FL 33140. © **305/531-5771**. Fax 305/673-1612. 254 units. Winter $109–$139 double. Off-season $95–$105 double. AE, MC, V. **Amenities:** Cafe, 2 bars; outdoor pool; exercise room. *In room:* A/C, TV, dataport, fridge, iron, safe.

INEXPENSIVE

Days Inn Oceanside *(Value)*   One of the most economical choices for travelers, this hotel has been refurbished in splashy pastels and bright lavenders. It's clean and cheap, and children under 17 stay free. A kosher Chinese restaurant is on the premises.

4299 Collins Ave., Miami Beach, FL 33140. ✆ **800/356-3017** or 305/673-1513. Fax 305/538-0727. 143 units. Winter $99–$119 double. Off-season $79–$99 double. AE, MC, V. Valet parking $12.50. Pets accepted. **Amenities:** 2 restaurants, lounge; pool; access to nearby watersports; concierge; room service; dry-cleaning service; laundry. *In room:* A/C, TV, dataport, fridge on request, coffeemakers in some rooms, iron, safe.

Suez Oceanfront Resort   The king of kitsch, the Las Vegas–like Suez is guarded by an undersized replica of Egypt's famed Sphinx—you can't miss it. Unfortunately, the Sphinx can't keep a quasi-seedy crowd from gathering here. The campy hotel does, however, offer newly renovated rooms on the beach, whereas most of the other old hotels have turned condo. Its location on Collins Avenue's trafficky, tacky motel row is convenient if your idea of convenience includes T-shirt shops, Denny's, and Walgreens. Nonetheless, the Suez is right on the beach, so if you stick to the back of the hotel, you'll appreciate it more. For the price, it's a decent choice. There's also a restaurant on the premises, though it's not very good.

18215 Collins Ave., Sunny Isles, FL 33160. ✆ **800/327-5278** or 305/932-0661. Fax 305/937-0058. www.suezresort.com. 200 units. Winter $95–$105 double. Off-season $70–$85 double. Kitchenettes $10–$15 extra. AE, DC, MC, V. Free parking. **Amenities:** Restaurant; outdoor heated pool; tennis courts; exercise room; coin-op washers and dryers. *In room:* A/C, TV, dataport, fridge, hair dryer, irons on request.

3 Key Biscayne

Locals call it the Key, and, technically, Key Biscayne is the northernmost island in the Florida Keys even though it is located in Miami. A relatively unknown area until an impeached Richard Nixon bought a home here in the '70s, Key Biscayne, at 1.25 square miles, is an affluent but hardly lively residential and recreational island known for its pricey homes, excellent beaches, and actor Andy Garcia, who makes his home here. The island is far enough from the mainland to make it feel semiprivate, yet close enough to downtown for guests to take advantage of everything Miami has to offer.

VERY EXPENSIVE

Ritz-Carlton Key Biscayne *(★★★)* *(Kids)*   Described by some as an oceanfront mansion, the Ritz-Carlton takes Key Biscayne to the height of luxury with 44 acres of tropical gardens, a 20,000-square-foot European-style spa, and a world-class tennis center under the direction of tennis pro Cliff Drysdale. Decorated in British-colonial style, the Ritz-Carlton looks as if it came straight out of Bermuda, with its impressive flower-laden landscaping. The Ritz Kids programs provide children ages 5 to 12 with fantastic activities, and the 1,200-foot beach-front offers everything from pure relaxation to fishing, boating, or windsurfing. Spacious and luxuriously appointed rooms are elegantly Floridian, featuring large balconies overlooking the ocean or the lush gardens. Unlike many behemoth hotels, the Ritz-Carlton is as much a part of the aesthetic value of the island as is its natural beauty, and its oceanfront Mediterranean-style restaurant, Aria, is exquisite. The best spa in Miami is also here, with 20,000 square feet of space that overlook the Atlantic Ocean and unheard-of treatments such as the Fountain of Youth Ocean Balance (in which you attain total relaxation while floating in the water) and the Key Lime Coconut Body Scrub.

Where to Stay in Key Biscayne, Downtown, Coral Gables, Coconut Grove & West Miami/Airport Area

Biltmore Hotel **8**
Biscayne Bay Marriott **27**
Clarion Hotel & Suites **22**
David William Hotel **9**
Days Inn **5, 6**
Don Shula's Hotel
  and Golf Club **4**
Doral Golf Resort and Spa **1**
Grove Isle Club and Resort **18**
Hampton Inn **13**
Hotel Inter-Continental Miami **24**
Hotel Place St. Michel **7**
Hyatt Regency
  Coral Gables **10**
Hyatt Regency at Miami
  Convention Center **23**
JW Marriott Hotel **19**
Mandarin Oriental, Miami **25**
Mayfair House Hotel **14**
Miami International
  Airport Hotel **2**
Miami River Inn **21**
Mutiny Hotel **15**
Omni Colonnade Hotel **11**
Riviera Court Motel **12**
Ritz-Carlton Coconut Grove **16**
Ritz-Carlton Key Biscayne **31**
Sheraton Biscayne Bay Hotel **20**
Silver Sands
  Beach Resort **29**
Sonesta Beach Resort
  Key Biscayne **30**
Turnberry Isle Resort
  and Club **28**
Wyndham Grand Bay Hotel **17**
Wyndham Hotel Miami **26**
Wyndham Miami Airport **3**

415 Grand Bay Dr., Key Biscayne, FL 33149. ☎ **800/241-3333** or 305/365-4500. Fax 305/365-4509. www.ritzcarlton.com. 402 units. Winter $440–$690 suite. Off-season $215–$405 suite. AE, DC, DISC, MC, V. Valet parking $23.43 per day. **Amenities:** Restaurant, pool grill, spa cafe, 3 bars; 2 outdoor heated pools; tennis center w/lessons available; health club & spa; watersports equipment; children's programs; 24-hr. room service; overnight laundry service. *In room:* A/C, TV, dataport, minibar, hair dryer, safe.

Silver Sands Beach Resort

If Key Biscayne is where you want to be and you don't want to pay the prices of the Sonesta next door, consider this quaint one-story motel. Everything is crisp and clean, and the pleasant staff will help with anything you may need, including babysitting. But despite the name, it's certainly no resort. Except for the beach and pool, you'll have to leave the premises for almost everything else, including food. The well-appointed rooms are very beachy, sporting a tropical motif and simple furnishings. Oceanfront suites have the added convenience of full kitchens, with stoves and pantries. You'll sit poolside with an unpretentious set of Latin-American families and Europeans who have come for a long and simple vacation—and get it.

301 Ocean Dr., Key Biscayne, FL 33149. ☎ **305/361-5441.** Fax 305/361-5477. 56 units. Winter $149–$349 double. Off-season $129–$309 double. Additional person $30. Weekly rates available. AE, DC, MC, V. Free parking. **Amenities:** Medium-sized pool; secretarial services; coin-op washers and dryers. *In room:* A/C, TV, VCRs in some rooms, kitchenette, fridge, microwave, coffeemaker.

Sonesta Beach Resort Key Biscayne 🎖🎖 (Kids)

The Sonesta is an idyllic, secluded resort on Key Biscayne—like a souped-up summer camp. Families and couples alike love this place for its oceanfront location and its many high-caliber amenities, which make it unlikely you'll want to venture off the property. Each of the plush 292 rooms, also recently upgraded, has a private balcony or terrace. There are also 12 one- and two-bedroom suites as well as fully furnished three- and four-bedroom vacation homes, with private pools, adjacent to the main hotel. Room 828 is particularly appealing, with its sweeping views of the ocean, comfortable (to say the least) king bed, and top-floor location.

Known for having the best piña coladas in the entire city, the pool and beach bars are popular with locals and vacationers alike. The hotel's Two Dragons restaurant is good, featuring Chinese, Thai, and Japanese food. A fantastic, free, and fully supervised kids' program (ages 3 to 12) will actually allow parents to have a vacation of their own. Although you may not want to leave the lush grounds, Bill Baggs State Recreation Area and the area's best beaches are nearby and worth the trip. Travelers here are only about 15 minutes from Miami Beach and even closer to the mainland and Coconut Grove.

A new Sonesta Hotel & Suites just opened in Coconut Grove, at 2889 McFarlane Rd. (☎ **305/529-2828**). With 300 rooms, many of which overlook Biscayne Bay, it is much smaller (and, for now at least, much cheaper) than it's sprawling Key Biscayne sister and, thankfully, it brings a much needed additional option to the hotel-challenged Coconut Grove.

350 Ocean Dr., Key Biscayne, FL 33149. ☎ **800/SONESTA** or 305/361-2021. Fax 305/361-3096. www. sonesta.com. 292 units. Winter $295–$465 double; $875–$1,475 suite. Off-season $195–$285 double; $650–$1,000 suite. 15% gratuity added to food and beverage bills. Special packages available. AE, DC, DISC, MC, V. Valet parking $12. **Amenities:** 4 restaurants, 2 bars, lounge; outdoor heated Olympic-sized pool; access to nearby golf; 7 tennis courts; fitness center; full-service spa; 2 waterfront Jacuzzis; extensive watersports equipment rental; bike and moped rental; children's programs; sports court; sailing lessons; shuttle service to shopping and entertainment; business center; salon; limited room service; laundry and dry-cleaning service. *In room:* A/C, TV, dataport, minibar, coffeemaker, hair dryer.

4 Downtown

If you've ever read Tom Wolfe's *Bonfire of the Vanities*, you may understand what downtown Miami is all about. If not, it's this simple: Take a wrong turn and you could find yourself in some serious trouble. Desolate and dangerous at night, downtown is trying to change its image, but it's a long, tedious process. Recently, however, part of the area has experienced a renaissance in terms of nightlife, with several popular dance clubs and bars opening up in the environs of NE 11th Street off Biscayne Boulevard. Most downtown hotels cater primarily to business travelers and pre- and postcruise passengers. Although business hotels are expensive, quality and service are of a high standard. Look for discounts and packages for the weekend, when offices are closed and rooms often go empty. If you're the kind of person who digs an urban setting, you may enjoy downtown, but if you're looking for shiny, happy Miami, you're in the wrong place (for now). As of press time, the developer of the Ritz-Carlton on South Beach was about to close a deal with downtown's shoddy DuPont Plaza, located on the sketchier side of the Miami River, in which millions of dollars would be invested to revamp the decrepit property, upgrading it into a classy lower-end hotel. Keep your eyes on this area.

VERY EXPENSIVE

Hotel Inter-Continental Miami ⚓ This hotel presents a serious catch-22: It's got a front-row view of all of Miami Beach, Biscayne Bay, the Miami River, and the Atlantic Ocean, but it is also located in downtown Miami. If it's a view that you want, then you should stay here, but if you're more interested in location, you may want to reconsider.

With the decidedly threatening presence of the hyperluxurious Mandarin Oriental just over the Brickell Bridge, the Inter-Continental had no choice but to keep up with the competition. A $34 million renovation has brought it up to speed, rendering it downtown proper's swankiest hotel. It boasts more marble than the Liberace Museum (both inside and out), but it is warmed by bold colors and a fancified Florida flavor. The lobby features a marble centerpiece sculpture by Henry Moore and is topped by a pleasing skylight. Plants, palm trees, and eclectic furnishings also add charm and enliven the otherwise stark space. Perfectly designed for business travelers, each room is outfitted with a desk and Internet-ready telephone lines, but is not fabulous. They're really just swankier versions of the rooms in a typical chain hotel, albeit a little more froufrou and elaborate, with marble bathrooms, upholstered seating areas and sit-in window sills. Some suites have fully equipped kitchenettes. Guests who stay in the Inter-Continental are big fish in the very small sea of desolate downtown Miami, but don't worry about your safety—this hotel is extremely secure.

100 Chopin Plaza, Miami, FL 33131. ✆ **800/327-3005** or 305/577-1000. Fax 305/577-0384. www.inter conti.com. 640 units. Winter $255–$335 double. Off-season $150–$245 double. Year-round $550–$3,000 suite. Additional person $20. Weekend and other packages available. AE, DC, DISC, MC, V. Valet parking $17. **Amenities:** 3 restaurants, 2 lounges; Olympic-size outdoor heated pool, access to nearby golf course; spa; concierge; tour desk; car-rental desk; large business center; shopping arcade; salon and barbershop; room service; coin-op washers and dryers; laundry and dry-cleaning service. *In room:* A/C, TV/VCR, CD player, minibar, hair dryer.

Mandarin Oriental, Miami ⚓⚓⚓ Corporate big shots finally have a high-end luxury hotel to stay in while wheeling and dealing their way through Miami. Catering to business travelers, conventioneers, and the occasional leisure traveler who doesn't mind spending in excess of $500 a night for a room, the swank Mandarin Oriental features a waterfront location, residential-style rooms with Asian touches (most with balconies), and several upscale dining and bar facilities. The waterfront view of the city is the hotel's best asset, both priceless and absolutely stunning. Much of the hotel's staff was flown in from Bangkok and Hong Kong to demonstrate the hotel's unique brand of superattentive Asian-inspired service. The hotel's two restaurants, the high-end Azul and the more casual Café Sambal, are up to Mandarin standards and are both wonderful, as is the 15,000-square-foot spa in which traditional Thai massages and Ayurvedic treatments are your tickets to nirvana.

500 Brickell Key Dr., Miami, FL 33131. ℂ 305/913-8288. Fax 305/913-8300. www.mandarinoriental.com. 329 units. $550–$575 double; $1,200–$4,000 suite. AE, DC, DISC, MC, V. Valet parking $24. **Amenities:** 2 restaurants, bar; outdoor pool; state-of-the-art health club; full-service spa; outdoor Jacuzzi; concierge; 24-hr. business center. *In room:* A/C, TV, dataport, minibar, hair dryer, iron, safe.

EXPENSIVE

Hyatt Regency at Miami Convention Center 😊😊
The Hyatt Regency is located just off the Miami River in the heart of downtown Miami. It shares space with the Miami Convention Center, the James L. Knight Convention Center Theater, an exhibition hall, and a 5,000-seat auditorium and concert hall. This hotel is perfect for large groups, business travelers, or basketball fanatics in town to see the Miami Heat play at the nearby American Airlines Arena. The People Mover and Metrorail are just blocks away, and water taxis are available at the front steps. Most of the spacious guest rooms have a balcony with a view of either the city or the bay.

400 SE Second Ave., Miami, FL 33131. ℂ 800/233-1234 or 305/358-1234. Fax 305/374-1728. www.miami.hyatt.com. 612 units. Winter $205–$250 double. Off-season $120–$205 double. AE, DC, DISC, MC, V. Valet parking $18. **Amenities:** Restaurant; outdoor pool; health club; extensive business center. *In room:* A/C, TV, dataport, coffeemaker, hair dryer, safe.

MODERATE

Biscayne Bay Marriott 😊
Just 7 miles east of the airport, the Biscayne Bay Marriott Hotel and Marina is on the sketchy outskirts of downtown Miami, yet it manages to create its own world of tranquility and entertainment. The 603-room hotel is equipped with a 220-slip full-service marina. Watersports rentals are available nearby. There's also 24-hour on-site security and valet parking. Some rooms face the bay, and some have balconies. The views are fantastic. If you want to stay in a Marriott, however, you may want to consider the newer JW Marriott (see below) on less desolate Brickell Avenue a few miles south.

1633 N. Bayshore Dr., Miami, FL 33132. ℂ 305/374-3900. Fax 305/375-0597. www.marriott.com. 600 units. Winter $194–$250 double. Off-season $124–$204 double. AE, DC, DISC, MC, V. Valet parking $15. **Amenities:** 3 restaurants, 2 lounges; pool; health club; Jacuzzi; concierge; business center; limited room service; coin-op washers and dryers; laundry and dry-cleaning service. *In room:* A/C, TV, dataport, minibar, coffeemaker, hair dryer.

JW Marriott Hotel 😊😊
Located smack in the middle of the business-oriented Brickell Avenue near downtown Miami, the JW Marriott is a *really* nice Marriott catering mostly to business travelers, but located conveniently enough between Coconut Grove and South Beach that it isn't a bad choice for vacationers, either. A small but elegant lobby features the classy, appropriately named Drake's Power Bar. The buzz of business deals being sealed amidst clouds of cigar smoke contributes to the smoky, but not staid, atmosphere here. Rooms are equipped with every amenity you might need. A lovely outdoor pool, fitness center, sauna, and

hot tub should become everybody's business at this hotel. Next door is the area's bustling brewery, Gordon Biersch, which attracts well-heeled, young professional types who gather for postwork revelry.

1111 Brickell Ave., Miami, FL 33131. ℂ **800/228-9290** or 305/374-1224. Fax 305/374-4211. www.marriott. com. Winter $219 deluxe room; $319 concierge room; $450 junior suite. Off-season $149 deluxe room; $189 concierge room; $350 junior suite. AE, DC, DISC, MC, V. Valet parking $18; self-parking $16. **Amenities:** 2 restaurants, bar; outdoor pool; health club; spa; sauna; concierge; tour desk; business center; laundry service. *In room:* A/C, TV, dataport (with free Internet access), minibar, coffeemaker, hair dryer, iron, safe.

Miami River Inn ★★★ *(Finds)* The Miami River Inn, listed on the National Register of Historic Places, is a quaint country-style hideaway (Miami's *only* bed-and-breakfast!) consisting of four cottages smack in the middle of downtown Miami. In fact, it's so hidden that most locals don't even know it exists, which only adds to its panache. Every room has hardwood floors and is uniquely furnished with antiques dating from 1908. In one room, you might find a hand-painted bathtub, a Singer sewing machine, and an armoire from the turn of the 20th century, restored to perfection. Thirty-eight rooms have private baths—4 have a shower only, 6 have a tub only, and 28 have a splendid shower-and-tub combo. One- and two-bedroom apartments are available as well. In the foyer, you can peruse a library filled with books about old Miami. It's close to public transportation, restaurants, and museums, and only 5 minutes from the business district.

118 SW South River Dr., Miami, FL 33130. ℂ **800/468-3589** or 305/325-0045. Fax 305/325-9227. www.miamiriverinn.com. 40 units. Winter $99–$229 double. Off-season $69–$109 double. Rates include continental breakfast. Additional person $15. AE, DC, DISC, MC, V. Free parking. Pets accepted for $25 per night. **Amenities:** Small, lushly landscaped swimming pool; access to nearby YMCA facilities; Jacuzzi; babysitting; coin-op washers and dryers; laundry and dry-cleaning service. *In room:* A/C, TV, hair dryer, iron.

Sheraton Biscayne Bay Hotel ★ This downtown hotel's waterfront location is its greatest asset. Nestled between Brickell Park and Biscayne Bay, the Sheraton is set back from the main road and surrounded by a pleasant bayfront walkway. Since a recent $14 million renovation, this Sheraton is especially recommendable. Its identical rooms are well furnished and comfortable. The hotel is popular with business travelers, but a fine choice for those who don't mind driving a few minutes to Miami's more populated areas.

495 Brickell Ave., Miami, FL 33131. ℂ **800/284-2000** or 305/373-6000. Fax 305/374-2279. www.sheraton. com. 598 units. Winter $199–$209 double; $225–$305 suite. Off-season $149–$175 double; $200–$250 suite. Additional person $10. Senior discounts and weekend and other packages available. AE, DC, DISC, MC, V. Self-parking $18. **Amenities:** Restaurant, bar; pool; exercise room. *In room:* AC, TV, dataport, fridges available on request, coffeemaker, hair dryer, iron.

INEXPENSIVE

Clarion Hotel & Suites ★ This hotel is especially designed for the seasoned business traveler. Its location in downtown Miami (right on the river) provides excellent access to the commercial world of nearby Brickell Avenue and the legal precincts in downtown. Due to its position adjoining the Hyatt, a Metromover station, and some major parking lots, this hotel does, however, lack a room with a view, which may be disheartening for some guests. The spacious and elegantly appointed guest rooms and suites offer many amenities, and the two-room apartment suites are ideal for extended stays.

100 SE 4th St., Miami, FL 33131. ℂ **800/838-6501** or 305/374-5100. Fax 305/381-9826. www.clarion miaconctr.com. 149 units. Year-round $99–$169 double. AE, DC, DISC, MC, V. Valet parking $15. **Amenities:** Restaurant, lounge; outdoor heated pool; exercise room; room service (7am–11:30pm); laundry service. *In room:* A/C, TV, dataport, coffeemaker, hair dryer.

5 Coral Gables

Translated appropriately as "City Beautiful," the Gables, as it's affectionately known, was one of Miami's original planned communities and is still among the city's prettiest, pedestrian-friendly (albeit preservation-obsessed) neighborhoods. Pristine with a European flair, Coral Gables is best known for its wide array of excellent upscale restaurants of various ethnicities, as well as a hotly contested megashopping complex featuring upscale stores such as Nordstrom (the quiet city didn't want to welcome new traffic).

If you're looking for luxury, Coral Gables has a number of wonderful hotels, but if you're on a tight budget, you may be better off elsewhere. Two popular and well-priced chain hotels in the area are a **Holiday Inn** (© **800/327-5476** or 305/667-5611) at 1350 S. Dixie Hwy., with rates between $75 and $125, and a **Howard Johnson** (© **800/446-4656** or 305/665-7501) at 1430 S. Dixie Hwy., with rates ranging from $65 to $95. Both are located directly across the street from the University of Miami and are popular with families and friends of students.

VERY EXPENSIVE

Biltmore Hotel 🏨🏨🏨   A romantic sense of Old World glamour combined with a rich history permeate the Biltmore as much as the pricey perfume of the guests who stay here. Built in 1926, it's the oldest Coral Gables hotel and a National Historical Landmark—one of only two operating hotels in Florida to receive that designation. Rising above the Spanish-style estate is a majestic 300-foot copper-clad tower, modeled after the Giralda bell tower in Seville and visible throughout the city. Over the years, the Biltmore has passed through many incarnations (including a post–World War II stint as a VA hospital), but it is now back to its original 1926 splendor. More intriguing than scary is the rumor that ghosts of wounded soldiers and even Al Capone, for whom the Everglades Suite is nicknamed, roam the halls here. But don't worry. The hotel is far from a haunted house. It is warm, welcoming, and extremely charming. Now under the management of the Westin Hotel group, the hotel boasts large Moorish-style rooms decorated with tasteful period reproductions and some high-tech amenities. The enormous lobby, with its 45-foot vaulted ceilings, makes a bold statement of elegance. Always a popular destination for golfers, including former President Clinton (who stays in the Al Capone suite), the Biltmore is situated on a lush, rolling 18-hole course that is as challenging as it is beautiful. The spa is fantastic and the enormous 21,000 square foot winding pool (surrounded by arched walkways and classical sculptures) is legendary—it's where a pre-*Tarzan* Johnny Weissmuller broke the world's swimming record. Even if you don't stay at the Biltmore Hotel, definitely take a tour of it to learn about its fascinating history and mystery. Call © **305/445-1926** for more information or see p. 183.

1200 Anastasia Ave., Coral Gables, FL 33134. © 800/727-1926 or 305/445-1926; Westin 800/228-3000. Fax 305/442-9496. www.biltmorehotel.com. 275 units. Winter $339–$509. Off-season $259–$479. Additional person $20. Special packages available. AE, DC, DISC, MC, V. Valet parking $14; free self-parking. **Amenities:** 5 restaurants, 2 bars; outdoor pool; 18-hole golf course; 10 lighted tennis courts; state-of-the-art health club; full-service spa; sauna; concierge; car rental through concierge; elaborate business center and secretarial services; salon; 24-hr. room service babysitting laundry and dry-cleaning service. *In room:* A/C, TV, VCR on request, fax, dataport, minibar, hair dryer, iron, safe; kitchenette in tower suite.

Hyatt Regency Coral Gables 🏨🏨   High on style, comfort, and price, this Hyatt is part of Coral Gables' Alhambra, an office-hotel complex with a

Mediterranean motif. The building itself is gorgeous, designed with pink stone, arched entrances, grand courtyards, and tile roofs. Most recently, the pool and lobby were beautifully renovated. Inside you'll find overstuffed chairs on marble floors surrounded by opulent antiques and chandeliers. The large guest rooms are comfortable, if uninspired. A few rooms have balconies. Though the hotel fails to authentically mimic something much older and much farther away, it is attractive in its newness and an excellent place from which to admire the more historic properties in the neighborhood.

50 Alhambra Plaza, Coral Gables, FL 33134. ⓒ 800/233-1234 or 305/441-1234. Fax 305/441-0520. www. hyatt.com. 242 units. Winter $340 double. Off-season $254 double. Year-round $375–$1,800 1-bedroom suite; $575–$2,050 2-bedroom suite. Additional person $25. Packages and senior discounts available. AE, MC, V. Valet parking $14; self-parking $11. **Amenities:** Restaurant, bar; large outdoor heated pool; nearby golf course; health club; Jacuzzi; 2 saunas; concierge; business center; limited room service; in-room massage; babysitting; same-day laundry and dry-cleaning service. *In room:* A/C, TV, fax in some rooms, dataport, minibar, coffeemaker, hair dryer, iron, safe.

EXPENSIVE

David William Hotel 𝒜𝒜 This sister hotel to the Biltmore shares many of the same amenities without the Biltmore's price. You can even take a shuttle to the Biltmore to play a round of golf, enjoy the health club and spa, play tennis, or take a dip in the pool. The luxurious one- and two-bedroom suites are extremely spacious and have eat-in kitchens for extended stays. For a spectacular view of Miami, go up to the roof and have a drink by the pool. The hotel, which has undergone a recent external renovation, is directly across the street from the Granada Golf Course, less than 5 miles from the airport, and only 20 minutes from Miami Beach. Donna's Bistro, a fusion restaurant with a homey feel, is spectacular. Executive chef Donna Wynter was the chef de cuisine at the Biltmore Hotel and has worked as a chef at New York's Tavern on the Green and Toscana Ristorante. If you want luxury without the price, this is your best alternative in the Gables.

700 Biltmore Way, Coral Gables, FL 33134. ⓒ **800/757-8073** or 305/445-7821. Fax 305/913-1943. www.davidwilliamhotel.com. 116 units. Winter $249–$489 double. Off-season $209–$269 double. AE, DISC, MC, V. Valet parking $9. **Amenities:** Restaurant, coffee shop, lounge, gourmet market; rooftop pool; limited room service. *In room:* A/C, TV, fax, kitchenette, minibar, coffeemaker, hair dryer, iron, safe.

Hotel Place St. Michel 𝒜𝒜𝒜 This European-style hotel in the heart of Coral Gables is one of the city's most romantic options. The accommodations and hospitality are straight out of Old World Europe, complete with dark wood-paneled walls, cozy beds, beautiful antiques, and a quiet elegance that seems startlingly out of place in trendy Miami. Everything here is charming—from the brass elevator and parquet floors to the paddle fans. One-of-a-kind furnishings make each room special. Bathrooms are on the smaller side but are hardly cramped. All have shower/tub combos except for two, which have either/or. If you're picky, request your preference. Guests are treated to fresh fruit baskets upon arrival and enjoy perfect service throughout their stay. The exceptional Restaurant St. Michel is a very romantic dining choice.

162 Alcazar Ave., Coral Gables, FL 33134. ⓒ **800/848-HOTEL** or 305/444-1666. Fax 305/529-0074. www.hotelplacestmichel.com. 27 units. Winter $165 double; $200 suite. Off-season $125 double; $160 suite. Additional person $10. Rates include continental breakfast and fruit basket upon arrival. AE, DC, MC, V. Self-parking $7. **Amenities:** Restaurant, lounge; access to nearby health club; concierge; room service; laundry and dry-cleaning service. *In room:* A/C, TV, dataport, hair dryer, iron (available upon request).

Omni Colonnade Hotel 𝒜 The Colonnade occupies part of a large historic building, originally built by Coral Gables' founder, George Merrick, in 1926.

Faithful to its original style, the hotel (popular with business travelers) is a successful amalgam of new and old, with an emphasis on modern conveniences. The structure stands 14 elegant stories high, although guest rooms occupy only four floors. The oversized rooms are worthy of the hotel's rates: They feature sitting areas, historic photographs, marble counters, gold-finished faucets, and solid wood furnishings. Thoughtful extras include complimentary shoeshines and champagne upon arrival. Doc Dammers Saloon and restaurant offers a good happy hour for the 30-something crowd. There's live entertainment on weekends.

180 Aragon Ave. (at Ponce de León and Miracle Mile), Coral Gables, FL 33134. ℭ **800/THE-OMNI** or 305/441-2600. Fax 305/445-3929. www.omnihotels.com. 157 units. Winter $215–$425 double. Off-season $165–$365 double. Free morning coffee and tea in lobby. Packages available. AE, DC, DISC, MC, V. Valet parking $10. **Amenities:** Restaurant; heated rooftop pool, small modern rooftop health club; Jacuzzi; concierge; tour desk; car-rental desk; shopping arcade; 24-hr. room service; in-room massage; babysitting; coin-op washers and dryers; same-day laundry and dry-cleaning service. In room: A/C, TV, VCR upon request, fax, dataport, minibar, coffeemaker, hair dryer, iron.

INEXPENSIVE

Riviera Court Motel   Besides the Holiday Inn down the road, this family-owned motel is the best discount option in the area. The comfortable and clean two-story property, dating from 1954, has a small pool and is set back from the road, so the rooms are all relatively quiet. Vending machines are the only choice for refreshments, but guests are near many great dining spots. You can also choose to stay in one of the efficiencies, which have fully stocked kitchens. For gossip mavens, this is the place where the pre-rehabilitated tennis star Jennifer Capriati was busted for drug possession many years ago.

5100 Riviera Dr. (on U.S. 1), Coral Gables, FL 33146. ℭ **800/368-8602** or 305/665-3528. 30 units. Winter $75–$88 double. Off-season $68–$80 double. 10% discount for seniors and AAA members. AE, DC, DISC, MC, V. **Amenities:** Pool. In room: A/C, TV.

6 Coconut Grove

This waterfront village hugs the shores of Biscayne Bay, just south of U.S. 1 and about 10 minutes from the beaches. Once a haven for hippies, head shops, and arty bohemian characters, the Grove succumbed to the inevitable temptations of commercialism and has become a Gap nation, featuring a host of fun, themed restaurants, bars, a megaplex, and lots of stores. Outside of the main shopping area, however, you will find the beautiful remnants of old Miami in the form of flora, fauna, and, of course, water.

Also see the last paragraph of the Sonesta Beach Resort Key Biscayne listing, on p. 102, for a review of the new Sonesta Hotel & Suites Coconut Grove.

VERY EXPENSIVE

Grove Isle Club and Resort ✦✦✦   Hidden away in the bougainvillea and lushness of the Grove, the Grove Isle Resort is off the beaten path on its own lushly landscaped 20-acre island, just outside the heart of Coconut Grove. The isolated exclusivity of this resort contributes to a country club vibe, though, for the most part, the people here aren't snooty; they just value their privacy and precious relaxation time. Everyone dresses in white and pastels, and if they're not on their way to a set of tennis, they're not in a rush to get anywhere. You'll step into rooms that are elegantly furnished with mosquito-netted canopy beds and a patio overlooking the bay. You'll need to reserve early here—rooms go very fast. Baleen, a fantastic yet pricey haute cuisinerie, serves fresh seafood and other regional specialties in an elegant dining room, or, better yet, outside on the water.

4 Grove Isle Dr., Coconut Grove, FL 33133. ℂ **800/88-GROVE** or 305/858-8300. Fax 305/854-6702. www.groveisle.com. 49 units. Winter $350–$495 suite. Off-season $295–$475 suite. Rates include breakfast. Additional person $20. AE, DC, MC, V. Valet parking $15. **Amenities:** Large outdoor heated pool; 12 outdoor tennis courts; deluxe health club; watersports rentals; concierge; secretarial services; salon; room service; in-room massage; babysitting; laundry and dry-cleaning service. *In room:* A/C, TV/VCR, video rental delivered to room for $5, dataport, minibar, hair dryer, iron, safe.

Mayfair House Hotel ★ *Overrated*

This Gaudí-esque hotel, located within the deserted streets of Mayfair Mall (an outdoor shopping area), certainly makes you feel removed from the mayhem in the surrounding streets of the Grove, but to me, it's somewhat desolate. Each guest unit has been individually designed and was renovated in 1998. No two rooms are alike, though each room has its own Roman tub or whirlpool and private terrace. Some suites are downright opulent and include a private outdoor Japanese-style hot tub. The top-floor terraces offer good views, and all are hidden from the street by leaves and latticework. Since the lobby is in a shopping mall, recreation is confined to the roof, where you'll find a small pool, sauna, and snack bar. NBA players have been known to stay here, as has one of Miami's more public residents, O. J. Simpson. If you're looking for complete seclusion, the Mayfair is fine, but, for the money, the airier Wyndham Grand Bay or Mutiny hotels are better choices (see below).

3000 Florida Ave., Coconut Grove, FL 33133. ℂ **800/433-4555** or 305/441-0000. Fax 305/441-1647. www.mayfairhousehotel.com. 179 units. Winter $289–$379 suite. Off-season $169–$379 suite. Year-round $800 penthouse. Packages available. AE, DC, DISC, MC, V. Valet parking $15; self-parking $6. **Amenities:** Restaurant, rooftop snack bar; private nightclub; outdoor pool; access to nearby health club; Jacuzzi; concierge; elaborate business center and secretarial services; 24-hr. room service; dry cleaning. *In room:* A/C, TV/VCR, fax, dataport, minibar, coffeemaker, hair dryer.

Mutiny Hotel ★★

En route to the center of the Grove, docked along Sail-boat Bay and the marina, lies this revamped hotel best known as the hangout for the *Miami Vice* set—drug kingpins, undercover cops, and other shady characters—during the mid-'80s. Now it caters to a much more legitimate clientele. Service and style are bountiful at the Mutiny, which somehow has avoided the nouveau-hotel hype and managed to stand on its own quiet merits without becoming part of the scene. The newly converted condos promise to be the best-kept secret in the Grove. The suites' British Colonial motif is warmed up with soft drapes, comfortable mattresses, and regal Old English furnishings. Each suite comes with a large bathroom (executive and two-bedroom suites have two bathrooms), full kitchen complete with china and complimentary coffee, and all the usual amenities associated with this class of hotel. The Mutiny is just a few blocks away from CocoWalk and the shops at Mayfair.

2951 S. Bayshore Dr., Miami, FL 33133. ℂ **888/868-8469** or 305/441-2100. Fax 305/441-2822. www.mutinyhotel.com. 120 suites. Winter $229–$799 1- and 2-bedroom suites. Off-season $179–$599 1- and 2-bedroom suites. Year-round $799–$1,799 1- and 2-bedroom penthouses. AE, DC, DISC, MC, V. Valet parking $16. **Amenities:** Restaurant; small outdoor heated pool with whirlpool; spa; health club; concierge; limited room service; babysitting; laundry and dry-cleaning service. *In room:* A/C, TV/VCR, dataport, kitchen, coffeemaker, hair dryer.

Ritz-Carlton Coconut Grove

The third and smallest of Miami's Ritz-Carlton hotels, scheduled to open in fall 2002, promises to be the most intimate of its properties, surrounded by 2 acres of tropical gardens and overlooking Biscayne Bay and the Miami skyline. Decorated in an Italian Renaissance design, the hotel's understated luxury will be a welcomed addition to an area known for its gaudiness. Expect the Ritz-Carlton standard of service and comfort.

2700 Tigertail Ave., Coconut Grove, FL 33133. (C) **800/241-3333** or 305/644-4680. Fax 305/644-4681. www.ritzcarlton.com. 115 units. Winter $385–$750 double. Off-season $245–$550 double. AE, DC, DISC, MC, V. Valet parking. **Amenities:** 2 restaurants, cigar bar; outdoor pool; health club; concierge, business center; 24-hr. room service. *In room:* A/C, TV, dataport, minibar, hair dryer.

Wyndham Grand Bay Hotel *★★★*   Grand in size and stature, the Grand Bay Hotel looks like it belongs in Acapulco with its ziggurat structure and tropical landscaping, but once you see the massive bright red sculpture/structure done by late Condé Nast editorial director Alexander Lieberman in the driveway, you know you're not in Mexico. Ultraluxurious, the Grand Bay is quietly elegant, and, as a result, has hosted the likes of privacy fanatics such as Michael Jackson. British singer George Michael filmed his "Careless Whisper" video here because of its sweeping views of Biscayne Bay. Rooms are superb, with views of the bay and the Coconut Grove Marina, and they're decorated in soft peach tones with a country French theme. Bathrooms are equally luxurious. Service is outstanding, and the clientele ranges from families to international jet-setters. Bice, a sublime Northern Italian restaurant, is the hotel's most popular dining option.

2669 S. Bayshore Dr., Coconut Grove, FL 33133. (C) **800/327-2788** or 305/858-9600. Fax 305/858-1532. www.wyndham.com. 181 units. Winter $359–$400 suite. Off-season $279–$349 suite. Additional person $20. AE, DC, MC, V. Valet parking $16. **Amenities:** 4 restaurants, lounge serving afternoon tea; indoor heated pool and outdoor pool; 24-hr. health club; Jacuzzi; sauna; concierge; business center; babysitting. *In room:* A/C, TV, CD player, fax, dataport, minibar, coffeemaker, hair dryer, iron, safe.

MODERATE

Hampton Inn   This very standard chain hotel is a welcome reprieve in an area otherwise known for very pricey accommodations. The rooms are nothing exciting, but the freebies, like local phone calls, parking, in-room movies, breakfast buffet, and hot drinks around the clock make this a real steal. Although there is no restaurant or bar, it is close to lots of both—only about half a mile to the heart of the Grove's shopping and retail area and about as far from Coral Gables. Rooms are brand new, sparkling clean, and larger than that of a typical motel. Located at the residential end of Brickell Avenue, it's a quiet, convenient location 15 minutes from South Beach and 5 minutes from Coconut Grove. If you'd rather save your money for dining and entertainment, this is a good bet.

2800 SW 28th Terrace (at U.S. 1 and SW 27th Ave.), Coconut Grove, FL 33133. (C) **888/287-3390** or 305/448-2800. Fax 305/442-8655. www.hampton-inn.com. 137 units. Winter $134–$154 double. Off-season $104–$124 double. Rates include continental breakfast buffet and local calls. AE, DC, DISC, MC, V. Free parking. **Amenities:** Large outdoor pool; Jacuzzi; exercise room. *In room:* A/C, TV, microwave on request.

7 West Miami/Airport Area

As Miami continues to grow at a rapid pace, expansion has begun westward, where land is plentiful. Several resorts have taken advantage of the space to build world-class tennis and golf courses. While there's no sea to swim in, a plethora of facilities makes up for the lack of an ocean view.

EXPENSIVE

Doral Golf Resort and Spa *★*   This recently renovated 650-acre golf and tennis resort is in the middle of nowhere, but with all it's got, it really is a destination in itself. While the pampering in the spa is nothing to sneer at, the next-door golf resort hosts world-class tournaments and boasts the Great White Course—the Southeast's first desert-scape course, designed by the Shark himself,

Greg Norman. *Note:* Repeat guests usually book the season well in advance. The Blue Lagoon water park features two 80,000-gallon pools with cascading waterfalls, a rock facade, and the 125-foot Blue Monster water slide. Rooms here, like the hotel itself, are spacious, all with private balconies, many overlooking a golf course or garden. Much-needed renovations to the rooms reveal a plantation-style decor with lots of wicker and wood. Spacious bathrooms are done up in marble. Enhancements to the golf courses, spa suites, and driving range have also brought the resort up to speed with its competition. The spa's restaurant serves tasty, healthy fare—so good you won't realize it's health food, actually. For a spa or golf vacation, the Doral is an ideal choice. Otherwise, consider investing your money in a hotel that's better located.

4400 NW 87th Ave., Miami, FL 33178. ✆ **800/71-DORAL** or 305/592-2000. Fax 305/594-4682. www.doral resort.com. 693 units. Winter $349 double; $439 suite; $565 1-bedroom suite; $909 2-bedroom suite. Off-season $155 double; $225 suite; $305 1-bedroom suite; $405 2-bedroom suite. Additional person $35. Golf and spa packages available. AE, DC, DISC, MC, V. Valet parking $15. **Amenities:** Restaurant, sports bar; 4 pools and a 125-ft. water slide; 5 golf courses and driving range; 10 tennis courts; health club & world-class spa; bike rental; concierge; business center; room service; babysitting; laundry and dry-cleaning service. *In room:* A/C, TV, CD player, dataport, minibar, coffeemaker, hair dryer, iron, safe.

MODERATE

Don Shula's Hotel and Golf Club
Guests come to Shula's mostly for the golf, but there's plenty here to keep nongolfers busy, too. Opened in 1992 to much fanfare from the sports and business community, Shula's resort is an all-encompassing oasis in the middle of the planned residential neighborhood of Miami Lakes, complete with a Main Street and nearby shopping facilities—a good thing, since the site is more than a 20-minute drive from anything. The guest rooms, located in the main building or surrounding the golf course, are plain but pretty in typical, uninspiring Florida decor—pastels, wicker, and light wood. As expected, the hotel's Athletic Club features state-of-the-art equipment and classes, but costs hotel guests $10 per day or $35 per week. The award-winning Shula's Steak House and the more casual Steak House Two get high rankings nationwide. They serve huge Angus beef steaks and seafood, which can be worked off with a round of golf the next day.

Main St., Miami Lakes, FL 33014. ✆ **800/24-SHULA** or 305/821-1150. Fax 305/820-8190. 330 units. Winter $129–$289 suite. Off-season $99–$209 suite. Additional person $10. Business packages available. AE, DC, MC, V. **Amenities:** 6 restaurants, 2 bars; 2 pools; 2 golf courses and a driving range; 9 tennis courts; health club; saunas; sporting courts. *In room:* A/C, TV/VCR.

Miami International Airport Hotel ⭐
I don't know of a nicer airport hotel, and you can't beat the convenience—it's actually in the airport at Concourse E. Every amenity of a first-class tourist hotel is here. The rooms are modern, clean, and spacious, with newly renovated furnishings, mattresses, fixtures, and carpeting. You might think you'd be deafened by the roar of the planes, but all of the rooms have been soundproofed and actually allow very little noise in. In addition, the hotel has modern security systems and is extremely safe.

Airport Terminal Concourse E (at the intersection of NW 20th St. and LeJeune Rd.; P.O. Box 997510), Miami, FL 33299-7510. ✆ **800/327-1276** or 305/871-4100. Fax 305/871-0800. www.miahotel.com. 260 units. Winter $179–]$650 double. Off-season $130–$270 double. Additional person $10. AE, DC, MC, V. Parking $10. **Amenities:** Restaurant, cocktail lounge; large rooftop pool; racquetball courts; well-equipped health club; Jacuzzi; sauna; concierge; tour desk; business center; limited room service; salon; laundry and dry-cleaning service. *In room:* A/C, TV, dataport, hair dryer, iron.

BARGAIN CHAINS

If you must stay near the airport, consider any of the dozens of moderately priced chain hotels. You'll find one of the cheapest and most recommendable options at either of the **Days Inn** locations at 7250 NW 11th St. or 4767 NW 36th St. (℃ **800/329-7466** or 305/888-3661), each about 2 miles from the airport. The larger property on 36th Street offers slightly cheaper rates with singles starting as low as $49. The 11th Street locale may charge more for weekends, but prices usually start at $70. Prices include free transportation from the airport.

A more luxurious option is the **Wyndham** at 3900 NW 21st St. (℃ **800/933-1100**), with rates from $100 to $225. There's also another location in downtown Miami at 1601 Biscayne Blvd. (℃ **800/WYNDHAM** or 305/374-0000). Rates there run from a high of $238 in season to $158 during the summer.

8 North Dade County

VERY EXPENSIVE

Turnberry Isle Resort & Club 👁👁👁 One of Miami's classiest resorts, this gorgeous 300-acre compound, owned by the Mandarin Oriental Hotel group, has every possible facility for active guests, particularly golfers. You'll pay a lot to stay here—but it's worth it. The main attractions are two Trent Jones courses, available only to members and guests of the hotel. A new seven-story Jasmine wing looks like a Mediterranean village surrounded by tropical gardens that are joined by covered marble walkways to the other wings. Treat yourself to a "Turnberry Retreat" at the Turnberry Spa, which recently underwent a $10 million renovation. The spa comprises three levels of deluxe pampering and includes aerobics and fitness classes, stress reduction, massage therapy, and a juice bar designed for complete rejuvenation. Impeccable service from check-in to checkout consistently brings loyal fans back to this resort for more. Its location in the well-manicured residential and shopping area of North Miami Beach known as Aventura means you'll find excellent shopping and some of the best dining in Miami right in the neighborhood. Unless you're into boating, the higher-priced resort rooms (instead of the yacht club) are where you'll want to stay; you'll be steps from the spa facilities and the renowned Veranda restaurant. The well-proportioned rooms are gorgeously tiled to match the Mediterranean-style architecture. The huge bathrooms even have a color TV mounted within reach of the whirlpool bathtubs and glass-walled showers. The only drawback to this hotel is that you'll need to take a shuttle to the beach.

19999 W. Country Club Dr., Aventura, FL 33180. ℃ **800/327-7028** or 305/936-2929. Fax 305/933-6560. www.turnberryisle.com. 395 units. Winter $395–$495 double; $605–$1,200 suite; $3,000–$4,200 penthouse. Off-season $175–$275 double; $375–$730 suite; $2,500–$3,500 penthouse. AE, DC, DISC, MC, V. Valet parking $12; free self-parking. **Amenities:** 6 restaurants, numerous bars and lounges; 2 outdoor pools; 2 golf courses; 2 tennis complexes, state-of-the-art spa, extensive watersports equipment rental, concierge, secretarial services; 24-hr. room service; babysitting. *In room:* A/C, TV/VCR, CD player, fax, dataport, minibar, fridge and coffeemaker on request, hair dryer.

6

Where to Dine in Miami

Don't be fooled by the plethora of superlean model types you're likely to see posing throughout Miami: Contrary to popular belief, dining in this city is as much a sport as the in-line skating on Ocean Drive. With over 6,000 restaurants to choose from, dining out in Miami has become a passionate pastime for locals and visitors alike. Our star chefs have fused Californian-Asian with Caribbean and Latin elements to create a world-class flavor all its own: *Floribbean*. Think mango chutney splashed over fresh swordfish or a spicy sushi sauce served alongside Peruvian ceviche.

Formerly synonymous with early-bird specials, Miami's new-wave cuisine, 10 years in the making, now rivals that of San Francisco—or even New York. Nouveau Cuban chef Douglas Rodriguez may have fled his Miami kitchen in favor of one in Manhattan, but other stellar chefs such as Mark Militello, Allen Susser, Norman van Aken, and Jonathan Eismann remain firmly planted in the city's culinary scene, fusing local ingredients into edible masterpieces. Indulging in this New World cuisine is not only high in calories, it's high in price. But if you can manage to splurge at least once, it'll be worth it.

Thanks to a thriving cafe society in both South Beach and Coconut Grove, you can also enjoy a moderately priced meal and linger for hours without having a waiter hover over you. In Little Havana, you can chow down on a meal that serves about six for less than $10. And since seafood is plentiful, it doesn't have to cost you an arm and a leg to enjoy the appendages of a crab or lobster. Don't be put off by the looks of our recommended seafood shacks in places such as Key Biscayne—oftentimes these spots get the best and freshest catches.

Whatever you're craving, Miami's got it—with the exception of decent Chinese food and a New York–style slice of pizza. If you're craving a scene with your steak, then South Beach is the place to be. Like many cities in Europe and Latin America, it is fashionable to dine late in South Beach, preferably after 9pm, sometimes as late as midnight. Service on South Beach is notoriously slow and arrogant, but it comes with the turf. (Of course, it is possible to find restaurants that defy the notoriety and actually pride themselves on friendly service.) On the mainland—especially in Coral Gables, and, more recently, downtown and on Brickell Avenue—you can also experience fine, creative dining without the pretense.

The biggest complaint when it comes to Miami dining isn't the haughtiness, but rather the dearth of truly moderately priced restaurants, especially in South Beach and Coral Gables. It's either really cheap or really expensive; the in-between somehow gets lost in the culinary shuffle. Quick-service diners don't really exist here as they do in other cosmopolitan areas. I've tried to cover a range of cuisines in a range of prices. But with new restaurants opening on a weekly basis, you're bound to find a savory array of dining choices on every budget.

Many restaurants keep extended hours in season (roughly December to April), and may close for lunch and/or dinner on Monday, when the traffic is slower. Always call ahead, since schedules do change.

Also, always look carefully at your bill—many South Beach restaurants include a 15% gratuity to your total due to the enormous influx of European tourists who are not accustomed to tipping. Keep in mind that this amount is the *suggested* amount and can be adjusted, either higher or lower, depending on your assessment of the service provided. Because of this tipping-included policy, South Beach wait staff are best known for their lax or inattentive service.

If you want to picnic on the beach or pick up some dessert, check out the gourmet-food shops, green markets, and bakeries listed under "Food" in chapter 8, "Miami Shopping."

1 Restaurants by Cuisine

AMERICAN

5061 Eaterie and Deli ✿ (Miami, $$, p. 147)

Atlantic Restaurant ✿✿ (Bal Harbour, $$$, p. 139)

Big Pink ✿ (South Beach, $$, p. 128)

Biscayne Miracle Mile Cafeteria ✿ (Coral Gables, $, p. 159)

Christy's ✿✿ (Coral Gables, $$$$, p. 156)

Curry's (Miami Beach, $, p. 142)

11th Street Diner (South Beach, $, p. 133)

The Forge Restaurant ✿✿✿ (Miami Beach, $$$$, p. 136)

Front Porch Café ✿ (South Beach, $, p. 133)

Granny Feelgood's (Downtown, $$, p. 148)

Here Comes the Sun ✿ (North Miami Beach, $, p. 144)

Joe Allen ✿✿ (South Beach, $$, p. 130)

News Café ✿ (South Beach, $, p. 134)

Nexxt Café ✿ (South Beach, $$, p. 132)

S&S Restaurant (Downtown, $, p. 149)

Sheldon's Drugs ✿ (Surfside, $, p. 142)

Shula's Steak House ✿✿ (Miami Beach, $$$$, p. 138)

Soyka Restaurant & Café ✿ (Downtown, $$, p. 149)

Tobacco Road (Downtown, $, p. 150)

Wilderness Grill (South Miami, $$, p. 160)

Van Dyke Cafe ✿ (South Beach, $$, p. 133)

AMERICAN PROGRESSIVE

Twelve Twenty ✿✿✿ (South Beach, $$$$, p. 125)

ASIAN

Spice ✿✿ (North Beach, $$, p. 141)

BARBECUE

Shorty's ✿ (South Miami, $, p. 161)

Jeffrey's ✿✿ (South Beach, $$, p. 129)

BRAZILIAN

Porcao ✿✿ (Downtown, $$$$, p. 146)

Wish ✿✿✿ (South Beach, $$$$, p. 126)

CANTONESE

Red Lantern ✿ (Coral Gables, $$, p. 156)

CEVICHE

Sushi Samba Dromo ✿✿✿ (South Beach, $$$, p. 127)

Key to Abbreviations: $$$$=Very Expensive $$$=Expensive $$=Moderate $=Inexpensive

Tambo 🎭🎭🎭 (South Beach, $$$, p. 128)

CHINESE

Christine Lee's 🎭🎭 (Sunny Isles, $$$, p. 139)

Kon Chau 🎭 (West Miami, $, p. 161)

Tropical Chinese 🎭🎭 (West Miami, $$$, p. 160)

COLOMBIAN

Mama Vieja 🎭 (South Beach, $$, p. 131)

CONTINENTAL

Crystal Café 🎭🎭🎭 (Miami Beach, $$$, p. 140)

Gordon Biersch Brewery Restaurant (Downtown, $$, p. 148)

Jeffrey's 🎭🎭 (South Beach, $$, p. 129)

Lagoon 🎭 (North Miami Beach, $$$, p. 143)

CREPES

Crepe Maker Café 🎭 (South Miami, $, p. 161)

CUBAN/LATIN FARE

La Carreta 🎭 (Little Havana, $, p. 152)

La Cibeles Café 🎭 (Downtown, $, p. 149)

La Esquina de Tejas Hondureña 🎭🎭 (Little Havana, $, p. 152)

Larios on the Beach 🎭 (South Beach, $$, p. 130)

Latin American Cafeteria 🎭🎭 (Downtown, $, p. 149)

Lincoln Road Café 🎭 (South Beach, $, p. 134)

Oasis (Key Biscayne, $, p. 154)

Puerto Sagua 🎭 (South Beach, $, p. 135)

Versailles 🎭🎭 (Little Havana, $, p. 152)

Yuca 🎭 (South Beach, $$$$, p. 126)

DELI

5061 Eaterie and Deli 🎭 (Miami, $$, p. 147)

Wolfie Cohen's Rascal House 🎭 (Sunny Isles, $$, p. 141)

DINER FARE

S&S Restaurant (Downtown, $, p. 149)

ECLECTIC

BED 🎭🎭 (South Beach, $$$$, p. 120)

Blue Door 🎭🎭 (South Beach, $$$$, p. 120)

Meza Fine Art Gallery Café 🎭🎭 (Coral Gables, $$, p. 158)

Tantra 🎭🎭🎭 (South Beach, $$$$, p. 124)

Touch 🎭🎭 (South Beach, $$$$, p. 125)

Wish 🎭🎭🎭 (South Beach, $$$$, p. 126)

ENGLISH TEA

Tea Room 🎭 (South Miami, $, p. 162)

FONDUE

Melting Pot (North Miami Beach, $$, p. 143)

FRENCH

5061 Eaterie & Deli 🎭 (Miami, $$, p. 147)

Brasserie Les Halles 🎭🎭 (Coral Gables, $$, p. 158)

Crepe Maker Café 🎭 (South Miami, $, p. 161)

Le Bouchon du Grove 🎭🎭 (Coconut Grove, $$$, p. 155)

Le Festival 🎭🎭 (Coral Gables, $$$$, p. 157)

L'Entrecote de Paris 🎭🎭 (South Beach, $$$, p. 127)

Provence Grill 🎭🎭 (Downtown, $$$, p. 147)

Wish 🎭🎭🎭 (South Beach, $$$$, p. 126)

FRENCH TROPICAL

Blue Door 🎭🎭 (South Beach, $$$$, p. 120)

FUSION

Sirena 🎭🎭🎭 (South Beach, $$$$, p. 124)

GERMAN

Dab Haus ✿ (South Beach, $, p. 133)

GLOBAL FUSION

Azul ✿✿✿ (Downtown, $$$$, p. 144)

GREEK

Daily Bread Marketplace (Coral Gables, $, p. 160)

The Greek Place (Surfside, $, p. 142)

HAITIAN

Tap Tap ✿ (South Beach, $$, p. 132)

HEALTH FOOD

Amos' Juice Bar (North Miami Beach, $, p. 143)

Granny Feelgood's (Downtown, $$, p. 148)

Here Comes the Sun ✿ (North Miami Beach, $, p. 144)

INDIAN

Anokha ✿✿✿ (Coconut Grove, $$$, p. 155)

House of India ✿ (Coral Gables, $$, p. 158)

INTERNATIONAL

Cafe Tu Tu Tango ✿ (Coconut Grove, $, p. 156)

IRISH PUB

John Martin's ✿ (Coral Gables, $$, p. 158)

ITALIAN

Bice ✿✿✿ (Coconut Grove, $$$$, p. 155)

Big Fish ✿✿ (Downtown, $$$, p. 146)

Cafe Prima Pasta ✿✿ (Miami Beach, $$, p. 140)

Cafe Ragazzi ✿✿ (Surfside, $$, p. 140)

Caffe Abbracci ✿✿ (Coral Gables, $$$, p. 157)

Carpaccio ✿ (Bal Harbour, $$$, p. 139)

Escopazzo ✿✿✿ (South Beach, $$$$, p. 121)

Joia Restaurant and Bar ✿✿ (South Beach, $$$, p. 126)

Laurenzo's Cafe ✿✿ (North Miami Beach, $, p. 144)

Macaluso's ✿✿✿ (South Beach, $$, p. 131)

Oggi Caffe ✿ (North Beach, $$, p. 141)

Osteria del Teatro ✿✿✿ (South Beach, $$$$, p. 123)

Paulo Luigi's Ristorante Italiana ✿ (Coconut Grove, $$, p. 155)

Perricone's Marketplace ✿ (Downtown, $, p. 149)

Spice ✿✿ (North Beach, $$, p. 141)

Spiga ✿✿ (South Beach, $$, p. 132)

Sport Café ✿ (South Beach, $, p. 136)

Stefano's ✿ (Key Biscayne, $$$, p. 153)

Tuscan Steak ✿✿✿ (South Beach, $$$$, p. 125)

JAPANESE

Sushi Samba Dromo ✿✿✿ (South Beach, $$$, p. 127)

MEDITERRANEAN

Balan's ✿✿ (South Beach, $$, p. 128)

Baleen ✿✿✿ (Coconut Grove, $$$$, p. 154)

Baraboo ✿✿ (North Beach, $$$, p. 139)

Lemon Twist ✿✿ (Miami Beach, $$, p. 140)

Macarena ✿✿ (South Beach, $$, p. 131)

Mark's South Beach ✿✿✿ (South Beach, $$$$, p. 122)

MEXICAN

El Rancho Grande ✿✿ (South Beach, $$, p. 129)

El Toro Taco Family Restaurant ✿✿✿ (Homestead, $, p. 161)

Mrs. Mendoza's Tacos al Carbon ✿ (South Beach, West Miami, $, p. 134)

San Loco Tacos ✿ (South Beach, $, p. 135)

Señor Frogs ☆ (Coconut Grove, $$, p. 156)

MIDDLE EASTERN
Sirena ☆☆☆ (South Beach, $$$$, p. 124)

NEW WORLD CARIBBEAN
Ortanique on the Mile ☆☆ (Coral Gables, $$, p. 159)

NEW WORLD CUISINE
Astor Place ☆☆ (South Beach, $$$$, p. 118)

Chef Allen's ☆☆☆ (North Miami Beach, $$$$, p. 142)

Crystal Café (Miami Beach, $$$, p. 140)

Mark's South Beach ☆☆☆ (South Beach, $$$$, p. 122)

Norman's ☆☆☆ (Coral Gables, $$$$, p. 157)

PAN-ASIAN
Bambu ☆☆ (South Beach, $$$$, p. 120)

China Grill ☆☆☆ (South Beach, $$$$, p. 121)

Nemo ☆☆☆ (South Beach, $$$$, p. 123)

Pacific Time ☆☆☆ (South Beach, $$$$, p. 123)

PIZZA
Piola ☆☆ (South Beach, $$, p. 132)

Pizza Rustica ☆ (South Beach, $, p. 135)

Pucci's Pizza (South Beach, $, p. 135)

SANDWICHES
La Sandwicherie (South Beach, $, p. 134)

Paninoteca ☆ (South Beach, Coral Gables, $, p. 134)

SEAFOOD
Baleen ☆☆☆ (Coconut Grove, $$$$, p. 154)

Bayside Seafood Restaurant and Hidden Cove Bar ☆ (Key Biscayne, $, p. 153)

Big Fish ☆☆ (Downtown, $$$, p. 146)

Bubba Gump Shrimp Co. (Downtown, $$, p. 147)

Fishbone Grille ☆☆ (Downtown, $$, p. 148)

Grillfish ☆☆ (South Beach, $$, p. 129)

Jimbo's (Key Biscayne, $, p. 154)

Joe's Seafood ☆ (Downtown, $$, p. 148)

Joe's Stone Crab Restaurant ☆☆ (South Beach, $$$$, p. 121)

Lagoon ☆ (North Miami Beach, $$$, p. 143)

Les Deux Fontaines ☆☆ (South Beach, $$, p. 130)

Monty's Stone Crab/Seafood House ☆ (South Beach, $$$$, p. 122)

Red Fish Grill ☆ (Coral Gables, $$, p. 159)

Rusty Pelican ☆ (Key Biscayne, $$$, p. 153)

Tambo ☆☆☆ (South Beach, $$$, p. 128)

SPANISH
Cafe Tu Tu Tango ☆ (Coconut Grove, $, p. 156)

Casa Juancho ☆☆ (Little Havana, $$$, p. 150)

Macarena ☆☆ (South Beach, $$, p. 131)

Puerto Sagua ☆ (South Beach, $, p. 135)

STEAK
Capital Grille ☆☆ (Downtown, $$$$, p. 144)

Christy's ☆☆ (Coral Gables, $$$$, p. 156)

The Forge Restaurant ☆☆☆ (Miami Beach, $$$$, p. 136)

Gaucho Room ☆☆☆ (South Beach, $$$$, p. 121)

Kiss ☆ (South Beach, $$$$, p. 122)

Morton's of Chicago ☆ (Downtown, $$$$, p. 146)

The Palm ☆☆ (Bay Harbor Island, $$$$, p. 138)

Shula's Steak House 🦞🦞 (Miami Beach, $$$$, p. 138)

Smith & Wollensky 🦞 (South Beach, $$$$, p. 124)

Tuscan Steak 🦞🦞🦞 (South Beach, $$$$, p. 125)

SUSHI

Bond St. Lounge 🦞🦞 (South Beach, $$, p. 129)

Nobu 🦞🦞🦞 (South Beach, $$$$, p. 123)

Shoji Sushi 🦞🦞🦞 (South Beach, $$$, p. 127)

Sushi Rock Café 🦞 (South Beach, $, p. 136)

Sushi Samba Dromo 🦞🦞🦞 (South Beach, $$$$, p. 127)

Tambo 🦞🦞🦞 (South Beach, $$$$, p. 128)

VIETNAMESE

Hy-Vong 🦞🦞 (Little Havana, $$, p. 152)

Miss Saigon Bistro 🦞🦞 (Coral Gables, $, p. 160)

2 South Beach

The renaissance of South Beach (which started in the early '90s and is still continuing, as classic cuisine gives in to mod-temptation by inevitably fusing with more chic, nouveau developments created by faithful followers and devotees of the Food Network school of cooking) has spawned dozens of first-rate restaurants. In fact, big-name restaurants from across the country have capitalized on South Beach's international appeal and opened, and continue to open, branches here with great success. A few old standbys remain from the *Miami Vice* days, but the flock of newcomers dominates the scene, with places going in and out of style as quickly as the tides.

The Lincoln Road area is packed with places offering good food and a great atmosphere. Since it's impossible to list them all, I recommend strolling and browsing. Most restaurants post a copy of their menu outside.

With very few exceptions, the places on Ocean Drive are crowded with tourists and priced accordingly. You'll do better to venture a little farther onto the pedestrian-friendly streets just west of Ocean Drive.

VERY EXPENSIVE

Astor Place 🦞🦞 NEW WORLD CUISINE   Caribbean cowboy chef Johnny Vinczenz has returned Astor Place to its original chic-chuck-wagon glory, whipping his chef's lasso into an epicurean frenzy with signature dishes straight from the American-Caribbean heartland: wild-mushroom pancake short stack with balsamic syrup, Jamaican jerk veal tenderloin, and wasabi skillet-seared tuna steak. Portions are huge and often enough for two to share. Appetizers are also generous in size, popular among the many lightweight model types who frequent the place. Desserts are glorious; chocoholics will be in heaven with the Cuarto de Chocolates featuring flourless chocolate cake, a chocolate dome, and peanut-butter chocolate bars. Sunday's Gospel Brunch is the ideal way to pay penance for your sins of the night before, but beware: The live gospel music is LOUD! Comfortable booths and soothing lighting give way to a scene that's reminiscent of a Hollywood movie premiere. Beware of whiplash-inducing situations, especially on weekend nights. Sitting in the booth next to you at any time could be Cameron Diaz, Oliver Stone, or Neve Campbell, among other luminaries for whom the food is comfort enough against the scene-sucking gawkers. *Note:* At press time, Astor Place was closed for renovations. Call before going to see if they've reopened (and to see whether or not they changed their menu).

Booked seat 6A, open return.

Rented red 4-wheel drive.

Reserved cabin, no running water.

Discovered space.

With over 700 airlines, 50,000 hotels, 50 rental car companies and
,000 cruise and vacation packages, you can create the perfect get-
way for you. Choose the car, the room, even the ground you walk on.

Travelocity.com
A Sabre Company
Go Virtually Anywhere.

Where to Dine in South Beach

Astor Place Bar and Grill **39**
Balan's **5**
Bambu **12**
BED **40**
Big Pink **53**
Blue Door **16**
Bond St. Lounge **14**
Café Cardozo **32**
China Grill **51**
Dab Haus **44**
Daily Bread Marketplace **54**
El Rancho Grande **21**
11th Street Diner **37**
Escopazzo **31**
Front Porch Café **28**
Gaucho Room **22**
Grillfish **25**
Jeffrey's **6**
Joe Allen **2**
Joe's Stone Crab
  Restaurant **57**
Joia Restaurant and Bar **56**
Kiss **17**
Larios on the Beach **41**
La Sandwicherie **26**
Les Deux Fontaines **33**
L'Entrecote de Paris **50**
Lincoln Road Café **7**
Macaluso's **3**
Macarena **29**
Mama Vieja **13**
Mark's South Beach **36**
Monty's Stone Crab/
  Seafood House **52**
Mrs. Mendoza's Tacos al
  Carbon **38**
Nemo **55**
News Café **45**
Nexxt Café **20**
Nobu **15**
Osteria del Teatro **24**
Pacific Time **10**
Paninoteca **12**
Piola **4**
Pizza Rustica **42**
Poppy **8**

Pucci's Pizza **4**
Puerto Sagua **47**
San Loco Tacos **27**
Shoji Sushi **55**
Smith & Wollensky **58**
Sirena **15**
Spiga **34**
Sport Café **46**
Sushi Rock Café **30**
Sushi Samba Dromo **19**
Tambo **1**
Tantra **23**
Tap Tap **48**
Touch **9**
Tuscan Steak **49**
Twelve Twenty **35**
Van Dyke Cafe **11**
Wish **43**
Yuca **18**

In the Hotel Astor, 956 Washington Ave., South Beach. ℂ 305/672-7217. Reservations recommended. Main courses $27–$36. AE, MC, V. Mon–Sat 7:30–11am and 11:30am–2:30pm; Sun–Thurs 7–11pm, Fri–Sat 7pm–midnight; Sunday Gospel Brunch noon–2:30pm.

Bambu 🏵🏵 PAN-ASIAN An Asian-inspired haute eatery and sushi palace, this restaurant (with bamboo floors and woven raffia drapes, which create a Zen-like setting) has become a haven to the who's who of Hollywood. The food has gone from mediocre and overpriced to excellent and overpriced since its up-and-coming chef Rob Boone decided to place more emphasis on the food rather than the atmosphere, with elaborate main-plate dishes such as soy-lacquered sea bass with Honshimaji mushrooms and shiso leaf tempura, sake-soaked prime beef ribeye with butter-poached shiitakes and spinach-stuffed carrots, and crispy-skin duck with mandarin griddle cakes and red-wine plum sauce. There's also a full sushi bar offering sometimes-fresh sashimi, tartares, and yakitori skewers. In addition to the model-caliber clientele that tends to inhabit the upstairs VIP lounge, the saketinis—martinis made with sake and cucumber—leave quite an impression. Don't even try to tip the hostess if you forgot to call ahead; you won't get in without a reservation. *Note:* Bambu closed for renovations in the summer of 2002. Call before going to see if they've reopened.

1661 Meridian Ave., South Beach. ℂ **305/531-4800.** Reservations required. Main courses $29–$38. AE, MC, V. Daily 7pm–midnight.

BED 🏵🏵 ECLECTIC BED—that's "Beverage. Entertainment. Dining"—is one of the most gimmicky dining lounges to land in South Beach in a very long time. When you walk inside, you'll feel as if you've entered a Buddhist temple. An array of inviting mosquito-netted beds awaits diners. You'll rest your head against soft cushiony pillows. A DJ spins Euro mood music and some techno. You'll have no problem appreciating the taste and aroma of the exquisite (and exquisitely priced) cuisine, featuring dishes such as macadamia-nut-crusted swordfish with black-bean daikon sprout salad and peanut sauce. For dessert, try the Ménage à Trois—peanut butter mousse, homemade jam, and brittle all under a "blanket" of chocolate—or take a Roll in the Sack—an apple-cinnamon Swiss roll in a phyllo sack with vanilla ice cream. Beware of crumbs in the sheets, as they aren't always changed between customers, and for the agoraphobic, do not go to BED on a weekend night—it's a nightmare. This restaurant gets my approval for the stellar food, not as a night-club-esque hangout.

929 Washington Ave., South Beach. ℂ **305/532-9070.** Fax 305/532-7757. Reservations required, accepted only on the day you plan to dine there. Main courses $32–$40. AE, DC, MC, V. Wed–Sun: first lay (no actual seats) 8:30pm; second lay 10:30pm. Lounge 11pm–3am.

Blue Door 🏵🏵 FRENCH TROPICAL It used to be that the Blue Door's greatest claim to fame was that Madonna was part owner. The food was unremarkable, but the eye candy was sickly sweet. When the material girl fled, so did others, leaving the Blue Door wide open for anything, as long as it was as fabulous as the hotel in which it sits. The most recent incarnation of the restaurant begs for superlatives more flattering than the standard "fabulous." The eye candy is still here, but now you have good reason to focus your eyes on the food rather than who's eating it. Thanks to award-winning chef Claude Troisgros (rhymes with foie gras)—a star in his own right—the menu frowns upon the ubiquitous fusion moniker in favor of a more classic French approach to tropical spices and ingredients. Ragout of Maine lobster in coconut-milk broth; sea bass with brown butter, cashews, and roasted hearts of palm; and ravioli stuffed with taro root mousseline are just a few of the Blue Door's tempting offerings.

Service can be snippy, slow, and, at times, downright rude, but the food makes up for what the restaurant lacks in hospitality.

In the Delano Hotel, 1685 Collins Ave., South Beach. ✆ 305/674-6400. Reservations recommended for dinner. Main courses $29–$46. AE, DC, MC, V. Daily 7am–11:30am, 11:30am–4pm, 7pm–midnight (late-night menu 3–7am).

China Grill 𝕬𝕬𝕬 PAN-ASIAN   Unless your surname is Pacino, DeNiro, or Winfrey (you get the idea), you might find yourself digging a hungry hole to China Grill at the gauche hour of 6pm or the indigestion-inducing hour of midnight. But with an incomparable, albeit dizzying, array of amply portioned dishes such as the outrageous crispy spinach, wasabi mashed potatoes, seared rare tuna in spicy Japanese pepper, broccoli rabe dumplings, lobster pancakes, and a sinfully delicious dessert sampler complete with sparklers, this hub of South Beach flash is well worth the wait. In fact, the wait is part of the China Grill experience. A coveted spot at the bar is headquarters for many of Miami's movers and shakers who come solely for the frenetic scene. On weekend nights, there's barely room to breathe. Keep in mind that China Grill is a family-style restaurant and that dishes are meant to be shared.

404 Washington Ave., South Beach ✆ 305/534-2211. Reservations strongly recommended. Main courses $25–$59. AE, DC, M, V. Mon–Thurs 11:45am–midnight; Fri 11:45am–1am, Sat 6pm–1am, Sun 6pm–midnight.

Escopazzo 𝕬𝕬𝕬 ITALIAN   Escopazzo means "crazy" in Italian, but the only sign of insanity in this primo Northern Italian eatery is the fact that it only seats 70. The wine bottles have it better—the restaurant's cellar holds 1,000 bottles of various vintages. Should you be so lucky to score a table at this romantic local favorite, you'll have trouble deciding between dishes that will have you swearing off the Olive Garden with your first bite. Among these are pappardelle with wild game and mushroom ragout, swordfish carpaccio, and braised leg of lamb with juniper berries, rosemary, and fennel. The hand-rolled pastas and risotto are near perfection. Eating here is like dining with a big Italian family—it's never boring (the menu changes five or six times a year), the service is excellent, and nobody's happy until you are blissfully full.

1311 Washington Ave., South Beach. ✆ 305/674-9450. Reservations required. Main courses $18–$28. AE, MC, V. Mon, Tues, and Thurs 6pm–midnight, Fri–Sat 6pm–1am, Sun 6–11pm.

Gaucho Room 𝕬𝕬𝕬 STEAK   This restaurant will set you back *mucho dinero*, but it is one of the best steak houses in the city. The Gaucho Room is a stunning Argentinean dining room that serves prime aged meats with unparalleled service. Argentine ribeye is marinated in garlic, herbs, and olive oil before being grilled and served on butcher blocks. *Warning:* Those with lighter palates should probably request light seasoning on their food.

In the Loews Hotel, 1601 Collins Ave. (St. Moritz Bldg.), South Beach. ✆ 305/604-5290. Reservations recommended. Main courses $22–$52. AE, MC, V. Daily 7pm–1am.

Joe's Stone Crab Restaurant 𝕬𝕬 SEAFOOD   Unless you grease the palms of one of the stone-faced maitre d's with some stone-cold cash, you'll be waiting for those famous claws for up to 2 hours—if not more. As much a Miami landmark as the beaches themselves, Joe's is a microcosm of the city, attracting everyone from T-shirted locals to a bejeweled Ivana Trump. Whatever you wear, however, will be eclipsed by a kitschy, unglamorous plastic bib that your waiter will tie on you unless you say otherwise. Open only during stone-crab season (Oct–May), Joe's reels in the crowds with the freshest, meatiest stone crabs and their essential accouterments: creamed spinach and excellent sweet potato fries.

The claws come in medium, large, or jumbo. Some say size doesn't matter; others swear by the jumbo (and more expensive) ones. Whatever you choose, pair them with a savory mustard sauce (a perfect mix of mayo and mustard) or hot butter. Not feeling crabby? The fried chicken and liver and onions on the regular menu are actually considered by many as far superior—they're definitely far cheaper—to the crabs. Oh, yeah, and save room for dessert. The Key lime pie here is the best in town. If you don't feel like waiting, try Joe's Takeaway, which is located next door to the restaurant—it's a lot quicker and just as tasty.

11 Washington Ave. (at Biscayne St., just south of 1st St.), South Beach. (✆) 305/673-0365, or 305/673-4611 for takeout. www.joesstonecrab.com. Reservations not accepted. Market price varies but averages $62.95 for a serving of jumbo crab claws, $38.95 for large claws. AE, DC, DISC, MC, V. Daily 11:30am–2:30pm; Sun–Thurs 5–10pm, Fri–Sat 5–11pm. Open mid-Oct to mid-May.

Kiss ⭐ STEAK   This is not your grandfather's steakhouse. Sure, you can order the same New York strip as at, say, the Palm, but at Kiss, you can also get a strip show with your strip steak. Yes, Kiss is a high-style, high-concept cabaret, with live entertainment that isn't necessarily as raw as you may like your meat, but it's certainly more sizzling than medium rare. The food is quite good here, especially the ridiculously priced Kiss exclusive magnum slow-roasted prime rib, served with a trio of sauces for $69.95, but you will be distracted by the circus-like atmosphere and cavalcade of club clowns who don't convene here for food, but for fanfare and, of course, lots of air kisses.

In the Albion Hotel, 301 Lincoln Rd., South Beach. (✆) 305/695-4445. Reservations recommended. Main courses $22–$52. AE, MC, V. Mon–Thurs 7pm–1am, Fri–Sat 7pm–2am. Lounge open until 3am weekdays, 4am weekends. Closed Sun.

Mark's South Beach ⭐⭐⭐ NEW WORLD/MEDITERRANEAN   Named after owner and chef Mark Militello, this is one of the best restaurants in all of Miami. A cozy, contemporary restaurant nestled in the basement of the quietly chic Hotel Nash, Mark's New World– and Mediterranean-influenced menu changes nightly. What doesn't change is the consistency and freshness of the restaurant's exquisite cuisine. The roasted rack of Colorado lamb with semolina gnocchi is exceptional and worth every bit of cholesterol it may have. Crispy-skin yellowtail snapper with shrimp, tomato, black olives, oregano, and crumbled feta cheese is in a school of its own. Desserts, including an impressive cheese cart, are outrageous, especially the pistachio cake with chocolate sorbet. Unlike many South Beach eating establishments, the knowledgeable servers are here because of their experience in the restaurant—not modeling—business.

In the Hotel Nash, 1120 Collins Ave., South Beach. (✆) 305/604-9050. Reservations recommended. Main courses $16–$38. AE, DC, DISC, MC, V. Sun–Thurs 7–11pm, Fri–Sat 7pm–midnight.

Monty's Stone Crab/Seafood House ⭐ SEAFOOD   This restaurant is the antithesis of South Beach trendiness, with scrappy wood floors and a very casual raw bar set outside around a large swimming pool. The best deal in town is still the all-you-can-eat stone crabs—about $40 for the large ones and $35 for the mediums. That's about the same price that Joe's, located 2 blocks away, charges for just three or four claws. (But don't order stone crabs in summer—they aren't as fresh.) Enjoy the incredible views and off-season fish specialties, including the Maryland she-crab soup, rich and creamy without too much thickener. Beware of Friday nights, when the happy-hour crowds convene around (and sometimes in) the pool for postwork revelry.

300 Alton Rd., South Beach. (✆) 305/673-3444. Reservations recommended. Main courses $20–$40. AE, DC, MC, V. Sun–Thurs 5:30–11pm, Fri–Sat 5:30pm–midnight.

Nemo ✦✦✦ PAN-ASIAN   What Wolfgang Puck is to foodies on the West Coast, Nemo's chef, Michael Schwartz, is to Miami. Hailing from Puck's lauded Chinois in L.A., Schwartz's Pan-Asian cuisine is masterful. Located on the quickly developing South Beach area known as SoFi ("South of Fifth Street"), Nemo is a funky, high-style eatery with an open kitchen and an outdoor court-yard canopied by trees and lined with an eclectic mix of model types, foodies, and Schwartz groupies. Among the reasons to eat in this restaurant, whose name is actually "omen" spelled backward: grilled Indian spiced pork chop; grilled local mahimahi with citrus and grilled sweet onion salad; kimchi glaze, basil and crispy potatoes; and an inspired dessert menu by Hedy Goldsmith that's not for the faint of calories. Seating inside is comfy cozy, but borders on cramped. On Sunday mornings, the open kitchen is converted into a buffet counter for the restaurant's unparalleled brunch. Be prepared for a wait; the crowd tends to spill out onto the street.

100 Collins Ave., South Beach. ✆ 305/532-4550. Reservations recommended. Main courses $22–$36; Sun brunch $26. AE, MC, V. Mon–Fri noon–3pm and 7pm–midnight, Sun 11am–3pm and 6–11pm. Valet parking $10.

Nobu ✦✦✦ SUSHI   When Madonna ate here, no one really noticed. Not because they were purposely trying not to notice, but because the real star at Nobu is the sushi. The raw facts: Nobu has been hailed as one of the best sushi restau-rants in the world, with always-packed eateries in New York, London, and Los Angeles. The Omakase, or Chef's Choice—a multicourse menu entirely up to the chef for $70 per person and up—gets consistent raves. And although you won't wait long for your food to be cooked, you will wait forever to score a table here.

At the Shore Club Hotel, 1901 Collins Ave., South Beach. ✆ 305/695-3100. Reservations for parties of six or more. Main courses $10–$30. AE, MC, V. Sun–Thurs 6pm–midnight, Fri–Sat 6pm–1am.

Osteria del Teatro ✦✦✦ ITALIAN   Located in an unassuming storefront beneath the ultrasceney crobar nightclub, it's hard to believe that Osteria del Teatro is the best Italian bistro on the beach. What it might be lacking in decor is certainly not absent in the elaborate cuisine. Regulars who swear by this place won't even bother looking at the menu; instead they concentrate on the enor-mous changing list of specials on the blackboard. You will definitely be faced with some tough choices: plump chicken breast sautéed with shallots and sun-dried tomatoes in champagne cream sauce; seafood baked with linguine, garlic, fresh tomatoes, and olive oil in parchment paper; or homemade ravioli stuffed with scallops and crab in lobster sauce. The regulars here are on a first-name basis with the waiters, who always seem to know what you're in the mood for.

1443 Washington Ave. (at Española Way), South Beach. ✆ 305/538-7850. Reservations recommended. Main courses $13–$34. AE, DC, MC, V. Mon–Sat 6pm–midnight. Closed Sept.

Pacific Time ✦✦✦ PAN-ASIAN   Chef and co-owner (and former model) Jonathan Eismann was awarded the Robert Mondavi Award for Culinary Excel-lence in June 1994, and his restaurant, Pacific Time, has been recognized by *Bon Appétit* and *Esquire* magazines as one of America's "Best New Restaurants." Eismann's dishes are stunning hybrids of Chinese, Japanese, Korean, Viet-namese, Mongolian, and Indonesian flavors. One of the best dishes is the Mongolian lamb salad, which has a lightly sweet, earthy taste with a crunchy kick of onion. For a main course, the ever-changing menu offers many locally caught fish specialties such as Szechuan grilled mahimahi served on a bed of shredded shallots and ginger with a sweet sake-infused sauce and tempura-dunked sweet potato slivers on the side. The famous chocolate bomb is every bit as decadent as they say, with hot bittersweet chocolate bursting from the cupcake-like center—order it as soon as you sit down. The wine list is quite extensive and includes red and white wines from Italy, France, the Napa Valley, Australia, Argentina, New Zealand, and South Africa. The restaurant's best deal is its pretheater menu, a three-course dinner for only $34.

915 Lincoln Rd. (between Jefferson and Michigan aves.), South Beach. ℂ 305/534-5979. Reservations recommended. Main courses $23.50–$32. AE, DC, MC, V. Sun–Thurs 6–11pm, Fri–Sat 6pm–midnight.

Sirena ✰✰✰ MIDDLE EASTERN/FUSION Inside this fantastic neo–Middle Eastern restaurant, you'll find an elegant ambiance of rich swirled marble on the floors and walls, and outside, an inviting, serene patio overlooking the Shore Club Hotel's pool area. Despite the fact that the patio is actually raw, unfinished concrete, it's quite sultry outside. But even hotter than the restaurant's well-heeled, hipster clientele is the cuisine. Sure, you'll pay a pretty price for it, but consider it to be the culinary version of plastic surgery—it's an investment in your taste buds. The hearts of palm salad with jalapeño dressing is one of the tastiest salads I've ever had, with enough bite to counterbalance the delicate, plump hearts of palm. The sautéed foie gras with black plums, the priciest appetizer not including the $95 beluga caviar, is exquisite. For main courses, skip the roasted lamb chops—they're disappointing—and head right to the cumin-spiced peppered filet of beef with crispy hearts of palm fries and arugula. Desserts are delicious, too. The praline rum fudge cake is outstanding. The restaurant is also open for equally delicious—and expensive—breakfast, brunch, and lunch. The Key lime pancakes are worth the splurge.

In the Shore Club Hotel, 1901 Collins Ave., South Beach. ℂ 305/695-3218. Reservations recommended. Main courses $17–$36. AE, DC, MC, V. Sun–Thurs 6–11pm, Fri–Sat 6pm–midnight.

Smith & Wollensky ✰ STEAK The menu here is basic, almost austere, with a few chicken and fish choices and beef served about a dozen ways. The classic is the sirloin, seared lightly and served naked. The veal chop is of Flintstonian proportion. Mediocre side dishes such as asparagus, baked potato, onion rings, creamed spinach, and hash browns are sold a la carte. Service is erratic, from highly professional to rudely aloof. Desserts are expertly prepared by pastry chef Marta Braunstein; Drunken Donuts and milk chocolate crème brûlée are an excellent way to finish off an already-decadent meal. You'll find much tastier steaks (at comparable prices) at the Forge or Tuscan Steak; for a less expensive yet no less delicious steak, check out nearby L'Entrecote de Paris. What Smith & Wollensky's got on them, however, is its fantastic waterfront location and an innovative American dim sum brunch every Sunday from 10:30am to 1:30pm, featuring 45 items such as salmon lollypops, steamed dumplings, mini beef Wellington, oysters Rockefeller, and bottomless cups of juice, coffee, mimosas, and bloody marys for $39.50 per person.

1 Washington Ave. (in South Pointe Park), South Beach. ℂ 305/673-2800. www.smithandwollensky.com. Reservations recommended. Main courses $20–$35; lobster $38. AE, DC, DISC, MC, V. Mon–Sat noon–2 am; Sunday brunch 11am–2pm.

Tantra ✰✰✰ ECLECTIC Marrakesh meets Miami Beach in this truly original, outrageously priced exotic outpost devoted to the ancient Indian tantric philosophy of tempting the senses with all things pleasurable. Begin with your surroundings: a sultry interior of soft grass (yes, it's real; they resod weekly) and starry lights overhead. In the front room by the bar, there are low-lying couches and pillow-lined booths bolstered by drapes that can be closed for privacy. Belly dancers mix with cocktail waitresses singing the praises of Tantra's special aphrodisiac cocktails and offering you a puff of Turkish tobacco from the communal hookah pipe (they insist it's clean, but I'd be wary). A private VIP room off to the side features a hammock and a peaceful spiritual soundtrack.

Tantra serves a combination of Middle Eastern, Mediterranean, and Indian dishes that really are divine. Consider the Tantra Love Apple (a ripe tomato layered with Laura Chenel goat cheese and basil oil, garnished with pomegranate seeds), or perhaps Nine Jewel Indian Spiced Rack of Lamb. The $52 filet mignon is delicious, but its price tag borders on obscene.

Don't come to Tantra looking for a serene vibe to match the setting and menu. Tantra practically turns into a nightclub after dinner, attracting a crowd of celebrities and scenesters.

1445 Pennsylvania Ave. (at Española Way), South Beach. ℂ 305/672-4765. Reservations required. Main courses $24–$48. AE, DC, DISC, MC, V. Daily 7pm–5am. Late-night menu 1am to closing.

Touch ⍟⍟ ECLECTIC   Despite the presence of the ubiquitous velvet ropes out front and the loud soundtrack inside, Touch is not a nightclub. Located on busy Lincoln Road, Touch works harder to be something of a tropical supper club, complete with faux palm trees.

The food is a mod Southwestern, with dishes as dolled up as the restaurant's interior. Specialties include delicious Canadian elk chop, seared and served with black plum salad, Frangelico corn custard and Merlot plum demi-glacé; a red-peppercorn-crusted ahi tuna; and a pan-seared filet with vegetable sauté, wasabi mashed potatoes, and candied ginger. Despite the air of haughtiness you may receive out front at the ropes, service is actually quite good. If the noise inside is too loud, and it often is, request a table outside, ensconced safely behind the ropes, where you can watch the passersby try to put their fingers on what, exactly, Touch portends to be.

910 Lincoln Rd., South Beach. ℂ 305/532-8003. Reservations required. Main courses $20–$75. AE, DC, MC, V. Sun–Thurs 7pm–midnight, Fri–Sat 7pm–1am.

Tuscan Steak ⍟⍟⍟ ITALIAN/STEAK   This excellent Northern Italian restaurant, a member of the China Grill scion, is all about meat served Italian style, in large family-style portions. With a rich wood interior, the atmosphere is reminiscent of the dining room of a well-connected family—ornate and very loud. The house salad is a massive undertaking of the classic antipasto, filled with shredded slices of salami and pepperoni, chunks of mozzarella, and a delicate vinaigrette. Be sure to order the sautéed spinach with garlic and the onion mashed potatoes with whichever steak you choose. All steaks are big enough for at least three people to share. The house specialty is a delicious T-bone steak served with pungent garlic purée. On any given weekend night, reservations are secondary to being friends with the ultratanned host, so expect a long wait for a table. The bar is the only place to wait . . . if you can find a spot there, and drinks are rather pricey. The background music is straight out of Studio 54 and so is the flashy crowd. Despite the long waits, after one meal here, you'll likely want to kiss the ring of the true boss of this culinary mob scene—the chef.

433 Washington Ave., South Beach. ℂ 305/534-2233. Reservations strongly recommended on weekends. Main courses $20–$65. Family-style meals are $50 per person, including appetizer and main course. AE, DISC, MC, V. Sun–Thurs 6pm–midnight, Fri–Sat 6pm–1am.

Twelve Twenty ⍟⍟⍟ AMERICAN PROGRESSIVE   Prepare to shell out a pretty penny for the very haute twist on American and international cuisine (portions are small and prices are big) that rolls out of this kitchen in the high and mighty Tides Hotel. The air of elegance (perhaps pickled by the scent of money) mixes with the fragrances of dishes such as the blue prawn risotto with black trumpet mushrooms and curry, and warm maple-and-bourbon-smoked salmon. Save room for dessert, because you will want to try the Baked Jamaica—a luscious concoction of coffee and banana macadamia ice creams, English toffee fudge, cinnamon meringue, and dark rum crème anglaise. Also worthy of dessert are the restaurant's signature Tropical Popsicle martinis, such as the apricot and ginger version that comes complete with a minipopsicle-cum-stirrer made of lychee; a pineapple basil martini comes with a Guanabana popsicle. Unlike the oft-harried atmospheres of other South Beach eateries, where scene serves as an aperitif, there really is no scene here other than a trickle of hotel guests who occasionally pass through the lobby. Despite its exposure, Twelve Twenty does offer a fair share of privacy, which is good for the number of business power meals it hosts.

In the Tides Hotel, 1220 Ocean Dr., South Beach. ℂ 305/604-5130. Reservations recommended. Main courses $26–$35. AE, MC, V. Sun–Thurs 7–11pm, Fri–Sat 7–midnight.

Wish ✿✿✿ ECLECTIC/BRAZILIAN/FRENCH   Wish got its start as a haute vegetarian restaurant, located in the stylish Todd Oldham–designed The Hotel. It was, and still is, a terrific setting (request an outside table in the serene, umbrellaed courtyard), but the foodies couldn't bear a meal without meat. First culinary whiz Andrea Curto came on board and redirected the meaty menu, and then passed her whisk onto E. Michael Reidt, one of *Food and Wine* magazine's "Ten Best New Chefs of 2001," whose own culinary wishes have come true in the form of fantastic French Brazilian cuisine. Two of Wish's finest are cachaca-marinated tuna over jicama quinoa salad on spicy charred watermelon, and pan-seared beef tenderloin on a truffled taro root purée with stewed carrots and grilled asparagus.

In The Hotel, 801 Collins Ave., South Beach. ℂ 305/531-2222. Reservations recommended. Main courses $16–$32. AE, DC, DISC, MC, V. Daily 6–10:30pm.

Yuca ✿ *Overrated* CUBAN   While the name, which stands for Young Upscale Cuban Americans, is correctly pronounced "*Yoo*-ka," it really should be called as it looks: "*Yuck-a.*" Overpriced and with a rude staff to boot, Yuca has been hailed as Miami's premier nouveau Cubano restaurant, and it was—when Douglas Rodriguez was helming the galley. When Rodriguez left, I think he took all the good stuff with him to New York's lauded Patria restaurant, but folks still flock here. The food is little more than greasy concoctions of Cuban food masking itself as nouveau under heavy beds of sauces and other foreign substances. What Yuca is good for, however, is live Latin entertainment in the upstairs lounge. There's a two-drink minimum—a small price compared to the cost of the food.

501 Lincoln Rd. (corner of Drexel), South Beach. ℂ 305/532-9822. Reservations recommended. Main courses $22–$40. AE, DC, DISC, MC, V. Mon–Sat noon–11pm, Sun noon–10pm.

EXPENSIVE

Joia Restaurant and Bar ✿✿ ITALIAN   Owned by Miami nightlife diva Ingrid Casares, famous for her friendship with Madonna, Joia exudes a cozy atmosphere of self-conscious camaraderie, with a few tables indoors and several outdoors in a large courtyard. On any given night you're bound to see celebrities such as Ben Stiller, Donald Trump, Rupert Everett, and, yes, Madonna. Without harping on the service too much (it's quite leisurely), the pasta here is among the freshest anywhere on the beach. The chef is a native Italian and he takes great pride in crafting the perfect pasta no matter who's eating it. There is a laundry list of appetizers, salads, and pastas. Recommended dishes include the *rigatoni al funghi*, a mushroom-lover's delight, with large tube pasta filled with shiitake and porcini mushrooms; the *gnocchi di zucca*, homemade potato-and-pumpkin dumplings in a tomato or cheese sauce; and the *bauletti di pollo al funghi*, a folded chicken breast stuffed with Fontina cheese, mushrooms, and sage. The wine list is also exquisite.

150 Ocean Dr., South Beach. ✆ **305/674-8871.** Reservations recommended. Main courses $12–$30. AE, DC, DISC, MC, V. Daily noon–4pm; Sun–Thurs 6pm–midnight, Fri–Sat 6pm–1am.

L'Entrecote de Paris ★★ FRENCH   New York's got the Statue of Liberty and Miami's got L'Entrecote de Paris. We don't complain. Everything in this little piece of Paris, a classy little (albeit recently expanded) bistro, is simple. For dinner, it's either steak, chicken, or seafood—I'd stick to the steaks, particularly the house special, L'Entrecote's French steak, with all-you-can-eat French fries (or *pommes frites*, rather). The salmon looks like spa cuisine, served with a pile of bald steamed potatoes and a salad with simple greens and an unmatchable vinaigrette. The steak, on the other hand, is the stuff cravings are made of, even if you're not a die-hard carnivore. Its salty sharp sauce is rich but not thick, and full of the beef's natural flavor. I loved the *profiteroles au chocolat*, a perfect puff pastry filled with vanilla ice cream and topped with a dark bittersweet chocolate sauce. Most diners are very Euro and pack a petit attitude. Servers, however, are superquick and professional, and almost friendly in a French kind of way, making up for the close quarters.

413 Washington Ave., South Beach. ✆ **305/673-1002.** Reservations recommended on weekends. Main courses $16–$24. DC, MC, V. Sun–Thurs 6:30pm–midnight, Fri–Sat 6pm–1am.

Shoji Sushi ★★★ SUSHI   Despite the sushi saturation on South Beach, Shoji stands apart from the typical sashimi-and-California-roll routine with expertly prepared, exquisitely fresh, and *innovative* top-notch rolls. The sleek sister to its next-door neighbor Nemo, Shoji is known for its authentic Japanese box sushi technique; the sushi, rice, and ingredients are packed into a tidy, tasty cake that won't crumble into your lap. Among the rolls I can't seem to get enough of here are the hamachi jalapeño—cilantro, daikon sprout, asparagus, avocado, and jalapeños—and the spicy lobster roll which consists of mango, avocado, scallion, shiso, salmon egg, and huge chunks of lobster. Wash it all down with the saketinis and my personal fave, the gingertini, which is made with ginger, vodka, triple sec, ginger ale, and pickled ginger juice.

100 Collins Ave., South Beach. ✆ **305/532-4245.** Reservations recommended. Main courses $13–$21. AE, MC, V. Mon–Fri noon–3pm; daily 6pm–1am. Valet parking $10.

Sushi Samba Dromo ★★★ SUSHI/CEVICHE   It's Brazilian, it's Peruvian, it's Japanese, it's super sushi! This multinational New York City import is definitely sceneworthy: it's a hipster's paradise. This stylish, sexy restaurant charges a pretty penny for some exotic sushi rolls such as the $14.50 soft-shell crab roll (a tasty combo of chives, jalapeño, and crab) and the $11.50 South Asian roll, with shrimp, tomato, cucumber, chives, cilantro, and onions. And while the sushi is top-notch, the sashimi ceviches are even better. An assortment of four—your choice of lobster, salmon, yellowtail, tuna, and fluke—is somewhat of a deal at $27, considering the fact that separately each can run you from $9 to $13.50. Main plates are equally exceptional, and while they have the usual haute dishes of snapper and Chilean sea bass, I'd try the churrasco a' Rio Grande, a divine assortment of meats served with rice, beans, collard greens, and chimichurri sauce. Sushi Samba Dromo is one of the area's newer places to be, be it for a sushi roll that may set you back your kid's college fund or a very potent pisco sour or sakegria. Come here for good food and an excellent scene.

600 Lincoln Rd., South Beach. ✆ 305/673-5337. Reservations recommended. Main courses $17–$27. AE, MC, V. Daily noon–2 am.

Tambo ✦✦✦ SUSHI/CEVICHE Nikkei is not just a name for a financial index, though if it were, in the case of this large, stylish, and dimly lit restaurant, it would be sky-high as far as cuisine is concerned. A hybrid of Japanese and Peruvian flavors, Tambo's Nikkei cuisine is exquisite. Skip the sushi here—there are too many other sushi restaurants in town to satisfy that craving—and go straight to the ceviches. Until Tambo, I was always very skeptical of the soupy mix of marinated, uncooked fish, sauces, and assorted ingredients. When I read the offerings on this menu, though, my eyes zoomed in on the Ceviche Timbo: fresh scallops marinated in lime juice, with red onion, orange, mango, ginger, garlic, cilantro, scotch bonnet, and choclo salsa criolla, and I knew I had to take the plunge. It was one of the best things my overworked palate has ever experienced. Fresh and bursting with flavor, it turned me into a ceviche convert. There's a total of 15 ceviches to choose from. I suggest the Degustacion de Ceviches—a variety pack, if you will—of three ceviches. The gorgeous, meticulous, food-as-art presentation is worthy of a photo shoot, but don't spend too much time gawking; it tastes as good, if not better, as it looks.

1801 Purdy Ave./Sunset Harbor Dr., South Beach. ✆ 305/ 535-2414. Reservations accepted. Main courses $21–$30. AE, MC, V, Disc, DC. Mon–Sat 6:30pm–2:30am. (Kitchen open until 12:30am).

MODERATE

Balan's ✦✦ MEDITERRANEAN Balan's provides undeniable evidence that the Brits actually do know a thing or two about cuisine. A direct import from London's hip Soho area, Balan's draws inspiration from various Mediterranean and Asian influences, labeling its cuisine "MediterAsian." With a brightly colored interior straight out of a mod '60s flick, Balan's is a local favorite among the gay and arty crowds. The moderately priced food is rather good here—especially the sweet-potato soufflé with leeks and roasted garlic; fried goat cheese, and portobello mushrooms; and the Chilean sea bass with roasted tomato. When in doubt, the restaurant's signature lobster club sandwich is always a good choice. Adding to the ambience is the restaurant's people-watching vantage point on Lincoln Road.

1022 Lincoln Rd. (between Lenox and Michigan), South Beach. ✆ 305/534-9191. Reservations not accepted. Main courses $8–$18. AE, DISC, MC, V. Sun–Thurs 8am–midnight, Fri–Sat 8am–1am.

Big Pink ✦ (Kids) AMERICAN "Real Food for Real People" is the motto to which this restaurant strictly adheres. Located on what used to be a gritty corner of Collins Avenue, Big Pink—owned by the folks at the higher-end Nemo—is quickly identified by a whimsical Pippi Longstocking–type mascot on a sign outside. Scooters and motorcycles line the streets surrounding the place, which is a favorite among beach bums, club kids, and those craving Big Pink's comforting and hugely portioned pizzas, sandwiches, salads, and hamburgers. The fare is above average at best, and the menu is massive, but it comes with a good dose of kitsch, such as their "gourmet" spin on the classic TV dinner, which is done perfectly, right down to the compartmentalized dessert. Televisions line the bar area and family-style table arrangement (there are several booths, too) promotes camaraderie among diners. Outdoor tables are available.

Even picky kids will like the food here and parents can enjoy the family-friendly atmosphere (not the norm for South Beach) without worrying if their kids are making too much noise.

157 Collins Ave., Miami Beach. ℭ 305/532-4700. Main courses $12.50–$19.95. AE, DC, MC, V. Sun and Thurs 8am–2am; Mon–Wed 8 am–midnight; Fri–Sat 8am–5am.

Bond St. Lounge ✦✦ SUSHI   A New York City import, the sceney Bond St. Lounge is located in the basement of the shabby chic Townhouse Hotel and is packing in hipsters as tightly as the crab meat in a California roll. Despite its tiny size, Bond St. Lounge's superfresh nigiri and sashimi and funky sushi rolls, such as the sun-dried tomato and avocado or the arugula crispy potato, are worth cramming in for. As the evening progresses, however, Bond St. becomes more of a bar scene than a restaurant, but sushi is always available at the bar to accompany your sake bloody mary.

Townhouse Hotel, 150 20th St., South Beach. ℭ 305/534-3800. Reservations not accepted. Sushi $6–$12. AE, MC, V. Daily 6pm–2am.

El Rancho Grande ✦✦ MEXICAN   Hidden just off Lincoln Road, El Rancho Grande was once a well-kept secret among devout Mexican food fanatics. It's not such a secret anymore. With a relatively restrained decor (clay pots, sponge-painted yellow walls), El Rancho Grande doesn't hold anything back when it comes to the cuisine. The Aztec Soup, a hot and spicy blend of chicken and tortilla strips, is some of the best I've had. Fresh, spicy salsa and expertly prepared, hugely portioned enchiladas, burritos, and fajitas are sensational. The scene is young and lively without being too rowdy. Margaritas are a little weak when frozen and better ordered on the rocks. Expect a wait at the small bar for your table, especially on weekends. Limited outdoor seating is available.

1626 Pennsylvania Ave., Miami Beach. ℭ 305/673-0480. Main courses $10–$19. AE, DC, MC, V. Daily 11am–11pm.

Grillfish ✦✦ SEAFOOD   From the beautiful Byzantine-style mural and the gleaming oak bar, you'd think you were eating in a much more expensive restaurant, but Grillfish manages to pay the exorbitant South Beach rent with the help of a loyal local following who come for fresh, simple seafood in a relaxed but upscale atmosphere.

The servers are friendly and know the menu well. The barroom seafood chowder is full of chunks of shellfish, as well as some fresh white fish fillets in a tomato broth. The small ear of corn, included with each entree, is about as close as you'll get to any type of vegetable offering besides the pedestrian salad. Still, at these prices, it's worth a visit to try some local fare including mako shark, swordfish, tuna, marlin, and wahoo. For the surf-and-turf lovers, Grillfish has taken the plunge into a meaty venture right next door, at Grillsteak (1438 Collins Ave., same hours, credit cards, price range, and reservation policy). The two get along with each other rather swimmingly.

1444 Collins Ave. (corner of Española Way), South Beach. ℭ 305/538-9908. www.grillfish.com. Reservations for 6 or more only. Main courses $9–$26. AE, DC, DISC, MC, V. Sun–Thurs 6pm–11pm, Fri–Sat 6pm–midnight.

Jeffrey's ✦✦ *Finds* CONTINENTAL/BISTRO   Some say this is the most romantic restaurant on the beach; South Beach's gay crowd certainly seems to agree. Old-fashioned lace curtains and candlelight are a welcome respite from the glitz and chrome of the rest of the island. Most people don't even realize this restaurant exists. But don't think that means there are empty tables. Jeffrey's certainly has its fair share of regulars.

You can choose a succulent ¾-pound burger, or try a hearty chicken breast marinated in balsamic sauce and served with freshly mashed sweet potatoes over spinach, on white lace tablecloths. Some of the better seafood options include the conch fritters and the meaty crab cakes. Macadamia-encrusted tilapia is exceptional. Most desserts are tasty (there's an old-fashioned dessert cart to tempt you), but the homemade tarte tatin, a caramelly deep-dish apple tart, is delicious.

1629 Michigan Ave., South Beach. © 305/673-0690. Reservations highly recommended. Main courses $12–$24. AE, DC, MC, V. Tues–Sat 6–11pm, Sun 5–10pm. Closed Sept.

Joe Allen ★★ *Finds* AMERICAN   It's hard to compete in a city with haute spots everywhere you look, but Joe Allen, a restaurant that has proven itself in both New York and London, has stood up to the challenge by establishing itself off the beaten path in possibly the only area of South Beach that has managed to remain impervious to trendiness and overdevelopment. Located on the bay side of the beach, Joe Allen is nestled in an unassuming building conspicuously devoid of neon lights, valet parkers, and fashionable pedestrians. Inside, however, one discovers a hidden jewel: a stark yet elegant interior and no-nonsense, fairly priced, ample-portioned dishes such as meatloaf, pizza, fresh fish, and salads. The scene has a homey feel flavored by locals looking to escape the hype without compromising quality.

1787 Purdy Ave./Sunset Harbor Dr. (3 blocks west of Alton Rd.), South Beach. © 305/531-7007. Reservations recommended, especially on weekends. Main courses $14.50–$25. MC, V. Mon–Fri 11:30am–11:45pm, Sat–Sun noon–11:45pm.

Larios on the Beach ★ *Overrated* CUBAN   If you're a fan of singer Gloria Estefan, you will definitely want to check out this restaurant, which she and her husband, Emilio, co-own; if not, you may want to reconsider, as the place is an absolute mob scene, especially on weekends. The classic Cuban dishes get a so-so rating from the Cubans, but a better one from those who aren't as well versed in the cuisine. The portions here are larger than life, as are some of the restaurant's patrons, who come here for the sidewalk scenery and the well-prepared black beans and rice. Inside, the restaurant turns into a makeshift salsa club, with music blaring over the animated conversations and the sounds of English clashing with Spanish. Because of its locale on Ocean Drive, Larios is a great place to bring someone who's never experienced the Cuban culture or tasted its cuisine.

820 Ocean Dr., South Beach. © 305/532-9577. Reservations recommended. Main courses $8–$27. AE, MC, V. Sun–Thurs 11:30am–midnight; Fri–Sat 11:30am–2am.

Les Deux Fontaines ★★ SEAFOOD   Les Deux Fontaines successfully sets an example for many South Beach eateries with superb service, fresh seafood (10 different kinds of local fish), and an ambience that transports you to a chic, far-off French countryside. Attached to the elegant Hotel Ocean, Les Deux Fontaines features an expansive courtyard, which contains the two fountains for which the place is named, and is lined with tables and wicker chairs straight out of the Left Bank. On any given day or night, live music adds to the charm. Inside, it's a bona fide French bistro, awash in soothing hues and alive with the scents of seafood dishes prepared any way you'd like. The crowd here ranges from tourists to locals looking to escape the fray of Ocean Drive. In addition to romantic evening dinners, Sunday brunches are extremely popular.

1230 Ocean Dr., South Beach. $\mathcal{C}$ **305/672-7878.** Reservations recommended. Main courses $10–$20. AE, DC, DISC, MC, V. Daily 7:30am–midnight.

Macaluso's ✸✸✸ ITALIAN   This restaurant epitomizes the Italians' love for—and mastery of—savory, plentiful, down-home Staten Island–style food. While the storefront restaurant is intimate and demure in nature, there's nothing delicate about the bold mix of flavors in every meat and pasta dish here. Catch the fantastic clam pie when in season—the portions are huge. Pricier items vary throughout the season, but will likely feature fresh fish handpicked by Chef (and owner) Michael, the Don of the kitchen, who is so accommodating he'll take special requests or even bring to your table a complimentary, signature meatball. If he doesn't, don't hesitate to ask you waiter for one; he'll be glad to bring it to you. Everyone will recommend perennial favorites such as the rigatoni and broccoli rabe. There are delicious desserts that range from homemade anisette cookies to Patricia Scott's pastries. The wine list is also good. The George Duboeuf Beaujolais at $22 a bottle is a steal, when you consider it comes nicely chilled with slices of luscious Georgia peaches, which make a great and affordable dessert by themselves.

1747 Alton Rd., Miami Beach. $\mathcal{C}$ **305/604-1811.** Main courses $14–$28; pizza $8–$13. AE, MC, V. Tues–Sat 6pm–midnight, Sun 6–11pm. After 10:30pm only pies are served. Closed Mon.

Macarena ✸✸ SPANISH/MEDITERRANEAN   This Macarena has long outlived its passé line-dance namesake and is rather hip, actually, looked after by a young crew of Spanish imports whose families own several popular restaurants in Madrid. Show up before 10pm and you're sure to get a table. After that time, especially on weekends, it's standing room only. The gorgeous Euro crowd shows up for foot-stomping flamenco (every Wednesday and Friday—call for show times) and an outrageous selection of tapas, as well as Miami's very best paella (order a large portion and share it among at least four people). The garlic shrimp are tasty and aromatic and the yellow squash stuffed with seafood and cheese is especially delicious. All the seafood, such as mussels in marinara sauce and clams in green sauce, is worth sampling. With such reasonable prices, you can taste lots of dishes and leave satisfied. Try some of the terrific sangria, made with slices of fresh fruit and a subtle tinge of sweet soda. Sidewalk seating is available on busy Washington Avenue, but the action is more entertaining inside.

1334 Washington Ave., South Beach. $\mathcal{C}$ **305/531-3440.** Reservations recommended on weekends. Main courses $14–$22; tapas $7–$10. AE, DC, MC, V. Sun–Thurs 7pm–midnight, Fri–Sat 7pm–1:30am.

Mama Vieja ✸ COLOMBIAN   This funky Colombian hangout looks like a total dive from the outside, but once inside you will want to dive right into the supremely fresh national specialties such as *pargo rojo estofado a la mama vieja* (red snapper stuffed with a supercreamy and delicate seafood sauce in a rice base). Brightly painted walls and elevated porches look out onto a large-screen TV showing music videos from the old country. The walls and ceilings are decorated with hundreds of hats that have been donated by customers and signed in exchange for a free meal. Bring in an interesting hat and mention it to the server before placing your order so that he or she can bring you to the attention of the owner. All the dishes here are worth trying and are so reasonably priced that it's easy to order a lot. Try to save room for the milky sweet desserts and a good strong coffee—you'll need it if you want to dance it off after at Lola, the very popular, unpretentious hot spot next door. If not, there's live music here, too.

235 23rd St. (just west of Collins Ave.), South Beach. ☎ **305/538-2400.** Main courses $4.95–$14.95. AE, DC, DISC, MC, V. Wed–Mon noon–midnight. Closed Tues.

Nexxt Café ☆ AMERICAN   Locals joke that this lively, always-packed outdoor cafe should be called Nexxt Year to reflect the awfully slow service that has become its unfortunate trademark. Service aside, Nexxt has made quite a splash on South Beach, attracting an evening crowd looking for nighttime revelry and a morning crowd on the weekends for a standing-room-only brunch sensation. The fresh food comes in lavish portions that could easily feed two; the salads are an especially good bargain. Start your meal with the calamari fritti—they're a lot fresher here than at most other local restaurants—or the popcorn shrimp, which are larger than you might expect. The burgers and sandwiches are similarly big, and the steaks are well worth a taste. They have coffees in tall, grande, and "maxxi." There are also plenty of coffee cocktails, mixed drinks, frozen beverages, and wines, giving this place a nice bar life, too.

700 Lincoln Rd. (off Euclid Ave.), South Beach. ☎ **305/532-6643.** Reservations accepted (no-shows will be charged $15 per seat). Main courses $12–$23. AE, MC, V. Daily 9am–1am.

Piola ☆☆ PIZZA   This hip Italian import miraculously transforms pizza from an eat-out-of-the-box, stuff-a-slice-into-your-mouth experience into a fun, sit-down meal that's hard to beat for the price, quality, and quantity. An unabridged menu of nearly 80 different kinds of pizzas-for-one that are really enough to share between two people is mind numbing and mouth watering. I suggest that you order several pizzas, depending on how many people you are dining with (two is more than enough for two, etc.). Start with the quattro formaggio pizza—brie, Gorgonzola, parmesan, and mozzarella—and then consider a funkier version, say, smoked salmon and caviar. All pizzas are thin crusted and full of flavor. Wait staff is extremely friendly, too, but be prepared for a lengthy wait, especially on weekend nights when the movie-going crowds next door spill over for a snack.

1625 Alton Rd., South Beach. ☎ **305/674-1660.** Reservations accepted. Main courses $7–$15. AE, DC, MC, V. Daily 6pm–1am.

Spiga ☆☆ ITALIAN   This intimate Italian restaurant is cool without being pretentious, concentrating on the food rather than the fanfare that has become central to so many South Beach eateries. Like the hotel in which it resides, Spiga's atmosphere is wonderfully low-key, making it a quiet favorite with locals and some luminaries. The complimentary bruschetta with grilled eggplant, served to you at one of the few tables inside or out, is the first of many culinary treats. The garlicky gnocchi with tomato and basil is an incredible illustration of how simple doesn't have to mean bland. The pungent Gorgonzola polenta appetizer is a meal in itself, and the risotto with bay scallops is a rousing display of culinary precision. The place is vaguely reminiscent of a Florentine trattoria, and if you stop to listen, you'll notice the prevailing language here is, in fact, Italian.

Hotel Impala, 1228 Collins Ave., South Beach. ☎ **305/534-0079.** Reservations accepted. Main courses $7–$20. AE, DC, MC, V. Daily 6pm–midnight.

Tap Tap ☆ HAITIAN   The whole place looks like an overgrown tap tap, a brightly painted jitney common in Haiti. Every inch is painted in vibrant neon hues (blue, pink, purple, and so on) and the atmosphere is always fun. It's where the Haiti-philes and Haitians, from journalists to politicians, hang out.

The *lanbi nan citron,* a tart, marinated conch salad, is perfect with a tall tropical drink and maybe some lightly grilled goat tidbits, which are served in a savory brown sauce and are less stringy than a typical goat dish. Another super-satisfying choice is the pumpkin soup, a rich brick-colored purée of subtly seasoned pumpkin with a dash of pepper. An excellent salad of avocado, mango, and watercress is a great finish. Soda junkies should definitely try the water-melon soda. For the ethnophobic, there's a rather tasty vegetable stew, but I strongly recommend the goat—it tastes just like chicken.

819 5th St. (between Jefferson and Meridian aves., next to the Shell Station), South Beach. ℂ 305/672-2898. Reservations accepted. Main courses $6–$17. AE, DC, DISC, MC, V. Mon–Thurs 5–11pm, Fri–Sat 5pm–midnight, Sun 5–10pm. Closed in Aug.

Van Dyke Cafe ✿ AMERICAN   The younger, jazzier sibling of Ocean Drive's News Café, the Van Dyke is similar in spirit and cuisine but different in attitude. Unlike the much scenier and much more touristy News Café, Van Dyke is a locals' favorite, at which people-watching is also premium but attitude is practically nonexistent. Both cafes have nearly the same menu, with decent salads, sandwiches, and omelets, but the Van Dyke's warm wood-floored interior, upstairs jazz bar, accessible parking, and intense chocolate soufflé make it a less taxing alternative. Also, unlike News, Van Dyke turns into a sizzling nightspot, featuring live jazz nearly every night of the week (a $5 cover charge is added to your bill if you sit at a table; the bar's free). Outside there's a vast tree-lined seating area.

846 Lincoln Rd., South Beach. ℂ 305/534-3600. Reservations recommended for dinner. Main courses $9–$17. AE, DC, MC, V. Daily 8am–2am.

INEXPENSIVE

Dab Haus ✿ GERMAN   This lively, often rowdy, ale house/restaurant turns out good German fare. The honey-garlic brie appetizer melted over hot French bread is irresistible and very pungent. A mug of one of the many German beers available here is the perfect accompaniment to the house specialties, which include veal bratwurst, *knodel mit pilzsauce* (bread dumplings served with a mushroom-wine sauce), and the ubiquitous wiener schnitzel. Capped off with a dessert of apple strudel or crepes, a meal here is like taking a trip to Germany, minus the jet lag.

852 Alton Rd., South Beach. ℂ 305/534-9557. Main courses $7–$17. MC, V. Sun–Thurs 4–11pm, Fri–Sat 4pm–midnight.

11th Street Diner AMERICAN   Like many of Miami's residents, this retro-diner is a transplant from the Northeast. Uprooted from its 1948 Wilkes-Barre, Penn., foundation, the actual structure was dismantled and rebuilt on a bustling corner of Washington Avenue. It's a popular round-the-clock spot that attracts a friendly yet motley crew of locals, club kids, and curious tourists and is well known for its slow service and greasy diner fare. Come in for breakfast and you'll find bleary-eyed patrons chowing down after a night of partying.

1065 Washington Ave., South Beach. ℂ 305/534-6373. Items $8–$15. AE, MC. Daily 24 hr.

Front Porch Café ✿ AMERICAN   Located in an unassuming, rather dreary-looking Art Deco hotel, the Front Porch Café is a relaxed local hangout known for cheap breakfasts. While some of the wait staff might be a bit sluggish (many are bartenders or club kids by night), it seems that nobody here is in a rush. If you are, this is *not* the place for you. Enjoy home-style French toast with bananas and walnuts, omelets, fresh fruit salads, pizzas, and classic breakfast pancakes that put IHOP to shame. Front Porch Café is also known for its daily dose of local gossip, which flows as freely as the syrup.

In the Penguin Hotel, 1418 Ocean Dr., South Beach. ℂ **305/531-8300.** Main courses $5–$16. AE, DC, DISC, MC, V. Daily 8:30am–10:30pm.

La Sandwicherie SANDWICHES   You can get mustard, mayo, or oil and vinegar on sandwiches elsewhere in town, but you'd be missing out on all the local flavor. This gourmet sandwich bar, open until the crack of dawn, caters to ravenous club kids, biker-types, and the body artists who work in the tattoo parlor next door. For many people, in fact, no night of clubbing is complete without capping it off with a turkey sub from La Sandwicherie.

229 14th St. (behind the Amoco station), South Beach. ℂ **305/532-8934.** Sandwiches and salads $6–$12. No credit cards. Daily 9am–5am. Delivery 9:30am–10pm.

Lincoln Road Café ⭐ *Value* CUBAN   A local favorite, this down-to-earth Cuban-accented cafe is very popular for its cheap breakfasts. For $6, you can indulge in a hearty portion of eggs any style, with bacon, ham, sausage, Cuban toast, and coffee. Lunch and dinner specials are delicious and very cheap as well; try the black beans and rice or a chicken fricassee with plantains. The few tables inside are usually passed up in favor of the several outdoors, but in the evenings the house is full inside and out, as talented Latin musicians perform out front.

941 Lincoln Rd., South Beach. ℂ **305/538-8066.** Items $6–$11. AE, DC, MC, V. Daily 8am–midnight.

Mrs. Mendoza's Tacos al Carbon ⭐ MEXICAN   Somehow this place manages to make Mexican food seem healthy with its flavorful, marinated char-broiled meats and fresh vegetarian selections. In addition to bountiful burritos, Mrs. Mendoza's is known for fabulous salsas, from mild to five-alarm spicy. Whereas San Loco Tacos (see below) is known for its clubby crowd, the atmospherically lacking Mrs. Mendoza's is better known for a low-frills clientele who know and want great Mexican food—not a scene. There's another location at 9739 NW 41st St. (the Doral Plaza) in West Miami (ℂ **305/477-5119**).

1040 Alton Rd., South Beach. ℂ **305/535-0808.** Main courses $3–$5. No credit cards. Mon–Sat 11am–10pm, Sun noon–10pm.

News Café ⭐ AMERICAN   In the late '80s, South Beach pioneer Mark Soyka opened this cafe on a depressed, decrepit Ocean Drive, sparking what some now call the South Beach renaissance. The thriving News has become part of Miami history and it still draws locals onto what has become the most tourist-ridden street in the area. Whether you come by foot, blade, Harley, or Ferrari, you should wait for an outside table, which is where you need to be to fully appreciate the experience. Service is notoriously slow and often arrogant (perhaps because the tip is included), but the menu, while not newsworthy, has some fairly good items, such as the Middle Eastern platter of hummus, tahini, tabouli, and grape leaves; hamburgers; and omelets. If it's not too busy, you can enjoy a leisurely cappuccino outside; creative types like to bring their laptops and sit here all day (or all night—this place is open 24 hours a day!). There's also an extensive collection of national and international newspapers and magazines at the in-house newsstand. News Café also opened another clone, Café Cardozo, at the Cardozo Hotel at 1300 Ocean Drive on South Beach in case 5 blocks is too much to walk to the original.

800 Ocean Dr., South Beach. ℂ **305/538-6397.** Items $5–$20. AE, DC, MC, V. Open 24 hr.

Paninoteca ⭐ SANDWICHES   A gourmet Italian-style sandwich shop with delicious offerings such as grilled veggies and goat cheese on focaccia, the only thing that's not so palatable about Paninoteca is the slow service. Consider takeout or a leisurely, very leisurely, snack. There's also a Coral Gables shop at 264 Miracle Mile, between Ponce de León Boulevard and Salzedo Street, ℂ **305/443-8388.**

809 Lincoln Rd., South Beach. ℂ **305/538-0058.** Sandwiches $7–$9. No credit cards. Sun–Thurs 11am–11pm, Fri–Sat 11am–midnight.

Pizza Rustica ⍟ PIZZA   Italians often scoff at the way Americans have mangled their recipe for pizza. But at Pizza Rustica, even the Italians marvel at these thin-crusted gourmet meals. This is the real deal—no thick, doughy, greasy concoctions here. Instead, Rustica features several delicious, huge slices of gourmet, authentically Tuscan-style pizza. Spinach and Gorgonzola cheese blend harmoniously with a brush of olive oil and garlic on a slate of the delicious, crispy dough. There's also a four-cheese, arugula, and rosemary potato slice, among others. Check out their new location at 1447 Washington Ave. (between 8th and 9th sts.), South Beach (ℂ **305/538-6009**).

863 Washington Ave., South Beach. ℂ **305/674-8244.** Slice $4. No credit cards. Daily 11am–6am.

Pucci's Pizza PIZZA   Pucci's was once the parlor of choice for a New York–style slice long before Washington Avenue became the victim of a pizza parlor influx (there are at least 10 within 5 blocks). And while it thrived in its former Washington Avenue locale, it definitely stands apart in its new location on Alton Road, where the only competition is Pizza Hut. But there's no comparison. While no one will go on the record, rumor has it that Pucci's imports New York water to make sure the dough is authentic. Slices are slinging until the wee hours, and for the weight conscious, there's even a low-fat version.

1608 Alton Rd., South Beach. ℂ **305/674-1110.** About $2 slice, $12 pie. No credit cards. Daily 11am–midnight.

Puerto Sagua ⍟ CUBAN/SPANISH   This brown-walled diner is one of the only old holdouts on South Beach. Its steady stream of regulars ranges from *abuelitos* (little old grandfathers) to hipsters who stop in after clubbing. It has endured because the food is good, if a little greasy. Some of the less heavy dishes are a superchunky fish soup with pieces of whole flaky grouper, chicken, and seafood paella, or marinated kingfish. Also good are most of the shrimp dishes, especially the shrimp in garlic sauce, which is served with white rice and salad.

This is one of the most reasonably priced places left on the beach for simple, hearty fare. Don't be intimidated by the hunched, older waiters in their white button shirts and black pants. Even if you don't speak Spanish, they're usually willing to do charades. Anyway, the extensive menu, which ranges from BLTs to grilled lobsters to yummy fried plantains, is translated into English. Hurry, before another boutique goes up in its place.

700 Collins Ave., South Beach. ℂ **305/673-1115.** Main courses $6–$24; sandwiches and salads $5–$10. AE, DC, MC, V. Daily 7:30am–2am.

San Loco Tacos ⍟ MEXICAN   There are no talking Chihuahuas to promote this excellent fast-food Mexican joint, but word of human mouth seems to do the trick. The food is served quickly, with no frills attached, but it's done very well and the place is open late—perfect for an after-clubbing bite. The guacamole is very fresh, and the tacos, burritos, enchiladas, and a host of other Mexican munchies are zesty, not skimpy, and really cheap. Salsa is not watered down or prepackaged and comes in mild, medium, or hot. There are a few tables inside, but most people prefer to pick up their chow and take it out with them.

235 14th St., South Beach. © **305/538-3009**. Items $2–$7. No credit cards. Sun–Thurs 11am–5am, Fri–Sat 11am–6am.

Sport Café ★ ITALIAN   When Sport Café first opened, way back when South Beach was still a fledgling in the trendoid business, it had a plain interior, wooden chairs, and a view of the parking lot. Televisions inside were tuned to soccer matches at all times—hence the name. The key to Sport's success was, and still is, its good, cheap, homemade Italian food—nothing fancy. Only now the cafe has moved up the block to a large corner space complete with private out-door garden. The restaurant might have moved on to better digs, but one thing remains the same: The food is still great and the soccer matches continue to kick the crowd into a European-style frenzy. Try the nightly specials, especially when the owners' mother is cooking her secret lasagna.

560 Washington Ave., South Beach. © **305/674-9700**. Reservations accepted for 4 or more. Main courses $5–$18; sandwiches and pizzas $6–$9. AE, MC, V. Daily noon–1am.

Sushi Rock Café ★ SUSHI   Perhaps it has something to do with its campy name, but for some reason almost every rock star that comes to town makes a requisite stop here for a sushi fix. Aerosmith's Joe Perry and Steven Tyler ate here almost every night during their Miami-based recording sessions, and David Lee Roth has been spotted here more than once. Sushi Rock is known for a sporadically fresh assortment of sushi, hand rolls, and traditional Japanese cui-sine; funky atmosphere; and hip late-night crowds. What diners are to ham-burgers, Sushi Rock is to raw fish—it's always consistent but will never appear on any "best of" lists.

1351 Collins Ave. (at 14th St.), South Beach. © **305/532-2133**. Items $4–$19. AE, DC, MC, V. Sun–Thurs noon–midnight, Fri–Sat 2pm–1am.

3 Miami Beach, North Beach, Surfside, Bal Harbour & Sunny Isles

The area north of the Art Deco District—from about 21st Street to 163rd Street—had its heyday in the 1950s when huge hotels and gambling halls blocked the view of the ocean. Now, many of the old hotels have been converted into condos or budget lodgings and the bay-front mansions have been renovated by and for wealthy entrepreneurs, families, and speculators. The area has many more residents, albeit seasonal, than visitors. On the culinary front, the result is a handful of superexpensive, traditional restaurants as well as a number of value-oriented spots.

VERY EXPENSIVE
The Forge Restaurant ★★★ STEAK/AMERICAN   English oak paneling and Tiffany glass suggest high prices and haute cuisine, and that's exactly what you get at the Forge. Each elegant dining room possesses its own character and features high ceilings, ornate chandeliers, and European artwork. The atmos-phere is elegant but not too stuffy. On Wednesday night (the party night here), however, it's pandemonium as the who's who of Miami society gather for din-ner, dancing, and schmoozing. Like the rest of the menu, appetizers are mostly classics, from beluga caviar to baked onion soup to shrimp cocktail and escar-got. When they're in season, order the stone crabs. For the main course, any of the seafood, chicken, or veal dishes are recommendable, but the Forge is espe-cially known for its award-winning steaks. Its wine selection is equally lauded—ask for a tour of the cellar.

Where to Dine in Miami Beach, North Beach, Surfside, Bal Harbour & Sunny Isles

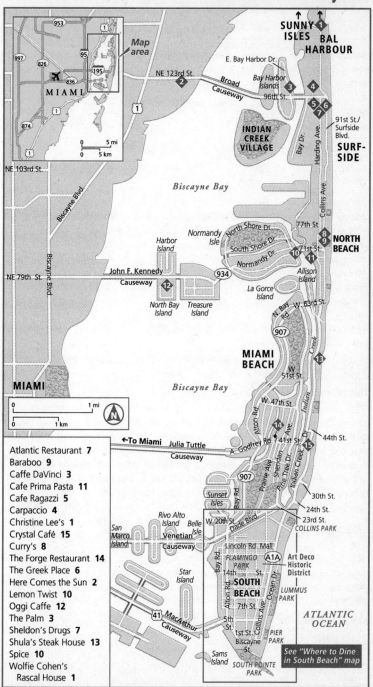

Atlantic Restaurant 7
Baraboo 9
Caffe DaVinci 3
Cafe Prima Pasta 11
Cafe Ragazzi 5
Carpaccio 4
Christine Lee's 1
Crystal Café 15
Curry's 8
The Forge Restaurant 14
The Greek Place 6
Here Comes the Sun 2
Lemon Twist 10
Oggi Caffe 12
The Palm 3
Sheldon's Drugs 7
Shula's Steak House 13
Spice 10
Wolfie Cohen's
   Rascal House 1

See "Where to Dine in South Beach" map

Kids Family-Friendly Restaurants

Baraboo *(see p. 139)* While the cuisine may be a bit funky for kids' palates, the wandering magicians and mimes are guaranteed to entertain the little ones, who will likely eat anything after the magician says "abracadabra."

Big Pink *(see p. 128)* One of South Beach's only family-friendly sit-down restaurants, Big Pink is a fun, noisy restaurant with a comprehensive menu consisting of macaroni and cheese, hamburgers, and other comfort foods guaranteed to satisfy the pickiest kids.

Bubba Gump Shrimp Co. *(see p. 147)* Named after the character from the motion picture *Forrest Gump,* this is a great place to bring the entire family on a lazy Sunday afternoon. You get to eat some good, moderately priced seafood, watch ships sail by on the bay, and shop at the Bayside Marketplace afterward. There's also a gift shop where you can buy Forrest Gump souvenirs, T-shirts, and caps. In Bayside Marketplace, 401 Biscayne Blvd. (at 4th Ave., north of the port of Miami); ✆ **305/379-8866.**

Wilderness Grill *(see p. 160)* Let the kids run wild in this noisy theme restaurant that serves as many sound effects as it does hamburgers. Shops at Sunset (57th and U.S. 1), 5701 Sunset Dr. #114; ✆ **305/ 740-3033.**

432 Arthur Godfrey Rd. (41st St.), Miami Beach. ✆ **305/538-8533.** Reservations required. Main courses $21–$55. AE, DC, MC, V. Sun–Thurs 6pm–midnight, Fri–Sat 6pm–1am.

The Palm 🟊🟊 STEAK   As sturdy as the tree that shares its name, the Palm is one of the country's most heralded steak houses, known for its Jurassic portions and no-nonsense service. Everything here is a la carte, and the prices add up quicker than the cholesterol courses through your veins. Both fish and meat are praiseworthy; the blackened swordfish steak is as hearty and massive as the filet mignon. Prime rib and New York strip are full of flavor as well and cooked to perfection. To complicate matters further, the veal and lamb chops are absolutely divine. For those who like a little surf with their turf, the lobsters here are truly freaks of nature, weighing in at 4 pounds and up. The food is prepared simply, but needs no enhancement. Sharing is encouraged unless you're a linebacker, and even they've been known to split a steak. Side dishes include salads, potatoes, and vegetables; be sure to try the superb creamed spinach.

9650 E. Bay Harbor Dr., Bay Harbor Island. ✆ **305/868-7256.** Reservations highly recommended. Main courses $18–$29. AE, DC, MC, V. Daily 5–11pm. From Collins Ave., turn west onto 96th St.; at Bal Harbour Shops, go over a small bridge, and turn right onto East Bay Harbor Dr. The restaurant is half a block down on the left.

Shula's Steak House 🟊🟊 AMERICAN/STEAK   Climb a sweeping staircase in the Alexander All-Suite Luxury Hotel and go through the glass hallway—designed like an atrium, so exotic flora and fauna beckon from both within and without—and you'll find yourself in this magnificent restaurant that has been acclaimed as one of the greatest steak houses in all of North America. If you're feeling adventurous, try the 48-ounce club (you can get your name engraved on a gold plaque if you can finish this absolutely *huge* piece of meat) or settle for the 20-ounce Kansas City strip or the 12-ounce filet mignon. Fresh seafood abounds when in season, and the oysters Rockefeller are a particularly good choice. The entertaining staff is very knowledgeable. The restaurant also has the No Name Lounge, where live piano music, premium spirits, and cigar smoking are available. There's another branch of Shula's at 7601 NW 154th St. (in Don Shula's Golf Club off the Palmetto Expressway; $©$ **305/820-8102**) in West Dade.

In the Alexander Hotel, 5225 Collins Ave., Miami Beach. $©$ **305/341-6565.** Reservations recommended. Main courses $18–$58. AE, DISC, MC, V. Daily 11am–3:30pm and 6–11pm. Free valet parking.

EXPENSIVE

Atlantic Restaurant ☆☆ AMERICAN   If you didn't know any better, you'd think you were in Nantucket at this comfortable blue-and-white beach-style restaurant designed to make you feel like you're eating in someone's guest house kitchen. The food, however, isn't your typical hamburger-and-hot-dog-on-the-grill fare. Sure, you can get all-American mac and cheese, but the Atlantic's version comes with truffles. Thanks to the Beach House Bal Harbour's owner, Jennifer Rubell, Atlantic gets delightfully kitschy with special themed-dinner nights such as the clam bake, in which a slew of fresh, all-you-can-eat seafood is yours for the taking. Same goes for the meat and potatoes night. Brunches are particularly delicious here, too, as is the poolside and oceanfront seating.

In the Beach House Bal Harbour Hotel, 9449 Collins Ave., Bal Harbour. $©$ **305/695-7930.** Reservations recommended, required on weekends. Main courses $9.50–$22. AE, DC, MC, V. Daily 7am–11pm.

Baraboo ☆☆ *Kids* MEDITERRANEAN   Baraboo, a crowded eatery in up-and-coming North Beach, is named for the small Wisconsin town that served as the original winter quarters of the Ringling Brothers Circus. Strolling mimes and magicians work the room, entertaining—or harassing, at times—diners who are indulging in the Mediterranean fare. Kids will love the distractions but will probably not like the adult food very much. Though not necessarily a theme restaurant, if they took away the clowning around, Baraboo could be a serious restaurant, featuring excellent ravioli with spinach, ricotta, and egg yolk; potato-crusted sea bass with saffron-sage sauce; and roasted Muscovy duck breast. If you prefer to remain outside the big top, there are several outdoor tables that will protect you from a wayward mime or magician.

7300 Ocean Terrace (at 73rd St. and Collins Ave.), North Beach. $©$ **305/867-4242.** Reservations recommended, required on weekends. Main courses $9–$39.95. AE, MC, V. Daily 5:30pm–1am.

Carpaccio ☆ ITALIAN   A favored spot for the ladies who lunch, Carpaccio's location in the ritzy Bal Harbour Shops is its tastiest aspect: It's definitely a place to see and be seen. Ask for specials rather than ordering off the regular menu; they're much more interesting—linguine lobster, snapper piccata, and veal chop any style—though they may be a bit pricier. Wear sunglasses to block the blinding glare of all the diamonds.

9700 Collins Ave. (97th St., in Bal Harbour Shops), Bal Harbour. $©$ **305/867-7777.** Reservations recommended. Main courses $15–$25; pastas $12–$15. AE, MC, V. Daily 11:30am–11pm.

Christine Lee's ☆☆ CHINESE   This Cantonese restaurant is a 35-year-old Miami staple that serves excellent but overpriced Chinese steak, shrimp and lobster sauce, and steak kew. Considering the dearth of good Chinese restaurants in Miami, this is a good choice if you absolutely *must* satisfy your cravings for Chinese, but it will definitely cost you more than it should.

17082 Collins Ave. (one block south of the Rascal House, in the RK strip mall, directly on Collins Ave.), Sunny Isles. ✆ **305/947-1717.** Reservations recommended. Main courses $6.95–$29. AE, DISC, MC, V. Daily 4–11pm; winter lunch 11am–3pm.

Crystal Café ★★★ CONTINENTAL/NEW WORLD   The setting is sparse, with a bottle of wine and Lucite salt and pepper grinders as the only centerpiece on each of the 15 or so tables. I promise you won't need the seasoning. Chef Klime has done it all with the help of his affable wife and a superb wait staff. Enjoy his unique sparkle at this little-known hideaway, which attracts stars like Julio Iglesias and other in-the-know gourmands.

With approximately 30 entrees, including a few nightly specials, each is beautifully presented and perfectly prepared. The shrimp-cake appetizer, for example, is the size of a bread plate and rests on top of a small mound of lightly sautéed watercress and mushrooms. Surrounding the delicately breaded disc are concentric circles of beautiful sauces. The veal Marsala is served in a luscious brown sauce thickened not with heavy cream or flour but with delicate vegetable broth and a hearty mix of mushrooms. The *osso buco* (an Italian dish consisting of veal shanks stewed in white wine with tomatoes, garlic, minced veggies, and more)) is a masterpiece.

726 41st St., Miami Beach. ✆ **305/673-8266.** Reservations recommended on weekends. Main courses $11–$25. AE, DC, DISC, MC, V. Tues–Thurs 5–10pm, Fri–Sat 5–11pm.

MODERATE

Cafe Prima Pasta ★★ ITALIAN   Proving that good things do come in small packages, this tiny corner cafe's home cooking draws nightly hordes of carbo-craving diners who don't seem to mind waiting for a table for upward of an hour, maybe more on weekends. The scent of garlic wafting into the street is guaranteed to kill any vampire, and it makes the wait for a table a bit more torturous. Other choice ingredients include the ripest, freshest tomatoes, the finest olive oil, mozzarella that melts in your mouth, and fish that puts some seafood restaurants to shame. The spicy garlic-and-oil dip that comes with the bread is hard to resist and will likely linger with you for days, like the memory of this fine meal. Though tables are packed in, the atmosphere still manages to be romantic.

414 71st St. (half a block east of the Byron movie theater), Miami Beach. ✆ **305/867-0106.** Reservations not accepted. Main courses $9–$19; pastas $7–$9. No credit cards. Mon–Thurs noon–midnight, Fri noon–1am, Sat 1pm–1am, Sun 5pm–midnight.

Cafe Ragazzi ★★ ITALIAN   This diminutive Italian cafe, with its rustic decor and a swift, knowledgeable wait staff, enjoys great success for its tasty simple pastas. The spicy puttanesca sauce with a subtle hint of fish is perfectly prepared. Also recommended is the salmon with radicchio. You can choose from many decent salads and carpacci, too. Lunch specials are a real steal at $7, including soup, salad, and daily pasta. Unlike Café Prima Pasta, Café Ragazzi is light on sceniness—people come here for the food only. Expect to wait on weekend nights.

9500 Harding Ave. (on corner of 95th St.), Surfside. ✆ **305/866-4495.** Reservations accepted for 4 or more. Main courses $9–$18. MC, V. Mon–Fri 11:30am–3pm; daily 5:30–11pm.

Lemon Twist ★★ MEDITERRANEAN   In addition to great Mediterranean fare, there is a twist to this place in the form of a complimentary shot of the eponymous house spirit (a lemon vodka shot). But that comes after your meal. To start, you will receive a bowl of perfectly marinated olives, which can endanger your appetite, so go easy on them. A soothing, mellow interior makes for a romantic dining experience, or, if you prefer, outdoor tables are available (though the street is hardly as scenic). In between, expect friendly service and excellent meat and pasta dishes at terrific prices. Specialties such as spinach lasagna with smoked salmon and shank of lamb caramelized with whole garlic are savored by a savvy crowd that has likely escaped South Beach for this refreshing change of scenery.

908 71st St. (off the 79th St. Causeway), Miami Beach/Normandy Isle. ℂ **305/868-2075.** Reservations recommended on weekends. Main courses $9–$18. AE, MC, V ($25 minimum). Tues–Sun 5:30pm–midnight. Closed July 4 weekend.

Oggi Caffe ✪ ITALIAN

Tucked away in a tiny strip mall on the 79th Street Causeway, this neighborhood favorite makes fresh pastas daily. Each one, from the agnolotti stuffed with fresh spinach and ricotta to the wire-thin spaghettini, is tender and tasty. A hearty *pasta e fagiola* is filled with beans and vegetables and could almost be a meal. I also recommend the daily soups, especially the creamy spinach soup when it's on the menu. Though you could fill up on the starters, the entrees, especially the grilled dishes, are superb. The salmon is served on a bed of spinach with a light lemon-butter sauce. The place is small and a bit rushed, but it's worth the slight discomfort for this authentic, moderately priced food. Another Oggi Caffe opened at 7921 NW 2nd Street in downtown Miami and a sister restaurant, Caffe DaVinci, 1009 Kane Concourse in Bay Harbor Islands, just west of Bal Harbour, has been attracting a faithful following for several years.

1740 79th St. Causeway (in the White Star shopping center next to the Bagel Café), North Beach. ℂ **305/866-1238.** Reservations recommended. Main courses $14–$25; pastas $9–$13. AE, DC, MC, V. Mon–Fri 11:30am–2:30pm; daily 6–11pm.

Spice ✪✪ ITALIAN/ASIAN

The owners of Cafe Prima Pasta decided that their excellent Italian fare needed a little Asian spice, so they opened this interesting restaurant to prove that the Italian-Asian combination does not have to be washed down with a Pepto-Bismol cocktail. (Actually, the menu's split down the middle, so you won't find mu shu lasagna or anything like that.) Though the Italian dishes on the menu are better—the seafood linguine is top-notch—the Asian items, such as the duck with soba noodles, aren't too shabby, either. And while the food here is quite good, even better is the restaurant's loungy atmosphere, which often features live music.

928 71st St., North Beach. ℂ **305/861-6707.** Reservations recommended. Main courses $8–$15. AE, DC, MC, V. Sun–Thurs 7pm–2am, Fri–Sat 7pm–5am.

Wolfie Cohen's Rascal House ✪ DELI

Open since 1954 and still going strong, this historic, nostalgic culinary extravaganza is one of Miami Beach's greatest traditions. Scooch into one of the ancient vinyl booths—which have hosted many a notorious bottom, from Frank Sinatra to mob boss Sam Giancana—and review the huge menu that's loaded with authentic Jewish staples. Consider the classic corned-beef sandwich, stuffed cabbage, brisket, or potato pancakes. If you're lucky, the waitress will give you a wax-paper doggy bag to wrap up the

---

Fun Fact **You Should Have Such Luck**

Since 1954, over 6.7 million stuffed cabbages, 750,000 chickens, and 26.5 million pickles have been consumed by over 100 million diners at the Rascal House.

---

leftover rolls and danish from your breadbasket. There is another Wolfie's in Boca Raton, at 2006 NW Executive Center Circle (© **561/982-8899**).

17190 Collins Ave. (at 163rd St.) Sunny Isles. © **305/947-4581**. Main courses $8–$30. AE, MC, V. Daily 7am–1am.

INEXPENSIVE

Curry's (Value) AMERICAN Established in 1937, this large dining room on the ocean side of Collins Avenue is one of Miami Beach's oldest, and kitschiest, restaurants. Neither the restaurant's name nor the tacky Polynesian wall decorations are indicative of its offerings, which are straightforwardly American and reminiscent of the area's heyday. Broiled and fried fish dishes are available, but the best selections, including steak, chicken, and ribs, come off the open charcoal grill perched by the front window. Prices are incredibly reasonable here, and include an appetizer, soup, or salad, as well as a potato or vegetable, dessert, and coffee or tea.

7433 Collins Ave., Miami Beach. © **305/866-1571**. Reservations accepted. Main courses (including appetizer and dessert) $10–$20. MC, V. Tues–Sun 4–10pm.

The Greek Place GREEK This little hole-in-the-wall diner with sparkling white walls and about 10 wooden stools serves fantastic Greek and American diner-style food. Daily specials like *pastitsio,* chicken *alcyone,* and roast turkey with all the fixings are big lunchtime draws for locals working in the area. Typical Greek dishes like shish kebab, souvlaki, and gyro are cooked to perfection as you wait. Even the hamburger, prime ground beef delicately spiced and freshly grilled, is wonderful.

233 95th St. (between Collins and Harding aves.), Surfside. © **305/866-9628**. Main courses $6–$7. No credit cards. Mon–Fri 10am–5pm, Sat 11am–3pm.

Sheldon's Drugs ★ (Value) AMERICAN This typical old-fashioned drugstore counter was a favorite breakfast spot of Isaac Bashevis Singer. Consider stopping into this historic site for a good piece of pie and a side of history. According to legend, the author was sitting at Sheldon's eating a bagel and eggs when his wife got the call in 1978 that he had won the Nobel Prize for Literature. The menu hasn't changed much since then. You can get eggs and oatmeal and a good tuna melt. A blue-plate special might be generic spaghetti and meatballs or grilled frankfurters. The food is pretty basic, but you can't beat the prices.

9501 Harding Ave., Surfside. © **305/866-6251**. Main courses $4–$8; soups and sandwiches $2–$5. AE, DISC, MC, V. Mon–Sat 7am–9pm, Sun 7am–4pm.

4 North Miami Beach

Although there aren't many hotels in North Dade, the population in the winter months explodes due to the onslaught of seasonal residents from the Northeast. A number of exclusive condominiums and country clubs, including William's Island, Turnberry, and the Jockey Club, breed a demanding clientele, many of whom dine out nightly. That's good news for visitors, who can find superior service and cuisine at value prices.

VERY EXPENSIVE

Chef Allen's ★★★ NEW WORLD CUISINE If anyone deserves to have a restaurant named after him, it's chef Allen Susser, winner of the esteemed James Beard Award for Best American Chef in the Southeast—the Academy Award of cuisine—and practically every other form of praise and honor awarded by the most discriminating palates. Chef Allen, the man, is royalty around here. Chef Allen, the restaurant, is his province, and foodies are his disciples. His platform? New World Cuisine and the harmony of exotic tropical fruits, spices, and vegetables. It is under Chef Allen's magic that ordinary Key limes and mangoes reappear in the form of succulent salsas and sauces. A traditional antipasto is transformed into a Caribbean one, with papaya-pineapple barbecue shrimp, jerk calamari, and charred rare tuna. Whole yellowtail in coconut milk and curry sauce is a particularly spectacular entree. Unlike other restaurants where location is key, Chef Allen's, located in the rear of a strip mall, could be in the desert, and hordes of people would still make the trek.

19088 NE 29th Ave. (at Biscayne Blvd.), North Miami Beach. ℂ 305/935-2900. Reservations recommended. Main courses $22–$40. AE, DC, MC, V. Sun–Thurs 6–10pm, Fri–Sat 6–11pm.

EXPENSIVE

Lagoon ✮ SEAFOOD/CONTINENTAL   This old bayfront fish house has been around since 1936. Major road construction nearby should have guaranteed its doom years ago, but the excellent view and incredible specials make it a worthwhile stop. If you can disregard the somewhat dirty bathrooms and nonchalant service, you'll find the best-priced juicy Maine lobsters around.

Yes, it's true! Lobster lovers can get two 1½ pounders for $22.95. Try them broiled with a light buttery seasoned coating. This dish is not only inexpensive but incredibly succulent, too. Side dishes include fresh vegetables, like broccoli or asparagus, as well as a huge baked potato, stuffed or plain.

488 Sunny Isles Blvd. (163rd St.), North Miami Beach. ℂ 305/947-6661. Reservations accepted. Main courses $12–$40; appetizers $6–$14. AE, MC, V. Daily 4:30–11pm. Happy hour daily 4:30–6pm.

MODERATE

Melting Pot FONDUE   Traditional fondue is supplemented by combination meat-and-fish dinners, which are served with one of almost a dozen different sauces. With its lace curtains and cozy booths, the Melting Pot can be quite romantic. To satisfy health-conscious diners, the owners have introduced a more wholesome version of fondue, in which you cook vegetables and meats in a low-fat broth. It tastes good, although this version is less fun than watching drippy cheese flow from the hot pot. Best of all, is dessert: chunks of fruit that you dip into a creamy chocolate fondue. No liquor is served here, but the wine list is extensive, and beer is available. A second Melting Pot is located at 11520 SW 72nd St. (Sunset Drive) in Kendall (ℂ **305/279-8816**).

In Sunny Isles Plaza shopping center, 3143 NE 163rd St. (between U.S. 1 and Collins Ave.), North Miami Beach. ℂ 305/947-2228. www.meltingpot.net. Reservations recommended on weekends. Appetizers $7.95 for 2. Fondues $11–$18. AE, DC, DISC, MC, V. Sun–Thurs 5:30–11pm, Fri–Sat 5:30pm–midnight.

INEXPENSIVE

Amos' Juice Bar HEALTH FOOD   This brightly painted stand in the middle of a busy road attracts a varied crowd, from young pony-tailed Europeans to bikers. If you don't mind a bit of car exhaust with your snapper sandwich, consider this North Dade landmark. The food is made on the premises and includes a great tuna salad, served in a pita with tons of crisp vegetables, including alfalfa sprouts, tomato, and lettuce. The hummus is also superb, although garlic lovers might want a hint more spark. You can also get a fresh smoothie or vegetable juice made on the spot.

18315 W. Dixie Hwy. (1 block west of Biscayne Blvd.), North Miami Beach. ℂ 305/935-9544. Sandwiches and salads $4–$6. No credit cards. Mon–Sat 8:30am–6:30pm.

Here Comes the Sun ☆ AMERICAN/HEALTH FOOD   One of Miami's first health-food spots, this bustling grocery-store-turned-diner serves hundreds of plates a night, mostly to blue-haired locals. It's noisy and hectic but worth it. In season, all types pack the place for a $7.95 special, served between 4 and 6:30pm, which includes an entree (you'll pick from more than 20 choices), soup or salad, coffee or tea, and a small frozen yogurt. Fresh grilled fish and chicken entrees are reliable and served with a nice array of vegetables. The miso burgers with "sun sauce" are a vegetarian's dream.

2188 NE 123rd St. (west of the Broad Causeway), North Miami Beach. ℂ 305/893-5711. Reservations recommended in season. Main courses $8–$14; early-bird special $7.95; sandwiches and salads $5–$11. AE, DC, DISC, MC, V. Mon–Sat 11am–8:30pm.

Laurenzo's Café ☆☆ ITALIAN   This recently expanded lunch counter in the middle of a chaotic grocery store has been serving delicious buffet lunches to the *paesanos* for years. New additions include an open kitchen and wood-burning pizza oven. A meeting place for the growing Italian population in Miami, the store has been open for more than 40 years. Daily specials usually include lasagna or eggplant parmigiana and two or three salad options. Also good are the rustic pizzas. Choose a wine from the vast selection and take your meal to go, or sit in the trellis-covered area amid busy shoppers buying their evening's groceries. You'll get to eavesdrop on some great conversations over your plastic tray of real Southern Italian–style cooking.

16385 W. Dixie Hwy. (south of corner of 163rd St.), North Miami Beach. ℂ 305/945-6381. Main courses $4–$8, salads $2–$5. No credit cards. Mon–Fri 11am–7:30pm, Sat 11am–7pm, Sun 11am–4pm.

5 Downtown Miami

Downtown Miami is a large sprawling area divided by the Brickell bridge into two distinct areas: Brickell Avenue and the bayfront area near Biscayne Boulevard. You shouldn't walk from one to the other—it's quite a distance and unsafe at night. Convenient Metromover stops do adjoin the areas, so for a quarter it's better to hop on the scenic sky tram (closed after midnight).

VERY EXPENSIVE

Azul ☆☆☆ GLOBAL FUSION   Executive chef Michelle Bernstein, Miami's wunderkind in the kitchen, creates a tour de force of international cuisine, inspired by Caribbean, French, Argentine, Asian, and even American flavors. Like a stunning designer gown, the restaurant's decor, with its waterfront view, high ceilings, walls burnished in copper, and silk-covered chairs, is complemented by sparkling jewels—in this case, the food. The *hamachi carpaccio* appetizer is a sumptuous arrangement of yellowtail (imported from Japan), shaved fennel, mixed greens, and cucumber. Entrees, or "plates of resistance" as they're called here, include braised langoustine open-faced ravioli; ginger-lemongrass-glazed Chilean sea bass served with black rice, kimchi, and Napa cabbage; and chicken with red Thai curry. Desserts range from fruity to chocolatey and shouldn't be skipped.

At the Mandarin Oriental, 500 Brickell Key Dr., Miami. ℂ 305/913-8254. Reservations strongly recommended. Main courses $24–$38. AE, DC, DISC, MC, V. Mon–Fri noon–3pm; Mon–Sat 7–11pm.

Capital Grille ☆☆ STEAK   This place reeks of power. Wine cellars filled with high-end classics, dark wood paneling, pristine white tablecloths, chandeliers, and marble floors all contribute to the clubby atmosphere. For an appetizer, start with the lobster and crab cakes. If you're not in the mood for beef or lobster, try

Where to Dine in Downtown Miami, Little Havana, Key Biscayne, Coconut Grove & Coral Gables

Anokha **33**	Paninoteca **29**
Azul **13**	Paolo Luigi's **35**
Baleen **19**	Perricone's Marketplace **14**
Bayside Seafood Restaurant and Hidden Cove Bar **17**	Porcao **12**
	Provence Grill **11**
Bice **36**	Red Fish Grill **32**
Big Fish **9**	The Red Lantern **33**
Biscayne Miracle Mile Cafeteria **28**	Rusty Pelican **16**
	S&S Restaurant **3**
Brasserie Les Halles **28**	Señor Frogs **33**
Bubba Gump Shrimp Co. **7**	Soyka Restaurant & Café **2**
Cafe Tu Tu Tango **34**	Stefano's **18**
Caffe Abbracci **30**	Tobacco Road **9**
Capital Grille **10**	Versailles **22**
Casa Juancho **21**	
Christy's **27**	
Daily Bread Marketplace **20**	
Fishbone Grille **9**	
5061 Eaterie & Deli **2**	
Franz & Joseph's in the Grove **33**	
Gordon Biersch Brewery Restaurant **14**	
Granny Feelgood's **6**	
House of India **25**	
Hy-Vong **22**	
Jimbo's **15**	
Joe's Seafood **5**	
John Martin's **29**	
La Carretta **22**	
La Cibeles Café **8**	
La Esquina de Tejas Hondureña **4**	
Latin American Cafeteria **31**	
Le Bouchon du Grove **33**	
Le Festival **23**	
Meza Fine Art Gallery Café **30**	
Miss Saigon Bistro **24**	
Morton's of Chicago **14**	
Norman's **26**	
Oasis **18**	
Oggi Café **1**	
Ortanique on the Mile **29**	

the pan-seared red snapper and asparagus covered with hollandaise. The wine cellars you're surrounded by are filled with about 5,000 bottles of wine—too extensive and rare to list. While some people prefer the more stalwart style and service of Morton's up the block, others find Capital to be a bit livelier. The food's pretty much the same between the two, though I find the steaks at Morton's to be a notch better; however, the atmosphere at the Capital Grille is *much* more inviting. Complimentary valet parking here as opposed to Morton's, which charges a fee, is another reason to visit.

444 Brickell Ave., Miami. ℂ 305/374-4500. Reservations recommended. Main courses $21–$35. AE, DC, DISC, MC, V. Mon–Fri 11:30am–3pm; Mon–Thurs 5–10:30pm; Fri 5–11pm; Sat 6–11pm; Sun 5–10pm.

Morton's of Chicago ⭐ STEAK   A private club-like ambience, with dark wood, leather booths, and tablecloths, makes Morton's of Chicago the preferred spot for major business transactions and quiet, romantic dinners. A vast menu includes a wide variety of excellent steaks and an award-winning menu consisting of shrimp Alexander, oysters on the half shell, sea scallops with apricot chutney, swordfish medallions with béarnaise sauce, and a dense, hot Godiva chocolate cake that's out of this world. Private dining rooms are perfect to carry on clandestine conversations and romantic liaisons. The open kitchen is probably the only thing here that's not private. At lunchtime, the power is tangible as business deals are sliced and diced as often as the steak is. At night, the scene is more elegant, attracting older sophisticates and pre- and post-theater crowds.

1200 Brickell Ave., Miami. ℂ **305/400-9990**. Reservations recommended. Main courses $20–$30. AE, DC, MC, V. Mon–Fri 11:30am–11pm, Sat 2:30–11pm, Sun 2:30–10pm.

Porcao ⭐⭐ BRAZILIAN   The name sounds eerily like "pork out," which is what you'll be doing at this exceptional Brazilian *churrascaria* (a Brazillian-style restaurant devoted mostly to meat—it's the Portuguese translation of steakhouse). For about $30, you can feast on salads and meats *after* you sample the unlimited gourmet buffet, which includes such fillers as pickled quail eggs, marinated onions, and an entire prosciutto. Do not stuff yourself here, as the next step is the meaty part: Choose as much lamb, filet mignon, chicken hearts, and steaks as you like, grilled, skewered, and sliced right at your table. Side dishes also come with the meal, including beans and rice and fried yucca.

801 Brickell Bay Dr., Miami. ℂ 305/373-2777. Reservations accepted. Prix fixe $31.50 per person, all you can eat. AE, DC, MC, V. Daily noon–midnight.

EXPENSIVE

Big Fish ⭐⭐ *Finds* SEAFOOD/ITALIAN   This scenic seafood shack on the Miami River is a real catch—if you can find it. Hard to locate but well worth the search, Big Fish's remote location keeps many people biting. In fact, Big Fish added some Italian options to its all-seafood menu in the hopes of luring more people, and that worked, too. Big Fish has a sweeping view of the Miami skyline and some of the freshest catch around; the pasta served with it is only a starchy diversion. But the spectacular setting may be the real draw, right there on the Miami River where freighters, fishing boats, dinghies, and sometimes yachts slink by to the amusement of the faithful diners who no longer have to fish around for a charming, serene seafood restaurant. Beware of Friday nights, when Big Fish turns into a big happy hour scene.

55 SW Miami Ave. Rd., Miami. ℂ 305/373-1770. Main courses $15–$28. AE, DC, MC, V. Daily 11am–11pm. Cross the Brickell Ave. Bridge heading south and take the first right on SW 5th St. The road narrows under a bridge. The restaurant is just on the other side.

Provence Grill ⚘⚘ FRENCH   This restaurant serves some of the best French meals this side of Toulouse. The brothers Cormouls-Houles use their prodigious culinary skills to assemble an affordable menu that allows the rest of us to know just how the French really live—and they do it, dare we say, with incredible panache. The grilled specialties, from chicken to salmon, are imbued with only the best seasonings and sauces. Sautéed mussels with garlic and chives are fabulous as a meal and as a dipping sauce for the crusty bread. Canard lovers will enjoy the grilled duck filet in a red port sauce. Real culinary adventurers should try the dessert menu—crème brûlée spiced with lavender (a local French favorite) is just one selection—which is truly a delight. A full bar outside brings you back from your French delusions of grandeur and returns you to a delightful downtown Miami state of mind with beautiful views of the downtown skyline.

1001 South Miami Ave., Miami. ⓒ 305/373-1940. Main courses $13.95–$21.95; appetizers $4.95–$6.95. AE, MC, V. Mon–Fri 11am–3pm; Sun–Thurs 5:30–10:30pm; Fri–Sat 5:30–11pm.

MODERATE

Bubba Gump Shrimp Co. SEAFOOD *Kids*   Inspired by the Tom Hanks megahit *Forrest Gump*, the Bubba Gump Shrimp Co. likens life not to a box of chocolates, but rather to a bucket o' shrimp. Located right on the water, this place offers lots of affordable, oddly named shrimp specials. For starters, try the Run Across America Sampler, which includes Bubba's Far Out Dip and Chips, New Orleans Peel n' Eat Shrimp, Texas Wild Wings, and Alabama Fried Shrimp for only $12.99. The Bubba's After the Storm Bucket of Boat Trash will trash your arteries with a deep-fried, albeit tasty, mix of shrimp, slipper lobster, and mahimahi. Lt. Dan's Drunken Shrimp is a delicious concoction of shrimp in bourbon sauce with spicy sausage and garlic mashed potatoes. A number of shrimpless salads and sandwiches are also on the menu. It's a fun place to bring the kids on a sunny afternoon. If you haven't stuffed yourself on shrimp, you may want to try the overly caloric Jenny's Strawberry Dream—pound cake layered with vanilla ice cream, surrounded by Jenny's "special sauce," and topped with fresh strawberry purée and whipped cream.

In Bayside Marketplace, 401 Biscayne Blvd. (at 4th Ave., north of the port of Miami), Miami. ⓒ 305/ 379-8866. Main courses $8–$18. AE, DC, DISC, MC, V. Sun–Thurs 11am–11pm, Fri–Sat 11am–midnight. Closed Thanksgiving and Dec 25.

5061 Eaterie & Deli ⚘ AMERICAN/FRENCH/DELI   This two-story, 1949 building on the up-and-coming 50s block of Biscayne Boulevard features a mind-numbing selection of generously portioned, uncomplicated cuisine (think American diner meets French bistro) with a lively, hip atmosphere to match. The urban industrial chic palette of muted tones, concrete floors, and subtle textures complement the leather sofas, animal-print recliners, and wooden chairs—all enhanced by an extensive menu and wine list. 5061 features a confusing selection of several types of fair-tasting cuisine—quiche, sandwiches, hamburgers, fish, pasta, salads—everything from cheese plates to cheeseburgers. Paté and terrine are made on site and are expertly prepared thanks to the fact that the restaurant's owner is Parisian. An open kitchen stretching 20 feet along the back wall creates a "set" emulating a live television cooking show with the restaurant patrons serving as the studio audience. There's a large bar downstairs with an excellent wine list, as well as a second-floor bookstore/cafe in which only travel, food, and wine books are sold.

5061 Biscayne Blvd. (at 50th St.), Miami. ⓒ 305/756-5051. Main courses $9.95–$29.95. AE, DC, MC, V. Daily 10:30am–11:30pm, deli 6:30am–8:30pm.

Fishbone Grille ★★ SEAFOOD   Fish are flying in the open kitchen of this extremely popular, reasonably priced seafood joint. Whether you take yours grilled, blackened, or sautéed, the chefs here work wonders with superfresh snapper, grouper, dolphin, tuna, sea bass, and shrimp, to name just a few. For nonfish eaters, there are delicious pizzas and an excellent New York strip steak. All meals come with salad and a fantastic slab of jalapeño cornbread. The interior is plain and simple; the only thing elaborate is the long list of daily specials.

650 S. Miami Ave., Miami. ✆ 305/530-1915. Reservations recommended for 6 or more. Main courses $9–$20. AE, DC, DISC, MC, V. Mon–Thurs 11:30am–10pm, Fri 11:30am–11pm, Sat 5–11pm, Sun 5:30–9pm.

Gordon Biersch Brewery Restaurant CONTINENTAL   Best known for its home-brewed lager beers and strict adherence to the 1516 German Purity Law (which mandates the use of only malt, hops, water, and yeast in the brewing process), Gordon Biersch is always buzzing with locals who cram into every bit of the restaurant's sprawling 10,800 square feet. The food, for a beer hall, is particularly good, but sometimes too exotic. There are the usual suspects—burgers and pizza—offset by heavier dishes such as chicken and andouille sausage gumbo and cashew chicken stir-fry. A popular lunch place for local businesspeople, Gordon Biersch is absolutely packed and oppressive on Friday nights, when happy hour turns into harassment hour.

1201 Brickell Ave. (next to the JW Marriott), Miami. ✆ 786/425-1130. Main courses $12–$20. AE, DC, MC, V. Sun–Thurs 11:30am–midnight, Fri–Sat 11:30am–2am.

Granny Feelgood's AMERICAN/HEALTH FOOD   Owner Irving Fields has been in the business of serving healthful food for more than 28 years, and his flagship store's offerings are priced right. Due to its proximity to the courthouse, there's a lot of legal-eagle traffic and networking going on here. Locals love Granny's for the fresh fish and poultry specials, a line of salads that define greenery and good health, and the always-impeccable service by a family-oriented staff who likes to get to know its clientele. Tourists swinging through downtown on the Metromover or just spinning by can munch healthily on anything from a brown rice and steamed vegetable plate to Granny's famous tuna-salad platter. The chef's identity is a secret, but I happen to know he was trained under local chef extraordinaire Allen Susser and also did a stint on nearby Fisher Island's swanky members-only restaurant, so the cuisine here will most definitely please the palate. Granny Feelgood's sells its own line of vitamins and herbal products.

25 W. Flagler St., Miami. ✆ 305/377-9600. Reservations not accepted. Main courses $9–$12. AE, MC, V. Mon–Fri 7am–5pm.

Joe's Seafood ★ (Finds) SEAFOOD   A good catch on the banks of the Miami River, Joe's Seafood (not to be confused with Joe's Stone Crab) has a great waterfront setting and a fairly simple yet tasty menu of fresh fish cooked in a number of ways—grilled, broiled, fried, or, the best in my opinion, in garlic or green sauce. Meals are quite the deal here, all coming with green salad or grouper soup and yellow rice or french fries. The complementary fish spread appetizer is also a nice touch. Because of this, not to mention the great, gritty ambiance that takes you away from neon, neo-Miami in favor of the old, seafaring days, there's usually a wait for a table.

400–404 NW N. River Drive, Miami. ✆ 305/381-9329. Reservations not accepted. Main courses $13.95–$22.95. AE, DC, DISC, MC, V. Daily 11am–10pm.

Soyka Restaurant & Café ☆ AMERICAN   Brought to us by the same man who owns the News and Van Dyke cafes in South Beach, Soyka is a much-needed addition (though it's easy to miss) to the seedy area known as the Biscayne Corridor. The motif inside is industrial chic, reminiscent of a souped-up warehouse you might find in New York. Lunches focus on burgers, sandwiches, and wood-fired oven pizzas. Dinners include simple fare such as an excellent, massive Cobb salad or more elaborate dishes such as the delicious turkey Salisbury steak. The bar area offers a few comfy couches and bar stools and tables on which to dine, if you prefer not to sit in the open dining room. A children's menu is available for both lunch and dinner. A lively crowd of bohemian Design District types, professionals, and singles gather here for a taste of urban life. On weekends, the place is packed and very loud. Do not expect an after-dinner stroll around the neighborhood—it's still too dangerous for pedestrian traffic. Head over the causeway to South Beach and stroll there.

5556 NE 4th Court (Design District, off of Biscayne Blvd. and 55th St.), Miami. ℂ 305/759-3117. Reservations recommended. Main courses $8–$26. AE, MC, V. Sun–Thurs 11am–11pm (bar open until midnight); Fri–Sat 11am–midnight (bar open until 1am). Happy hour Mon–Fri 4–7pm.

INEXPENSIVE

La Cibeles Café ☆ ⓥalue CUBAN   This typical Latin diner serves some of the best food in town. Just by looking at the line that runs out the door every afternoon between noon and 2pm, you can see that you're not the first to discover it. For about $5, you can have a huge and filling meal. Pay attention to the daily lunch specials and go with them. A pounded, tender chicken breast *(pechuga)* is smothered in sautéed onions and served with rice and beans and a salad. The trout and the roast pork are both very good. When available, try the *ropa vieja,* a shredded beef dish delicately spiced and served with peas and rice.

105 NE 3rd Ave. (1 block west of Biscayne Blvd.), Miami. ℂ 305/577-3454. No credit cards. Main courses $5–$9. Mon–Sat 7:30am–7:30pm.

Latin American Cafeteria ☆☆ CUBAN   The name may sound a bit generic, but this no-frills indoor-outdoor cafeteria has the best Cuban sandwiches in the entire city. They're big enough for lunch and a doggy-bagged dinner, too. Service is fast, prices are cheap, but be forewarned: English is truly a second language at this chain, so have patience. It's worth it.

9796 Coral Way, Miami. ℂ 305/226-2393. AE, MC, V. Main courses $5–$9. Daily 7:30am–11pm.

Perricone's Marketplace ☆ ITALIAN   A large selection of groceries and wine, plus an outdoor porch and patio for dining, make this one of the most welcoming spots downtown. Its rustic setting in the midst of downtown is a fantastic respite from city life. Sundays offer buffet brunches and all-you-can-eat dinners, too. But it's most popular weekdays at noon, when the suits show up for delectable sandwiches, quick and delicious pastas, and hearty salads.

15 SE 10th St. (corner of S. Miami Ave.), Miami. ℂ 305/374-9693. Sandwiches $6.95–$8.25; pastas $11.50–$16.95. AE, MC, V. Sun–Mon 7:30am–10:30pm, Tues–Sat 7:30am–midnight.

S&S Restaurant AMERICAN/DINER FARE   This tiny chrome-and-linoleum-counter restaurant in the middle of downtown looks like a truck stop. But locals have been coming back since it opened in 1938. Expect a wait at lunchtime while the mostly male clientele, from lawyers to linemen, wait patiently for huge quantities of old-fashioned fast food. Although the neighborhood has become pretty undesirable, the food—basic diner fare with some excellent stews and soups—hasn't changed in years. In addition to cheap break-fasts, the diner serves up some of the best comfort food in Miami.

1757 NE 2nd Ave., Miami. ℂ 305/373-4291. Main courses $5–$11. No credit cards. Mon–Fri 6am–4pm, Sat–Sun 6am–2 or 2:30pm (later on Heat basketball game nights).

Tobacco Road AMERICAN   Miami's oldest bar is a bluesy Route 66–inspired institution favored by barflies, professionals, and anyone else who wishes to indulge in good and greasy bar fare—chicken wings, nachos, and so on—for a reasonable price in a down-home, gritty but charming atmosphere. The burgers are also good—particularly the Death Burger, a deliciously unhealthy combo of choice sirloin topped with grilled onions, jalapeños, and pepper-jack cheese—bring on the Tums! Also a live music venue, the Road, as it is known by locals, is well traveled, especially during Friday's happy hour and Tuesday's lobster night, when 100 1¼-pound lobsters go for only $10.99 apiece.

626 S. Miami Ave. ℂ 305/374-1198. Main courses $7–$10. AE, DC, MC, V. Mon–Sat 11:30am–5am, Sun noon–5am. Cover charge $5 Fri–Sat night.

6 Little Havana

The main artery of Little Havana is a busy commercial strip called Southwest 8th Street, or *Calle Ocho*. Auto-body shops, cigar factories, and furniture stores line this street, and on every corner there seems to be a pass-through window serving superstrong Cuban coffee and snacks. In addition, many of the Cuban, Dominican, Nicaraguan, Peruvian, and other Latin American immigrants have opened full-scale restaurants ranging from intimate candlelit establishments to bustling stand-up lunch counters.

EXPENSIVE

Casa Juancho ✿✿ SPANISH   A generous taste of Spain comes to Miami in the form of the cavernous Casa Juancho, which looks like it escaped from a

---

Cuban Coffee

Despite the more than dozen Starbucks that dot the Miami landscape, locals still rely on the many Cuban cafeterias for their daily caffeine fix. Beware of the many establishments throughout Miami that serve espresso masked as Cuban coffee. For the real deal, go to the most popular—and most animated—Cuban cafeterias: **La Carreta** and **Versailles** (see below).

Cuban coffee is a longstanding tradition in Miami. You'll find it served from the takeout windows of hundreds of *cafeterías* or *luncherías* around town, especially in Little Havana, Downtown, Hialeah, and the beaches. Depending on where you are and what you want, you'll spend between 40¢ and $1.50 per cup.

The best *café Cubano* has a rich layer of foam on top formed when the hot espresso shoots from the machine into the sugar below. The result is the caramelly, sweet, potent concoction that's a favorite of locals of all nationalities.

To partake, you've just got to learn how to ask for it *en español*.

From Ceviche to Picadillo: Latin Cuisine at a Glance

In Little Havana and wondering what to eat? Many restaurants list menu items in English for the benefit of *norteamericano* diners. In case they don't, though, here are translations and suggestions for filling and delicious meals:

Arroz con pollo   Roast chicken served with saffron-seasoned yellow rice and diced vegetables.

Café Cubano   Very strong black coffee, served in thimble-size cups with lots of sugar. It's a real eye-opener.

Camarones   Shrimp.

Ceviche   Raw fish seasoned with spice and vegetables and marinated in vinegar and citrus to "cook" it.

Croquetas   Golden-fried croquettes of ham, chicken, or fish.

Paella   A Spanish dish of chicken, sausage, seafood, and pork mixed with saffron rice and peas.

Palomilla   Thinly sliced beef, similar to American minute steak, usually served with onions, parsley, and a mountain of french fries.

Pan Cubano   Long, white crusty Cuban bread. Ask for it *tostada* (toasted and flattened on a grill with lots of butter.

Picadillo   A rich stew of ground meat, brown gravy, peas, pimientos, raisins, and olives.

Plátano   A deep-fried, soft, mildly sweet banana.

Pollo asado   Roasted chicken with onions and a crispy skin.

Ropa vieja   A shredded beef stew whose name literally means "old clothes."

Sopa de pollo   Chicken soup, usually with noodles or rice.

Tapas   A general name for Spanish-style hors d'oeuvres, served in grazing-size portions.

production of *Don Quixote*. The numerous dining rooms are decorated with traditional Spanish furnishings and enlivened nightly by strolling Spanish musicians who tend to be annoying and expect tips—do not encourage them to play at your table; you'll hear them loud and clear from other tables, trust me. Try not to be frustrated with the older staff that doesn't speak English or respond quickly to your subtle glance—the food's worth the frustration. Your best bet is to order lots of *tapas*, small dishes of Spanish finger food. Some of the best include mixed seafood vinaigrette, fresh shrimp in hot garlic sauce, and fried calamari rings. A few entrees stand out, like roast suckling pig, baby eels in garlic and olive oil, and Iberian-style snapper.

2436 SW 8th St. (just east of SW 27th Ave.), Little Havana. (© 305/642-2452. Reservations recommended, but not accepted on Fri–Sat after 8pm. Main courses $15–$34; tapas $6–$8. AE, DC, DISC, MC, V. Sun–Thurs noon–midnight; Fri–Sat noon–1am.

MODERATE

Hy-Vong ★★ VIETNAMESE   A must in Little Havana, expect to wait hours for a table, and don't even think of mumbling a complaint. Despite the poor service, it's worth it. Vietnamese cuisine combines the best of Asian and French cooking with spectacular results. Food at Hy-Vong is elegantly simple and super-spicy. Appetizers include small, tightly packed Vietnamese spring rolls and kimchi, a spicy, fermented cabbage. Star entrees include pastry-enclosed chicken with watercress-cream-cheese sauce and fish in tangy mango sauce.

Enjoy the wait with a traditional Vietnamese beer and lots of company. Outside this tiny storefront restaurant, you'll meet interesting students, musicians, and foodies who come for the large delicious portions.

3458 SW 8th St. (between 34th and 35th aves.), Little Havana. ✆ 305/446-3674. Reservations accepted for parties of 5 or more. Main courses $9–$19. AE, MC, DISC, V. Tues–Sun 6–11pm. Closed 2 weeks in Aug.

INEXPENSIVE

La Carreta ★ CUBAN   This cavernous family-style restaurant is filled with relics of an old farm and college kids eating *medianoches* (midnight sandwiches with ham, cheese, and pickles) after partying all night. Waitresses are brusque but efficient and will help Anglos along who may not know the lingo. The menu is vast and very authentic, but is known for its sandwiches and smaller items. Try the *sopa de pollo,* a rich golden stock loaded with chunks of chicken and fresh vegetables, or the *ropa vieja,* a shredded beef stew in thick brown sauce. Because of its immense popularity and low prices, La Carreta has opened seven branches throughout Miami, including a counter in the Miami airport. Check the White Pages for other locations.

3632 SW 8th St., Little Havana. ✆ 305/444-7501. Main courses $5–$22. AE, DC, DISC, MC, V. Daily 24 hr.

La Esquina de Tejas Hondureña ★★ (Value) CUBAN   Best known as the diner where Ronald Reagan ate during his 1983 campaign in Miami, La Esquina de Tejas Hondureña has gained a national reputation for its great food and low prices. There's a shrine dedicated to the former president in the "Presidential Quarters," and the menu even has his signed autograph and the presidential seal of approval. This Cuban restaurant was recently bought by Hondurans, who serve its excellent food in either a Cuban or Honduran style, depending on what you choose. For instance, if you order the traditional Cuban steak dish, *carne asada,* you can choose it if you want it prepared Cuban style (fried) or Honduran style (grilled). There is also a completely new Honduran menu to choose from, featuring tacos, enchiladas, and *baleadas* (flour tortillas with butter, refried beans, and cheese). You must try the *arroz a la marinera,* the Cuban version of Spanish paella. It's filled with clams, oysters, mussels, lobster, shrimp, squid, snapper, stone crab, and scallops cooked in fresh seafood broth. If you're not in the mood for seafood, try the *vaca frita,* a grilled, shredded flank steak served with moro rice (black beans cooked with white rice) and *maduros* (sweet, fried plantains). Another house specialty is the *masas de puerco fritas,* a pork tender-loin cut in chunks, roasted, and then quickly deep-fried and served with mojo, grilled onions, garlic, olive oil, and bitter orange. You won't regret a trip here.

101 SW 12th Ave., Little Havana. ✆ 305/545-0337. Daily specials $7–$15; appetizers 75¢–$5.50. AE, MC, V. Daily 8am–5pm.

Versailles ★★ CUBAN   Versailles is the meeting place of Miami's Cuban power brokers, who convene daily over *cafe con leche* to discuss the future of the exiles' fate. A glorified diner, the place sparkles with glass, chandeliers, murals, and mirrors meant to evoke the French palace. There's nothing fancy here—nothing French, either—just straightforward food from the home country. The menu is a veritable survey of Cuban cooking and includes specialties such as Moors and Christians (flavorful black beans with white rice), ropa vieja (shredded beef stew), and fried whole fish. Whereas La Esquina de Tejas Hondureña is known more for its food and Ronald Reagan than its atmosphere, Versailles is the place to come for mucho helpings of Cuban kitsch. With its late hours, it's also the perfect place to come after spending your night in Little Havana.

3555 SW 8th St., Little Havana. ✆ **305/444-0240**. Soup and salad $2–$10; main courses $5–$20. DC, DISC, MC, V. Mon–Thurs 8am–2am, Fri 8am–3:30am, Sat 8am–4:30am, Sun 9am–1am.

7 Key Biscayne

Key Biscayne has some of the world's nicest beaches, hotels, and parks, yet it is not known for great food. Locals, or "Key rats" as they're known, tend to go off-island for meals or takeout, but here are some of the best on-the-island choices.

EXPENSIVE

Rusty Pelican ✯ SEAFOOD   The Pelican's private tropical walkway leads over a lush waterfall into one of the most romantic dining rooms in the city, located right on beautiful blue-green Biscayne Bay. The restaurant's windows look out over the water onto the sparkling stalagmites of Miami's magnificent downtown. Inside, quiet wicker paddle fans whirl overhead and saltwater fish swim in pretty tableside aquariums. The restaurant's surf-and-turf menu features conservatively prepared prime steaks, veal, shrimp, and lobster. The food is good, but the atmosphere—the reason why you're here—is even better, especially at sunset, when the view over the city is magical.

3201 Rickenbacker Causeway, Key Biscayne. ✆ **305/361-3818**. Reservations recommended. Main courses $16–$22. AE, DC, MC, V. Daily 11:30am–4pm, Sun–Thurs 5–11pm, Fri–Sat 5pm–midnight.

Stefano's ✯ ITALIAN   For its cheesy mid-'80s ambience, Stefano's has no match. Its restaurant and disco share the same strobe-lit atmosphere. Food is traditional and reliable, if a little pricey. You'll find an older country-club crowd here in the evenings, enjoying steaks, pastas, and seafood. Among the best entrees are the flavorful *risotto frutti di mare* (saffron risotto with shrimp, clams, mussels, and calamari) and the very cheesy lasagna.

After 7:30pm, the band starts playing American pop and Latin favorites. Some nights you feel as if you've accidentally happened upon your long-lost cousin's wedding, as you watch the parade of taffeta dresses and tipsy uncles.

24 Crandon Blvd., Key Biscayne. ✆ **305/361-7007**. Reservations recommended on weekends. Main courses $11–$29; appetizers $8–$12. AE, DC, MC, V. Sun–Thurs 5–11pm, Fri–Sat 5pm–5am. Disco open later Sun–Thurs.

INEXPENSIVE

Bayside Seafood Restaurant and Hidden Cove Bar ✯ *Finds* SEAFOOD
Known by locals as "the Hut," this ramshackle restaurant and bar is a laid-back outdoor tiki hut and terrace that serves pretty good sandwiches and fish platters on paper plates. A blackboard lists the latest catches, which can be prepared blackened, fried, broiled, or in a garlic sauce. The fish dip is wonderfully smoky and moist, if a little heavy on mayonnaise. Local fishers and yachties share this rustic outpost with equal enthusiasm and loyalty. A completely new air-conditioned area for those who can't stand the heat is a welcome addition, as are

the new deck and spruced-up decor. But behind it all, it's nothing fancier than a hut—if it was anything else, it wouldn't be nearly as appealing.

3501 Rickenbacker Causeway, Key Biscayne. ✆ 305/361-0808. Reservations accepted for 15 or more. Appetizers, salads, and sandwiches $4.50–$8; platters $7–$13. AE, MC, V. Daily 11:30am until closing (which varies).

Jimbo's *(Finds)* SEAFOOD   Locals like to keep quiet about Jimbo's, a ramshackle seafood shack that started as a gathering spot for fishermen and has since become the quintessential South Florida watering hole, snack bar, and hangout for those in the know. If ever Miami had a backwoods, this was it, right down to the smoldering garbage can, stray dogs, and chickens. Do *not* get dressed up to come here—you will get dirty. Go to the bathroom before you get here, too, because the porta-potties are absolutely rancid. Grab yourself a dollar can of beer (there's only beer, water, and soda, but you are allowed to bring your own choice of drink if you want) from the cooler and take in the view of the tropical lagoon where they shot *Flipper.* You may even see a manatee or two. Vacant shacks that served as backdrops for films such as *True Lies* surround this hidden enclave, which attracts everyone from shrimpers and politicians to well-oiled beach bums. Oddly enough, there's even a bocce court here, and the owner, Jimbo, may challenge you to a game. Play if you must, but word has it he never loses. Jimbo's smoked fish—marlin or salmon—is the best in town, but be forewarned: There are no utensils or napkins. When I asked for some, the woman said, "Lady, this is a place where you eat with your hands." I couldn't have said it better.

Off the Rickenbacker Causeway at Sewerline Rd., Virginia Key. ✆ 305/361-7026. Smoked fish about $4. No credit cards. Daily 6am–6:30pm. Head south on the main road towards Key Biscayne, make a left just after the MAST Academy (there will be a sign that says Virginia Key), tell the person in the toll booth you're going to Jimbo's, and he'll point you in the right direction.

Oasis *(Value)* CUBAN   Everyone, from the city's mayor to the local handymen, meet for delicious paella and Cuban sandwiches at this little shack. They gather outside, around the little takeout window, or inside at the few tables for superpowerful *cafesitos* and rich *croquetas.* It's slightly dingy, but the food is good and cheap.

19 Harbor Dr. (on corner of Crandon), Key Biscayne. ✆ 305/361-5709. Main courses $4–$12; sandwiches $3–$4. No credit cards. Daily 6am–9pm.

8 Coconut Grove

Coconut Grove was long known as the artists' haven of Miami, but the rush of developers trying to cash in on the laid-back charm of this old settlement has turned it into something of an overgrown mall. Still, there are several great dining spots both in and out of the confines of Mayfair or CocoWalk.

VERY EXPENSIVE

Baleen ✿✿✿ SEAFOOD/MEDITERRANEAN   While the prices aren't lean, the cuisine here is worth every pricey, precious penny. Oversized crab cakes, oak-smoked diver scallops, and steak-house-quality meats are among Baleen's excellent offerings. The lobster bisque is the best on Biscayne Bay. Everything here is a la carte, so order wisely, as it tends to add up quicker than you can put your fork down. The restaurant's spectacular waterfront setting makes Baleen a true knockout. Brunch is particularly noteworthy as well.

4 Grove Isle Dr. (in the Grove Isle Hotel), Coconut Grove. ✆ 305/858-8300. Reservations recommended. Main courses $18–$34. AE, DC, MC, V. Sun–Wed 7am–10pm, Thurs–Sat 7am–11pm.

Bice ✪✪✪ ITALIAN   Upon entering the dining room here, you feel as if you're sailing on a grand ocean liner, with several cozy tables and booths, high ceilings, and a glorious view of the hotel's sprawling waterfall and pool area. Knowledgeable and friendly servers complement the comprehensive Italian menu. Every appetizer sounds so good that it's almost impossible to decide. Beef carpaccio is a delight with hearts of palm and Reggiano cheese; a colorful grilled vegetable pyramid consists of gargantuan portions of meaty portobello mushrooms, fresh asparagus, and peppers with bursts of mouthwatering goat cheese lying within; Maryland crab cakes with the perfect hint of lemon are exceptional. For main courses, the pastas, homemade and extremely fresh, are eclipsed by a heavenly slab of Nebraska filet mignon with peppercorn sauce and a tower of french fries and onion rings. The veal chop is also sublime. For dessert, the crème brûlée and coffee gelato are delicious. Unlike many chichi restaurants, especially those found within swanky hotels, all dishes at Bice are generous in portion—huge, actually—and the only thing stuffy about dining here is how you'll feel after indulging.

2669 S. Bayshore Dr. (in the Grand Bay Hotel), Coconut Grove. ℂ 305/860-0960. Reservations recommended. Main courses $12–$37. AE, MC, V. Daily 7–11am, 11:30am–3pm, and 6–11pm.

EXPENSIVE

Anokha ✪✪✪ INDIAN   This is the best Indian restaurant in Miami. Anokha's motto is "a guest is equal to God and should be treated as such," and they do stick to it. The food here is from the gods, with fantastic tandooris, curries, and stews. The restaurant's location at the end of a quiet stretch of Coconut Grove is especially enticing because it prevents the throngs of pedestrians from overtaking what some people consider a diamond in the rough.

3195 Commodore Plaza (between Main Hwy. and Grand Ave.), Coconut Grove. ℂ 786/552-1030. Main courses $10–$30. AE, DC, MC, V. Tues–Sun 11:30am–10:30pm.

Le Bouchon du Grove ✪✪ FRENCH   This very authentic, exceptional bistro is French right down to the wait staff who may only speak French to you, forgetting that they are in the heart of Coconut Grove, U.S.A. But it matters not. The food, prepared by an animated French (what else?) chef, is superb. An excellent starter is the wonderful *gratinée Lyonnaise* (traditional French onion soup). Fish is brought in fresh daily; try the Chilean sea bass when in season *(filet de loup poele)*. Though it is slightly heavy on the oil, it is delivered with succulent artichokes, tomato confit, and seasoned roasted garlic that is a gastronomic triumph. The *carre d'agneau roti* (roasted rack of lamb with Provence herbs) is served warm and tender, with an excellent amount of seasoning. There is also an excellent selection of pricey but doable French and American red and white wines.

3430 Main Highway, Coconut Grove. ℂ 305/448-6060. Reservations recommended. Main courses $18–$25. AE, MC, V. Mon–Fri 10am–3pm; Mon–Thurs 5–11pm, Fri 5pm–midnight, Sat 8am–midnight, Sun 8am–11pm.

MODERATE

Paulo Luigi's ✪ ITALIAN   Paulo Luigi's serves rich dishes that include cold and hot appetizers, homemade soups and salads, pastas, and pizzas. Owners Paul and Lola Shalaj, restaurant entrepreneurs for the past 27 years, have gained and kept a large devoted clientele with their tasty light Italian cuisine, generous portions, and friendly environment that has served as the perfect fine-dining hideaway for both local and national customers alike.

A favorite is the *jumbo rigatti rubino*, a chicken dish with a side of sausages, asparagus, and portobello mushrooms in light marinara sauce. There's also *chicken Marsala, linguine al frutti di mare* (for poultry and seafood lovers), and a special children's menu.

3324 Virginia St., Coconut Grove. ✆ 305/445-9000. Reservations recommended. Main courses $9–$17. AE, MC, V. Daily noon–4pm and 5–11pm; Fri–Sat 5pm–1am.

Red Lantern 🐸 CANTONESE Miami is not known for having good Chinese food, but this popular Chinese spot is better than most. Specialties include shark's fin with chicken and steamed whole snapper with black-bean sauce. There's also an assortment of vegetarian dishes and some excellent soups. My favorite is the clay-pot stew of chicken in ginger broth. Although the atmosphere is nothing to speak of, the varied menu and interesting preparation keep locals happy and make a meal here worthwhile.

3176 Commodore Plaza (Grand Ave.), Coconut Grove. ✆ 305/529-9998. Main courses $8–$20. AE, DC, DISC, MC, V. Mon–Thurs 11:30am–11pm, Fri 11:30am–midnight, Sat 4pm–midnight, Sun 5–11pm.

Señor Frogs 🐸 MEXICAN Filled with a collegiate crowd, this restaurant is known for a raucous good time, a mariachi band, and powerful margaritas. The food at this rocking cantina is a bit too cheesy, but it's tasty, if not exactly authentic. The mole enchiladas, with 14 different kinds of mild chiles mixed with chocolate, is as flavorful as any I've tasted. Almost everything is served with rice and beans in quantities so large that few diners are able to finish.

3480 Main Hwy., Coconut Grove. ✆ 305/448-0999. Reservations not accepted. Main courses $12–$17. AE, DC, MC, V. Mon–Sat 11:30am–2am, Sun 11:30am–1am.

INEXPENSIVE

Cafe Tu Tu Tango 🐸 SPANISH/INTERNATIONAL This restaurant in the bustling CocoWalk is designed to look like a disheveled artist's loft. Dozens of original paintings—some only half-finished—hang on the walls and on studio easels. Seating is either inside, among the clutter, or outdoors, overlooking the Grove's main drag. Flamenco and other Latin-inspired tunes complement a menu with a decidedly Spanish flare. Hummus spread on rosemary flat bread and baked goat cheese in marinara sauce are two good starters. Entrees include roast duck with dried cranberries, toasted pine nuts, and goat cheese, plus Cajun chicken egg rolls filled with corn, cheddar cheese, and tomato salsa. Pastas, ribs, fish, and pizzas round out the eclectic offerings, and several visits have proved each consistently good. Try the sweet, potent sangria and enjoy the warm, lively atmosphere from a seat with a view.

3015 Grand Ave. (on the second floor of CocoWalk), Coconut Grove. ✆ 305/529-2222. Reservations not accepted. Tapas $3–$9.50. AE, MC, V. Sun–Wed 11:30am–midnight, Thurs 11:30am–1am, Fri–Sat 11:30am–2am.

9 Coral Gables

Coral Gables is a foodie's paradise—a city in which you certainly won't go hungry. What Starbucks is to most major cities, excellent gourmet and ethnic restaurants are to Coral Gables, where there's a restaurant on every corner, and everywhere in between.

VERY EXPENSIVE

Christy's 🐸🐸 STEAK/AMERICAN Power is palpable at this elegant English-style restaurant where an ex-president could be sitting at one table and a rock star at another. But Christy's is the kind of place where conversations are at a hush and no one seems to care whom they're sitting next to. The selling point here, rather, is the corn-fed beef and calf's liver, not to mention the broiled lamb chops, prime rib of beef with horseradish sauce, teriyaki-marinated filet mignon, and perfectly tossed Caesar salad. Baked sweet potatoes and a sublime blackout cake are also yours for the taking. For a little drama, order the cruise-ship-esque baked Alaska. It livens up the staid place. Just like a fine wine or the typical Christy's customer, the meat here is aged a long time. A landmark since 1978, Christy's has thrived amid the comings and goings of neighboring nouveau Coral Gables restaurants. Located on a nondescript corner, you know you've arrived at the right place if you can count the Rolls Royces parked out front.

3101 Ponce de León Blvd., Coral Gables. ✆ **305/446-1400.** Reservations recommended. Main courses $20–$35. AE, DC, MC, V. Mon–Thurs 11:30am–10pm, Fri 11:30am–11pm, Sat 5–11pm, Sun 5–10pm.

Le Festival ★★ FRENCH   Le Festival's contemporary pink awning hangs over one of Miami's most traditional Spanish-style buildings, hinting at the unusual combination of cuisine and decor that awaits inside. The modern dining rooms, enlivened with New French features and furnishings, belie the traditional highlights of a well-planned menu.

Shrimp and crab cocktails, fresh pâtés, and an unusual cheese soufflé are star appetizers. Both meat and fish are either simply seared with herbs and spices or doused in wine and cream sauces. Dessert can be a delight if you plan ahead: Grand Marnier and chocolate soufflés are individually prepared and must be ordered at the same time as the entrees. There's also a wide selection of other homemade sweets. If you go on a Monday, you'll get a complimentary soufflé. Not a bad way to start the week.

2120 Salzedo St. (right above Alhambra Circle), Coral Gables. ✆ **305/442-8545.** Reservations required for dinner. Main courses $30–$60. AE, DC, DISC, MC, V. Mon–Fri 11:45am–2:30pm; Mon–Thurs 6–10:30pm, Fri–Sat 6–11pm.

Norman's ★★★ NEW WORLD CUISINE   *Gourmet* magazine called Norman's the best restaurant in South Florida, but many disagree: They think it's the best restaurant in the entire United States. Gifted chef and cookbook author Norman van Aken takes New World Cuisine (which, along with chef Allen Susser, he helped create) to another plateau with dishes that have landed him on such shows as the Discovery Channel's *Great Chefs of the South* and on the wish lists of gourmands everywhere. The open kitchen invites you to marvel at the mastery that lands on your plate in the form of pan-roasted swordfish with black-bean *muneta;* stuffed baby bell pepper in cumin-scented tomato broth with avocado *crema;* chargrilled New York strip steak with *chimichurri* sabayon, *pommes frites,* and Creole-mustard-spiced caramelized red onions; plantain-crusted dolphin; or chicken and tiny shrimp paella with garbanzo beans and chorizo mojo, to name a few.

The staff is adoring and professional and the atmosphere is tasteful without being too formal. The portions are realistic, but still, be careful not to overdo it. You'll want to try some of the funky, fantastic desserts.

21 Almeria Ave. (between Douglas and Ponce de León), Coral Gables. ✆ **305/446-6767.** Reservations highly recommended. Main courses $22–$38. AE, DC, MC, V. Mon–Thurs 6–10:30pm, Fri–Sat 6–11pm. Bar opens at 5:30pm.

EXPENSIVE

Caffe Abbracci ★★ ITALIAN   You'll understand why this restaurant's name means "hugs" in Italian the moment you enter the dark romantic enclave: Your appetite will be embraced by the savory scents of fantastic Italian cuisine wafting through the restaurant. The homemade black-and-red ravioli filled with lobster in pink sauce, risotto with porcini and portobello mushrooms, and the house specialty—grilled veal chop topped with tricolor salad—are irresistible and perhaps the culinary equivalent of a warm, embracing hug. A cozy bar and lounge was added recently to further encourage the warm and fuzzy feelings.

318 Aragon Ave. (1 block north of Miracle Mile, between Salzedo St. and Le Jeune Rd.), Coral Gables. ① **305/441-0700.** Reservations recommended for dinner. Main courses $16–$26.50; pastas $15.50–$19.50. AE, DC, MC, V. Mon–Fri 11:30am–3pm, Sun–Thurs 6–11:30pm, Fri–Sat 6pm–12:30am.

MODERATE

Brasserie Les Halles ☆☆ FRENCH   Known especially for its fine steaks and delicious salads, this very welcome addition to the Coral Gables dining scene became popular as soon as it opened in 1997 and has since continued to do a brisk business. The modest and moderately priced menu is particularly welcome in an area of overpriced, stuffy restaurants. For starters, try the mussels in white wine sauce and the escargot. For a main course, the duck confit is an unusual and rich choice. Pieces of duck meat wrapped in duck fat are slow-cooked and served on salad frissé with baby potatoes with garlic. Service by the young French staff is polite but a bit slow. The tables tend to be a little too close, although there is a lovely private balcony space overlooking the long, thin dining room where large groups can gather.

2415 Ponce de León Blvd. (at Miracle Mile), Coral Gables. ① **305/461-1099.** Reservations recommended on weekends. Main courses $12.50–$22.50. AE, DC, DISC, MC, V. Daily 11:30am–midnight.

House of India ☆ INDIAN   House of India's curries, kormas, and kabobs are very good, but the restaurant's well-priced all-you-can-eat lunch buffet is unsurpassed. All the favorites are on display, including tandoori chicken, naan, and various meat and vegetarian curries, as well as rice and dal (lentils). This place isn't fancy and could use a good scrub-down (in fact, I've heard it described as a "greasy spoon"), but the service is excellent and the food is good enough to keep you from staring at your surroundings.

22 Merrick Way (near Douglas and Coral Way, 1 block north of Miracle Mile), Coral Gables. ① **305/444-2348.** Reservations recommended. Main courses $8–$17. AE, DC, DISC, MC, V. Daily 11:30am–3pm; Sun–Thurs 5–10pm, Fri–Sat 5–11pm.

John Martin's ☆ IRISH PUB   Forest green and dark wood give way to a very intimate publike atmosphere in which local businesspeople and barflies alike come to hoist a pint or two. The menu offers some tasty British specialties (not necessarily an oxymoron!), such as bangers and mash and shepherd's pie, as well as Irish lamb stew and corned beef and cabbage.

Of course, to wash it down, you'll want to try one of the ales on tap or one of the more than 20 single-malt scotches. The crowd is upscale and chatty, as is the young wait staff. Check out happy hour on weeknights, plus the Sunday brunch with loads of hand-carved meats and seafood.

253 Miracle Mile, Coral Gables. ① **305/445-3777.** Reservations recommended on weekends. Main courses $9–$20; sandwiches and salads $5–$16. AE, DC, DISC, MC, V. Mon–Thurs 11:30am–midnight, Fri–Sat 11:30am–1am, Sun noon–10pm.

Meza Fine Art Gallery Café ☆☆ ECLECTIC   This unique restaurant is located in a sleek, arty atmosphere featuring paintings, performance artists, and a multimedia array of talent—very Warhol. As eclectic as the art and artists who convene here, the menu is varied, with accents on Mediterranean and Italian, featuring well-priced, well-prepared dishes such as pan-seared tuna with sesame crust and balsamic vinegar reduction, and a delicious grilled churrasco skirt steak with chimichurri. Over 500 wines by the bottle and 78 by the glass make Meza an oenophile's favorite. Live music nightly from jazz and Latin to electronica brings out a motley crew of youngsters who look as if they stepped out of a Gap ad. A lively bar scene attracts a 30s-and-under crowd on late weekend nights. Earlier in the evenings, Meza caters to an older, more sophisticated dining crowd.

275 Giralda Ave., Coral Gables. ⓒ 305/461-2723. Reservations accepted. Main courses $6.95–$13.95. Three-course twilight dinner served Mon–Sat 6–8pm for $15.95 per person, including glass of wine. AE, DC, DISC, MC, V. Restaurant Mon–Fri noon–3pm, Mon–Sun 6–10:30pm. Bar Mon–Sun 5pm–2am.

Ortanique on the Mile 🎀 NEW WORLD CARIBBEAN You'll be greeted as you walk in by soft spiderlike lights and canopied mosquito netting that will make you wonder whether you're on a secluded island or inside one of King Tut's temples. Chef Cindy Hutson has truly perfected her tantalizing New World Caribbean menu. For starters, an absolute must is the pumpkin bisque with a hint of pepper sherry. Afterward, move on to the tropical mango salad with fresh marinated Sable hearts of palm, julienne mango, baby field greens, toasted Caribbean candied pecans, and passion-fruit vinaigrette. For an entree, I recommend the pan-sautéed Bahamian black grouper marinated in teriyaki and sesame oil. It's served with an ortanique (an orange-like fruit) orange liqueur sauce and topped with steamed seasoned chayote, zucchini, and carrots on a lemon-orange boniato sweet-plantain mash. For dessert, try the chocolate mango tower—layers of brownie, chocolate mango mousse, meringue, and sponge cake, accompanied by mango sorbet and tropical fruit salsa. Entrees may not be cheap, but they're a lot less than airfare to the islands, from where most, if not all, the ingredients used here hail.

278 Miracle Mile (next to Actor's Playhouse), Coral Gables. ⓒ 305/446-7710. Reservations requested. Main courses $11–$29. AE, DC, MC, V. Mon–Tues 6–10pm, Wed–Sat 6–11pm, Sun 5:30–9:30pm.

Red Fish Grill 🎀 SEAFOOD Hidden away at the edge of the saltwater lagoon in lush and tropical Matheson Hammock Park, Red Fish Grill is a decent seafood restaurant, but people don't come here for the food. Judging by the ambiance alone, the restaurant deserves four stars, but because the food is just okay (fish is either greasy or dry), it only gets one. But that's okay. Romantic, hard to find and truly reminiscent of Old Miami, Red Fish Grill makes up for its lack of flavor with its hard-to-beat, majestic setting.

In Matheson Hammock Park, 9610 Old Cutler Road., Coral Gables. ⓒ 305/668-8788. Reservations accepted. Main courses $15–$25. AE, DC, DISC, MC, V. Tues–Thurs 6pm–10pm, Fri–Sun 5pm–10pm. Enter Matheson Hammock Park, stay on the main road until you see the restaurant's parking lot.

INEXPENSIVE
Biscayne Miracle Mile Cafeteria 🎀 *Value* AMERICAN Here you'll find no bar, no music, and no flowers on the tables—just great Southern-style cooking at unbelievably low prices. The menu changes, but roast beef, baked fish, and barbecued ribs are typical entrees, few of which exceed $5.

Food is picked up cafeteria style and brought to one of the many unadorned Formica tables. The restaurant is always busy. The kitschy 1950s decor is an asset in this last of the old-fashioned cafeterias, where the gold-clad staff is proud and attentive. Enjoy it while it lasts.

147 Miracle Mile, Coral Gables. ⓒ 305/444-9005. Main courses $3.50–$4.50. MC, V. Daily 11am–8:30pm.

Daily Bread Marketplace GREEK This place is great for takeout food and homemade breads. The falafel and gyro sandwiches are large, fresh, and filling. The spinach pie for less than $1 is also recommended, though it's short on spinach and heavy on pastry. Salads, including luscious tabouli, hummus, and eggplant, are also worth a go. To take in or eat out, the Middle Eastern fare here is a real treat, especially in an area so filled with fancy French and Cuban fare. Plus, you can pick up hard-to-find groceries such as grape leaves, fresh olives, couscous, fresh nuts, and pita bread. A South Beach location has opened at 840 1st St. (at Alton Rd.) ℂ **305/673-2252.**

2400 SW 27th St. (off U.S. 1 under the monorail), Coral Gables. ℂ **305/856-0363** or 305/856-0366. Sandwiches and salads $3–$6. MC, V. Mon–Sat 8am–8pm, Sun 11am–5pm.

Miss Saigon Bistro ☆☆ VIETNAMESE Unlike Andrew Lloyd Webber's bombastic Broadway show, this Miss Saigon is small, quiet, and not at all flashy. Servers at this family-run restaurant—among them, Rick, the owners' son—will graciously offer to recommend dishes or even to custom-make something for you. The menu is varied and reasonably priced and the portions are huge—large enough to share. Noodle dishes and soup bowls are hearty and flavorful; caramelized prawns are fantastic, as is the whole snapper with lemongrass and ginger sauce. Despite the fact that there are few tables inside and a hungry crowd usually gathers outside in the street, they will not at all rush you through your meal, which is worth savoring.

146 Giralda Ave. (at Ponce de León and 37th Ave.), Coral Gables. ℂ **305/446-8006.** Main courses $4–$17. AE, DC, DISC, MC, V. Mon–Thurs 11am–3pm and 5:30–10pm, Fri–Sat 5:30–11pm, Sun 5:30–10pm.

10 South Miami & West Miami

Though mostly residential, these areas nonetheless have several eating establishments worth the drive.

EXPENSIVE

Tropical Chinese ☆☆ CHINESE This strip mall restaurant way out there in West Miami Dade is hailed as the best Chinese restaurant in the city. While the food is indeed very good—certainly more interesting than at your typical beef-and-broccoli shop—it still seems somewhat overpriced. Garlic spinach and prawns in a clay pot is delicious with the perfect mix of garlic cloves, mushrooms, and fresh spinach, but it's not cheap at $16.99. And unlike most Chinese restaurants, the dishes here are not large enough to share. Sunday afternoon dim sum is extremely popular and lines often snake around the shopping center.

7991 Bird Rd., West Miami. ℂ **305/262-7576.** Reservations highly recommended. Main courses $10–$25. AE, DC, MC, V. Mon–Fri 11:30am–10:30pm, Sat 11am–10:30pm, Sun 10:30am–10pm. Take U.S. 1 to Bird Rd. and go west on Bird, all the way down to 78th Ave. The restaurant is between 78th and 79th on Bird Rd. on the north side of the road.

MODERATE

Wilderness Grill (Kids) AMERICAN A cross between Outback Steakhouse and the Rainforest Café, this theme restaurant caters to kids with sound effects, rolling lights simulating lightning, and aquariums and terrariums that abound with exotic flora and fauna. The varied menu has everything from salads to emu steak. It's all okay, but not great. Try the Adelaide BBQ chicken; it's slow roasted in a tasty sauce and is a bargain at $12.95. Children's menus, which double as coloring books, are also available. *Note:* If you are an adult and attend without children, don't be surprised to find them a part of the wilderness wildlife.

Shops at Sunset (57th and U.S. 1), 5701 Sunset Dr., #114, South Miami. © **305/740-3033.** Main courses $8–$21. AE, MC, V. Sun–Thurs 11:30am–10pm, Fri–Sat 11:30am–midnight. Bar open until 1am on weekends.

INEXPENSIVE

Crepe Maker Café ⭐ *Kids* CREPES/FRENCH   Create your own delicious

crepes at this little French cafe. You can choose from ham, tuna, black olives, red peppers, capers, artichoke hearts, and pine nuts. Some of the best combinations include a Philly cheese steak with mushrooms and a classic cordon bleu. Delicious dessert crepes have ice cream, strawberries, peaches, walnuts, and pineapples. Enjoy your crepe fresh off the griddle at the counter or on a barstool. The soups are also delicious. Kids can run around in a small play area, too.

8269 SW 124th St., South Miami. © **305/233-4458** or 305/233-1113. Crepes $3–$7.50. No credit cards. Sun and Tues–Thurs 10:30am–8:30pm, Fri–Sat 10:30am–10:30pm. Crepe cart in CocoWalk Tues–Wed 4–10pm, Sun and Thurs 11am–11pm, Fri–Sat 11am–1am. Take U.S. 1 south to 124th St. and make a left. Restaurant is on the north side of street, across from the park.

El Toro Taco Family Restaurant ⭐⭐ *Finds* MEXICAN   Until I discovered

this Mexican oasis in the midst of South Florida farmland, I'd never had good enough reason to leave my quasi-cosmopolitan confines in Miami for rural Homestead way down south. This 96-seat family-run restaurant has put major miles on my car since I first stumbled upon it a few years ago when I was lost and very hungry. Fabulous, and I mean fabulous, Mexican fare, from the usual tacos, enchiladas, and burritos drenched with the freshest and zestiest salsa this side of Baja, is what you'll find here in abundance. It may sound odd to travel from a big city with tons of restaurants to farm country for Mexican food, but trust me, it's so cheap and delicious, it's worth the trip.

1 S. Krome Ave., Homestead © **305/245-8182.** Main courses $1.39–$8.75. DISC, MC, V. Tues–Sun 11am–9pm. Take 836 West (Dolphin Expressway) toward Miami International Airport. Take Florida Turnpike South Ramp toward Florida City/Key West. Take U.S. 41/SW 8th St. exit (#25) and turn left onto SW 8th St. Take SW 8th St. to Krome Ave. (⅕ mile) and turn left.

Kon Chau ⭐ CHINESE/DIM SUM   Don't be put off by the rather

unappealing shopping center in which this cheap dim sum place is located. If you want fancy plastic chopsticks and fancy prices, go up the block to Tropical Chinese. If you want delicious dim sum at ridiculously low prices, Kon Chau is where you'll find it. A simple checklist allows you to choose as much of whatever you want, from savory steamed shrimp dumplings to airy pork buns, for as little as $1 a piece, all day long. They also have regular dishes if you don't want dim sum.

8376 Bird Rd., West Miami. © **305/553-7799.** Items $1 and up. MC, V. Mon–Sat 11am–10pm, Sun 10am–10pm. Take Bird Rd. West to 83rd St. Restaurant is between 83rd and 84th sts. on the south side of the road, in a Dunkin Donuts shopping center.

Shorty's ⭐ BARBECUE   A Miami tradition since 1951, this honky-tonk of

a log cabin is still serving some of the best ribs and chicken in South Florida. People line up for the smoke-flavored, slow-cooked meat that's so tender it seems to fall off the bone. The secret, however, is to ask for your order with sweet sauce. The regular stuff tastes bland and bottled. All the side dishes, including the coleslaw, corn on the cob, and baked beans, look commercial but are necessary to complete the experience. This is a jeans and T-shirt kind of place, but you may want to wear an elastic waistband, as overeating is not uncommon.

A second Shorty's is located in Davie at 5989 S. University Dr. (© **305/944-0348**).

9200 S. Dixie Hwy. (between U.S. 1 and Dadeland Blvd.), South Miami. © **305/670-7732.** Main courses $5–$9. DISC, MC, V. Mon–Thurs 11am–10pm, Fri–Sat 11am–11pm.

Tea Room ⚘ ENGLISH TEA Do stop in for a spot of tea at this recently rebuilt tearoom in historic Cauley Square off U.S. 1. The little lace-curtained room is an unusual site in this heavily industrial area better known for its warehouses than its doilies.

Try one of the simple sandwiches, such as the turkey club with potato salad and a small lettuce garnish, or onion soup full of rich brown broth and stringy cheese. Daily specials, such as spinach and mushroom quiche, and delectable desserts are a must before beginning your explorations of the old antiques and art shops in this little enclave of civility down south.

12310 SW 224th St. (at Cauley Square), South Miami. © **305/258-0044.** Sandwiches and salads $7–$12; soups $3–$4. AE, DISC, MC, V. Mon–Sat 11am–4pm. Take 836 West (Dolphin Expressway) toward Miami International Airport. Take Palmetto Expressway South ramp toward Coral Way. Merge onto 826 South. Follow signs to Florida Turnpike toward Homestead. Take Turnpike South and exit at Caribbean Blvd. (#12). Go about a mile on Caribbean Blvd. Turn left on S. Dixie Hwy. and then right at SW 224th St. Then turn left onto Old Dixie Hwy. and a slight right onto SW 224th St. The restaurant is at Cauley Square Center.

7

What to See & Do in Miami

If there's one thing Miami doesn't have, it's an identity crisis. In fact, it's the city's vibrant, multifaceted personality that attracts millions each year, from all over the world. South Beach may be on the top of many Miami to-do lists, but the rest of the city, a fascinating assemblage of multicultural neighborhoods, should not be overlooked or neglected. Once considered "God's Waiting Room," the Magic City now attracts an eclectic mix of old and young, celebs and plebes, American and international, and geek and chic with an equally varied roster of activities.

For starters, Miami boasts some of the most natural beauty there is, with blinding blue waters, fine, sandy beaches, and lush tropical parks. The city's man-made brilliance, in the form of Crayola-colored architecture, never seems to fade in Miami's unique Art Deco District. For cultural variation, you can also experience the tastes, sounds, and rhythms of Cuba in Little Havana.

As in any metropolis, however, there are areas that aren't as great as others. Downtown Miami, for instance, is in the throes of a major, albeit slow, renaissance, in which the sketchier, warehouse sections of the city are being transformed into hubs of all things hip. In contrast to this development, however, are the still poverty-stricken areas of downtown such as Overtown, Liberty City, and Little Haiti. While it's obvious to advise you to exercise caution when exploring the less-traveled parts of the city, we would also be remiss in telling you to bypass them completely.

Lose yourself in the city's nature and its neighborhoods, and, best of all, its people—a sassy collection of artists and intellectuals, beach bums and international transplants, dolled-up drag queens and bodies beautiful. No wonder celebrities love to vacation here—the spotlight is on the city and its residents. And unlike most stars, Miami is always ready for its close-up. With so much to do and see, Miami is a virtual amusement park that's bound to entertain all those who pass through its palm-lined gates.

1 Miami's Beaches

Perhaps Miami's most popular attraction is its incredible 35-mile stretch of beachfront, which runs from the tip of South Beach north to Sunny Isles and circles Key Biscayne and the numerous other pristine islands dotting the

Impressions

Miami was like paradise. We had never been anywhere where there were palm trees. . . . We'd never seen a policeman with a gun, and those Miami cops did look pretty groovy.

—Paul McCartney in *The Beatles Anthology*

Atlantic. The characteristics of Miami's many beaches are as varied as the city's population: There are beaches for swimming, socializing, or serenity; for family, seniors, or gay singles; some to make you forget you're in the city, others darkened by huge condominiums. Whatever type of beach vacation you're looking for, you'll find it in one of Miami's two distinct beach areas: Miami Beach and Key Biscayne.

MIAMI BEACH'S BEACHES   Collins Avenue fronts more than a dozen miles of white-sand beach and blue-green waters from 1st to 192nd streets. Although most of this stretch is lined with a solid wall of hotels and condos, beach access is plentiful. There are lots of public beaches here, wide and well maintained, complete with lifeguards, bathroom facilities, concession stands, and metered parking (bring lots of quarters). Except for a thin strip close to the water, most of the sand is hard-packed—the result of a $10 million Army Corps of Engineers Beach Rebuilding Project meant to protect buildings from the effects of eroding sand.

In general, the beaches on this barrier island (all on the eastern, ocean side of the island) become less crowded the farther north you go. A wooden boardwalk runs along the hotel side of the beach from 21st to 46th streets—about 1½ miles—offering a terrific sun-and-surf experience without getting sand in your shoes. Aside from "The Best Beaches," listed below, Miami's lifeguard-protected public beaches include 21st Street, at the beginning of the boardwalk; 35th Street, popular with an older crowd; 46th Street, next to the Fontainebleau Hilton; 53rd Street, a narrower, more sedate beach; 64th Street, one of the quietest strips around; and 72nd Street, a local old-timers' spot.

KEY BISCAYNE'S BEACHES   If Miami Beach doesn't provide the privacy you're looking for, try Virginia Key and Key Biscayne. Crossing the Rickenbacker Causeway ($1 toll), however, can be a lengthy process, especially on weekends, when beach bums and tan-o-rexics flock to the Key. The 5 miles of public beach there, however, are blessed with softer sand and are less developed and more laid-back than the hotel-laden strips to the north.

THE BEST BEACHES
Here are my picks:

- **Best Party Beach:** In Key Biscayne, **Crandon Park Beach,** on Crandon Boulevard, is National Lampoon's *Vacation* on the sand. It's got a diverse crowd consisting of dedicated beach bums and lots of leisure-seeking families,

---

Fun Fact **From Desert Island to Fantasy Island**

Miami Beach wasn't always a beachfront playground. In fact, it was a deserted island until the late 1800s, when a developer started a coconut farm there. That action sparked an interest in many other developers, including John Collins (for whom Collins Avenue is named), who began growing avocados. Other visionaries admired Collins's success and eventually joined him, establishing a ferry service and dredging parts of the bay to make the island more accessible. In 1921, Collins built a 2½-mile bridge linking downtown Miami to Miami Beach, creating excellent accessibility *and* the longest wooden bridge in the world. Today Miami Beach has six links to the mainland.

Miami Area Attractions & Beaches

Amelia Earhart Park **5**
American Airlines Arena **17**
American Police Hall of Fame
  and Museum **14**
Barnacle State Historic Site **31**
Bayfront Park **21**
Bayside Marketplace **20**
Bill Baggs Cape Florida State
  Recreation Center **40**
Biltmore Hotel **26**
CocoWalk **29**
Coral Castle **38**
Crandon Park Golf Course **35**
Diaspora Vibe Art Gallery **12**
Doral Park Golf and Country Club **10**
Fairchild Tropical Garden **39**
Fisher Island **23**
Freedom Tower **17**
GameWorks **34**
Golf Club of Miami **1**
Gulfstream Park **4**
Haulover Marina **7**
Haulover Park Beach **7**
Hialeah Park **9**
Historical Museum
  of Southern Florida **18**

IMAX Theatre at Sunset Place **34**
The Kampong **30**
Latin American Art Museum **25**
Lowe Art Museum **33**
Marjory Stoneman Douglas
  Biscayne Nature Center **36**
Miami Art Museum **19**
Miami Jai Alai Fronton **11**
Miami Metrozoo **38**
Miami Museum of Science and
  Space Transit Planetarium **33**
Miami Seaquarium **32**
Miami-Dade Cultural Center
  (Miami Art Museum &
  the Historical Museum
  of Southern Florida) **18**
Miccosukee Indian Gaming **38**
Monkey Jungle **38**
Museum of Contemporary Art
  (MOCA) **6**
National Hurricane Center **24**
Oleta River State Recreation Area **4**
Parrot Jungle and Gardens **37**
  (until fall 2002);
  22 (from winter of 2003)

Preston B. Bird and Mary Heinlein
  Fruit and Spice Park **38**
Pro Player Stadium **2**
Rubell Family Art Collection **13**
The Scott Rakow Youth Center **15**
Sea Grass Adventures **36**
Spanish Monastery Cloisters **3**
Tropical Park **28**
United in Elián House **16**
Venetian Pool **27**
The Vizcaya Museum and Gardens **38**
World Chess Hall of Fame and Sidney
  Samole Chess Museum **38**

set to a soundtrack of salsa, disco, and reggae music blaring from a number of competing stereos. With 3 miles of oceanfront beach, bathrooms, changing facilities, 493 acres of park, 75 grills, 3 parking lots, several soccer and softball fields, and a public 18-hole championship golf course, Crandon is like a theme park on the sand. Admission is $2 per vehicle. It's open daily from 8am to sunset.

- **Best Beach for People-Watching: Lummus Park Beach,** a.k.a. Glitter Beach, runs along Ocean Drive from about 6th to 14th streets on South Beach. It's the best place to go if you're seeking entertainment as well as a great tan. On any day of the week, you might spy models primping for a photo shoot, nearly naked (topless is legal here) sun-worshippers avoiding tan lines, and an assembly line of washboard abs off of which you could (but shouldn't) bounce your bottle of sunscreen. Bathrooms and changing facilities are available on the beach, but don't expect to have a Cindy Crawford encounter in one of these. Most people tend to prefer using the somewhat drier, cleaner bathrooms of the restaurants on Ocean Drive.

- **Best Swimming Beach:** The **85th Street Beach,** along Collins Avenue, is the best place to swim away from the maddening crowds. It's one of Miami's only stretches of sand with no condos or hotels looming over sunbathers. Lifeguards patrol the area throughout the day and bathrooms are available, though they are not exactly the benchmark of cleanliness.

- **Best Windsurfing Beach: Hobie Beach,** on the side of the causeway leading to Key Biscayne, is not really a beach, but an inlet with predictable winds and a number of places where you can rent windsurfers. Bathrooms are available.

- **Best Shell-Hunting Beach:** You'll find plenty of colorful shells at **Bal Harbour Beach,** Collins Avenue at 96th Street. There's also an exercise course and good shade—but no lifeguards, bathrooms, or changing facilities.

- **Best (Ahem) All-Around Tanning Beach:** For that all-over tan, head to **Haulover Beach,** just north of the Bal Harbour border, and join nudists from around the world in a top-to-bottom tanning session. Should you choose to keep your swimsuit on, however, there are changing rooms and bathrooms.

- **Best Surfing Beach: Haulover Beach Park,** just over the causeway from Bal Harbour, seems to get Miami's biggest swells. Go early to avoid getting mauled by the aggressive young locals prepping for Maui.

- **Best Scenic Beach: Matheson Hammock Park Beach,** at 9610 Old Cutler Road in South Miami (© **305/665-5475**), is the epitome of tranquility, tucked away off of scenic Old Cutler Road in South Miami. And while it's scenic, it's not too much of a scene. It's a great beach for those seeking "alone time." Bathrooms and changing facilities are available.

- **Best Family Beach:** Because of its man-made lagoon, which is fed naturally by the tidal movement of the adjacent Biscayne Bay, the waters of **Matheson Hammock Park Beach** are extremely calm, not to mention safe and secluded enough for families to keep an eye on the kids.

- **Best Beach for Seculusion: Virginia Key on Key Biscayne,** where people go when they don't want to be found. It's also incredibly picturesque.

South Beach Attractions & Outdoor Activity Suppliers/Shops

To Central Miami Beach ↗

The Bass Museum of Art

22nd St
COLLINS PARK
20th St.
19th St.

Miami Beach Convention Center

Dade Boulevard
Convention Center Dr.
18th St.
17th St.

Venetian Causeway
BELLE ISLAND
Dade Boulevard

Lincoln Road Mall
Lincoln Rd.

HISTORIC ART DECO DISTRICT

16th St.
15th St.

Española Way

Biscayne Bay

14th St.
Miami Beach Post Office
13th St.
12th St.
11th St.
Beach Patrol Station
10th St.
9th St.
8th St.
7th St.
6th St.
5th St.
4th St.
3rd St.
2nd St.
1st St.
Commerce St.
Biscayne St.

FLAMINGO PARK

ATLANTIC OCEAN

LUMMUS PARK

Art Deco Welcome Center

SOUTH POINTE PARK

Government Cut

FISHER ISLAND

Purdy Ave.
Bay Rd.
West Ave.
Alton Rd.
Lenox Ave.
Michigan Ave.
Jefferson Ave.
Meridian Ave.
Michigan Ave.
Drexel Ave.
Washington Ave.
Collins Ave.
James Ave.
Ocean Dr.
Euclid Ave.
Pennsylvania Ave.
Collins Ave.
Washington Ave.
Ocean Dr.

0   1/4 mi
0   1/4 km

N

Art Center/South Florida **8**
Art Deco Welcome Center **19**
Bass Museum of Art **1**
Collins Park **3**
Colony Theater **6**
The Community Church **11**
Crunch **15**
Estefan Enterprises **20**
Fritz's Skate Shop **9**
Holocaust Memorial **4**
Jackie Gleason Theater
  of the Performing Arts **12**
Jose Cuervo Underwater Bar **23**
Lincoln Theater **10**
Lummus Park Beach **16**
Mermaid Sculpture **12**
Miami Beach Bicycle Center **21**
Miami Beach Botanical Garden **5**
Miami Beach Cultural Park **2**
Miami Beach Post Office **14**
Miami Beach Public Courts
  at Flamingo Park **13**
Miami Beach Regional Library **2**
Morris Lapidus Sculptures **12**
1928 Sterling Building **7**
Sanford L. Ziff Jewish Museum
  of Florida **22**
Versace Mansion **18**
Wolfsonian-Florida
  International University **17**

2 The Art Deco District (South Beach)

"You know what they used to say? 'Who's Art?'" recalls Art Deco revivalist Dona Zemo, "You'd say, 'This is an Art Deco building,' and they'd say, 'Really, who is Art?' These people thought 'Art Deco' was some guy's name."

How things have changed. This guy Art has become one of the most popular Florida attractions since, well, that mouse Mickey. The district is roughly bounded by the Atlantic Ocean on the east, Alton Road on the west, 6th Street to the south, and Dade Boulevard (along the Collins Canal) to the north.

Simply put, Art Deco is a style of architecture that, in its heyday of the 1920s and '30s, used to be considered ultramodern. Today, fans of the style consider it retro-fabulous. And while some people may not consider the style fabulous, it's undoubtedly retro. According to the experts, Art Deco made its debut in 1925 in an exposition in Paris in which it set a stylistic tone, with buildings based on early neoclassical styles with the application of exotic motifs like flora, fauna, and fountains based on geometric patterns. In Miami, Art Deco is marked by the pastel-hued buildings that line South Beach and Miami Beach. But it's a lot more than just color. If you look carefully, you will see the intricacies and impressive craftsmanship that went into each building back in the day—which, in Miami's case, was the '20s, '30s, and '40s, and now, thanks to intensive restoration, today.

Most of the finest examples of the whimsical Art Deco style are concentrated along three parallel streets—Ocean Drive, Collins Avenue, and Washington Avenue—from about 6th to 23rd streets.

After years of neglect and calls for the wholesale demolition of its buildings, South Beach got a new lease on life in 1979. Under the leadership of Barbara Baer Capitman, a dedicated crusader for the Art Deco region, and the Miami Design Preservation League, founded by Baer Capitman and five friends, an area made up of an estimated 800 buildings was granted a listing on the National Register of Historic Places. Designers then began highlighting long-lost architectural details with soft sherbet shades of peach, periwinkle, turquoise, and purple. Developers soon moved in, and the full-scale refurbishment of the area's hotels was under way.

Not everyone was pleased, though. Former Miami Beach commissioner Abe Resnick said, "I love old buildings. But these Art Deco buildings are 40, 50 years old. They aren't historic. They aren't special. We shouldn't be forced to keep them." But Miami Beach kept those buildings, and Resnick lost his seat on the commission.

Today, hundreds of new establishments—hotels, restaurants, and nightclubs—have renovated, or are in the process of renovating, these older, historical buildings and are moving in, making South Beach on the cutting edge of Miami's cultural and nightlife scene.

EXPLORING THE AREA

If you're touring this unique neighborhood on your own, start at the **Art Deco Welcome Center,** 1001 Ocean Dr. (*C* **305/531-3484**), which is run by the Miami Design Preservation League. The only beachside building across from the Clevelander Hotel and bar, the center gives away lots of informational material, including maps and pamphlets, and runs guided tours about the neighborhood. Art Deco books (including *The Art Deco Guide,* an informative compendium of all the buildings here), T-shirts, postcards, mugs, and other paraphernalia are for sale. It's open Monday to Saturday from 9am to 6pm, sometimes later.

⎛Finds⎞ Walking by Design

The Miami Design Preservation League offers several tours of Miami Beach's historic architecture, which all leave from the Art Deco Welcome Center, located at 1001 Ocean Dr. in Miami Beach. A self-guided audio tour (available 7 days a week, from 10am to 4pm) turns the streets into a virtual outdoor museum, taking you through Miami Beach's Art Deco district at your own leisure, with tours in several languages for just $10 per person. Guided tours conducted by local historians and architects offer an in-depth look at the structures and their history. The 90-minute Ocean Drive and Beyond tour (offered every Saturday at 10:30am) takes you through the district, pointing out the differences between Mediterranean Revival and Art Deco for $15 per person. If you're not blinded by neon, the Thursday night Art Deco District Up-to-Date tour (leaving at 6:30pm) will whisk you around for 90 minutes, making note of how certain local hot spots were architecturally famous way before the likes of Madonna and co. entered the scene. Cost is $15. For more information on tours or reservations, call ⓒ **305/672-2014.**

Take a stroll along **Ocean Drive** for the best view of sidewalk cafes, bars, colorful hotels, and even more colorful people. Another great place for a walk is **Lincoln Road,** which is lined with boutiques, large chain stores, cafes, and funky art and antiques stores. The Community Church, at the corner of Lincoln Road and Drexel Avenue, is the neighborhood's first church and one of its oldest surviving buildings, dating from 1921.

3 Miami's Museum & Art Scene

Miami has never been known as a cultural mecca as far as museums are concerned. Though several exhibition spaces have made forays into collecting nationally acclaimed work, limited support and political infighting have made it a difficult proposition. Recently, however, things have changed as museums such as the Wolfsonian, the Museum of Contemporary Art, the Bass Museum of Art, and the Miami Art Museum have gotten on the bandwagon, boasting collections and exhibitions high on the list of art aficionados. It's now safe to say that world-class exhibitions start here. Listed below are the most lauded museums that have become a part of the city's cultural heritage, and as such, are as diverse as the city itself. For gallery lovers, see "Specialized Tours" in section 6 of this chapter for scheduled gallery walks.

IN SOUTH BEACH

Work continues to proceed on the **Miami Beach Cultural Park,** which comprises a trio of arts buildings on Collins Park and Park Avenue (off Collins Avenue), bounded by 21st to 23rd streets—the newly expanded Bass Museum of Art (see below), the new Arquitectonica-designed home of the Miami City Ballet, and the Miami Beach Regional Library, which broke ground in January 2001 and will have a special focus on the arts. Collins Park, the former site of the Miami Beach Library, will return to its original incarnation as an open space extending to the Atlantic, but it will also be the site of large sculpture installations and cultural activities planned jointly by the organizations that share the space.

Roadside Attractions

The following examples of public art and prized architecture are great photo opportunities and worth visiting if you're in the area.

- **Versace Mansion (Amsterdam Palace):** Morbid curiosity has led hordes of people—tourists and locals—to this, the only private home on Ocean Drive. If you can get past the fact that the late designer was murdered on the steps of this palatial estate, you should definitely observe the intricate Italian architecture that makes this house stand out from its streamlined deco neighbors. Built in the 1930s as a replica of Christopher Columbus's son's palace in Santo Domingo, the house was originally called Casa Casuarina (House of the Pine), but was rechristened the Amsterdam Palace in 1935 when George Amsterdam purchased it. While there were rumors that the mansion was to be turned into a Versace museum, it was, instead, purchased by a private citizen from Texas. Located at the northwest corner of Ocean Drive and 11th Street, South Beach.

- **Estefan Enterprises:** Miami's royal family—Gloria and Emilio Estefan—may reside on private Star Island, but the headquarters of their musical empire is located in a whimsical building designed by the world-famous Arquitectonica architecture company. Its facade is carved with color-lined waves and fanciful shapes. But don't get caught up in the design, as you may miss an opportunity to run into the next Ricky Martin or even Gloria herself. The address is 420 Jefferson Ave. (at 5th Street), Miami Beach.

- **Miami Beach Post Office:** Usually known for long lines and surly people, post offices are rarely considered a must-see, but this one's an

ArtCenter/South Florida ★ Not exactly a museum in the classic sense of the word, ArtCenter/South Florida is a multichambered space where local artists display their works in all mediums—from photography and sculpture to video and just about anything else that might exemplify their artistic nature. Admission is free and it's quite fun to mosey through the space viewing the various artists at work in their studios. Of course, all the art is for sale, but there's no pressure to buy. If you call ahead, you can schedule a guided tour of all the studios, which will give you extra insight into the exhibits. Otherwise, just wander and enjoy.

800–924 Lincoln Rd. (at Meridian Ave.), South Beach. ✆ 305/674-8278. www.artcentersf.org. Free admission. Daily 11am–11pm.

Bass Museum of Art ★★★ The Bass Museum of Art has expanded and received a dramatically new look, rendering it Miami's most progressive art museum. World-renowned Japanese architect Arata Isozaki designed the magnificent new facility, which has triple the former exhibition space, and added an outdoor sculpture terrace, a museum cafe and courtyard, and a museum shop, among other improvements. In addition to providing space in which to show the permanent collection, exhibitions of a scale and quality not previously seen in Miami will now be featured at the Bass. The museum's permanent collection exception. Built in 1937, this historic Depression-era modern-style building features a fabulous rotunda. Utterly Floridian are the coral steps that lead to the entrance. In addition to the requisite mailboxes, stamp machines, and wanted posters, inside, an intricate sun motif surrounds a lantern hanging from the ceiling, which illuminates an epic mural that depicts some of South Florida's history. One glimpse of this magnificent building and you'll rethink the meaning of "going postal." Find it at 1300 Washington Ave., Miami Beach.

- **Mermaid Sculpture:** A pop-art masterpiece designed by Roy Lichtenstein, this sculpture captures the buoyant spirit of Miami Beach and its environs. It's in front of the Jackie Gleason Theater of the Performing Arts, 1700 Washington Ave., Miami Beach.

- **Morris Lapidus on Lincoln Road:** Famed designer/architect, the late Morris Lapidus—the "high priest of high kitsch"—who is best known for the Fontainebleau Hotel, created a series of sculptures that are angular, whimsical, and quirky, competing with the equally amusing mix of pedestrians who flock to Lincoln Road. In addition to the sculptures on Lincoln Road (at Washington Avenue), which you can't miss, Lapidus also created the Colony Theater, 1040 Lincoln Rd., which was built by Paramount in 1943; the 1928 Sterling Building, 927 Lincoln Rd., whose glass blocks and blue neon are required evening viewing; and the Lincoln Theater, 555 Lincoln Rd., which features a remarkable tropical bas-relief.

includes European paintings from the 15th through the early 20th centuries with special emphasis on Northern European art of the Renaissance and baroque periods, including Dutch and Flemish masters such as Bol, Flinck, Rubens, and Jordaens. In 2001 an art lab opened, making it possible for all aspiring artists to create their own masterpieces on computers for free or a nominal charge.

2121 Park Ave. (1 block west of Collins Ave.), South Beach. © 305/673-7530. www.bassmuseum.org. Admission $6 adults, $4 students and seniors, free for children 6 and under. Tues–Wed and Fri–Sat 10am–5pm, Thurs 10am–9pm, Sun 11am–5pm. Closed Mon.

Holocaust Memorial ★★★   This heart-wrenching memorial is hard to miss and would be a shame to overlook. The powerful centerpiece, Kenneth Triester's *Sculpture of Love & Anguish,* depicts victims of the concentration camps crawling up a giant, yearning hand, stretching up to the sky, marked with an Auschwitz number tattoo. Along the reflecting pool is the story of the Holocaust, told in cut marble slabs. Inside the center of the memorial is a tableau that is one of the most solemn and moving tributes to the millions of Jews who lost their lives in the Holocaust I've seen. You can walk through an open hallway lined with photographs and the names of concentration camps and their victims. From the street, you'll see the outstretched arm, but do stop and tour the sculpture at ground level.

Miami Art Galleries

Miami's finest art galleries are located within walking distance of one another in Coral Gables along Ponce de León Boulevard, extending from U.S. 1 to Bird Road. Still others are clustered in Bal Harbour's ritzy shopping district, on 96th Street off of Collins Avenue, right near the Bal Harbour Shops. Unfortunately, South Beach's Lincoln Road, which once had dozens of galleries, now has only a few—a result of soaring rents.

Also check out the burgeoning art scene in the Design District north of downtown just west of Biscayne Boulevard around 40th Street. Listed below is a selection of galleries both in and out of these areas.

If you happen to be in town on the first Friday of the month, you should take the free trolley tour of the Coral Gables Art District. The tour runs from 7 to 10pm; meet at Elite (listed below) or at any of the other participating galleries in the area. See p. 184 for more information.

Barbara Gillman Gallery This gallery's ongoing exhibit of jazz photographer Herman Leonard's fantastic black-and-white photographs of legends such as Billie Holiday and Frank Sinatra has been so popular it hasn't changed in years. In addition to the works of Leonard and other renowned artists such as Andres Serrano, Andy Warhol, and James Rosenquist, the gallery displays the work of new local talent. 5582 NE 4th Court #5, Miami. ✆ 305/759-9155.

Britto Central Some people liken local Brazilian artist Romero Britto to Andy Warhol because of his colorful, whimsical paintings of young children and animals, among other things. Serious art lovers, however, consider Britto's cartoonish works more along the lines of a second-rate Walt Disney. You decide. 818 Lincoln Rd., South Beach. ✆ 305/531-8821.

Elite Fine Art Touted as one of the finest galleries in Miami, Elite features modern and contemporary Latin American painters and sculptors such as Angel Hurtado, Olga Sinclair, and Gina Pellon, among others. 3140 Ponce de León Blvd., Coral Gables. ✆ 305/448-3800.

Evelyn S. Poole Ltd. Known as the finest of the fine antiques collections, the Poole assortment of European 17th-, 18th-, and 19th-century decorative furniture and accessories is housed in 5,000 square feet of space in the newly revived Decorator's Row. 3925 N. Miami Ave., Miami. ✆ 305/573-7463.

Meza Fine Art Gallery Café ⓕⁱⁿᵈˢ Dine amidst fine works of art in this funky gallery and cafe that specializes in Latin American artists, including Carlos Betancourt, Javier Marin, and Gloria Lorenzo. 275 Giralda Ave., Coral Gables. ✆ 305/461-2723.

Tower Theater This renovated movie theater in Little Havana features highly regarded Cuban art such as Carlos Navarro's *Cosas Cubanas (Cuban Things)*. 1508 SW 8th St., Little Havana. ✆ 305/443-5415.

Wallflower Gallery ⓕⁱⁿᵈˢ Funky, eclectic, and reminiscent of Andy Warhol's Factory, the Wallflower Gallery features an assortment of exhibits from local artists from erotica to exotica and everything in between. Performance art and live music are also featured here. 10 NE 3rd St., Miami. ✆ 305/579-0069.

1933 Meridian Ave. (at Dade Blvd.), South Beach. ℂ **305/538-1663**. http://miami.travelape.com/attractions/
holocaust-memorial/. Free admission. Daily 9am–9pm.

Sanford L. Ziff Jewish Museum of Florida ⭐   Chronicling over 230 years
of Jewish heritage and experiences in Florida, the Jewish Museum presents a fascinating look at religion and culture through films, lectures, and exhibits such as
"Mosaic: Jewish Life in Florida," which features over 500 photos and artifacts
documenting the Jewish experience in Florida since 1763. The museum is
housed in a former synagogue.

301 Washington Ave., South Beach. ℂ **305/672-5044**. www.jewishmuseum.com. $5 adults, $4 seniors and
students, $10 families. Free admission Sat. Tues–Sun 10am–5pm. Closed Mondays and Jewish holidays.

Wolfsonian-Florida International University ⭐⭐⭐ *Finds*   Mitchell Wolf-
son Jr., heir to a family fortune built on movie theaters, was known as an eccentric, but I'd call him a pack rat. A premier collector of propaganda and
advertising art, Wolfson was spending so much money storing his booty that he
decided to buy the warehouse that was housing it. It ultimately held more than
70,000 of his items, from controversial Nazi propaganda to King Farouk of
Egypt's match collection. Thrown in the eclectic mix are also zany works from
great modernists such as Charles Eames and Marcel Duchamp. He then gave
this incredibly diverse collection to Florida International University. The former
1927 storage facility has been transformed into a museum that is the envy of
curators around the world. The museum is unquestionably fascinating and hosts
lectures and rather swinging events surrounding particular exhibits.

1001 Washington Ave., South Beach. ℂ **305/531-1001**. www.wolfsonian.fiu.edu. Admission $5 adults;
$3.50 seniors, students with ID, and children 6–12; by donation Thurs 6–9pm. Mon, Tues, Fri, and Sat
11am–6pm, Thurs 11am–9pm, Sun noon–5pm.

American Police Hall of Fame and Museum   This strange museum
appeals mostly to those fascinated by police and their gadgetry. Once inside,
you'll find a combination of reality and fantasy that's part thoughtful tribute,
part Hollywood-style drama. Just past the car featured in the motion picture
Blade Runner is a mock prison cell, in which visitors can take pictures of themselves pretending they're doing 5 to 10. Also on hand are execution devices,
including a guillotine and an electric chair (whose controversial use was recently
abolished in Florida). In the entry is a touching memorial to the more than
7,000 American police officers who have lost their lives in the line of duty. Even
if you don't go inside, you can't miss the museum, which has a real police car
attached to its facade. Unfortunately, at press time, it was announced that some-
time in 2003, the museum would be moving out of Miami and up to Titusville,
in central Florida. Call for more information and to see if the museum is still in
Miami when you're there.

Finds Eyeing the Storm

For Weather Channel fanatics and those who are just curious, the **National
Hurricane Center** offers free tours before and after hurricane season, from
January 15 through May 15, explaining everything from keeping track of
storms to the history of some of the nation's most notorious and devas-
tating hurricanes. Reservations required. Florida International University, 11691
SW 17th St., South Florida. ℂ **305/229-4470**. Free Admission.

3801 Biscayne Blvd., Miami. © 305/573-0070. www.aphf.org. Admission $12 adults, $9 seniors over 61, $6 children 11 and under, free for law enforcement officers and family survivors. Daily 10am–5:30pm. Go north on U.S. 1 from downtown; it's the building with police car affixed to its side. Parking in the back.

Diaspora Vibe Art Gallery 🎯🎯

This art complex, housed in an old bakery, is a funky artist hangout and is the home to some of the greatest artworks of Miami's diverse Caribbean, Latin American, and African-American cultures. The gallery has two seasons of shows, often focusing on emerging artists. During the winter, three artists are selected by the gallery to travel to and exhibit their works in Paris. On the last Friday of every month, from May through October, the gallery holds its fabulous "Final Fridays." A new artist's work is spotlighted inside, while outside in the courtyard are live music performances and readings of poetry and folk tales. Delicious Caribbean cuisine is also served. The who's who of Miami's cognoscenti gather here to recharge their cultural batteries.

561 NW 32nd St., Studio 48 (Bakehouse Art Complex), Miami. © 305/759-1110. www.diasporavibe.com. Free admission. "Final Fridays" events $15. Mon–Fri by appointment; Sat–Sun 1–6pm; Final Fridays events May–Oct last Fri of the month 7–11pm.

Latin American Art Museum

In addition to the permanent collection of contemporary artists from Spain and Latin America, this 3,500-square-foot museum hosts monthly exhibitions of works from Latin America and the Caribbean Basin. Usually, the exhibitions focus on a theme, such as international women or surrealism. It's not a major attraction, but worth a stop if you're interested in Latin American art. On the same block, you'll find great design stores and a few other galleries.

2206 SW 8th St., Little Havana. © 305/644-1127. Free admission. Tues–Fri 11am–5pm, Sat 11am–4pm. Second Friday of every month, 6:30pm–10pm. Closed Aug and major holidays.

Lowe Art Museum 🎯🎯

Located on the University of Miami campus, the Lowe Art Museum has a dazzling collection of 8,000 works that include American paintings, Latin American art, Navajo and Pueblo Indian textiles, and Renaissance and baroque art. Traveling exhibits such as *Rolling Stone* magazine's photo collection also stop here. For the most part, the Lowe is known for its collection of Greek and Roman antiquities, and, as compared to the more modern MOCA, Bass, and Miami Art Museum, features mostly European and international art hailing back to ancient times.

University of Miami, 1301 Stanford Dr. (at Ponce de León Blvd.), Coral Gables. © 305/284-3603. www.lowe museum.org. Admission $5 adults, $3 seniors and student with ID. Donation day is first Tues of the month. Tues, Wed, Fri, and Sat 10am–5pm, Thurs noon–7pm, Sun noon–5pm.

Miami Art Museum at the Miami–Dade Cultural Center 🎯🎯🎯

The Miami Art Museum (MAM) features an eclectic mix of modern and contemporary works by such artists as Eric Fischl, Max Beckmann, Jim Dine, and Stuart Davis. Rotating exhibitions span the ages and styles, and often focus on Latin American or Caribbean artists. There are also fantastic themed exhibits such as the Andy Warhol exhibit, which featured all-night films by the artist, make-your-own pop art, cocktail hours, and parties with local deejays. JAM at MAM is the museum's popular happy hour, which takes place the second Thursday of the month and is tied in to a particular exhibit. Almost as artistic as the works inside the museum is the composite sketch of the people—young and old—who attend these events.

The Miami–Dade Cultural Center, where the museum is housed, is a fortresslike complex designed by Phillip Johnson. In addition to the acclaimed Miami Art Museum, the center houses the main branch of the Miami–Dade

Public Library, which sometimes features art and cultural exhibits, and the Historical Museum of Southern Florida, which highlights the fascinating history of the area. Unfortunately, the plaza onto which the complex opens is home to many of downtown Miami's homeless population, which makes it a bit off-putting but not dangerous.

101 W. Flagler St., Miami. ⓒ **305/375-3000**. www.miamiartmuseum.org. Admission $5 adults, $2.50 seniors and students, free for children under 12. Tues–Fri 10am–5pm; third Thurs of each month 10am–9pm; Sat–Sun noon–5pm. Closed major holidays. From I-95 south, exit at Orange Bowl–NW 8th St. and continue south to NW 2nd St.; turn left at NW 2nd St. and go 1½ blocks to NW 2nd Ave.; turn right.

Miami Museum of Science and Space Transit Planetarium ★★ *Kids* The Museum of Science features more than 140 hands-on exhibits that explore the mysteries of the universe. Live demonstrations and collections of rare natural history specimens make a visit here fun and informative. Many of the demos involve audience participation, which can be lots of fun for willing and able kids and adults alike. There is also the Wildlife Center, with more than 175 live reptiles and birds of prey. The adjacent Space Transit Planetarium projects astronomy and laser shows as well as interactive demonstrations of upcoming computer technology and cyberspace features. Call, or visit their website, for a list of upcoming exhibits and laser shows.

3280 S. Miami Ave. (just south of the Rickenbacker Causeway), Coconut Grove. ⓒ **305/646-4200** for general information or 305/854-2222 for planetarium show times. www.miamisci.org. $10 adults, $8 seniors and students, $6 children 3–12, free for children 2 and under; laser shows $6 adults, $3 seniors and children 3–12. After 4:30pm, ticket prices are half price. 25% discount for AAA members. Ticket prices include entrance to all museum galleries, planetarium shows, and the Wildlife Center. Museum of Science, daily 10am–6pm; call for planetarium show times (last show is at 4pm weekdays and 5pm on weekends). Closed on Thanksgiving and Christmas Day.

Museum of Contemporary Art (MOCA) ★★★   MOCA boasts an impressive collection of internationally acclaimed art with a local flavor. It is also known for its forward thinking and ability to discover and highlight new artists. A high-tech screening facility allows for film presentations to complement the exhibitions. You can see works by Jasper Johns, Roy Lichtenstein, Larry Rivers, Duane Michaels, and Claes Oldenberg, plus there are special exhibitions by such artists as Yoko Ono, Sigmar Polke, John Baldessari, and Goya. Guided tours are offered in English, Spanish, French, Creole, Portuguese, German, and Italian.

770 NE 125th St., North Miami. ⓒ **305/893-6211**. Fax 305/891-1472. www.mocanomi.org. Admission $5 adults, $3 seniors and students with ID, free for children 12 and under. Tues by donation. Tues–Sat 11am–5pm, Sun noon–5pm. Closed Mon and major holidays.

Rubell Family Art Collection ★★★ *Finds*   This impressive collection, owned by the Miami hotelier family, the Rubells, is housed in a two-story 40,000-square-foot former Drug Enforcement Agency warehouse in a sketchy area

---

Checkmate

The World Chess Hall of Fame and Sidney Samole Chess Museum, 13755 SW 119th Ave. in South Miami (ⓒ **786/242-4255**), is eye-catching, housed in a 45-foot-tall chessboard-like structure and featuring an interactive history of chess; an introduction to famous and celebrity players; computer-simulated, fully participatory games and challenges; tournament spaces; rare artifacts; an IBM Deep Blue feature; and a short film called *Chess Experience*.

north of downtown Miami. The building looks like a fortress, which is fitting: Inside is a priceless collection of more than a thousand works of contemporary art, by the likes of Keith Haring, Damien Hirst, Julian Schnabel, Jean-Michel Basquiat, Paul McCarthy, Charles Ray, and Cindy Sherman. But be forewarned: Some of the art is extremely graphic and may be off-putting to some. The gallery changes exhibitions twice yearly and there is a seasonal program of lectures, artists' talks, and performances by prominent artists. As of press time, the gallery was looking to move to a larger space nearby toward the end of 2002 to accommodate this ever-growing, ever-impressive collection.

95 NW 29th St. (on the corner of NW 1st Ave. near the Design District), Miami. ✆ 305/573-6090. Free admission. Thurs–Sat 9am–9pm and by appointment.

4 Historic Homes & Sites

South Beach's well-touted Art Deco District is but one of many colorful neighborhoods that can boast dazzling architecture. The rediscovery of the entire Biscayne Corridor (from downtown to about 80th Street and Biscayne Boulevard) has given light to a host of ancillary neighborhoods on either side that are filled with Mediterranean-style homes and Frank Lloyd Wright gems. Coral Gables is home to many large and beautiful homes, mansions, and churches that reflect architecture from the 1920s, '30s, and '40s. Some of the homes, or portions of their structures, have been created from coral rock and shells. The Biltmore Hotel is also filled with history. See p. 183 for information on touring the hotel.

Barnacle State Historic Site 🎯🎯 The former home of naval architect and early settler Ralph Middleton Munroe is now a museum in the heart of Coconut Grove. It's the oldest house in Miami and it rests on its original foundation, which sits on 5 acres of hardwood and landscaped lawns. The house's quiet surroundings, wide porches, and period furnishings illustrate how Miami's first snowbird lived in the days before condo-mania and luxury hotels. Enthusiastic and knowledgeable state park employees offer a wealth of historical information to those interested in quiet, low-tech attractions like this one. Call for details on the fabulous monthly moonlight concerts during which folk, blues, or classical music is presented and picnicking is encouraged.

3485 Main Hwy. (1 block south of Commodore Plaza), Coconut Grove. ✆ 305/448-9445. Fax 305/448-7484. Admission $1. Concerts $5, free for children under 10. Fri–Mon 9am–4pm. Tours Fri–Sun at 10am, 11:30am, 1pm, and 2:30pm. From downtown Miami, take U.S. 1 south to 27th Ave., make a left, and continue to S. Bayshore Dr.; then make a right, follow to the intersection of Main Hwy., and turn left.

Coral Castle 🎯🎯 *Finds* There's plenty of competition, but Coral Castle is probably the strangest attraction in Florida. In 1923, the story goes, a 26-year-old crazed Latvian, suffering from unrequited love of a 16-year-old who left him

---

A Glimpse into the Past

Coconut Grove's link to the Bahamas dates from before the turn of the 20th century, when islanders came to the area to work in a newly opened hotel called the Peacock Inn. Bahamian-style wooden homes built by these early settlers still stand on Charles Street. Goombay, the lively annual Bahamian festival, celebrates the Grove's Caribbean link and has become one of the largest black heritage street festivals in America. (See p. 21 for more information.)

Freedom Tower

Driving north on Biscayne Boulevard in downtown Miami, one may be distracted by the traffic, the neon lights coming from the Bayside Marketplace, or the behemoth cruise ships docked at the port. But perhaps the most dramatic presence on this heavily trafficked stretch of downtown is the Freedom Tower, 600 Biscayne Blvd. at NE 6th Street, built in 1925 and modeled after the Giralda Tower in Spain. Once home to the now-defunct *Miami Daily News* and *Metropolis* newspapers, the Freedom Tower was sold in 1957 to the U.S. General Services Administration, which used the building to process over 500,000 Cubans fleeing the island once Castro took over.

When the government left the building in 1974, the Freedom Tower was abandoned until 1997, when former Cuban American National Foundation chairman Jorge Mas Canosa bought the building for $4.2 million, vowing to preserve it as Miami's version of the Statue of Liberty. With over $30 million being invested in the building, it reopened as the Cuban American National Foundation headquarters, which the executive director envisions as the place in which a trade agreement with Cuba will be signed once the communist government falls. In the meantime, the building will also house a museum dedicated to the history of Cubans in the United States. For hours, directions, and more information, call ✆ **305/592-7768.**

at the altar, immigrated to South Miami and spent the next 25 years of his life carving huge boulders into a prehistoric-looking roofless "castle." It seems impossible that one rather short man could have done all this, but there are scores of affidavits on display from neighbors who swear it happened. Apparently, experts have studied this phenomenon to help figure out how the Great Pyramids and Stonehenge were built. Rocker Billy Idol was said to have been inspired by this place to write his song "Sweet 16." An interesting 25-minute audio tour guides you through the spot, now in the National Register of Historic Places. Although Coral Castle is overpriced and undermaintained, it's worth a visit when in the area, which is about 37 miles from Miami.

28655 S. Dixie Hwy., Homestead. ✆ 305/248-6345. www.coralcastle.com. Admission $9.75 adults, $6.50 seniors, $5 children 7–12. Daily 7am–9pm. Take 836 West (Dolphin Expressway) toward Miami International Airport. Merge onto 826 South (Palmetto Expressway) and take it to the Florida Turnpike toward Homestead. Take the 288th St. exit (#5) and then take a right on South Dixie Hwy., a left on SW 157th Ave., and then a sharp left back onto South Dixie Hwy. Coral Castle is about .05 miles down on the left side of the street.

Spanish Monastery Cloisters ✮✮✮ *(Finds)* Did you know that the alleged oldest building in the Western Hemisphere dates from 1133 and is located in Miami? The Spanish Monastery Cloisters were first erected in Segovia, Spain. Centuries later, newspaper magnate William Randolph Hearst purchased and brought them to America in pieces. The carefully numbered stones were quarantined for years until they were finally reassembled on the present site in 1954. It has often been used as a backdrop for movies and commercials and is a very popular tourist attraction.

16711 W. Dixie Hwy. (at NE 167th St.), North Miami Beach. ✆ 305/945-1461. monastery@earthlink.net. Admission $5 adults, $2.50 seniors, $2 children 3–12. Mon–Sat 9am–5pm, Sun 1–5pm.

United in Elián House   It was only a matter of time. After Elián González was rescued from a raft off the coast of Fort Lauderdale in November 1999, he lived

(C) Digging Miami

Until the controversial discovery of the archaeological site known as the Miami River Circle, the oldest existing artifacts in the city were presumed to have existed in the closets of Miami's retirement homes. In September 1998, during a routine archeological investigation on the mouth of the Miami River, several unusual and unique features were discovered cut into the bedrock: a prehistoric circular structure, 38 feet in diameter, with intentional markings of the cardinal directions as well as a 5-foot-long shark and two stone axes, suggesting the circle had ceremonial significance to Miami's earliest inhabitants—the Tequesta Indians. Radiocarbon tests confirm that the circle is about 2,000 years old.

While some have theorized that the circle is a calendar or Miami's own version of Stonehenge, most scholars believe that the discovery represents the foundation of a circular structure, perhaps a council house or a chief's house. Expert scientists, archeologists, and scholars who have made visits to the site indicate that the circle is of local, regional, and national significance. Local preservationists formed an organization, Save the Miami Circle, to ensure that developers don't raze the circle to make way for condominiums. For now, the circle remains put and the mystery continues. See www.savethecircle.org for more information.

in this modest, now famous, Little Havana house with relatives for five months before being reunited with his father and returned to Cuba in a storm of controversy. For Cuban nationals, the house became a shrine and the boy became a symbol for their struggle. There are collages of Elián all over the house; there's also trash in the yard as if someone still actually lives there. Apparently there was no time to clean up before the throngs of curiosity seekers came and the place was turned into a museum. Visitors receive a sticker with "the picture" of when the boy was seized by Federal marshals and returned to his father—a day of infamy in Cuban-American history. See where Elián lived, played, breathed, and ate. See Elián's toys. See where the international media camped out for five months. See where relatives cried for the cameras. You get the picture.

2319 NW 2nd St., Little Havana. No tel. Sunday 10am–6pm. Free admission.

Venetian Pool ★★★ *Kids*   Miami's most beautiful and unusual swimming pool, dating from 1924, is hidden behind pastel stucco walls and is honored with a listing in the National Register of Historic Places. Underground artesian wells feed the free-form lagoon, which is shaded by three-story Spanish porticos and features both fountains and waterfalls. It can be cold in the winter months. During summer, the pool's 800,000 gallons of water are drained and refilled nightly thanks to an underground aquifer, ensuring a cool, *clean* swim. Visitors are free to swim and sunbathe here, just as Esther Williams and Johnny Weissmuller did decades ago. For a modest fee, you or your children can learn to swim during special summer programs.

2701 DeSoto Blvd. (at Toledo St.), Coral Gables. (C) 305/460-5356. www.venetianpool.com. Admission and hours vary seasonally. Nov–Mar $5.50 for those 13 and older, $2.50 children under 13; April–Oct, $8.50 for those 13 and older, $4.50 children under 13. Children must be 3 years old and provide proof of age with birth certificate, or 38 inches tall to enter. Hours are at least 11am–4:30pm, but are often longer. Call for more information.

The Vizcaya Museum and Gardens ✪✪✪   Sometimes referred to as the "Hearst Castle of the East," this magnificent villa is more Gatsby-esque than anything else you'll find in Miami. It was built in 1916 as a winter retreat for James Deering, co-founder and former vice president of International Harvester. The industrialist was fascinated by 16th-century art and architecture and his ornate mansion, which took 1,000 artisans 5 years to build, became a celebration of that period. If you love antiques, this place is a dream come true, packed with European relics and works of art from the 16th to the 19th centuries. Most of the original furnishings, including dishes and paintings, are still intact. You will see very early versions of a telephone switchboard, central vacuum cleaning system, elevators, and fire sprinklers. A free guided tour of the 34 furnished rooms on the first floor takes about 45 minutes. The second floor, which consists mostly of bedrooms, is open to tour on your own. The spectacularly opulent villa wraps itself around a central courtyard. Outside, lush formal gardens, accented with statuary, balustrades, and decorative urns, front an enormous swath of Biscayne Bay. Definitely take the tour of the rooms, but immediately thereafter, you will want to wander and get lost in the resplendent gardens.

3251 S. Miami Ave. (just south of Rickenbacker Causeway), North Coconut Grove. ℂ 305/250-9133. www. vizcayamuseum.com. Admission $10 adults, $5 children 6–12, free for children 5 and under. Villa daily 9:30am–5pm (ticket booth closes at 4:30pm); gardens daily 9:30am–5:30pm.

5 Nature Preserves, Parks & Gardens

The Miami area is a great place for outdoors types, with beaches, parks, nature preserves, and gardens galore. For information on South Florida's two national parks, the Everglades and Biscayne National Park, see chapter 10.

The **Amelia Earhart Park,** 401 E. 65th St., Hialeah (ℂ **305/685-8389**), is the only real reason to travel to industrial, traffic-riddled Hialeah. The park has five lakes stocked with bass and bream for fishing; playgrounds; picnic facilities; and a big red barn that houses cows, sheep, and goats for petting and ponies for riding. There's also a country store and dozens of old-time farm activities like horseshoeing, sugarcane processing, and more. Parking is free on weekdays and $3.50 per car on weekends. Open daily from 9am to sunset. To drive here, take I-95 north to the NW 103rd Street exit, go west to East 4th Avenue, and then turn right. Parking is 1½ miles down the street. Depending on traffic, Hialeah is about a half hour from downtown Miami.

At the historic **Bill Baggs Cape Florida State Park** ✪, 1200 Crandon Blvd. (ℂ **305/361-5811**), at the southern tip of Key Biscayne about 20 minutes from downtown Miami, you can explore the unfettered wilds and enjoy some of the most secluded beaches in Miami. There's also a historic lighthouse that was built in 1825, which is the oldest lighthouse in South Florida. The lighthouse was damaged during the Second Seminole War (1836) and again in 1861 during the Civil War. Out of commission for a while, in 1978 the U.S. Coast Guard restored it to working lighthouse condition. A rental shack leases bikes, hydrobikes, kayaks, and many more water toys. It's a great place to picnic, and a newly constructed restaurant serves homemade Latin food, including great fish soups and sandwiches. Just be careful that the raccoons don't get your lunch—the furry black-eyed beasts are everywhere. Wildlife aside, however, Bill Baggs has been consistently rated as one of the top 10 beaches in the U.S. for its 1¼ miles of wide, sandy beaches and its secluded, serene atmosphere. Admission is $4 per car with up to eight people. Open daily from 8am to sunset. Tours of the lighthouse are available every Thursday through Monday at 10am and 1pm. Arrive at least half an hour early to sign up—there is only room for 10 people on each. Take I-95 to the Rickenbacker Causeway and take that all the way to the end.

Fairchild Tropical Garden ✿✿✿, at 10901 Old Cutler Rd. in South Miami (© **305/667-1651;** www.ftg.org), is the largest of its kind in the continental United States. A veritable rain forest of both rare and exotic plants, as well as 11 lakes and countless meadows, are spread across 83 acres. Palmettos, vine pergola, palm glades, and other unique species create a scenic, lush environment. More than 100 species of birds have been spotted at the garden (ask for a checklist at the front gate), and it's home to a variety of animals. You should not miss the 30-minute narrated tram tour (tours leave on the hour from 10am to 3pm weekdays and 10am to 4pm on weekends) to learn about the various flowers and trees on the grounds. There is also a museum, a cafe, a picnic area, and a gift shop with fantastic books on gardening, cooking, and edible gifts. The 2-acre rain-forest exhibit, Windows to the Tropics, will save you a trip to the Amazon. Expect to spend a minimum of 2 hours here.

Admission is $8 for adults and free for children 12 and under accompanied by an adult. Open daily, except Dec. 25, from 9:30am to 4:30pm. Take I-95 south to U.S. 1, turn left onto Le Jeune Road, and follow it straight to the traffic circle; from there, take Old Cutler Road 2 miles to the park.

You might remember the pink flamingos at **Hialeah Park** ✿, 2200 E. 4th Ave., Hialeah (© **305/885-8000;** www.hialeahpark.com), from *Miami Vice*. This famous flamingo colony is the largest of its kind. The track (which no longer hosts races), listed on the National Register of Historic Places, is one of the most beautiful in the world, featuring old-fashioned stands and acres of immaculately manicured grounds. It is open to the public, for free, to tour around and see the spectacular grounds. Call before going as hours can be erratic.

Located on Biscayne Bay in Coconut Grove (4013 Douglas Rd.; www.ntbg. org/kampong.html), the **Kampong** ✿✿ is a 7-acre botanical garden featuring a stunning array of flowering trees and tropical fruit trees including mango, avocado, and pomelos. In the early 1900s, noted plant explorer David Fairchild traveled the world seeking rare plants of economic and aesthetic value that might be cultivated in the United States. In 1928, he and his wife, Marian (daughter of Alexander Graham Bell), built a two-story residence here (listed on the National Register of Historic Places) amid some of his collections, borrowing the Malaysian word *kampong* for his home in a garden. In the 1960s, the Fairchilds sold the Kampong to Catherine Hauberg Sweeney, who donated the property to the National Tropical Botanical Garden to promote and preserve this South Florida treasure. It's a must-see for those interested in horticulture. Tours are by appointment only, from Monday to Friday. For tour information, call © **305/442-7169.** Admission is $10 a person. Take U.S. 1 to Douglas Road (SW 37th Ave.). Go east on Douglas Road for about a mile. The Kampong will be on your left.

Named after the late champion of the Everglades, the **Marjory Stoneman Douglas Biscayne Nature Center** ✿, 6767 Crandon Blvd., Key Biscayne (© **305/361-6767;** www.biscaynenaturecenter.org), has just moved into a brand-new $4 million facility and offers hands-on marine exploration, hikes through coastal hammocks, bike trips, and beach walks. Local environmentalists and historians lead intriguing trips through the local habitat. Call to reserve a spot on a regularly scheduled weekend tour or program. Be sure to wear comfortable closed-toe shoes for hikes through wet or rocky terrain. Open daily 10am to 7pm Memorial Day through Labor Day; daily 10am to 4pm the rest of year. Admission to park is $4 per person; admission to nature center free. Call for weekend programs. To get there, take I-95 to the Rickenbacker Causeway Exit (#1) and take the causeway all the way until it becomes Crandon Boulevard. The center is on the east side of the street (the Atlantic Ocean side). Driving time is about 25 minutes from downtown Miami.

Because so many people are so focused on the beach itself, the **Miami Beach Botanical Garden,** 2000 Convention Center Dr., Miami Beach (© **305/ 673-7256**), remains, for the most part, a secret garden. The lush, tropical 4½-acre garden is a fabulous, all-natural retreat from the hustle and bustle of the silicone-enhanced city. Open Monday through Friday from 8:30am to 5pm, Saturday and Sunday from 9:30am to 5pm. Admission is free.

The **Oleta River State Recreation Area** 🎯🎯, 3400 NE 163rd St., North Miami (© **305/919-1846**), consists of 993 acres—the largest urban park in the state—on Biscayne Bay. The beauty of the Oleta River combined with the fact that you're essentially in the middle of a city makes this park especially worth visiting. With miles of bicycle and canoe trails, a sandy swimming beach, shaded picnic pavilions, and a fishing pier, Oleta River State Recreation Area offers visitors an outstanding outdoor recreational experience cloistered from the confines of the big city. Open daily from 8am to sunset. Admission for pedestrians and cyclists is $1 per person; by car: driver plus car, $2; driver plus up to 7 passengers and car, $4. Take 1-95 to exit 17 (SR 826 East), and go all the way east until just before the causeway. The park entrance is on your right. Driving time from downtown Miami is about a half hour.

A testament to Miami's unusual climate, the **Preston B. Bird and Mary Heinlein Fruit and Spice Park** 🎯, 24801 SW 187th Ave., Homestead (© **305/ 247-5727**), harbors rare fruit trees that cannot survive elsewhere in the country. If a volunteer is available, you'll learn some fascinating things about this 30-acre living plant museum, where the most exotic varieties of fruits and spices—ackee, mango, Ugli fruits, carambola, and breadfruit—grow on strange-looking trees with unpronounceable names. There are also original coral rock buildings dating back to 1912. An art festival here in January is among the park's most popular—and populated—events.

The best part? You're free to take anything that *naturally* falls to the ground. You'll also find samples of interesting fruits and jellies made from the park's bounty as well as exotic ingredients and cookbooks in the gift store.

Admission to the spice park is $3.50 for adults and $1 for children under 12. It's open daily from 10am to 5pm; closed major holidays. Tours are included in the price of admission and are offered at 11am, 1pm, and 2:30pm. Take U.S. 1 south, turn right on SW 248th Street, and go straight for 5 miles to SW 187th Avenue. The drive from Miami should take 45 minutes to an hour.

Tropical Park, 7900 SW 40th St. in West Miami (© **305/226-8315**), has it all. Enjoy a game of tennis and racquetball for a minimal fee, or swim and sun yourself on the secluded little lake. You can use the fishing pond for free, and they'll even supply you with the rods and bait. If you catch anything, however, you're on your own. Open daily from sunrise to sunset. Admission is free. To get there, go west on Bird Road until you reach the overpass for the Palmetto Expressway (826). The park is on the left-hand side immediately after the overpass.

6 Sightseeing Cruises & Organized Tours

BOAT & CRUISE-SHIP TOURS

You don't need a boating license or a zillion-dollar yacht to explore Miami by boat. Thanks to several enterprising companies, boat tours are easy to find, affordable, and are an excellent way to see the city from a more liquid perspective.

Bay Escape 🐦 This 1-hour air-conditioned cruise will take you past Millionaires' Row and the Venetian Islands (see below box) for just $10. There's also a food stand and cash bar. The tours are bilingual.

Bayside Marketplace Marina, 401 Biscayne Blvd., Downtown. ℂ **305/373-7001.** All tickets $10; free for children 12 and under. Millionaires' Row tour daily 1, 3, 5, and 7pm. Evening party cruise (music and cash bar) Fri–Sat 9–11pm.

Heritage Miami II Topsail Schooner This relaxing ride aboard Miami's only tall ship is a fun way to see the city, since it's on a schooner (as opposed to the other tour company's cruising boats), which gives you more of a feel of the water. The 2-hour cruise passes by Villa Vizcaya, Coconut Grove, and Key Biscayne and puts you in sight of Miami's spectacular skyline and island homes. Call to make sure the ship is running on schedule. On Friday, Saturday, and Sunday evenings, there are 1-hour tours to see the lights of the city, leaving at 6:30pm, for $10 per person.

Bayside Marketplace Marina, 401 Biscayne Blvd., Downtown. ℂ **305/442-9697.** Fax 305/442-0119. Tickets for day tours $15 adults, $10 children 12 and under. Sept–May only. Tours leave daily at 1:30, 4, and 6:30pm and Fri–Sun also at 9, 10, and 11pm.

Water Taxi 🐦🐦🐦 *Value* Not exactly a tour, per se, the Water Taxi is a cheap and fantastic way to see the city via local waterways. The two major routes run between Bayside Marketplace and the 5th Street Marina on South Beach; the second is basically a downtown water shuttle service between the various hotels in downtown as well as the Port of Miami, the Hard Rock Cafe at Bayside, East Coast Fisheries, and Fisher Island. Cost is $7 one way, $12 round trip, and $15 for an all-day pass. The Bayside/South Beach trip is the best one to take because there aren't as many stops.

ℂ **305/467-6677.** www.watertaxi.com.

Moments Venice in Miami

You don't have to endure jet lag and time zone differences to enjoy the beauty of Italy. Located just off Miami Beach, Florida's own Venetian Islands (NE 15th Street and Dade Boulevard) were joined together in 1926 by a bascule bridge known as the Venetian Causeway. A series of 12 bridges connecting the Venetian Islands and stretching between Miami and Miami Beach feature octagonal concrete entrance towers, which give you a great view of the water. The oldest causeway in metropolitan Miami, the Venetian is rickety in a charming way, featuring fantastic views of the city and the mammoth cruise ships docked at the port, not to mention a glimpse of some of Miami's most beautiful waterfront homes. Bikers and joggers especially love the Venetian causeway because of limited traffic and beautiful scenery.

Tips **Go Ahead, Act Like a Tourist!**

The Miami Tourist Bus may sound like a savvy traveler's worst nightmare, but if you want to see the city London-style on a double-decker diesel bus *and* get a tan, this is your best bet. Running daily from Aventura to Miami's Kendall suburb, the bus allows unlimited hop-on/hop-off service at popular stops such as Sunset Place, CocoWalk, and Bayside, and has onboard commentary and history as you're being driven through the city. The bus also takes you through the Art Deco District and the tony Bal Harbour Shops, all for a $20 day pass. Weeklong passes are also available for $45. For more information, call © **305/573-8687** or log onto www.miami touristbus.com.

SIGHTSEEING TOURS

While there are several sightseeing tour operators in Miami, most, unfortunately, either don't speak English or are just plain shoddy. The following is the one we'd recommend:

Miami Nice Excursion Travel and Service ⊛ Pick your destination, and the Miami Nice tours will take you to the Everglades, Fort Lauderdale, South Beach, the Seaquarium, Key West, Cape Canaveral, or wherever else you desire. The best trip for first-timers is the City Tour, a comprehensive tour of the entire city and its various neighborhoods. If you've got the time, you will definitely want to add on a side trip to the Everglades and/or Key West (though I suggest exploring the Everglades on your own). Included in most Miami trips is a fairly comprehensive city tour narrated by a knowledgeable guide. The company is one of the oldest in town.

18430 Collins Ave., Miami Beach. © **305/949-9180**. http://miaminicetours.com. Tours are $29–$55 adults, $25 children. Daily 7am–10pm. Call ahead for directions to various pickup areas.

SPECIALIZED TOURS

In addition to those listed below, a great option for seeing the city is to take a tour led by **Dr. Paul George.** Dr. George is a history teacher at Miami–Dade Community College and a historian at the Historical Museum of Southern Florida. He also happens to be "Mr. Miami." There's a set calendar of tours (including the Murder, Mystery, and Mayhem Bus Tour detailed below), and all of them are fascinating to South Florida buffs. Tours focus on neighborhoods, such as Little Havana, Brickell Avenue, or Key Biscayne, and on themes, such as Miami cemeteries and the Miami River. The often long-winded discussions can be a bit much for those who just want a quick look around, but Dr. George certainly knows his stuff. The cost is $15 to $25; reservations are required (© **305/ 375-1621**). Tours leave from the Historical Museum at 101 W. Flagler St., Downtown.

Biltmore Hotel Tour ⊛⊛⊛ *(Value* Take advantage of these free Sunday walking tours to enjoy the hotel's beautiful grounds. The Biltmore is chock-full of history and mystery, including a few ghosts; go out there and see for yourself. In addition, there are also free weekly fireside sessions that are open to the public and presented by Miami Storytellers. Learn about the hotel's early days and rich stories of the city's past. These wonderful sessions are held in the main lobby by the fireplace and are accompanied by a glass of champagne. Call ahead to confirm.

1200 Anastasia Ave., Coral Gables. ✆ **305/445-1926.** www.biltmorehotel.com. Free admission. Tours depart on Sun at 1:30, 2:30, and 3:30pm. Call for times of storytelling sessions.

Coral Gables Art and Gallery Tour ★★★ *Value*   This is a fabulous and *free* event that draws art aficionados and the generally curious to sip wine and analyze the various works of art displayed in the many galleries of Coral Gables featuring American folk, African, Native American, and Latin art and photography. On the first Friday of every month, art lovers are shuttled to more than 20 galleries that participate in Gables Night. Pick one up from outside any of the galleries in the area. Most galleries are on Ponce de León Boulevard, between SW 40th and SW 24th streets. The vans run continuously from 7 to 10pm.

Various locations in Coral Gables. For more information, call Elite Fine Art (✆ **305/448-3800**), or stop by any of the galleries in the area. Free. First Fri of the month 7–10pm.

Miami Design Preservation League ★★   On Thursday evenings and Saturday mornings, the Design Preservation League sponsors walking tours that offer a fascinating inside look at the city's historic Art Deco District. Tour-goers meet for a 1½-hour walk through some of America's most exuberantly "architectured" buildings. The league led the fight to designate this area a National Historic District and is proud to share the splendid locale with visitors. Also, see p. 168 for more information.

Art Deco Welcome Center, 1001 Ocean Dr., South Beach. ✆ **305/672-2014.** www.mdpl.org. Walking tours $10 per person. Tours leave Sat at 10:30am and Thurs at 6:30pm. Self-guided audio tours also available daily for $10. No reservations necessary. Call ahead for updated schedules.

Murder, Mystery, and Mayhem Bus Tour ★★★   Visit the past by video and bus to Miami-Dade's most celebrated crimes and criminals from the 1800s to the present. From the murder spree of the Ashley Gang to the most notorious murders and crimes of our century, including the murder of designer Gianni Versace, historian Paul George conducts a most fascinating 3-hour tour of scandalous proportions.

Leaves Sat at 10pm from the Dade Cultural Center, 101 W. Flagler St., Miami. Tickets $35. Advance reservations required; call ✆ **305/375-1621.**

Second Thursdays: Miami Beach Arts Night ★★★ *Value*   The artistic equivalent of a triathlon, this free cultural open house in Miami Beach takes place on the second Thursday of every month at various venues throughout the city. Hear a string quartet at an area church and then hop on the shuttle for a Haitian dance performance at the Miami Beach Recreation Center. A celebration of the arts, Second Thursdays are a wonderful way to explore the rich and diverse cultures that make the city such a fascinating melting pot.

Various venues. ✆ **305/673-7600.** www.2ndthursdays.com. Free. Second Thurs of every month 6–9pm.

7 Watersports

There are many ways to get well acquainted with Miami's wet look. Choose your own adventure from the suggestions listed below.

BOATING

Private rental outfits include **Boat Rental Plus,** 2400 Collins Ave., Miami Beach (✆ **305/534-4307**), where 50-horsepower 18-foot powerboats rent for some of the best prices on the beach. There's a 2-hour minimum and rates go from $99 to $449, including taxes and gas. They also have great specials on Sundays. A $250 cash or credit card deposit is required. Cruising is permitted only in and around Biscayne Bay. Ocean access is prohibited. Renters must be over 21. The rental office is at 23rd Street, on the inland waterway in Miami Beach. It's open daily from 10am to sunset. If you want a specific type of boat, call ahead to reserve. Otherwise, show up and take what's available.

Club Nautico of Coconut Grove, 2560 S. Bayshore Dr. (© **305/858-6258**), rents high-quality powerboats for fishing, water-skiing, diving, and cruising in the bay or ocean. All boats are Coast Guard equipped, with VHF radios and safety gear. Rates range from $199 for 4 hours and $299 for 8 hours, to as much as $419 on weekends. Club Nautico is open daily from 9am to 5pm (weather permitting). Other locations include the Crandon Park Marina, 4000 Crandon Blvd., Key Biscayne (© **305/361-9217**), with the same rates and hours as the Coconut Grove location; and the Miami Beach Marina, Pier E, 300 Alton Rd., South Beach (© **305/673-2502**), where rates range from $229 for 4 hours and from $299 for 8 hours. Nautico on Miami Beach is open daily from 9am to 5pm. For money-saving coupons, log on to www.boatrent.com.

JET SKIS/WAVERUNNERS

Don't miss a chance to tour the islands on the back of your own powerful water-craft. Bravery is, however, a prerequisite, as Miami's waterways are full of speeding jet-skiers and boaters who think they're in the Indy 500. Many beachfront concessionaires rent a variety of these popular (and loud) water scooters. The latest models are fast and smooth. Try **Tony's Jet Ski Rentals,** 3601 Rickenbacker Causeway, Key Biscayne (© **305/361-8280**), one of the city's largest rental shops, located on a private beach in the Miami Marine Stadium lagoon. There are three models available accommodating up to three people. Rates range from $45 for a half hour to $80 for a full hour, depending on the number of riders. Tony's is open daily from 10:30am to 6:30pm.

KAYAKING

The laid-back **Urban Trails Kayak Company** rents boats at 10800 Collins Ave. in South Beach (© **305/947-1302**). The outfitters here give interested explorers a map to take with them and quick instructions on how to work the paddles and boats. They also operate very scenic 4-hour guided tours through rivers with mangroves and islands as your destination—less than 10 people on the tour costs $45 per person; more than 10 people costs $35 per person. These must be booked in advance. Rates are $8 an hour, $20 for up to 4 hours, and $25 for over 4 hours. Tandems (for two people) are $12 an hour, $30 for up to 4 hours, and $35 for the day. Open daily from 9am to 5pm.

SAILING

You can rent sailboats and catamarans through the beachfront concessions desk of several top resorts, such as the Doral Golf Resort and Spa and Dezerland Beach Resort Hotel (see p. 110 and p. 98).

Sailboats of Key Biscayne Rentals and Sailing School, in the Crandon Marina (next to Sundays on the Bay), 4000 Crandon Blvd., Key Biscayne (© **305/361-0328** days, 305/279-7424 evenings), can also get you out on the water. A 22-foot sailboat rents for $27 an hour or $81 for a half day. A Cat-25 or J24 is available for $35 an hour or $110 for a half day. If you've always had a dream to win the America's Cup but can't sail, the able teachers at Sailboats will get you started. They offer a 10-hour course over 5 days for $300 for one person or $400 for you and a buddy.

Shake-a-Leg, 2600 Bayshore Dr., Coconut Grove (© **305/858-5550**), is a membership-mostly sailing and boating organization that caters to the physically challenged by offering unique sailing programs specifically designed for those with physical disabilities. The program offers instructional lessons on kayaking and sailing and features certified instructors who will work with the student as they develop boating skills at their own pace. Shake-a-Leg members also welcome non-physically disabled volunteers for activities on and off the water. It costs $60 for nonmembers to rent a boat for 3 hours; free for volunteers and members of Shake-a-Leg. Open Wednesday through Sunday from 9am to 5pm.

SCUBA DIVING & SNORKELING

In 1981, the U.S. government began a wide-scale project designed to increase the number of habitats available to marine organisms. One of the program's major accomplishments has been the creation of nearby artificial reefs, which have attracted all kinds of tropical plants, fish, and animals. In addition, Biscayne National Park (see "Biscayne National Park," in chapter 10, "The Everglades & Biscayne National Park") offers a protected marine environment just south of downtown.

Several dive shops around the city offer organized weekend outings, either to the reefs or to one of over a dozen old shipwrecks around Miami's shores. Check "Divers" in the Yellow Pages for rental equipment and for a full list of undersea tour operators.

Diver's Paradise of Key Biscayne, 4000 Crandon Blvd. (© **305/361-3483**), offers two dive expeditions daily to the more than 30 wrecks and artificial reefs off the coast of Miami Beach and Key Biscayne. You can take a 3-day certification course for $399, which includes all the dives and gear. If you already have your C-card, a dive trip costs about $90 if you need equipment and only $35 if you bring your own gear. It's open Monday to Friday from 10am to 6pm and Saturday and Sunday from 8am to 6pm. Call ahead for times and locations of dives. For snorkeling, they will also set you up with equipment and maps on where to see the best underwater sights. Rental for mask, fins, and snorkel is $15.

South Beach Divers, 850 Washington Ave., Miami Beach (© **305/531-6110**) will also be happy to tell you where to go under the sea and will provide you with rental equipment as well for $30, which includes the mask, fins, and snorkel. They also do dive trips to Key Largo three times a week and do dives off Miami on Sundays at $95 for a two-tank dive.

WINDSURFING

Many hotels rent windsurfers to their guests, but if yours doesn't have a water-sports concession stand, head for Key Biscayne.

⸨Finds⸩ Miami's Best Dive Bar

In May 2000, Jose Cuervo Tequila company celebrated Cinco de Mayo—or, as their clever marketing staff deemed it, Sinko de Mayo—by submerging an actual, $45,000 full-size margarita bar and six stools about 200 yards offshore from Ocean Drive and 3rd Street. Known as the Jose Cuervo Underwater Bar, the bar is 8 feet high and made of concrete and steel, lying 20 feet below the ocean's surface. Now an official artificial reef, it's one of South Beach's coolest—and most hidden—wreck-reational watering holes.

Sailboards Miami, Rickenbacker Causeway, Key Biscayne (© **305/361-SAIL**), operates out of big yellow trucks on Hobie Beach, the most popular wind-surfing spot in the city. For those who've never ridden a board but want to try it, they offer a 2-hour lesson for $69 that's guaranteed to turn you into a wave warrior or you get your money back. After that, you can rent a board for $26 an hour or $38 for 2 hours. If you want to make a day of it, a 10-hour prepaid card costs $150. These cards require you to prepay, but they also reduce the price by about $70 for the day. You can use the card all year, until the time on it runs out. Open daily from 10am to 5:30pm. Make your first right after the tollbooth (at the beginning of the causeway—you can't miss it) to find the outfitters.

8 More Ways to Play, Indoors & Out

BIKING

The cement promenade on the southern tip of South Beach is a great place to ride. Biking up the beach (on either the beach or along the beach on a cement pathway—which is a lot easier!) is great for surf, sun, sand, exercise, and people-watching—just be sure to keep your eyes on the road, as the scenery can be most distracting. Most of the big beach hotels rent bicycles, as does the **Miami Beach Bicycle Center,** 601 5th Street, South Beach (© **305/674-0150**), which charges $5 per hour or $14 per day. It's open Monday to Saturday from 10am to 7pm, Sunday from 10am to 5pm.

Bikers can also enjoy more than 130 miles of paved paths throughout Miami. The beautiful and quiet streets of Coral Gables and Coconut Grove are great for bicyclists. Several bike trails are spread throughout these neighborhoods, where old trees form canopies over wide, flat roads lined with grand homes and quaint street markers.

The terrain in Key Biscayne is perfect for biking, especially along the park and beach roads. If you don't mind the sound of cars whooshing by your bike lane, **Rickenbacker Causeway** is also fantastic, since it is one of the only bikeable inclines in Miami from which you get fantastic elevated views. However, be warned that this is a grueling ride, especially going up the causeway. **Key Biking,** 61 Harbor Dr., Key Biscayne (© **305/361-0061**), rents mountain bikes for $5 an hour or $15 a day. It's open Monday through Friday from 10am to 7pm, Saturday from 10am to 6pm, and Sunday from 11am to 4pm.

If you want to avoid the traffic altogether, head out to **Shark Valley** in the Everglades National Park—one of South Florida's most scenic bicycle trails and a favorite haunt of city-weary locals. For more information, see chapter 10.

For a decent list of trail suggestions throughout South Florida, visit www.geocities.com/floutdoorzone/bike.html. *Biking note:* Children under the age of 16 are required by Florida law to wear a helmet, which can be purchased at any bike store or retail outlet selling biking supplies.

FISHING

Fishing licenses are required in Florida. If you go out with one of the fishing charter boats listed below, you are automatically accredited, because the companies are. If you go out on your own, however, you must have a Florida fishing license, which costs $16.50. Call © **888/FISH-FLORIDA** for more information.

Some of the best surf casting in the city can be had at **Haulover Beach Park** at Collins Avenue and 105th Street, where there's a bait-and-tackle shop right on the pier. **South Pointe Park,** at the southern tip of Miami Beach, is another

C A Berry Good Time

South Florida's farming region has been steadily shrinking in the face of industrial expansion, but you'll still find several spots where you can get back to nature while indulging in a local gastronomic delight—picking your own produce at the "U-Pic-'Em" farms that dot South Dade's landscape. Depending on what's in season, you can get everything from fresh herbs and vegetables to a mélange of citrus fruits and berries. During berry season—January to April—it's not uncommon to see hardy pickers leaving the groves with hands and faces that are stained a tale-telling crimson and garnished with happy smiles. On your way through South Dade, keep an eye out for the bright red "U-Pic-'Em" signs.

There are also a number of fantastic fruit stands in the region.

Burr's Berry Farms, 12741 SW 216th St. (*C* **305/251-0145**), located in the township of Goulds about an hour from downtown Miami, has created a sensation with their fabulous strawberry milk shakes. To get there, go south on U.S. 1 and turn right on SW 216th Street. The fruit stand is about 1 mile west. Open daily from 9am to 5:30pm.

For fresh fruit in a tasty pastry or tart, head over to **Knaus Berry Farm** at 15980 SW 248th St. (*C* **305/247-0668**), in an area known as the Redlands. Some people erroneously call this farm an Amish farm, but in actuality it's run by a sect of German Baptists. The stand offers items ranging from fresh flowers to homemade ice cream, but be sure to indulge in one of their famous homemade cinnamon buns. Be prepared to wait on a long line to stock up—people flock here from as far away as Palm Beach. Head south on U.S. 1 and turn right on 248th Street. The stand is 2½ miles further on the left-hand side. Open Monday through Saturday from 8am to 5:30pm.

popular fishing spot and features a long pier, comfortable benches, and a great view of the ships passing through Government Cut, the deep channel made when the port of Miami was dug.

You can also do some deep-sea fishing in the Miami area. One bargain outfitter, the **Kelley Fishing Fleet,** at the Haulover Marina, 10800 Collins Ave. (at 108th St.), Miami Beach (*C* **305/945-3801**), has half-day, full-day, and night fishing aboard diesel-powered "party boats." The fleet's emphasis on drifting is geared toward trolling and bottom fishing for snapper, sailfish, and mackerel. Half-day and night fishing trips are $29 for adults and $20 for children up to 10 years old; full-day trips are $40 for adults and $25 for children; Prices are $5 cheaper if you have your own rod. Daily departures are scheduled at 9am, 1:45pm, and 8pm; reservations are recommended.

Also at the Haulover Marina is the charter boat *Helen C* (10800 Collins Ave.; *C* **305/947-4081**). Although there's no shortage of private charter boats here, Capt. Dawn Mergelsberg is a good pick, since she puts individuals together to get a full boat. Her *Helen* is a twin-engine 55-footer, equipped for big-game "monster" fish like marlin, tuna, dolphin fish, shark, and sailfish. The cost is $85 per person. Private, full-day trips are available for groups of six people per vessel and cost $800. Group rates and specials are also available. Sailings are scheduled for 8am to noon and 1 to 5pm daily; call for reservations. Children are welcome.

Key Biscayne offers deep-sea fishing to those willing to get their hands dirty and pay a bundle. The competition among the boats is fierce, but the prices are basically the same no matter which you choose. The going rate is about $400 to $450 for a half day and $600 to $700 for a full day of fishing. These rates are usually for a party of up to six, and the boats supply you with rods and bait as well as instruction for first-timers. Some will take you out to the Upper Keys if the fish aren't biting in Miami.

You might also consider the following boats, all of which sail out of the Key Biscayne marina and are in relatively good shape and nicer than most out there: *Sunny Boy III* (© 305/361-2217), *Queen B* (© 305/361-2528), and *L & H* (© 305/361-9318). Call for reservations.

Bridge fishing in Biscayne Bay is also popular in Miami; you'll see people with poles over almost every waterway. But look carefully for signs telling you whether it's legal to do so wherever you are. Some bridges forbid fishing.

GAMBLING

Although gambling is technically illegal in Miami, there are plenty of loopholes that allow all kinds of wagering. Gamblers can try their luck at offshore casinos or on shore at bingo, jai alai, card rooms, horse tracks, dog races, and Native American reservations.

Especially popular is **Miccosukee Indian Gaming,** 500 SW 177th Ave. (off S.R. 41, in West Miami on the outskirts of the Everglades; © **800/741-4600** or 305/222-4600), where a touch of Vegas meets West Miami. This tacky casino isn't Caesar's Palace, but you can play tab slots, high-speed bingo (watch out for the serious blue-haired players who will scoff if you make too much noise or if you win before they do), and even poker (with a $10 maximum pot). With more than 85,000 square feet of playing space, the complex even offers overnight accommodations for those who can't get enough of the thrill and don't want to make the hour-long trip back to downtown Miami. Take the Florida Turnpike South towards Florida City/Key West. Take the SW 8th Street Exit (#25) and turn left onto SW 8th Street. Drive for about 3½ miles and then turn left onto Krome Avenue. You can't miss it—it's the only thing there!

Recently, many of Miami's sketchier gambling cruise operators have been shut down. The classiest and most legit gambling cruise still in business is the *Casino Princesa,* which docks behind the Hard Rock Cafe in Bayside Marketplace. This 200-foot, $15 million yacht has more than 200 slot machines, 32 tables, a restaurant, and four lounges in 10,000 square feet of gaming space on two

---

Tips **A Fisherman's Friend**

The Biscayne Bay area is prime tarpon fishing country and a pretty good spot for a lot of other trophy sportfish: snook, bonefish, dolphin fish, and sailfish. For a fee, local guides are happy to show you the hot spots and make sure you reel one in. One such guide is **Capt. David Parsons** (© 305/ 968-9603), who owns a great 28-foot boat, *Hakuna Matata.* He knows where the fish are biting, and will take you from Biscayne Bay to the Atlantic Ocean in search of the best catch of the day for a steep $550 for four people, including rods, gear, and bait. All you bring is food/drink.

decks. It's also a major bargain (unless, of course, you lose) at $10.95 per person. Ships sail for 4½ hours from 12:30 to 5pm daily and also from 7:30pm to midnight on weekend nights. They will also pick you up at your hotel. Call ℂ **305/379-5825** for updated schedules.

GOLF

There are more than 50 private and public golf courses in the Miami area. Contact the **Greater Miami Convention and Visitors Bureau** (ℂ **800/933-8448**; www.miamiandbeaches.com) for a list of courses and costs.

The best hotel courses in Miami are found at the **Doral Golf Resort and Spa** (see p. 110), home of the legendary Blue Monster course as well as the Gold Course, designed by Raymond Floyd; the Great White Shark Course; and the Silver Course, refinished by Jerry Pate.

Other hotels with excellent golf courses include the **Turnberry Isle Resort & Club** (see p. 112), with two Robert Trent Jones–designed courses for guests and members, and the **Biltmore Hotel** ⊛⊛ (see p. 106), which is my pick for best public golf course, because of its modest greens fees and an 18-hole par-71 course located on the hotel's spectacular grounds. It must be good: Despite his penchant for privacy, former President Bill Clinton prefers teeing off at this course over any other in Miami!

Otherwise, the following represent some of the area's best public courses. **Crandon Park Golf Course,** formerly known as the Links, 6700 Crandon Blvd., Key Biscayne (ℂ **305/361-9129**), is the number one ranked municipal course in the state and one of the top five in the country. The park is situated on 200 bayfront acres and offers a pro shop, rentals, lessons, carts, and a lighted driving range. The course is open daily from dawn to dusk; greens fees (including cart) are $86 per person during the winter and $45 per person during the summer. Special twilight rates are available.

One of the most popular courses among real enthusiasts is the semi-private **Doral Park Golf and Country Club,** 5001 NW 104th Ave., West Miami (ℂ **305/591-8800**); it's not related to the Doral Hotel or spa. Call to book in advance, since this challenging 18-holer is extremely popular. The course is open from 6:30am to 6pm during the winter and until 7pm during the summer. Cart and greens fees vary, so call ℂ **305/594-0954** for information.

Known as one of the best in the city, the **Golf Club of Miami,** 6801 Miami Gardens Dr., at NW 68th Avenue, North Miami (ℂ **305/829-8456**), has three 18-hole courses of varying degrees of difficulty. You'll encounter lush fairways, rolling greens, and some history to boot. The west course, designed in 1961 by Robert Trent Jones and updated in the 1990s by the PGA, was where Jack Nicklaus played his first professional tournament and Lee Trevino won his first professional championship. The course is open daily from 6:30am to sunset. Cart and greens fees are $45 to $75 per person during the winter, and $20 to $34 per person during the summer. Special twilight rates are available.

⸜Tips **Par for the Course**

You can get information about most Florida courses, including current greens fees and reserve tee times, through **Tee Times USA**, P.O. Box 641, Flagler Beach, FL 32136 (ℂ **800/374-8633**, 888/465-3567, or 904/439-0001; fax 904/439-0099; www.teetimesusa.com). This company also publishes a vacation guide that includes many stay-and-play golf packages.

Golfers looking for some cheap practice time will appreciate **Haulover Park Beach,** 10800 Collins Ave., Miami Beach (© **305/940-6719**), in a pretty bay-side location. The longest hole on this par-27 course is 125 yards. It's open daily from 7:30am to 5:30pm during the winter, and until 7:30pm during the summer. Greens fees are $5 per person during the winter and $4 per person during the summer. Handcarts cost $1.40.

HEALTH CLUBS

Being situated in a very body-conscious city, many of Miami's hotels have state-of-the-art gyms. The **David Barton Gym** at the Delano Hotel, the **Spa of Eden** at the Eden Roc Hotel, and the fitness center at the **Biltmore Hotel** are just some examples of the impressive and state-of-the-art equipment and facilities some Miami hotels can boast. Guests of hotels with health clubs can usually use the equipment for free (though not at the Delano's gym, where guests have to pay $15 a day!). Although many of Miami's full-service hotels have fitness centers and may be convenient, you can't always count on them in less-upscale establishments or in the small Art Deco District hotels. Instead, you may want to turn to the several health clubs around the city that will take in nonmembers on a daily basis. For **Bally's Total Fitness,** dial © **800/777-1117** to find the clubs closest to where you'll be staying. (There are no outlets on the beaches; most are in South Miami.) One of the most popular clubs, which welcomes walk-in guests is **Crunch,** 1253 Washington Ave., South Beach (© **305/674-8222**), where you might work out on the top-of-the-line equipment with Cindy Crawford, Madonna, or any of a number of supermodels when they're in town. Use of the facility is $18 daily or $65 weekly. It keeps late hours, especially in season, when it's often open until midnight.

IN-LINE SKATING

Miami's consistently flat terrain makes in-line skating a breeze. Lincoln Road, for example, is a virtual skating rink as bladers compete with bikers and walkers for a slab of slate. But the city's heavy traffic and construction do make it tough to find long routes suitable for blading.

Because of the popularity of blading and skateboarding, the city has passed a law prohibiting skating on the west side (the cafe-lined strip) of Ocean Drive in the evenings, as well as a law that all bladers must skate slowly and safely. Also, if you're going to partake in the sport, remember to keep a pair of sandals or sneakers with you, since many area shops won't allow you inside with skates on.

Despite all the rules, you can still have fun, and the following rental outfit can help chart an interesting course for you and supply you with all the necessary gear. In South Beach, **Fritz's Skate Shop,** 726 Lincoln Rd. Mall (© **305/532-1954**), rents top-quality skates, including safety pads, for $8 per hour, $24 per day, and $34 overnight. If you're an in-line skater newbie, an instructor will hold your hand for $25 an hour. The shop also stocks lots of gear and clothing.

SWIMMING

There is no shortage of water in the Miami area. See the Venetian Pool listing (p. 178) and the "Miami's Beaches" section earlier in this chapter for descriptions of good swimming options.

TENNIS

Hundreds of tennis courts in South Florida are open to the public for a minimal fee. Most courts operate on a first-come, first-served basis, and are open

On Location in Miami

With its warm weather, picturesque skylines, and gorgeous sunsets, Miami is the perfect setting for making movies.

Since the earliest days of the film industry, Miami has had a starring role in some of America's most celebrated celluloid classics, from the Marx Brothers' first feature, *The Cocoanuts* (1929), to the 1941 classic, *Citizen Kane,* which used the spectacular South Florida coastline as the setting for Kane's own Hearst Castle, Xanadu. As the film industry evolved and productions became more elaborate, Miami was thrice seized by a suave international man of intrigue known as Bond, James Bond, in *Dr. No, Live and Let Die,* and *Goldfinger.* In the past 5 years, there were over 60 major motion pictures filmed in Miami–Dade County, from action flicks like *True Lies* and *Any Given Sunday* to comedies such as *There's Something About Mary* and dramas such as *Random Hearts.*

At any given time of day—or night—actors, directors, and film crews can be spotted on the sands and streets of Miami working on what may be the next blockbuster to hit the big screen. Watching a film being shot is fun, free entertainment. Unfortunately, filming schedules are not publicized, so keep an eye out for CREW signs posted throughout the city and check with hotel personnel, who are usually up-to-date on who's in town shooting what. Who knows? You could be discovered!

from sunrise to sunset. For information and directions, call the **City of Miami Beach Recreation, Culture, and Parks Department** (© 305/673-7730) or the **City of Miami Parks and Recreation Department** (© 305/575-5256).

Of the 590 public tennis courts throughout Miami, the three hard courts and seven clay courts at the **Key Biscayne Tennis Association,** 6702 Crandon Blvd. (© 305/361-5263), are the best and most beautiful. Because of this, they often get crowded on weekends. You'll play on the same courts as Lendl, Graf, Evert, McEnroe, and other greats; this is also the venue for one of the world's biggest annual tennis events, the NASDAQ 100 Open (see p. 21). There's a pleasant, if limited, pro shop, plus many good pros. Only four courts are lit at night, but if you reserve at least 48 hours in advance, you can usually take your pick. They cost $6 per person per hour. Courts are open daily from 8am to 9pm.

Other courts are pretty run of the mill and can be found in most neighborhoods. I do, however, recommend the **Miami Beach public courts at Flamingo Park,** 1001 12th St. in South Beach (© 305/673-7761), where there are 19 clay courts that cost $2.50 per person an hour during the day and $3 per person an hour at night. It's first come, first serve.

Hotels with the best tennis facilities are the Biltmore, Turnberry Isle Resort and Spa, the Doral Resort and Spa, and the Inn and Spa at Fisher Island. See chapter 5, "Where to Stay in Miami," for information about these accommodations.

9 Spectator Sports

Check the *Miami Herald*'s sports section for a daily listing of local events and the paper's Friday "Weekend" section for comprehensive coverage and in-depth reports. For last-minute tickets, call the venue directly, since many season ticket holders sell singles and return unused tickets. Expensive tickets are available from brokers or individuals listed in the classified sections of the local papers. Some tickets are also available through **Ticketmaster** (© **305/358-5885**).

BASEBALL

The **Florida Marlins** shocked the sports world in 1997 when they became the youngest expansion team to win a World Series, but then floundered as their star players were sold off by former owner Wayne Huizenga. As long as the rebuilding process continues and the Marlins continue to struggle, tickets are easy to come by. If you're interested in catching a game, be warned: The summer heat in Miami can be unbearable, even in the evenings.

Home games are held at the **Pro Player Stadium,** 2267 NW 199th St., North Miami Beach (© **305/626-7426**). Tickets range from $4 to $50. Box office hours are Monday to Friday from 8:30am to 6pm, Saturday from 8:30am to 4pm, and before games; tickets are also available through Ticketmaster. The team currently holds spring training in Melbourne, FL.

BASKETBALL

The **Miami Heat** (© **305/577-HEAT** or 305/835-7000), now led by celebrity coach Pat Riley, made its NBA debut in November 1988 and their games remain one of Miami's hottest tickets. Courtside seats are full of visiting celebrities from Puff Daddy to Madonna. The season lasts from October to April, with most games beginning at 7:30pm. They play in the brand-new waterfront **American Airlines Arena** located downtown on Biscayne Boulevard. Tickets are $14 to $50. Box office hours are Monday to Friday from 10am to 4pm (until 8pm on game nights); tickets are also available through Ticketmaster.

FOOTBALL

Miami's golden boys are the **Miami Dolphins,** the city's most recognizable team, followed by thousands of "dolfans." The team plays at least eight home games during the season, between September and December, at **Pro Player Stadium,** 2267 NW 199th St., North Miami Beach (© **305/620-2578**). Tickets cost between $20 and $40. The box office is open Monday to Friday from 8:30am to 5:30pm; tickets are also available through Ticketmaster.

HORSE RACING

Located on the Dade–Broward County border in Hallandale (just north of North Miami Beach/Aventura) is **Gulfstream Park,** at U.S. 1 and Hallandale Beach Boulevard (© **305/931-7223;** www.gulfstreampark.com), South Florida's very own version of the Kentucky Derby, albeit not as sceney. This horse track is a haven for serious gamblers and voyeurs alike. Large purses and important races are commonplace at this sprawling suburban course, and the track is typically crowded, especially during its amusing and entertaining concert series from January to April featuring has-beens and one-hit wonders such as Cindy Lauper, REO Speedwagon, and Bryan Adams on the front lawn for just $5. Call for schedules. Admission is $3 to the grandstand and $5 to the clubhouse; parking is free. From January through March, post times are Wednesday to Monday at 1pm.

You might remember the pink flamingos at **Hialeah Park** ✿, 2200 E. 4th Ave., Hialeah (© **305/885-8000;** www.hialeahpark.com), from *Miami Vice.* This famous flamingo colony is the largest of its kind. The track, listed on the National Register of Historic Places, is one of the most beautiful in the world, featuring old-fashioned stands and acres of immaculately manicured grounds. It is open to the public, for free, to tour around and see the spectacular grounds.

ICE HOCKEY

The young **Florida Panthers** (© **954/835-7000**) have already made history. In the 1994–95 season, they played in the Stanley Cup finals, and they have amassed a legion of fans who love them. Much to the disappointment of Miamians, they moved to a new venue in Sunrise, the next county north of Miami–Dade, more than an hour from downtown Miami. Call for directions and ticket information.

JAI ALAI

Jai alai, sort of a Spanish-style indoor lacrosse, was introduced to Miami in 1924 and is regularly played in two Miami-area frontons (the buildings in which jai alai is played). Although the sport has roots stemming from ancient Egypt, the game, as it's now played, was invented by Basque peasants in the Pyrenees Mountains during the 17th century.

Players use woven baskets, called *cestas,* to hurl balls, called *pelotas,* at speeds that sometimes exceed 170 mph. Spectators, who are protected behind a wall of glass, place bets on the evening's players. The Florida Gaming Corporation owns the jai alai operations throughout the state, making betting on this sport as legal as buying a lottery ticket.

The **Miami Jai Alai Fronton,** 3500 NW 37th Ave., at NW 35th Street (© **305/633-6400**), is America's oldest fronton, dating from 1926. It schedules 13 games per night, which typically last 10 to 20 minutes, but can occasionally go much longer. Admission is $1 to the grandstand, $5 to the clubhouse. There are year-round games on Monday and Wednesday to Saturday at 7pm, and matinees on Monday, Wednesday, and Saturday at noon. This is the main location where jai alai is played in Miami. The other South Florida jai alai venue is in Dania, near the Fort Lauderdale Hollywood International Airport. See p. 316 for more information on **Dania Jai Alai.**

Jai Alai Explained

Jai alai originated in the Basque country of Northern Spain, where players used to use church walls as their courts. The game looks very much like lacrosse, actually, with rules very similar to handball or tennis. The game is played on a court with numbered lines. What makes the game totally unique, however, is the requirement that the ball must be returned in one continuous motion. The server must bounce the ball behind the serving line and with the basket, must hurl the ball to the front wall, with the aim being that, upon rebound, the ball will bounce between lines 4 and 7. If it doesn't, it is an under or over serve and the other team receives a point.

10 Cruises & Other Caribbean Getaways

Cruising has come a long way since the days of bingo, shuffleboard, and even the delusional *Love Boat*. Whether you prefer megaships with rock-climbing walls or a smaller, less elaborate ship that just sails you to your destination, a floating vacation can be a very enticing option for people traveling to South Florida. The proximity to the Caribbean makes a 3-, 4-, or 7-day cruise an excellent diversion from the hustle and bustle of the big city.

If you want to catch a weekend in the Caribbean while you're in South Florida but aren't enthralled with the idea of boat travel, there are a number of air packages available as well. Travel to Cuba is severely restricted from Miami (or anywhere in the United States) for all but those who have obtained licenses from the U.S. State Department (see details at www.destinationcuba.com/whocanvisit.htm), although many people choose to go there from Mexico, Jamaica, or the Bahamas.

The following sections aren't intended to be detailed descriptions of the cruising and package options available out of Miami and the Keys—that would fill up an entire book on its own—but they will give you a good overview of the cruising and package picture.

CRUISES

The Port of Miami is the world's busiest cruise-ship port, with a passenger load of close to 3 million annually. The popularity of these cruises shows no sign of tapering off, and the trend in ships is toward bigger, more luxurious liners. Usually all-inclusive, cruises offer value and simplicity compared to other vacation options. Most of the Caribbean-bound cruise ships sail weekly out of the Port of Miami. They are relatively inexpensive, can be booked without advance notice, and make for an excellent excursion.

The Port of Miami is very close to downtown Miami, but the most popular pre- and postcruise destination in Miami is South Beach (about a 10-minute ride from the port), because of its proximity to the port and the fact that it's a relatively small (and walkable) area full of nightlife, beaches, hotels, and restaurants (see the South Beach sections of this book). If you're just looking for a quick overnight stay, your best bet may be one of the downtown-area hotels, which are closest to the port. The only two in the immediate area that I'd recommend, however, are the Hotel Inter-Continental Miami (see p. 103), which is literally up the block from the port, or the Biscayne Bay Marriott (see p. 104), located about 5 minutes away. For food and shopping, Bayside Marketplace (see p. 209) is within walking distance of the port. For other restaurants in this area, check the "Downtown Miami" section of chapter 6, "Where to Dine in Miami," beginning on p. 144. Cabs are abundant at the port. A ride to the airport should cost about $25 and a ride to South Beach should be about $10.

All the shorter cruises (3 and 4 days) are well equipped for gambling. Their casinos open as soon as the ship clears U.S. waters—typically 45 minutes after leaving port. Usually, four full-size meals are served daily, with portions so huge they're impossible to finish. Games, movies, and other onboard activities ensure you're always busy. Passengers can board up to 2 hours before departure for meals, games, and cocktails.

There are dozens of cruises from which to choose—from 1-day excursions to a trip around the world. You can get a full list of options from the **Metro-Dade**

Seaport Department, 1015 North America Way, Miami, FL 33132 (© **305/ 371-7678**). It's open Monday through Friday from 8am to 5pm.

The cruise lines and ships listed below offer 3-, 4-, and 7-night cruises to the Caribbean, Key West, and other longer itineraries that often change. If you want more information, contact the individual line, or, for Bahamas cruises, call the **Bahamas Tourist Office,** 19495 Biscayne Blvd., Suite 809, Aventura, FL 33180 (© **305/932-0051**). All passengers must travel with a passport or proof of citizenship for reentry into the United States.

For detailed information on Caribbean cruises, pick up a copy of *Frommer's Caribbean Cruises & Ports of Call.*

Carnival Cruise Lines (© **800/327-9501** or 305/599-2200; www.carnival. com) has 3- and 4-day cruises to Key West and the Caribbean as well as 7-day excursions that include stops in Mexico, Jamaica, and the Cayman Islands. Carnival's ships are appropriately known as "Fun Ships," catering to a young party-hearty crowd. There's also a smoke-free ship called the *Paradise.* Cruises usually depart from Miami Friday through Monday. Prices range from $400 to $3,000 (lower rates are usually available, depending on season), not including port charges, which can be as high as $200 per person.

Cunard (© **800/528-6273** or 305/463-3000; www.cunardline.com), which moved here in late 1997, is known for its Old World elegance and caters to an older, sophisticated crowd. If you're looking for Internet cafes and ice-skating rinks, Cunard isn't for you. This line's Miami ships include the legendary throwback from the halcyon days of the mighty luxe ocean liner, *Queen Elizabeth II,* as well as the *Queen Mary II.* Itineraries are usually at least 10 days long, though there are some that last 6 days, such as the jazz, fine arts, and big-band cruises. Prices start at $3,300 per person.

Norwegian Cruise Line (© **800/327-7030** or 305/436-0866; www.ncl.com) has four ships based in Miami during the winter months and usually one in the summer. NCL is known for having the most flexible dining setup at sea, with open-seating and casual dress codes. A mixture of young and older crowds can be found on their ships. Ships go to Key West, the Bahamas, and the Western Caribbean. Its shortest cruises are 3 days; the longest—from Miami to France— is 15 days. Rates range from $199 per person for an inside cabin on the shortest cruises to $4,500 per person for the best cabin on the transcontinental journey.

Royal Caribbean International (© **800/327-6700** or 305/539-6000; www. rccl.com), one of the premier lines in Miami, has about half a dozen ships departing Miami at any given time. The Port of Miami actually had to renovate three cruise terminals in 1999—at a price of $60 million—to accommodate Royal Caribbean's 142,000-ton ship *Voyager of the Seas,* which boasts an ice-skating rink and a rock-climbing wall, among other theme-parklike diversions. *Explorer of the Seas* and *Adventure of the Seas* are the line's second and third theme parks at sea, also featuring extreme sports and an assortment of high-tech activities. As a result, RCI caters to a young and old(er), active crowd as well as families with children. The line mostly offers Caribbean cruises and some Bahamas destinations. The *Legend of the Seas* and the *Splendor of the Seas* offer 3- and 4-night Bahamas trips as for as low as less than $100 per person per day, to as high as $7,500 per person for an 11-night cruise through the Caribbean.

FLIGHTS & WEEKEND PACKAGES

For those who want a quick getaway to the Caribbean without the experience of cruising, many airlines and hotels team up to offer affordable weekend packages.

For example, the Bahamas' most entertaining and family-friendly resort, the **Atlantis** on Paradise Island (© **888-528-7155;** www.atlantis.com), is a tropical theme park offering extensive watersports plus an active casino. Reasonably priced 3-day packages start at about $390, depending on departure date. (It's generally cheaper to fly midweek.) Flights on **Continental Airlines** (© **800/ 786-7202**) depart at least twice daily from Miami International. You can also choose to stay in the company's other luxurious resorts: the **Paradise Beach Resort** or the **Ocean Club.** Book package deals through **Paradise Island Vacations** (© 800/722-7466).

Other groups that arrange competitively priced packages include **American Flyaway Vacations,** operated by American Airlines (© 800/321-2121); **Bahamas Air** (© 800/222-4262 or 305/593-1910); and **Chalks Ocean Airways** (© 305/371-8628). Call for rates, since they vary dramatically throughout the year and also depend on what type of accommodations you choose. Keep your eye on the travel section of the *Miami Herald* as well, as special deals and packages are almost always advertised.

11 Animal Parks

For a tropical climate, Miami's got a lot of nontropical animals to see, and we're not talking about the motorists on I-95. Everything from dolphins and alligators to lions, tigers, and bears call Miami home (most in parks, some in nature). Call the parks to inquire about discount packages or coupons, which may be offered at area retail stores or in local papers.

Miami Metrozoo ★★ *Kids* This 290-acre, sparsely landscaped complex (it was devastated by Hurricane Andrew) is quite a distance from Miami proper and the beaches—about 45 minutes—but worth the trip. Isolated and never really crowded, it's also completely cageless—animals are kept at bay by cleverly designed moats. This is a fantastic spot to take younger kids (the older ones seem bored and unstimulated here); there's a wonderful petting zoo and play area, and the zoo offers several daily programs designed to educate and entertain. Mufasa and Simba (of Disney fame) were modeled on a couple of Metrozoo's lions. Other residents include two rare white Bengal tigers, a Komodo dragon, rare koala bears, a number of kangaroos, and an African meerkat. The air-conditioned Zoofari Monorail tour offers visitors a nice overview of the park. An Andean Condor exhibit opened in 2000, and the zoo is always upgrading its facilities, including the impressive aviary. *Note:* The distance between animal habitats can be great, so you'll be doing *a lot* of walking here. For this reason, there are benches and shaded gazebos strategically positioned throughout the zoo so you can rest when you need to. Also, because the zoo can be miserably hot during summer months, plan these visits in the early morning or late afternoon. Expect to spend about 3 hours here.

12400 SW 152nd St., South Miami. © 305/251-0400. www.zsf.org. Admission $8.95 adults, $4.75 children 3–12. Daily 9:30am–5:30pm (ticket booth closes at 4pm). Free parking. From U.S. 1 south, turn right on SW 152nd St. and follow signs about 3 miles to the entrance.

Miami Seaquarium ★ *Kids* *Overrated* If you've been to Orlando's SeaWorld, you may be disappointed with Miami's version, which is considerably smaller and not as well maintained. It's hardly a sprawling seaquarium, but you will want to arrive early to enjoy the effects of its mild splash. You'll need at least 3 hours to tour the 35-acre oceanarium and see all four daily shows starring a number of showy ocean mammals. You can cut your visit to 2 hours if you limit your shows to the better, albeit corny, Flipper Show and Killer Whale Show. The highly regarded Water and Dolphin Exploration Program (WADE) allows visitors to touch and swim with dolphins in the Flipper Lagoon. The program costs $125 per person and is offered twice daily, Wednesday through Sunday. Children must be at least 52 inches tall to participate. Reservations are necessary for this program. Call ☎ **305/365-2501** in advance for reservations.

4400 Rickenbacker Causeway (south side), en route to Key Biscayne. ☎ 305/361-5705. www.miami seaquarium.com. Admission $23.95 adults, $18.95 children 3–9, free for children under 3. Daily 9:30am–6pm (ticket booth closes at 4:30pm).

Monkey Jungle ✸ *Overrated*   Personally, I think this place is disgusting. It reeks, the monkeys are either sleeping or in heat, and it's really far from the city, even farther than the zoo. But if primates are your thing and you'd rather pass on the zoo, you'll be in paradise. You'll see rare Brazilian golden lion tamarins and Asian macaques. There are no cages to restrain the antics of the monkeys as they swing, chatter, and play their way into your heart. Screened-in trails wind through acres of "jungle," and daily shows feature the talents of the park's most progressive pupils. People who go here are not monkeying around—many of the park's frequent visitors are scientists and anthropologists. Despite the smell, however, I must admit that I found myself thoroughly amused by the animal antics at the Orangutans' Asiatic Ape Exhibit. Newer exhibits include the Cameroon Jungle and the Lemurs of Madagascar. If you can stand the humidity, the smell, and the bugs (flies, mosquitoes, etc.), expect to spend about 2 hours here. The park's website sometimes offers downloadable discount coupons, so if you have Internet access, take a look before you visit.

14805 SW 216th St., South Miami. ☎ 305/235-1611. www.monkeyjungle.com. Admission $15.95 adults, $12.95 seniors and active-duty military, $9.95 children 4–12. Daily 9:30am–5pm (tickets sold until 4pm). Take U.S. 1 south to SW 216th St., or from Florida Turnpike, take exit 11 and follow the signs.

Parrot Jungle and Gardens ✸✸ *Kids*   This Miami institution will take flight from its current location in South Miami in the fall of 2002 and head north in the winter of 2003 to a new $46 million home on Watson Island, along the MacArthur Causeway near Miami Beach. While the island will double as a protected bird sanctuary, the jungle's soon-to-be former digs in the heart of South Miami in a circa-1900 coral rock structure are a lot more charming and kitschier. The new 18.6-acre park will feature an Everglades exhibit, a petting zoo, and several theaters, jungle trails, and aviaries. Watch your heads because flying above are hundreds of parrots, macaws, peacocks, cockatoos, and flamingos. Continuous shows star roller-skating cockatoos, card-playing macaws, and numerous stunt-happy parrots. There are also tortoises, iguanas, and a rare albino alligator on exhibit. The park's website sometimes offers downloadable discount coupons, so if you have Internet access, take a look before you visit.

Until the move: 11000 SW 57th Ave., Southern Miami–Dade County. ☎ 305/666-7834. After the move: 1111 Parrot Jungle Trail, Watson Island (on the north side of MacArthur Causeway/I-395). ☎ 305/372-3822. www.parrotjungle.com. Admission $15.95 adults, $13.95 seniors, $10.95 children 3–10. Daily 9:30am–6pm. Cafe opens at 8am. Take U.S. 1 south and turn left at SW 57th Ave., or exit Kendall Dr. from the Florida Turnpike and turn right on SW 57th Ave.

Sea Grass Adventures ✸ *Value Kids*   Even better than the Seaquarium is Sea Grass Adventures, in which a naturalist from the Marjory Stoneman Douglas Biscayne Nature Center will introduce kids and adults to an amazing variety of creatures that live in the sea grass beds of the Bear Cut Nature Preserve near Crandon Beach on Key Biscayne. Not just a walking tour, you will be able to wade in the water with your guide and catch an assortment of sea life in nets provided by the guides. At the end of the program, participants gather on the beach while the guide explains what everyone's just caught, passing the creatures around in miniature viewing tanks. Call for available dates and reservations.

Marjory Stoneman Douglas Biscayne Nature Center, 6767 Crandon Blvd., Key Biscayne. (℗ 305/361-6767. $10 per person. Daily 10am–4pm.

12 Video Arcades & Entertainment Centers

GameWorks (★ (Kids)   Steven Spielberg's SEGA GameWorks in the Shops at Sunset Place has become the hottest place for young adults to play. You'll see kids, Gen-Xers, and baby boomers fighting off dinosaurs from *Jurassic Park,* racing in the Indy 500, swooshing down a snowy ski trail, throwing darts, and shooting pool in this sleek multilevel playground. The young at heart will find the perfect combination of vintage arcade games, high-tech videos, virtual-reality arenas, pool tables, food, and cocktails in this playground occupying more than 33,000 square feet. The GameWorks Grill serves up everything from gourmet salads to pizzas and burgers. Bring lots—and we mean lots—of change.

5701 Sunset Dr., South Miami. (℗ 305/667-4263. www.gameworks.com. Sun–Wed 11am–midnight, Thurs–Sat 11am–2am. Games 50¢–$5.

IMAX Theatre at Sunset Place (★ (Kids)   Utilizing high-tech film techniques, six-story-high screens, and wraparound digital sound, this unique movie experience really makes you feel like you're part of the action. Films tend to be on the more educational side, but kids won't mind because the effects are outstanding. Also available is a 3-D theater that really tempts you to reach out and touch the images.

5701 Sunset Dr., South Miami. (℗ 305/663-4629. www.imax.com/miami. $9 adults, $8 seniors and students, $7 children under 12. Shows daily 11am–11pm. Call for schedule.

The Scott Rakow Youth Center (★ (Kids)   This center is a hidden treasure on Miami Beach. The two-story facility boasts an ice-skating rink, bowling alleys, a basketball court, gymnasium equipment, and full-time supervision for kids in the fourth grade and up. Call for a complete schedule of organized events. The only drag is that it's not open to adults (except on Sunday, family day).

2700 Sheridan Ave., Miami Beach. (℗ 305/673-7767. Admission is $1.50 per day for children 9 to 17. Daily 2–8:30pm.

8

Miami Shopping

Miami is one of the world's premier shopping cities; more than 10 million visitors came here last year and they spent in excess of $13 billion. People come to Miami from all over—from Latin America to Hong Kong—in search of some products that are all-American (i.e., Levi's, Nikes, etc.).

So if you're not into sunbathing and outdoor activities, or you just can't take the heat, you'll be in good company in one of Miami's many malls—and you are not likely to emerge empty-handed. In addition to the strip malls, Miami offers a choice of megamalls, from the upscale Shops at Sunset to the mammoth Aventura Mall to the ritzy Bal Harbour Shops (just to name a few).

Miami also offers more unique shopping spots, such as Bayside's Marketplace, where you can buy such eclectic items as handcrafted tropical birds or jewelry made of precious stones, and Little Havana, where you can buy hand-rolled cigars and *guayabera* shirts.

You may want to order the Greater Miami Convention and Visitors Bureau's "Shop Miami: A Guide to a Tropical Shopping Adventure." Although it is limited to details on the bureau's paying members, it provides some good advice and otherwise unpublished discount offers. The glossy little pamphlet is printed in English, Spanish, and Portuguese and provides information about transportation from hotels, translation services, and shipping. Call ✆ **800/ 283-2707** or 305/539-3034 for more information.

1 The Shopping Scene

Below, you'll find descriptions of some of the more popular retail areas, where many stores are conveniently clustered together to make browsing easier.

As a general rule, shop hours are Monday through Saturday from 10am to 6pm and Sunday from noon to 5pm. Many stores stay open late (until 9pm or so) one night of the week (usually Thursday). Shops in Coconut Grove are open until 9pm Sunday through Thursday and even later on Friday and Saturday nights. South Beach's stores also stay open later—as late as midnight. Department stores and shopping malls also keep longer hours, with most staying open from 10am to 9 or 10pm Monday through Saturday, and noon to 6pm on Sunday. With all these variations, call ahead to specific stores to find out what their hours are.

The 6.5% state and local sales tax is added to the price of all nonfood purchases. Food and beverage in hotels and restaurants are taxed via the resort tax, which is 3% in Miami/South Beach and Bal Harbour, 4% in Surfside, and 2% in the rest of Miami–Dade County.

Most Miami stores can wrap your purchase and ship it anywhere in the world via United Parcel Service (UPS). If they can't, you can send it yourself, either

Miami's Shopping Scene

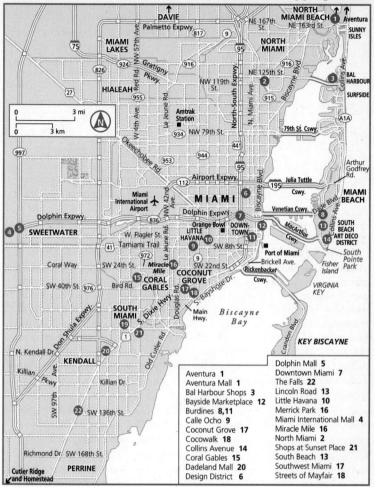

Aventura **1**
Aventura Mall **1**
Bal Harbour Shops **3**
Bayside Marketplace **12**
Burdines **8,11**
Calle Ocho **9**
Coconut Grove **17**
Cocowalk **18**
Collins Avenue **14**
Coral Gables **15**
Dadeland Mall **20**
Design District **6**

Dolphin Mall **5**
Downtown Miami **7**
The Falls **22**
Lincoln Road **13**
Little Havana **10**
Merrick Park **16**
Miami International Mall **4**
Miracle Mile **16**
North Miami **2**
Shops at Sunset Place **21**
South Beach **13**
Southwest Miami **17**
Streets of Mayfair **18**

through UPS (☎ **800/742-5877**) or through the U.S. Mail (see the Post Office Section under "Fast Facts: Miami" in chapter 4, "Getting to Know Miami").

SHOPPING AREAS

Most of Miami's shopping happens at the many megamalls scattered from one end of the county to the other; however, there is also some excellent boutique shopping and browsing to be done in the following areas (see "The Neighborhoods in Brief" in chapter 4 for more information):

AVENTURA On Biscayne Boulevard between Miami Gardens Drive and the county line at Hallandale Beach Boulevard is a 2-mile stretch of major retail stores including Best Buy, Borders, Circuit City, Linens N' Things, Marshall's, Sports Authority, and more. Also here is the mammoth Aventura Mall, housing a fabulous collection of shops and restaurants.

Impressions

Someday . . . Miami will become the great center of South American trade.

—Julia Tuttle, Miami's founder, 1896

CALLE OCHO   For a taste of Little Havana, take a walk down 8th Street between SW 27th Avenue and SW 12th Avenue, where you'll find some lively street life and many shops selling cigars, baked goods, shoes, furniture, and record stores specializing in Latin music. For help, take your Spanish dictionary.

COCONUT GROVE   Downtown Coconut Grove, centered on Main Highway and Grand Avenue and branching onto the adjoining streets, is one of Miami's most pedestrian-friendly zones. The Grove's wide sidewalks, lined with cafes and boutiques, can provide hours of browsing pleasure. Coconut Grove is best known for its chain stores (Gap, Banana Republic, etc.) and some funky holdovers from the days when the Grove was a bit more bohemian, plus excellent sidewalk cafes centered on CocoWalk and the Streets of Mayfair.

MIRACLE MILE (CORAL GABLES)   Actually only a half-mile long, this central shopping street was an integral part of George Merrick's original city plan. Today, the strip still enjoys popularity, especially for its bridal stores, ladies' shops, haberdashers, and gift shops. Recently, newer chain stores, like Barnes & Noble, Old Navy, and Starbucks, have been appearing on the Mile. **Merrick Park,** a mammoth, 850,000-square-foot upscale outdoor shopping complex between Ponce de León Boulevard and Le Jeune Road, just off the Mile, opened in the Fall of 2002 with Nordstrom, Neiman Marcus, Armani, and Yves St. Laurent on board, to name a few.

DOWNTOWN MIAMI   If you're looking for discounts on all types of goods—especially watches, fabric, buttons, lace, shoes, luggage, and leather—Flagler Street, just west of Biscayne Boulevard, is the best place to start. I wouldn't necessarily recommend buying expensive items here, as many stores seem to be on the shady side and do not understand the word *warranty.* However, you can still have fun here as long as you are a savvy shopper and don't mind haggling with people who may not have the firmest grasp on the English language. Most signs are printed in English, Spanish, and Portuguese; however, many shopkeepers may not be entirely fluent in English.

SOUTH BEACH ☆   Slowly but surely South Beach has come into its own as far as shopping is concerned. While the requisite stores—Gap, Banana Republic, et al.—have anchored here, several higher-end stores have also opened on the southern blocks of Collins Avenue, which has become the Madison Avenue of Miami. For the hippest clothing boutiques (including Armani and Armani Exchange, Ralph Lauren, Versace, Benetton, Agnes B, Guess?, Club Monaco, Kenneth Cole, and Nicole Miller, among others), stroll along this pretty strip of the Art Deco District.

For those who are interested in a little more fun with their shopping, consider South Beach's legendary Lincoln Road. This pedestrian mall, originally designed in 1957 by Morris Lapidus, recently underwent a multimillion-dollar renovation, restoring it to its former glory. Here, shoppers find an array of clothing, books, tchotchkes, and art as well as a menagerie of sidewalk cafes flanked on one end by a multiplex movie theater, and at the other, the Atlantic Ocean.

2 Shopping A to Z

ANTIQUES/COLLECTIBLES

Miami's antiques shops are scattered in small pockets around the city. Many that feature lower-priced furniture can be found in North Miami, in the 1600 block of NE 123rd Street, near West Dixie Highway. About a dozen shops sell china, silver, glass, furniture, and paintings. But you'll find the bulk of the better antiques in Coral Gables and in Southwest Miami along Bird Road between 64th and 66th avenues and between 72nd and 74th avenues. For international collections from Bali to France, check out the burgeoning scene in the Design District centered on Northeast 40th Street west of 1st Avenue. Miami also hosts several large antiques shows each year. In October and November, the most prestigious one—the **Antique Show**—hits the Miami Beach Convention Center (© **305/754-4931**). Exhibitors from all over come to display their wares, including jewelry. There's also a decent monthly show at the **Coconut Grove Convention Center** (© **305/444-8454**). Miami's huge concentration of Art Deco buildings from the '20s and '30s makes this the place to find the best selections of Deco furnishings and decorations. A word to the serious collectors: Dania Beach, up in Broward County (see chapter 12, "The Gold Coast: Hallandale to the Palm Beaches") about half an hour from downtown Miami, is the best place for antiques (it's known as the antique capital of South Florida), so you may want to consider browsing in Miami and shopping up there.

Architectural Antiques   A great place to browse—if you don't mind a little dust—this huge warehouse has an impressive stash of ironwork, bronzes, paintings, lamps, furniture, and sculptures which have been salvaged from estates worldwide. Don't be surprised to find odd items, too, like an old British phone booth or a pair of gargoyles off an ancient church. 2500 SW 28th Lane (just west of U.S. 1), Miami. © 305/285-1330. archantique@earthlink.net.

Miami Twice   While they are not technically antiques yet, the Old Florida furniture and decorations from the '30s, '40s, and '50s are great fun (and collectible). In addition to loads of Deco memorabilia, there are also vintage clothes, shoes, and jewelry. 6562 SW 40th St., South Miami. © 305/666-0127. Fax 305/661-1142.

Modernism Gallery   Specializing in 20th-century furnishings from Gilbert Rohde, Noguchi, and Heywood Wakefield, this shop has some of the most beautiful examples of Deco goods from France and the United States. If they don't have what you're looking for, ask. They possess the amazing ability to find the rarest items. 1622 Ponce de León Blvd., Coral Gables. © 888/217-2760.

Senzatempo *(Finds)*   If the names Charles Eames, George Nelson, or Gio Ponti mean anything to you, then this is where you'll want to visit. There's retro, Euro fabulous designer furniture and decorative arts from 1930 to 1960, as well as collectible watches, timepieces, and clocks. 1655 Meridian Ave. (at Lincoln Rd.), South Beach. © 305/534-5588. www.senzatempo.com.

ART GALLERIES

See p. 172 in chapter 7, "What to See & Do in Miami," for a list of some of the art galleries in the greater Miami area.

BOOKS

Barnes & Noble *(Kids)*   With half a dozen outlets in the area (Aventura, South Miami, Kendall, etc.) and more on the way, this huge chain offers anything readers could ask for, including a comfortable cafe, a large children's section, and tons of magazines. Plus, the chain gives you a 10% discount on all bestsellers and has incredible closeout specials. They often schedule readings with noted authors, too. Of the Miami-area locations, this branch has an especially nice little scene, featuring local intellectuals, students, and professors from the nearby University of Miami. 152 Miracle Mile, Coral Gables. ✆ 305/446-4152. www.bn.com.

Books & Books   A dedicated following turns out to browse at this warm and wonderful little independent shop. Enjoy the upstairs antiquarian room, which specializes in art books and first editions. If that's not enough intellectual stimulation for you, the shop hosts free lectures from noted authors, experts, and personalities almost nightly, from Monica Lewinsky to Martin Amis. At another location (933 Lincoln Rd., South Beach; ✆ 305/532-3222), you'll rub elbows with tanned and buffed South Beach bookworms sipping cappuccinos at the Russian Bear Cafe inside the store. This branch stocks a large selection of gay literature and also features lectures. 265 Aragon Ave., Coral Gables. ✆ 305/442-4408. www.booksandbooks.com.

Kafka's Cyberkafe   Check your e-mail and surf the Web while you sip a latte or snack on a sandwich or pastry with friendly neighborhood regulars. This popular used bookstore also stocks a wide range of foreign and domestic magazines and caters to an international-youth-hostel-type crowd. 1464 Washington Ave., South Beach. ✆ 305/673-9669.

CIGARS

Although it is illegal to bring Cuban cigars into the United States, somehow, forbidden *Cohibas* show up at every dinner party and nightclub in town. Not that I condone it, but if you hang around the cigar smokers in town, no doubt one will be able to tell you where you can get some of the highly prized contraband. Be careful, however, of counterfeits, which are typically Dominican cigars posing as Cubans. Cuban cigars are illegal and unless you go down a sketchy alley to buy one from a dealer (think of it as shady as a drug deal), you are going to be smoking Dominican ones.

The stores listed below sell excellent hand-rolled cigars made with domestic- and foreign-grown tobacco. Many of the *viejos* (old men) got their training in Cuba working for the government-owned factories in the heyday of Cuban cigars.

La Gloria Cubana   This tiny storefront shop employs about 45 veteran Cuban rollers who sit all day rolling the very popular torpedoes and other critically acclaimed blends. They're usually backordered, but it's worth stopping in: They will sell you a box and show you around. 1106 SW 8th St., Little Havana. ✆ 305/858-4162.

Mike's Cigars *(Finds*   Mike's recently moved to this new location, but it's one of the oldest and best smoke shops in town. Since 1950, Mike's has been selling the best from Honduras, the Dominican Republic, and Jamaica, as well as the very hot local brand, La Gloria Cubana. Many say it has the best prices, too. Mike's has the biggest selection of cigars in town and the employees speak English. 1030 Kane Concourse (at 96th St.), Bay Harbor Island. ✆ 305/866-2277. www.mikescigars.com.

COSMETICS, FRAGRANCES, BEAUTY PRODUCTS & A SALON

Brownes & Co. *(Finds*   Designed to look like an old-fashioned apothecary, this recently expanded beauty emporium combines the best selection of makeup and hair products—MAC, Shu Uemura, Kiehl's, Stila, Molton Brown, Francois Nars, and Dr. Hauschka, just to name a few—with lots of delicious-smelling bath and body stuff, plus a full-service beauty salon. Feel free to browse and sample here, as perfume-spritzing salespeople won't bother you. If you do need help, the staff is a collection of experts when it comes to beauty and hair products. Upstairs is the renowned salon, Some Like It Hot, in which you can get fabulously coiffed, colored, buffed, and waxed. If you do want to get waxed, make sure to ask for the city's best waxer, Latecia. 841 Lincoln Rd., South Beach. © 305-532-8703. www.brownesbeauty.com.

Sephora   The Disney World of makeup, Sephora offers a dizzying array of cosmetics, perfumes, and styling products. Unlike Brownes & Co., however, personal service and attentiveness is at a minimum. Because there are so many products, shopping here can be a harrowing experience. Two locations: 721 Collins Ave., South Beach © 305/532-0728, or 2982 Grand Ave., Coconut Grove © 305/448-3003.

FASHION: CLOTHING & ACCESSORIES

Miami didn't become a fashion capital until—believe it or not—the pastel-hued, Armani-clad cops on *Miami Vice* had their close-ups on the tube. Before that, Miami was all about old men in white patent leather shoes and well-tanned women in bikinis. How things have changed! Miami is now a fashion mecca in its own right, with some of the same high-end stores you'd find on Rue de Fauborg St. Honore in Paris or Bond Street in London. You'll find all the chichi labels, including Prada and Gucci, right here at the posh Bal Harbour Shops. For funkier frocks, South Beach is the place, where designers such as Cynthia Rowley, Betsey Johnson, and Giorgio Armani compete for window shoppers with local up-and-coming designers, some of whom design for drag queens and club kids only. The strip on Collins Avenue between 7th and 10th streets has become quite upscale, including such shops as Armani Exchange and Nicole Miller, along with the inescapable Gap and Banana Republic. Of course, there's also more mainstream (and affordable) shopping in the plethora of malls and outdoor shopping and entertainment complexes that are sprinkled throughout the city (see the section on malls below).

UNISEX

Agnes B   This fabulous French import features unique women's, men's, and children's high fashion at high prices. If you don't have carte blanche, however, the best buy in the store is the one-of-a-kind Agnes B perfume, in a lovely heart bottle, for just $20. 640 Collins Ave., South Beach. © 305/604-8705.

Base   A beautiful store featuring one-of-a-kind clothing made in St. Vincent that's light, breezy, fashionable, and, of course, pricey. Keep on the lookout for excellent sales. 939 Lincoln Rd., South Beach. © 305/531-4982.

Glitzy Tartz   The name alone says it all. This outlandish boutique features everything you'd want if you were a go-go boy or girl, in vinyl, mesh, and lamé—all in several sizes way too tight to accentuate the, uh, positive. 1251 Washington Ave., South Beach. © 305/535-0068.

Island Trading   Part of music mogul Chris Blackwell's empire, Island sells everything you'd need to wear in a tropical resort town: batik sarongs, sandals, sundresses, bathing suits, cropped tops, and more. Many of the unique styles are created on the premises by a team of young, innovative designers. 1332 Ocean Dr., South Beach. © 305/673-6300.

Laundry Industry If you're colorblind, from New York, or just can't be bothered with coordinating your colors, Laundry Industry is for you, with the most chic (and priciest) black-and-white-only threads for men and women this side of SoHo. 666 Collins Ave., South Beach. © 305/531-2277.

Urban Outfitters It took a while for this urban outpost to hit Miami, but once it did, it became a favorite for the young hipster set who favor T-shirts that say "Princess" instead of Prada. Cheapish, utilitarian, and funky, Urban Outfitters is an excellent place to pick up a pair of used jeans or some funky tchotchkes for your apartment. Two locations: 653 Collins Ave., South Beach © 305/535-9726, or Shops at Sunset, 5701 SW 72nd St., South Miami © 305/663-1536.

WOMEN'S

Alice's Day Off For beachwear, Alice's is the place. Season after season, you'll find pretty and flattering floral patterns and many flashy bikinis. If an itsy-bitsy bikini is not your style, Alice's also has a range of more modest cuts. Three locations: Miami International Mall, 1455 NW 107th Ave., Miami © 305/477-0393; Dadeland Mall, 7223 SW 88th St., Miami © 305/663-7299; and 5900 SW 72nd St., South Miami © 305/284-0301. www.alicesdayoff.com.

Belinda's This German designer makes some of the most beautiful and intricate teddies, nightgowns, and wedding dresses. The styles are a little too Stevie Nicks for me, but the creations are absolutely worth admiring. The prices are appropriately high. 827 Washington Ave., South Beach. © 305/532-0068.

Betsey Johnson Wacky, spirited New York designer Betsey Johnson offers outrageous, funky, and very loud clothes for young women. 805 Washington Ave., South Beach. © 305/673-0023. www.betseyjohnson.com.

Intermix Pretty young things can get all dolled up thanks to Intermix's fun assortment of hip women's fashions, from Stella McCartney's pricey rhinestone T-shirts to the latest jeans worn by everyone at the MTV Awards. 634 Collins Ave., South Beach. © 305/531-5950.

La Perla The only store in Florida that specializes in superluxurious Italian intimate apparel. Of course, you could fly to Milan for the price of a few bras and a nightgown, but you can't find better quality. 9700 Collins Ave. (in the Bal Harbour Shops), Bal Harbour. © 305/864-2070.

Place Vendome For cheap and funky club clothes from zebra-print pants to bright, shiny tops. Two locations: 934 Lincoln Rd., South Beach © 305/673-4005, and Aventura Mall, North Miami Beach © 305/932-8931.

Therapy Opened by Ellen Lansburgh, who ran successful shops in Aspen and New York that catered to a famous clientele, this intimate boutique offers one-of-a-kind pieces. The clothes, made of luxurious fabrics such as silk, taffeta, and tulle, are elegant and comfortable and are all the rage for the ladies-who-lunch crowd. 1065 Kane Concourse, Bay Harbor Islands. © 305/861-6900.

MEN'S

Giorgio's One of the finest custom men's stores in Miami, Giorgio's features an extensive line of Italian suits and all the latest by Canelli. 208 Miracle Mile, Coral Gables. © 305/448-4302.

La Casa de las Guayaberas *(Finds* Miami's premier purveyor of the traditional yet retro-hip Cuban shirt known as the *guayabera*—a loose-fitting, pleated, button-down shirt—was founded by Ramon Puig, who emigrated to Miami over 40 years ago. He still uses the same scissors he did back then, only now he's joined by a team of seamstresses who hand-sew 20 shirts a day in all colors and styles. Prices range from $15 to $375. 5840 SW 8th St., Little Havana. © 305/266-9683.

Wilke Rodriguez   Miami designer Eddie Rodriguez is a Latin Hugo Boss, with high-fashion suits in linens and light wool blends made especially for warmer climates. Cool T-shirts, shorts, and jackets are also part of this line, which is a local status symbol for many of Miami's fashion-conscious males. Prices range from the high $50s for T-shirts to $275 and up for jackets. 801 Washington Ave., South Beach. © 305/534-4030.

CHILDREN'S

Most department stores have extensive children's sections. But if you can't find what you are looking for, consider one of the many Baby Gaps or Gap Kids outlets around town or try one of the specialty boutiques listed here.

French Kids Inc. *(Finds*   Although this former South Miami boutique conducts most of its business on the Internet now (www.frenchkids.com), a little-known secret is that they still have a Miami warehouse from which their beautiful imported (and expensive) clothes for newborns to teenagers are sold. Open only by appointment on Saturdays, which is worth it since the clothes are slightly discounted at this warehouse and the kids get to try everything on. 4906 SW 74th Court., South Miami. E-mail for appointment: info@frenchkids.com.

Roland Children's Wear   You'll find a unique assortment of kid's clothes for dress-up or playtime. They specialize in cute, funky stuff. 450 41st St., Miami Beach. © 305/531-0130.

ACCESSORIES

Crybaby   Like a shop straight off of Melrose in Los Angeles or Magazine Street in New Orleans, this funky, kitschy tchotchke store carries whimsical toys, accessories, gifts, and clothing bearing the likenesses of the queen of kitsch, Hello Kitty, and much more, made by neo-pop artists such as Paul Frank (whose work entails Julius the monkey!). 6669 Biscayne Blvd., Miami. © 305/754-4279.

SEE   This fantastic eyewear store features an enormous selection of stylish specs all priced at $169, including your prescription. The staff is patient and knowledgeable. 921 Lincoln Rd., South Beach. © 305/672-6622.

Simons and Green   Fantastic sterling silver jewelry, leather goods, and other assorted high-end tchotchkes and gift items are what you'll find in this quaint mainstay on South Miami's Sunset Drive. 5842 Sunset Dr., South Miami. © 305/667-1692.

FOOD

There are dozens of ethnic markets in Miami, from Cuban *bodegas* to Jamaican import shops and Guyanese produce stands. Check the phone book under grocers for listings. I've listed a few of the biggest and best markets in town that sell prepared foods as well as staple items. On Saturday mornings, vendors set up stands loaded with papayas, melons, tomatoes, and citrus, as well as cookies, ice creams, and sandwiches on South Beach's Lincoln Road.

Biga Bakery   You'll be happy to pay upward of $6 a loaf when you sink your teeth into these inimitable Old World–style breads. Also, most of the locations have a to-die-for prepared-food counter serving up everything from chicken curry salad to hummus and pot pies. Pastries and cakes are as gorgeous as they are delicious. 305 Alcazar, Coral Gables. © 305/446-2111. Check phone book for other locations.

Epicure This is the closest thing Miami Beach has got to the famed Balducci's or Dean & DeLuca. Here, you'll find not only fine wines, cheeses, meats, fish, and juices, but some of the best produce, such as portobello mushrooms the size of a yarmulke. This neighborhood landmark is best known for supplying the Jewish residents of the beach with all their Jewish favorites, such as matzo ball soup, gefilte fish, and deli items. Prices are steep, but generally worth it. The cakes in particular are rich and decadent, and a rather large one doesn't cost more than $10. 1656 Alton Rd., Miami Beach. ✆ **305/672-1861.**

Gardner's Market Anything a gourmet or novice cook could desire can be found here. One of the oldest and best grocery stores in Miami, Gardner's now has three locations, all of which offer great takeout and the freshest produce. 7301 Red Rd., South Miami ✆ **305/667-9953;** 8287 SW 124th St., Pinecrest ✆ **305/255-2468;** 651 Brickell Key Dr., Downtown ✆ **305/371-3701.**

Joe's Takeaway If you don't want to wait 2 hours to get your paws on Joe's Stone Crab's meaty claws, let Joe's, Miami's stone-crab institution (see p. 121), ship you stone crabs anywhere in the country, but only during the season, which runs from mid-October through mid-May. 227 Biscayne St., South Beach. ✆ **800/780-CRAB** or 305/673-0365.

La Brioche Doree This tiny storefront off 41st Street is packed most mornings with French expatriates and visitors who crave the real thing. There are luscious pastries and breads, plus soup and sandwiches at lunch. No one makes a better croissant. 4017 Prairie Ave., Miami Beach. ✆ **305/538-4770.**

Laurenzo's Italian Supermarket and Farmer's Market Anything Italian you want—homemade ravioli, hand-cut imported Romano cheese, plus fresh fish and meats—can be found here. Laurenzo's also offers one of the most comprehensive wine selections in the city. Be sure to see the neighboring store full of just-picked herbs, salad greens, and vegetables from around the world. A daily Farmer's Market is open from 7am to 6pm. Incredible daily specials lure thrifty shoppers from all over the city. 16385 and 16445 W. Dixie Hwy., North Miami Beach. ✆ **305/945-6381** or 305/944-5052.

JEWELRY
For name designers like Gucci and Tiffany & Co., go to the Bal Harbour Shops (see "Malls," below).

International Jeweler's Exchange At least 50 reputable jewelers hustle their wares from individual counters at one of the city's most active jewelry centers. Haggle your brains out for excellent prices on timeless antiques from Tiffany's, Cartier, or Bulgari, or on unique designs you can create yourself. 18861 Biscayne Blvd. (in the Fashion Island), North Miami Beach. ✆ **305/931-7032.**

Seybold Building Jewelers who specialize in an assortment of goods (diamonds, gems, watches, rings, etc.) gather here daily to sell diamonds and gold. With 300 jewelry stores located inside this independently owned and operated multilevel treasure chest, the glare is blinding as you enter. Here, you'll be sure to see handsome and up-to-date designs, but not too many bargains. 36 NE 1st St., Downtown. ✆ **305/374-7922.**

MALLS
There are so many malls in Miami and more being built all the time that it would be impossible to mention them all. What follows is a list of the biggest and most popular.

You can find any number of nationally known department stores including Saks Fifth Avenue, Macy's, Lord & Taylor, Sears, and JCPenney in the Miami malls listed below, but Miami's own is **Burdines,** at 22 E. Flagler St., Downtown (© **305/835-5151**) and 1675 Meridian Ave. (just off Lincoln Rd.) in South Beach (© **305/674-6311**). One of the oldest and largest department stores in Florida, Burdines specializes in good-quality home furnishings and fashions.

Aventura Mall *(Kids)*   A multimillion-dollar makeover has made this spot one of the premier places to shop in South Florida. With more than 2.3 million square feet of space, this airy, Mediterranean-style mall has a 24-screen movie theater and more than 250 stores, including megastores JCPenney, Lord & Taylor, Macy's, Bloomingdale's, Sears, and Burdines. The mall offers moderate to high-priced merchandise and is extremely popular with families. A large indoor playground, Adventurer's Cove, is a great spot for kids, and the mall frequently offers activities and entertainment for children. There are numerous theme restaurants and a food court that eschews the usual suspects in favor of local operations. 19501 Biscayne Blvd. (at 197th St. near the Dade–Broward County line), Aventura. © 305/935-1110. www.shopaventuramall.com.

Bal Harbour Shops   One of the most prestigious fashion meccas in the country, Bal Harbour offers the best-quality goods from the finest names. Giorgio Armani, Dolce & Gabbana, Christian Dior, Fendi, Joan & David, Krizia, Rodier, Gucci, Brooks Brothers, Waterford, Cartier, H. Stern, Tourneau, and many others are sandwiched between Neiman Marcus and a newly expanded Saks Fifth Avenue. Well-dressed shoppers stroll in a pleasant open-air emporium featuring several good cafes, covered walkways, and lush greenery. Parking costs $1 an hour with a validated ticket. You can stamp your own at the entrance to Saks Fifth Avenue, even if you don't make a purchase. 9700 Collins Ave. (on 97th St., opposite the Sheraton Bal Harbour Hotel), Bal Harbour. © 305/866-0311. www.balharbour shops.com.

Bayside Marketplace   A popular stop for cruise-ship passengers, this touristy waterfront marketplace is filled with the usual suspects of chain stores as well as a slew of tacky gift shops and carts hawking assorted junk in the heart of downtown Miami. The second-floor food court is stocked with dozens of fast-food choices and bars. Most of the restaurants and bars stay open later than the stores. There's Lomardi's Conga Bar, Dick's Last Resort, Hard Rock Cafe, Fat Tuesday, Sharkey's, and Let's Make a Daiquiri. Parking is $1 per hour. While we wouldn't recommend you necessarily drop big money at Bayside, you should go by just for the view (of Biscayne Bay and the Miami skyline) alone. In June you can watch the Opsail sailboat show, and in February, the Miami Sailboat Show, where sailboats dock in the area and make the view even nicer. Beware of the adjacent amphitheater known as Bayfront Park, which usually hosts large-scale concerts and festivals, causing major pedestrian and vehicle traffic jams. 401 Biscayne Blvd., Downtown. © 305/577-3344. www.baysidemarketplace.com.

CocoWalk   CocoWalk is a lovely outdoor Mediterranean-style mall with the usual fare of Americana: Gap, Banana Republic, etc. Its open-air style architecture is inviting not only for shoppers but also for friends or spouses of shoppers who'd prefer to sit at an outdoor cafe while said shopper is busy in the fitting room. A multiplex movie theater is also here, which comes in handy when there are big sales going on and the stores are mobbed. 3015 Grand Ave., Coconut Grove. © 305/444-0777. www.cocowalk.com.

Dadeland Mall One of the county's first malls, Dadeland features more than 175 specialty shops, anchored by four large department stores: Burdines, JCPenney, Lord & Taylor, and Saks Fifth Avenue. Sixteen restaurants serve from the adjacent Treats Food Court. New retail stores are constantly springing up around this centerpiece of South Miami suburbia. If you're not in the area, however, the mall is not worth the trek. Additionally, many non-Spanish-speaking people are put off by Dadeland because of the predominance of Spanish-speaking store employees. 7535 N. Kendall Dr. (intersection of U.S. 1 and SW 88th St., 15 minutes south of Downtown), Kendall. ℂ 305/665-6226.

Dolphin Mall As if Miami needed another mall, this $250 million megamall and amusement park rivals Broward County's monstrous Sawgrass Mills outlet. The 1.4-million-square-foot outlet mall features outlets such as Off Saks (Fifth Avenue), plus several discount shops, a 28-screen movie theater, and, not to be outdone by the Mall of America in Minnesota, a roller coaster. Florida Turnpike at S.R. 836, West Miami. ℂ 305/365-7446.

The Falls Traffic to this mall borders on brutal, but once you get there, you'll feel a slight sense of serenity. Tropical waterfalls are the setting for this outdoor shopping center with dozens of moderately priced and slightly upscale shops. Miami's first Bloomingdale's is here, as are Polo, Ralph Lauren, Caswell-Massey, and more than 60 other specialty shops. A recent renovation added Macy's, Crate & Barrel, Brooks Brothers, and Pottery Barn, among others. If you are planning to visit any of the nearby attractions, which include Metro Zoo and Monkey Jungle, check with customer service for information on discount packages. 8888 Howard Dr. (at the intersection of U.S. 1 and 136th St., about 3 miles south of Dadeland Mall), Kendall. ℂ 305/255-4570. www.shopthefalls.com.

Sawgrass Mills Just as some people need to take a tranquilizer to fly, others need one to traipse through this mammoth mall—the largest outlet mall in the country. Depending on what type of shopper you are, this experience can either be blissful or overwhelming. If you've got the patience, it is worth setting aside a day to do the entire place. Though it's located in Broward County, it is a phenomenon that attracts thousands of tourists and locals sniffing out bargains. From Miami, buses run three times daily; the trip takes just under an hour. Call **Coach USA** (ℂ 305/887-6223) for exact pickup points at major hotels. The price is $10 for a round-trip ticket. If you are driving, take I-95 north to 595 west to Flamingo Road. Exit and turn right, driving 2 miles to Sunrise Boulevard. You can't miss this monster on the left. Parking is free, but don't forget where you parked your car or you might spend a day looking for it. 12801 W. Sunrise Blvd., Sunrise (west of Fort Lauderdale). ℂ 954/846-2300. www.millscorp.com.

Shops at Sunset Place Completed in early 1999 at a cost of over $140 million, this sprawling outdoor shopping complex offers more than just shopping. Visitors experience high-tech special effects, such as daily tropical storms (minus the rain) and the electronic chatter of birds and crickets. In addition to a 24-screen movie complex and an IMAX theater, there's a GameWorks (Steven Spielberg's Disney-esque playground for kids and adults), a Virgin Records store, and a NikeTown as well as mall standards such as Victoria's Secret, Gap, Urban Outfitters, bebe, etc. 5701 Sunset Dr. (at 57th Ave. and U.S. 1, near Red Rd.), South Miami. ℂ 305/663-0482.

Streets of Mayfair This sleepy, desolate, labyrinthine shopping area conceals a movie theater, several top-quality shops, a bookstore, restaurants, art galleries, bars, and nightclubs. It was meant to compete with the CocoWalk shopping complex (just across the street), but its structure is very mazelike. Though it is open air, it is not wide open like CocoWalk and pales in comparison to that more populated neighbor. 2911 Grand Ave. (just east of Commodore Plaza), Coconut Grove. © 305/448-1700.

MUSIC STORES

Blue Note Records *(Finds*   Here for more than 18 years, Blue Note is music to the ears of music fanatics with a good selection of hard-to-find progressive and underground music. There are new, used, and discounted CDs and old vinyl, too. Call to find out about performances. Some great names show up occasionally. A second location features jazz and LPs only. 16401 NE 15th Ave., North Miami Beach. © 305/940-3394. For jazz/LPs: 2299 NE 164th St., North Miami Beach © 305/354-4563. www.bluenoterecords.com.

Casino Records Inc.   The young, hip salespeople here speak English and tend to be music buffs. This store has the largest selection of Latin music in Miami, including pop icons such as Willy Chirino, Gloria Estefan, Albita, and local boy Nil Lara. Their slogan translates to "If we don't have it, forget it." Believe me, they've got it. 1208 SW 8th St., Little Havana. © 305/856-6888.

Esperanto Music *(Finds*   According to the experts, this independently owned record store boasts the city's best collection of Cuban and Latin music. 513 Lincoln Rd., Miami Beach. © 305/ 534-2003.

Revolution Records and CDs   Here you'll find a quaint and fairly well-organized collection of CDs, from hard-to-find jazz to original recordings of Buddy Rich. They'll search for anything and let you hear whatever you like. 1620 Alton Rd., Miami Beach. © 305/673-6464.

Yesterday and Today Records *(Finds*   This is Miami's most unique and well-stocked store for vinyl—you know, the audio dinosaur that went out with the Victrola? Y & T, as it's known, is a collector's heaven, featuring every genre of music imaginable on every format. Chances are, you could find some eight-track tapes, too. 7902 NW 36th St., Miami. © 305/468-0311.

SPORTS EQUIPMENT

People-watching seems to be the number-one sport in South Florida, but for the more athletic pursuits, consider the shops listed below. One of the area's largest sport's equipment chains is the **Sports Authority,** with at least six locations throughout the county. Check the White Pages for details.

Alf's Golf Shop   This is the best pro shop around. The knowledgeable staff can help you with equipment for golfers of every level, and the neighboring golf course offers discounts to Alf's clients. Two locations: 524 Arthur Godfrey Rd., Miami Beach © 305/673-6568, and 15369 S. Dixie Hwy., Miami, © 305/378-6086.

Bass Pro Shops Outdoor World   Fishing and sports enthusiasts must head north to Broward County to see this huge retail complex, which offers demonstrations in such sports as fly-fishing and archery, classes in marine safety, and every conceivable gadget you could ask for. 200 Gulf Stream Way (west side of I-95), Dania Beach. © 954/929-7710.

Bird's Surf Shop   If you're a hard-core surfer—or just want to look like one—head to Bird's Surf Shop. Although Miami doesn't regularly get huge swells, if you're here during the winter and one should happen to hit, you'll be ready. The shop carries more than 150 boards. Call its surf line (© 305/947-7170) to find the best waves from South Beach to Cape Hatteras and even the Bahamas and Florida's West Coast. 250 Sunny Isles Blvd., North Miami Beach. ℂ 305/940-0929.

Edwin Watts Golf Shops   One of 30 Edwin Watts shops throughout the Southeast, this full-service golf retail shop is one of the most popular in Miami. You can find it all, including clothing, pro-line equipment, gloves, bags, balls, videos, and books. Plus, you can get coupons for discounted greens fees on many courses. 15100 N. Biscayne Blvd., North Miami Beach. ℂ 305/944-2925.

Island Water Sports   You'll find everything from booties to gloves to baggies and tanks. Check in here before you rent that WaveRunner or windsurfer. 16231 Biscayne Blvd., North Miami. ℂ 305/944-0104.

Golf Headquarters *Finds*   This chain store guarantees the lowest prices on golf equipment and accessories. There's more than 6,000 square feet of store here; you can even practice your swing at an indoor driving range, where a radar gun will clock your speed. 7930 NW 36th Ave. (near the airport), Miami. ℂ 305/593-2999.

X-Isle Surf Shop   Prices are slightly higher at this beach location, but you'll find the hottest styles and equipment. They also offer surfboard rental. Free surf report at ℂ **305/534-7873.** 437 Washington Ave., South Beach. ℂ 305/673-5900.

THRIFT STORES/RESALE SHOPS

Children's Exchange *Kids*   Selling everything from layettes to overalls, this pleasant little shop is chock-full of good Florida-style stuff for kids to wear to the beach and in the heat. 1415 Sunset Dr., Coral Gables. ℂ 305/666-6235.

Douglas Gardens Jewish Home and Hospital Thrift Shop   Prices here are no longer the major bargain they once were, but for housewares and books, you can do all right. Call to see if they are offering any specials for seniors or students. 5713 NW 27th Ave., North Miami Beach. ℂ 305/638-1900.

Rags to Riches   This is an old-time consignment shop where you might find some decent rags, and maybe even some riches. Though not as upscale as it used to be, this place is still a good spot for costume jewelry and shoes. 12577 Biscayne Blvd., North Miami. ℂ 305/891-8981.

Red White & Blue *Finds*   Miami's best-kept secret is this mammoth thrift store that is meticulously organized and well stocked. You've got to search for great stuff, but it is there. There are especially good deals on children's clothes and housewares. 12640 NE 6th Ave., North Miami. ℂ 305/893-1104.

9

Miami After Dark

With all the hype, you'd expect Miami to have long outlived its 15 minutes of fame by now. But you'd be wrong. Miami's nightlife, especially in South Beach, is hotter than ever before—and still getting hotter.

Practically every club in the area has installed closely guarded velvet ropes to create an air of exclusivity. Don't be fooled or intimidated by them— *anyone* can go clubbing in the Magic City, and throughout this chapter, I've provided tips to ensure you gain entry to the venue you want to go to.

South Beach is certainly Miami's uncontested nocturnal nucleus, but more and more diverse areas, such as the Design District, South Miami, and even Little Havana, are increasingly providing fun alternatives without the ludicrous cover charges, "fashionably late" hours of operation (things don't typically get started on South Beach until after 11pm), the lack of sufficient self-parking, and outrageous drink prices that come standard in South Beach.

And while South Beach dances to a more electronic beat, other parts of Miami dance to a Latin beat—from salsa and merengue to tango and cha cha. However, if you're looking for a less frenetic good time, Miami's bar scene offers something for everyone, from haute hotel bars to sleek, loungey watering holes.

If the possibility of a celebrity sighting doesn't fulfill your cultural needs, Miami also offers a variety of first-rate diversions in theater, music, and dance, including a world-class ballet under the aegis of Edward Villella, a recognized symphony, and a talented opera company.

For up-to-date listing information, and to make sure time hasn't elapsed for the club of the moment, check the *Miami Herald's* "Weekend" section, which runs on Friday, or the more comprehensive listings in *New Times,* Miami's free alternative weekly, available each Wednesday, or visit www. miami.citysearch.com online.

1 Bars & Lounges

There are countless bars in and around Miami, with the highest concentration on trendy South Beach. The selection listed here is a mere sample. Keep in mind that many of the popular bars—and the easiest to get into—are in hotels. For a clubbier scene, if you don't mind making your way through hordes of inebriated club kids, a stroll on Washington Avenue will provide you with ample insight into what's hot and what's not. Just hold onto your bags. It's not dangerous, but occasionally, a few shady types manage to slip into the crowd. Another very important tip when in a club: *Never put your drink down out of your sight*—there have been unfortunate incidents in which drinks have been spiked with illegal chemical substances. For a less hard-core, collegiate nightlife, head to Coconut Grove. Most require proof that you are over 21 to enter. Oh, yes, and when going out in South Beach, make sure to take a so-called disco nap, as things don't

Impressions
Miami is where neon goes to die.

—Lenny Bruce

get going until at least 11pm. If you go earlier, be prepared to face an empty bar or club. Off of South Beach and in hotel bars in general, the hours are fashionably earlier, with the action starting as early as, say, 7pm.

Blue A very laid-back, very locals scene set to a sultry soundtrack of deep soul and house music has Miami's hipsters feeling the blues on a nightly basis from 10pm to 5am. Before you whip out the St. John's Wort, dive into this so-not-trendy-it's-trendy lounge, in which the pervasive color blue will actually heighten your spirits as an eclectic haze of models, locals, and lounge lizards gather to commiserate in their dreaded trendy status. 222 Española Way (between Washington and Collins aves.), South Beach. © 305/534-1009. No cover.

Clevelander If wet T-shirt contests and a fraternity party atmosphere are your thing, then this Ocean Drive mainstay is your kind of place. Popular with tourists and locals who like to pretend they're tourists, the Clevelander attracts a lively, sporty, adults-only crowd (the burly bouncers *will* confiscate fake IDs) who have no interest in being part of a scene, but, rather, taking in the very revealing scenery. A great time to check out the Clevelander is on a weekend afternoon, when beach Barbies and Kens line the bar for a post-tanning beer or frozen cocktail. 1020 Ocean Dr., South Beach. © 305/531-3485. No cover.

Forge The Forge lounge hosts an unusual mix of the uptight and those who wear their clothes too tight. It's also where surgically altered ladies look for their cigar-chomping sugar daddies in a setting that somehow reminds me of *Dynasty*. Call well in advance if you want to watch the parade of characters from a dinner table (see p. 136). The Forge people also own a ritzier nightclub (which is attached to the club), reminiscent of a cruise-ship lounge, called Jimmy'z (they say it's a private club, but if you dine at the restaurant or are acquainted with someone in the know, you can get in). 432 41st St., Miami Beach. © 305/538-8533. No cover (though door policy tends to be a bit exclusive; dress up and you should have no problem).

Fox's Sherron Inn *(Finds* The spirit of Frank Sinatra is alive and well at this dark and smoky watering hole that dates back to 1946. Everything down to the vinyl booths and the red lights make Fox's a retro fabulous dive bar. Cheap drinks, couples cozily huddling in booths, and a seasoned staff of bartenders and barflies make Fox's the perfect place to retreat from the trenches of trendiness. Oh, and the food's actually good here, too. 6030 S. Dixie Hwy. (at 62nd Ave.), South Miami. © 305/661-9201. No cover.

Laundry Bar The only place in Miami where it's okay to let friends drink and dry. Laundry Bar features working washers, dryers, a fully stocked bar, and several other distractions to help make doing your laundry a fun rather than a dreaded chore. It's also one of the only bars on South Beach open from 7am to 5am daily. Thursdays seem to be laundry night on South Beach, when a DJ spins the best in house music. On Wednesdays and Fridays, gospel diva Marvel Epps (formerly of the Astor Place restaurant's Gospel Brunch fame) sings live to an always packed and lively house. And although it's most popular with the gay community, Laundry Bar draws a mixed crowd; on weekends, the place is

South Beach After Dark

Academy **24**
Añoranzas Taberna **1**
Billboard Live **18**
Blue **20**
Bond St Lounge **4**
Books & Books **11**
Clevelander **27**
Colony Theater **10**
Crobar **19**
Jackie Gleason Theater of
  the Performing Arts **8**
Jazid **22**
La Sandwicherie **23**
Laundry Bar **9**
Level **24**
Liquid **17**
Loading Zone **21**
Lobby Bar at the Hotel Astor **28**
Lola **2**
Mac's Club Deuce **23**
Mango's Tropical Café **29**
Marlin Bar **25**
Miami City Ballet **3**
Mynt **5**
New World Symphony **14**
News Café **30**
Nikki Beach Club **33**
Ophelia and Juan Jr Roca Center **3**
Opium Garden **32**
Purdy Lounge **6**
Rain **1**
Rose Bar at the Delano **16**
Rumi **15**
San Loco Tacos **23**
Score **13**
1771 **7**
Twist **26**
Upstairs at the Van Dyke Café **12**
Wet Willie's **31**

packed like an overloaded washing machine. Daily happy hours (5–7pm) with two-for-one drinks allow you to save your change for the washing machines. 721 Lincoln Lane (behind Burdines off Lincoln Rd.), South Beach. © 305/531-7700. www.laundry-bar.com. No cover.

Lola *(Finds* Lola redefines the neighborhood bar, striking the perfect balance between chill and chic. This bar, located away from the South Beach mayhem, is a showgirl in her own right—a swank, sultry lounge where people are encouraged to come as they are, leaving the attitude at home. Attracting a mixed crowd of gay, straight, young, and old(er), Lola reinvents itself each night with DJs spinning everything from retro '80s music to hard rock and classic oldies. On Tuesdays, the bar's most popular—and populated—night, it gets mobbed inside and outside, so they tend to keep a crowd at the ropes before letting them all in like cattle. 247 23rd St., South Beach. © 305/695-8697. No cover.

Mac's Club Deuce Standing on its own amidst an oasis of trendiness, Mac's Club Deuce is the quintessential dive bar, with cheap drinks and a cast of characters ranging from your typical barfly to your atypical drag queen. It's got a well-stocked jukebox, friendly bartenders, a pool table, and best of all, it's an insomniac's dream, open daily from 8am to 5am. 222 14th St., South Beach. © 305/673-9537. No cover.

Mynt This hyper-stylish, hip lounge is reminiscent of a space-age cafeteria. A massive 6,000-square-foot space, Mynt is nothing more than a huge living room in which models, celebrities, and assorted hangers-on bask in the green glow to the beats of very loud lounge and dance music. If you want to dance—or move, for that matter, this is not the place in which to do so. It's all about striking a pose in here. 1921 Collins Ave., South Beach. © 786/276-6132. Cover $10–$20.

Piccadilly Garden Lounge *(Finds* Hardly anyone in Miami knows that this completely off-the-beaten-path Design District lounge exists, which makes it that much cooler. A young, alternative crowd (bordering on Gothic) gathers in this garden every Saturday night for what is known as Pop Life, a musical homage to the sounds of British pop and alternative music. While the dank interior resembles a stuffy old Holiday Inn lounge, the music and the crowd is very mod. 35 NE 40th St., Design District. © 305/573-8221. Cover $5 Sat.

Purdy Lounge With the exception of a wall of lava lamps, Purdy is not unlike your best friend's basement, featuring a pool table and a slew of board games such as Operation to keep the attention-deficit disordered from getting bored.

Moments Stargazing

The most popular places for celebrity sightings include Cameron Diaz's Bambu restaurant, Tantra, the lobby bar at the Hotel Astor, poolside at the Delano, and the Level and crobar nightclubs. Miami Heat basketball games are also star magnets.

Swank Hotel Bars

Long gone are the days of the old-school Holiday Inn lounges. In fact, some hotels seem to spend more money on their bars than they do on their bedding. That aside, hotel barhopping is very popular in Miami. Here's my list of the best:

Rose Bar at the Delano (see below) for seeing and being seen.

Lobby bar at the Hotel Astor, 956 Washington Ave., South Beach (© 305/672-1402), to bask in a flattering light with a sophisticated, not snotty, crowd.

Marlin Bar at the Marlin hotel, 1200 Collins Ave., South Beach (© 305/673-8373), to experience what is known as Caribbean chic.

Bond St. Lounge at the Townhouse hotel, 150 20th St., South Beach (© 305/534-3800), a New York import, is a tiny bar/lounge which also serves food; it's known for excellent sushi and a hip, chic jet-set crowd.

Harry's American Bar at the Eden Roc Resort, 4525 Collins Ave., Miami Beach (© 305/674-5568), a throwback to the days of Miami Beach kitsch, when Liza, Sammy, and Frank were splashing around at the pool.

Because it's a no-nonsense bar with relatively cheap cocktails (by South Beach standards), Purdy gets away with not having a star DJ or fancy bass-heavy Bose sound system. A CD player somehow does the trick. With no cover and no attitude, a line is inevitable, so be prepared to wait. Saturday night has become the preferred night for locals, while Friday night happy hour draws a young professional crowd on the prowl. 1811 Purdy Ave./Sunset Harbor, South Beach. © 305/531-4622. No cover.

Rose Bar at the Delano If every rose has its thorn, the thorn at this painfully chic hotel bar is the excruciatingly high-priced cocktails. Otherwise, the crowd here is full of the so-called glitterati, fabulatti, and other assorted poseurs who view life through (Italian-made) rose-colored glasses. 1685 Collins Ave., South Beach. © 305/672-2000. No cover.

Wet Willie's With such telling drinks as Call a Cab, this beachfront oasis is not the place to go if you have a long drive ahead of you. A well-liked pre-and postbeach hangout, Wet Willie's inspires serious drinking. Popular with the Harley Davidson set, tourists, and beachcombers, this bar is best known for its rooftop patio (get there early if you plan to get a seat) and its half-nude bikini beauties. 760 Ocean Dr., South Beach. © 305/532-5650. No cover.

2 Dance Clubs, Live Music, the Gay & Lesbian Scene & Latin Clubs

DANCE CLUBS

Clubs are as much a cottage industry in Miami as is, say, cheese in Wisconsin. Clubland, as its known, is not just a nocturnal theme park but a way of life for some. On any given night in Miami, there's something going on—no excuses are needed to throw a party here. Short of throwing a glammy event for the grand opening of a new gas station, Miami is very party hearty, celebrating everything

---

Tips **Ground Rules: Stepping Out in Miami**

• Nightlife on South Beach doesn't really get going until after 11pm. As a result, you may want to consider taking what is known as a disco nap so that you'll be fully charged until the wee hours.

• If you're unsure of what to wear out on South Beach, your safest bet will be anything black.

• Do *not* try to tip the doormen manning the velvet ropes. That will only make you look desperate and you'll find yourself standing outside for what will seem like an ungodly amount of time. Instead, try to land your name on the ever-present guest lists by calling the club early in the day yourself, or, better yet, having the concierge at your hotel do it for you. Concierges have connections. If you don't have connections and you find yourself without a concierge, then act assertive, not surly, at the velvet rope, and your patience will usually be rewarded with admittance. If all else fails—for men, especially— surround yourself with a few leggy model types and you'll be noticed quicker.

• Finally, have fun. It may look like serious business when you're on the outside, but once you're in, it's another story. Attacking Clubland with a sense of humor is the best approach to a successful, memorable evening out.

---

from the fact that it's Tuesday night to the debut of a hot new DJ. Within this very bizarre after-dark community, a very colorful assortment of characters emerge, from your (a)typical nine-to-fivers to shady characters who have reinvented themselves as hot shots on the club circuit. While this scene of seeing and being seen may not be your cup of Absolut, it's certainly never boring.

The club music played on Miami's ever-evolving social circuit is good enough to get even the most rhythmically challenged wallflowers dancing. To keep things fresh in Clubland, local promoters throw one-nighters, which are essentially parties with various themes or motifs, from funk to fashion. Because these change so often, we can't possibly list them here. Word of mouth, local advertising, and listings in the free weekly *New Times,* miami.citysearch.com, or the "Weekend" section of the *Miami Herald* are the best ways to find out about these ever-changing events.

Before you get all decked out to hit the town as soon as the sun sets, consider the fact that Miami is a very late town. Things generally don't get started before 11pm. The Catch-22 here is that if you don't arrive on South Beach early enough, you may find yourself driving around aimlessly for parking, as it is very limited outside of absurd $20 valet charges. Municipal lots fill up quickly, so your best bet is to arrive on South Beach somewhat early and kill time by strolling around, having something to eat, or sipping a cocktail in a hotel bar. Another advantage of arriving a bit earlier than the crowds is that some clubs don't charge a cover before 11pm or midnight, which could save you a wad of cash over time. Most clubs are open every night of the week, though some are only open Thursday to Sunday and others are only open Monday though

Saturday. Call ahead to get all of this information as up-to-date as possible: Things change very quickly around here. Cover charges are very haphazard, too. If you're not on the ubiquitous guest list (ask your concierge to put you on the list—he or she has the ability to do so, which won't help you with the wait to get in, but will eliminate the cover charge), you may have to fork over a ridiculous $20 to walk past the ropes. Don't fret, though. There are many clubs and bars that have no cover charge—they just make up for it by charging $13 for a martini!

Note: As with anything on Miami's nocturnal circuit, call in advance to make sure that the dance club you're planning to go to hasn't become a video arcade.

Bermuda Bar and Grill This North Miami Beach spot is a sanctuary for those who'd rather not deal with the hustle, bustle, and hassle of driving and parking in South Beach or Coconut Grove. Bermuda Bar is a mega dance club that is often frequented by young suburban professionals. Good pizzas and grilled foods are available, too. It's usually open until the sun comes up. Wednesday's ladies nights are particularly popular, when women drink free and men are at their mercy. 3509 NE 163rd St., North Miami Beach. *℃* 305/945-0196. Cover $0–$10. No cover before 9pm. Open Wed–Sat.

Bongo's Cuban Café Gloria Estefan's latest hit in the restaurant business pays homage to the sites, sounds, and cuisine of pre-Castro Cuba. Bongo's is a mammoth restaurant attached to the American Airlines Arena in downtown Miami. On Friday and Saturday after 11:30pm, it's transformed from a friendly family restaurant into the city's hottest 21-and-over salsa nightclub. Cover charge at that time is a hefty $20, but consider it your ticket to what happens to be an astounding show of some of the best salsa dancers in the city. Prepare yourself for standing room only. At the American Airlines Arena, 601 Biscayne Blvd., Downtown Miami. *℃* 786/777-2100. Cover $20.

Club Space Clubland hits the mainland with this cavernous downtown warehouse of a club. With over 30,000 square feet of dance space, you can spin around a la Stevie Nicks (albeit to a techno beat) without having to worry about banging into someone. However, after hours (around 2am), Club Space packs them in. While Saturday caters to a more homogeneous and gay crowd, Friday is a free-for-all. Conveniently, the club often runs shuttles from the beach. Call for more information, as it doesn't have a concrete schedule. 142 NE 11th St., Miami. *℃* 305/372-9378. Cover $0–$20.

Haute Off the Press

Just as this book was going to press, a few nocturnal South Beach haute spots opened to pretty impressive reviews. While, once again, we emphasize the fact that you should always check in advance to see if a place is still open, it seems that the new house-music dance club **Spin** (320 Lincoln Rd., South Beach; *℃* 305/532-8899) and the buzz-worthy lounge **Honey** (645 Washington Ave.; *℃* 305/604-8222) may outlast the flash-in-the-pan status and actually stick around long enough for you to check them out. Don't be surprised, however, if you find that either space has a new name, new concept, or new management. After just three weeks of its grand opening, Spin lost one of its head honchos to another club. (Sigh.) Just another night in Clubland.

Impressions
Working the door teaches you a lot about human nature.
                                    —A former South Beach doorman

crobar *(Finds* Still haunted by the ghost of clubs past, the space formerly known as the Cameo Theatre is now possessed by the mod, millennial, industrial spirit that is crobar. With its intense, dance-heavy sound system, an industrially chic ambience, and crowds big enough to scare away any memories of a sadly abandoned Cameo, this Chicago import has raised the bar on South Beach nightlife with crazy theme nights (the monthly Sex night is particularly, uh, stimulating), top-name DJs, and the occasional celebrity appearance. On Sunday, the club hosts an extremely popular gay night known as Anthem. (See "The Gay & Lesbian Scene," below.) 1445 Washington Ave., South Beach. ✆ 305/531-8225. www.crobarmiami.com. Cover $25.

Level Overdone and some say overhyped, Level takes the notion of South Beach excess even further with its outlet-mall-sized, 40,000-square-foot space featuring four dance floors, three levels, five rooms, and nine bars. Like a video game, your status here is determined by which level you can land on. If you befriend one of the club's owners, you may end up at the top. Leveling out the competition, this club has cornered the market on parties and events, throwing one nearly every night. Because it is the largest club on the beach, the velvet rope scene can be quite harassing, but if you call in advance, the accommodating staff will usually put you on the guest list, which means you don't have to pay the cover, though you will still have to wait in line. Friday night is a very popular gay night, while the rest of the week attracts a mixed crowd of straights, gays, and somewhere-in-betweens. Celebs love Level because it has so many VIP rooms. 1235 Washington Ave., South Beach. ✆ 305/532-1525. www.levelnightclub.com. Cover $20–$30.

Liquid Way back when, during South Beach's halcyon days, before Madonna became a mother and stopped her clubbing ways, Liquid was the Studio 54 of the south, and everyone who was anyone showed up here to show off. Then one of the club's owners was arrested for his alleged "family" connections and Liquid dried up. In late 2001, Liquid was resurrected by a completely new owner in a completely different space. Without Madonna, however, Liquid is just your generic dance club, just a ghost of a legend that no one who experienced the original has any desire to visit. 1532 Washington Ave., South Beach. ✆ 305/531-9411. Cover $10–$20.

Living Room Downtown The downtown satellite of a now defunct South Beach club that was formerly the hautest of the hot (especially amongst European jet-setters), the Living Room Downtown is nearly as velvety chic as its original incarnation, only there's a twist: This one has a 24-hour liquor license. *Note:* This place is not for the weary. 60 NE 11th St., Downtown. ✆ 305/342-7421. Cover $10–$20.

Nikki Beach Club *(Finds* What the Playboy Mansion is to Hollywood, the Nikki Beach Club is to South Beach. This place is the product of local nightlife royalty Tommy Pooch and Eric Omores. Half-naked ladies and men actually venture into the daylight on Sundays (around 4pm, which is ungodly in this town) to see, be seen, and, at times, be obscene. At night, it's very Brady

Bunch–goes-to-Hawaii seeming, with a sexy tiki hut/Polynesian theme/style, albeit rated R. The Sunday afternoon beach party is almost legendary and worth a glimpse—that is, if you can get in. This is not your equal-opportunity beach club. Egos are easily shattered, as surly doormen are known to reject those who don't drive up in a Ferrari. Also located within this bastion of hedonism is the superhot **Pearl,** a mod-ish, 380-seat, orange-hued restaurant and lounge that features a continental menu created by Nikki chef Brian Rutherford. But you'd do better to forget the food and go for the eye candy. 101 Ocean Dr., South Beach. ℂ 305/538-1111. Cover $10–$20.

Opium Garden   Housed in the massive, open-air space formerly known as Amnesia, Opium Garden is a highly addictive nocturnal habit for those looking for a combination of sexy dance music, scantily clad dancers, and, for the masochists out there, an oppressive door policy in which two sets of velvet ropes are set up to keep those deemed unworthy out of this see-and-be-sceney den of inequity. 136 Collins Ave., South Beach. ℂ 305/531-5535. Cover $10–$30.

Rain   A very minimalist dance club/lounge, Rain is a great night spot for many reasons. First and foremost, its location off the beachy path is ideal for those who insist on clubbing and driving. Ample parking in the area definitely makes up for the fact that you'll pay upwards of $9 for a cocktail. Second, the music's great. Local DJ Mark Leventhal's Tuesday night funkfest known as Home Cookin' is particularly fun and comes complete with a free barbecue. If you don't feel like dancing, outdoor and indoor lounging space is aplenty. 323 23rd St., South Beach. ℂ 786/295-9540. Cover $10–$30.

Rumi   Named after a 13th-century Sufi mystic, South Beach's first upscale supper club is command central for hipsters hailing from all coasts. Designed by hot NYC designers Nancy Mah and Scott Kester, Rumi is an urbane oasis of reds, tans, and chocolates, reminiscent of the golden age of supper clubs of the '30s and '40s. This bi-level space features intimate lounge areas as well as private and public dining rooms, in which haute Floribbean cuisine is served until around 11pm, when the tables conspicuously disappear and give way to a neo-Zen-like stomping ground for South Beach's chic elite. Make sure to check out the queen-sized Murphy bed that snaps down from the wall to make room for late-night lounging. As long as you can get past the velvet ropes (by either looking pretty, being on the guest list, or just getting the doorman on a good day), there is no cover to bask in this bastion of South Beach scene-dom. 330 Lincoln Rd., South Beach. ℂ 305/672-4353. www.rumimiami.com. No cover.

LIVE MUSIC

Unfortunately, Miami's live music scene is not thriving. Instead of local bands garnering devoted fans, local DJs are more admired, skyrocketing much more easily to fame—thanks to the city's lauded dance-club scene. However, there are

---

Rock 'n' Bowl

Inspired by the alcohol-free rave dance parties of the '90s, Rave Bowling at **Cloverleaf Lanes,** 17601 NW 2nd Ave., North Dade (ℂ 305/652-4197), keeps teens off the streets, but in the gutters. Low lighting, glow-in-the-dark pins, and loud music keep things rolling every Friday and Saturday night from 8:30pm until 3am. Games are $4.50 each; shoes and balls are an extra $2.

still several places that strive to bring Miami up to speed as far as live music is concerned. You just have to look—and listen—for it a bit more carefully. The following is a list of places you can, from time to time, catch some live acts, be it a DJ or an aspiring Nirvana.

Billboard Live   Affiliated with the national music industry magazine, this mammoth dance club, bar, recording studio, and live music venue is much cooler than its chain-ish name implies. Although at press time the live acts haven't necessarily been major headliners (Macy Gray was supposed to kick off a tour here, but then canceled with no reason), the acoustics in this multilevel club are exceptional, as is the Saturday night DJ-ed dance scene and Sunday afternoon, mostly gay Tea Dance Disco parties. The club's first-floor patio restaurant is also a great alternative to the thumping club vibe. 1501 Collins Ave., South Beach. ✆ 305/538-2251. Cover $0–$20.

Churchill's Hideaway *(Finds)*   British expatriate Dave Daniels couldn't live in Miami without a true English-style pub, so he opened Churchill's Hideaway, the city's premier space for live rock music. Filthy and located in a rather unsavory neighborhood, Churchill's is committed to promoting and extending the lifeline of the lagging local music scene. A fun no-frills crowd hangs out here. Bring earplugs with you, as it is deafening once the music starts. 5501 NE 2nd Ave., Little Haiti. ✆ 305/757-1807. Cover $0–$5.

Jazid *(Finds)*   Smoky, sultry, and illuminated by flickering candelabras, Jazid is the kind of place where you'd expect to hear Sade's "Smooth Operator" on constant rotation. Instead, however, you'll hear live jazz (sometimes on acid), soul, and funk. Past surprise performers at Jazid include former Smashing Pumpkin's front man Billy Corgan. An eclectic mix of mellow folk convenes here for a much necessary respite from the surrounding Washington Avenue mayhem. 1342 Washington Ave., South Beach. ✆ 305/673-9372. No cover.

Tobacco Road   Al Capone used to hang out here when it was a speakeasy. Now, locals flock here to see local bands perform, as well as national acts such as George Clinton and the P-Funk All-Stars, Koko Taylor, and the Radiators. Tobacco Road (the proud owner of Miami's very first liquor license) is small and gritty and meant to be that way. Escape the smoke and sweat in the backyard patio, where air is a welcome commodity. The downright cheap nightly specials, such as the $11 lobster on Tuesday, are quite good and are served until 2am; the bar is open until 5am. 626 S. Miami Ave. (over the Miami Ave. Bridge near Brickell Ave.), Downtown. ✆ 305/374-1198. Cover $5 Fri–Sat.

Upstairs at the Van Dyke Cafe *(Finds)*   The cafe's jazz bar, located on the second floor, resembles a classy speakeasy in which local jazz performers play to an intimate, enthusiastic crowd of mostly adults and sophisticated young things, who often huddle at the small tables until the wee hours. 846 Lincoln Rd., Miami Beach. ✆ 305/534-3600. Cover $3–$6 for a seat; no cover at the bar.

THE GAY & LESBIAN SCENE

Miami and the beaches have long been host to what is called a "first-tier" gay community. Similar to the Big Apple, the Bay Area, or LaLa land, Miami has had a large alternative community since the days when Anita Bryant used her citrus power to boycott the rise in political activism by gays in the early '70s. Well, things have changed and Miami–Dade now has a gay rights ordinance.

Newcomers intending to party in any bar, whether downtown or certainly on the beach, will want to check ahead for the schedule, as all clubs must have a gay or lesbian night to pay their rent. Miami Beach, in fact, is a capital of the gay circuit party scene, rivaling San Francisco, Palm Springs, and even the mighty Sydney, Australia, for tourist dollars.

Academy   Hordes of gay men (and some women) join the Academy at Level every Friday, when the dance floor is packed with wall-to-wall hard bodies. 1235 Washington Ave., South Beach. ℂ **305/532-1525.** Cover $20–$30.

Anthem   Sunday nights at crobar sing the gay anthem with this hyperpopular one-nighter featuring Miami's own superstar DJ Abel. 1445 Washington Ave., South Beach. ℂ **877/CRO-SOBE** or 305/531-5027. Cover $25.

Cactus Bar & Grill   Somewhere, over the causeway, there is life beyond South Beach—that is, for Miami's gay society. Housed in a large two-story space, Cactus attracts a mix of unpretentious, professional, and very attractive men and women. There's something for everyone here, whether it's the indoor pool tables, the outdoor swimming pool, or drinks that are considerably cheaper than on South Beach. Friday evening happy hours and Sunday afternoon Tea Dances are a virtual cattle call, attracting hordes of folks looking to quench their thirst for fun at Miami's sprawling urban oasis. 2401 Biscayne Blvd., Downtown. ℂ **305/438-0662.** No cover.

Loading Zone   A leather and Levi bar known for its cruisability, pool tables, movies, and pitchers of beer. There's also an in-house leather store for the kinky shopper. Open daily 10pm to 5am. 1426 Alton Rd., South Beach. ℂ **305/531-5623.** Cover $15–$20.

O-Zone   This is the zone of choice for gay men with an aversion to South Beach's cruisy, scene-heavy vibes. It's known for a heavily Latin crowd (mixed with a few college boys from nearby University of Miami) and fantastic, outlandish drag shows on the weekends. 6620 SW 57th Ave. (Red Rd.), South Miami. ℂ **305/667-2888.** No cover for men on Sat; other nights $5–$10.

1771   For those seeking liberation from the cookie-cutter mold of run-of-the-mill, Saturday-night dance clubs, this place, formerly known as Salvation, is where you'll find it. Housed in an old warehouse, 1771 is spacious but always filled to capacity with shirtless, sweaty circuit boys dancing themselves into oblivion. Major DJs spin here, and, at times, divas sing here, such as Bette Midler, who did a rare and ribald cabaret performance to an SRO audience. You can't blame the owners for charging $20 to get in when you see this bevy of beautiful boys. Only open on Saturday nights. 1771 West Ave., South Beach. ℂ **305/673-6508.** Cover $20.

Score   There's a reason this Lincoln Road hotbed of gay social activity is called Score. In addition to the huge pick-up scene, Score offers a multitude of bars, dance floors, lounge-like areas, and outdoor tables in case you need to come up for air. Sunday afternoon Tea Dances are legendary here. 727 Lincoln Rd., South Beach. ℂ **305/535-1111.** No cover.

Twist   One of the most popular bars (and hideaways) on South Beach, this recently expanded bar (which is literally right across the street from the police station) has a casual yet lively local atmosphere. 1057 Washington Ave., South Beach. ℂ **305/538-9478.** No cover.

LATIN CLUBS

Considering that Hispanics make up a large part of Miami's population and that there's a huge influx of Spanish-speaking visitors, it's no surprise that there are some great Latin nightclubs in the city.

The Rhythm Is Gonna Get You

Are you feeling shy about hitting a Latin club because you fear your two left feet will stand out? Then take a few lessons from one of the following dance companies or dance teachers. They offer individual and group lessons to dancers of any origin who are willing to learn. These folks have made it their mission to teach merengue and flamenco to non-Latinos and Latino left-foots and are among the most reliable, consistent, and popular ones in Miami. So what are you waiting for?

Thursday and Friday nights at **Bongo's Cuban Café** (American Airlines Arena, 601 Biscayne Blvd., Downtown; © 786/777-2100) are an amazing showcase of some of the city's best salsa dancers, but amateurs need not be intimidated thanks to the instructors at Latin Groove Dance Studios, who are on hand to help you with your two left feet.

At **Ballet Flamenco La Rosa** (in the Performing Arts Network building, 13126 W. Dixie Hwy., North Miami; © 305/899-7730), you can learn to flamenco, salsa, or merengue. This is the only professional flamenco company in the area. If you're feeling shy, $50 will buy you a private lesson; otherwise, it's $10 for a group lesson.

Nobody salsas like **Luz Pinto** (© 305/868-9418), and she also knows how to teach the basics with patience and humor. She charges between $40 and $55 for a private lesson for up to four people and $10 per person for a group lesson. A good introduction is her multi-level group class at 7pm Sunday evenings at the PAN building. Although she teaches everything from ballroom to merengue, her specialty is Casino-style salsa, popularized in the 1950s in Cuba, Luz's homeland. A mix between disco and country square dancing, Casino-style salsa is all the rage in Latin clubs in town. Good students may be able to convince Luz, for an extra fee, to chaperone a trip to a nightclub to show off their moves. Ask her for more information.

Angel Arroya has been teaching salsa to the clueless out of his home (at 16467 NE 27th Ave., North Miami Beach; © 305/949-7799) for the past 10 years. Just $10 will buy you an hour's time in his "school." He traditionally teaches Monday and Wednesday nights, but call ahead to check for any schedule changes.

Plus, with the meteoric rise of the international music scene based in Miami, many international stars come through the offices of MTV Latino, SONY International, and a multitude of Latin TV studios based in Miami—and they're all looking for a good club scene on weekends. Most of the Anglo clubs also reserve at least 1 night a week for Latin rhythms.

Añoranzas Taberna You've heard of *son?* Hear it here—along with salsa, cumbia, merengue, vallenato, and house music. This neighborhood Latin disco and nightclub gets going after hours with a wild strobe-lit atmosphere. If you don't know how to do it, just wait. You'll have plenty of willing teachers on hand. Open Friday to Sunday from 8pm to 5am. 241 23rd St. (1 block west of Collins Ave.), South Beach. © 305/538-1196. No cover.

Casa Panza *(Finds* This *casa* is one of Little Havana's liveliest and most popular nightspots. Every Tuesday, Thursday, and Saturday night, Casa Panza, in the heart of Little Havana, becomes the House of Flamenco, with shows at 8 and 11pm. You can either enjoy a flamenco show or strap on your own dancing shoes and participate in the celebration. Enjoy a fantastic Spanish meal before the show, or just a glass of sangria before you start stomping. Open until 4am, Casa Panza is a hot spot for young Latin club kids, and, occasionally, a few older folks who are so taken by the music and the scene that they've failed to realize that it's well past their bedtime. 1620 SW 8th St. (Calle Ocho), Little Havana. (*C*) 305/643-5343. No cover.

Hoy Como Ayer Formerly known as Cafe Nostalgia, the Little Havana hangout dedicated to reminiscing about Old Cuba, Hoy Como Ayer is like the Brady Bunch of Latin hangouts—while it was extremely popular with old timers in its Cafe Nostalgia incarnation, it is now experiencing a resurgence among the younger generation, seeking their own brand of Nostalgia. Its Thursday night party, Fuacata (slang for "Pow!"), is a magnet for artsy Latin hipsters, featuring classic Cuban music mixed in with modern DJ-spun sound effects. Open Thursday to Sunday from 9pm to 4am. 2212 SW 8th St. (Calle Ocho), Little Havana. (*C*) 305/541-2631. Cover $10 Thurs–Sun.

La Covacha *(Finds* This hut, located virtually in the middle of nowhere (West Miami), is the hottest Latin joint in the entire city. Sunday features the best in Latin rock, with local and international acts. But the shack is really jumping on weekend nights when the place is open until 5am. Friday is *the* night here, so much so that the owners had to place a red velvet rope out front to maintain some semblance of order. It's an amusing sight—a velvet rope guarding a shack—but once you get in, you'll understand the need for it. Do not wear silk here, as you *will* sweat. 10730 NW 25th St. (at NW 107th Ave.), West Miami. (*C*) 305/594-3717. Cover $0–$10.

Mango's Tropical Café Claustrophobic types do not want to go near Mango's. Ever. One of the most popular spots on Ocean Drive, this outdoor enclave of Latin liveliness shakes with the intensity of a Richter-busting earthquake. Welcome and *bienvenido,* Mango's is *Cabaret,* Latin style. Nightly live Brazilian and other Latin music, not to mention scantily clad male and female dancers, draw huge gawking crowds in from the sidewalk. But pay attention to the music if you can: Incognito international musicians often lose their anonymity and jam with the house band on stage. Open daily from 11am to 5am. 900 Ocean Dr., South Beach. (*C*) 305/673-4422. Cover $5–$15.

3 The Performing Arts

Highbrows and culture vultures complain that there is a dearth of decent cultural offerings in Miami. What do locals tell them? Go back to New York! In all seriousness, however, in recent years, Miami's performing arts scene has improved greatly. The city's Broadway Series features Tony Award–winning shows (the touring versions, of course), which aren't always Broadway caliber, but they are usually pretty good and not nearly as pricey. Local arts groups such as the Miami Light Project, a not-for-profit cultural organization that presents live performances by innovative dance, music, and theater artists, have had huge success in attracting big-name artists such as Nina Simone and Philip Glass to Miami. In addition, a burgeoning bohemian movement in Little Havana has given way to performance spaces that have become nightclubs in their own right.

THEATER

The **Actors' Playhouse,** a musical theater at the newly restored Miracle Theater at 280 Miracle Mile, Coral Gables (© **305/444-9293;** www.actorsplayhouse. org), is a grand 1948 Art Deco movie palace with a 600-seat main theater and a smaller theater/rehearsal hall that hosts a number of excellent musicals for children throughout the year. In addition to these two rooms, the Playhouse recently added a 300-seat children's balcony theater. Tickets run from $26 to $50.

The **Coconut Grove Playhouse,** 3500 Main Hwy., Coconut Grove (© **305/ 442-4000;** www.cgplayhouse.com), was also a former movie house, built in 1927 in an ornate Spanish rococo style. Today, this respected venue is known for its original and innovative staging of both international and local dramas and musicals. The house's second, more intimate Encore Room is well suited to alternative and experimental productions. Tickets run from $37 to $42.

The **Gables Stage** at the Biltmore Hotel, Anastasia Avenue, Coral Gables (© **305/445-1119**), stages at least one Shakespearean play, one classic, and one contemporary piece a year. This well-regarded theater usually tries to secure the rights to a national or local premiere as well. Tickets cost $22 and $28; $10 and $17 for students and seniors.

The **Jerry Herman Ring Theatre** is on the main campus of the University of Miami in Coral Gables (© **305/284-3355**). The University's Department of Theater Arts uses this stage for advanced-student productions of comedies, dramas, and musicals. Faculty and guest actors are regularly featured, as are contemporary works by local playwrights. Performances are usually scheduled Tuesday through Saturday during the academic year. In the summer, don't miss Summer Shorts, a selection of superb one-acts. Tickets sell for $5 to $20.

The **New Theater,** 65 Almeria Ave., Coral Gables (© **305/443-5909**), prides itself on showing world-renowned works from America and Europe. As the name implies, you'll find mostly contemporary plays, with a few classics thrown in for variety. Performances are staged Thursday to Sunday year-round. Tickets are $20 on weekdays, $25 weekends. If tickets are available on the day of the performance—and they usually are—students pay half price.

CLASSICAL MUSIC

In addition to a number of local orchestras and operas (see below), which regularly offer quality music and world-renowned guest artists, each year brings a slew of classical music special events and touring artists to Miami. The Concert Association of Florida (CAF), © **305/532-3491,** produces one of the most important and longest-running series. Known for more than a quarter of a century for its high-caliber, star-packed schedules, CAF regularly arranges the best "serious" music concerts for the city. Season after season, the schedules are punctuated by world-renowned dance companies and seasoned virtuosi like Itzhak Perlman, Andre Watts, and Kathleen Battle. Since CAF does not have its own space, performances are usually scheduled in the Miami–Dade County Auditorium or the Jackie Gleason Theater of the Performing Arts (see the "Major Venues" section below). The season lasts from October through April, and ticket prices range from $20 to $70.

Florida Philharmonic Orchestra South Florida's premier symphony orchestra, under the direction of James Judd, presents a full season of classical and pops programs interspersed with several children's and contemporary popular music performances. The Philharmonic performs downtown in the

Gusman Center for the Performing Arts and at the Miami–Dade County Auditorium (see the "Major Venues" section below). 1243 University Dr., Miami. © 800/226-1812 or 305/476-1234. Tickets $15–$60. When extra tickets are available, students are admitted free on day of performance.

Miami Chamber Symphony   This professional orchestra is a small, subscription-series orchestra that's not affiliated with any major arts organizations and is therefore an inexpensive alternative to the high-priced classical venues. Renowned international soloists perform regularly. The season runs October to May, and most concerts are held in the Gusman Concert Hall, on the University of Miami campus. 5690 N. Kendall Dr., Kendall. © 305/858-3500. Tickets $12–$30.

New World Symphony   This organization, led by artistic director Michael Tilson Thomas, is a stepping stone for gifted young musicians seeking professional careers. The orchestra specializes in ambitious, innovative, energetic performances and often features renowned guest soloists and conductors. The symphony's season lasts from October to May, during which time there are many free concerts. 541 Lincoln Rd., South Beach. © 305/673-3331. www.nws.org. Tickets free–$58. Rush tickets (remaining tickets sold 1 hr. before performance) $20. Students $10 (1 hr. before concerts; limited seating).

OPERA

Florida Grand Opera   Around for over 60 years, this company regularly features singers from top houses in both America and Europe. All productions are sung in their original language and staged with projected English supertitles. Tickets become scarce when Placido Domingo or Luciano Pavarotti (who made his American debut here in 1965) comes to town. The opera's season runs roughly from November to April, with five performances each week. A new multimillion-dollar headquarters for the opera is scheduled to open in mid-2004; until then, performances take place at the Miami–Dade County Auditorium and the Broward Center for the Performing Arts, about 40 minutes from downtown Miami. Box office: 1200 Coral Way, Southwest Miami. © 800/741-1010. www.fgo.org. Tickets $19–$145. Student discounts available.

DANCE

Several local dance companies train and perform in the Greater Miami area. In addition, top traveling troupes regularly stop at the venues listed below. Keep your eyes open for special events and guest artists.

Ballet Flamenco La Rosa   For a taste of local Latin flavor, see this lively troupe perform impressive flamenco and other styles of Latin dance on Miami stages. (They also teach Latin dancing—see the "The Rhythm Is Gonna Get You" box above.) 13126 W. Dixie Hwy., North Miami, © 305/899-7729. Tickets $25 at door, $20 in advance, $18 for students and seniors.

Miami City Ballet   This artistically acclaimed and innovative company, directed by Edward Villella, features a repertoire of more than 60 ballets, many by George Balanchine, and has had more than 20 world premieres. The company moved into a new $7.5 million headquarters in January 2000—the Ophelia and Juan Jr. Roca Center at the Collins Park Cultural Center in Miami Beach. This three-story center features eight rehearsal rooms, a ballet school, a boutique, and ticket offices. The City Ballet season runs from September to April. Ophelia and Juan Jr. Roca Center, Collins Ave. and 22nd St., South Beach. © 305/532-4880 or 305/532-7713 for box office. Tickets $17–$50.

MAJOR VENUES

The **Colony Theater,** on Lincoln Road in South Beach (© **305/674-1026**), has become an architectural showpiece of the Art Deco District. This multipurpose 465-seat theater stages performances by the Miami City Ballet and the Ballet Flamenco La Rosa as well as off-Broadway shows and other special events. The Colony closed in July 2002 for 16 months for a $4.3 million renovation that will add wing and fly space, improve handicapped access, and restore the lobby to its original art deco look.

At the **Miami–Dade County Auditorium,** West Flagler Street at 29th Avenue, Southwest Miami (© **305/547-5414**), performers gripe about the lack of space, but for patrons, this 2,430-seat auditorium is the only Miami space in which you can hear the opera—for now. A multimillion-dollar performing arts center downtown has been in the works for years (see below). For now, though, the Miami–Dade County Auditorium is home to the city's Florida Grand Opera, and it also stages productions by the Concert Association of Florida, many programs in Spanish, and a variety of other shows.

At the 1,700-seat **Gusman Center for the Performing Arts,** 174 E. Flagler St., Downtown (© **305/372-0925**), seating is tight, and so is funding, but the sound is superb. In addition to hosting the Florida Philharmonic Orchestra and the Miami Film Festival, the elegant Gusman Center features pop concerts, plays, film screenings, and special events. The auditorium was built as the Olympia Theater in 1926, and its ornate palace interior is typical of that era, complete with fancy columns, a huge pipe organ, and twinkling "stars" on the ceiling.

Not to be confused with the Gusman Center (above), the **Gusman Concert Hall,** 1314 Miller Dr., at 14th Street, Coral Gables (© **305/284-6477**), is a roomy 600-seat hall that gives a stage to the Miami Chamber Symphony and a varied program of university recitals.

The elegant **Jackie Gleason Theater of the Performing Arts (TOPA),** located in South Beach at Washington Avenue and 17th Street (© **305/673-7300**), is the home of the Miami Beach Broadway Series, which has recently presented *Rent, Phantom of the Opera,* and *Les Misérables.* This 2,705-seat hall also hosts other big-budget Broadway shows, classical music concerts, and dance performances.

At press time, the city granted a budget in excess of $200 million for its official Performing Arts Center. Planned are a 2,400-seat ballet/opera house and a 2,000-seat concert hall for the Florida Philharmonic Orchestra, Florida Grand Opera, New World Symphony, Miami City Ballet, and a major concert series. Designed by world-renowned architect Cesar Pelli, it will be the focal point of a planned Arts, Media, and Entertainment District in mid-Miami. The complex will be wrapped in limestone, slate, decorative stone, stainless steel, glass curtain walls, and tropical landscaping, and is slated to be complete in mid-2004. For more information, check out the center's website at www.pacfmiami.org.

4 Cinemas, the Literary Scene, Spectator Sports & More

CINEMAS

In addition to the annual Miami Film Festival in February and other, smaller film events (See "South Florida Calendar of Events," in chapter 2, "Planning Your Trip to South Florida"), Miami has nearly as many multiplex cinemas as it does palm trees. And for good reason. When it rains in Miami, what else is there to do besides go to the movies, a museum, or the mall? But if 40 screens of *Jurassic Park III* isn't your idea of a day at the movies, consider the following arty theaters, known for playing lots of subtitled, foreign films as well as those that get bumped off the big screen by the Jurassic Parks of the celluloid world.

Absinthe Cinemateque, 235 Alcazar Ave., Coral Gables (© **305/446-7144**), is a small one-screen theater that shows good movies, often Spanish-language films, without the hustle and bustle of the crowded multiplexes. The Alcazar shows the more artsy of the major films as well as some obscure independents. Tickets are $6.

Astor Art Cinema, 4120 Laguna St. (© **305/443-6777**), is an oasis in the midst of a desert of Cineplex Odeons and AMCs in Coral Gables. This quaint double theater hosts foreign, classic, independent, and art films and serves decent popcorn, too. Tickets are $5.

The **Bill Cosford Cinema,** at the University of Miami, is located on the second floor of the memorial building off Campo Sano Avenue (© **305/284-4861**). This well-endowed little theater was recently revamped and boasts high-tech projectors, new air-conditioning, and a new decor. It sponsors independent films as well as lectures by visiting filmmakers and movie stars. Andy Garcia and Antonio Banderas are a few of the big names this theater has attracted. It also hosts the African-American Film Festival, a Student Film Festival, and collaborations with the Fort Lauderdale Festival (a very small film festival). Admission is $5.

The **Mercury Theatre,** Biscayne Boulevard at 55th Street, Miami (© **305/759-8809**), is the city's newest art house cinema, showing classic and contemporary films from all over the world. Tickets are $8 or $6 for seniors and matinees.

THE LITERARY SCENE

Books & Books, in Coral Gables at 265 Aragon Ave. and in Miami Beach at 933 Lincoln Rd., hosts readings almost every night and is known for attracting such top authors as Colleen McCullough, Jamaica Kincaid, and Martin Amis. For details on their free readings, call © **305/442-4408.**

To hear more about what's happening on Miami's literary scene, tune into the "Cover to Cover" radio show, broadcast at 8pm on Mondays on public radio station WLRN (91.3 FM).

Warhol Redux?

Miami's **Artemis Performance Network** sets the stage for the city's creative types with eclectic venues and events dedicated to and showcasing the local arts community. A network of performing artists, visual artists, musicians, presenters, educators, and administrators, Artemis is backed by the support of the Miami–Dade County Cultural Affairs Council, among others. Responsible for turning Little Havana into a bohemian hangout, Artemis sponsors most of its events at a loftlike performance space simply known as PS 742, at 742 SW 16th Ave. in Little Havana (© **305/643-6611**), in which events such as Surreal Saturdays (first Saturday of every month) feature a funky roster of spoken word, multimedia, and musical artists. Locals have compared the scene at PS 742 to that of New York City's East Village, circa 1980.

SPECTATOR SPORTS

For information on watching baseball, basketball, football, horse racing, ice hockey, and jai alai (many of these games are at night), please see the "Spectator Sports" section of chapter 7, "What to See & Do in Miami," beginning on p. 193.

5 Late-Night Bites

Although some dining spots in Miami stop serving at 10pm, many are open very late or even around the clock—especially on weekends. So, if it's 4am and you need a quick bite after clubbing, don't fret. There are a vast number of pizza places lining Washington Avenue in South Beach that are open past 6am. Especially good are **La Sandwicherie,** 229 14th St. (behind the Amoco station; © 305/532-8934), which serves up a great late-night sandwich until 5am; and its next-door neighbor **San Loco Tacos** (235 14th St.; © **305/538-3009**), which slings tacos until 5am on weeknights and 6am on weekends. Another place of note for night owls is the **News Café,** 800 Ocean Dr. (© **305/538-6397**), a trendy and well-priced cafe that has an enormous menu offering great all-day breakfasts, Middle Eastern platters, fruit bowls, or steak and potatoes—and everything is served 24 hours a day. In Coconut Grove, there's another crowded News Café, 2901 Florida Ave. (behind Mayfair; © 305/774-6397), serving up the same fresh food around the clock. If your night out was at one of the Latin clubs around town, stop in at **Versailles,** 3555 SW 8th St. (© **305/444-0240**), in Little Havana. What else but a Cuban *medianoche* (midnight sandwich) will do? It's not open all night, but its hours extend well past midnight—usually until 3 or 4am on weekends—to cater to gangs of revelers, young and old.

For a more thorough listing of Miami's most notable restaurants, please see chapter 6, "Where to Dine in Miami."

10

The Everglades & Biscayne National Park

Miami has been called the "gateway to the world" because its port leads the pack in passengers heading to the Caribbean and to Latin America. But tourists should also take some time out to see the wild plant and animal life in the swampy Everglades and the underwater treasures of Biscayne National Park.

1 A Glimpse of Everglades National Park ✶✶

35 miles SW of Miami

Before going, my conception of the Everglades was that it was one big swamp swarming with ominous creatures. For someone who'd rather endure an endless series of root canals than audition for a role on *Survivor* (the closest I'd ever been to nature was sleep-away camp), the Everglades may as well have been the *Never*-glades. That is, until I finally decided to venture there. To my surprise, and contrary to popular belief, the Everglades isn't really a swamp at all, but one of the country's most fascinating natural resources. Imagine a shallow river of grass protected by canopies of lush mangroves and you've got the Everglades, where primitive wildlife peacefully coexists with awe-struck visitors.

For first-timers or those with dubious athletic skills, the best way to see the 'Glades is probably via airboats, which actually aren't allowed in the park proper but cut through the saw grass on the park's outskirts, taking you past countless birds, alligators, crocodiles, deer, and raccoons. A walk on one of the park's many trails will provide you with a different vantage point; up-close interaction with an assortment of tame wildlife. But the absolute best way to see the 'Glades is via canoe, where you can get incredibly close to nature. Whichever method you choose, I guarantee you will marvel at the sheer beauty of the Everglades. In addition to the multitude of mosquito bites (the bugs seem to be immune to repellent—wear long pants and cover your arms, if possible), an Everglades experience will definitely contribute to a newfound appreciation for Florida's natural (and beautiful) wonderland.

This vast and unusual ecosystem is actually a shallow, 40-mile-wide, slow-moving river. Rarely more than knee-deep, the water is the lifeblood of this wilderness, and the subtle shifts in water level dictate the life cycle of the native plants and animals. Most folks viewed the Everglades as a worthless swamp until Marjory Stoneman Douglas (who fought tirelessly to save this fragile resource until her death in 1998 at the age of 108) focused attention on the area with her moving and insightful book *The Everglades: River of Grass,* published in 1947.

In that same year, 1.5 million acres—less than 20% of the Everglades' wilderness—were established as Everglades National Park. At that time, few

Everglades National Park

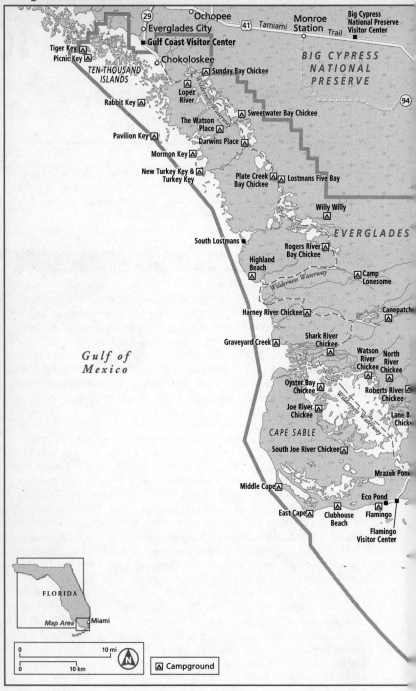

Tiger Key 🔺
Picnic Key 🔺

TEN THOUSAND ISLANDS

29
Ochopee
Everglades City
Gulf Coast Visitor Center
Chokoloskee

Sunday Bay Chickee 🔺

41 Tamiami Trail
Monroe Station
Big Cypress National Preserve Visitor Center

BIG CYPRESS NATIONAL PRESERVE

94

Lopez River 🔺
Rabbit Key 🔺
The Watson Place 🔺
Pavilion Key 🔺
Darwins Place 🔺
Mormon Key 🔺
New Turkey Key & Turkey Key 🔺

Sweetwater Bay Chickee 🔺

Plate Creek Bay Chickee 🔺 Lostmans Five Bay

Willy Willy 🔺

EVERGLADES

South Lostmans ■

Rogers River Bay Chickee 🔺

Highland Beach 🔺

Wilderness Waterway

Camp Lonesome 🔺

Harney River Chickee 🔺

Canepatch 🔺

Graveyard Creek 🔺

Shark River Chickee 🔺

Watson River Chickee 🔺
North River Chickee 🔺

Gulf of Mexico

Oyster Bay Chickee 🔺

Roberts River Chickee 🔺

Joe River Chickee 🔺

Wilderness Waterway

Lane B. Chick

CAPE SABLE

South Joe River Chickee 🔺

Mrazek Pond

Middle Cape 🔺

Eco Pond ■
Flamingo

East Cape 🔺
Clubhouse Beach

Flamingo Visitor Center

FLORIDA

Map Area
Miami

0 ——— 10 mi
0 ——— 10 km

N

🔺 Campground

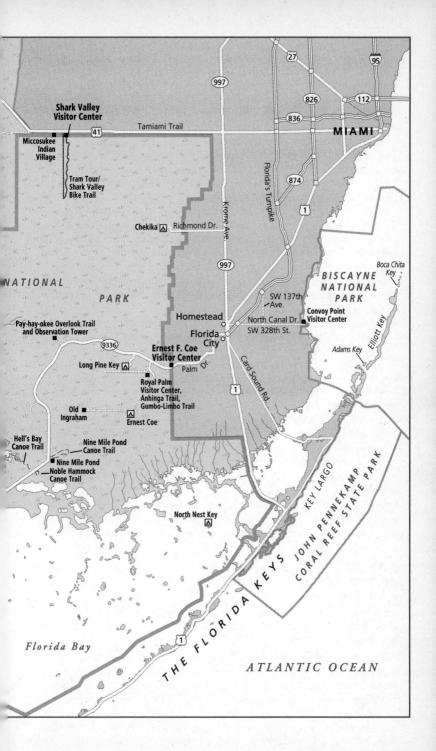

Shark Valley
Visitor Center

Miccosukee
Indian
Village

Tamiami Trail

Tram Tour/
Shark Valley
Bike Trail

MIAMI

Chekika · Richmond Dr.

NATIONAL

PARK

Florida's Turnpike

Krome Ave.

BISCAYNE
NATIONAL
PARK

Boca Chita
Key

Pay-hay-okee Overlook Trail
and Observation Tower

Homestead

SW 137th
Ave.

North Canal Dr.

Convoy Point
Visitor Center

Florida
City

SW 328th St.

Elliott Key

Ernest F. Coe
Visitor Center

Long Pine Key

Palm Dr.

Adams Key

Royal Palm
Visitor Center,
Anhinga Trail,
Gumbo-Limbo Trail

Card Sound Rd.

Old
Ingraham

Ernest Coe

Hell's Bay
Canoe Trail

Nine Mile Pond
Canoe Trail

KEY LARGO

Nine Mile Pond

Noble Hammock
Canoe Trail

North Nest Key

JOHN PENNEKAMP
CORAL REEF STATE PARK

THE FLORIDA KEYS

Florida Bay

ATLANTIC OCEAN

lawmakers understood how neighboring ecosystems relate to each other. Consequently, the park is heavily affected by surrounding territories and is at the butt end of every environmental insult that occurs upstream in Miami. Recently, environmental activists have succeeded in persuading politicians to enact legislation to clean up the pollution that has threatened this unusual ecosystem ever since the days when heavy industry—most notably the sugar industry—first moved into the area.

While there has been a marked decrease in the indigenous wildlife here, Everglades National Park nevertheless remains one of the few places where you can see dozens of endangered species in their natural habitat, including the swallowtail butterfly, American crocodile, leatherback turtle, southern bald eagle, West Indian manatee, and Florida panther.

Take your time on the trails, and a hypnotic beauty begins to unfold. Follow the rustling of a bush, and you might see a small green tree frog or tiny brown anole lizard, with its bright-red spotted throat. Crane your neck to see around a bend and discover a delicate, brightly painted mule-ear orchid.

The slow and subtle splendor of this exotic land may not be immediately appealing to kids raised on video games and rapid-fire commercials, but they'll certainly remember the experience and thank you for it later. Meanwhile, you'll find plenty of dramatic fun around the park, such as airboat rides, alligator wrestling, and biking to keep the kids satisfied for at least a day.

In the 1800s, before the southern Everglades were designated a national park, the only inhabited piece of this wilderness was a quiet fishing village called Flamingo. Accessible only by boat and leveled every few years by hurricanes, the mosquito-infested town never grew very popular. When the 38-mile-long road from Florida City was completed in 1922, many of those who did live here fled to someplace either more or less remote. Today, Flamingo is a center for visitor activities and is the main jumping-off point for backcountry camping and exploration. It is also now home to National Park Service and concessionaire employees and their families. Some 1,400 residents still live in this small enclave in the eastern section of the park, though the local agency governing the area has recently begun a buyout program so the area can be returned to its original state.

> **Lazy River**
> It takes a month for 1 gallon of water to move through Everglades National Park.

JUST THE FACTS

GETTING THERE & ACCESS POINTS   Although the Everglades may seem overwhelmingly large and unapproachable, it's easy to get to the park's two main areas—the northern section, which is accessible via Shark Valley and Everglades City, or the southern section, accessible through the Ernest F. Coe Visitor Center, near Homestead and Florida City.

Northern Entrances   A popular day trip for Miamians, **Shark Valley,** a 13-mile paved road ending at an observation tower overlooking the pulsating heart of the Everglades, is the easiest and most scenic way to explore the Everglades. Just 25 miles west of the Florida Turnpike, Shark Valley is best reached via the Tamiami Trail, South Florida's pre-Turnpike, two-lane road that cuts across the southern part of the state along the park's northern border. Roadside attractions (boat rides and alligator farms, for example) along the trail are operated by the

Miccosukee Indian Village and are fun and worth a quick stop. An excellent tram tour (leaving from the Shark Valley Visitor Center) goes deep into the park along a trail that's also terrific for biking. This is also the best way to reach the park's only accommodation (and full-service outfitters), the Flamingo Lodge. Shark Valley is about an hour's drive from Miami.

A little less than 10 miles west along the Tamiami Trail from Shark Valley, you'll discover the **Big Cypress National Preserve,** in which stretches of vibrant green cypress and pine trees make for a fabulous Kodak moment. If you pick up State Road 29 and head south from the Tamiami Trail, you'll hit a modified version of civilization in the form of Everglades City (where the Everglades meets the Gulf of Mexico) and see another entrance to the park and the **Gulf Coast Visitor Center.** To reach Shark Valley from Miami: Go west on I-395 to State Road 821 south (the Florida Turnpike). Take the U.S. 41/SW 8th Street (Tamiami Trail) exit. The Shark Valley entrance is just 25 miles west. To get to Everglades City, continue west on the Tamiami Trail and head south on State Road 29. Everglades City is approximately a 2½-hour drive from Miami, but because it is scenic, it may take longer if you stop or slow down to view your surroundings.

Southern Entrance Via Homestead & Florida City   If you're in a rush to hit the 'Glades and don't care about the scenic route, this is your best bet. Just southeast of Homestead and Florida City, off of State Road 9336, the southern access to the park will bring you directly to the Ernest F. Coe Visitor Center. Right inside the park, 4 miles beyond the Ernest F. Coe Visitor Center, is the Royal Palm Visitor Center, which is the starting point for the two most popular walking trails—Gumbo Limbo and Anhinga, on which you will witness a plethora of birds and wildlife roam freely, unperturbed by their human voyeurs. If you go 13 miles west of the Ernest F. Coe Visitor Center, you will hit the Pa-hay-okee Overlook Trail, which is worth a trek across the boardwalk to reach the observation tower. Overhead you'll spot vultures and hawks hovering protectively amidst a resplendent, picturesque, bird's-eye view of the Everglades. To get to the Southern entrance from Miami: Go west on I-395 to State Road 821 south (Florida Turnpike). The Turnpike will end in Florida City. Take your first right turn through the center of town (you can't miss it) and follow the signs to the park entrance on State Road 9336. The Ernest F. Coe Visitor Center is about 1½ hours from Miami.

VISITOR CENTERS & INFORMATION   General inquiries and specific questions should be directed to **Everglades National Park Headquarters,** 40001 S.R. 9336, Homestead, FL 33034 (© **305/242-7700**). Ask for a copy of *Parks and Preserves,* a free newspaper that's filled with up-to-date information about goings-on in the Everglades. Headquarters is staffed by helpful phone operators daily from 8:30am until 4:30pm. You can also try www.nps.gov/ever/visit/index.htm or www.florida-everglades.com.

Note that all hours listed are for the high season, generally November through May. During the slow summer months, many offices and outfitters keep abbreviated hours. Always call ahead to confirm hours of operation.

Thirty-eight miles from the main entrance, at the park's southern access, is the **Flamingo Visitor Center,** which offers natural history exhibits and information on Flamingo's visitor services.

Especially since its recent expansion, the **Ernest F. Coe Visitor Center,** located at the park headquarters' entrance west of Homestead and Florida City, is the best place for gathering information for your trip. In addition to information on tours and boat rentals, and free brochures outlining trails, wildlife, and activities, you will also find state-of-the-art educational displays, films, and interactive exhibits. A gift shop sells postcards, film, unusual gift items, an impressive selection of books about the Everglades, and a supply of your most important gear: insect repellent. The shop is open from 8am until 5pm daily.

The **Royal Palm Visitor Center,** a small nature museum located 3 miles past the park's main entrance, is a smaller information center. The museum is not great (there are displays with recorded messages interpreting the park's ecosystem), but the center is the departure point for the popular Anhinga and Gumbo Limbo Trails. The center is open daily from 8am until 4pm.

Knowledgeable rangers, who provide brochures and personal insight into the park's activities, also staff the **Shark Valley Visitor Center,** at the park's northern entrance, and the **Flamingo Visitor Center.** Both are open from 8:30am until 5pm.

ENTRANCE FEES, PERMITS & REGULATIONS   Permits and passes can be purchased only at the main park entrance, the Chekika entrance, or the Shark Valley entrance stations.

Even if you are just visiting the park for an afternoon, you'll need to buy a 7-day permit, which costs $10 per vehicle. Pedestrians and cyclists are charged $5 each and $4 at Shark Valley.

An Everglades Park Pass, valid for a year's worth of unlimited admissions, is available for $20. U.S. citizens may purchase a 12-month Golden Eagle Passport for $65, which is valid for entrance into any U.S. national park. U.S. citizens aged 62 and older pay only $10 for a Golden Age Passport—that's valid for life. A Golden Access Passport is available free to U.S. citizens with disabilities.

Permits are required for campers to stay overnight either in the backcountry or in the primitive campsites. See information about camping in "Where to Stay," later in this chapter.

Those who want to fish without a charter captain must obtain a standard State of Florida saltwater fishing license. These are available in the park at Flamingo Lodge or at any tackle shop or sporting goods store nearby. Nonresidents will pay $17 for a 7-day license or $7 for 3 days. Florida residents can get a fishing license good for the whole year for $14. Snook and crawfish licenses must be purchased separately at a cost of $2.

Charter captains carry vessel licenses that cover all paying passengers, but ask to be sure. Fishing licenses are available at various bait-and-tackle shops outside the park at the same rates as those offered inside the park. A good one nearby is **Don's Bait & Tackle,** located at 30710 S. Federal Hwy., in Homestead right on U.S. 1 (© **305/247-6616**). *Note:* Most of the area's freshwater fishing, limited to murky canals and artificial lakes near housing developments, is hardly worth the trouble when so much good saltwater fishing is available.

Firearms are not allowed anywhere in the park.

SEASONS   There are two distinct seasons in the Everglades: high season and mosquito season. High season is also dry season and lasts from late November to May. Despite the bizarre cold and wet weather patterns that El Niño brought in 1998, most winters here are warm, sunny, and breezy—a good combination for keeping the bugs away. This is the best time to visit because low water levels attract the largest variety of wading birds and their predators. As the dry season wanes, wildlife follows the receding water; and by the end of May, the only living things you are sure to spot will cause you to itch. The worst, called "no-see-ums," are not even swattable. If you choose to visit during the buggy season, be vigilant in applying bug spray.

Also, realize that many establishments and operators either close or curtail offerings in the summer, so always call ahead to check schedules.

RANGER PROGRAMS   More than 50 ranger programs, free with admission, are offered each month during high season and give visitors an opportunity to gain an expert's perspective. Ranger-led walks and talks are offered year-round from the Royal Palm Visitor Center, west of the main entrance, and at the Flamingo and Gulf Coast visitor centers as well as the Shark Valley Visitor Center during the winter months. Park rangers tend to be helpful, well informed, and good-humored. Some programs occur regularly, such as Royal Palm Visitor Center's Glade Glimpses, a walking tour during which rangers point out flora and fauna and discuss issues affecting the Everglade's survival. These tours are scheduled at 12:30pm daily. The Anhinga Ambles, a similar program that takes place on the Anhinga Trail, starts at 10:30am or 3:30pm daily. Since times, programs, and locations vary from month to month, check a schedule, available at any of the visitor centers (see above).

SAFETY   There are many dangers inherent in this vast wilderness area. *Always* let someone know your itinerary before you set out on an extended hike. It's mandatory that you file an itinerary when camping overnight in the backcountry (which you can do when you apply for your overnight permit at either the Flamingo Visitor Center or the Gulf Coast Visitor Center). When you're on the water, watch for weather changes; severe thunderstorms and high winds often develop rapidly. Swimming is not recommended because of the presence of alligators, sharks, and barracudas. Watch out for the region's four indigenous poisonous snakes: diamondback and pygmy rattlesnakes, coral snakes (identifiable by their colorful rings), and water moccasins (which swim on the surface of the water). Again, bring insect repellent to ward off mosquitoes and biting flies. First aid is available from park rangers. The nearest hospital is in Homestead, 10 miles from the park's main entrance.

SEEING THE HIGHLIGHTS

Shark Valley, a 13-mile paved road (ideal for biking) through the park, provides a fine introduction to the wonder of the Everglades, but don't plan on spending more than a few hours there. Bicycling or taking a guided tram tour (see p. 241) are fantastic ways to see the park's highlights.

If you want to see a greater array of plant and animal life, make sure that you venture into the park through the main entrance, pick up a trail map, and dedicate at least a day to exploring from there.

Stop first along the Anhinga and Gumbo Limbo trails, which start right next to one another, 3 miles from the park's main entrance. These trails provide a thorough introduction to Everglades flora and fauna and are highly recommended to first-time visitors. Each of them is ½ mile round-trip. **Gumbo Limbo Trail** (my pick for best walking trail in the Everglades) meanders through a gorgeous shaded, junglelike hammock of gumbo limbo trees, royal palms, ferns, orchids, air plants, and a general blanket of vegetation, though it doesn't put you in close contact with much wildlife. **Anhinga Trail** is one of the most popular trails in the park because there's more water and wildlife in this area of the park than in most parts of the Everglades, especially during dry season. Alligators, lizards, turtles, river otters, herons, egrets, and other animals abound, making this one of the best

Island Hopping

Beginning at Marco Island and heading south into the Everglades, there are a whopping 10,000 islands, whose primary residents are the same red mangrove trees that can be found throughout the Everglades. Often called "walking trees" because of their roots, mangrove trees arch above the ground like crouched legs.

trails for seeing wildlife. Arrive early to spot the widest selection of exotic birds (like the Anhinga bird, the trail's namesake, a large black fishing bird so accustomed to humans that many of them build their nests in plain view). Take your time—at least an hour is recommended for each trail. Both are wheelchair accessible. If you treat the trails and modern boardwalk as pathways to get through quickly, rather than destinations to experience and savor slowly, you'll miss out on the still beauty and hidden treasures that await.

If you want to get closer to nature, a few hours in a canoe along any of the trails allows paddlers the chance to sense the park's fluid motion and to become a part of the ecosphere. Visitors who choose this option end up feeling more like explorers than merely observers. (See "Sports & Outdoor Activities," below.)

No matter which option you choose (and there are many), I strongly recommend staying for the 7pm program, available during high season at the Long Pine Key Amphitheater. This talk and slide show, given by one of the park's rangers, will give you a detailed overview of the park's history, natural resources, wildlife, and threats to its survival.

SPORTS & OUTDOOR ACTIVITIES

BIKING   The relatively flat 38-mile-long paved Main Park Road is great for biking because of the multitude of hardwood hammocks (treelike islands or dense stands of hardwood trees that grow only a few inches above land) and a dwarf cypress forest (stunted and thinly distributed cypress trees, which grow in poor soil on drier land), but Shark Valley is the best biking trail by far. Expect to spend 2 to 3 hours along either.

If the park isn't flooded from excess rain (which it often is, especially in spring), Shark Valley in Everglades National Park is South Florida's most scenic bicycle trail. Many locals haul their bikes out to the 'Glades for a relaxing day of wilderness-trail riding. You'll share the flat paved road only with other bikers and a menagerie of wildlife. (Don't be surprised to see a gator lounging in the sun or a deer munching on some grass. Otters, turtles, alligators, and snakes are common companions in the Shark Valley area.) There are no shortcuts, so if you become tired or are unable to complete the entire 15-mile trip, turn around and return on the same road.

Those who love to mountain bike, and who prefer solitude, might check out the **Southern Glades Trail,** a 14-mile-long unpaved trail opened in late 1998 that is lined with native trees and teeming with wildlife such as deer, alligators, and the occasional snake. The remote trail runs along the C-111 canal, off State Road 9336 and Southwest 217th Street.

You can rent bikes at the Flamingo Lodge, Marina, and Outpost Resort (see "Where to Stay," below) for $17 per 24 hours, $14 per full day, $8.50 per half day (any 4-hr. period), and $3 per hour. A $50 deposit is required for each rental. Rentals can be picked up from 7am and the bikes have to be returned by

5pm. Bicycles are also available from Shark Valley Tram Tours, at the park's Shark Valley entrance (© **305/221-8455**), for $4.75 per hour; rentals can be picked up anytime between 8:30am and 3pm and must be returned by 4pm.

BIRD-WATCHING   More than 350 species of birds make their homes in the Everglades. Tropical birds from the Caribbean and temperate species from North America can be found here, along with exotics that have blown in from more distant regions. Eco and Mrazek ponds, located near Flamingo, are two of the best places for birding, especially in early morning or late afternoon in the dry winter months. Pick up a free birding checklist from a visitor center (see "Just the Facts," earlier in this chapter), and ask there what's been spotted in recent days.

CANOEING   Canoeing through the Everglades may be one of the most serene, surprisingly diverse adventures you'll ever have. From a canoe (where you're incredibly close to the water level), your vantage point is priceless. Canoers in the Glades can coexist with the gators and birds there in a way no one else can; they behave as if you are part of the ecosystem—something that can't happen on an airboat. A ranger-guided boat tour is your best bet and costs $19.95, plus a required deposit. As always, a ranger will help you understand the surroundings and give you an education on what you're seeing.

Everglades National Park's longest "trails" are designed for boat and canoe travel, and many are marked as clearly as walking trails. The **Noble Hammock Canoe Trail,** a 2-mile loop, takes 1 to 2 hours and is recommended for beginning canoers. The **Hell's Bay Canoe Trail,** a 3- to 6-mile course for hardier paddlers, takes 2 to 6 hours, depending on how far you choose to go. Park rangers can recommend other trails that best suit your abilities, time limitations, and interests.

You can rent a canoe at the Flamingo Lodge, Marina, and Outpost Resort (see p. 242) for $40 for 24 hours, $32 per full day, $22 per half day (any 4-hr. period), and $8 per hour. They also have family canoes that rent for $12, $30, $40, and $50, respectively. Skiffs, kayaks, and tandem kayaks are also available. The concessionaire will shuttle your party to the trailhead of your choice and pick you up afterward. Rental facilities are open daily from 6am to 8pm.

Overnight canoe rentals are available for $50 to $60. During ideal weather conditions (stay away during bug season!), you can paddle right out to the Gulf and camp on the beach. However, Gulf waters at beach sites can be extremely rough and people in small watercraft such as a canoe should exercise caution.

You can also take a canoe tour from the Parks Docks on Chokoloskee Causeway on State Road 29, a half-mile south of the traffic circle at the ranger station in Everglades City. Call Everglades National Park Boat Tours at © **800/445-7724.**

FISHING   About one-third of Everglades National Park is open water. Freshwater fishing is popular in brackish **Nine-Mile Pond** (25 miles from the main entrance) and other spots along the Main Park Road, but because of the high mercury levels found in the Everglades, freshwater fishers are warned not to eat their catch. Before casting, check in at a visitor center, as many of the park's lakes are preserved for observation only. Fishing licenses are required. See "Just the Facts," earlier in this chapter.

Saltwater anglers will find snapper and sea trout plentiful. Charter boats and guides are available at Flamingo Lodge, Marina, and Outpost Resort (see "Where to Stay," below). Phone for information and reservations.

MOTORBOATING Motorboating around the Everglades seems like a great way to see plants and animals in remote habitats, and, indeed, is an interesting and fulfilling experience as you throttle into nature. However, environmentalists are taking stock of the damage motorboats (especially airboats) inflict on the delicate ecosystem. If you choose to motor, remember that most of the areas near land are "no wake" zones and that, for the protection of nesting birds, landing is prohibited on most of the little mangrove islands. Motorboating is allowed in certain areas such as Florida Bay, the backcountry toward Everglades City, and the Ten Thousand Islands area. In all the freshwater lakes, however, motorboats are prohibited if they're above five horsepower. There's a long list of restrictions and restricted areas, so get a copy of the park's boating rules from Everglades National Park Headquarters before setting out (see "Just the Facts," earlier in the chapter).

The Everglades' only marina—accommodating about 50 boats with electric and water hookups—is the Flamingo Lodge, Marina, and Outpost Resort, in Flamingo. The well-marked channel to the Flamingo is accessible to boats with a maximum 4-foot draft and is open year-round. Reservations can be made through the marina store (© **941/695-3101**, ext. 304). Skiffs with 15-horsepower motors are available for rent. These low-power boats cost $90 per day, $65 per half day (any 5-hr. period), and $22 per hour. A $125 deposit is required.

ORGANIZED TOURS

AIRBOAT TOURS Shallow-draft, fan-powered airboats were invented in the Everglades by frog hunters who were tired of poling through the brushes. Airboats cut through the saw grass and are sort of like hydraulic boats in which at high enough speeds, the boat actually lifts above the saw grass and into the air. And even though airboats are the most efficient (not to mention fast and fun!) way to get around, they are not permitted in the park (these shallow-bottom runabouts tend to inflict severe damage on animals and plants). Just outside the boundaries of the Everglades, however, you'll find a number of outfitters offering rides. (If you choose to ride on one, you should consider bringing earplugs; these high-speed boats are loud.)

Airboat rides are offered at the **Miccosukee Indian Village,** just west of the Shark Valley entrance on U.S. 41/the Tamiami Trail (© **305/223-8380**). Native American guides will take you through the reserve's swampy brushes at high speeds and stop along the way to point out alligators, native plants, and exotic birds. The price is $10. However, *be warned and advised:* we are not recommending this particular outfit over the many others you're sure to see along the way—they are merely the ones closest to the Shark Valley entrance. While the Miccosukee can offer excellent tours, we've also received complaints about both their tours (taking visitors along a canal instead of above the sawgrass) and their tour guides (not pointing out wildlife or talking much at all). Because the Miccosukee Indian Village is, essentially, a tourist spot, complete with a souvenir-laden shopping area, be wary of the fact that the airboat tours given here may not be 100 percent authentic.

Nevertheless, the ones offered by the reservation can be campy and kitschy fun—if you get a good guide. The situation isn't going to be any different anywhere else: As always, the quality of your tour is only going to be as good as the quality of your tour guide, and there's almost no way of judging that before you lay down your money and go. That said, the best boat rides in the Everglades seem to be in Everglades City and anywhere that's off the Indian Reservation.

At Home in the Everglades

The Everglades offers a protective area in which an eclectic mix of mammals and reptiles can flourish. One such mammal is the endangered sea cow, or manatee, which typically inhabits saltwater, except during winter months when it migrates to the rivers and springs for warmth. It is an amorphous-looking, gray-toned creature with no distinct shape; it can grow to 13 feet in length and 1,300 pounds. Although their size is intimidating, they are extremely timid mammals.

Also sharing space among the mangroves, and found in most bodies of water in the Everglades, are the ubiquitous alligators, reminiscent of a half-submerged log. When I was on a boat ride, the boat captain baited an alligator with a chunk of raw meat and the gator swam right up to the boat. I did not remain calm, even though the captain assured us that it wouldn't jump into the boat. Alas, he was right, but it's a frightening feeling akin to a 3-D movie, which you should not try to duplicate. If an alligator approaches you, *do nothing.* Use your common sense and either stand still or walk (not run) away. Do not touch them or they will attack! The alligator is a protected species in the state, but a designated alligator-hunting season, done on a lottery system, exists to control the population.

The **Everglades Alligator Farm,** 4 miles south of Palm Drive/State Route 9336 and on Southwest 192nd Avenue (© **305/247-2628**), offers half-hour guided airboat tours from 9am until 6pm daily. The price, which includes admission to the park, is $14.50 for adults, $8 for children.

MOTORBOAT TOURS Both Florida Bay and backcountry tours are offered at the Flamingo Lodge, Marina, and Outpost Resort (see "Where to Stay," below). Florida Bay tours cruise nearby estuaries and sandbars, while six-passenger backcountry boats visit smaller sloughs. Passengers can expect to see birds and a variety of other animals (raccoons, wild pigs, etc.). Both are available in 1½- and 2-hour versions that cost an average of $16 for adults, $8 for children, under 6 free. Tours depart throughout the day, and reservations are recommended. There are also charter-fishing and sightseeing boats that can be booked through the resort's main reservation number (© **941/695-3101**).

TRAM TOURS At the park's Shark Valley entrance, open-air tram buses take visitors on 2-hour naturalist-led tours that delve 7½ miles into the wilderness. At the trail's midsection, passengers can disembark and climb a 65-foot observation tower that offers good views of the 'Glades, though the tower on the Pahay-okee trail is better. Visitors will see plenty of wildlife and endless acres of saw grass. Tours run November to April only, daily from 9am to 4pm, and are sometimes stalled by flooding or particularly heavy mosquito infestation. Reservations are recommended from December to March. The cost is $9.30 for adults, $5.15 for children 12 and under, and $8.25 for seniors. For further information, contact the **Shark Valley Tram Tours** at © **305/221-8455.**

SHOPPING

You won't find big malls or lots of boutiques in this area, although there is an outlet center nearby, the **Keys Factory Shops** (© **305/248-4727**), at 250 E. Palm Dr. (where the Florida Turnpike meets U.S. 1), in Florida City, with more than 60 stores, including Nike Factory, Bass Co., Levi's, OshKosh, and Izod. You can pick up a free coupon booklet (called the Come Back Pack) from the Customer Service Center, which includes coupons good for discounts at the outlet center. It's open Monday to Saturday until 9pm, Sundays until 6pm.

A necessary stop and a good place for a refreshment is one of Florida's best-known fruit stands: **Robert Is Here** (© **305/246-1592**). Robert has been selling his homegrown treats for nearly 40 years at the corner of Southwest 344th Street (Palm Drive) and Southwest 192nd Avenue. Here, you'll find the freshest pineapples, bananas, papayas, mangos, and melons anywhere, as well as his famous shakes in unusual flavors like Key lime, coconut, orange, and cantaloupe. Exotic fruits, bottled jellies, hot sauces, and salad dressings are also available. This is a great place to pick up culinary souvenirs and sample otherwise unavailable goodies. Open daily 8am until 7pm.

Along Tamiami Trail, there are several roadside shops hawking Native American handicrafts, including one at the **Miccosukee Indian Village** (© **305/ 223-8380**), just west of the Shark Valley entrance. At nearly every one of these shops, you'll find the same stock of feathered dreamcatchers, stuffed alligator heads and claws, turquoise jewelry, and other trinkets. Be sure to take note of the unique, colorful, handmade cloth Miccosukee dolls.

WHERE TO STAY

The only lodging in the park proper is the Flamingo Lodge, a fairly priced and very recommendable option. However, there are a few hotels just outside the park that are even cheaper, like the Miccosukee Resort and Convention Center (500 SW 177th Ave.; © **877/242-6464** or 305/221-8623; www.miccosukee. com), on the northern edge of the park, which is really just a step above a Holiday Inn, with just standard guest rooms. However, if you're here, you're not likely to spend that much time in your room. Tourists like this hotel for its gambling casino, expansive meeting and banquet facilities, spa services, great children's programs, entertainment, and excursions to the Florida Everglades.

And although bugs can be a major nuisance, especially in the warm months, camping is really the way to go in this very primitive environment, since it's the best way to fully experience South Florida's wilderness.

LODGING IN EVERGLADES NATIONAL PARK

Flamingo Lodge, Marina, and Outpost Resort 🐾🐾 The Flamingo Lodge is the only lodging actually located within the boundaries of Everglades National Park. This woodsy, sprawling complex offers rooms (overlooking the Florida Bay) in either a two-story simple motel or the lodge. Either option feels very much like being at summer camp, with a few more amenities. Rooms are your standard, cookie-cutter motel-style rooms, with functional bathrooms. No luxury here, but it's nonetheless a comfort for those who'd rather not experience the great outdoors while they sleep. More interesting than the actual motel, however, are the visitors who crop up on the lawn—alligators, raccoons, and other nomadic creatures. The hotel is open year-round, although the restaurant (see "Where to Dine in and Around the Park," below) closes in the summer.

1 Flamingo Lodge Hwy., Flamingo, FL 33034. © **800/600-3813** or 941/695-3101. Fax 941/695-3921. www. flamingolodge.com. 127 units. Winter from $95 double; $99–$135 cottage; $110–$145 suite. Off-season $65–$79 double; $59 cottage; call for suite rates. Rates for cottages or suites are for 1 to 4 people. Free for children under 18 in parents' room. Continental breakfast included in rates from May to October. AE, DC, DISC, MC. Take Florida Tpk. south to Florida City; exit on U.S. 1. At 4-way intersection, turn right onto Palm Dr.; continue for 3 miles and turn left at Robert Is Here fruit stand. Turn right at the 3-way intersection. The

park entrance is 3 miles ahead. Continue for about 38 more miles to reach lodge. **Amenities:** Waterside bar and restaurant; freshwater swimming pool; convenience store; bike, canoe, and kayak rentals; marina with boat tours; boat rentals; houseboat and fishing charters; coin-op washers and dryers. *In room:* A/C, TV in standard rooms and suites but not in cottages, kitchen in cottages and suites only.

CAMPING & HOUSEBOATING IN THE EVERGLADES

Campgrounds are available year round in Flamingo, Chekika, and Long Pine Key. All three have drinking water, picnic tables, charcoal grills, bathrooms, tent and trailer pads, and welcome RVs, though there are no electrical hook-ups. Flamingo has cold-water showers, Chekika has free hot showers, and Flamingo offers hot showers for $3. Private ground fires are not permitted, but supervised campfire programs are conducted during winter months. Chekika campers must register before 5pm, after which time the gates are locked and only registered campers are allowed access. Long Pine Key and Flamingo are much more popular and require reservations in advance. Reservations may be made through the National Park Reservations Service at ✆ **800/365-CAMP.** Campsites are $14 per night with a 14-day consecutive-stay limit, 30 days a year maximum.

Camping is also available in the **backcountry** (those remote areas accessible only by boat, foot, or canoe—basically most of the park) year-round on a first-come, first-served basis. Campers must register with park rangers and also get a free permit (see section on "Safety," earlier in this chapter) in person or by telephone no less than 24 hours before the start of their trip. For more information, contact the Gulf Coast Visitor Center (✆ **941/695-3311**) or the Flamingo Visitor Center (✆ **941/695-2945**), which are the only two places that give out these permits. Once you have one, camping sites cost $10 for 1 to 6 people, $20 for 7 to 12 people, and $30 for more than 13 people. Campers can use only designated campsites, which are plentiful and well marked on visitor maps.

Many backcountry sites are *chickee huts*—covered wooden platforms (with toilets) on stilts. They're accessible only by canoe and can accommodate free-standing tents (without stakes). Ground sites are located along interior bays and rivers, and beach camping is also popular. In summer especially, mosquito repellent is necessary gear.

Houseboat rentals are one of the park's best-kept secrets. Available through the Flamingo Lodge, Marina, and Outpost Resort, motorized houseboats make it possible to explore some of the park's more remote regions without having to worry about being back by nightfall. You can choose from two different types of houseboats. The first, a 40-foot pontoon boat, sleeps six to eight people in a single large room that's separated by a central head (bathroom) and shower. There's a small galley (kitchen) that contains a refrigerator, stove, oven, and charcoal grill. Prices aren't cheap, unless you are with a good-sized group. It rents for between $340 and $475 for 2 nights (there is a 2-night minimum in high season).

The newer, sleeker Gibson fiberglass boats sleep six and have toilets and showers, air-conditioning, electric stoves, and a full rooftop sundeck. These rent for $575 for 2 nights (the 2-night minimum lasts all year long). With either boat, the seventh night is free when renting for a full week.

Boating experience is helpful but not mandatory, as the boats only cruise up to 6 miles per hour and are surprisingly easy to use. In-season, reservations should be made months in advance; call ✆ **800/600-3813** or 941/695-3101.

LODGING IN EVERGLADES CITY

Since Everglades City is 35 miles southeast of Naples and 83 miles west of Miami, many people choose to explore this western entrance to Everglades

National Park, located off the Tamiami Trail, on State Road 29. An annual seafood festival held the first weekend in February is a major event that draws hordes of people. Everglades City (the gateway to the Ten Thousand Islands), where the 'Glades meets the Gulf of Mexico, is the closest thing you'll get to civilization in South Florida's swampy frontier, with a few tourist traps—er, shops, a restaurant, and two bed-and-breakfasts.

Ivey House B&B ★★ *Finds*   Housed in what used to be a recreational center for the men who built the Tamiami Trail, the Ivey House offers three types of accommodations. In the original house, there are 10 small rooms that share communal bathrooms (one each for women and men). One private cottage consists of two bedrooms, a full kitchen, a private bathroom, and a screened-in porch. The Ivey's new inn (opened in 2001) adds 17 rooms (with private bathrooms) that face a courtyard with a screened-in shallow "conversation" pool. During the summer, however, the mosquitoes are out in full force and a trip to the pool could leave you with multiple bites as it did me (screens or not). Bring bug spray!

Owners Sandee and David Harraden are extremely knowledgeable about the Everglades, and usually the guests are as well. A living-room area offers guests the opportunity to mingle. A typical continental breakfast is available from 7 to 9am only. Boxed lunches, stored in a cooler so you can bring them along for your Everglades excursions, are offered for $9.50 each. Dinners may be available by the time you go. Call to get more information. The Ivey House is closed in September. *Note:* No smoking in any of the buildings.

107 Camellia St., Everglades City, FL 34139 ⓒ **941/695-3299.** Fax 941/695-4155. www.iveyhouse.com. 28 units. Winter $60–$85 main house (older rooms); $125–$155 (cottage, 2-night minimum); $100 and up for one of the newer rooms. Off-season $50–$70 main house; $90–$105 cottage; $90 and up for newer rooms. MC, V. **Amenities:** Restaurant; small pool; free use of bikes; Everglades excursions available. *In room:* AC (all rooms), TV, fridge (inn and cottage), kitchen (cottage only).

On the Banks of the Everglades ★★★ *Finds*   This very cute bed-and-breakfast is right on the money, as far as kitsch is concerned. On the Banks of the Everglades is a fabulous retreat from the lush greenery of the swampy Everglades to the even more lush greenery of money. Located in a building that was formerly the first bank established in Collier County, in 1923, money is this place's premise, but it won't cost you too much to stay here. Rooms such as the Trust Room, the Checking Department, and the Stocks and Bond Room are clean and comfortable (though bathrooms are down the hall) and are all located on the floor where banking used to be done until 1962. All other rooms, such as the Mortgage Loan Department, Savings Department, and Dividends Department do have bathrooms. Perhaps the best parts about the place, besides the congenial service, are that breakfast is served in the bank's fully restored vault and that original artifacts from the bank are still visible, such as the 3,000-pound cannonball safe. Unlike a real bank, however, the knowledgeable staff at the inn are happy to give free advice on what to do in the area.

201 W. Broadway, Everglades City, FL 34139 ⓒ **888/431-1977** or 941/695-3151. Fax 941/695-3335. www. banksoftheeverglades.com. 10 units, 6 with private bathroom. $85 (shared bathroom); $153–$160 (private bathroom). Rates include continental breakfast. AE, DISC, MC, V. Closed July–Oct. **Amenities:** Free use of bikes; Everglades excursions available. *In room:* AC, TV.

Rod & Gun Lodge ★   This rustic old white clapboard house has plenty of history and all kinds of activities for sports enthusiasts, including a swimming pool, bicycle rentals, tennis center, and nearby boat rentals and private fishing guides.

Sitting on the banks of the sleepy Barron River, the Rod & Gun Lodge was orig-inally built as a private residence nearly 170 years ago, but Barron Collier turned it into a cozy hunting lodge in the 1920s. President Herbert Hoover vacationed here after his 1928 election victory, and President Harry S. Truman flew in to sign Everglades National Park into existence in 1947 and stayed over as well. Other guests have included President Richard Nixon, Burt Reynolds, and Mick Jagger. The public rooms are beautifully paneled and hung with tarpon, wild boar, deer antlers, and other trophies. Guest rooms in this single-story building are unfussy but perfectly comfortable. Out by the swimming pool and river-bank, a screened veranda with ceiling fans offers a pleasant place for a libation. The excellent seafood restaurant serves breakfast, lunch, and dinner. The entire property is nonsmoking. *Note:* No credit cards are accepted.

Riverside Dr. and Broadway (P.O. Box 190), Everglades City, FL 34139. © **941/695-2101.** 17 units, all with bathroom (some with shower only). Winter $95 single or double. Off-season $75 single or double. No credit cards. Closed after July 4th for the summer. **Amenities:** Restaurant; pool; tennis courts; bicycle rentals. *In room:* A/C, TV.

NEARBY IN HOMESTEAD & FLORIDA CITY

Homestead and Florida City, two adjacent towns that were almost blown off the map by Hurricane Andrew in 1992, have come back better than before. Located about 10 miles from the park's main entrance, along U.S. 1, 35 miles south of Miami, these somewhat rural towns offer several budget lodging options, including a handful of chain hotels. There is a **Days Inn** (© **305/245-1260**) in Homestead and a **Hampton Inn** (© **800/426-7866** or 305/247-8833) right off the turnpike in Florida City. However, the best option is listed below.

Best Western Gateway to the Keys   This two-story standard motel offers contemporary style and comfort about 10 miles from the park's main entrance. A decent-sized pool and a small spa make it an attractive option to some. Each identical standard room has bright, tropical bedspreads and oversized picture windows. The suites offer convenient extras like a microwave, coffeemaker, an extra sink, and a small fridge. Clean and conveniently located, the only draw-back is that in season, there is often a 3-day minimum stay requirement. You'd do best to call the local reservation line (© **305/246-5100**) instead of the toll-free number—on several occasions, the hotel made an exception to the rule while the central reservation line was not able to do the same.

411 S. Krome Ave. (U.S. 1), Florida City, FL 33034. © **800/528-1234** or 305/246-5100. Fax 305/242-0056. www.bestwestern.com. 114 units. Winter from $91–$109. Off-season from $71–$89. Rates include conti-nental breakfast. During races and the very high season, there may be a 3-night minimum stay. AE, DC, DISC, MC, V. **Amenities:** Pool; spa; laundry and dry cleaning. *In room:* A/C, TV, dataport, fridge, coffeemaker, hair dryer.

WHERE TO DINE IN & AROUND THE PARK

You won't find fancy nouvelle cuisine in this suburbanized farm country, but there are plenty of fast-food chains along U.S. 1 and a few old favorites worth a taste, listed below.

Here for nearly a quarter of a century, **El Toro Taco Family Restaurant** (see p. 161) at 1 S. Krome Ave. (near Mowry Drive and Campbell Drive; © **305/ 245-8182**) opens daily at 9:30am and stays crowded until at least 9pm most days. The fresh grilled meats, tacos, burritos, salsas, guacamole, and stews are all mild and delicious. No matter how big your appetite, it's hard to spend more than $12 per person at this Mexican outpost. Bring your own beer or wine.

Housed in a squat, one-story, windowless stone building that looks something like a medieval fort, the **Capri Restaurant,** 935 N. Krome Ave., Florida City (© **305/247-1542**), has been serving hearty Italian-American fare since 1958. Great pastas and salads complement a full menu (portions are big) of meat and fish dishes. They serve lunch and dinner every day (except Sunday) until 11pm.

The **Miccosukee Restaurant** (© **305/223-8380**), just west of the Shark Valley entrance on the Tamiami Trail (U.S. 41), serves authentic pumpkin bread, fry bread, fish, and not-so-authentic Native American interpretations of tacos and fried chicken. It's worth a stop for brunch, lunch, or dinner.

In Everglades City, the **Oyster House** (© **941/695-2073**) on Chokoloskee Causeway (Highway 29 south), is a large but homey seafood restaurant with modest prices, excellent service, and a fantastic view of the Ten Thousand Islands. Try the hush puppies.

Once inside the Everglades, you'll want to eat at the only restaurant within the boundaries of this huge park, the **Flamingo Restaurant** (© **941/695-3101**). Located in the Flamingo Lodge (see "Where to Stay," earlier in this chapter), this is a very civilized and affordable restaurant. Besides the spectacular view of Florida Bay and numerous Keys from the large, airy dining room, you'll also find fresh fish that is grilled, blackened, or deep-fried. Dinner entrees come with salad or conch chowder, and steamed vegetables, black beans, and rice or baked potato. The large menu has something for everyone, including basic and very tasty sandwiches, pastas, burgers, and salads. A kids' menu offers standard choices like hot dogs, grilled cheese, or fried shrimp for less than $6. Prices are surprisingly moderate, with full meals starting at about $11 and going no higher than $22. You may need reservations for dinner, however, especially in season.

2 Biscayne National Park ⭐

35 miles S of Miami, 21 miles E of Everglades National Park

With only about 500,000 visitors each year (mostly boaters and divers), the unusual Biscayne National Park is one of the least-crowded parks in the country. Perhaps that's because the park is a little more difficult than most to access—more than 95% of its 181,500 acres are underwater.

The park's significance was first formally acknowledged in 1968 when, in an unprecedented move (and against intense pressure from developers), President Lyndon B. Johnson signed a bill to conserve the barrier islands off South Florida's east coast as a national monument—a protected status that's just a rung below national park. After being twice enlarged, once in 1974 and again in 1980, the waters and land surrounding the northernmost coral reef in North America became a full-fledged national park—the largest of its kind in the country.

To be fully appreciated, Biscayne National Park should be thought of more as a preserve than as a destination. I suggest using your time here to explore underwater life, of course, but also to relax.

The park consists of 44 islands, but only a few of them are open to visitors. The most popular one is **Elliott Key,** which has campsites and a visitor center plus freshwater showers (cold water only), restrooms, trails, and a buoyed swim area. It's located about 9 miles from **Convoy Point,** the park's official headquarters on land. During Columbus Day weekend, there is a very popular regatta in which a lively crowd of party people gathers—sometimes in the nude—to celebrate the long weekend. If you'd prefer to rough it a little more, the 29-acre island known as **Boca Chita Key,** once an exclusive haven for yachters, has now become a popular spot for all manner of boaters. Visitors can enjoy camping and tour the island's restored historic buildings, including the county's second-largest lighthouse and a tiny chapel.

The park's small mainland mangrove shoreline and keys are best explored by boat. Its extensive reef system is renowned by divers and snorkelers worldwide.

JUST THE FACTS

GETTING THERE & ACCESS POINTS   Convoy Point, the park's mainland entrance, is located 9 miles east of Homestead. To reach the park from Miami, take the Florida Turnpike to the Tallahassee Road (SW 137th Ave.) exit. Turn left, then left again at North Canal Drive (SW 328th St.) and follow signs to the park. Another option is to rent a speedboat in Miami and cruise south for about an hour and a half. If you're coming from U.S. 1, whether you're heading north or south, turn east at North Canal Drive (SW 328th St.). The entrance is approximately 9 miles away. The rest of the park is accessible only by boat.

Most of Biscayne National Park is accessible only to boaters. Because of that, mooring buoys abound, since it is illegal to anchor on coral. When no buoys are available, boaters must anchor on sand or on the new docks surrounding the small harbor off of Boca Chita. Boats can also dock there overnight for $15. Even the most experienced boaters should carry updated nautical charts of the area, which are available at Convoy Point. The waters are often murky, making the abundant reefs and sandbars difficult to detect—and there are more interesting ways to spend a day than waiting for the tide to rise. There's a boat launch at adjacent Homestead Bayfront Park, and 66 slips on Elliott Key, available free on a first-come, first-served basis.

Transportation to and from the visitor center to Elliot Key costs $24.95 round trip per person and takes about an hour. This is a convenient option, ensuring that you don't get lost on some deserted island by boating there yourself. Call for a seasonal schedule (✆ **305/230-1100**).

VISITOR CENTERS & INFORMATION   The **Convoy Point Visitor Center,** 9700 SW 328th St., Homestead, FL 33033-5634, at the park's main entrance (✆ **305/230-7275;** fax 305/230-1190; www.biscayne.national-park. com), is the natural starting point for any venture into the park without a boat. In addition to providing comprehensive information about the park, on request, rangers will show you a short video on the park, its natural surroundings, and what you may see. Open Monday to Friday from 8:30am to 4:30pm and Saturday and Sunday from 8:30am to 5pm.

For information on transportation, glass-bottom boat tours, and snorkeling and scuba diving expeditions, contact the park concessionaire, **Biscayne National Underwater Park, Inc.,** P.O. Box 1270, Homestead, FL 33030 (✆ **305/230-1100;** fax 305/230-1120; captsaw@bellsouth.net). The company is open daily from 8:30am to 5pm and later in winter.

ENTRANCE FEES & PERMITS   Entering Biscayne National Park is free. There is a $15-per-night overnight docking fee at both Boca Chita Key Harbor and Elliott Key Harbor ($7.50 per night for holders of Golden Age or Golden Access Passports). See p. 187 for information on fishing permits. Backcountry camping permits are free and can be picked up from the Convoy Point Visitor Center. For information on fees and permits, call the park ranger at ✆ **305/ 230-1144.**

SEEING THE HIGHLIGHTS

Since the park is primarily underwater, the only way to truly experience it is with snorkel or scuba gear. Beneath the surface of Biscayne National Park, the aquatic universe pulses with multicolored life: Bright parrotfish and angelfish, gently rocking sea fans, and coral labyrinths abound. See the "Snorkeling & Scuba Diving" section below for more information. Afterward, take a picnic out to Elliott Key and taste the crisp salt air blowing off the Atlantic. Or head to Boca Chita, an intriguing island, once the private playground of wealthy yachters.

SPORTS & OUTDOOR ACTIVITIES

CANOEING & KAYAKING   Biscayne National Park offers excellent canoeing, both along the coast and across the open water to nearby mangroves and artificial islands that dot the longest uninterrupted shoreline in the state of Florida. Since tides can be strong, only experienced canoeists should attempt to paddle far from shore. If you do plan to go far, first obtain a tide table from the visitor center (see "Just the Facts," above) and paddle with the current. Free ranger-led canoe tours are scheduled every Saturday, from 9am to noon; phone for information. You can rent a canoe at the park's concession stand; rates are $8 an hour or $22 for 4 hours. Kayakers will have to bring their own boats but are welcome to explore the same quiet routes. Call ✆ **305/230-1100** for reservations, information, ranger tours, and boat rentals.

FISHING   Ocean fishing is excellent year-round at Biscayne National Park; many people cast their lines right from the breakwater jetty at Convoy Point. A fishing license is required (see p. 187). Bait is not available in Biscayne National Park but is sold in adjacent Homestead Bayfront Park. Stone crabs and Florida lobsters can be found here, but you're allowed to catch these only on the ocean side when they're in season. There are strict limitations on size, season, number, and method of take (including spearfishing) for both fresh- and saltwater fishing. The latest regulations are available at most marinas, bait-and-tackle shops, and at the park's visitor centers. Or you can contact the **Florida Game and Fresh Water Fish Commission,** Bryant Building, 620 S. Meridian St., Tallahassee, FL 32399-1600 (✆ **904/488-1960**).

HIKING & EXPLORING   Since the majority of this park is underwater, hiking is not the main attraction here, but, nonetheless, there are some interesting sights and trails. At Convoy Point, you can walk along the 370-foot boardwalk and along the half-mile jetty that serves as a breakwater for the park's harbor. From there, you can usually see brown pelicans, little blue herons, snowy egrets, and a few exotic fish.

Elliott Key is accessible only by boat, but once you're there, you have two good trail options. True to its name, the Loop Trail makes a 1½-mile circle from the bayside visitor center, through a hardwood hammock and mangroves, to an elevated oceanside boardwalk. It's likely that you'll see purple and orange land crabs scurrying around the mangrove roots.

Reopened in 1998, Boca Chita Key was once the playground for wealthy tycoons, and it still offers the peaceful beauty that attracted elite anglers from cold climates. Many of the historical buildings are still intact, including an ornamental lighthouse, which was never put into use.

Take advantage of the tours, usually led by a park ranger and available every Sunday at 1pm. The tour, including the boat trip, takes about 3 hours. The price is $19.95 for adults and $9.95 for children. However, call in advance to see if the sea is calm enough for the boat trip—the boats won't run in rough seas.

Fun Fact **Navigational Hazards**

Boca Chita Key's lighthouse was built by Honeywell Corporation tycoon Mark Honeywell, who owned the Key from 1937 through 1945 as a land-mark and navigational tool for his boat captain. Built out of coral rock with interior stairs designed to resemble something out of King Arthur's round table days, the lighthouse was lit, but never registered properly with the Lighthouse Service, which informed Honeywell that the lighthouse was not charted and, as a result, was considered a navigational hazard rather than a tool (since it was built on the western side of the island in the path of shallow reefs, boaters would have followed the beacon only to go aground). The lighthouse's lights were extinguished, leaving nothing more than a monument to Honeywell's belief in living by his own rules.

SNORKELING & SCUBA DIVING   The clear, warm waters of Biscayne National Park are packed with colorful tropical fish that swim in the offshore reefs. If you don't have your own gear or don't want to lug it the park, you can rent or buy snorkeling and scuba gear at the full-service dive shop at Convoy Point. Rates are in line with dive shops on the mainland.

The best way to see the park from underwater is to take a snorkeling or scuba diving tour operated by **Biscayne National Underwater Park, Inc.** (✆ **305/ 230-1100**). Snorkeling tours depart at 1:30pm daily, last about 3 hours, and cost $29.95 per person, including equipment. They also run weekend two-tank dives for certified divers. The price is $44.95 per person, including two tanks and weights. Reef dives depart on Saturdays and wall dives depart on Sundays. Make your reservations in advance. The shop is open daily from 9am to 5pm.

SWIMMING   You can swim at the protected beaches of Elliott Key, Boca Chita Key, and adjacent Homestead Bayfront Park, but none of these match the width or softness of other South Florida beaches. Check the water conditions before heading into the sea: The strong currents that make this a popular desti-nation for windsurfers and sailors can be dangerous, even for strong swimmers. Homestead Bayfront Park is really just a marina located next to Biscayne National Park, but it does have a beach and picnic facilities as well as fishing areas and a playground. It's located at Convoy Point, 9698 SW 328th St., Homestead,(✆ **305/230-3033**).

GLASS-BOTTOM BOAT TOURS

If you prefer not to dive, the best way to see the sites is on a glass-bottom boat tour. **Biscayne National Underwater Park, Inc.** (✆ **305/230-1100**) offers daily trips to view some of the country's most beautiful coral reefs and tropical fish. Boats depart year-round from Convoy Point at 10am and stay out for about 3 hours. At $19.95 for adults, $17.95 for seniors, and $9.95 for children 12 and under, the scenic and informative tours are well worth the price. Boats carry fewer than 50 passengers; reservations are almost always necessary.

WHERE TO STAY

Besides campsites, there are no facilities available for overnight guests to this watery park. Most noncamping visitors come for an afternoon, on their way to the Keys, and stay overnight in nearby Homestead, where there are many national chain hotels and other affordable lodgings (see p. 245).

CAMPING

Although you won't find hotels or lodges in Biscayne National Park, it does have some of the state's most pristine campsites. Since they are inaccessible by motor vehicle, you'll be sure to avoid the mass of RVs so prevalent in many of the state's other campgrounds. Sites are on Elliott Key and Boca Chita (also see p. 246) and can only be reached by boat. If you don't have your own, call ℂ **305/ 230-1100** to arrange a drop-off. Transportation to and from the visitor center costs $21 per person. Boca Chita only has saltwater toilets; Elliot Key has fresh water, but is otherwise no less primitive. With a backcountry permit available free from the visitor's center, you can pitch your tent somewhere even more private. Ask for a map at the visitor center, and be sure to bring plenty of bug spray. Sites cost $10 a night for up to six persons staying in one or two tents.

Backcountry camping is only allowed on Elliot Key, which is a very popular spot (accessible only by boat) for boaters and campers. It is approximately 9 miles from Convoy Point Visitors Center and offers hiking trails, fresh water, boat slips, showers, and restrooms. While there, don't miss the Old Road, a 7-mile tropical hammock trail that runs the length of Elliott Key. This trail is one of the few places left in the world to see the highly endangered Schaus swallowtail butterfly, recognizable by its black wings with diagonal yellow bands. They're usually out from late April through July.

11

The Keys & the Dry Tortugas

The drive from Miami to the Keys is a slow descent into an unusual but breathtaking American ecosystem: On either side of you, for miles ahead, lies nothing but emerald waters. (On weekends, however, you will also see plenty of traffic.) Strung out across the Atlantic Ocean like loose strands of cultured pearls, more than 400 islands make up this 150-mile-long chain of the Keys.

Despite the usually calm landscape, these rocky islands can be treacherous, as a series of tropical storms, hurricanes, and tornadoes reminded residents in the summer and fall of 1998, when millions of dollars of damage were inflicted. The exposed coast has always posed dangers to those on land as well as at sea.

When Spanish explorers Juan Ponce de León and Antonio de Herrera sailed amid these craggy, dangerous rocks in 1513, they and their men dubbed the string of islands "Los Martires" (The Martyrs), because they thought the rocks looked like men suffering in the surf. It wasn't until the early 1800s that rugged and ambitious pioneers, who amassed great wealth by salvaging cargo from ships sunk nearby, settled the larger islands (legend has it that these shipwrecks were sometimes caused by the "wreckers," who occasionally removed navigational markers from the shallows to lure unwitting captains aground). At the height of the salvaging mania (in the 1830s), Key West boasted the highest per-capita income in the country.

However, wars, fires, hurricanes, mosquitoes, and the Depression took their toll on these resilient islands in the early part of this century, causing wild swings between fortune and poverty. In 1938, the spectacular Overseas Highway (U.S. 1) was finally completed atop the ruins of Henry Flagler's railroad (which was destroyed by a hurricane in 1935, leaving only bits and pieces still found today), opening the region to tourists, who had never before been able to drive to this seabound destination. These days, the highway connects more than 30 of the populated islands in the Keys. The hundreds of small, undeveloped islands that surround these "mainline" keys are known locally as the "backcountry" and are home to dozens of exotic animals and plants. Therein lie some of the most renowned outdoor sporting opportunities, from bonefishing to spearfishing and—at appropriate times of the year—diving for lobsters. To get to the backcountry, you must take to the water—a vital part of any trip to the Keys. Whether you fish, snorkel, dive, or just cruise, include some time on a boat in your itinerary; otherwise, you haven't truly seen the Keys.

Of course, people go to the Keys for the peaceful waters and the year-round warmth, but the sea and the teeming life beneath it are the main attractions here: Countless species of brilliantly colored fish can be found swimming in the ocean, and you'll discover a stunning abundance of tropical and exotic plants, birds, and reptiles.

The warm, shallow waters (waters are deeper and rougher on the eastern/Atlantic side of the Keys) nurture living coral that supports a complex, delicate ecosystem of plants and animals—sponges, anemones, jellyfish, crabs, rays, sharks, turtles, snails, lobsters, and thousands of types of fish. This vibrant underwater habitat thrives on one of the only living tropical reefs in the entire North American continent. As a result, anglers, divers, snorkelers, and watersports enthusiasts of all kinds come to explore.

Heavy traffic has taken its toll on this fragile ecoscape, but conservation efforts are underway (traffic laws are strictly enforced on Deer Key, for example, due to deer crossings). In fact, environmental efforts in the Keys exceed those in many other high-traffic visitor destinations.

Although the atmosphere throughout the Keys is that of a laid-back beach town, don't expect to find many impressive beaches here, especially after the damaging effects of the tropical storms and hurricanes in 1998. Beaches are mostly found in a few private resorts, though there are some small, sandy beaches in John Pennekamp State Park, Bahia Honda State Park, and in Key West. One great exception is Sombrero Beach in Marathon (see p. 256), which is well maintained by Monroe County and is larger and considerably nicer than other beaches in the Keys. Sombrero Beach features a beachfront park, picnic facilities, a playground, and a protected cove at the west end of the beach for children.

The Keys are divided into three sections, both geographically and in this chapter. The Upper and Middle Keys are closest to the Florida mainland, so they are popular with weekend warriors who come by boat or car to fish or relax in towns like Key Largo, Islamorada, and Marathon. Further on, just beyond the impressive Seven-Mile Bridge (which actually measures only 6½ miles), are the Lower Keys, a small, unspoiled swath of islands teeming with wildlife. Here, in the protected regions of the Lower Keys, is where you're most likely to catch sight of the area's many endangered animals—with patience, you may spot the rare eagle, egret, or Key deer. You should also keep an eye out for alligators, turtles, rabbits, and a huge variety of birds.

Key West, the most renowned—and last—island in the Lower Keys, is literally at the end of the road. The southernmost point in the United States (made famous by the Nobel Prize winner Ernest Hemingway), this tiny island is the most popular destination in the Florida Keys, overrun with cruise-ship passengers and day-trippers, as well as franchises and T-shirt shops. More than 1.6 million visitors pass through each year. Still, this "Conch Republic" has a tightly knit community of permanent residents who cling fiercely to their live-and-let-live attitude—an atmosphere that has made Key West famously popular with painters, writers, and free spirits.

The last section in this chapter is devoted to the Dry Tortugas, a national park located 68 nautical miles from Key West.

⌐Tips Don't Be Fooled

Avoid the many "Tourist Information Centers" that dot the main highway. Most are private companies hired to lure visitors to specific lodgings or outfitters. You're better off sticking with the official, not-for-profit centers that are extremely well located and staffed.

The Florida Keys

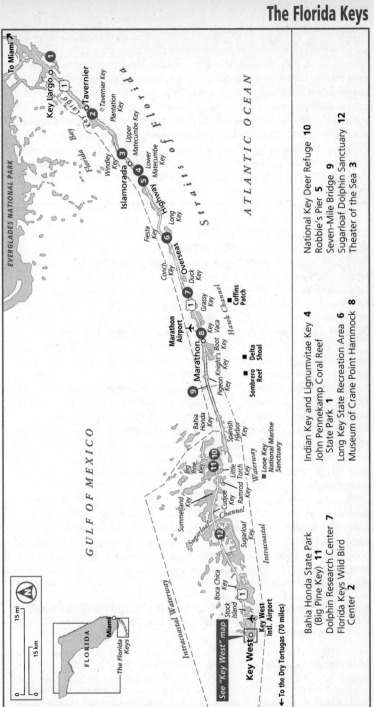

To Miami

EVERGLADES NATIONAL PARK

GULF OF MEXICO

Key Largo ○
Tavernier
Tavernier Key
Plantation Key
Upper Matecumbe Key
Islamorada
Lower Matecumbe Key
Windley Key
Florida Bay
Fiesta Key
Long Key
Overseas
Conch Key
Duck Key
Grassy Key
Coffins Patch
Hawk Channel
Marathon Airport
Marathon
Key Vaca
Knight's Boot Key
Pigeon Key
Sombrero Reef
Delta Shoal
Bahia Honda Key
Spanish Harbor Key
Looe Key National Marine Sanctuary
Big Pine Key
Little Torch Key
Ramrod Key
Summerland Key
Cudjoe Key
Sugarloaf Channel
Sugarloaf Key
Boca Chica Key
Stock Island
Key West Intl. Airport
Key West ○

Florida Keys
Straits of Florida
ATLANTIC OCEAN

Intracoastal Waterway
Intracoastal

← To the Dry Tortugas (70 miles)

See "Key West" map

FLORIDA
Miami
The Florida Keys

0   15 mi
0   15 km

Bahia Honda State Park (Big Pine Key) **11**
Dolphin Research Center **7**
Florida Keys Wild Bird Center **2**

Indian Key and Lignumvitae Key **4**
John Pennekamp Coral Reef State Park **1**
Long Key State Recreation Area **6**
Museum of Crane Point Hammock **8**

National Key Deer Refuge **10**
Robbie's Pier **5**
Seven-Mile Bridge **9**
Sugarloaf Dolphin Sanctuary **12**
Theater of the Sea **3**

Moments **No Place Like Homestead**

On its own, there's not much to the waterfront shack that is Alabama Jack's. The bar serves beer and wine only, and the restaurant specializes in greasy bar fare. But this quintessential Old Floridian dive, located between Homestead and Key Largo, is a colorful must on the drive south. Hordes of Harley Davidson bikers, local Miamians, barflies, and anglers flock here with much devotion, and the views of the mangroves are spectacular. To get there, pick up Card Sound Road (the old Route 1) a few miles after you pass Homestead, heading toward Key Largo. Alabama Jack's is on the right-hand side and can't be missed. 5800 Card Sound Rd., Homestead. ✆ 305/ 248-8741.

EXPLORING THE KEYS BY CAR

After you have gotten off the Florida Turnpike and landed on U.S. 1, which is also known as the Overseas Highway (see "Getting There," under "Essentials," below), you'll have no trouble negotiating these narrow islands, since it is the only main road connecting the Keys. The scenic, lazy drive from Miami can be very enjoyable if you have the patience to linger and explore the diverse towns and islands along the way. If you have the time, I recommend allowing at least 2 days to work your way down to Key West and 3 or more days once there.

Most of U.S. 1 is a narrow, two-lane highway, with some wider passing zones along the way. The speed limit is usually 55 mph; it's 35 to 45 mph on Big Pine Key and in some commercial areas. Despite the protestations of island residents, there has been talk of expanding the highway, but plans have not been finalized. Even on the narrow road, you can usually get from downtown Miami to Key Largo in just over an hour. If you're determined to drive straight through to Key West, allow at least 3½ hours. Weekend travel is another matter entirely: When the roads are jammed with travelers from the mainland, the trip could take upward of 5 to 6 hours (when there's an accident, traffic is at an absolute standstill). If at all possible, I strongly urge you to avoid driving anywhere in the Keys on Friday afternoons or Sunday evenings.

To find an address in the Keys, don't bother looking for building numbers; most addresses (except in Key West and parts of Marathon) are delineated by mile markers (MM), small green signs on the roadside, which announce the distance from Key West. The markers start at number 127, just south of the Florida mainland. The zero marker is in Key West, at the corner of Whitehead and Fleming streets. Addresses in this chapter are accompanied by a mile marker (MM) designation when appropriate.

---

1 The Upper & Middle Keys: Key Largo ✦/✦ to Marathon ✦

58 miles SW of Miami

The Upper Keys are a popular, year-round refuge for South Floridians who take advantage of the islands' proximity to the mainland. This is the fishing and diving capital of America, and the swarms of outfitters and billboards never let you forget it.

Key Largo, once called Rock Harbor but renamed to capitalize on the success of the 1948 Humphrey Bogart film (which wasn't actually filmed there), is the largest Key and is more developed than its neighbors to the south. Dozens of chain hotels, restaurants, and tourist information centers service the many water enthusiasts who come to explore the nation's first underwater state park, **John Pennekamp Coral Reef State Park,** and its adjacent marine sanctuary. **Islamorada,** the unofficial capital of the Upper Keys, offers the area's best atmosphere, food, fishing, entertainment, and lodging. It's an unofficial "party capital" for mainlanders seeking a quick tropical excursion. Here (Islamorada is actually composed of four islands), nature lovers can enjoy walking trails, historic explorations, and big-purse fishing tournaments. For a more tranquil, quieter, less party-hearty Keys experience, all other Keys besides Key West and Islamorada are better choices. **Marathon,** smack in the middle of the Florida Keys, is one of the most populated Keys and is known as the heart of the Keys. It is part fishing village, part tourist center, and part nature preserve. This area's highly developed infrastructure includes resort hotels, a commercial airport, and a highway that expands to four lanes.

ESSENTIALS

GETTING THERE   From Miami International Airport (there is also an airport in Marathon), take Le Jeune Road (Northwest 42nd Ave.) to Route 836 west. Follow signs to the Florida Turnpike South (about 7 miles). The turnpike extension connects with U.S. 1 in Florida City. Continue south on U.S. 1. For a scenic option, weather permitting, take Card Sound Road south of Florida City, a backcountry drive that reconnects with U.S. 1 in upper Key Largo. The view from the Card Sound Bridge is spectacular and well worth the dollar toll.

If you're coming from Florida's west coast, take Alligator Alley to the Miami exit and then turn south onto the turnpike extension. The turnpike will end in Florida City, at which time you will be dumped directly onto the one-lane road, U.S. 1, that leads to the Keys. Have plenty of quarters (at least $10 worth, round trip) for the tolls.

Greyhound (© 800/231-2222; www.greyhound.com) has three buses leaving Miami for Key West every day, which also stop in Key Largo, Tavernier, Islamorada, Marathon, Big Pine Key, Cudjoe Key, Sugarloaf, and Big Coppitt on their way south. Prices range up from about $13 to $32 one way and take between an hour and 40 minutes to 4 hours and 40 minutes, depending on how far south you're going. Seats fill quickly in season, so come early. It's first come, first served.

VISITOR INFORMATION   Make sure you get your information from official, not-for-profit centers. The **Key Largo Chamber of Commerce,** U.S. 1 at MM 106, Key Largo, FL 33037 (© 800/822-1088 or 305/451-1414; fax 305/451-4726; www.keylargo.org), runs an excellent facility, with free direct-dial phones and plenty of brochures. Headquartered in a handsome clapboard house, the chamber operates as an information clearinghouse for all of the Keys and is open daily from 9am to 6pm.

The **Islamorada Chamber of Commerce,** housed in an actual little red caboose, U.S. 1 at MM 82.5, P.O. Box 915, Islamorada, FL 33036 (© 800/322-5397 or 305/664-4503; fax 305/664-4289; www.islamoradachamber.com), also offers maps and literature on the Upper Keys.

You can't miss the big blue Visitors Center at MM 53.5, the **Greater Marathon Chamber of Commerce,** 12222 Overseas Hwy., Marathon, FL 33050 (© 800/262-7284 or 305/743-5417; fax 305/289-0183; www.florida keysmarathon.com). Here, you can receive free information on local events, festivals, shows, attractions, dining, and lodging.

OUTDOOR SIGHTS & ACTIVITIES

Anne's Beach (at MM 73.5, on Lower Matecumbe Key, at the Southwest end of Islamorada) is really more of a picnic spot than a full-fledged beach, but die-hard suntanners still congregate on this lovely but tiny strip of coarse sand that was damaged beyond recognition during the series of storms in 1998. Plans are in place to reconstruct the boardwalk and huts, but at press time, work had not yet started.

A better choice for real beaching is **Sombrero Beach** 🏖🏖 in Marathon at the end of Sombrero Beach Road (near MM 50). This wide swath of uncluttered beachfront actually benefited from Hurricane George in September 1998 with generous deposits of extra sand and a facelift courtesy of the Monroe County Tourist Development Council. More than 90 feet of sand is dotted with palms, Australian pines, and royal poincianas as well as with barbecue grills, clean bathrooms, and some brand new tiki huts for relaxing in the shade.

If you want to see the Keys in their natural state, before modern development, you must venture off the highway and take to the water. Two backcountry islands that offer a glimpse of the "real" Keys are **Indian Key** and **Lignumvitae Key** 🏖🏖🏖. Visitors come to these to relax and enjoy the islands' colorful birds and lush hammocks (elevated pieces of land above a marsh).

Named for the lignum vitae ("wood of life") trees found there, **Lignumvitae Key** supports a virgin tropical forest, the kind that once thrived on most of the Upper Keys. Over the years, human settlers imported "exotic" plants and animals to the Keys, irrevocably changing the botanical makeup of many backcountry islands and threatening much of the indigenous wildlife. Over the past 25 years, however, the Florida Department of Natural Resources has successfully removed most of the exotic vegetation from this Key, leaving this 280-acre site much as it existed in the 18th century. The island also holds the Matheson House, a historic house built in 1919 that has survived numerous hurricanes. You can go inside the house, but this is only interesting if you have a hankering for coral rock, which the house is made out of. It's now a museum dedicated to the history, nature, and topography of the area. More interesting is actually seeing the area via the Botanical Gardens, which surround the house and are a state preserve. Lignumvitae Key has a visitor's center at MM 88.5 (𝒞 **305/664-2540**).

Indian Key, a much smaller island on the Atlantic side of Islamorada, was occupied by Native Americans for thousands of years before European settlers arrived. The 10-acre historic site was also the original seat of Dade County before the Civil War. Interestingly, from an archeological standpoint, you can see the ruins of the previous settlement and tour the lush grounds on well-marked trails. Off Indian Key Fill, Overseas Hwy., MM 79. To get information about Indian Key, call the Florida Park Service at 𝒞 **305/664-4815** or check out www.dep.state.fl.us/parks/district5/indiankey/index.asp.

If you want to see both islands, plan to spend at least half a day. To get there, you can rent your own powerboat at **Robbie's Rent-A-Boat,** U.S. 1 at MM 77.5 on the bay side (see p. 261) on Islamorada. It's then a $1 admission fee to each island, which includes an informative hour-long guided tour by park rangers. This is a good option if you are a confident boater.

However, I also recommend taking Robbie's **ferry service.** A visit to one island costs $15, $10 for kids 12 and under, which includes the $1 park admission; trips to both islands cost $25 per person. (If you have time for only one island, make it Lignumvitae.) Not only is the ferry more economical, but it's easier to enjoy the natural beauty of the islands when you aren't negotiating the shallow reefs along the way. The runabouts, which carry up to six people, depart from Robbie's Pier Thursday to Monday at 9am and 1pm for Indian Key, and at 10am and 2pm for Lignumvitae Key. In the busy season, you may need to book as early as 2 days before departure. Call ℂ **305/664-4815** for information from the park service or ℂ **305/664-9814** for Robbie's.

Crane Point Hammock 🐾🐾 *Finds* *Kids*   Crane Point Hammock is a little-known but worthwhile stop, especially for those interested in the rich botanical and archaeological history of the Keys. This privately owned 64-acre nature area is considered one of the most important historical sites in the Keys. It contains what is probably the last virgin thatch-palm hammock in North America as well as a rainforest exhibit and an archaeological dig site with pre-Columbian and prehistoric Bahamian artifacts.

Also headquarters for the Florida Keys Land and Sea Trust, the hammock's impressive nature museum has simple, informative displays of the Keys' wildlife, including a walk-through replica of a coral-reef cave and life-size dioramas with tropical birds and Key deer. Kids can participate in art projects, see 6-foot-long iguanas, climb through a scaled-down pirate ship, and touch a variety of indigenous aquatic and landlubbing creatures.

5550 Overseas Hwy. (MM 50), Marathon. ℂ **305/743-9100**. Admission $7.50 for adults, $6 for seniors over 64, $4 for students, and free for children under 6. Mon–Sat 9am–5pm, Sun noon–5pm.

Pigeon Key 🐾🐾   At the curve of the old bridge on Pigeon Key is an intriguing historical site that has been under renovation since late 1993. This 5-mile-long island was once the camp for the crew that built the old railway in the early part of the century and later served as housing for the bridge builders. From here, your vista includes both the vestiges of Henry Flagler's old Seven-Mile Bridge as well as the one on which traffic presently soars, many old wooden cottages, and a truly tranquil stretch of lush foliage and sea. If you miss the shuttle tour from the Pigeon Key Visitor Center or would rather walk or bike to the site, it's about 2½ miles. You may want to bring a picnic to enjoy after a brief self-guided walking tour of the Key and museum visit of what has become an homage to Flagler's railroad, featuring artifacts and photographs of the old bridge. There is also an informative 28-minute video of the island's history offered every hour starting at 10am. Parking is available at the Knight's Key end of the bridge, at MM 48, or at the Visitors Center at mile marker 47, on the ocean side.

East end of the Seven-Mile Bridge near MM 47, Marathon. ℂ **305/743-5999**. Open 9am–5pm; shuttle tours run every hour 10am–4pm. Admission $8.50, $5 for children under 13. Price includes shuttle transportation from the Visitors Center.

Seven-Mile Bridge 🐾🐾🐾   A stop at the Seven-Mile Bridge is a rewarding and relaxing break from the drive south. Built alongside the ruins of oil magnate Henry Flagler's incredible Overseas Railroad, the "new" bridge (between MM 40 and 47) is considered an architectural feat. The wide arched span, completed in 1985 at a cost of more than $45 million, is impressive, and its apex is the highest point in the Keys. The new bridge and its now-defunct neighbor provide an excellent vantage point from which to view the stunning waters of the Keys. In the daytime, you may want to walk, jog, or bike along the scenic 4-mile stretch of old bridge, or join local anglers, who catch barracuda, yellowtail, and dolphin (the fish, not the mammal) on what is known as "the longest fishing pier in the world." Parking is available on both sides of the bridge.

Between MM 40 and 47 on U.S. 1. ℂ **305/289-0025**.

Fun Fact Bridge Mix

The Seven-Mile Bridge is the longest fragmented (unconnected pieces) bridge in the world. Completed in 1985, it was constructed parallel to the original bridge, part of Henry Flagler's Florida East Coast Railroad, which served as the original link to the Lower Keys. Some people may recognize the remnants of the old bridge from the Arnold Schwarzenegger film *True Lies*. Others fearfully contemplate whether a wrong turn would lead them to the old bridge instead of the new one. Not to worry: The old bridge is closed to cars and has been transformed into the world's longest fishing pier.

VISITING WITH THE ANIMALS

Dolphin Research Center ★★★ *Kids*   If you've always wanted to touch, swim, or play with dolphins, this is the place to do it. Of the three such centers in the continental United States (all located in the Keys), the Dolphin Research Center is the most organized and informative. Although some people argue that training dolphins is cruel and selfish, this is one of the most respected institutions that study and protect the mammals. Knowledgeable trainers at the Dolphin Research Center will also tell you that the dolphins need stimulation and enjoy human contact. They certainly seem to. They nuzzle and seem to smile and kiss the lucky few that get to swim with them in the daily program. The "family" of 15 dolphins swims in a 90,000-square-foot natural saltwater pool carved out of the shoreline.

If you can't get into the swim program, you can still take the interesting hourlong walking tour of the facilities or sign up for a class in hand signals or feed the dolphins from docks. Because the Dolphin Encounter swimming program is the most popular, reservations must be made at least 1 month in advance. The cost is $135 per person. If you're not brave enough to swim with the dolphins or you have a child under 12 (not permitted to swim with dolphins), try the Dolphin Splash program, in which participants stand on an elevated platform from which to "meet and greet" the dolphins. A height requirement of 44 inches is enforced, and an adult must hold up children under the required height. Cost for this program is $75 per person; free for children under 3.

U.S. 1 at MM 59 (on the bay side), Marathon. ✆ **305/289-1121.** Swim with the dolphins, $135 per person. Call on the first day of the month to book for the following month. Educational walking tours 5 times daily: 10am, 11am, 12:30pm, 2pm, and 3:30pm. Admission $15 adults, $12.50 seniors, $10 children 4–12, free for children 3 and under. Daily 9:30am–4pm.

Florida Keys Wild Bird Center ★   Wander through lush canopies of mangroves on narrow wooden walkways to see some of the Keys' most famous residents—the large variety of native birds, including broad-wing hawks, great blue and white herons, roseate spoonbills, white ibis, cattle egrets, and a number of pelicans. This not-for-profit center operates as a hospital for the many birds that have been injured by accident or disease. Visit at feeding time, usually about 3:30pm, when you can watch the staff feed the hundreds of hungry beaks.

U.S. 1 at MM 93.6 Bayside, Tavernier. ✆ **305/852-4486.** fkwbc@reefnet.com. Donations suggested. Daily 8:30am–6pm.

Robbie's Pier ★★★ *Value*   One of the best and definitely one of the cheapest attractions in the Upper Keys is the famed Robbie's Pier. Here, the fierce steely tarpons, a prized catch for backcountry anglers, have been gathering for the past 20 years. You may recognize these prehistoric-looking giants that grow up to 200 pounds; many are displayed as trophies and mounted on local restaurant walls. To see them live, head to Robbie's Pier, where tens and sometimes hundreds of these behemoths circle the shallow waters waiting for you to feed them. Kayak tours promise an even closer glimpse.

U.S. 1 at MM 77.5, Islamorada. ✆ 305/664-9814. Admission $1. Bucket of fish $2. Daily 8am–5pm. Look for the Hungry Tarpon restaurant sign on the right after the Indian Key channel.

Theater of the Sea ✿ *Kids*   Established in 1946, the Theater of the Sea is one of the world's oldest marine zoos. Recently refurbished, with newly paved walkways, landscaping, and an on-site photo service, the park's dolphin and sea lion shows are entertaining and informative, especially for children who can also see sharks, sea turtles, and tropical fish. If you want to swim with dolphins and you haven't booked well in advance, this is the place you may be able to get into with just a few hours, or days, notice as opposed to the more rigid Dolphin Research Center (see above) in Marathon. (While the Dolphin Research Center is a legitimate, scientific establishment, this is more of a theme-park attraction. That's not to say the dolphins are mistreated, but it's just not as, say, educational and professional as it is at the Dolphin Research Center.) Theater of the Sea also permits you to swim with the sea lions and stingrays. Children under 5 are not permitted to participate. There are also 4-hour adventure and snorkel cruises, $60 for adults and $35 for children, in which you can learn about the history and ecology of the marine environment. The facility also serves as a haven for dozens of stray cats that have free run of the grounds and gift shop.

U.S. 1 at MM 84.5, Islamorada. ✆ 305/664-2431. www.theaterofthesea.com. Admission $17.75 adults, $11.25 children 3–12. Dolphin swim $135; sea lion swim $90; stingray swim $40 per person. Reservations a must. Daily 9:30am–5:45pm (ticket office closes at 4pm).

TWO EXCEPTIONAL STATE PARKS

One of the best places to discover the diverse ecosystem of the Upper Keys is in its most famous park, **John Pennekamp Coral Reef State Park** ✿✿✿, located on U.S. 1 at MM 102.5, in Key Largo (✆ **305/451-1202**). Named for a former *Miami Herald* editor and conservationist, the 188-square-mile park is the nation's first undersea preserve: it's a sanctuary for part of the only living coral reef in the continental United States. The original plans for Everglades National Park included this part of the reef within its boundaries, but opposition from local homeowners made its inclusion politically impossible.

Because the water is extremely shallow, the 40 species of coral and more than 650 species of fish here are particularly accessible to divers, snorkelers, and glass-bottomed-boat passengers. Your first stop should be the Visitors Center, which is full of educational fish tanks and a mammoth 30,000-gallon saltwater aquarium that re-creates a reef ecosystem. At the adjacent dive shop, you can rent snorkeling and diving equipment and join one of the boat trips that depart for the reef throughout the day. Visitors can also rent motorboats, sailboats, Windsurfers, and canoes. The 2-hour glass-bottomed-boat tour is the best way to see the coral reefs if you don't want to get wet. Watch for the lobsters and other sea life residing in the fairly shallow ridge walls beneath the coastal waters. But remember: These are protected waters, so don't remove anything from the water.

Canoeing around the park's narrow mangrove channels and tidal creeks is also popular. You can go on your own in a rented canoe or, in winter, sign up for a tour led by a local naturalist. Hikers have two short trails from which to choose:

a boardwalk through the mangroves and a dirt trail through a tropical hardwood hammock. Ranger-led walks are usually scheduled daily from the end of November to April. Phone (© **305/451-1202**) for information and reservations.

Park admission is $2.50 per vehicle for one occupant; for two or more, it is $4 per vehicle, plus 50¢ per passenger; $1.50 per pedestrian or bicyclist. On busy weekend days, there's often a line of cars to get into the park. On your way into the park, ask the ranger for a map. Glass-bottomed-boat tours cost $18 for adults and $10 for children 11 and under. Snorkeling tours are $25.95 for adults and $19.95 for children 17 and under, including equipment. Sailing and snorkeling tours are $31.95 for adults, $26.95 for children 17 and under, including equipment. Canoes rent for $10 per hour. For experienced boaters only, four different-sized Reef boats (powerboats) rent for $27.50 to $50 per hour, with cheaper half-day and full-day rates available; call © **305/451-6325** for more information. A $400 deposit (and up depending on boat size, starting at a 22 ft. boat) is required. The park's boat rental is open daily from 8am to 5pm—the last boat rented is at 3pm; phone for tour and dive times. Reservations are recommended for all of the above. Also, see below for more options on diving, fishing, and snorkeling these reefs.

Long Key State Recreation Area ✮✮✮, U.S. 1 at MM 68, Long Key (© **305/664-4815**), is one of the best places in the Middle Keys for hiking, camping, snorkeling, and canoeing. This 965-acre site is situated atop the remains of an ancient coral reef. At the entrance gate, ask for a free flyer describing the local trails and wildlife.

There are three nature trails that can be explored via foot or canoe; the Golden Orb Trail is a 40-minute walk through mostly just plants, the Layton Trail is a 15-minute walk along the bay, and the Long Key Canoe Trail glides along a shallow water lagoon. Campsites are located along the Atlantic Ocean and the swimming, snorkeling, and saltwater fishing (license required) are top-notch here. Educational programs on the aforementioned are available, too, for novices. Snorkeling is shallow and on the shoreline of the Atlantic Ocean. The nearest place to rent snorkeling equipment is Holiday Isle, 84001 U.S. 1, Islamorada (© **800/327-7070**).

The park's excellent 1½-mile canoe trail is also short and sweet, allowing visitors to loop around the mangroves in about an hour. You can rent canoes at the trailhead for about $4 per hour. Long Key is also a great spot to stop for a picnic if you get hungry on your way to Key West.

Railroad builder Henry Flagler created the Long Key Fishing Club here in 1906, and the waters surrounding the park are still popular with game fishers. In summer, sea turtles lumber onto the protected coast to lay their eggs, all lined up on the coast. It's a big event, and educational programs are available to view this phenomenon.

Admission is $3.25 per car plus 50¢ per person (except for the Layton Trail, which is free). Open daily from 8am to sunset.

WATERSPORTS FROM A TO Z

There are literally hundreds of outfitters in the Keys who will arrange all kinds of water activities, from cave dives to parasailing. If those recommended below are booked up or unreachable, ask the local chamber of commerce for a list of qualified members.

BOATING   In addition to the rental shops in the state parks, you will find dozens of outfitters along U.S. 1 offering a range of runabouts and skiffs for

The 10 "Keymandments"

The Keys have always attracted independent spirits, from Ernest Hemingway and Tennessee Williams to Jimmy Buffett, Zane Grey, and local hero Mel Fisher. Writers, artists, and freethinkers have long drifted down here to escape.

Although you'll generally find a very laid-back and tolerant code of behavior in the Keys, some rules do exist. Be sure to respect the 10 "Keymandments" while you're here, or suffer the consequences.

- Don't anchor on a reef. (Reefs are alive.)
- Don't feed the animals. (They'll want to follow you home, and you can't keep them.)
- Don't trash our place (or we'll send Bubba to trash yours).
- Don't touch the coral. (After all, you don't even know them. Some pose a mild risk of injury as well.)
- Don't speed (especially on Big Pine Key, where deer reside and tar-and-feathering is still practiced).
- Don't catch more fish than you can eat. (Better yet, let them go. Some of them support schools.)
- Don't collect conch. (This species is protected by Bubba.)
- Don't disturb the bird nests. (They find it very annoying.)
- Don't damage the sea grass. (And don't even think about making a skirt out of it.)
- Don't drink and drive on land or sea. (There's absolutely nothing funny about it.)

boaters of any experience level. **Captain Pip's,** U.S. 1 at MM 47.5, Marathon (© **800/707-1692** or 305/743-4403), rents 18- to 24-foot motorboats with 90- to 225-horsepower engines for $130 to $225 per day. Overnight accommodations are available and include a free boat rental; 2-night minimum $220 to $255; weekly $1,190 to $1,890. Rooms are Key West comfortable and charming, with ceiling fans, tile floors, and pine paneling. But the best part about it is that every room comes with an 18- to 21-foot boat for your use during your stay.

Robbie's Rent-a-Boat, U.S. 1 at MM 77.5, Islamorada (© **305/664-9814**), rents 14- to 27-foot motorboats with engines ranging from 15 to 200 horsepower. Boat rentals are $70 to $205 for a half day and $90 to $295 for a full day.

CANOEING & KAYAKING   I can think of no better way to explore the uninhabited, shallow backcountry on the Gulf side of the Keys than by kayak or canoe, since you can reach places big boats just can't get to because of their large draft. Sometimes manatees will even cuddle up to the boats, thinking them another friendly species.

Many area hotels rent kayaks and canoes to guests, as do the outfitters listed here. **Florida Bay Outfitters,** U.S. 1 at MM 104, Key Largo (© **305/451-3018**), rents canoes and sea kayaks for use in and around John Pennekamp Coral Reef State Park for $20 to $40 for a half day and $35 to $55 for a whole day. Canoes cost $25 for a half day and $35 for a whole day. **Coral Reef Park Co.,** on U.S. 1 at MM 102.5, Key Largo (© **305/451-1621**), rents canoes and kayaks for $8 per hour, $28 for a half day; most canoes are sit-on-tops.

DIVING & SNORKELING   The **Florida Keys Dive Center,** on U.S. 1 at MM 90.5, Tavernier (© **305/852-4599**), takes snorkelers and divers to the reefs of John Pennekamp Coral Reef State Park and environs every day. PADI (Professional Association of Diving Instructors) training courses are also available for the uninitiated. Tours leave at 8am and 12:30pm and cost $25 per person to snorkel (plus $8 rental fee for mask, snorkel, and fins) and $59 per person to dive (plus an extra $20 if you need to rent all the gear).

At **Hall's Dive Center & Career Institute,** U.S. 1 at MM 48.5, Marathon (© **305/743-5929**), snorkelers and divers can choose to dive at Looe Key, Sombrero Reef, Delta Shoal, Content Key, and Coffins Patch. Tours are scheduled daily at 9am and 1pm. You will spend 1 hour at each of two sites per tour. If you mention this book, you will get a special discounted rate ($5–$10 off) of $30 per person to snorkel (additional gear is $11) and $40 per person to dive (tanks are $8.50 each).

With **SNUBA Tours of Key Largo** (© **305/451-6391**; www.pennekamp. com/sw/snuba.htm), you can dive down to 20 feet attached to a comfortable breathing apparatus that really gives you the feeling of scuba diving without having to be certified. You can tour shallow coral reefs teeming with hundreds of colorful fish and plant life, from sea turtles to moray eels. Reservations are required; call to find out where and when to meet. A 2- to 3-hour underwater tour (typically 1–4pm) costs $75, including all equipment. If you have never dived before, you may require a 1-hour lesson in the pool, which costs an additional $45.

FISHING   **Robbie's Partyboats & Charters,** on U.S. 1 at MM 84.5, Islamorada (© **305/664-8070** or 305/664-4196), located at the south end of the Holiday Isle Docks, offers day and night deep-sea and reef fishing trips aboard a 65-foot party boat. Big-game fishing charters are also available, and "splits" are arranged for solo fishers. Party-boat fishing costs $25 for a half-day morning tour (rod and reel rental $3); it's $15 extra if you want to go back out on an afternoon tour. Charters run $400 for a half day, $600 for a full day; splits begin at $65 per person. Phone for information and reservations.

Bud n' Mary's Fishing Marina, on U.S. 1 at MM 79.8, Islamorada (© **800/742-7945** or 305/664-2461), one of the largest marinas between Miami and Key West, is packed with sailors offering guided backcountry fishing charters. This is the place to go if you want to stalk tarpon, bonefish, and snapper. If the seas are not too rough, deep-sea and coral fishing trips can also be arranged. Charters cost $500 to $550 for a half day, $750 to $800 for a full day, and splits begin at $125 per person.

The Bounty Hunter, 15th Street at Burdine's Marina, Marathon (© **305/743-2446**), offers full- and half-day outings. For 28 years, Captain Brock Hook's huge sign has boasted, "No fish, no pay." You're guaranteed to catch something, or your money back! Choose your prey from shark, barracuda, sailfish, or whatever else is running. Prices are $400 for a half day, $500 for three-quarters of a day, and $600 for a full day. Rates are for groups of no more than six people.

Tips **Boat Choices**

For a more enjoyable time, ask for a sit-inside boat—you'll stay drier. Also, a fiberglass (as opposed to plastic) boat with a rudder is generally more stable and easier to maneuver.

Acquaint Yourself

Fans of stone crabs can get further acquainted with those seasonal crustaceans thanks to Keys Fisheries' 3-hour tours aboard 40- to 50-foot vessels, which leave from Marathon. The tour includes views of fishermen as they collect crabs from traps and process their claws. The $425 tour cost includes up to six passengers and up to 6 pounds of fresh claws iced for travel or prepared at a dockside restaurant. Stone-crab season is from October 15 to May 15. Call ℂ 305/743-4353 or check the Web at www. keysfisheries.com for more information.

SHOPPING

On your way to the Keys, you'll find an outlet center, the **Prime Outlets at Florida City** (ℂ 305/248-4727), at 250 E. Palm Dr. (where the Florida Turnpike meets U.S. Hwy. 1), in Florida City. The center holds more than 60 stores, including Nike Factory, Bass Co., Levi's, OshKosh, and Izod. Travelers can pick up a free discount coupon booklet called the Come Back Pack from the Customer Service Center. The outlet is open Monday to Saturday from 10am to 9pm, Sunday from 11am to 6pm.

The Upper and Middle Keys have no shortage of tacky tourist shops selling shells and T-shirts (the ubiquitous "beads and trinkets") and other hokey souvenirs, but for real Keys-style shopping, check out the weekend **flea markets.** The best, the Key Largo Storage/Flea Market, is held every Saturday and Sunday bayside at MM 103.5 (ℂ 305/451-0677). Dozens of vendors open their stalls from 9am until 4 or 5pm, selling every imaginable sort of antiques, T-shirts, plants, shoes, books, toys, and games, as well as a hearty dose of good old-fashioned junk. Also decent is the Grassy Key Flea Market, at MM 60, on the ocean side. The rest, however, are pretty schlocky.

A mecca for fishing and sports enthusiasts, the **World Wide Sportsman** (ℂ 305/664-4615) at MM 81.5, is not only the largest fishing store in the Keys, but also a meeting place for anglers from all over the world. Every possible gizmo and gadget, plus hundreds of T-shirts, hats, books, and gift items, are displayed in its more than 25,000 square feet. The salespeople are knowledgeable and eager to help. Travel specialists can even arrange for charter trips and backcountry tours. The store is open daily from 7am until 8:30pm.

WHERE TO STAY

U.S. 1 is lined with chain hotels in all price ranges. In the Upper Keys, the best moderately priced option is the **Ramada Limited Resort & Casino** (ℂ 800/ THE-KEYS or 305/451-3939) at MM 100, off of U.S. 1 in Key Largo, which has three pools and a casino boat and is just 3 miles from John Pennekamp Coral Reef State Park. Another good option in the Upper Keys is **Islamorada Days Inn,** U.S. 1 at MM 82.5 (ℂ 800/DAYS-INN or 305/664-3681). In the Middle Keys, the **Wellesley Inn** at 13351 Overseas Hwy., MM 54 in Marathon (ℂ 305/743-8550) also offers reasonably priced oceanside rooms.

Since the real beauty of the Keys lies mostly beyond the highways, there is no better way to see this area than by boat. Why not stay in a floating hotel? Especially if traveling with a group, houseboats can be economical. To rent a houseboat, call Ruth and Michael Sullivan at **Smilin' Island Houseboat Rentals,**

MM 99.5, Key Largo (✆ **305/451-1930**). Rates are from $750 to $1,350 for 3 nights. Boats accommodate up to six people.

For land options, consider the below recommendations.

VERY EXPENSIVE

Cheeca Lodge & Spa ✿✿✿ *(Kids)*   Luxurious and relaxing Cheeca has been hosting celebrities, royalty, and politicians since its opening in 1949. Guests now enjoy the luxury of the Cheeca's freshly renovated and remodeled rooms. Each of the 203 units offers all the amenities of a world-class resort in a very laid-back setting. You may not feel compelled to leave the sprawling grounds, but it's good to know that the hotel is conveniently situated near the best restaurants and nightlife. Located on 27 acres of beachfront property (the 1,100-foot palm-lined beach is truly idyllic), this rambling resort is known for its excellent sports facilities, including one of the only golf courses in the Upper Keys. All rooms are spacious and have small balconies. The nicer ones overlook the ocean and have large marble bathrooms. Rooms by the golf course have showers, not bathtubs, and overlook man-made lagoons. The Atlantic's Edge restaurant is one of the best in the Upper Keys (see p. 269). In May 2001, the state-of-the-art Avanyu health spa and fitness center opened. Children 6 to 12 can have their own customized vacation with Camp Cheeca's organized activities and events.

U.S. 1 at MM 82 (P.O. Box 527), Islamorada, FL 33036. ✆ **800/327-2888** or 305/664-4651. Fax 305/664-2893. www.cheeca.com. 203 units. Winter $149–$650 double; $219–$1,600 suite. Off-season $129–$475 double; $189–$1,225 suite. AE, DC, DISC, MC, V. **Amenities:** 2 restaurants, 2 lounges (1 pool side); 3 outdoor heated pools, kids' pool; 9-hole, par-3 golf course; 6 lighted tennis courts; Jacuzzi, 5 hot tubs; access to nearby health club; watersports equipment rental; bike rental; children's nature programs; concierge; tour desk; car-rental desk; room service; in-room massage; babysitting; dry-cleaning and laundry services; nature trails. *In room:* A/C, TV/VCR, CD player, dataport, kitchenette (in suites), minibar, coffeemaker, hair dryer.

Hawk's Cay Resort ✿✿✿ *(Kids)*   Located on its own 60-acre island in the Middle Keys, this resort has a relaxed and casual island atmosphere. If it's recreation you're looking for, Hawk's Cay is far superior to the more luxurious Cheeca Lodge. It offers an impressive array of activities—sailing, fishing, snorkeling, and water-skiing to name a few—and the unique opportunity to frolic in a special pool reserved for swimming with dolphins. (You'll need to reserve a spot well in advance for the dolphins—there's a waiting list.) The rooms are large and newly renovated, with island-style furniture, and each opens onto a private balcony with ocean or tropical views (pricing varies depending on the view). The large bathrooms are well appointed and have granite countertops. The clubhouse has an exercise room, whirlpool, and steam room. In addition to a lagoon and several pools for families, the resort boasts a secluded pool for adults only. Organized children's activities, including special marine and ecologically inspired programs, will keep your little ones busy while you relax.

61 Hawk's Cay Blvd. at MM 61, Duck Key, Fl 33050. ✆ **888/814-9104** or 305/743-7000. Fax 305/743-5215. www.hawkscay.com. 176 units. Winter $240–$395 double; $445–$1100 suite. Off-season $200–$325 double; $375–$1,000 suite. Packages available. AE, DC, DISC, MC, V. **Amenities:** 3 restaurants, lounge; outdoor heated pool, adults-only private pool; 18-hole putting course, nearby golf course (transportation available); 8 tennis courts (2 lighted); small exercise room; Jacuzzi; watersports equipment rental; bike rental; children's programs ($25–$35 per child); game room; concierge; limited room service; in-room massage. *In room:* A/C, TV/VCR, fridge, iron, coffeemaker, hair dryer.

Westin Beach Resort ✿✿   In addition to a $3 million overhaul, the resort distinguishes itself by its secluded yet convenient location—it's set back on 12 private acres of gumbo-limbo and hardwood trees, making it invisible from the busy highway. Despite its hideaway location, the sprawling pink-and-blue four-story complex is surprisingly large: Two wings that face 1,200 feet of the Florida Bay flank a three-story atrium lobby. The large guest rooms all have private balconies overlooking either the bay or nature trails and are immaculate and fairly large—your typical, upscale-ish Westin room. The suites are twice the size of standard rooms with double-size balconies and better quality wicker furnishings. Ten suites feature private spa tubs and particularly luxurious bathrooms with adjustable showerheads, bidets, and lots of room for toiletries.

U.S. 1 at MM 97, Key Largo, FL 33037. ℂ 800/728-2738, 800/539-5274, or 305/852-5553. Fax 305/852-8669. www.keylargoresort.com. 200 units. Winter $189–$389; Jacuzzi suites start at $369. Off-season $109–$369; Jacuzzi suites start at $279. AE, DC, DISC, MC, V. **Amenities:** 2 restaurants, snack bar; 2 outdoor heated swimming pools; 2 lighted tennis courts; exercise room; Jacuzzi; watersports equipment rentals; bike rental; children's programs; concierge; secretarial services; 24-hr. room service; dry-cleaning and laundry services; in-room massage; babysitting; nature trails. *In room:* A/C, TV, dataport, minibar, coffeemaker, hair dryer, iron.

EXPENSIVE

Jules' Undersea Lodge 🐠🐠🐠 *(Finds)*   Staying here is certainly an experience of a lifetime—if you're brave enough to take the plunge. Originally built as a research lab in the 1970s, this small underwater compartment (which rests on pillars on the ocean floor) now operates as a two-room hotel. As expensive as it is unusual, Jules' is most popular with diving honeymooners. To get inside, guests swim 21 feet under the structure and pop up into the unit through a 4-by-6-foot "moon pool" that gurgles soothingly all night long. The 30-foot-deep underwater suite consists of two separate bedrooms that share a common living area. Room service will deliver your meals, daily newspapers, even a late-night pizza in waterproof containers at no extra charge.

51 Shoreland Dr., Key Largo, FL 33037. ℂ 305/451-2353. Fax 305/451-4789. www.jul.com. 2 units. $250–$350 per person. Rates include breakfast and dinner as well as all equipment and unlimited scuba diving in the lagoon for certified divers. Packages available. AE, DISC, MC, V. From U.S. 1 S., at MM 103.2, turn left onto Transylvania Ave., across from the Central Plaza shopping mall. **Amenities:** Entertainment center; dining area. *In room:* A/C, telephone, kitchenette.

Marriott Key Largo Bay Beach Resort 🐠🐠   While hardly quaint, this amenities-laden 17-acre complex has everything an active or resting traveler could want, including a private beach, a new European health spa, a small, nine-hole putting course, and tennis courts. All guests are also welcome to sail for free on a gambling cruise ship that anchors in international waters from 2pm until 2am daily. Rooms are decorated in a pleasant, if generic, tropical style, and most have balconies overlooking the stunning Florida Bay. The enormous suites can easily sleep a family of five, and all have large wraparound terraces and big sitting areas.

103800 Overseas Hwy. at MM 103, Key Largo, FL 33037. ℂ 800/932-9332 or 305/453-0000. Fax 305/453-0093. www.marriottkeylargo.com. 153 units. Winter $289–$649. Off-season $209–$449. AE, DC, MC, V. **Amenities:** Restaurant, snack bar; large outdoor pool; access to nearby tennis and racquetball courts; health center and spa, Jacuzzi; watersports equipment rentals; bike rental; children's programs; game room; concierge; business center; limited room service; in-room massage; babysitting; dry-cleaning and laundry services; nature trail. *In room:* A/C, TV, VCR on request, dataport, minibar, coffeemaker, hair dryer, iron, safe.

The Moorings 🐠🐠🐠 *(Finds)*   Staying at the Moorings is more like staying at a secluded beach house than at a hotel. You'll never see another soul on this 18-acre resort if you choose not to. There isn't even maid service unless you request it. The romantic whitewashed units, from cozy cottages to three-bedroom houses, are spacious and modestly decorated. All have full kitchens (though there are 2 restaurants within walking distance), and most have washers and dryers. Some have CD players and VCRs; ask when you book. The real reason to come to this resort is to relax on the more than 1,000-foot beach (one of the only real beaches around). There are a hard tennis court, a few kayaks and windsurfers, but absolutely no motorized water vehicles in the waters surrounding the hotel, making it completely quiet and tranquil. There is no room service or restaurant (although Morada Bay across the street is excellent). This is a place for people who like each other a lot. Leave the kids at home unless they are extremely well behaved and not easily bored.

123 Beach Rd. near MM 81.5 on the ocean side, Islamorada, FL 33036. ℂ 305/664-4708. Fax 305/664-4242. www.themooringsvillage.com. 18 cottages. Winter $200–$250 small cottages; $475 1-bedroom house; $3,325–$7,875 weekly oceanfront house. Off-season daily $185–$225 small cottages; $375 1-bedroom house; $2,625–$6,650 weekly oceanfront house. 2-night minimum for smaller cottages; 1-week minimum for larger cottages. MC, V. **Amenities:** Large outdoor heated pool; tennis court; watersports equipment rental. *In room:* A/C, TV, kitchen, coffeemaker, hair dryer.

MODERATE

Banana Bay Resort & Marina 🍌🍌 *(Finds)* It doesn't look like much from the sign-cluttered Overseas Highway, but when you enter the lush grounds of Banana Bay, you will realize you're in one of the most bucolic and best-run properties in the Upper Keys. Built in the early 1950s as a place for fisherman to stay during extended fishing trips, the resort is a beachfront maze of two-story buildings hidden among banyans and palms. The rooms are moderately sized, and many have private balconies where you can enjoy your complimentary coffee and newspaper every morning. Recent additions to the hotel include a recreational activity area with horseshoe pits, a bocce court, picnic areas with barbecue grills, and a giant lawn chessboard. The hotel's kitschy restaurant serves three meals a day, indoors or poolside. This resort is family friendly, but if you're looking for an adults-only resort, there's also a Banana Bay Resort in Key West (ℂ **305/296-6925**) that doesn't allow children.

U.S. 1 at MM 49.5, Marathon, FL 33050. ℂ 800/BANANA-1 or 305/743-3500. Fax 305/743-2670. www.bananabay.com. 60 units. Winter $125–$250 double. Off-season $85–$175 double. Rates include continental breakfast. 3- and 7-night honeymoon & wedding packages available. AE, DC, DISC, MC, V. **Amenities:** Restaurant, 3 bars; small beach and snorkel area; pool; tennis courts; health club; Jacuzzi; watersports rental; charter fishing; sailing and diving; self-service Laundromat. *In room:* A/C, TV, dataport, fridge, hair dryer, iron.

Conch Key Cottages 🍌🍌 *(Finds)* Here's your chance to play castaway in the Keys. Occupying its own private micro-island just off U.S. 1, Conch Key Cottages is a comfortable hideaway run by live-in owners Ron Wilson and Wayne Byrnes, who are constantly fixing and adding to their unique property. This is a place to get away from it all; the cottages aren't located close to much, except maybe one or two interesting eateries. The cabins overlook their own stretch of natural, but very small, private beach and have a screened-in porch, cozy bedroom, bathroom, hammock, barbecue grill, and a two-person kayak. Request one of the two-bedroom cottages—especially if you are traveling with the family. They are the most spacious and are well designed, practically tailor-made, for couples or families. On the other side of the pool are a handful of efficiency apartments (all with fully equipped kitchens) that are similarly outfitted, but enjoy no beach frontage.

Near U.S. 1 at MM 62.3, Marathon, FL 33050. ℂ 800/330-1577 or 305/289-1377. Fax 305/743-8207. www.conchkeycottages.com. 12 cottages. Dec 15–Sept 8 $110–$288; Sept 9–Dec 14 $74–$215. DISC, MC, V. **Amenities:** Pool; complimentary kayaks; laundry facilities. *In room:* A/C, TV, kitchen, coffeemaker. No phone.

Faro Blanco Marine Resort 🍌 Spanning both sides of the Overseas Highway and all on waterfront property, this huge, two-shore marina and hotel complex offers something for every taste. Free-standing camp-style cottages with a small bedroom are the resort's least expensive accommodations, but they are in dire need of rehabilitation. Old appliances and a musty odor make them the least desirable units on the property. The houseboats are the best choice and value. Permanently tethered (so tightly moored, you hardly move at all, even in the roughest weather) in a tranquil marina, these white rectangular boats look like floating mobile homes and are uniformly clean, fresh, and recommendable, with four hotel rooms to each boat. They have colonial American-style furnishings, fully equipped kitchenettes, front and back porches, and water, water everywhere. The resort's condos have three bedrooms, two baths, and terraces. Finally, there are two unusual rental units located in a lighthouse on the pier. Circular staircases, unusually shaped immaculate rooms and showers, and nautical decor make it a unique place to stay, but some guests might find it claustrophobic.

1996 Overseas Hwy., U.S. 1 at MM 48.5, Marathon, FL 33050. © 800/759-3276 or 305/743-9018. Fax 305/ 866-5235. 123 units. 31 houseboats with 4 units each. Winter $89–$150 cottage; $109–$200 houseboat; $185 lighthouse; $267–$327 condo. Off-season $79–$119 cottage; $99–$178 houseboat; $145 lighthouse; $215–$263 condo. AE, DISC, MC, V. **Amenities:** 4 restaurants, 2 lounges; Olympic-size pool; fully equipped dive shop; barbecue and picnic areas; playground. *In room:* A/C, TV.

Holiday Isle Resort ⚓   A huge resort complex encompassing five restaurants, several lounges, tiki huts, a large marina, many retail shops, and four distinct (if not distinctive) hotels, the Holiday Isle is one of the biggest resorts in the Keys. It attracts a Spring Break kind of crowd year-round. Its Tiki Bar claims to have invented the rumrunner drink (151-proof rum, blackberry brandy, banana liqueur, grenadine, and lime juice), and there's no reason to doubt it. Hordes of partiers are attracted to the resort's nonstop merrymaking, live music, and beachfront bars. As a result, some of the accommodations can be noisy. Rooms can be bare-bones budget to oceanfront luxury, as the broad range of prices reflects. Even the nicest rooms could use a good cleaning. El Capitan and Harbor Lights, two of the least expensive hotels on the property, are both austere. Like the other hotels here, rooms could use a thorough rehab. Howard Johnson's, another Holiday Isle property, is a little farther from the action and a tad more civilized. If you plan to be here for a few days, choose an efficiency or a suite; both have kitchenettes.

U.S. 1 at MM 84, Islamorada, FL 33036. © 800/327-7070 or 305/664-2321. Fax 305/664-2703. www. holidayisle.com. 199 units. Winter $130–$290 double; $290–$420 suite. Off-season $110–$240 double; $240–$410 suite. AE, DISC, MC, V. **Amenities:** 5 restaurants, 12 bars; 3 outdoor heated pools, kids' pool; Jacuzzi; kids programs; laundry facilities; watersports equipment rentals. *In room:* A/C, TV, fridge, hair dryer.

Kona Kai Resort & Gallery ⚓⚓   Unique to the Upper Keys, this little haven, with just 11 units, is both casual and elegant. Quaint rooms and complete suites dot the lushly landscaped 2-acre property, which boasts a large variety of native vegetation like palms, bougainvillea, and ferns, plus an impressive collection of fruit-bearing trees, such as carambola, passion fruit, banana, Key lime, guava, and coconut, which you can sample. An orchid house has over 250 beautiful flowers. Lounge chairs, hammocks, a Jacuzzi, and a compact beach are available for those who just want to relax (no phones in the rooms make relaxing imperative), while the owners will organize excursions to the Everglades, the backcountry, or wherever for the more adventurous. All the rooms are very private and simply furnished; bathroom amenities are fabulous, with lotions, soaps, and shampoos made from tropical fruits. For meals, you'll need to visit a nearby restaurant—there are three within walking distance and several more a short drive away. Smoking is not permitted in the rooms. An art gallery featuring work by American and international painters, photographers, and sculptors doubles as the property's office and lobby. Even if you are not staying here, stop in to see the artwork.

97802 Overseas Hwy. (U.S. 1 at MM 97.8), Key Largo, FL 33037. ✆ 800/365-7829 or 305/852-7200. Fax 305/852-4629. www.konakairesort.com. 11 units. Winter $196–$233 double; $257–$658 1- to 2-bedroom suite. Off-season $108–$129 double; $143–$433 1- to 2-bedroom suite. AE, DISC, MC, V. Children under 16 not permitted. Closed Sept. **Amenities:** Heated pool; tennis court; spa, Jacuzzi; watersports equipment rental; boat ramp/dockage; concierge; in-room massage and facials. *In room:* A/C, TV, fridge, hair dryer; kitchen, VCR, CD player (suites only). No phone.

Lime Tree Bay Resort Motel   The Lime Tree Bay Resort is the only hotel in the tiny town of Layton (population 183). Midway between Islamorada and Marathon, the hotel is only steps from Long Key State Recreation Area. It's situated on a very pretty piece of waterfront graced with hundreds of mature palm trees and lots of other tropical foliage. Motel rooms and efficiencies have tiny bathrooms with standing showers but are clean and well maintained. The best deal is the two-bedroom bayview cottage. The large living area with new fixtures and furnishings leads out to a large private deck where you can enjoy a view of the Gulf from your hammock. A full kitchen and two full bathrooms make it a comfortable space for six people. Fifteen efficiencies and suites have kitchenettes.

U.S. 1 at MM 68.5 in Layton, Long Key, FL 33001. ✆ 800/723-4519 or 305/664-4740. Fax 305/664-0750. www.limetreebayresort.com. 30 units. Winter $102–$235 double. Off-season $79–$215 double. AE, DC, DISC, MC, V. **Amenities:** Restaurant; small outdoor pool; tennis court; Jacuzzi; watersports equipment rental. *In room:* A/C, TV, dataport, kitchenette (in some units).

INEXPENSIVE

Bay Harbor Lodge ✮   A small, simple retreat that's big on charm, the Bay Harbor Lodge is an extraordinarily welcoming place. The lodge is far from fancy, though it features new windows and paint, and the widely ranging accommodations are not created equal. The motel rooms are small and ordinary in decor, but even the least expensive is recommendable. The efficiencies are larger motel rooms with fully equipped kitchenettes. The oceanfront cottages are larger still, have full kitchens, and represent one of the best values in the Keys. The vinyl-covered furnishings and old-fashioned wallpaper won't win any design awards, but elegance isn't what the "real" Keys are about. The 1½ lush acres of grounds are planted with banana trees and have an outdoor heated pool and several small barbecue grills. A small beach is ideal for some quiet sunning and relaxation. Guests are free to use the rowboats, paddleboats, canoes, kayaks, and snorkeling equipment. Bring your own beach towels.

97702 Overseas Hwy., U.S. 1 at MM 97.7 (off the southbound lane of U.S. 1), Key Largo, FL 33037. ✆ 800/385-0986 or 305/852-5695. www.thefloridakeys.com/bayharborlodge. 16 units. Winter $75–$165 double; $95–$165 cottage. Off-season $65–$95 double; $95–$105 cottage. MC, V. **Amenities:** Freshwater pool; watersports equipment rental. *In room:* A/C, TV, fridge, microwave, coffeemaker, hair dryer.

Ragged Edge Resort ✮✮   This small oceanfront property's 11 units are spread out along more than half a dozen gorgeous, grassy waterfront acres. All are immaculately clean and comfortable, and most are outfitted with full kitchens and tasteful furnishings. There's no bar, restaurant, or staff to speak of, but the retreat's affable owner, Jackie Barnes, is happy to lend you bicycles or good advice on the area's offerings. A large dock attracts boaters and a good variety of local and migratory birds.

243 Treasure Harbor Rd. (near MM 86.5), Islamorada, FL 33036. ✆ 800/436-2023 or 305/852-5389. www.ragged-edge.com. 11 units. Winter $69–$189. Off-season $49–$132. AE, MC, V. **Amenities:** Outdoor pool; free use of bikes; Laundromat. *In room:* A/C, kitchen (most units), fridge, coffeemaker.

CAMPING

John Pennekamp Coral Reef State Park ★★ One of Florida's best parks (see p. 259), Pennekamp offers 47 well-separated campsites, half of which are available by advance reservation, the rest distributed on a first-come, first-served basis. The tent sites are small but well equipped with bathrooms, hot water, and showers. Note that the local environment provides fertile breeding grounds for insects, particularly in the late summer, so bring insect repellent or you will be sorry. Two man-made beaches and a small lagoon nearby attract many large wading birds. Reservations are held until 5pm, and the park must be notified of late arrival by phone on the check-in date. Pennekamp opens at 8am and closes around sundown.

U.S. 1 at MM 102.5 (P.O. Box 487), Key Largo, FL 33037. ℂ **305/451-1202.** 47 campsites. Reservations can be made in advance by calling Reserve America (ℂ **800/326-3521.** $24 (without electricity)–$26 (with electricity) per site. Park entry $4 per vehicle (50¢ for each additional person). Yearly permits and passes available. AE, DISC, MC, V. No pets.

Long Key State Park ★ The Upper Keys' other main state park is more secluded than its northern neighbor—and more popular. All sites are located oceanside and surrounded by narrow rows of trees and nearby toilet and bathroom facilities. Reserve well in advance, especially in winter.

U.S. 1 at MM 67.5 (P.O. Box 776), Long Key, FL 33001. ℂ **305/664-4815.** 60 oceanfront sites. $24–$26 per site for 1–4 people. $3.25 per vehicle. AE, DISC, MC, V. No pets.

WHERE TO DINE

Although not known as a culinary hot spot (though always improving), the Upper and Middle Keys do offer some excellent restaurants, most of which specialize in seafood. Often, visitors (especially those who fish) take advantage of accommodations that have kitchen facilities and cook their own meals. Some restaurants will even clean and cook your catch, for a fee.

VERY EXPENSIVE

Atlantic's Edge ★★★ SEAFOOD/REGIONAL Ask for a table by the oceanfront window to feel really privileged at this restaurant, the most elegant in the Keys. Although the service and food are generally first rate, don't get dressed up—a sports coat for men will be fine but isn't necessary. You can choose from an innovative, varied menu, which offers several choices of fresh fish, steak, chicken, and pastas. The crab cakes, made with stone crab when in season, are the very best in the Keys; served on a warm salad of baby greens with a mild sauce of red peppers, they're the stuff cravings are made of. Other excellent dishes include a Thai-spiced fresh baby snapper and the vegetarian angel-hair pasta with mushrooms, asparagus, and peppers in a rich broth. Service can sometimes be less than efficient but is always courteous and professional.

In the Cheeca Lodge, U.S. 1 at MM 82, Islamorada. ℂ **305/664-4651.** Reservations recommended. Main courses $20–$36. AE, DC, DISC, MC, V. Daily 6–10pm.

EXPENSIVE

Barracuda Grill ★★ SEAFOOD Owned by Lance Hill and his wife, Jan (a former sous chef at Little Palm Island, see p. 277), this small, casual spot serves excellent seafood, steaks, and chops, but unfortunately, it's only open for dinner. Some of the favorite dishes are the Caicos gold conch and mangrove snapper and mango. Try the Tipsy Olives appetizer, marinated in gin or vodka, to kick-start your meal. For fans of spicy food, try the red-hot calamari. Decorated with barracuda-themed art, the restaurant also features a well-priced American wine list with lots of California vintages.

U.S. 1 at MM 49.5 (bayside), Marathon. ✆ 305/743-3314. Main courses $10–$26. AE, MC, V. Mon–Sat 6–10pm.

Marker 88 ✿✿✿ SEAFOOD/REGIONAL   An institution in the Upper Keys, Marker 88 has been pleasing locals and visitors for dinner since it opened in the early 1970s. Chef-owner Andre Mueller fuses tropical fruit and fish with such items as crabmeat stuffing, asparagus, tomatoes, lemons, olives, capers, and mushrooms to make the most delectable and innovative seafood dishes around. Taking full advantage of his island location, Andre offers dozens of seafood selections, including Keys lobster, Bahamas conch, Florida Bay stone crabs, Gulf Coast shrimp, and an impressive variety of fish from around the country. After you've figured out what kind of seafood to have, you can choose from a dozen styles of preparation. The Keys' standard style is meunière, which is a subtle, tasty sauce of lemon and parsley. Although everything looks tempting, don't over-order—portions are huge. The waitresses, who are pleasant enough, require a bit of patience, but the food—not to mention the spectacular Gulf views from the outdoor bar and tables—is worth it.

U.S. 1 at MM 88 (bayside), Islamorada. ✆ 305/852-9315. Reservations suggested. Main courses $14–$33. AE, DC, DISC, MC, V. Tues–Sun 5–11pm. Closed in Sept.

Morada Bay Beach Cafe ✿✿ CARIBBEAN/AMERICAN   This lovely bayside bistro offers superfresh, innovative seafood as well as more basic offerings, such as chicken salads, fajitas, and hamburgers. Salads such as the Sunshine Salad are large and lavished with slices of avocado, mango, and tomato. When in season, delicious raw oysters are imported from Long Island. Fish dishes are always fresh and served in a number of styles; I like mine jerked with a peppery coating and nearly black finish. If you can't decide, share a few items from the tapas menu: jumbo shrimp cocktails, fried calamari, conch fritters, smoked fish dip, or a charcuterie of sausage and ham on country bread. Located at the same address is Pierre's Restaurant (✆ **305/664-3225**), a New World cuisine fine-dining restaurant that's a bit pricier (main courses $24–$37), but worth a splurge.

U.S. 1 at MM 81.6, Islamorada. ✆ 305/664-0604. Reservations recommended for large groups. Main courses $17–$28. AE, DISC, MC, V. Daily 11:30am–10pm.

MODERATE

Green Turtle Inn ✿✿ SEAFOOD   The Green Turtle Inn was established in 1947 as a place where anglers and travelers to and from Key West could stop for local delicacies made from sea turtles harvested in local waters. It has become the quintessential Keys eatery, with a friendly, local flavor and delicious and *different* fare, such as turtle steaks, soups, and chowders. Alligator steak is also popular and, yes, it does taste like chicken. Campy house pianist Tina Martin has become somewhat of a local celebrity, but it's really the turtle chowder for which the Inn has become best known. The restaurant also has a cannery so you can take some of the chowder to your friends who won't believe how good it is until they taste it for themselves.

U.S. 1 at MM 81.5, Islamorada. ✆ **305/664-9031**. Main courses $13.50–$21.95. AE, DISC, MC, V. Tues–Sun noon–10pm.

Lazy Days Oceanfront Bar and Seafood Grill ✿ SEAFOOD/AMERICAN   Opened in 1992, the Lazy Days quickly became one of the most popular restaurants around, mostly because of its large portions and lively atmosphere. Dining

The Truth About Keys Cuisine

There are few world-class chefs in the Florida Keys, but that's not to say the food isn't great. Restaurants here serve very fresh fish and a few local specialties—most notably conch fritters and chowder, Key lime pie, and stone-crab claws and lobster when they're in season.

Although a commercial net-fishing ban has diminished the stock of once-abundant fish in these parts, even the humblest of restaurants can be counted on to take full advantage of the gastronomic treasures of their own backyard. The Keys have everything a cook could want: the Atlantic and the Gulf of Mexico for impeccably fresh seafood; a tropical climate for year-round farm-stand produce (including great tomatoes, beans, berries, and citrus fruit), and a freshwater swamp for rustic delicacies such as alligator, frog legs, and hearts of palm.

Conch fritters and chowder are mainstays on most tourist-oriented menus. Because the queen conch was listed as an endangered species by the U.S. government in 1985, however, the conch in your dish was most likely shipped fresh-frozen from the Bahamas or the Caribbean.

Key lime pie consists of the juice of tiny yellow Key limes (a fruit unique to South Florida), along with condensed milk, all in a graham cracker crust. Experts debate whether the true Key lime pie should have a whipped cream or a meringue topping, but all agree that the filling should be yellow, *never* green.

Another unique offering, the **Florida lobster** is an entirely different species from the more common Maine variety and has a sweeter meat. It's also known as the "Spiny" lobster because of all the bumps on its shell. You'll see only the tails on the menu because the Florida lobster has no claws.

Stone crabs are even better—succulent, sweet, tender, and very meaty. They've been written about and talked about by kings, presidents, and poets. Although you'll find them on nearly every menu in season (from October until May), consider buying a few pounds of jumbos at the fish store to take to the beach in a cooler. Don't forget to ask to have them cracked for you, and get a cup of creamy mustard sauce for dipping. Topped off with a cold bottle of champagne, there is no better meal. (You'll be glad to know that after their claws are harvested, the crabs grow new ones, thus ensuring a long-lasting supply of these unique delicacies.)

on the oceanfront outdoor veranda is highly recommended. Meals are pricier than the casual dining room would suggest, but the food is good enough and the menu varied. Steamed clams with garlic and bell peppers make a tempting appetizer. The menu focuses on—what else?—seafood, but you can also find good pasta dishes such as linguine with littleneck clams. Most main courses come with baked potato, vegetables, a tossed salad, and French bread, making appetizers redundant.

U.S. 1 at MM 79.9, Islamorada. (C) 305/664-5256. Main courses $11–$29.95. AE, DISC, MC, V. Wed–Sun 11:30am–10pm.

Lorelei Restaurant and Cabana Bar *☆☆* SEAFOOD/BAR FOOD   Don't resist the siren call of the enormous, sparkling roadside mermaid—you won't be dashed onto the rocks. This big old fish house and bar is a great place for a snack, a meal, or a beer. Inside, a good-value menu focuses mainly on seafood. When in season, lobsters are the way to go. For $20, you can get a good-sized tail—at least a 1-pounder—prepared any way you like. Other fare includes the standard clam chowder, fried shrimp, and doughy conch fritters. Salads and soups are hearty and satisfying. For those tired of fish, the menu also offers a few beef selections. The outside bar has live music every evening, and you can order snacks and light meals from a limited menu that is satisfying and well priced.

U.S. 1 at MM 82, Islamorada. ☎ 305/664-4656. Reservations not usually required. Main courses $12–$24. AE, DC, DISC, MC, V. Daily 7am–10:30pm. Outside bar serves breakfast 7–11am; lunch/appetizer menu 11am–9pm. Bar closes at midnight.

INEXPENSIVE

Calypso's *☆* SEAFOOD   The awning still bears the name of the former restaurant, Demar's, but the food here is all Todd Lollis's, an inspired young chef who looks like he might be more comfortable at a Grateful Dead concert than in a kitchen, but who turns out inventive seafood dishes in a casual and rustic waterside setting. If it's available, try the butter pecan sauce over whatever fish is freshest. Don't miss the white-wine sangria, full of tangy oranges and limes and topped with a dash of cinnamon. The prices are surprisingly reasonable, but the service can be a little more laid-back than you're used to. The toughest part is finding the place. From the south, turn right at the blinking yellow lights near MM 99.5 to Ocean Bay Drive and then turn right. Look for the blue-vinyl-sided building on the left.

1 Seagate Blvd. (near MM 99.5), Key Largo. ☎ 305/451-0600. Main courses $9–$18. MC, V. Wed–Mon 11:30am–10pm, Fri–Sat until 11pm.

Islamorada Fish Company *☆☆* SEAFOOD   The original Islamorada Fish Company has been selling seafood out of its roadside shack since 1948. It's still the best place to pick up a cooler of stone-crab claws in season (mid-October through April). Also great are the fried-fish sandwiches, served with melted American cheese, fried onions, and coleslaw. A few hundred yards up the road (at MM 81.6) is Islamorada Fish Company Restaurant & Bakery, the newer establishment, which looks like an average diner but has a selection of fantastic seafood and pastas. It's also the place for breakfast. Locals gather for politics and gossip as well as delicious grits, oatmeal, omelets, and homemade pastries. ☎ **305/664-8363;** open Thursday to Tuesday 6am to 9pm, Wednesday 6am to 2pm.

U.S. 1 at MM 81.5 (up the street from Cheeca Lodge), Islamorada. ☎ **800/258-2559** or 305/664-9271. www.islamoradafishco.com. Reservations not accepted. Main courses $8–$27; appetizers $4–$7. DISC, MC, V. Sun–Thurs 11am–9pm, Fri–Sat 11am–10pm.

Time Out Barbecue *☆☆* BARBECUE   This barbecue joint serves up hot and hearty old-fashioned barbecue that is among the best around. According to management, the secret is in the slow cooking—more than 10 hours for the melt-in-your-mouth soft pork sandwich. Topped off with delicious, not-too-creamy coleslaw and sweet baked beans, any of the many offerings are worth a stop. You can grab a seat at the picnic table on the grassy lawn next to the Trading Post.

U.S. 1 at MM 81.5 (oceanside). ☎ **305/664-8911.** Sandwiches $4.25–$6; rib and chicken platters to share $7–$15. MC, V. Daily 11am–10pm.

THE UPPER & MIDDLE KEYS AFTER DARK

Nightlife in the Upper Keys tends to start before the sun goes down, often at noon, since most people—visitors and locals alike—are on vacation. Also, many anglers and sports-minded folk go to bed early.

Hog Heaven opened in the early 1990s, the joint venture of some young locals tired of tourist traps. Located at MM 85.3, just off the main road on the ocean side in Islamorada (© 305/664-9669), it's a welcome respite from the neon-colored cocktail circuit. This whitewashed biker bar offers a waterside view and diversions that include big-screen TVs and video games. The food isn't bad, either. The atmosphere is cliquish since most patrons are regulars, so start up a game of pool or skeet to break the ice. Open 11am to 4am daily.

No trip to the Keys is complete without a stop at the **Tiki Bar at the Holiday Isle Resort,** U.S. 1 at MM 84, Islamorada (© 800/327-7070 or 305/664-2321). Hundreds of revelers visit this oceanside spot for drinks and dancing at any time of day, but the live rock music starts at 8:30pm. (See "Where to Stay," earlier in this chapter.) The thatched-roof Tiki Bar draws a high-energy but laid-back mix of thirsty people, all in pursuit of a good time. In the afternoon and early evening (when everyone is either sunburned, drunk, or just happy to be dancing to live reggae), head for **Kokomo's,** just next door. Kokomo's often closes at 7:30pm on weekends (5:30pm on weekdays), so get there early. For information, call the Holiday Isle Resort.

Locals and tourists mingle at the outdoor cabana bar at **Lorelei** (see "Where to Dine," above). Most evenings after 5pm, you'll find local bands playing on a thatched-roof stage—mainly rock and roll, reggae, and sometimes blues.

Woody's Saloon and Restaurant, on U.S. 1 at MM 82, Islamorada (© 305/664-4335), is a lively, wacky, loud, gritty, raunchy, local legend of a place serving up mediocre pizzas and live bands almost every night. The house band, Big Dick and the Extenders, showcases a 300-pound Native American who does a lewd, rude, and crude routine of jokes and songs starting at 9pm, Tuesday through Sunday. He is a legend. By the way, don't think you're lucky if you are offered the front table: It's the target seat for Big Dick's haranguing. Avoid the lame karaoke performance on Sunday and Monday evenings. There's a small cover charge most nights. Drink specials, contests, and the legendary Big Dick keep this place packed until 4am almost every night. *Note:* This place is not for the faint of heart (or tact!), but more for those of the Howard Stern school of nightlife.

For a more subdued atmosphere, try the handsome stained glass and mahogany wood bar and club at **Zane Grey's** (on the second floor of World Wide Sportsman at MM 81.5). Outside, enjoy a view of the calm waters of the bay; inside, soak up the history of some real longtime anglers. It is open from 11am to 11pm, and later on weekends. Call to find out who is playing on weekends (© 305/664-4244), when there is live entertainment and no cover charge.

2 The Lower Keys: Big Pine Key to Coppitt Key

128 miles SW of Miami

Unlike their neighbors to the north and south, the Lower Keys (including Big Pine, Sugarloaf, and Summerland) are devoid of rowdy Spring Break crowds, boast few T-shirt and trinket shops, and have almost no late-night bars. What they do offer are the very best opportunities to enjoy the vast natural resources on land and water that make the area so rich. Stay overnight in the Lower Keys, rent a boat, and explore the reefs—it might be the most memorable part of your trip.

ESSENTIALS

GETTING THERE   See "Essentials" for the Upper and Middle Keys (p. 255) and continue south on U.S. 1. The Lower Keys start at the end of the Seven-Mile Bridge. There are also airports in Marathon and Key West.

VISITOR INFORMATION   The **Big Pine and Lower Keys Chamber of Commerce,** on the ocean side of U.S. 1 at MM 31 (P.O. Box 430511), Big Pine Key, FL 33043 (© **800/872-3722** or 305/872-2411; fax 305/872-0752; www. lowerkeyschamber.com), is open Monday through Friday from 9am to 5pm and Saturday from 9am to 3pm. The pleasant staff will help with anything a traveler may need. Call, write, or stop in for a comprehensive, detailed information packet.

WHAT TO SEE & DO

Once the centerpiece (these days, it's Big Pine Key) of the Lower Keys and still a great asset is **Bahia Honda State Park** ⍟, U.S. 1 at MM 37.5, Big Pine Key (© **305/872-2353**), which, even after the violent storms of 1998, has one of the most beautiful coastlines in South Florida. Bahia Honda (pronounced *Bah*-ya) is a great place for hiking, bird watching, swimming, snorkeling, and fishing. The 524-acre park encompasses a wide variety of ecosystems, including coastal mangroves, beach dunes, and tropical hammocks. There are miles of trails packed with unusual plants and animals and a small white beach. Shaded sea-side picnic areas are fitted with tables and grills. Although the beach is never wider than 5 feet even at low tide, this is the Lower Keys' best beach area.

True to its name (Spanish for "deep bay"), the park has relatively deep waters close to shore, and they are perfect for snorkeling and diving. Easy offshore snor-keling here gives even novices a chance to lie suspended in warm water and sim-ply observe diverse marine life passing by. Or else head to the stunning reefs at Looe Key, where the coral and fish are more vibrant than anywhere else in the United States. Snorkeling trips go from the Bahia Honda concessions to Looe Key National Marine Sanctuary (4 miles off shore). They depart twice daily from March through September and cost $25.95 for adults, $20.95 for youths 6 to 14, and are free for children 5 and under. Call © **305/872-3210** for a schedule.

Admission to the park is $4 per vehicle (plus 50¢ per person), $1.50 per pedestrian or bicyclist, free for children 5 and under. If you are alone in a car, you'll pay only $2.50. Open daily from 8am to sunset.

The most famous residents of the Lower Keys are the tiny Key deer. Of the estimated 300 existing in the world, two-thirds live on Big Pine Key's **National Key Deer Refuge** ⍟. To get your bearings, stop by the rangers' office at the Winn-Dixie Shopping Plaza near MM 30.5 off U.S. 1. They'll give you an informative brochure and map of the area. The refuge is open Monday through Friday from 8am to 5pm.

If the office is closed, head out to the Blue Hole, a former rock quarry now filled with the fresh water that's vital to the deer's survival. To get there, turn right at Big Pine Key's only traffic light onto Key Deer Boulevard (take the left fork immediately after the turn) and continue 1½ miles to the observation-site parking lot, on your left. The half-mile **Watson Hammock Trail,** about a third of a mile past the Blue Hole, is the refuge's only marked footpath. Try coming out to the footpath in the early morning or late evening to catch a glimpse of

Failed Ingenuity

The only man-made attraction in the Lower Keys is the **Sugarloaf Bat Tower,** off U.S. 1 at MM 17 (next to Sugarloaf Airport on the bay side). In a vain effort to battle the ubiquitous troublesome mosquitoes in the Lower Keys, developer Clyde Perkey built this odd structure to lure bug-eating bats. Despite his alluring design and a pungent bat aphrodisiac, his guests never showed. Since 1929, this wooden, flat-topped, 45-foot-high pyramid has stood empty and deserted, except for the occasional tourist who stops to wonder what it is. There is no sign or marker to commemorate this odd remnant of ingenuity. It's worth a 5-minute detour to see it. To get there, turn right at the Sugarloaf Airport sign and then right again onto the dirt road that begins just before the airport gate; the tower is about 100 yards ahead.

these gentle, dog-sized deer. There is an observation deck there from which you can watch and photograph the protected species. They are more active in cool hours and in cooler times of the year. Refuge lands are open daily from half an hour before sunrise to half an hour after sunset. Don't be surprised to see a lazy alligator warming itself in the sun, particularly in outlying areas around the Blue Hole. If you do see a gator, do not go near it, do not touch it, and do not provoke it. Keep your distance and if you must get a photo, use a zoom lens. Also, whatever you do, do not feed the deer—it will threaten their survival. Call the **park office** (C **305/872-2239**) to find out about the infrequent free tours of the refuge, scheduled throughout the year.

OUTDOOR PURSUITS

BICYCLING   If you have your own bike, or if your lodging offers a rental (many do), the Lower Keys are a great place to get off busy U.S. 1 to explore the beautiful back roads. On Big Pine Key, cruise along Key Deer Boulevard (at MM 30). Those with fat tires can ride into the National Key Deer Refuge.

BIRD-WATCHING   Bring your birding books. A stopping point for migratory birds on the Eastern Flyway, the Lower Keys are populated with many West Indian bird species, especially during spring and fall. The small vegetated islands of the Keys are the only nesting sites in the United States for the great white heron and the white-crowned pigeon. They're also some of the very few breeding places for the reddish egret, the roseate spoonbill, the mangrove cuckoo, and the black-whiskered vireo. Look for them on Bahia Honda Key and the many uninhabited islands nearby.

BOATING   Dozens of shops rent powerboats for fishing and reef exploring. Most also rent tackle, sell bait, and have charter captains available. **Bud Boats,** at the Old Wooden Bridge Fishing Camp and Marina, MM 30 in Big Pine Key (C **305/872-9165**), has a wide selection of well-maintained boats. Depending on the size, rentals cost between $70 and $250 for a day, between $50 and $130 for a half day. Another good option is **Jaybird's Powerboats,** U.S. 1 at MM 33, Big Pine Key (C **305/872-8500**). They rent for full days only. Prices start at $155 for a 19-footer.

CANOEING & KAYAKING   The Overseas Highway (U.S. 1) touches on only a few dozen of the many hundreds of islands that make up the Keys. To really see the Lower Keys, rent a kayak or canoe—perfect for these shallow waters. **Reflections Kayak Nature Tours,** operating out of Parmer's Resort, on U.S. 1 at MM 28.5, Little Torch Key (© **305/872-2896**), offers fully outfitted backcountry wildlife tours, either on your own or with an expert. The expert, Mike Wedeking, a former U.S. Forest Service guide, keeps up an engaging discussion describing the area's fish, sponges, coral, osprey, hawks, eagles, alligators, raccoons, and deer. The 3-hour tours cost $49 per person and include spring water, fresh fruit, granola bars, and use of binoculars. Bring a towel and sea sandals or sneakers.

FISHING   A day spent fishing, either in the shallow backcountry or in the deep sea, is a great way to ensure yourself a fresh fish dinner, or you can release your catch and just appreciate the challenge. Whichever you choose, **Larry Threlkeld's Strike Zone Charters,** U.S. 1 at MM 29.5, Big Pine Key (© **305/ 872-9863**), is the charter service to call. Prices for fishing boats start at $450 for a half day and $595 for a full day. If you have enough anglers to share the price, it isn't too steep. They may also be able to match you with other interested visitors.

HIKING   You can hike throughout the flat marshy Keys, on both marked trails and meandering coastlines. The best places to trek through nature are **Bahia Honda State Park** at MM 29.5 and **National Key Deer Refuge** at MM 30 (for more information on both, see "What to See & Do," above). Bahia Honda Park has a free brochure describing an excellent self-guided tour along the Silver Palm Nature Trail. You'll traverse hammocks, mangroves, and sand dunes and cross a lagoon. The walk (which is less than a mile) explores a great cross-section of the natural habitat in the Lower Keys and can be done in under half an hour.

SNORKELING & DIVING   Snorkelers and divers should not miss the Keys' most dramatic reefs at the **Looe Key National Marine Sanctuary.** Here, you'll see more than 150 varieties of hard and soft coral—some, centuries old—as well as every type of tropical fish, including gold-and-blue parrot fish, moray eels, barracudas, French angels, and tarpon. **Looe Key Dive Center,** U.S. 1 at MM 27.5, Ramrod Key (© **305/872-2215**), offers a mind-blowing 5-hour tour aboard a 45-foot catamaran with two shallow 1-hour dives for snorkelers and scuba divers. Snorkelers pay $22.50, and divers with their own equipment pay $35; on Wednesdays and Saturdays you can do a fascinating dive to the *Adolphus Busch Sr.,* a shipwreck sunk off Looe Key in 100 feet of water, for $40. Good-quality rentals are available. (See "What to See & Do," above, for other diving options.)

SHOPPING
Certainly not known for great shopping, the Lower Keys do happen to be home to many talented visual artists, particularly those who specialize in depicting their natural surroundings. The **Artists in Paradise Gallery,** on Big Pine Key in the Winn-Dixie Shopping Plaza, near MM 30.5, 1 block north of U.S. 1 at the traffic light (© **305/872-1828**), displays a changing selection of watercolors, oils, photos, and sculptures. This cooperative gallery displays the work of more than a dozen artists who share the task of watching the store. Hours are usually daily from 10am to 6pm.

WHERE TO STAY
There are a number of cheap, fairly unappealing fish shacks along the highway for those who want bare-bones accommodations. So far, there are no national

hotel chains in the Lower Keys. For information on lodging in cabins or trailers at local campgrounds, see "Camping," below.

VERY EXPENSIVE

Little Palm Island ★★★   This exclusive island escape—host to presidents and royalty—is not just a place to stay while in the Lower Keys; it is a destination all its own. Built on a private 5-acre island, it's accessible only by boat. Guests stay in thatched-roof duplexes amid lush foliage and flowering tropical plants. Many villas have ocean views and private sundecks with rope hammocks. Inside, the romantic suites have all the comforts and conveniences of a luxurious contemporary beach cottage, but without telephones, TVs, or alarm clocks. As if its location weren't idyllic enough, a new full-service spa recently opened on the island. Note that on the breezeless south side of the island, mosquitoes can be a problem, even in the winter. (So bring spray and lightweight, long-sleeved clothing.) Known for its innovative and pricey food, Little Palm also hosts visitors just for dinner or lunch. If you are staying on the island, opt for the full American plan, which includes three meals a day for about $140 per person. If you pay a la carte, you could spend that much just on dinner. At these prices, Little Palm appeals to those who aren't keeping track.

Launch is at the ocean side of U.S. 1 at MM 28.5, Little Torch Key, FL 33042. ✆ 800/343-8567 or 305/872-2524. Fax 305/872-4843. www.littlepalmisland.com. 28 bungalows, 2 deluxe suites. Winter $795–$1,695 per couple. Off-season $695–$1,595 per couple. Rates include transportation to and from the island and unlimited (nonmotorized) watersports. Meal plans include 2 meals daily for $125 per person per day, 3 meals at $140 per person. AE, DC, DISC, MC, V. No children under 16. **Amenities:** Restaurant, bar; 2 pools (1 outdoor with small waterfall, 1 indoor); health club and spa; jogging trail; extensive watersports equipment rental; concierge; courtesy van from Key West or Marathon airport; ferry service to and from the mainland; limited room service; in-room massage; dry-cleaning and laundry services. *In room:* A/C, dataport, Jacuzzi, minibar, coffeemaker, hair dryer. No phone.

MODERATE

Deer Run Bed and Breakfast ★★ (Finds)   Located directly on the beach, Sue Abbott's small, homey, smoke-free B&B is a real find. One upstairs and two downstairs guest rooms are comfortably furnished with queen-size beds, good closets, and touch-sensitive lamps. Rattan and 1970s-style chairs and couches furnish the living room, along with 13 birds and three cats. Breakfast, which is served on a pretty, fenced-in porch, is cooked to order by Sue herself. The wooded area around the property is full of Key deer, which are often spotted on the beach as well. A hot tub overlooking the ocean is especially nice. Ask to use one of the bikes to explore nearby nature trails.

Long Beach Dr. (P.O. Box 431), Big Pine Key, FL 33043. ✆ 305/872-2015. Fax 305/872-2842. deerrunbb@aol.com. 3 units. Winter from $165 double. Off-season from $95 double. Rates include full American breakfast. No credit cards. From U.S. 1 S., turn left at the Big Pine Fishing Lodge (MM 33); continue for about 2 miles. No children under 16. **Amenities:** Jacuzzi; free use of bikes. *In room:* A/C, TV.

INEXPENSIVE

Parmer's Resort ★★   Parmer's, a fixture here for more than 20 years, is well known for its charming hospitality and helpful staff. This downscale resort offers modest but comfortable cottages, each of them unique. Some are waterfront, many have kitchenettes, and others are just a bedroom. Room 26, a.k.a. Wahoo, a one-bedroom efficiency, is especially nice, with a small sitting area that faces the water. Room 6, a small efficiency, has a kitchenette and an especially large bathroom. The rooms have been recently updated—and are consistently very clean. Many can be combined to accommodate large families. The hotel's waterfront location almost makes up for the fact that you must pay extra for maid service.

Barry Ave. (P.O. Box 430665), near MM 28.5, Little Torch Key, FL 33043. © **305/872-2157.** Fax 305/872-2014. www.parmersresort.com. 45 units. Winter $75–$220 double; from $105 efficiency. Off-season $55–$85 double; $75–$150 efficiency. Rates include continental breakfast. AE, DISC, MC, V. From U.S. 1, turn right onto Barry Ave. Resort is a ½ mile down on the right. **Amenities:** Heated pool; boat ramp; bike rental; coin-op washers and dryers. *In room:* A/C, TV.

CAMPING

Bahia Honda State Park ⓡⓡ (© 305/872-2353; www.abfla.com/parks/BahiaHonda/bahiahonda.html) offers some of the best camping in the Keys. It is as loaded with facilities and activities as it is with campers. However, don't be discouraged by its popularity—this park encompasses more than 500 acres of land, 80 campsites spread throughout three areas, and six spacious and comfortable cabin units (fitting six people each) that were reconstructed between 2000 and 2001. Cabins hold up to eight guests and come complete with linens, kitchenettes, and utensils as well as a wraparound terrace, barbecue pit, and rocking chairs.

For one to four people, camping here costs about $25 per site without electricity and $26 with electricity. Depending on the season, cabin prices change: Prices range from $50 to $110. Additional people (over four) cost $6 each. MasterCard and Visa are accepted.

Another excellent value can be found at the **KOA Sugarloaf Key Resort** ⓡⓡ, near MM 20. This oceanside facility has 200 fully equipped sites, with water, electricity, and sewer, which rent for about $70 a night (no-hook-up sites cost about $38). Or pitch a tent on the 5 acres of lush waterfront property. This site is especially nice because of its private beaches, access to diving, snorkeling, and boating, and its grounds are nice and well maintained. The resort also rents travel trailers. The 22-foot Dutchman sleeps six and is equipped with eating and cooking utensils. It costs about $100 a day. More luxurious trailers go for $160 a day. All major credit cards are accepted. For details, write them at P.O. Box 420469, Summerland Key, FL 33042 (© **800/562-7731** or 305/745-3549; fax 305/745-9889; www.koa.com).

WHERE TO DINE

There aren't many fine dining options in the Lower Keys, with the exception of the dining room at Little Palm Island Resort, MM 285, Little Torch Key, (© **305/872-2551**), in which you'll be wowed with gourmet French Caribbean fare that looks like a meal but eats like a vacation. You need to take a ferry to this chichi private resort island, on which you can indulge in the exquisite oceanside restaurant, even if you're not staying over. If you don't have the chance to get there, try the following, worth a stop for those passing through.

MODERATE

Mangrove Mama's Restaurant SEAFOOD/CARIBBEAN As the dedicated locals who come daily for happy hour will tell you, this is a true Lower Keys institution and a dive (the restaurant is a shack that used to have a gas pump as well as a grill) in the best sense of the word. Guests share the property with some miniature horses (out back) and stray cats. A handful of simple tables, inside and out, are shaded by banana trees and palm fronds. Fish is the menu's mainstay, although soups, salads, sandwiches, and omelets are also good. Grilled teriyaki chicken and club sandwiches are tasty alternatives to fish, as are meatless chef's salads and spicy barbecued baby-back ribs.

U.S. 1 at MM 20, Sugarloaf Key. © 305/745-3030. Main courses $10–$20; lunch $6–$9; brunch $5–$7. MC, V. Daily 11:30am–10pm (11am in season).

Monte's SEAFOOD   Certainly nobody goes to this restaurant/fish market for its atmosphere: Plastic place settings rest on plastic-covered picnic-style tables in a screen-enclosed dining patio. But Monte's doesn't need great atmosphere, since it has survived for more than 20 years on its very good and incredibly fresh food. The day's catch may include shark, tuna, lobsters, stone crabs, or shrimp.

U.S. 1 at MM 25, Summerland Key. (**305/745-3731**. Main courses $13–$17; lunch $6–$10. No credit cards. Mon–Sat 9am–10pm, Sun 10am–9pm.

INEXPENSIVE

Coco's Kitchen ☆ CUBAN/AMERICAN   This tiny storefront has been dishing out black beans, rice, and shredded beef to fans of Cuban cuisine for more than 10 years. The owners, who are actually from Nicaragua, cook not only superior Cuban food but also some local specialties, Italian food, and Caribbean food. Specialties include fried shrimp, whole fried yellowtail, and Cuban-style roast pork (available only on Saturdays). The best bet is the daily special, which may be roasted pork or fresh grouper, served with rice and beans or salad and crispy fries. Top off the huge, cheap meal with a rich caramel-soaked flan.

283 Key Deer Blvd. (in the Winn-Dixie Shopping Center), Big Pine Key. (**305/872-4495**. Main courses $6–$14.79; breakfast $2–$5. MC, V. Mon–Sat 7am–7:30pm. Turn right at the traffic light near MM 30.5. Stay in the left lane.

No Name Pub PUB FOOD/PIZZA   This funky old bar out in the boonies serves snacks and sandwiches until 11pm on most nights, and drinks until midnight. Pizzas are tasty—thick-crusted and supercheesy. Try one topped with local shrimps, or consider a bowl of chili with all the fixings—hearty and cheap. Everything is served on paper plates. Locals hang out at the rustic bar, one of the Florida Keys' oldest, drinking beer and listening to a jukebox heavy with 1980s selections. The decor, if you can call it that, is basic—the walls and ceilings are plastered with thousands of autographed dollar bills.

¼ mile south of No Name Bridge on N. Watson Blvd., Big Pine Key. (**305/872-9115**. Pizzas $6–$18; subs $5. MC, V. 11am–11pm. Turn right at Big Pine's only traffic light (near MM 30.5) onto Key Deer Blvd. Turn right on Watson Blvd. At stop sign, turn left. Look for a small wooden sign on the left marking the spot.

THE LOWER KEYS AFTER DARK

Although the mellow islands of the lower Keys aren't exactly known for wild nightlife, there are some friendly bars and restaurants where locals and tourists gather to hang out and drink.

One of the most scenic is **Sandbar** ((**305/872-9989**), a wide-open breezy wooden house built on slender stilts and overlooking a wide channel on Barry Avenue (near MM 28.5). It attracts an odd mix of bikers and blue-hairs daily from 11am until 10pm and is a great place to overhear local gossip and colorful metaphors. Pool tables are the main attraction, but there's also live music some nights. The drinks are reasonably priced, and the food isn't too bad, either. For another fun bar scene, see **No Name Pub,** listed above in "Where to Dine."

3 Key West ☆☆☆

159 miles SW of Miami

There are two schools of thought on Key West—one is that it has become way too commercial, and the other is that it's still a place where one can go and not worry about being prim, proper, or even well groomed. I think it's a bizarre fusion of both—a fascinating look at small town America in which people truly live by the (off)beat of their own drum, albeit one with a Gap and Banana Republic thrown in to bring you back to some reality. The locals, or "conchs" (pronounced *conks*), and the developers here have been at odds for years. This once low-key island has been thoroughly commercialized—there's a Hard Rock Cafe smack in the middle of Duval Street and thousands of cruise-ship passengers descend on Mallory Square each day. It's definitely not the seedy town Hemingway and his cronies once called their own. Or is it?

Laid-back Key West still exists, but it's now found in different places: the backyard of a popular guesthouse, for example, or an art gallery, a secret garden, or the hip hangouts of Bahama Village. Fortunately there are plenty of these, and Key West's greatest historic charm is found just off the beaten path. Don't be afraid to explore these residential areas, as conchs are notoriously friendly. In fact, exploring the side streets always seems to yield a new discovery of some sort. Of course, there are always the calm waters of the Atlantic and the Gulf of Mexico all around.

The heart of town offers party people a good time—that is, if your idea of a good time is the smell of stale beer, loud music, and hardly shy revelers. Here, you'll find good restaurants, fun bars, live music, rickshaw rides, and lots of shopping. Key West is still very gay-centric, except during the time of Spring Break. Same-sex couples walking hand in hand are the norm here, and if you're not open-minded and would prefer to avoid this scene, just look for the ubiquitous rainbow flag hanging outside of gay establishments and you'll know what to expect. For the most part, however, the scene is extremely mixed and colorful. If partying isn't your thing, then avoid Duval Street (the Bourbon Street of South Florida) at all costs. Instead, take in the scenery at a dockside bar or oceanside Jacuzzi. Whatever you do, don't bother with a watch or tie—this is the home of the perennial vacation.

ESSENTIALS

GETTING THERE   For directions by car, see "Essentials," for the Upper and Middle Keys (p. 255) and continue south on U.S. 1. When entering Key West, stay in the far-right lane onto North Roosevelt Boulevard, which becomes Truman Avenue in Old Town. Continue for a few blocks, and you will find yourself on Duval Street ⍟, in the heart of the city. If you stay to the left, you'll also reach the city center after passing the airport and the remnants of historic houseboat row, where a motley collection of boats once made up one of Key West's most interesting neighborhoods.

Several regional airlines fly nonstop (about 55 min.) from Miami to Key West; fares are about $120 to $300 round-trip. **American Eagle, Continental, Delta,** and **US Airways Express** land at **Key West International Airport,** South Roosevelt Boulevard (© **305/296-5439**), on the southeastern corner of the island.

Greyhound (© **800/231-2222;** www.greyhound.com) has buses leaving Miami for Key West every day for about $30 to $32 one way and $57 to $60 round trip. Seats fill up in season, so come early. The ride takes about 4½ hours.

GETTING AROUND   With limited parking, narrow streets, and congested traffic, driving in Old Town Key West is more of a pain than a convenience. Unless you're staying in one of the more remote accommodations, consider trading in the car for a bicycle. The island is small and as flat as a board, which makes it easy to negotiate, especially away from the crowded downtown area.

Key West

Many tourists also choose to cruise by moped, an option that can make navigating the streets risky, especially since there are no helmet laws in Key West. So be careful and spend the extra few bucks to rent a helmet; hundreds of visitors are seriously injured each year.

Rates for simple one-speed cruisers start at about $8 per day (from $40 per week). Mopeds start at about $12 for 2 hours, $25 per day, and $100 per week. The best shops include the **Bicycle Center** at 523 Truman Ave. (© **305/294-4556**); the **Moped Hospital,** 601 Truman Ave. (© **305/296-3344**); and **Tropical Bicycles & Scooter Rentals** at 1300 Duval St. (© **305/294-8136**). The **Bike Shop,** 1110 Truman Ave. (© **305/294-1073**), rents mountain bikes for $12 per day ($60 per week). Cruisers go for $8 per day and $40 per week. A $150 deposit is required for cruisers, $250 for mountain bikes.

PARKING Parking in Key West's Old Town is particularly limited, but there is a well-placed **municipal parking lot** at Simonton and Angela streets, just behind the firehouse and police station. If you have brought a car, you may want to stash it here while you enjoy the very walkable downtown part of Key West.

VISITOR INFORMATION The **Florida Keys and Key West Visitors Bureau,** P.O. Box 1147, Key West, FL 33041 (© **800/FLA-KEYS;** www.keywest.com), offers a free vacation kit packed with visitor information. The **Key West Chamber of Commerce,** 402 Wall St., Key West, FL 33040 (© **800/527-8539** or 305/294-2587; www.keywestchamber.com), also offers both general and specialized information. The lobby is open daily from 8:30am to 6pm; phones are answered from 8am to 8pm. The **Key West Visitors Center** is the area's best for information on accommodations, goings-on, and restaurants; the number is © **800/LAST-KEY.** It's open weekdays from 8am to 5:30pm and weekends from 8:30am to 5pm. Gay travelers will want to call the **Key West Business Guild** (© **305/294-4603**), which represents more than 50 guest houses and B&Bs in town, as well as many other gay-owned businesses (ask for its color brochure), or **Good Times Travel** (© **305/294-0980**), which will set up lodging and package tours on the island.

ORIENTATION A mere 2-by-4-mile island, Key West is simple to navigate, even though there is no real order to the arrangement of streets and avenues. As you enter town on U.S. 1 (also called Roosevelt Blvd.), you will see most of the moderately priced chain hotels and fast-food restaurants. The better restaurants, shops, and outfitters are crammed onto Duval Street, the main thoroughfare of Key West's Old Town. Surrounding streets contain many inns and lodges in picturesque Victorian/Bahamian homes. On the southern side of the island is the coral beach area and some of the larger resort hotels.

The area called Bahama Village has only recently become known to tourists. With several newly opened, trendy restaurants and guesthouses, this hippie-ish neighborhood, complete with street-roaming chickens and cats, is the most urban and rough you'll find in the Keys. You might see a few seedy drug dealings on street corners, but it's nothing to be overly concerned with: It looks worse than it is and resident business owners tend to keep a vigilant eye on the neighborhood. The area is actually quite funky and should be a welcome diversion from the Duvalian mainstream.

SEEING THE SIGHTS

Before shelling out big bucks for any of the dozens of worthwhile attractions in Key West, I recommend getting an overview on either of the two comprehensive island tours, the **Conch Tour Train** or the **Old Town Trolley** (see "Organized Tours," later in the chapter). There are simply too many attractions and historic houses to list. I've highlighted my favorites below but encourage you to seek out others.

Audubon House & Tropical Gardens ⋆⋆   This well-preserved home, dating from the early 19th century, stands as a prime example of early Key West architecture. Named after renowned painter and bird expert John James Audubon, who was said to have visited the house in 1832, the graceful two-story home is a peaceful retreat from the bustle of Old Town. Included in the price of admission is a self-guided audio tour that lasts about half an hour and spotlights rare Audubon prints, gorgeous antiques, historical photos, and lush tropical gardens. With voices of several characters from the house's past, the tour never gets boring—although it is at times a bit hokey. Even if you don't want to spend the time and money to explore the grounds and home, check out the impressive gift shop, which sells a variety of fine mementos at reasonable prices.

205 Whitehead St. (between Greene and Caroline sts.) ⓒ **305/294-2116.** Admission $8.50 adults, $3.50 children 6–12. Daily 9:30am–5pm (last admission at 4:30pm). Discounts for students and AAA and AARP members.

Ernest Hemingway Home and Museum ⋆   Hemingway's particularly handsome stone Spanish Colonial house, built in 1851, was one of the first on the island to be fitted with indoor plumbing and a built-in fireplace, and it contains the first swimming pool built on Key West. The author owned the home from 1931 until his death in 1961, and he lived there with about 50 cats, whose descendants, including the famed six-toed cats, still roam the premises. It was during those years that the Nobel Prize winner wrote some of his most famous works, including *For Whom the Bell Tolls, A Farewell to Arms,* and *The Snows of Kilimanjaro.* Fans may want to take the optional half-hour tour, where you'll see rooms of his house with glass cabinets that store certain artifacts, books, and pieces of mail addressed to him. It's interesting (to an extent) and included in the price of admission. If you don't take the tour or have no literary interest in Hemingway, the admission price is really a waste of money. If you're feline phobic, beware: There are cats everywhere.

907 Whitehead St. (between Truman Ave. and Olivia St.) ⓒ **305/294-1136.** Fax 305/294-2755. www.hemingwayhome.com. Admission $9 adults, $5 children. Daily 9am–5pm. Limited parking.

Harry S. Truman Little White House Museum ⋆⋆   President Harry Truman used to refer to the White House as the "Great White Jail." On temporary leave from the big house, Truman discovered the serenity of Key West and made his escape to what became known as the Little White House, which is open to the public for touring. The house is fully restored, and the exhibits document Truman's time in the Keys. Tours are every 15 minutes and last between 45 and 50 minutes. For fans of all things Oval Office–related, there's a presidential gift shop on the premises.

111 Front St., Key West. ⓒ **305/294-9911.** www.trumanlittlewhitehouse.com. Admission $10 adults, $5 children under 12. Daily 9am–4:30pm.

Impressions

I've a notion to move the Capitol to Key West and just stay.
                                                    —President Harry S. Truman

Key West Cemetery ★★★ *(Finds)*   This funky, picturesque cemetery is the epitome of the quirky Key West image, as irreverent as it is humorous. Many tombs are stacked several high, condominium style—the rocky soil made digging 6 feet under nearly impossible for early settlers. Headstones reflect residents' lighthearted attitudes toward life and death. I TOLD YOU I WAS SICK is one of the more famous epitaphs, as is the tongue-in-cheek widow's inscription AT LEAST I KNOW WHERE HE'S SLEEPING TONIGHT. There's a fun 1½-tour that's full of history and local lore, but if you want to save some money and just read the amusing inscriptions, it's free to walk through.

Entrance at the corner of Margaret and Angela sts. ℂ 305/294-WALK for tour reservations. Free admission. Tour $18 adults, $10 kids 12 and under. Daily dawn to dusk.

East Martello Museum and Gallery   Adjacent to the airport, the East Martello Museum is located in a Civil War–era brick fort that itself is worth a visit. The museum contains a bizarre variety of exhibits that collectively do a thorough job of interpreting the city's intriguing past. Historical artifacts include model ships, a deep-sea diver's wooden air pump, a crude raft from a Cuban boat lift, a supposedly haunted doll, a Key West–style children's playhouse from 1918, and a horse-drawn hearse. Exhibits illustrate the Keys' history of salvaging, sponging, and cigar making. After seeing the galleries (should take about 45 minutes to an hour), climb a steep spiral staircase to the top of a lookout tower for good views over the island and ocean. A member of the Key West Art and Historical Society, East Martello has two cousins, the Key West Museum of Art and History, 281 Front St., (ℂ **305/295-6616**) and the Key West Lighthouse Museum, 938 Whitehead St., (ℂ **305/294-0012**).

3501 S. Roosevelt Blvd. ℂ 305/296-3913. Admission $6 adults, $4 seniors, $3 children 8–12, free for children 7 and under. Daily 9:30am–5pm (last admission is at 4pm).

Key West Aquarium ★★ *(Kids)*   The oldest attraction on the island, the Key West Aquarium is a modest but fascinating exhibit. A long hallway of eye-level displays showcase dozens of varieties of fish and crustaceans. You'll see delicate sea horses swaying in the backlit tanks. Kids can touch sea cucumbers and sea anemones in a shallow tank in the entryway. If you can, catch one of the free guided tours, where you can witness the dramatic feeding frenzy of the sharks, tarpon, barracudas, stingrays, and turtles. Expect to spend about an hour to an hour and a half here.

1 Whitehead St. (at Mallory Sq.) ℂ 305/296-2051. www.keywestaquarium.com. Admission $9 adults, $4.50 children 4–12, free for children under 4. Tickets are good for 2 consecutive days. Look for discount coupons at local hotels, at Duval St. kiosks, and from trolley and train tours. Daily 10am–6pm; tours at 11am, 1pm, 3pm, and 4pm.

Key West Lighthouse Museum ★   When the Key West Lighthouse opened in 1848, many locals mourned. Its bright warning to ships signaled the end of a profitable era for wreckers, the pirate salvagers who looted reef-stricken ships. The story of this and other Keys lighthouses is illustrated in a small museum that was formerly the keeper's quarters. When radar and sonar made the lighthouse obsolete, it was opened to visitors as a tourist attraction. It's worth mustering the energy to climb the 88 claustrophobic steps to the top, where you'll be rewarded with magnificent panoramic views of Key West and the ocean.

938 Whitehead St. ℂ 305/294-0012. Admission $8 adults, $4 children 7–12, free for children 6 and under. Daily 9:30am–5pm (last admission at 4:30pm).

Going, Going, Gone: Where to Catch the Famous Key West Sunset

A tradition in Key West, the Sunset Celebration can be relaxing or overwhelming, depending on your vantage point. If you're in town, you must check out this ritual at least once. Every evening, locals and visitors gather at the docks behind Mallory Square (at the western-most end of Whitehead Street) to celebrate the day gone by. Secure a spot on the docks early to experience the carnival of portrait artists, acrobats, food vendors, animal acts, and other performers trading on the island's Bohemian image. But the carnival atmosphere isn't for everyone: In season, the crowd can be overwhelming, especially when the cruise ships are in port. Also, hold onto your bags and wallets as the tight crowds make Mallory Square at sunset prime pick-pocketing territory.

A more refined choice is the Hilton's **Sunset Deck** (© **305/294-4000**), a luxurious second-floor bar on Front Street, right next door to Mallory Square. From the civilized calm of a casual bar, you can look down on the mayhem with a drink in hand.

Also near the Mallory madness is the **Ocean Key Resort's** bar. This long open-air pier serves up drinks and decent bar food against a dra-matic pink- and yellow-streaked sky. It's located at the very tip of Duval Street (© **800/328-9815** or 305/296-7701).

For the very best potent cocktails and great bar food on an outside patio or enclosed lounge, try **Pier House Resort and Caribbean Spa's Havana Docks** at 1 Duval St. (© **305/296-4600**). There's usually live music and a lively gathering of visitors enjoying this island's bounty. The bar is right on the water and is a prime sunset viewing spot.

Key West's Shipwreck Historeum   You'll see more impressive artifacts at nearby Mel Fisher's museum, but for the morbidly curious, shipwrecks should rank right up there with car wrecks. For those of you who can't help but look, this museum is the place to be for everything you ever wanted to know about shipwrecks and more. See movies, artifacts, and a real life wrecker, who will be more than happy to indulge your curiosity of the wrecking industry that preoc-cupied the early pioneers of Key West. Depending on your level of interest, you can expect to spend up to 2 hours here.

1 Whitehead St. (at Mallory Sq.) © 305/292-8990. Fax 305/292-5536. Admission $8 adults, $4 children 4–12. Shows daily every half-hour 9:45am–4:45pm.

Mel Fisher Maritime Heritage Museum 🔑🔑🔑   This museum honors local hero Mel Fisher, whose death in 1998 was mourned throughout South Florida, and who, along with a crew of other salvagers, found a multimillion-dollar treas-ure trove in 1985 aboard the wreck of the Spanish galleon *Nuestra Señora de Atocha*. If you're into diving, pirates, and sunken treasures, check out this small informative museum, full of doubloons, pieces of eight, emeralds, and solid-gold bars. A 1700 English merchant slave ship, the only tangible evidence of the transatlantic slave trade, is on view on the museum's second floor. A dated but informative film provides a good background for Fisher's incredible story.

200 Greene St. ℂ **305/294-2633.** Admission $7.50 adults, $3.75 children 6–12, free for children 5 and under. Daily 9:30am–5pm. Take U.S. 1 to Whitehead St. and turn left on Greene.

Memorial Sculpture Garden ⚄ Installed in 1997, this impressive sculpture garden contains a large monument to the wreckers who made Key West rich more than a century ago. Also on display are 36 bronze busts of the island's most colorful leaders and characters: There's Harry Truman, Henry Flagler, and, of course, Ernest Hemingway, all mounted on elegant coral columns.

Front Street, near Mallory Square. Free admission.

Oldest House/Wrecker's Museum ⚄ Dating from 1829, this old New England Bahama House has survived pirates, hurricanes, fires, warfare, and economic ups and downs. The 1½-story home was designed by a ship's carpenter and incorporates many features from maritime architecture, including portholes and a ship's hatch designed for ventilation before the advent of air-conditioning. Especially interesting is the detached kitchen building outfitted with a brick "beehive" oven and vintage cooking utensils. Although not a must-see on the Key West tour, history and architecture buffs will appreciate the finely preserved details and the glimpse of a slower, easier time in the island's life.

322 Duval St. ℂ **305/294-9502.** Admission $5 adults; $1 children 6–12; free for children 5 and under. Daily 10am–4pm.

ORGANIZED TOURS

BY TROLLEY-BUS & TRAM Yes, it's more than a bit hokey to sit on this 60-foot tram of yellow cars, but it's worth it—at least once. The city's whole story is packed into a neat, 90-minute package on the **Conch Tour Train,** which covers the island and all its rich, raunchy history. Operating since 1958, the trains are open-air, which can make the ride uncomfortable in bad weather. The "train's" engine is a propane-powered Jeep disguised as a locomotive. Tours depart from both Mallory Square and the Welcome Center, near where U.S. 1 becomes North Roosevelt Boulevard, on the less developed side of the island. For more information, contact the **Conch** at (ℂ **305/294-5161**). The cost is $18 for adults, $9 for children 4 to 12, and free for children 3 and under. Daily departures are every half-hour from 9am to 4:30pm.

⎛*Moments* **A Great Escape**

Many people complain that Key West's quirky, quaint panache has been lost to the vulture of capitalism, evidenced in the glut of T-shirt shops and tacky bars. But that's not entirely so. For a quiet respite, visit the Key West Botanical Gardens, a little-known slice of serenity tucked between the Aqueduct Authority plant and the Key West Golf Course. The 11-acre gardens—maintained by volunteers and funded by donations—contain the last hardwood hammock in Key West, plus a colorful representation of wildflowers, butterflies, and birds. A genetically cloned tree is the latest addition to the gardens. Although the gardens received a terrible blow from the storms of 1998, the calm remains within them. Botanical Garden Way and College Rd., Stock Island. Free admission. Daily 8am–sunset. Follow College Rd.; then turn right just past Bayshore Manor.

Literary Key West

Counting Ernest Hemingway and Tennessee Williams among your denizens would give any city the right to call itself a literary mecca. But over the years, tiny Key West has been home—or at least home away from home—to dozens of literary types who are drawn to some combination of its gentle pace, tropical atmosphere, and lighthearted mood (not to mention its lingering reputation for an oft-ribald lifestyle). Writers have long known that more than a few muses prowl the tree-laden streets of Key West.

Robert Frost first visited Key West in 1934 and stayed here for the remainder of his life. In the early 20th century, writers like John Dewey, Archibald MacLeish, John Dos Passos, Wallace Stevens, and S. J. Perelman were drawn to the island.

Even as Key West boomed and busted and boomed again, and despite the island's growing popularity with world travelers, writers continued to move to Key West or visit with such regularity that they were deemed honorary "conchs." Novelists Phil Caputo, Tom McGuane, Jim Harrison, John Hershey, Alison Lurie, and Robert Stone were among these.

Of course, one of Key West's favorite sons also earned a spot in the annals of local literary history. Famous for his good-time, tropical-laced music, Jimmy Buffett was also a surprisingly well-received novelist in the 1990s. Although Buffett now makes the infinitely ritzier Palm Beach his Florida home, his presence is still felt in virtually every corner of Key West.

But it is Nobel Prize–winner and avid outdoorsman Ernest Hemingway who is most identified with Key West. Much of the island has changed since he lived here from 1931 to 1961. Even the famous Sloppy Joe's bar, which Hemingway frequented mostly from 1933 to 1937, has changed locations (reportedly without closing—customers supposedly picked up their drinks and whatever else from the bar they could carry and brought it all down the block to the new location, and service resumed with barely a blink!). Fortunately, The Ernest Hemingway Home and Museum (see p. 283) has been lovingly preserved. But perhaps to get the best feel for what Hemingway loved most about Key West, visit the docks at Garrison Bight. It is from there that Hemingway and his many famous (and infamous) friends and contemporaries departed for Caribbean ports of call and for sport upon the sea.

Key West pays homage to its literary legacy with the annual January Key West Literary Seminar. For information, call ℰ 888/293-9291 or visit www.keywestliteraryseminar.org.

The **Old Town Trolley** is the choice in bad weather or if you are staying at one of the many hotels on its route. Humorous drivers maintain a running commentary as the enclosed tram loops around the island's streets past all the major sights. Trolleys depart from Mallory Square and other points around the island, including many area hotels. For details, call © **305/296-6688.** Tours are $18 for adults, $9 for children 4 to 12, and free for children 3 and under. Departures are daily every half-hour (though not always on the half-hour) from 9am to 4:45pm. Whichever you choose, these historic trivia-packed tours are well worth the price of admission.

BY AIR Proclaimed by the mayor as "the official air force of the Conch Republic," **Island Airplane Tours,** at Key West Airport, 3469 S. Roosevelt Blvd. (© **305/294-8687**), offers windy rides in its open-cockpit 1940 Waco biplanes that take you over the reefs and around the islands. Thrill seekers—and only they—will also enjoy a spin in the company's S2-B aerobatics airplane, which does loops, rolls, and sideways figure eights. Company owner Fred Cabanas was "decorated" in 1991, after he spotted a Cuban airman defecting to the United States in a Russian-built MIG fighter. Sightseeing flights cost $50 to $200, depending on the duration.

BY BOAT The pride of Key West, *Fireball,* at 0 Duval St. (© **305/296-6293;** fax 305/294-8704), is a 58-foot glass-bottomed catamaran that goes on both day (noon, 2pm, 4pm) coral-reef tours and evening sunset cruises. Reef trips cost $25 per person; sunset cruises (4:30pm) are $30 per person and include snacks, sodas, and a glass of champagne. Kids sail for half-price.

   Schooner *Western Union* (© **305/292-9830**) was built in 1939 and served as a cable-repair vessel until it was designated the flagship of the city of Key West and began day, sunset, and charter sailings. Sunset sailings are especially memorable and include entertainment, cocktails, and a cannon fire. Prices vary.

OTHER TOURS For a lively look at Key West, try a 2-hour tour of the island's five **most famous pubs.** It starts daily at 2:30pm, lasts 1½ hours, costs $21, and includes four drinks. Another fun tour is the 1-mile, 90-minute **nightly ghost tour,** leaving at 8pm from the Holiday Inn La Concha, 430 Duval St. Cost is $18 for adults and $10 for children under 12. This spooky and interesting tour gives participants insight into many old island legends. The Key West Tour Association offers both tours. Finally, there's a cemetery tour (see p. 284), which leaves daily at 10:30am (© **305/294-WALK**). It's creepy, spooky, and all together kooky, as it approaches death with a sense of humor.

Parrotheads on Parade

For Jimmy Buffett fans, or Parrotheads, as they're also known, there's a fabulous tour that shouldn't be missed. **Trails of Margaritaville (© 305/292-2040)** is an amusing 90-minute walking tour providing fans with an officially sanctioned peek at the stomping grounds of Buffett's carefree days in Key West back in the 1970s. Decked out in full Parrothead regalia—Hawaiian shirts and parrot hats—the informative and often hilarious guides lead you past the hangouts and other highpoints of Buffett's Key West, spinning yarns about the musician, and Key West in general. The tour departs daily at 4pm from **Captain Tony's Saloon** (428 Greene St.), where Buffett used to hang out and perform, and ends at, you guessed it, Margaritaville Cafe on Duval Street. Tour tickets are $18 for adults, $15 for locals with ID, and $10 for children. Bring cash or travelers checks; no credit cards accepted. Reservations are required at least 2 days in advance.

OUTDOOR PURSUITS

BEACHES   Unlike the rest of the Keys, you'll actually find a few small beaches here, although they don't compare with the state's wide natural wonders up the coast: A narrow rocky beach is typical of the Key's beaches. Here are your options: **Smathers Beach,** off South Roosevelt Boulevard west of the airport; **Higgs Beach,** along Atlantic Boulevard between White Street and Reynolds Road; and **Fort Zachary Beach,** located off the western end of Southard Boulevard.

A magnet for partying teenagers, **Smathers Beach** is Key West's largest and most overpopulated beach. Despite the number of rowdy teens, the beach is actually quite clean and it looks lovely since its renovation in the spring of 2000. If you go early enough in the morning, you may notice some people sleeping on the beach from the night before.

Higgs Beach is a favorite among Key West's gay crowds, but what many people don't know is that beneath the sand is an unmarked cemetery of African slaves who died while waiting for freedom. Higgs has a playground and tennis courts and is near the minute Rest Beach, which is actually hidden by the White Street Pier.

Although there is an entrance fee ($3.75 per car, plus more for each passenger), I recommend the beach at **Fort Zachary,** since it also includes a great historical fort, a Civil War museum, and a large picnic area with tables, barbecue grills, bathrooms, and showers. Plus, large trees scattered across 87 acres provide shade for those who are reluctant to bake in the sun. Hurricane George damaged the vulnerable point in 1998, but replanting of native vegetation has made it even better than before.

BICYCLING & MOPEDING   A popular mode of transportation for locals and visitors, bikes and mopeds are available at many rental outlets in the city (see p. 282). Escape the hectic downtown scene and explore the island's scenic side streets by heading away from Duval Street toward South Roosevelt Boulevard and the beachside enclaves along the way.

DIVING   One of the area's largest scuba schools, **Dive Key West Inc.,** 3128 N. Roosevelt Blvd. (© **800/426-0707** or 305/296-3823; fax 305/296-0609; www.divekeywest.com), offers instruction on all levels and its dive boats take participants to scuba and snorkel sites on nearby reefs.

Wreck dives and night dives are two of the special offerings of **Lost Reef Adventures,** 261 Margaret St. (© **800/952-2749** or 305/296-9737). Regularly scheduled runs and private charters can be arranged. Phone for departure information.

Also see **Mosquito Coast Outfitters,** under "Kayaking," below.

FISHING   As any angler will tell you, there's no fishing like Keys fishing. Key West has it all: bonefish, tarpon, dolphin, tuna, grouper, cobia, and more. Sharks, too.

Step aboard a small exposed skiff for an incredibly diverse day of fishing. In the morning, you can head offshore for sailfish or dolphin (the fish, not the mammal), and then by afternoon, get closer to land for a shot at tarpon, permit, grouper, or snapper. Here in Key West, you can probably pick up more cobia— one of the best fighting and eating fish around—than anywhere else in the world. For a real fight, ask your skipper to go for the tarpon—the greatest fighting fish there is, famous for its dramatic "tail walk" on the water after it's hooked. Shark fishing is also popular.

Tips Reel Deals

When looking for the best deals on fishing excursions, know that the bookers from the kiosks in town generally take 20% of a captain's fee in addition to an extra monthly fee. You can usually save yourself money by booking directly with a captain or going straight to one of the docks.

You'll find plenty of competition among the charter fishing boats in and around Mallory Square. You can negotiate a good deal at **Charter Boat Row,** 1801 N. Roosevelt Ave. (across from the Shell station), home to more than 30 charter fishing and party boats. Just show up to arrange your outing, or call **Garrison Bite Marina** (© 305/292-8167) for details.

The advantage of the smaller, more expensive charter boats is that you can call the shots. They'll take you where you want to go, to fish for what you want to catch. These "light tackles" are also easier to maneuver, which means you can go to backcountry spots for tarpon and bonefish, as well as out to the open ocean for tuna and dolphin. You'll really be able to feel the fish, and you'll get some good fights. Larger boats, for up to six or seven people, are cheaper and are best for kingfish, billfish, and sailfish. Consider Captain Vinnie Argiro's **Heavy Hitters Charters** (© 305/745-6665) if you want a light-tackle experience. For a larger boat, try Captain Henry Otto's 44-foot *Sunday,* docked at the Hyatt in Key West (© 305/294-7052).

The huge commercial party boats are more for sightseeing than serious angling, though you can get lucky and get a few bites at one of the fishing holes. One especially good deal is the *Gulfstream III* (© 305/296-8494), an all-day charter that goes out daily from 9:30am until 4pm. You'll pay $35, plus $3 for a rod and reel. It's $25 for kids under 12. This 65-foot party boat usually has at least 30 other anglers. Bring your own cooler or buy snacks on the boat. Beer and wine are allowed.

Serious anglers should consider the light-tackle boats that leave from **Oceanside Marina** (© 305/294-4676) on Stock Island, at 5950 Peninsula Ave., 1½ miles off U.S. 1. It's a 20-minute drive from Old Town on the Atlantic side. There are more than 30 light-tackle guides, which range from flatbed backcountry skiffs to 28-foot open boats. There are also a few larger charters and a party boat that goes to the Dry Tortugas. Call for details.

For a light-tackle outing with a very colorful Key West flair, call **Captain Bruce Cronin** at © 305/294-4929 or **Captain Kenny Harris** at © 305/294-8843,** two of the more famous (and pricey) captains working these docks for over 20 years. You'll pay from $550 for a full day, usually about 8am until 4pm, and from $400 for a half day.

GOLF A relative newcomer in terms of local recreation, golf is gaining in popularity here as it is in many visitor destinations. The area's only public club is **Key West Golf Club** (© 305/294-5232), an 18-hole course located at the entrance to the island of Key West at MM 4.5 (turn onto College Rd. to the course entrance). Designed by Rees Jones, the course has plenty of mangroves and water hazards on its 6,526 yards. It's open to the public and has a new pro shop. Call ahead for tee-time reservations. The fee is $140 per player, including cart.

KAYAKING **Mosquito Coast Outfitters,** housed in a woodsy wine bar at 1017 Duval St. (© 305/294-7178), operates a first-rate kayaking and snorkeling tour every day as long as the weather is mild. The tours depart at 9am sharp (returns around 3pm) and cost $45 per person. Included in the price are snacks, soft drinks, and a guided tour of the mangrove-studded islands of Sugar Key or Geiger Key just north of Key West. The tour is primarily for kayaking, but you will have the opportunity to get in the water for snorkeling, if you're interested.

SHOPPING

You'll find all kinds of unique gifts and souvenirs in Key West, from coconut postcards to Key lime pies. On Duval Street, T-shirt shops outnumber almost any other business. If you must get a wearable memento, be careful of unscrupulous salespeople. Despite efforts to curtail the practice, many shops have been known to rip off unwitting shoppers. It pays to check the prices and the exchange rate before signing any sales slips. You are entitled to a written estimate of any T-shirt work before you pay for it.

At Mallory Square is the **Clinton Street Market,** an overly air-conditioned mall of kiosks and stalls designed for the many cruise-ship passengers who never venture beyond this supercommercial zone. Amid the dreck are some delicious coffee and candy shops and some high-priced hats and shoes. There's also a free and clean restroom.

Once the main industry of Key West, cigar making is enjoying renewed success at the handful of factories that survived the slow years. Stroll through **"Cigar Alley"** (while on Green St., go 2 blocks west and you'll hit Cigar Alley, also known as Pirate's Alley), where you will find *viejitos* (little old men) rolling fat stogies just as they used to do in their homeland across the Florida Straits. Stop at the **Key West Cigar Factory,** at 308 Front St. (© 305/294-3470), for an excellent selection of imported and locally rolled smokes, including the famous El Hemingway. Remember, buying or selling Cuban-made cigars is illegal. Shops advertising "Cuban cigars" are usually referring to domestic cigars made from tobacco grown from seeds that were brought from Cuba decades ago. To be fair, though, many premium cigars today are grown from Cuban-seed tobacco—only it is grown in Latin America and the Caribbean, not Cuba.

If you are looking for local or Caribbean art, you will find nearly a dozen galleries and shops clustered on Duval Street between Catherine and Fleming streets. You'll also find some excellent shops scattered on the side streets. One worth seeking out is the **Haitian Art Co.,** 600 Frances St. (© 305/296-8932), where you can browse through room upon room of original paintings from well-known and obscure Haitian artists in a range of prices from a few dollars to a few thousand. Also, check out **Cuba, Cuba!** at 814 Duval St. (© 305/295-9442), where you'll

---

Fun Fact Conch If You Love Key West

Ever wonder how Key West got the nickname "the Conch Republic"? In 1982, the U.S. Border Patrol set up a roadblock on U.S. 1 to search for illegal aliens and drugs. This maneuver effectively slowed passage from the Keys to the mainland and damaged the economy (albeit temporarily). In response, Key West mayor Dennis Wardlow collaborated with five businessmen and established the so-called Conch Republic, declaring Key West's independence from—and war on—the U.S. The roadblock was removed, but the moniker stuck.

find paintings, sculpture, and photos by Cuban artists as well as books and art from the island.

A favorite stop in the Keys is the deliciously fragrant **Key West Aloe** at 524 Front St., between Simonton and Duval streets (© **305/294-5592**). Since 1971, this shop has been selling a simple line of bath products, including lotions, shampoos, and soothing balms for those who want a reminder of the tropical breezes once they're back home. At the main shop (open until 8pm), you can find great gift baskets, tropical perfumes, and candies and cookies, too. In addition to frangipani, vanilla, and hibiscus scents, sample Key West for Men, a unique and alluringly musky bestseller.

For foodies, the **Key Lime Pie Co.** (© **305/294-6567**) is so popular for its pies, cookies, and pretty much anything you can think of made with Key lime (candles, soaps, lotions), that there are two on the tiny island. One is at 701 Caroline St. and the other is at 424 Greene St. From sweet to spicy, **Peppers of Key West** (© **305/295-9333**) at 602 Greene St. is a hot-sauce lover's heaven, with hundreds of variations of sauce from brutally spicy to mild. Grab a seat at the tasting bar and be prepared to let your taste buds sizzle.

Literature and music buffs will appreciate the many bookshops and record stores on the island. **Key West Island Bookstore** (© **305/294-2904**) at 513 Fleming St. carries new, used, and rare books and specializes in fiction by residents of the Keys, including Hemingway, Tennessee Williams, Shel Silverstein, Ann Beattie, Richard Wilbur, and John Hersey. **Flaming Maggie's** (© **305/294-3931**) at 830 Fleming St. carries a wide selection of gay books. Both shops are open daily.

One of the area's newer and funkier shops is the combination museum and gift shop called **Reworx,** just behind the quirky gift gallery **Pandemonium** and the mosaic car at 825 Duval St. (© **305/294-0351.** Actually, this is Pandemonium's number, but the owners are friends. For Reworx, ask for Valerie.) Mammoth functional art made from salvaged metal parts is on display, and smaller works from recycled material are on sale. Admission to the adjacent museum of industrial art from recycled items is $7 for adults, $5 for children aged 5 to 12, and well worth it.

Also worth checking out in the newly revitalized Bahama Village section of town are the shops along Petronia Street between Thomas and Whitehead streets. Especially interesting is **Maskerville** (© **305/293-6937**), which sells a variety of feather-laden artwork from masks to lampshades. Just next door is **Hello Gorgeous,** at 315 Petronia St. (© **305/294-1770**), which carries unique clothing, shoes, and jewelry for women and impersonators (the name comes from one of Barbra Streisand's more memorable lines).

Off the beaten track at 814 Fleming St. (© **305/294-7901**) is the **Helio Gallery Store,** featuring locally made crafts and fine art.

For anything else, from bed linens to candlesticks to clothing, go to downtown's oldest and most renowned department store, **Fast Buck Freddie's,** at 500 Duval St. (© **305/294-2007**). For the same merchandise at reduced prices, try **Half Buck Freddie's** ⊕, 726 Caroline St. (© **305/294-2007**), where you can shop for out-of-season bargains and "rejects" from the main store.

WHERE TO STAY

You'll find a wide variety of places to stay in Key West, from resorts with all the amenities to seaside motels, quaint bed-and-breakfasts, and clothing-optional guesthouses. Unless you're in town during Key West's most popular holidays—Fantasy Fest (around Halloween), where Mardi Gras meets South Florida for the

NC-17 set; Hemingway Days (in July), where Papa is seemingly and eerily alive and well; and Christmas and New Year's—or for a big fishing tournament (many are held from October to December) or boat-racing tourney, you can almost always find a place to stay at the last minute. However, you may want to book early, especially in winter, when prime properties fill up and many require 2- or 3-night minimum stays. Prices at these times are also extremely high. Finding a decent room for under $100 a night is a real trick.

Another suggestion, and my recommendation, is to call **Vacation Key West** (© **800/595-5397** or 305/295-9500; www.vacationkw.com), which is a wholesaler that offers discounts of 20% to 30% and is skilled at finding last-minute deals. They represent mostly larger hotels and motels but can also place visitors in guesthouses. The phones are answered weekdays from 9am to 6pm and Saturday from 11am to 2pm. The **Key West Innkeepers Association,** P.O. Box 6172, Key West, FL 33041 (© **800/492-1911** or 305/292-3600), can also help find lodging in any price range from its dozens of members and affiliates.

Gay travelers will want to call the **Key West Business Guild** (© **305/294-4603**), which represents more than 50 guest houses and B&Bs in town, as well as many other gay-owned businesses. Be advised that most gay guesthouses have a clothing-optional policy. One of the most elegant and popular ones is **Big Ruby's** (© **800/477-7829** or 305/296-2323; rates start at $145 for a double during peak season and $85 during off season) at 409 Appelrouth Lane (a little alley just off Duval Street). A low cluster of buildings surrounds a lushly landscaped courtyard where a hearty breakfast is served each morning and wine is poured at dusk. The mostly male guests hang out by a good-sized pool, tanning in the buff. Also popular is **Oasis** at 823 Fleming St. (© **305/296-2131;** rates in winter are $169–$229 and $109–$169 in summer), which is superclean and friendly, with a central location and a 14-seat hot tub.

Another luxurious property is the **Florida Key Guesthouse** at 412 Frances St. (© **305/296-4719;** rates are $225 in season and $125 during the off-season), which is more romantic and traditionally decorated and welcomes many lesbian travelers as well. *Out and About* gave it a five-star rating. For women only, **Pearl's Rainbow,** 525 United St. (© **800/74-WOMYN** or 305/292-1450) is a large, fairly well-maintained guesthouse with lots of privacy and amenities, including two pools and two hot tubs. Rates in season range from $109 to $229.

VERY EXPENSIVE

Hilton Key West Resort and Marina ☆☆   Completed in fall 1996, this Hilton, which saw a light room renovation in 2001, is a truly luxurious addition to downtown's hotel scene, situated at the very end of Duval Street in the middle of all of Old Town's action. The sparkling rooms are large and well appointed, with all the modern conveniences. Choose a suite in the main building if you want a large Jacuzzi in your living room. Otherwise, the marina building has great views. The secluded beach is great for an escape from the Duval Street frenzy. Flagler's, the elegant indoor dining room, offers ample breakfasts and a huge Sunday brunch.

Hilton's gorgeous **Sunset Key Guest Cottages** ☆☆☆, with whitewashed interiors, picture windows, and fabulous views, are located 100 yards offshore on Sunset Key and are accessible only by private launch. Check in at the Hilton and take a 10-minute cruise to the island, where there are no cars, only a gourmet grocery, restaurant, bar, and free-form tropical pool with whirlpool jets. Sunset guests also have access to all watersports at the Hilton. Cottages are equipped with full kitchens, high-tech entertainment centers, and one, two, or three massive bedrooms. For true luxe when staying in a cottage, consider hiring a private chef for a meal or two.

245 Front St. (at the end of Duval St.), Key West, FL 33040. © **800/221-2424** or 305/294-4000. Fax 305/294-4086. www.keywestresort.hilton.com. 215 units. Winter $299–$525 double; $375–$800 suite. Off-season $195–$425 double; $300–$800 suite. 37 Sunset Key Cottages, up to 5 people: winter $575–$1,825; off-season $325–$1,095. Private chef: $75 per person plus additional chef/hotel fees, tax, and gratuities. AE, DC, DISC, MC, V. Self parking $7, valet parking $10. **Amenities:** 2 restaurants, pool bar; outdoor heated pool; health club; Jacuzzi; watersports equipment rental; full-service marina; bike rental; game room; concierge; business center; limited room service; in-room massage; dry-cleaning service; self-service laundry. *In room:* A/C, TV, dataport, minibar, coffeemaker, hair dryer, iron.

Pier House Resort and Caribbean Spa 🐾🐾   Pier House is one of the area's best resort choices, offering luxurious rooms, top-notch service, and a full-service spa. If you're looking for something a bit more intimate than the Wyndham Reach, Pier House is an ideal choice. Its location—at the foot of Duval Street and just steps from Mallory Docks—is the envy of every hotel on the island. Set back from the busy street, on a short strip of beach, this hotel is a welcome oasis of calm. The accommodations here vary tremendously, from relatively simple business-style rooms to romantic guest quarters complete with integrated stereo systems and whirlpool tubs. Their best waterfront suites and rooms have recently been renovated. Although every accommodation has either a balcony or a patio, not all overlook the water. My favorites, in the two-story spa building, don't have any view at all. But what they lack in scenery, they make up for in opulence; each well-appointed spa room has a sitting area and a huge Jacuzzi bathroom.

1 Duval St. (near Mallory Docks), Key West, FL 33040. © **800/327-8340** or 305/296-4600. Fax 305/296-9085. www.pierhouse.com. 142 units. Winter $245–$410 double. Off-season $200–$355 double. AE, DC, MC, V. **Amenities:** 3 restaurants, 3 bars; heated swimming pool; full-service spa and fitness center; private beach; 2 Jacuzzis; sauna; watersports equipment rentals; moped and bike rental; concierge; limited room service; in-room massage; babysitting; laundry services. *In room:* A/C, TV, dataport, minibar, coffeemaker, hair dryer, iron.

Wyndham Casa Marina Resort 🐾🐾 *Kids*   Located on Kokomo Beach, Key West's largest private beach, the Casa Marina Resort (built in 1921) is one of the island's most desirable. The setting couldn't be more idyllic, and to further complement its surroundings, the hotel itself is luxurious with beamed ceilings, polished pine floors, and French Provincial furniture. Rooms are comfortable and soothing; the best ones are those with oceanfront balconies or French doors overlooking the oceanfront lawn. The pools are gorgeous with stunning views of the Atlantic. Families love the Casa Marina for its Kid's Retreat, which runs Thursday through Sunday and offers full- and half-day programs ($35 full day; $25 half-day), with activities such as swimming, arts and crafts, and sports. Evening activities (movies, campfires, cookouts) are available for the whole family. In 2001, the hotel spent $2 million on renovating Flagler's, its 1920s-style surf-and-turf restaurant.

1500 Reynolds St., Key West, FL 33040 © **800/626-0777** or 305/296-3535. www.casamarinakeywest.com. 311 units. Winter $269–$799; off-season $169–$799. AE, MC, DC, DISC, MC, V. From Key West International Airport, go west on Roosevelt Blvd. 1 mile to Atlantic Blvd. and turn left. Go 1 mile to Reynolds St. and turn right. Hotel is on left. **Amenities:** 2 restaurants; 2 outdoor pools; lighted tennis court; exercise room; sauna; watersports equipment rental; bike and moped rental; children's programs; concierge; tour desk; courtesy airport transportation; massage; babysitting. *In room:* A/C, TV, coffeemaker, hair dryer.

Wyndham Reach Resort 🐾🐾   Unlike Wyndham's Casa Marina resort, the Reach is better suited to adults only and not families. The location here can be either a highlight or a drawback; it's a 5-minute walk away from the center of the Duval Street action. Supported by stilts that leave the entire ground floor for

---

Fun Fact **Did You Know**

Rumor has it that the very first Key lime pie ever created was made at the turn of the 19th century in the Curry Mansion's kitchen by Mr. Curry's cook, Aunt Sally.

---

car parking, the hotel offers four floors of rooms designed around atriums. The wonderful guest rooms are large and feature tile floors and sturdy wicker furnishings. Each has a vanity area separate from the bathroom. The rooms are so nice you can easily forgive the small closets and diminutive dressers. All have sliding glass doors that open onto balconies, and some have ocean views. The grounds are amply planted with palms and surround a small pool area. There's also a private pier for fishing and tanning. The protected waters are tame and shallow. For steak lovers, there's Shula's on the Beach, a Keys sibling to Miami's lauded Don Shula's Steakhouse.

1435 Simonton St., Key West, FL 33040. © 800/874-4118. For reservations © 800/996-3426. Fax 305/296-4633. www.wyndham.com/reachresort. 150 units. Winter $259–$469 single or double. Off-season $159–$369 single or double. AE, DC, DISC, MC, V. **Amenities:** 2 restaurants, bar; outdoor heated swimming pool; nearby tennis and golf; health club and spa; watersports equipment rental; bike rental, concierge; tour desk, business center; salon; room service; in-room massage; babysitting; dry cleaning. *In room:* A/C, TV, minibar, fridge, coffeemaker.

EXPENSIVE

Curry Mansion Inn ☆☆ *(Finds* This wonderfully charismatic inn is the former home of the island's first millionaire, a once penniless Bahamian immigrant who made a fortune as a pirate. Owned today by innkeepers Al and Edith Amsterdam, the Curry Mansion is now on the National Register of Historic Places; you won't feel like you're staying in a museum, but rather in a wonderfully warm home. Rooms are very sparsely decorated, with white wicker furniture, four-poster wooden beds, and pink walls, in which Key West minimalism meets Victorian. The pool, located in the house's courtyard, is open 24 hours for those who enjoy midnight swimming. The dining room is reminiscent of a Victorian dollhouse, with rich wood floors and furnishings and elegant table settings. Every morning there's a delicious European-style breakfast buffet and at night, cocktail parties. There's also a really nice patio out back, on which, from time to time, there's live entertainment.

511 Caroline St., Key West, FL 33040. © 800/253-3466 or 305/294-5349. Fax 305/294-4093. www.curry mansion.com. 28 units. Winter $150–$375 double. Off-season $130–$250 double. No children under 12. Rates include European breakfast buffet. AE, DC, MC, V. **Amenities:** Dining room; swimming pool; bike rental, concierge. *In room:* A/C, TV, minibar.

Island City House Hotel ☆☆ A small resort unto itself, the Island City House consists of three separate and unique buildings that share a common junglelike patio and pool. The first building, unimaginatively called the Island City House building, is a historic three-story wooden structure with wraparound verandas that allow guests to walk around the entire edifice on any floor. The warmly dressed old-fashioned interiors here include wood floors and many antique furnishings. Many rooms have full-size kitchens. The tile bathrooms could use more counter space, and the room lighting isn't always perfect, but eccentricities are part of this hotel's charm.

The unpainted wooden Cigar House has particularly large bedrooms, similar in ambience to those in the Island City House. The Arch House is the least appealing of the three buildings, but still recommended. Built of Dade County pine, the Arch House's cozy bedrooms are furnished in wicker and rattan and come with small kitchens and bathrooms.

411 William St., Key West, FL 33040. ☎ **800/634-8230** or 305/294-5702. Fax 305/294-1289. www.island cityhouse.com. 24 units. Winter $175–$315; off-season $115–$210. Rates include breakfast. AE, DC, DISC, MC, V. **Amenities:** Outdoor heated pool; Jacuzzi; access to nearby health club; bike rental; concierge; in-room massage; babysitting; dry-cleaning and laundry services; self-service Laundromat. *In room:* A/C, TV, kitchens, coffeemaker, hair dryer.

Marquesa Hotel ★★★ *(Finds)* The Marquesa offers the charm of a small historic hotel coupled with the amenities of a large resort. It encompasses four buildings, two swimming pools, and a three-stage waterfall that cascades into a lily pond. Two of the hotel's houses are luxuriously restored Victorian homes whose rooms are outfitted with extraplush antiques and oversize contemporary furniture. The rooms in the two other newly constructed buildings are even more opulent; many have four-poster wrought-iron beds with bright floral spreads. The green marble bathrooms in the new building are lush and spacious; those in the older building are also nice, but not nearly as huge and luxe. The decor is simple, elegant, and spotless. These are the only hotel rooms I have ever seen that I would love to have in my own home. The hotel also boasts one of Key West's most elegant restaurants, the Cafe Marquesa.

600 Fleming St. (at Simonton St.), Key West, FL 33040. ☎ **800/869-4631** or 305/292-1919. Fax 305/294-2121. www.marquesa.com. 27 units. Winter $260–$395 double. Off-season $170–$285 double. No children under 12. AE, DC, MC, V. **Amenities:** Restaurant; 2 outdoor swimming pools (1 is heated); access to nearby health club; bike rental; concierge; limited room service. *In room:* A/C, TV, dataport, minibar, hair dryer.

Weatherstation Inn ★ *(Finds)* Originally built in 1912 as a weather station, this beautifully restored and meticulously maintained two-story, Renaissance-style inn is located just 2 blocks from Duval Street. It's situated on the tropical grounds of the former Old Navy Yard, now an exclusive and very private gated community. Harry Truman, Eisenhower, and JFK have all visited the station. Spacious and uncluttered, each room is uniquely furnished to complement the interior architecture: hardwood floors, tall sash windows, and high ceilings. The large modern bathrooms are especially appealing. Enjoy a complimentary continental breakfast by the pool among the flowers. The staff is friendly and accommodating.

57 Front St., Key West, FL 33040. ☎ **800/815-2707** or 305/294-7277. Fax 305/294-0544. www.weather stationinn.com. 8 units. Winter $195–$315 double. Off-season $150–$215 double. Rates include continental breakfast. AE, MC, V. **Amenities:** Outdoor pool; concierge. *In room:* A/C, TV, dataport, hair dryer.

MODERATE

Chelsea House ★ Despite its decidedly English name, the Chelsea House is all-American, a term that in Key West isn't code for "conservative." Chelsea House caters to a mixed gay/straight clientele and displays its liberal philosophy most prominently on the clothing-optional sundeck. One of only a few guest houses in Key West that offer TVs, VCRs, private bathrooms, and kitchenettes in each guest room, Chelsea House has a large number of repeat visitors. The apartments come with full kitchens and separate living areas, as well as palm-shaded balconies in back. The bathrooms and closets could be bigger, but both are adequate and serviceable. When weather permits, which is almost always, breakfast is served outside by the pool.

707 Truman Ave., Key West, FL 33040. ☎ **800/845-8859** or 305/296-2211. Fax 305/296-4822. www.chelsea housekw.com. 20 units. Winter $135–$245 double. Off-season $85–$135 double. Rates include breakfast. AE, DC, DISC, MC, V. Private parking. Children 17 and under not accepted. Pets accepted; $15 per night.

Amenities: Outdoor pool; access to nearby health club; bike rental; concierge. *In room:* A/C, TV/VCR, fax, kitchenette, fridge, hair dryer, iron.

La Pensione ★★ This classic bed-and-breakfast, located in the 1891 home of a former cigar executive, distinguishes itself from other similar inns by its extreme attention to details. The friendly and knowledgeable staff treats the stunning home and its guests with extraordinary care. The comfortable rooms all have air-conditioning, ceiling fans, king-size beds, and private bathrooms. Many also have French doors opening onto spacious verandas. Although the rooms have no phones or televisions, the distractions of Duval Street, only steps away, should keep you adequately occupied during your visit. Breakfast, which includes made-to-order Belgian waffles, fresh fruit, and a variety of breads or muffins, can be taken on the wraparound porch or at the communal dining table.

809 Truman Ave. (between Windsor and Margaret sts.), Key West, FL 33040. ℂ **800/893-1193** or 305/292-9923. Fax 305/296-6509. www.lapensione.com. 9 units. Winter from $178 double. Off-season from $98 double. Rates include breakfast. No children accepted. There's a 10% discount for readers who mention this book. AE, DC, DISC, MC, V. **Amenities:** Outdoor pool; access to nearby health club; bike rental. *In room:* A/C. No phone.

Southernmost Point Guest House ★★ *Finds* *Kids* One of the few inns that actually welcome children and pets, this romantic and historic guest house is a real find. The antiseptically clean rooms are not as fancy as the house's ornate 1885 exterior, but each is unique and includes some combination of basic beds and couches and a hodgepodge of furnishings, including futon couches, high-back wicker chairs, and plenty of mismatched throw rugs. Room 5 is best; situated upstairs, it has a private porch, an ocean view, and windows that let in lots of light. Every room has fresh flowers, a refrigerator, and a full decanter of sherry. Mona Santiago, the hotel's kind, laid-back owner, provides chairs and towels that can be brought to the beach, which is just a block away. Plus, guests can help themselves to free wine as they soak in the 14-seat hot tub. Kids will enjoy the swings in the backyard and the pet rabbits.

1327 Duval St., Key West, FL 33040. ℂ **305/294-0715.** Fax 305/296-0641. www.southernmostpoint.com. 6 units. Winter $105–$250; off-season $65–$165. Rates include breakfast. AE, MC, V. Pets accepted $5 in summer, $10 in winter. **Amenities:** Garden pool; hot tub; laundry facilities; barbecue grills. *In room:* A/C, TV/VCR, coffeemaker, hair dryer, iron.

Westwinds Inn ★ A close second to staying in your own private 19th-century clapboard, tin-roofed house is this tranquil inn, located just 4 blocks from Duval Street in the historic Seaport district. Lush landscaping—banana stalks, mango, and Spanish lime trees—keeps the inn extremely private and secluded, and at times, you do feel as if you're alone. And that's not a scary thing—it's absolutely fabulous. Two pools, one heated in the winter, are offset by alcoves, fountains, and the extremely well-maintained white-washed inn, which is actually composed of five separate houses. Rooms are Key West comfortable, with wicker furnishings and fans, and all have private bathrooms. Families are welcome, but children under 12 are not. All rooms are nonsmoking.

914 Eaton St., Key West, FL 33040. ℂ **800/788-4150** or 305/296-4440. Fax 305/293-9031. www.westwinds keywest.com. 26 units. Winter $90–$150; off-season $70–$120. Rates include continental breakfast. DISC, MC, V. **Amenities:** 2 pools (1 heated); bike rental; self-service laundry. *In room:* A/C (some rooms have TVs and kitchenettes).

INEXPENSIVE

Abaco Inn ★ *Value* This tidy little guest house is situated on a secluded lane just off Duval Street. Although there is no pool or view, the three simple but comfortable rooms are well stocked, immaculate, and charming. Each room has a sizeable private bathroom, queen bed, and a twin-size Murphy bed. Once the home of a cigar maker, the house dates from the early 1900s. Now it is owned and operated by George Fontana, a friendly and knowledgeable tour guide and writer. Look for his column on local characters in the *Key West Citizen*. You can't beat the price in this superconvenient location. No smoking is allowed on the property.

415 Julia St. (between Truman Ave. and Virginia St.), Key West, FL 33040. ② 800/358-6307 or 305/296-2212. Fax 305/295-0349. www.abaco-inn.com. 3 units. Winter from $99–$109 double. Off-season from $69 double. 4-day minimum stay in season. Additional person $15 extra. AE, DISC, MC, V. **Amenities:** Bike rental; concierge. *In room:* A/C, TV, microwave, fridge, coffeemaker, hair dryer.

Angelina Guest House 🏵🏵 This youth-hostel-type guest house is about the cheapest in town and conveniently located near a hot, hippie restaurant called Blue Heaven (see "Where to Dine," below). It is generally safe and full of character. The rooms are all furnished differently in a modest style, recently upgraded with new decor. Only three rooms do not have private baths. Two rooms have full kitchens, and one has a microwave and small refrigerator; there are no televisions or telephones. A gorgeous lagoon-style heated pool with waterfall and tropical landscaping was an excellent addition. Even better are the poolside hammocks—get out there early, they go quickly! Even though the Angelina is sparse, it's a great place to crash if you are on the cheap. Many repeat guests consider "this old house" their home away from home.

302 Angela St. (at the corner of Thomas St.), Key West, FL 33040. ② 888/303-4480 or 305/294-4480. Fax 305/272-0681. www.angelinaguesthouse.com. 15 units. Winter $75–$149; off-season $49–$95. Rates include continental breakfast. DISC, MC, V. **Amenities:** Outdoor heated pool; concierge. *In room:* A/C, hair dryer, iron.

The Grand 🏵🏵 *Finds* Don't expect cabbies or locals to know about this well-kept secret, located in a modest residential section of Old Town, about 5 blocks from Duval Street. It's got almost everything you could want, including a very moderate price tag. Proprietor Elizabeth Rose goes out of her way to provide any and all services for her appreciative guests. All rooms have private bathrooms, air-conditioning, and private entrances. Room no. 2 on the backside of the house is the best deal; it's small, but it has a porch and the most privacy. Suites are a real steal, too. The large two-room units come with a complete kitchen. This place is undoubtedly the best bargain in town.

1116 Grinnell St. (between Virginia and Catherine sts.), Key West, FL 33040. ② 888/947-2630 or 305/294-0590. Fax 305/294-0477. www.thegrandguesthouse.com. 10 units. Winter $98–$188; off-season $88–$118. Rates include continental breakfast. AE, DISC, MC, V. **Amenities:** Bike and scooter rental; concierge. *In room:* A/C, TV/VCR, fridge.

Grand Key Resort 🏵 *Finds* If you don't mind staying on the quiet "other" side of the island, a 10-minute cab ride away from Duval Street, the Grand Key Resort is an excellent choice, not to mention value. An ecologically conscious resort, Grand Key has been renovated with eco-sensitive materials as well as an interior created to conserve energy, reduce waste, and preserve the area's natural resources. Rooms are clean and comfortable, with some looking out onto the spacious pool area, which is surrounded by an unsightly empty lot of mangroves and marshes. The hotel's restaurant is also very good, but for excitement, you will need to look elsewhere.

3990 South Roosevelt Blvd., Key West, FL 33040. ② 888/310-1540 or 305/293-1818. Fax 305/296-6962. www.grandkeyresort.com. 216 units. Winter $179–$489; off-season $125–$420. Rates include continental breakfast. AE, DISC, MC, V. Free parking. **Amenities:** Restaurant, tiki bar and lounge; pool; concierge;

meeting rooms; limited room service. *In room:* A/C, TV/Web TV, Sony Playstation, dataport, minibar, coffee-maker, hair dryer.

Key West International Hostel & Seashell Motel   This well-run afford-able hostel is a 3-minute walk to the beach and to Old Town. Very busy with European backpackers, it's a great place to meet people. The dorm rooms are dark and sparse, but clean enough. The higher-priced motel rooms are a good deal, especially those equipped with full kitchens. The common area room has been upgraded, and a two-bedroom suite has been added for those looking to upgrade a bit. Amenities include a pool table under a tiki roof, and bicycle rentals for $8 per day. There's also cheap food available for breakfast, lunch, and dinner as well as discounted prices for snorkeling, diving, and sunset cruises.

718 South St., Key West, FL 33040. © **800/51-HOSTEL** or 305/296-5719. Fax 305/296-0672. www.keywest hostel.com. 100 units. Year-round members $19.50, nonmembers $22.50. Motel units $75–$105 in season; $55–$85 off-season. MC, V. **Amenities:** Bike rental; kitchen. *In room:* A/C, TV, fridge, coffeemaker, hair dryer; dorm rooms only have A/C.

WHERE TO DINE

With its share of the usual drive-through fast-food franchises (mostly up on Roosevelt Boulevard) and Duval Street succumbing to the lure of a Hard Rock Cafe, you might be surprised to learn that, over the years, an upscale and high-quality dining scene has begun to thrive in Key West. Wander Old Town or the newly spruced-up Bahama Village and browse menus after you have exhausted the list of my picks below.

If you don't feel like venturing out, call **We Deliver** (© **305/293-0078**), a service that will bring you anything you want from any of the area's restaurants or stores for a small fee (between $3 and $6). We Deliver operates between 3 and 11pm. If you are staying in a condominium or efficiency, you may want to stock your refrigerator with groceries, beer, wine, and snacks from the area's oldest gro-cer, **Fausto's Food Palace.** Open since 1926, there are now two locations: 1105 White St. and 522 Fleming St. The Fleming Street location will deliver (© **305/294-5221** or 305/296-5663). Fausto's has a $25 delivery minimum.

VERY EXPENSIVE

Cafe des Artistes ★★★ FRENCH   Open for nearly 2 decades, the Cafe des Artistes' impressive longevity is the result of its winning combination of food and atmosphere. The fact that it was once part of a hotel built in 1935 by Al Capone's bookkeeper adds to its allure, but it's really the food that people come for. Tradi-tional French meals benefit from a subtle tropical twist. Start with the duck-liver paté, made with fresh truffles and old cognac, or Maryland crabmeat served with an artichoke heart and herbed tomato confit. Ask about the escargot du jour. Nouvelle and traditional French entrees include lobster flambé with mango and basil, and wine-basted lamb chops rubbed with rosemary and ginger.

1007 Simonton St. (near Truman Ave.). © **305/294-7100.** Reservations recommended. Main courses $25–$38. AE, MC, V. Daily 6–11pm.

Café Marquesa ★★★ CONTEMPORARY AMERICAN   If you're looking for fabulous dining in Key West, this is the place. The intimate 50-seat restaurant is something to look at, but it's really the food that you'll want to admire. Spe-cialties include peppercorn-dusted seared yellowfin tuna with saffron risotto; grilled Florida lobster tail and diver sea scallops with Thai basil sauce, black Thai rice, and Asian vegetables; and an almost-perfect feta and pinenut-crusted rack of lamb with rosemary demi-glacé, creamy polenta, and eggplant caponata. If you're looking to splurge, financially and gastronomically, this is the place.

The Marquesa Hotel, 600 Fleming St. © **305/292-1919**. Reservations highly recommended. Main courses $20–$36. AE, DC, MC, V. Daily 7–11pm summer; 6–11pm winter. No smoking.

Louie's Backyard ★★ CARIBBEAN   Nestled amid blooming bougainvillea on a lush slice of the Gulf, Louie's remains one of the most romantic restaurants on earth. Famed chef Norman Van Aiken of Norman's in Miami brought his talents farther south and started what has become one of the finest dining spots in the Keys. As a result, this is one of the hardest places to score a reservation: Either call way in advance or hope that your hotel concierge has some pull. After dinner, sit at the dockside bar and watch the waves crash, almost touching your feet, while enjoying a cocktail at sunset. You can't go wrong with the fresh catch of the day or any seafood dish for that matter. The weekend brunches are also great. Even if you can't stay for dinner, go for lunch; this is one dining experience you won't want to miss.

700 Waddell Ave. © **305/294-1061**. Reservations highly recommended. Main courses $25–$30; lunch $8–$15. AE, DC, MC, V. Daily 11:30am–3pm and 6–10:30pm.

One Duval ★★★ CARIBBEAN   The waterfront setting of this restaurant at the Pier House Resort is beautiful, but you may be too distracted to notice the views when you taste the food, which executive chef Will Greenwood describes as New Calypso Harvest. One of the best restaurants in Key West, One Duval blends the ingredients of the Caribbean and Florida with an innovative twist. For starters, the crabmeat stuffed in phyllo dough is outstanding, not to mention filling, and the goat cheese soufflé is rich and incredibly hedonistic. For main courses, the smoked cured pork chop with Captain Morgan spiced rum sauce is a best bet, as is the ponzu marinated yellowfin tuna tartare and avocado mousse timbale served in a macadamia-nut-cilantro jus. The Key lime pie with meringue is a must-have. Service is friendly and hyper-professional, and it's not the kind of restaurant they rush you out of. Eat first, then sit back and digest the views. You don't want to miss any of what this fine restaurant has to offer.

1 Duval Street. © **305/296-4600**. Reservations highly recommended. Main courses $25–$30. AE, DC, MC, V. Daily 6–10:30pm.

EXPENSIVE

Antonia's ★★ REGIONAL ITALIAN   The food is great, but the atmosphere is a bit fussy for Key West. If you don't have a reservation in-season, don't bother. Still, if you are organized and don't mind paying high prices for dishes that go for much less elsewhere, try this old favorite. From the perfectly seasoned homemade focaccia to an exemplary crème brûlée, this elegant little standout is amazingly consistent. The menu includes a small selection of classics, such as *zuppa di pesce*, rack of lamb in a rosemary sauce, and veal Marsala. However, the way to go is with the nightly specials. You can't go wrong with any of the handmade pastas. And the owners, Antonia Berto and Phillip Smith, travel to Italy every year to research recipes, so you can be sure you're getting an authentic taste of Italy in small-town Key West.

615 Duval St. © **305/294-6565**. Fax 305/294-3888. Reservations suggested. Main courses $20–$28; pastas $13–$18. AE, DC, MC, V. Daily 6–11pm.

Bagatelle ★★★ SEAFOOD/TROPICAL   Reserve a seat at the elegant second-floor veranda overlooking Duval Street's mayhem. From the calm above, you may want to start your meal with the excellent herb-and-garlic-stuffed whole artichoke or the sashimilike seared tuna rolled in black peppercorns. Also recommended is a lightly creamy garlic-herb pasta topped with Gulf shrimp,

Florida lobster, and mushrooms. The best chicken and beef dishes are given a tropical treatment: grilled with papaya, ginger, and soy.

115 Duval St. (*C*) **305/296-6609.** Reservations recommended. Main courses $14–$21; lunch $5–$10. AE, DISC, MC, V. Sun–Thurs 11:30am–10pm, Fri–Sat 11:30am–11pm.

La Trattoria *R* ITALIAN Have a true Italian feast in a relaxed atmosphere. Each dish here is prepared and presented according to old, Italian tradition and is cooked to order. The antipasti are scrumptious. Try the delicious baked breadcrumb-stuffed mushroom caps; they're firm yet tender. The stuffed eggplant with ricotta and roasted peppers is light and flavorful. Or have the seafood salad of shrimp, calamari, and mussels, fish-market fresh and tasty. The pasta dishes are also great: Try the *penne Venezia,* with mushrooms, sun-dried tomatoes, and crabmeat, or the cannelloni stuffed with veal and spinach. For dessert, don't skip the homemade tiramisu; it's light yet full-flavored. The dining room is spacious but still intimate, and the waiters are friendly and informative. Before you leave, be sure to visit Virgilio's, the restaurant's very own cocktail lounge with live jazz until 2am.

524 Duval St. (*C*) **305/296-1075.** Pasta $10–$17; main courses $17–$22. AE, DC, DISC, MC, V. Daily 5:30–11pm.

Mangoes *RRR* FLORIBBEAN This restaurant's large brick patio, shaded by overgrown banyan trees, is so alluring to passersby that it's packed almost every night of the week. Many people don't realize how pricey the meals can be here because, upon first glance, it looks like a casual Duval Street cafe, but both its prices and cuisine are a notch above casual. Appetizers include conch chowder laced with sherry, lobster dumplings with tangy Key lime sauce, and grilled shrimp cocktail with spicy mango chutney. Spicy sausage with black beans and rice, crispy curried chicken, and local snapper with passion-fruit sauce are typical among the entrees, but the Garlic and Lime Pinks—a half pound of Key West pink shrimp seasoned and grilled with a roasted garlic and Key lime glaze—are the menu's best offering by far. The Cuban Coffee Pork is definitely a different take on roast pork, rubbed with Cuban coffee and grilled with a vanilla-bean butter sauce and banana black-currant chutney. Even though it is right on tourist-laden Duval Street, Mangoes enjoys a good reputation among locals and stands out from the rest of the greasy bar bar fare found there.

700 Duval St. (at Angela St.) (*C*) **305/292-4606.** Reservations recommended for parties of 6 or more. Main courses $12–$26; pizzas $10–$13; lunch $7–$14. AE, DC, DISC, MC, V. Daily 11am–midnight; pizza until 1am.

MODERATE
Alonzo's Oyster Bar *R* SEAFOOD Alonzo's Oyster Bar offers good seafood in a casual setting. It's located on the ground floor of the A&B Lobster House at the end of Front Street in the marina. To start off your meal, try the steamed beer shrimp—tantalizingly fresh jumbo shrimp in a garlic, Old Bay, beer, and cayenne pepper sauce. A house specialty is white clam chili, a delicious mix of tender clams, white beans, and potatoes served with a dollop of sour cream. An excellent entree is the pan-fried lobster cakes, served with sweet-corn mashed potatoes, chipotle gravy, and roasted-corn salsa. Alonzo's is the casual section of the A&B Lobster House; if you want to dress up, go upstairs for their "fine dining." The staff is cheerful and informative, and the service is very good.

231 Margaret St. (*C*) **305/294-5880.** Appetizers $5–$8; main courses $11–$17. MC, V. Daily 11am–11pm.

Banana Cafe *RRR* *Finds* FRENCH Although neither as elaborate as Cafe des Artistes nor quite as casual as Blue Heaven, Banana Café is open for three meals a day and benefits from a French country cafe look and feel. It's an upscale local eatery that's been discovered by savvy visitors on the less congested end of Duval Street and kept its loyal clientele with affordable prices and delightful, light preparations. Banana Café's crepes are legendary on the island for breakfast or lunch, and fresh quality ingredients and a French-themed menu bring daytime diners back for the casual, classy, tropical-influenced dinner menu. Every Thursday night, there's live jazz.

1211 Duval St. ℂ **305/294-7227.** Main courses $4.79–$23; breakfast and lunch $2–$8.50. AE, DC, MC, V. Daily 8am–11pm.

Blue Heaven 🗛 *Finds* SEAFOOD/AMERICAN/NATURAL   This little hippie-run gallery and restaurant has become the place to be in Key West—and with good reason. Be prepared to wait in line. The food here is some of the best in town, especially for breakfast. You can enjoy homemade granola, huge tropical fruit pancakes, and seafood Benedict. Dinners are just as good and run the gamut from fresh-caught fish dishes to Jamaican-style jerk chicken, curried soups, and vegetarian stews. But if you're a neat freak, don't bother. Some people are put off by the dirt floors and roaming cats and birds, but frankly, it adds to the charm. The building used to be a bordello, where Hemingway was said to hang out watching cockfights. It's still lively there, but not that lively!

305 Petronia St. ℂ **305/296-8666.** Main courses $10–$30; lunch $6–$14; breakfast $5–$11. DISC, MC, V. Daily 8am–11:30am, noon–3pm, and 6pm–10:30pm; Sun brunch 8am–1pm. Closed mid-Sept to early Oct.

Mangia, Mangia 🗛 *Value* ITALIAN/AMERICAN   Locals appreciate that they can get good, inexpensive food here in a town filled with tourist traps. Off the beaten track, in a little corner storefront, this great Chicago-style pasta place serves some of the best Italian food in the Keys. The family-run restaurant offers superb homemade pastas of every description, including one of the tastiest marinaras around. The simple grilled chicken breast brushed with olive oil and sprinkled with pepper is another good choice, as is the Picadillo Pasta—black bean pasta shells smothered in a Cuban-inspired sauce with meat, tomatoes, olives, capers, and spices. You wouldn't know it from the glossy glass front room, but there's a fantastic little outdoor patio dotted with twinkling pepper lights and lots of plants. You can relax out back with a glass of one of their excellent wines—they're said to have the largest selection in the Keys—or homemade beer while you wait for your table.

900 Southard St. (at Margaret St.). ℂ **305/294-2469.** Reservations not accepted. Main courses $9–$15. AE, MC, V. Daily 5:30–10pm.

Pepe's *Finds* AMERICAN   This old dive has been serving good, basic food for nearly a century. Steaks and Apalachicola Bay oysters are the big draw for regulars who appreciate the rustic barroom setting and historic photos on the walls. Look for original scenes of Key West in 1909, when Pepe's first opened. If the weather is nice, choose a seat on the patio under a stunning mahogany tree. Burgers, fish sandwiches, and standard chili satisfy hearty eaters. Buttery sautéed mushrooms and rich mashed potatoes are the best comfort food in Key West. Stop by early for breakfast when you can get old-fashioned chipped beef on toast and all the usual egg dishes. In the evening, there are reasonably priced cocktails on the deck.

806 Caroline St. (between Margaret and Williams sts.). ℂ **305/294-7192.** Main courses $13–$22; breakfast $2–$9; lunch $5–$9. DISC, MC, V. Daily 6:30am–10:30pm.

Turtle Kraals Wildlife Grill 🗛 *Finds* SOUTHWESTERN/SEAFOOD You'll join lots of locals in this out-of-the-way converted warehouse with indoor and dockside seating that serves innovative seafood at great prices. Try the twin lobster tails stuffed with mango and crabmeat, or any of the big quesadillas or fajitas. Kids will like the wildlife exhibits and the very cheesy menu. Blues bands play most nights.

213 Margaret St. (corner of Caroline St.). ℭ **305/294-2640.** Main courses $10–$20. DISC, MC, V. Mon–Thurs 11am–10:30pm, Fri–Sat 11am–11pm, Sun noon–10:30pm; bar closes at midnight.

INEXPENSIVE

Anthony's Cafe 🟊 ITALIAN DELI/ROTISSERIE   Although owned and operated by a Greek import, this rustic Italian-style trattoria is a welcome addition to an area crowded with more expensive and less delicious options. Fragrant roasted chicken and overstuffed sandwiches on fresh baked bread are the best choices. Also good are the many salads and daily specials.

1111 Duval St. (at Amelia St.). ℭ **305/296-8899.** Breakfast $2–$5; sandwiches and salads $5.50–$7 with a side; hot plates $8–$13. Cash only. Daily 8am–10pm.

Bahama Mama's Kitchen 🟊🟊 BAHAMIAN   Sit outside under an umbrella and enjoy the authentic Bahamian dishes made from recipes that have been handed down through owner Corey's family for the past 150 years. Prepared fresh daily, all dishes are created with their special Bahamian seasonings. Try the coconut shrimp butterflied, soaked in coconut oil, battered with egg, and then rolled in fresh shredded coconut and deep-fried. The fresh catch of the day comes blackened, broiled, or fried and is served with island plantains, shrimp hash cakes, and crab rice. The service is good and the staff is friendly.

In the Bahama Village Market, 324 Petronia St. ℭ **305/294-3355.** Appetizers $4–$7; main courses $9–$13. MC, V. Daily 11am–10pm.

The Deli DINER/AMERICAN   In operation since 1950, this family-owned corner eatery has kept up with the times. It's really more of a diner than a deli and has a vast menu with all kinds of hearty options, from meatloaf to yellowtail snapper. The seafood options are pretty good. A daily selection of more than a dozen vegetables includes the usual diner choices of beets, corn, and coleslaw with some distinctly Caribbean additions, such as rice and beans and fried plantains. Most dinners include a choice of two vegetables and homemade biscuits or corn bread. Breakfasts are made to order and attract a loyal following of locals. The Deli also offers ice cream sundaes and gourmet coffees.

531 Truman Ave. (corner of Truman Ave. and Simonton St.). ℭ **305/294-1464.** Full meals $7–$23; sandwiches $3–$8. DISC, MC, V. Daily 7:30am–10pm.

El Siboney Restaurant 🟊 *Value* CUBAN   For good, cheap Cuban food, stop at this corner dive that looks more like a gas station than a diner. Be prepared, however, to wait like the locals for succulent roast pork, Cuban sandwiches, grilled chicken, and *ropa vieja* (a stewlike dish of beef, onion, garlic, and tomatoes), all served with heaps of rice and beans.

900 Catherine St. (at Margaret St.). ℭ **305/296-4184.** Main courses $5–$13. No credit cards. Mon–Sat 11am–9:30pm.

PT's Late Night 🟊 *Finds* AMERICAN   This place is worth knowing about not only because it's one of the only places in town serving food past 10pm, but also because it happens to serve good food at extremely reasonable prices. PT's is more like a sports bar than a restaurant, and service can be a bit slow and brusque, but you'll enjoy their heaping plates of nachos, sizzling fajitas served with all the trimmings, and superfresh salads—so big they can be a meal in themselves.

920 Caroline St. (at the corner of Margaret St.). (305/296-4245. Main courses $6.95–$14.95. DISC, MC, V. Daily 11am–4am.

KEY WEST AFTER DARK

Duval Street is the Bourbon Street of Florida. Amid the T-shirt shops and clothing boutiques, you'll find bar after bar serving neon-colored frozen drinks to revelers who bounce from one to the next from noon till dawn. Bands and crowds vary from night to night and season to season. Your best bet is to start at Truman Avenue and head up Duval to check them out for yourself. Cover charges are rare, except in gay clubs (see "The Gay Scene" section below), so stop into a dozen and see which you like. For the most part, Key West is a late-night town, and bars and clubs don't close until around 3 or 4am.

Captain Tony's Saloon   Just around the corner from Duval's beaten path, this smoky old wooden bar (see "The Legend of Captain Tony" box) is about as authentic as you'll find. It comes complete with old-time regulars who remember the island before cruise ships docked here; they say Hemingway drank, caroused, and even wrote here. The owner, Captain Tony Tarracino, a former controversial Key West mayor—immortalized in Jimmy Buffett's "Last Mango in Paradise"—has recently capitalized on the success of this once-quaint tavern by franchising the place. 428 Greene St. (305/294-1838.

Durty Harry's   This large complex features live rock bands almost every night. You can wander to one of the many outdoor bars or head up to Upstairs at Rick's, an indoor/outdoor dance club that gets going late. For the more racy singles or couples, there is also the Red Garter, a pocket-sized strip club. The hawker outside reminds couples, in case they've forgotten, that "the family that strips together sticks together." 208 Duval St. (305/296-4890.

Epoch   Until an arsonist put an end to the legend in 1995, this former gay club was the place to dance to everything from techno to house and disco to reggae. Now expanded to include seven bars, an even bigger dance floor, a huge outside deck overlooking Duval Street, and a new state-of-the-art sound system, this is a better-than-ever choice for people of any orientation who can appreciate a good time. 623 Duval St. (305/296-8521.

The Legend of Captain Tony

Captain Tony Tarracino, proprietor of Captain Tony's Saloon, 428 Greene St. ((305/294-1838), was a Key West legend even before Jimmy Buffet immortalized him in "The Last Mango in Paris." Notwithstanding Mr. Buffet's influence, you won't find a cheeseburger in paradise at Captain Tony's, because they don't serve food. They do, however, serve mind-erasing cocktails and visions of old Key West. The walls and ceiling are adorned with, among other colorful things, old photos of the old Captain, a tombstone, an old horn, and a tree that actually grows out of the ceiling. The music is loud; the patrons louder.

The legendary Captain also happens to be the ex-mayor of Key West and everybody's favorite barkeep. If you really want a sublime experience, ask the crusty old Captain (if you're lucky enough to catch a glimpse of him, probably drinking out of a mug containing some sort of dark liquor) anything about love, life, or even libations and he'll be happy to indulge you with his off-the-cuff philosophies.

Jimmy Buffett's Margaritaville Cafe   This cafe, named after another Key West legend, is a worthwhile stop. Although Mr. Buffett moved to glitzy Palm Beach years ago, his name is still attracting large crowds. This kitschy restaurant/bar/gift shop features live bands every night—from rock to blues to reggae and everything in between. The touristy cafe is furnished with plenty of Buffett memorabilia, including gold records, photos, and drawings. The margaritas are high priced but tasty, but the cheeseburgers aren't worth singing about. 500 Duval St. ℂ 305/292-1435.

Sloppy Joe's   You'll have to stop in here just to say you did. Scholars and drunks debate whether this is the same Sloppy Joe's that Hemingway wrote about, but there's no argument that this classic bar's early 20th-century wooden ceiling and cracked tile floors are Key West originals. There's live music nightly as well as a cigar room and martini bar. 201 Duval St. ℂ 305/294-5717, ext. 10. www.sloppyjoes.com.

Wax   Wax oozes a cosmopolitan ambiance, looking as if it were shipped down from New York, with its blood-red interior, very hip, loungy atmosphere, and excellent DJ'ed dance music. Though it has a more elegant atmosphere than any other place on the island, Wax's patrons (it's where all the locals go to avoid tourists) dress down. 422 Applerouth Lane. ℂ 305/296-6667.

THE GAY SCENE

Key West's bohemian live-and-let live atmosphere extends to its thriving and quirky gay community. Since Tennessee Williams and before, Key West has provided the perfect backdrop to a gay scene unlike that of many large urban areas. Seamlessly blended with the prevailing culture, there is no "gay ghetto" in Key West, where alternative lifestyles are embraced and even celebrated.

Although restaurants and businesses welcome visitors without discrimination, nightlife *is* inevitably nightlife. In Key West, the best music and dancing can be found at the predominantly gay clubs. While many of the area's other hot spots are geared toward tourists who like to imbibe, the gay clubs are for those who want to rave, gay or not. Covers vary, but are rarely more than $10.

Two adjacent popular late-night spots are the **801 Bourbon Bar/One Saloon** (801 Duval St. and 514 Petronia St. ℂ 305/294-9349 for both), featuring great drag and lots more disco. A mostly male clientele frequents this hot spot from 9pm until 4am. Another Duval Street favorite is **Diva's**, at 711 Duval St. (℃ 305/292-8500), where you might catch drag queens belting out torch songs or judges voting on the best package in the wet-jockey-shorts contest.

Sunday nights are fun at two local spots. **Tea by the Sea,** on the pier at the Atlantic Shores Motel, 510 South St. (℃ 800/520-3559), attracts a faithful following of regulars and visitors alike. The clothing-optional pool is always an attraction. Show up after 7:30pm. Better known around town as La-Te-Da, **La Terraza de Marti,** the former Key West home of Cuban exile Jose Marti, at 1125 Duval St. (ℂ 305/296-6706), is a great spot to gather poolside for the best martini in town—but don't bother with the food. Just upstairs from there is the **Crystal Room** (ℂ 305/296-6706), with a high-caliber cabaret performance featuring the popular Randy Roberts in the winter.

4 The Dry Tortugas ★★

70 miles W of Key West

Few people realize that the Florida Keys don't end at Key West, since about 70 miles west of there is a chain of seven small islands known as the Dry Tortugas.

As long as you have come this far, you might wish to visit them, especially if you're into bird watching, which is their primary draw.

Ponce de León, who discovered this far-flung cluster of coral keys in 1513, named them Las Tortugas because of the many sea turtles, which still flock to the area during the nesting season in the warm summer months. Oceanic charts later carried the preface "dry" to warn mariners that fresh water was unavailable here. Modern intervention has made drinking water available, but little else.

These undeveloped islands make a great day trip for travelers interested in seeing the natural anomalies of the Florida Keys—especially the birds. The Dry Tortugas are nesting grounds and roosting sites for thousands of tropical and subtropical oceanic birds. Visitors will also find a historical fort, good fishing, and terrific snorkeling around shallow reefs.

GETTING THERE

BY BOAT The **Yankee Fleet,** based in Key West (© **800/634-0939** or 305/ 294-7009), offers day trips from Key West for sightseeing, snorkeling, or both. Cruises leave daily for the 3-hour journey at 7:30am from the Land's End Marina at Margaret Street and travel to Garden Key. Breakfast is served on board. Once on the island, you can join a guided tour of Fort Jefferson or explore it on your own. Boats return to Key West by 7pm. Tours cost $109 per person, including breakfast, lunch, dinner, and snorkeling equipment; $69 for children 16 and under; $99 for seniors, students, and military personnel. Phone for reservations.

The **Sunny Days Catamarans'** *Fast Cat* (© **800/236-7937;** 305/292-6100) is faster, quieter, and more high tech than the loud Yankee fleet, as well as a better value. Included in the $95 round-trip adult fare ($65 for children) is a continental breakfast and a buffet lunch with cold cuts, fresh veggies, fruits, salads, unlimited sodas and water, plus an island tour and a snorkeling excursion to a shipwreck in 5 to 20 feet of water. The high-speed power cat leaves Key West for Garden Key at 8am and returns by 6pm.

BY PLANE **Seaplanes of Key West,** based at Key West Airport (© **800/950-2-FLY** or 305/294-0709), offers daily excursions. Weather permitting, flights depart at 8am, 10am, noon, and 2pm. The 40-minute trip at about 500 feet offers a great introduction to the Dry Tortugas. Fares, which include snorkeling equipment and a cooler for use on the island, start at $179 for adults, $129 for kids 12 and under, $99 for kids 6 and under for a half-day; and $305 for adults, $225 for kids 12 and under, and $170 for kids 6 and under for a full day. Bring a bathing suit, snorkeling equipment, and some snacks to enjoy on these remote and beautiful islands. If you want to stay overnight at Fort Jefferson, it costs $329 for adults, $235 for kids 12 and under, and $179 for kids 6 and under.

EXPLORING THE DRY TORTUGAS

Of the seven islands that make up the Dry Tortugas, Garden Key is the most visited, because it is where Fort Jefferson and the visitor center are located. Loggerhead Key, Middle Key, and East Key are only open during the day and are for hiking. Bush Key is for the birds—literally! It's a nesting area for birds only, though it is open from October to January for special excursions. Hospital and Long Keys are closed to the public.

Fort Jefferson, a huge six-sided 19th-century fortress, is built almost at the water's edge of Garden Key, giving the appearance that it floats in the middle of the sea. The monumental structure is surrounded by formidable 8-foot-thick walls that rise up from the sand to a height of nearly 50 feet. Impressive arch-ways, stonework, and parapets make this 150-year-old monument a grand sight. With the invention of the rifled cannon, the fort's masonry construction became obsolete, and the building was never completed. For 10 years, however, from 1863 to 1873, Fort Jefferson served as a prison, a kind of "Alcatraz East." Among its prisoners were four of the "Lincoln Conspirators," including Samuel A. Mudd, the doctor who set the broken leg of fugitive assassin John Wilkes Booth. In 1935, Fort Jefferson became a national monument administered by the National Park Service. For more information about Fort Jefferson and the Dry Tortugas, call the **Everglades National Park Service** at © **305/242-7700** or visit www.fortjefferson.com. Fort Jefferson is open during daylight hours on Garden Key, and there is a self-guiding trail that interprets the history of human presence in the Dry Tortugas while leading visitors through the fort.

OUTDOOR PURSUITS

BIRD-WATCHING   Bring your binoculars and your bird books: Bird watch-ing is *the* reason to visit this little cluster of tropical islands. The Dry Tortugas, uniquely situated in the middle of the migration flyway between North and South America, serve as an important rest stop for the more than 200 winged varieties that pass through here annually. The season peaks from mid-March to mid-May, when thousands of birds show up, but many species from the West Indies can be found here year-round.

DIVING & SNORKELING   The warm, clear, shallow waters of the Dry Tor-tugas produce optimum conditions for snorkeling and scuba diving. Four endangered species of sea turtles—the green, leatherback, Atlantic ridley, and hawksbill—can be found here, along with a myriad of marine species. The region just outside the seawall of Fort Jefferson is excellent for underwater tour-ing; an abundant variety of fish, coral, and more live in just 3 or 4 feet of water.

FISHING   Fishing for snapper, tarpon, grouper, and other fish used to be pop-ular here until July of 2001, when a federal law closed off all fishing in a 90-square-mile tract of open ocean called the Tortugas North and a 61-square-mile tract of open ocean called the Tortugas South. The ban basically prohibits all fishing in order to preserve the dwindling population of fish (a result of com-mercial fishermen and environmental factors). Instead, head to Key West.

CAMPING

The rustic beauty of tiny Garden Key (the only island of the Dry Tortugas where campers are allowed to pitch their tent) is a camper's dream. Don't worry about sharing your site with noisy RVs or motor homes; they can't get here. The abun-dance of birds doesn't make it quiet, but camping here—a stone's throw from the water—is as picturesque as it gets. Picnic tables, cooking grills, and toilets are provided, but there are no showers. All supplies must be packed in and out. Sites are $3 per person per night and are available on a first-come, first-served basis. With only 10 sites, they book up fast. For more information, call the **National Park Service** (© **305/242-7700**).

12

The Gold Coast:
Hallandale to the Palm Beaches

Named not for the sun-kissed skin of the area's residents but for the gold salvaged from shipwrecks off its coastline, the Gold Coast embraces more than 60 miles of beautiful Atlantic shoreline—from the pristine sands of Jupiter in northern Palm Beach County to the legendary strip of beaches in Fort Lauderdale.

If you haven't visited the cities along Florida's southeastern coast in the last few years, you'll be amazed at how much has changed. Miles of sprawling grassland and empty lots have been replaced with luxurious resorts and high-rise condominiums. Taking advantage of their close proximity to Miami, the cities that make up the Gold Coast have attracted millions looking to escape crowded sidewalks, traffic jams, and the everyday routines of big-city life.

Fortunately, amid all the building, much of the natural treasure of the Gold Coast remains. There are 300 miles of Intracoastal Waterway, not to mention Fort Lauderdale's Venetian-inspired canals. And the unspoiled splendor of the Everglades is just a few miles inland.

The most popular areas in the Gold Coast are Fort Lauderdale, Boca Raton, and Palm Beach. While Fort Lauderdale is a favored beachfront destination, Boca Raton and Palm Beach are better known for their country club lifestyles and excellent shopping. Further north is the quietly popular Jupiter, best known for spring training at the Roger Dean Stadium and for former resident Burt Reynolds. In between these better-traveled destinations are a few things worth stopping for . . . but not much. Driving north along the coastline is one of the best ways to fully appreciate what the Gold Coast is all about—it's a perspective you certainly won't find in a shopping mall.

Tourists come here by the droves, but they aren't the only people coming; thousands of transplants, fleeing the increasing population influx in Miami and the frigid winters up North, have made this area their home. As a result, there has been a construction boom in the existing cities and even westward, into the swampy areas of the Everglades. More than 20 homes per day are being built in Broward County alone. There has also been a great revitalization of several downtown areas, including Hollywood, Fort Lauderdale, and West Palm Beach. These once-desolate urban centers have been spruced up and now attract more young travelers and families than ever before.

Unfortunately, like its neighbors to the south, the Gold Coast can be prohibitively hot and buggy in the summer. The good news is that bargains are plentiful in the summer months (May–Oct), when many locals take advantage of package deals and uncrowded resorts.

The Gold Coast

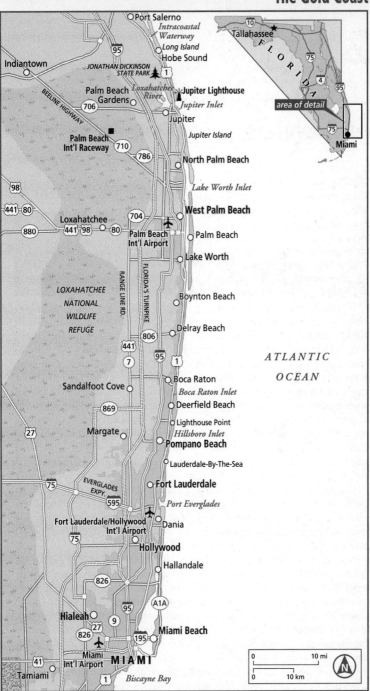

Port Salerno

Intracoastal Waterway

Long Island

Hobe Sound

Indiantown

95

JONATHAN DICKINSON STATE PARK

1

BEELINE HIGHWAY

Palm Beach Gardens

Loxahatchee River

Jupiter Lighthouse

Jupiter Inlet

Jupiter

706

Palm Beach Int'l Raceway

710

786

Jupiter Island

North Palm Beach

98

441 80

880

441 98

Loxahatchee

80

704

Lake Worth Inlet

West Palm Beach

Palm Beach Int'l Airport

Palm Beach

Lake Worth

RANGE LINE RD.

FLORIDA'S TURNPIKE

LOXAHATCHEE NATIONAL WILDLIFE REFUGE

Boynton Beach

806

441

7

Delray Beach

95

1

27

Sandalfoot Cove

Boca Raton

Boca Raton Inlet

869

Deerfield Beach

Margate

Lighthouse Point

Hillsboro Inlet

Pompano Beach

Lauderdale-By-The-Sea

75

EVERGLADES EXPY.

595

Fort Lauderdale

Port Everglades

Fort Lauderdale/Hollywood Int'l Airport

Dania

75

Hollywood

Hallandale

826

95

A1A

Hialeah

27

9

826

195

Miami Beach

41

Miami Int'l Airport

MIAMI

Tamiami

1

Biscayne Bay

ATLANTIC OCEAN

Tallahassee

F L O R I D A

10

75

4

95

area of detail

75

Miami

0   10 mi

0   10 km

N

For the purposes of this chapter, the Gold Coast will consist of the towns of Hallandale, Hollywood, Pompano Beach, Fort Lauderdale, Dania, Deerfield, Boca Raton, Delray Beach, Boynton Beach, and the Palm Beaches.

EXPLORING THE GOLD COAST BY CAR

Like most of South Florida, the Gold Coast consists of a mainland and an adjacent strip of barrier islands. You'll have to check the maps to keep track of the many bridges that allow access to the islands where most of the tourist activity is centered. Interstate 95, which runs north-south, is the area's main highway. Farther west is the Florida Turnpike, a toll road that can be worth the expense since the speed limit is higher and it is often less congested than I-95. Also on the mainland is U.S. 1, which generally runs parallel to I-95 (to the east) and is a narrower thoroughfare mostly crowded with strip malls and seedy hotels.

I recommend taking Florida A1A, a slow oceanside road that connects the long, thin islands of Florida's whole east coast. Although the road is narrow, it is the most scenic and forces you into the relaxed atmosphere of these resort towns.

1 Broward County: Hallandale & Hollywood ⬧ to Fort Lauderdale ⬧⬧

23 miles N of Miami

Until the 2000 presidential election fiasco, most people had never heard of Broward County. Less exposed than the highly hyped Miami, Broward County is a lot calmer and, according to some, a lot friendlier than the Magic City. In fact, a friendly rivalry exists between residents of Miami–Dade County and Broward County. Miamians consider themselves more sophisticated and cosmopolitan than their northern neighbors who, in turn, dismiss the alleged sophistication as snobbery and actually prefer their own county's gentler pace.

With more than 23 miles of beachfront and 300 miles of navigable waterways, Broward County is also a great outdoor destination. Scattered amid the shopping malls, condominiums, and tourist traps is a beautiful landscape lined with hundreds of parks, golf courses, tennis courts, and, of course, beaches.

The City of Hallandale Beach is a small, peaceful oceanfront town located just north of Dade County's Aventura. Condos are the predominant landmarks in Hallandale, which is still pretty much a retirement community, although the revamped multimillion-dollar Westin Diplomat Resort is trying to revitalize and liven up the area. Just north of Hallandale is the more energetic, but not-yet-thriving Hollywood.

Like many other small American towns, South Florida's city of Hollywood has been working on redeveloping its downtown area for years. Once a sleepy community wedged between Fort Lauderdale and Miami, Hollywood is now a bustling area of 1.5 million people belonging to an array of ethnic and racial identities: from white and African American, to people of Jamaican, Chinese, and Dominican descent. (*Money* magazine trumpeted the self-described "City of the Future" as having an ethnic makeup that mirrors what America will look like by the year 2022.)

A spate of redevelopment has made the pedestrian-friendly center along Hollywood Boulevard and Harrison Street, east of Dixie Highway, a popular destination for travelers and locals alike. Some predict Hollywood will be South

Fort Lauderdale, Hollywood & Pompano Beach Area

Armadillo Cafe **28**
Banyan Marina Resort **20**
Bass Pro Shops Outdoor World **32**
Beach Place **15**
Blue Seas Courtyard **9**
Bonnet House **14**
Boomers **34**
Brasserie Las Olas **23**
Broward Mall **26**
Butterfly World **1**
Cap's Place Island Restaurant **2**
Courtyard Villa on the Ocean **10**
Creolina's **25**
Dania Jai Alai **33**
Darrel & Oliver's Cafe Maxx **3**
Dave & Busters **36**
Emerald Hills **35**
The Floridian Restaurant **21**
Fort Lauderdale Beach
    Promenade **13**
Fort Lauderdale Stadium **7**

Florida's next big destination—South Beach without the attitude, traffic jams, and parking nightmares. While the prediction is a dubious one, Hollywood is definitely awakening from its long slumber. Prices are a fraction of other tourist areas, and a quasi-bohemian vibe is apparent in the galleries, clubs, and restaurants that dot the new "strip." Its gritty undercurrent, however, prevents it from becoming too trendy.

Fort Lauderdale, and its well-known strip of beaches, restaurants, bars, and souvenir shops, has also undergone a major transformation. Once famous (or infamous) for the annual mayhem it hosted during Spring Break, this area is now attracting a more affluent, better-behaved yachting crowd.

In addition to beautiful wide beaches, the city, also known as the Venice of America, has more than 300 miles of navigable waterways and innumerable canals, which permit thousands of residents to anchor boats in their backyards. Boating is not just a hobby here; it's a lifestyle. Visitors can easily get on the water, too, by renting a boat or simply hailing a moderately priced water taxi.

Huge cruise ships also take advantage of Florida's deepest harbor, Port Everglades, whose name is somewhat misleading because it is not part of the Florida Everglades. The seaport is actually located on the southeastern coast of the Florida peninsula, near the Fort Lauderdale Hollywood International Airport on the outskirts of Hollywood and Dania Beach. Port Everglades is the second-busiest cruise-ship base in Florida after Miami and one of the top five in the world. For further information on cruises, see chapter 7, "What to See & Do in Miami," and consult *Frommer's Caribbean Cruises & Ports of Call.*

ESSENTIALS

GETTING THERE   If you're driving from Miami, it's a straight shot north to Hollywood or Fort Lauderdale. Visitors on their way to or from Orlando should take the Florida Turnpike to Exit 53, 54, 58, or 62, depending on the location of your accommodations.

The **Fort Lauderdale Hollywood International Airport** is small, easy to negotiate, and located just 15 minutes from both of the downtown areas it services.

Amtrak (© **800/USA-RAIL**) stations are at 200 SW 21st Terrace (Broward Boulevard and I-95), Fort Lauderdale (© **954/587-6692**), and 3001 Hollywood Blvd., Hollywood (© **954/921-4517**).

VISITOR INFORMATION   The **Greater Fort Lauderdale Convention & Visitors Bureau,** 1850 Eller Dr., Suite 303 (off I-95 and I-595 east), Fort Lauderdale, FL 33316 (© **954/765-4466;** fax 954/765-4467; www.sunny.org), is an excellent resource for area information in English, Spanish, and French. I highly recommend calling them in advance to request a free comprehensive guide covering events, accommodations, and sightseeing in Broward County. In addition, once you are in town, you can call an **information line** (© **954/527-5600**) to get easy-to-follow directions, travel advice, and assistance from multilingual operators who staff a round-the-clock help line. Also available for brochures, information, and vacation packages in Fort Lauderdale are operators at Greater Than Ever Fort Lauderdale (© **800/22-SUNNY**).

The **Greater Hollywood Chamber of Commerce,** 330 N. Federal Hwy. (on the corner of U.S. 1 and Taylor Street), Hollywood, FL 33020 (© **954/ 923-4000;** fax 954/923-8737), is open Monday through Friday from 8:30am to 5pm. Here you'll find the lowdown on all of Hollywood's events, attractions, restaurants, hotels, and tours.

BEACHES

The southern part of the Gold Coast, Broward County, has the region's most popular and amenities-laden beaches, which stretch for more than 23 miles. Most do not charge for access, though all are well maintained. Here's a selection of some of the county's best from south to north.

Hollywood Beach, stretching from Sheridan Street to Georgia Street, is a major attraction in the city of Hollywood, a virtual carnival with a motley assortment of young hipsters, big families, and sunburned tourists who dodge bicyclers and skaters along the rows of tacky souvenir shops, T-shirt shops, game rooms, snack bars, beer stands, hotels, and miniature golf courses. The 3-mile-long Hollywood Beach **Boardwalk,** modeled after Atlantic City's legendary boardwalk, is Hollywood's most popular beachfront pedestrian thoroughfare, a cement promenade that's 30 feet wide and stretches along the shoreline. Popular with runners, skaters, and cruisers, the boardwalk is also renowned as a hangout for thousands of retirement-age snowbirds who get together for frequent dances and shows at a faded outdoor amphitheater. Despite efforts to clear out a seedy element, the area remains a haven for drunks and scammers, so keep alert.

If you tire of the hectic diversity that defines Hollywood's boardwalk, enjoy the natural beauty of the beach itself, which is wide and clean. There are lifeguards, showers, bathroom facilities, and public areas for picnics and parties.

The **Fort Lauderdale Beach Promenade,** along the beach, underwent a $26 million renovation, and it looks fantastic. It's especially peaceful in the mornings when there's just a smattering of joggers and walkers, but even at its most crowded on the weekend, the expansive promenade provides room for everyone. Note, however, that the beach is hardly pristine; it is across the street from an uninterrupted stretch of hotels, bars, and retail outlets. Also nearby is a megaretail and dining complex, Beach Place, on Florida A1A, midway between Las Olas Boulevard and Sunrise Boulevard (see "Shopping & Browsing," later in this chapter for more information).

Just across the road, on the sand, most days you will find hard-core volleyballers, who welcome anyone with a good spike, and an inviting ocean welcoming swimmers of any level. The unusually clear waters are under the careful watch of some of Florida's best-looking lifeguards. Freshen up afterward in any of the clean showers and restrooms conveniently located along the strip. Pets have been banned from most of the beach in order to maintain the impressive cleanliness not commonly associated with such highly trafficked public beaches; a designated pet area exists away from the main sunbathing areas.

Especially on weekends, parking along the oceanside meters is nearly impossible to find. Try biking, skating, or hitching a ride on the water taxi instead. The strip is located on A1A, between SE 17th Street and Sunrise Boulevard.

Dania Beach's **John U. Lloyd Beach State Park,** 6503 N. Ocean Dr., Dania (© **954/923-2833**) is 251 acres of barrier island between the Atlantic Ocean and the Intracoastal Waterway, from Port Everglades on the north to Dania on the south. Its natural setting contrasts sharply with the urban development of Fort Lauderdale. Lloyd Beach, one of Broward County's most important nesting beaches for sea turtles, produces some 10,000 hatchlings a year. The park's broad, flat beach is popular for swimming and sunning. Self-guided nature trails are great for those who are too restless to sunbathe.

Turtle Trail

In June and July, the John U. Lloyd beach is crawling with nature lovers who come for the spectacular Sea Turtle Awareness Program. Park rangers begin the evening with a lecture and slide show while scouts search the beach for nesting loggerhead sea turtles. If a turtle is located—plenty of them usually are—a beach walk is conducted, where participants can see the turtles nesting and, sometimes, hatching their eggs. The program begins at 9pm. Call ℂ **954/923-2833** for reservations. Comfortable walking shoes and insect repellent are recommended. The park entrance fee of $2 to $4 per carload applies.

ACTIVE PURSUITS

BOATING   Often called the "yachting capital of the world," Fort Lauderdale provides ample opportunity for visitors to get out on the water, either along the Intracoastal Waterway or on the open ocean. If your hotel doesn't rent boats, try **Bill's Sunrise Watersports,** 2025 E. Sunrise Blvd., Fort Lauderdale (ℂ **954/ 462-8962**). They will outfit you with a variety of craft, including jet skis, WaveRunners, 13-foot Cigarette boats, 15-foot jet boats, and 8-foot power-boats, year-round. Bill's is open daily from 9am to 6pm. Rates start at $50 per half-hour for WaveRunners, $75 to $85 for boats (for 2 hr., with a 2-hr. minimum), and $65 for parasailing solo ($120 for a tandem flight). Parasailing lasts about 1 hour and 15 minutes, with four flights a day taking off.

CRUISES   The **Jungle Queen,** 801 Sea Breeze Blvd. (3 blocks south of Las Olas Boulevard on A1A), in the Bahia Mar Yacht Center, Fort Lauderdale (ℂ **954/462-5596**), a Mississippi River–style steamer, is one of Fort Lauderdale's best-known attractions, cruising up and down the New River. All-you-can-eat dinner cruises and 3-hour sightseeing tours take visitors past Millionaires' Row, Old Fort Lauderdale, and the new downtown. Cruises depart nightly at 7pm and cost $29 for adults and $15 for children 12 and under. Sightseeing tours are scheduled daily at 10am and 2pm and cost $13.75 for adults and $8.75 for children 10 and under.

If you're interested in gambling, several casino boat companies operate day cruises out of Port Everglades and offer blackjack, slots, and poker. **Discovery Cruise Lines** (ℂ **800/937-4477**) has daily cruises to the Bahamas, where you can gamble, eat, and party for 5 to 6 hours (you have about 3 hr. in the Bahamas to go to the straw market or to do even more gambling) for about $120. The price includes breakfast, lunch, and dinner, but drinks cost extra.

Sea Escape (ℂ **800/327-2005** or 954/453-3333) also launches daily casino cruises 13 times a week. But these don't travel more than a few miles offshore. These trips "to nowhere" depart from Monday to Thursday from 11am to 4:30pm and 7:30pm to 12:30am. The party cruises offer buffet meals and full casinos for $30 to $40 a person. I'd recommend spending an additional $20 for a cabin (do not expect *Love Boat* luxe here), so you can stretch out and relax in between hands. Even though the cruises don't go far from the coast, 5 or 6 hours is a long time to spend at sea, especially if the weather is rough. Evening cruises, which return at 1:30am on weekends, cost $48 and offer full buffet dinners and a Las Vegas–style show. Port charges are included, although you must pay a $3 departure tax and $2.65 passenger charge. This is one of the best deals you'll find. Sea Escape also has a new 2- and 3-night cruise option, where visitors can go to Nassau, the Bahamas, for as little as $199 per person with all meals included.

FISHING Completed in 1999 at a cost of more than $32 million, the **IGFA (International Game Fish Association) World Fishing Center** at 300 Gulf Stream Way (© 954/922-4212) in Dania Beach is an angler's paradise. One of the highlights of this museum, library, and park is the virtual-reality fishing simulator, which allows visitors to actually reel in their own computer-generated catch. Also included in the 3-acre park are displays of antique fishing gear, record catches, famous anglers, various vessels, and a wetlands lab. To get a list of local captains and guides, call **IGFA headquarters** (© 954/927-2628) and ask for the librarian. Admission is $5 for adults, $4 for children between 3 and 12, and free for children under 3. On the grounds is also **Bass Pro Shops Outdoor World,** a huge multifloor retail complex situated on a 3-acre lake.

GAME PARKS **Boomers,** at 1801 NW 1st St., east of I-95 between the Griffin and Sterling road exits, in Dania, is good for kids during the day—at night, the park attracts a rowdy bunch of teenagers. The newest addition to the park is a wooden roller coaster (the thrills are high, but the lines are long). With a massive 24-hour video arcade, five challenging miniature-golf greens, go-carts and NASCAR racing, batting cages, and a huge sky coaster, this place provides exhaustive entertainment. Call for prices and hours (© 954/921-1411).

For adults who love video games but can't deal with hordes of kids, there's **Dave & Busters** at 3000 Oakwood Blvd. in Hollywood, just off the Sheridan Street exit of I-95 (© 954/923-5505). This complex is basically an adult Chuck E. Cheese's—it features tons of video games, a full bar and sit-down restaurant, as well as a more casual spot with table service. On weekends Dave & Busters is packed with young adults on dates and rowdy groups of guys of all ages. An admission of $3 is charged only on Friday and Saturday after 10pm. D&B's opens weekdays at 11am and weekends at 11:30am and usually closes by 1am.

GameWorks, the mega-arcade of Hollywood movie mogul Steven Spielberg, is located in the Sawgrass Mills outlet center (see p. 320) and features a high-tech

---

Kids Wild Things

Deerfield Island Park (on the ocean, 2 miles south of the Palm Beaches), surrounded by the Intracoastal Waterway and two canals, is accessible only by boat. The heavily wooded 56-acre site includes an 8½-acre mangrove swamp and is home to the gopher tortoise. The park also serves as a nesting place for squirrels, raccoons, and armadillos. Visitors can hike the park's two main trails. The park is good for kids, because it's an urban wilderness with a rustic Tom Sawyer–esque adventure feel. Picnic areas with grills and tables are available on a first-come, first-serve basis, and there is also a small playground. A free boat shuttle transports visitors to the island hourly, but book early as the shuttle fills up quickly. Call for times and reservations. The shuttle takes off from the Sullivan Park boat dock. To get there from I-95, head east on Hillsboro Boulevard past Federal Highway and then north (left) on Riverview Road to the park. 1720 Deerfield Island Park, Deerfield Beach, © 954/360-1320. Open Wednesday to Sunday from 9am to 5pm.

Remnants of the Past

Any diving outfit in Jupiter beach will take you to the spot where the remnants of a shipwreck from a 16th- or 17th-century Spanish galleon lie. Discovered in 1988 by Jupiter lifeguard Peter Leo, who on his morning swim came across an anchor and a cannon, the wreck has since produced 10 more cannons and over 10,000 gold and silver coins. However, should you come across more coins, you won't be able to throw them in your piggy bank—Leo owns the mining rights to the wreck. This is a more historic dive than the Mercedes, since it's an actual wreck and not one that was intentionally submerged for divers.

playground with video games that appeal to adults and kids, from virtual reality to arcade standards to interactive games, plus a restaurant and full bar.

GOLF More than 50 golf courses in all price ranges compete for players. Some of the best include **Emerald Hills** at 4100 North Hills Dr., Hollywood, just west of I-95 between Sterling Road and Sheridan Street. This beauty consistently lands on the "best of" lists of golf writers throughout the country. The 18th hole, on a two-tier green, is the challenging course's signature; it's surrounded by water and is more than a bit rough. The course is pricey—greens fees start at $75. Call © **954/961-4000** for tee times. For one of Broward's best municipal challenges, try the 18-holer at the **Orangebrook Golf Course** at 400 Entrada Dr. in Hollywood (© **954/967-GOLF**). Built in 1937, this is one of the state's oldest courses and one of the area's best bargains. Morning and noon rates range from $21 to $33. After 2pm, you can play for less than $20, including a cart. Men must wear collared shirts to play here, and no spikes are allowed.

SCUBA DIVING In Broward County, the best wreck dive is the *Mercedes I,* a 197-foot freighter that washed up in the backyard of a Palm Beach socialite in 1984 and was sunk for divers the following year off Pompano Beach. The artificial reef, filled with colorful sponges, spiny lobsters, and barracudas, is located 97 feet below the surface, a mile offshore between Oakland Park Boulevard and Sunrise Boulevard. Dozens of reputable dive shops line the beach. Ask at your hotel for a nearby recommendation or contact **Lauderdale Undersea Adventures,** 1525 S. Andrews Ave., Fort Lauderdale (© **954/462-3400**).

SPECTATOR SPORTS Baseball fans can get their fix at the **Fort Lauderdale Stadium,** 5301 NW 12th Ave. (© **954/938-4980**), where the Baltimore Orioles play spring training exhibition games starting in early March; call © **954/776-1921** for tickets. General admission is $6, a spot in the grandstand $9, kids 14 and under $3, and box seats $12. During the season, the Florida Marlins play just south of Hallandale at the **Pro Player Stadium** near the Dade–Broward County line. Call Ticketmaster for tickets (© **305/358-5885**), which range from $4 to $50. Tickets go on sale in January.

Pompano Park Racing, 1800 SW 3rd St., Pompano Beach (© **954/972-2000**), features parimutuel harness racing from October to early August. Grandstand admission is free; clubhouse admission is $2.

Jai alai, a sort of Spanish-style indoor lacrosse, was introduced to Florida in 1924 and still draws big crowds who bet on the fast-paced action. Broward's only fronton, **Dania Jai Alai,** 301 E. Dania Beach Blvd. at the intersection of A1A and U.S. 1 (© **954/920-1511** or 954/426-4330), is a great place to spend an afternoon or evening.

Wrapped around an artificial lake, **Gulfstream Park,** at U.S. 1 and Hallandale Beach Boulevard, Hallandale (© **954/454-7000**), is pretty and popular. Large purses and important horse races are commonplace at this recently refurbished suburban course, and the track is often crowded. It hosts the Florida Derby each March. Call for schedules. Admission is $3 to the grandstand, and $5 to the clubhouse. Parking is free. From January 3 to March 15, post times are Wednesday to Monday at 1pm, and the doors open at 11am. Many weekends feature live concerts by well-known musicians.

In the sport of ice hockey, the young Florida Panthers (© **954/835-7000**) have already made history. In the 1994–95 season, they played in the Stanley Cup finals, and the fans love them. They play in Sunrise at the **National Car Rental Center** at 2555 NW 137th Way. Tickets range from $14 to $100. Call for directions and ticket information.

TENNIS   There are hundreds of courts in Broward County, and plenty are accessible to the public. Many are at resorts and hotels. If not at yours, try one of these. Famous as the spot where Chris Evert got in her early serves, the **Jimmy Evert Tennis Center,** 701 NE 12th Ave. (off Sunrise Boulevard), Fort Lauderdale (© **954/828-5378**), has 18 clay and 3 hard courts (15 lighted). Her coach and father, James Evert, still teaches young players here, though he is very picky about whom he'll accept. Nonresidents of Fort Lauderdale pay $3.50 (singles) to $4.50 (doubles) per hour. Reservations are accepted after 2pm for the following day but cost an extra $3. Lights are also an extra $3 per hour and are available only for the clay courts. At the **Marina Bay Resort,** 2175 S.R. 84, west of I-95 in Fort Lauderdale (© **954/791-7600**), visitors can play for free on one of nine hard courts on a first-come, first-served basis. Three are lighted at night.

SEEING THE SIGHTS

Museum of Discovery & Science ⚛⚛ *(Kids*   This museum's high-tech, interactive approach to education proves that science can equal fun. Adults won't feel as if they're in a kiddie museum, either. During the week, school groups meander through the cavernous two-story modern building. Kids 7 and under enjoy navigating their way through the excellent explorations in the "Discovery Center." Florida Ecoscapes is particularly interesting, with a living coral reef, bees, bats, frogs, turtles, and alligators. Most weekend nights, you'll find a diverse crowd ranging from hip high-school kids to 30-somethings enjoying a rock film in the IMAX 3-D theater, which also shows short, science-related, supersize films daily. Out front, see the 52-foot-tall Great Gravity Clock, located in the museum's atrium, the largest kinetic-energy sculpture in the state. Call for changing exhibits.

401 SW 2nd St., Fort Lauderdale. © 954/467-6637. www.mods.org. Museum admission (includes admission to 1 IMAX film) $13 adults, $12 seniors, $11 children 3–12. Mon–Sat 10am–5pm, Sun noon–6pm. Movie theaters stay open later. From I-95, exit on Broward Blvd. E. Continue to SW 5th Ave.; turn right, garage on right.

Billie Swamp Safari ⚛ *(Kids*   Billie Swamp Safari is an up-close and personal view of the Seminole Indians' 2,200-acre Big Cypress Reservation. There are daily tours into reservation wetlands, hardwood hammocks, and areas where wildlife (seemingly strategically placed deer, water buffalo, bison, wild hogs, ornery ostriches, rare birds, and alligators) reside. Tours are provided aboard swamp buggies, customized motorized vehicles specially designed to provide visitors with an elevated view of the frontier while comfortably riding through the wetlands and cypress heads. For the more adventurous, you may want to take a fast-moving airboat ride or trek through a nature trail. Airboat rides run about

One If by Land, Taxi If by Sea

Plan to spend at least an afternoon or evening cruising Fort Lauderdale's 300 miles of waterways in the only way you can: by boat. The **Water Taxi of Fort Lauderdale (℃ 954/467-6677)** is one of the greatest innovations for water lovers since those cool Velcro sandals. A trusty fleet of older port boats serves the dual purpose of transporting and entertaining visitors as they cruise through "the Venice of America."

Taxis operate on demand and also along a fairly regular route, carrying up to 48 passengers. If you stay at a hotel on the route, you can be picked up at your hotel, usually within 15 minutes of calling, and then be shuttled to any of the dozens of restaurants, bars, and attractions on or near the waterfront. If you aren't sure where you want to go, ask one of the personable captains, who can point out historic and fun spots along the way.

For a day cruise with the kids, make a stop at the Museum of Discovery & Science, where you can catch an IMAX film or just enjoy the current educational exhibits. Then, if you are up for a walk, head across the 3-mile-long Riverwalk, a scenic palm-lined walkway along the New River where you can enjoy your picnic lunch; or try one of the restaurants dotting the way to Las Olas Boulevard and the Las Olas Riverfront. When you are ready for some shopping or a sit-down meal, reboard and head to Beach Place at Las Olas Boulevard and Cortez Street in the heart of Fort Lauderdale's most famous strip. Stop for refreshments at Casablanca Café, (3049 Alhambra St., ℃ 954/764-3500), an oceanfront American restaurant located in a beautiful historic home.

In the evening, the water taxi is ideal for bar-hopping—no worrying about parking or choosing a designated driver. Make your first stop at Shooters, where professionals, boaters, and tourists share the large lively patio for a popular happy hour from 5 to 7pm on weekdays. Right next door is Bootlegger's, featuring more than 70 beers at an outside bar. Later debark at O'Hara's, in the downtown section of Las Olas Boulevard (see "The Hollywood & Fort Lauderdale Area After Dark" section later in this chapter), where you'll hear a great mix of live jazz and blues.

Starting daily from 10am, boats usually run until midnight and until 2am on weekends, depending on the weather. The cost is $7.50 per person per trip, $14 round-trip, and $16 for a full day. Children under 12 ride for half-price and free on Sundays. Opt for the all-day pass; it's worth it.

20 minutes and are $8 less than the 1-hour long Swamp Buggy tours. A stop at an alligator farm reeks of Disney, but kids won't care. You can also stay overnight in a native tiki hut if you're really looking to immerse yourself in the culture.

Big Cypress Reservation, 1½-hr. drive west of Fort Lauderdale. ℃ 800/949-6101. Free admission. Boat tours $10–$20. Daily 8am–8pm. Airboats depart every 30 min.; last ride at 4:30pm.

Bonnet House 𝒜𝒜𝒜   This historic 35-acre plantation home and estate, accessible by guided tour only, will provide you with a fantastic glimpse of old South Florida. Built in 1921, the sprawling two-story waterfront home (surrounded with formal tropical gardens) is really the backdrop of a love story, which the very chatty volunteer guides will share with you if you ask. Some have actually lunched with the former resident of the house, the late Evelyn Bartlett, the wife of world-acclaimed artist Frederic Clay Bartlett. The worthwhile 1¼-hour tour brings you quirky people, whimsical artwork, lush grounds, and interesting design. Inquire about the literary walks and science workshops, which are offered regularly on the grounds.

900 N. Birch Rd. (1 block west of the ocean, south of Sunrise Blvd.), Fort Lauderdale. ℂ 954/563-5393. www.bonnethouse.org. Admission $9 adults, $8 seniors, $7 students under 18, free for children 6 and under. Tours Wed–Fri 10am–1:30pm, Sat–Sun 12:30pm–2:30pm.

Butterfly World *Kids*   One of the world's largest butterfly breeders, Butterfly World cultivates more than 150 species of these colorful and delicate insects. In the park's walk-through, screened-in laboratory, visitors can see thousands of caterpillars and watch newborn butterflies emerge from their cocoons and flutter around as they learn to fly. There's also a new, separate aviary dedicated to lorikeets (the "clowns" of the bird world, because they are quite animated and very colorful), which offers visitors the opportunity to hand-feed the birds.

Tradewinds Park S., 3600 W. Sample Rd., Coconut Creek (west of the Florida Tpk.). ℂ **954/977-4400.** www. butterflyworld.com. Admission $13.95 adults, $8.95 children 4–12, free for children 3 and under. Mon–Sat 9am–5pm, Sun 1–5pm; last admission at 4pm. Directions: From I-95, exit at Sample Road and head west until you reach Tradewinds Park on the south side of Sample Road. Enter the park and the butterfly house is inside, straight ahead, about a third of a mile.

International Swimming Hall of Fame and Aquatic Complex ★   Olympic diver Greg Louganis dove here, and you will want to take your best Olympic plunge, too, when you see the two very inviting 10-lane, 50-meter pools. Fortunately you can, for just $3, so bring your bathing suit. For inspiration, take in a swim flick (featuring Esther Williams and other aquatic stars) at the complex's theater or visit the comprehensive exhibition of medals, photos, and other memorabilia of swimming contests past.

1 Hall of Fame Dr., Fort Lauderdale. ℂ **954/462-6536** or 954/828-4580 for the pool. $3 for museum, $3 for pool. Family rate $5. Museum open daily from 9am–7pm. Pool open daily 8am–4pm; closed late December to mid-January.

Stranahan House ★★★   In a town whose history is younger than many of its residents, visitors may want to take a minute to see Fort Lauderdale's very oldest standing structure and a prime example of classic Florida Frontier architecture. Built in 1901 by the "father of Fort Lauderdale," Frank Stranahan, this house once served as a trading post for Seminole trappers who came here to sell pelts. It's been a post office, town hall, and general store, and now is a worthwhile little museum of South Florida pioneer life, containing turn-of-the-last-century furnishings and historical photos of the area. It is also the site of occasional concerts and social functions. Call for details.

335 SE 6th Ave. (Las Olas Blvd. at the New River Tunnel), Fort Lauderdale. ℂ **954/524-4736.** www. stranahanhouse.com. Admission $5 adults, $3 students and children. Wed–Sat 10am–4pm, Sun 1–4pm. Tours are on the hour; last tour at 3pm. Accessible by water taxi.

SHOPPING & BROWSING

It's all about malls in Broward County. And while most of the best shopping is located within Fort Lauderdale proper, there are other areas in the county also worth browsing.

Dania is known as the Antique Capital of the South because within 1 square mile of Federal Highway, the city has over a hundred dealers selling everything from small collectibles to fine antiques. **R. Cook & Co.,** 44 N. Federal Hwy. (© **954/922-1118**), for instance, deals in vintage Louis Vuitton, plus exotic skins once owned by Ernest Hemingway (who was an avid sportsman and hunter) and antique scientific instruments, among other things. **Louis Kleinman Collectibles,** 60 N. Federal Hwy. (© **954/920-2801**), boasts a large collection of china, including Limoges porcelain pillboxes. **Iris Fields of Dania,** 60 N. Federal Hwy. (© **954/926-5658**), features a fabulous collection of antique perfume bottles. **Daddy's Inc.,** 19 N. Federal Hwy. (© **954/920-4001**) has a huge selection of Tiffany lamps, furniture, watercolors, silver, and gold.

For bargain mavens, there's a strip of "fashion" stores on Hallandale Beach Boulevard's "Schmatta Row," east of Dixie Highway and the railroad tracks, where off-brand shoes, bags, and jewelry are sold at deep discounts. Hollywood Boulevard also offers some interesting shops with everything from Indonesian artifacts to used and rare books, leather bustiers, and handmade hats. Dozens of shops line the pedestrian-friendly strip just west of Young Circle. The art galleries are clustered along Harrison Street, just east of Dixie Highway.

The area's only beachfront mall, **Beach Place,** is in Fort Lauderdale on A1A just north of Las Olas Boulevard. The recipient of a $1.6 million face-lift in 2001, this 100,000-square-foot giant sports the usual chains like Sunglass Hut, Limited Express, Banana Republic, and Gap, as well as lots of popular bars and restaurants. While it used to be all the rage with the Spring Break set, Beach Place is now aiming for a much more upscale clientele, adding many new higher-end stores and restaurants.

Other more traditional malls include the upscale **Galleria,** at Sunrise Boulevard near the Fort Lauderdale Beach, and **Broward Mall,** west of I-95 on Broward Boulevard, in Plantation.

If you are looking for unusual boutiques, especially art galleries, head to trendy Las Olas Boulevard ⊛ (located west of A1A and a block east of Federal Highway/U.S. 1, off of SE 8th St.), where there are hundreds of shops with alluring window decorations (like kitchen utensils posing as modern-art sculptures) and intriguing merchandise such as mural-size oil paintings.

On the edge of the Arts and Science District is **Las Olas Riverfront,** a retail complex with 260,000 square feet of restaurants, clothing stores, arcades, and a multiplex movie theater.

Lord & Taylor has a little-known clearance center where discounts on new clothing for women, kids, and men can be as much as 75%. If you can handle open dressing rooms, overstuffed racks, and surly sales help, the Lord & Taylor Clearance Center is a great find at 6820 N. University Dr. in Tamarac. You may want to call © **954/720-1915** to find out about special events, when prices are lowered even further.

The Fort Lauderdale Swap Shop, 3291 W. Sunrise Blvd. (© **954/791-SWAP**), is one of the world's largest flea markets. I think it's rather schlocky, actually. In addition to endless acres of vendors hawking everything from electronics to underwear, there's a miniature amusement park, a 13-screen drive-in movie theater, weekend concerts, and even a free daily circus complete with elephants, horse shows, high-wire acts, and clowns.

The monster of all outlet malls is **Sawgrass Mills,** 12801 W. Sunrise Blvd., Sunrise (© **800-FL-MILLS** or 954/846-2350; fax 954/846-2312). Since the most recent expansion, completed in mid-1999 and adding more than 30 new designer outlet stores, this behemoth (shaped like a Florida alligator) now holds more than 300 shops, kiosks, a 24-screen movie theater, and many restaurants and bars, including a Hard Rock Cafe. Make sure you note which section you parked in, as it is nearly impossible to locate your car in the equally mammoth, labyrinthine parking lot. The enclosed area covers nearly 2.5 million square feet over 50 acres—there's no way to see it all in a day. Wear your most comfortable shoes, or buy an extra pair while you're there! Stores include Donna Karan Company Store, Levi's Outlet, Sunglass Hut, Ann Taylor Loft, and Barney's New York, all selling goods at between 20% and 80% below retail. Label-conscious shoppers are especially impressed with Off Fifth, the Saks Fifth Avenue outlet store, and Last Call, the Neiman-Marcus clearance center. You may want to invest in a coupon booklet ($5), which entitles you to even greater discounts at many of the mall's stores and restaurants as well as area attractions. A booklet is good for up to a year and can be turned in for an updated booklet at no charge. To get there, take I-95 to I-595 west to the Flamingo Road exit, turn right, and drive 2 miles to Sunrise Boulevard; you will see the large complex on the left. From the Florida Turnpike, exit Sunrise Boulevard west.

Fishing enthusiasts won't want to miss **Bass Pro Shops Outdoor World** (200 Gulfstream Way, Dania Beach; ℂ **954/929-7710**), a sprawling retail complex just west of I-95, where you can buy anything from yachts to lures.

WHERE TO STAY

The Fort Lauderdale beach has a hotel or motel on nearly every block, and they range from the run-down to the luxurious. Both the **Howard Johnson** (ℂ **800/327-8578** or 954/563-2451), at 700 N. Atlantic Blvd. (on A1A, south of Sunrise Boulevard), and the **Days Inn** (ℂ **800/329-7466** or 954/462-0444), at 435 N. Atlantic Blvd. (A1A), offer clean oceanside rooms starting at about $150.

In Hollywood, where prices are generally cheaper, the **Holiday Inn** at 101 N. Ocean Blvd. (ℂ **954/921-0990**) operates a full-service hotel right on the ocean. With prices starting at around $110 in season and discounts for AAA members, it's a great deal. **Howard Johnson** (ℂ **800/423-9867** or 954/925-1411) has a good location right on the beach at 2501 N. Ocean Dr. (I-95 to Sheridan Street east to A1A south).

Extended Stay America/Crossland Economy Studios (ℂ **800/398-7829**) has four superclean properties in Fort Lauderdale and offers year-round rates as low as $49 a night and $159 per week. The studios are designed with business travelers in mind. Each includes free local calls, a dataport, a kitchenette, a recliner, and a well-lit desk.

Especially for rentals for a few weeks or months, call **Florida Sunbreak** (ℂ **800-SUNBREAK**). Or call the **South Florida Hotel Network** (ℂ **800/538-3616**) for help in finding small inns and lodges in any price range. Also, check out the annual list of small lodgings compiled by the **Greater Fort Lauderdale Convention & Visitors Bureau** (ℂ **954/765-4466**). It is especially helpful for those looking for privately owned, charming, and affordable lodgings.

VERY EXPENSIVE

Hyatt Regency Pier Sixty-Six ★★ Located on 22 tropical acres on the Intracoastal Waterway, this resort is best known for its world-class marina and its rooftop lounge that spins every 66 minutes. If you experience vertigo after sitting in the revolving lounge, an invigorating body or skincare treatment at the hotel's intimate, private, exquisite European Spa LXVI will help relocate your sense of balance. Equally invigorating are the hotel's recreational amenities, which include a sprawling three-pool complex with a 40-person hydrotherapy pool, tennis courts, and an aquatic center complete with every watersport imaginable. The hotel's California Cafe is a popular, eclectic eatery. After a recent renovation, the tropical-style rooms are spruced up with cherry-wood furnishings and bathrooms with marble floors and granite vanities. All rooms have balconies with views of the Intracoastal and the hotel's lushly landscaped gardens. Suites come with Jacuzzi, wet bar, living room, dining room, and exceptional views.

2301 SE 17th St. Causeway, Fort Lauderdale, FL 33316. ℭ **800/233-1234** or 954/525-6666. Fax 954/728-3541. www.hyatt.com. 380 units. Winter $289 double. Off-season $229 double. Year-round from $1,000 suite. AE, DC, DISC, MC, V. Valet parking $10; self-parking $8 a day. **Amenities:** 3 restaurants, 3 bars; 2 swimming pools; 2 lighted clay tennis courts; spa; watersports equipment rental; bike rental; children's center/programs; concierge; tour desk; courtesy car; business center; shopping arcade; salon; 24-hr. room service; babysitting; dry-cleaning and laundry services; self-service laundry. *In room:* A/C, TV, dataport, minibar, coffeemaker, hair dryer.

Marriott's Harbor Beach 🏵🏵🏵   This resort is loaded with the same amenities as Pier Sixty-Six but with a more secluded setting, located on 16 oceanfront acres just south of Fort Lauderdale's strip. Everything in this place is huge—from the guest rooms and suites to the 8,000-square-foot swimming pool to the $8 million 24,000-square-foot European spa. A huge 1999 renovation added a bit more personality to the formerly stale guest rooms and suites. Accommodations now feature marble, deep crown molding, and all-new bathrooms with granite vanities, Italian marble flooring, and wrap-around mirrors. A revamped lobby affords sweeping ocean views. All rooms open onto private balconies overlooking either the ocean or the Intracoastal Waterway. The hotel's 3030 Ocean is an excellent seafood restaurant and raw bar; Riva, a Mediterranean-style, oceanfront eatery, is also top-notch. Return guests include many convention groups and families who enjoy the space and the great location off the beaten strip.

3030 Holiday Dr., Fort Lauderdale, FL 33316. ℭ **800/222-6543** or 954/525-4000. Fax 954/766-6193. www.marriottharborbeach.com. 659 units. Winter $259–$429 double. Off-season $99–$279 double. Year-round from $600 suite. AE, DC, DISC, MC, V. Valet parking $10. From I-95, exit on I-595 east to U.S. 1 N.; proceed to SE 17th St.; make a right and go over the Intracoastal bridge past 3 traffic lights to Holiday Dr.; turn right. **Amenities:** 4 restaurants, 2 bars; outdoor heated pool; 5 clay tennis courts; health club; European-style spa; extensive watersports equipment; bike rental; children's center and programs; game room; concierge; tour desk; courtesy car; business center; salon, 24-hr. room service; in-room massage; babysitting; laundry services and self-service laundry. *In room:* A/C, TV, dataport, minibar, coffeemaker, hair dryer.

The Westin Diplomat Resort & Spa 🏵   In its day, the Hollywood Diplomat was a swanky affair, an oceanfront playground attending to a host of celebs that included Sinatra and co. The new Diplomat, which opened in February of 2002, was built on the site of the original to the tune of $600 million.

This is a 1,060-room full-service beach resort that's loaded with amenities. The hotel's main building is a 39-story oceanfront tower surrounded by 8 acres of man-made lakes. A gorgeous bridged, glass-bottomed swimming pool with cascading waterfalls, private cabanas, and a slew of watersports and activities adds a tropical touch. Rooms are a cross between a subtle boutique hotel and an Art Deco throwback, with dark woods, hand-cut marble and, most impressive, the 10-layer Heavenly Bed, a Westin trademark with custom designed pillow top mattresses and a very cushy down blanket (crank up the A/C!). Dining options are resortlike in quantity and quality. A fine-dining steakhouse is very elegant looking, and several more casual options are available. A South Beach–style nightclub is also on site—convenient, considering there is no nightlife in the surrounding area unless you go north to downtown Hollywood or south to South Beach. At press time, construction on the hotel's shopping and entertainment complex across the street was still ongoing.

The Diplomat's Country Club and Spa opened in March 2000 and is modeled after an Italian villa, with 60 luxurious guest rooms, yacht slips, a 155-acre golf course, and a world-class spa and tennis club. The 30,000-square-foot spa has 17 treatment rooms, spa pool, spa menu, and an extensive selection of treatments.

Although the hotel is attached to a newly built, massive convention center, the Diplomat is so mammoth that you may never come into contact with the name-tagged conventioneers sharing the hotel with you.

3555 S. Ocean Dr. (A1A), Hollywood, FL 33019. ℭ **800/327-1212** or 954/457-2000. www.diplomatresort. com. 1,060 units. Winter $285–$370; off-season $195–$315. AE, DC, DISC, MC, V. Valet parking $16. **Amenities:** 8 restaurants; 3 lounges; 2 pools; golf course; 10 clay tennis courts; health club and spa; watersports equipment rental. *In room:* A/C, TV/Web TV, fax, dataport, minibar, coffeemaker, hair dryer.

Wyndham Resort and Spa ☽

This resort couldn't be any more remote, not to mention a long way from any water or beaches; but if you're looking for a purely spa and/or golf vacation—for which there are many packages available—it's not a bad choice. Located in an unoriginal planned community known as Weston, the resort is located on a man-made lake and golf course. Rooms are spacious and bathrooms are huge, all overlooking the lake or golf course.

250 Racquet Club Rd., Fort Lauderdale, FL 33326. ℭ **800/996-3426** or 954/389-3300. Fax 954/384-6878. www.wyndham.com. 496 units. Winter from $209–$289; off-season $134–$249. Golf and spa packages (with or without meals) $265–$305 per person based on double occupancy. AE, DC, DISC, MC, V. Valet parking $8. From I-95, exit at I-595, driving west to 136th Ave., S.R. 84; turn left to Bonaventure Blvd. Make a right to Racquet Club Rd. From W. I-75, exit 12 (Arvida Parkway), continue west to Weston Blvd.; turn right and proceed to Saddle Club Rd. Turn left to Bonaventure Blvd.; make a right to Racquet Club Rd. **Amenities:** 4 restaurants (nutritionist services available), 2 bars; 5 swimming pools; 2 championship golf courses; 15 lighted tennis courts; spa; Jacuzzi; sauna; children's programs; concierge; tour desk; business center; 24-hr. room service; in-room massage; dry-cleaning and laundry services; courtesy car. *In room:* A/C, TV, dataport, kitchenette in some suites, minibar, coffeemaker, hair dryer.

EXPENSIVE

Lago Mar Resort and Club ☽☽☽ *Kids*

A charming lobby with a rock fireplace and saltwater aquarium sets the tone of this utterly inviting resort, a casually elegant piece of Old Florida that occupies its own little island between Lake Mayan and the Atlantic. Lago Mar guests have access to the broadest and best strip of beach in the entire city, not to mention the wonderful bougainvillea-lined, 9,000-square-foot swimming lagoon. Lago Mar is very family oriented, with lots of facilities and supervised activities for children, especially during Spring Break and Christmas vacations. Service is spectacular. The rooms and suites have Mediterranean or Key West influences and are well appointed—but it's likely you won't be spending much time inside. As of January 2002, a full-service spa will offer a wide array of pampering treatments, steam rooms, and a 1,000-square-foot exercise facility may come in handy after you indulge in the hotel's Northern Italian restaurant, Acquario, worth a visit even if you don't stay here.

1700 S. Ocean Lane, Fort Lauderdale, FL 33316. ℭ **800/524-6627** or 954/523-6511. Fax 954/524-6627. www.lagomar.com. 212 units. Winter $195 double; from $295 suite. Off-season $100–$135 double; from $135 suite. AE, DC, MC, V. Free valet parking. From Federal Hwy. (U.S. 1), turn east onto SE 17th St. Causeway; turn right onto Mayan Dr.; turn right again onto S. Ocean Dr.; turn left onto Grace Dr.; then left again onto S. Ocean Lane to the hotel. **Amenities:** 4 restaurants, cocktail lounge, wine room; outdoor pool and lagoon; 2 tennis courts; exercise room; watersports equipment rental, children's programs during holiday periods, game room, concierge; tour desk; business center; 24-hr. room service; dry-cleaning and laundry services. *In room:* A/C, TV, dataport, hair dryer; kitchenette, coffeemaker in some units.

Pillars Hotel ☽☽☽ *Finds*

It took me a while to discover this hotel and, apparently, that's exactly the point. One of Fort Lauderdale's best-kept secrets, if not the best, Pillars Hotel transports you from the neon-hued flash and splash of Fort Lauderdale's strip and takes you to a two-story British Colonial, Caribbean-style retreat tucked away on the bustling Intracoastal Waterway. With just 23 rooms, you feel as if you have the grand house all to yourself, albeit with white-tablecloth room service, an Eden-istic courtyard with free-form pool, lush land-scaping, access to a water taxi, and signing privileges at nearby restaurants and spa. Rooms are luxurious and loaded with amenities such as private-label bath products, ultraplush bedding and, if you're so inclined, a private masseuse to iron out your personal kinks. Upon arrival, you will be greeted with a welcome cocktail, and there's always free iced tea at the pool in case you're thirsty. A library area, with grand piano and over 500 books and videos, is at your dis-posal, as is pretty much anything you request here. The quintessential Fort Lauderdale retreat, the Pillars is the zenith of Fort Lauderdale accommodations. There are four suites, and all rooms are nonsmoking.

111 N. Birch Road, Fort Lauderdale, FL 33304 (✆ **954/467-9639.** Fax 954/763-2845. www.pillarshotel.com. 23 units. Winter $189–$259 double; $279–$389 suite. Off-season $119–$199 double; $189[nd[$349 suite. AE, MC, DC, DISC, V. Complementary off-street parking. **Amenities:** Waterfront pool; sun deck; 24-hr. concierge; 24-hr. room service; signing privileges at Max's Beach Place restaurant; water-taxi service; pre-ferred rates at beachfront and downtown health clubs; business services; in-room massage; same-day laun-dry service. *In room:* AC, TV/VCR, dataport, minibar, hair dryer, iron, safe.

Riverside Hotel 🎔🎔 A touch of New Orleans hits Fort Lauderdale's popular Las Olas Boulevard in the form of this charming, six-story 1936 hotel. There's no beach here, but the hotel is located on the sleepy and scenic New River, cap-turing the essence of that ever-elusive Old Florida. Guest rooms are a bit nicer than the public areas (outfitted in Mexican tile and wicker furnishings) and are spacious and well maintained. Details like intricately tiled bathrooms and old-style furniture enhance the charm of the otherwise stark building. The best rooms face the New River, but it's hard to see the water past the parking lot and trees. Twelve rooms offer king-size beds with mirrored canopies and flowing drapes. There are also seven elegantly decorated suites with wet bars and French doors that lead to private balconies. The hotel has two restaurants worth trying: Indigo, a fantastic Asian/Indonesian restaurant in the hotel lobby (see "Where to Dine," below), and the Grill Room, for Old World elegance.

620 E. Las Olas Blvd., Fort Lauderdale, FL 33301. (✆ **800/325-3280** or 954/467-0671. Fax 954/462-2148. www.riversidehotel.com. 217 units. Winter $179–$369 suite. Off-season $124–$339 suite. Special packages are available; discount for online bookings. AE, DC, MC, V. Valet parking $8–$10. From I-95, exit onto Broward Blvd.; turn right onto Federal Hwy. (U.S. 1), then left onto Las Olas Blvd. **Amenities:** 2 restaurants; outdoor pool; concierge; secretarial services; limited room service; babysitting; dry-cleaning and laundry services. *In room:* A/C, TV, dataport, minibar, fridge, coffeemaker, hair dryer, iron.

MODERATE

Banyan Marina Resort 🎔🎔 These fabulous waterfront apartments, located on a beautifully landscaped residential island, may have you vowing never to stay in a hotel again. They're intimate, charming, *and* reasonably priced. Built around a stunning 75-year-old banyan tree, the Banyan Marina Resort is located directly on the active canals halfway between Fort Lauderdale's downtown and the beach. When available, you'll choose between one- and two-bedroom apart-ments, which have been recently renovated. All are comfortable and spacious, with French doors, full kitchens, and living rooms. The best part of staying here, besides your gracious and knowledgeable hosts, Dagmar and Peter Neufeldt, is that the convenient water taxi will find you here and take you anywhere you want to be, day or night. There is a small outdoor heated pool and a marina for those with boats in tow. In 1998, the Neufeldts were honored by a local campaign to enhance the area, Broward Beautiful, winning first place for the past three years in a row in the category of small multifamily dwellings.

111 Isle of Venice, Fort Lauderdale, FL 33301. ℂ 954/524-4430. Fax 954/764-4870. www.banyanmarina. com. 10 units. Winter $95–$250 apt. Off-season $60–$170 apt. Weekly and monthly rates available. MC, V. Free parking. To get there from I-95, exit Broward Blvd. E.; cross U.S. 1 and turn right on SE 15th Ave. At the first traffic light (Las Olas Blvd.), turn left. Turn left at the third island (Isle of Venice). **Amenities:** Restaurant; pool; dock. *In room:* A/C, TV, dataport, kitchen, coffeemaker, hair dryer.

Courtyard Villa on the Ocean ✿✿   Nestled between a bunch of larger hotels, this small, eight-room historic hotel offers a romantic getaway right on the beach. It recently underwent a complete renovation, adding 19th-century antique reproduction furnishings to its charmed setting. Courtyard Villa offers spacious oceanfront efficiencies with private balconies, larger suites overlooking the pool, and full 2-bedroom apartments. Rooms are plush with chenille bedspreads and carved four-poster beds; fully equipped kitchenettes are an added convenience. The tiled bathrooms have strong hot showers to wash off the beach sand. Room 8 is especially nice, with French doors that open to a private balcony overlooking the ocean. Relax in the hotel's unique heated pool/spa or on the second-floor sundeck. You can also swim off the beach to a living reef just 50 feet offshore. Scuba diving instruction is available on premises.

4312 El Mar Dr., Lauderdale-by-the-Sea, FL 33308. ℂ 800/291-3560 or 954/776-1164. Fax 954/491-0768. www.courtyardvilla.com. 10 units. Winter $159 double; $250 2-bedroom. Off-season $105 double; $150 2-bedroom. Rates include full breakfast. AE, MC, V. Pets under 35 lbs. are accepted with a $200 deposit, must be caged while outside; no pit bulls, Dobermans, or Rottweilers. **Amenities:** Outdoor heated pool; Jacuzzi; scuba instruction; free use of bikes; limited room service; free laptop use with Internet service. *In room:* A/C, TV/VCR, kitchenette, coffeemaker, hair dryer.

La Casa Del Mar ✿✿ *(Finds)*   The 10 theme rooms in this Spanish-Mediterranean B&B, situated right on the beach, are splendid, with private baths, each decorated in a motif inspired by an artist (such as Monet), regional style (such as Southwestern), or star (Judy Garland). Enjoy exquisite personal service by the English- and German-speaking co-owners. A delicious, home-cooked buffet-style breakfast is served in the main house but can be enjoyed outdoors under a mango tree in the resplendent garden. The swimming pool is large for such a small accommodation and is a great place to mingle at a late afternoon wine-and-cheese party with the other guests, who range from young couples to savvy European travelers. Best of all, it's a deal and a pretty well-kept secret.

3003 Granada St., Fort Lauderdale, FL 33304. ℂ 954/467-2037. Fax 954/467-7439. www.lacasadelmar. com. 10 units. Winter $110–$145; off-season $80–$100. Rates include breakfast. AE, MC, V. **Amenities:** Outdoor pool. *In room:* A/C, TV/VCR, fridge.

Traders Ocean Resort ✿   Located directly on the beach, this recently renovated hotel is not luxurious, but its service is superb, amenities are plentiful, and its atmosphere is completely conducive to a most relaxing vacation. Rooms are large and comfortable, and many feature ocean views. An outdoor tiki bar, often with live entertainment, provides further encouragement to unwind. The hotel attracts a mostly mature crowd, but if it's a tranquil vacation you're after, Traders may make a loyal customer out of you, regardless of your age.

1600 S. Ocean Blvd, Lauderdale-by-the-Sea, FL 33062. ℂ 800/325-5220 or 954/941-8400. Fax 954/941-1024. www.tradersresort.com. 93 units. Winter $95–$239; off-season $79–$139. AE, DC, DISC, MC, V. **Amenities:** Restaurant, lounge, tiki bar; freshwater heated outdoor pool; extensive watersports equipment rental; shuffleboard; volleyball; concierge; massage. *In room:* A/C, TV.

INEXPENSIVE

Blue Seas Courtyard ✿ (Finds) This 1940s motel will take you back to the days of Old Florida, thanks to a careful restoration and renovation. Rooms are large and bright, with full kitchens, huge bathrooms, terra-cotta tiles, Haitian and Peruvian art, and Southwest and Danish furnishings. Outside are a brick pool, flowing fountains, and lounges and tables facing the gardens or even the ocean, which is just a block away.

4525 El Mar Dr., Lauderdale-by-the-Sea, FL 33308. (✆) **877/225-8373** or 954/772-6337. Fax 954/772-6337. www.blueseascourtyard.com. 12 units. Winter $64–$94; off-season $60–$69. Free parking. MC, V. **Amenities:** Heated pool; access to nearby tennis court; nearby children's playground; coin laundry. *In room:* A/C, TV.

Ronny Dee Resort Motel ✿ The good news is that this family-owned motel is just 100 yards from the beach and extremely affordable. The bad news is that it's located on busy Florida A1A. Popular with European guests, this two-story yellow motel is wrapped around a central swimming pool; its guest rooms are wood-paneled (suburban style) and filled with an eclectic mix of furniture. A new coat of paint and new flooring helped to spruce up the place recently. It's clean but not overflowing with all the creature comforts of other chain motels.

717 S. Ocean Blvd., Pompano Beach, FL 33062. (✆) **954/943-3020.** Fax 954/783-5112. 35 units. Winter $49–$72 double; from $390 efficiency. Off-season $35–$41 double: from $249 efficiency. AE, MC, V. From I-95, exit Atlantic Blvd. E. to A1A N. **Amenities:** Outdoor heated pool; game room. *In room:* A/C, TV, dataport, fridge.

Sea Downs (and the Bougainvillea) ✿✿ This bargain accommodation is often booked months in advance by returning guests who want to be directly on the beach without paying a fortune. The hosts of this superclean 1950s motel live on the premises and keep things running smoothly. Renovations completed in 1997 have replaced bathroom fixtures, and many rooms have been redecorated here and at the owner's other even less expensive property next door, the 11-unit Bougainvillea. Guests at both hotels share the Sea Downs' pool.

2900 N. Surf Rd., Hollywood, FL 33019. (✆) **954/923-4968.** Fax 954/923-8747. www.seadowns.com or www.bougainvilleahollywood.com. 12 units. Winter $80–$135 daily; $511–$875 weekly. Off-season $52–$99 daily; $315–$651 weekly. No credit cards accepted. From I-95, exit Sheridan St. E. to A1A, go south.; drive ½ mile to Coolidge St.; turn left. **Amenities:** Freshwater outdoor pool; concierge; laundry facilities. *In room:* A/C, TV, dataport, kitchen, fridge, coffeemaker.

WHERE TO DINE

It took a while for a more sophisticated, varied Epicurean scene to reach these shores, but Fort Lauderdale, and to some extent Hollywood, finally have several fine restaurants. Increasingly, ethnic options are joining the legions of surf-and-turferies that have dominated the area for so long. **Las Olas Boulevard** has so many eateries that the city has put a moratorium on the opening of new restaurants on the 2-mile-long street.

VERY EXPENSIVE

Darrel & Oliver's Cafe Maxx ✿✿ FLORIDIAN/NEW WORLD Despite its bleak location in an unassuming storefront, Darrel & Oliver's Cafe Maxx is one of the best restaurants in Broward County. When it opened in 1984, it was the first restaurant to have an open kitchen, and what a stir that caused! Now, instead of focusing on the kitchen, it's what comes out of it that's a marvel. Consider pecan-crusted chicken breasts with honey-lime-roasted sweet potatoes, caramelized apples, and onion; sweet onion-crusted yellowtail snapper with Madeira sauce; or a macadamia-pesto-crusted veal chop.

2601 E. Atlantic Blvd., Pompano Beach. ℂ **954/782-0606.** Fax 954/782-0648. Reservations recommended. Main courses $18–$39. AE, DC, DISC, MC, V. Mon–Thurs 5:30–10:30pm, Fri–Sat 5:30–11pm, Sun 5:30–10pm. From I-95, exit at Atlantic Blvd. E. The restaurant is 3 lights east of Federal Hwy.

Left Bank ✸✸✸ FRENCH   Regulars complain that the usually brilliant Provençal cuisine at the Left Bank has suffered now that Jean-Pierre Brehier has joined the celebrity-chef bandwagon. I think they just miss him—Brehier's sous-chefs handle his menu like pros. Compared with other chefs who flee the galley for the Food Network, Brehier is still very much devoted to his own kitchen. Left Bank provides an elegant, romantic atmosphere that's bolstered by dark woods and large murals—perfect for Valentine's Day or an anniversary. Skip the Japanese-influenced seared tuna and Thai peanut Chilean sea bass, and go totally French with the French onion soup and grilled baby veal rack with grilled shrimp, herb potato mash, and Cabernet sauce, or the herb-crusted roasted filet mignon with blue-cheese-stuffed red potatoes and Cabernet sauce. Jackets are not required here, but are recommended.

214 SE 6th Ave. (north of Las Olas Blvd.), Fort Lauderdale. ℂ **954/462-5376.** Reservations strongly recommended. Main courses $25–$33. AE, DC, MC, V. Sun and Tues–Thurs 5:30–9:30pm, Fri–Sat 5:30–10pm. Closed Mon.

Mark's Las Olas ✸✸✸ NEW WORLD CUISINE   Before star chef Mark Militello hit Las Olas Boulevard, there was really no reason to dine here. However, once he opened the doors to his sleek, modern restaurant, he opened the eyes and mouths of discriminating Fort Lauderdale gourmands to his excellent New World cuisine. Grilled spiny lobster, with applewood-smoked bacon-conch sauce, sweet plantain mash, and conch fritters, is possibly the best item on the menu. If the kitchen is out of it—they tend to run out quickly—everything else on the menu, from the tuna pizza to the wood-oven-roasted salmon, is delicious. Save room for a chocolate dessert—any one will do.

1032 E. Las Olas Blvd., Fort Lauderdale. ℂ **954/463-1000.** Reservations suggested. Main courses $14–$30. Mon–Fri 11:30am–2:30pm; Mon–Thurs 6–10:30pm; Fri–Sat 6–11pm; Sun 6–10pm. AE, DC, MC, V.

EXPENSIVE

Armadillo Cafe ✸✸✸ SOUTHWESTERN   The city of Davie may be best known for farmland and rodeos, but it's also celebrated for this outstanding Southwestern restaurant, which attracts city slickers from all over South Florida. The Armadillo recently moved from its strip-mall digs to a much larger space to accommodate all the foodies who flock here in search of porcini-dusted sea bass and lobster quesadillas, among other things. At press time, a more casual off-shoot, Armadillo Cafe 2.0, was slated to open, offering lunch and dinner.

3400 S. University Dr., Davie. ℂ **954/791-5104.** Reservations essential. Main courses $16.95–$28.95. AE, DC, DISC, MC, V. Mon–Thurs 5–10pm, Fri–Sun 5–11pm.

Himmarshee Bar & Grille ✸ AMERICAN   Located on a popular street of bars frequented by Fort Lauderdale's young professionals, Himmarshee Bar & Grille is known for its cool scene and its cuisine. A mezzanine bar upstairs is ideal for people-watching; outdoor tables, if you can score one, are tight but strategically situated in front of all the street's action. On Friday and Saturday nights, in particular, it's difficult to get a table here. However, if you can deal with cramming into the bar, it's worth a cocktail or two. The wine list is particularly impressive, and the grilled sirloin burger with creamy basil Gorgonzola is a delicious meal in itself for only $7.50.

210 SW 2nd St. (south of Broward Blvd., west of U.S. 1), Fort Lauderdale. ℂ **954/524-1818.** Reservations recommended. Main courses $12–$24. AE, MC, V. Mon–Fri 11:30am–2:30pm; Sun–Thurs 6–10:30pm; Fri–Sat 6–11:30pm.

Hobo's Fish Joint ★★ SEAFOOD   Huge portions of extremely fresh fish are prepared in more than a dozen ways at this steakhouse-style restaurant with wood floors and white tablecloths. Despite the fact that it's located away from the ocean in the utterly suburban enclave of Coral Springs, this joint is worth the trip. Some even say it's the best seafood in Broward County. I say it's a tough call between here and the Sunfish Grill (see below). See for yourself with the littleneck clams in garlic bouillon or Chilean sea bass oreganato on a bed of orzo.

10317 Royal Palm Blvd. (at Coral Springs Dr.), Coral Springs. ℂ **954/346-5484.** Reservations for 6 or more. Main courses $17–$27. AE, MC, V. Mon–Thurs 5:30–9:30pm, Fri–Sat 5:30–10:30pm, Sun 5:30–9pm. From I-95, exit at Commercial Blvd., go west to University Dr., turn right and then about a mile up, take a left on Royal Palm Blvd.

Sunfish Grill ★★★ SEAFOOD   Unlike its fellow contemporary seafood restaurants, the Sunfish Grill chooses to focus on fish, not fusion. Chef Anthony Sindaco doesn't want to be a star, either. He'd prefer to leave the spotlight on his fantastic fish dishes, which are possibly the freshest in town thanks to the fact that he buys his fish at local markets and often from well-known local fisherman who appear at his back door with their catches of the day. The shrimp bisque cappuccino is a deliciously rich soup served in a demitasse cup—because it's that rich. Conch fritters are purely spectacular, not full of filler. Chilean sea bass, expertly cooked with roasted fennel, saffron potatoes, and a caramelized onion broth, is wonderful, but the best thing in my opinion was the seared tuna resting on a bed of mushroom and oxtail ragout with garlic mashed potatoes. It's not your typical Japanese-style seared tuna; it's better. In fact, almost everything at the Sunfish Grill is better than most seafood restaurants.

2771 E. Atlantic Blvd., Pompano Beach. ℂ **954/788-2434.** Reservations accepted. Main courses $17–$28. AE, MC, V. Mon–Thurs 6–9:30pm, Fri–Sat 6–10:30pm. Closed Sun.

MODERATE

Brasserie Las Olas ★ AMERICAN   This is the News Café of Fort Lauderdale, owned by the same man who spread the News and its uncomplicated café cuisine in Miami way back when. Located on the bottom floor of an office building and just over the bridge from the Broward County Courthouse, the Brasserie is a big power lunch spot, with high ceilings and high noise levels. Food is simple, from pizza to pasta, with some comfort food thrown in the mix. The calve's liver with caramelized onions and the balsamic-marinated pork chop are excellent choices if pizza with Gorgonzola and bacon sounds too simple for you. Desserts and coffees are plenty, and just like its Miami sibling, the Brasserie won't frown if you just prefer to order a cappuccino rather than an entire meal.

333 Las Olas Blvd., Fort Lauderdale. ℂ **954/779-7374.** Reservations for 6 or more. Main courses $8–$17. AE, DC, DISC, MC, V. Mon–Fri 11am–11pm, Sat–Sun 9am–11pm.

Cap's Place Island Restaurant ★★★ *Finds* SEAFOOD   Opened in 1928 by a bootlegger who ran in the same circles as gangster Meyer Lansky, this barge-turned-restaurant is one of South Florida's best-kept secrets. Although it's no longer a rumrunning restaurant and gambling casino, its illustrious past (FDR and Winston Churchill dined here—together) landed it a coveted spot on the National Register of Historic Places. To get there, you have to take a ferryboat, provided by the restaurant. The ride across the Intracoastal is not long and it definitely adds to the Cap's Place experience. And the food's good, too! Traditional seafood dishes such as Florida or Maine lobster, clams linguine, clams casino, and oysters Rockefeller will take you back to the days when a soprano was thought to be just an opera singer.

2765 NE 28th Court, Lighthouse Point. ⓒ **954/941-0418.** Reservations accepted. Main courses $20–$25. MC, V. Daily 5:30pm–midnight. To get to Cap's Place motor launch from I-95, exit at Copan's Road and go east to U.S. 1 (Federal Highway). At NE 24th St., turn right and follow the double lines and signs to the Lighthouse Point Yacht Basin and Marina (8 miles north of Fort Lauderdale). From there, follow a Cap's Place sign pointing you to the shuttle.

Creolina's ⭐⭐ CREOLE   You'll find authentic Louisiana Creole cuisine at this small but very popular restaurant, situated along the Riverwalk. Try the shrimp jambalaya with shrimp sausage and vegetables in a rich brown Cajun sauce served over rice, or the crayfish étouffée with crayfish tail simmered in a mellow Cajun sauce and served over rice. The mashed potatoes are homemade, and the delicious fresh-squeezed lemonade is made daily. There is also a terrific New Orleans Sunday brunch. Ask to sit in sassy Rosie's section.

209 SW 2nd St., Fort Lauderdale. ⓒ **954/524-2003.** Appetizers $4–$9; main courses $13–$18. AE, MC, V. Tue–Fri 11am–2:30pm and 5–10pm; Fri–Sat 5–11pm; Sun–Mon 5–9pm.

Indigo ⭐⭐ SOUTHEAST ASIAN/ECLECTIC   It seems a little strange to chow down on southeast Asian food in an utterly New Orleans–style hotel, but this is South Florida—the wackier, the better. This not-so-traditional meal begins with a basket of pappadams, puffy nan bread, and shrimp puff bread. Next might be a superrich grilled vegetable cassoulet au gratin and a fried rice dish with shallots, corn, and asparagus; or nan pizzas covered with such toppings as onions, shiitake mushrooms, goat cheese, spinach, eggplant, garlic, curried tomato, and pine nuts. Particularly good is the meaty soy and portobello mushroom combination wrapped in fluffy puff pastry and served with a delicate broccoli sauce. Sounds like a lot of activity going on in one dish, but like the restaurant itself, somehow it all works.

In the Riverside Hotel, 620 E. Las Olas Blvd., Fort Lauderdale. ⓒ **954/467-0671.** Reservations only for groups of 6 or more. Main courses $12–$22. AE, DC, DISC, MC, V. Daily 7am–9:45pm.

Sugar Reef ⭐⭐ FRENCH VIETNAMESE   I could go on about the restaurant's priceless, unobstructed ocean view, but the menu of Mediterranean, Caribbean, and French-Vietnamese dishes is just as outstanding. A pleasant tropical decor is bolstered by the fresh air wafting in from the Atlantic through the open windows. Seafood bouillabaisse in green curry and coconut broth and pork loin Benedict—layers of jerk-spiced pork and hollandaise sauce—are among the restaurant's most popular dishes. The restaurant puts a savory spin on duck, roasted and topped with sweet chile and papaya salsa.

600 N. Surf Rd. (on the broadwalk just north of Hollywood Blvd.), Hollywood. ⓒ **954/922-1119.** Reservations for 6 or more. Main courses $10–$24; sandwiches and salads $4–$9. AE, DISC, MC, V. Mon 4–10:30pm; Tues–Thurs 11am–10:30pm; Fri–Sun 11am–11pm (sometimes later in winter).

Tarpon Bend ⭐⭐ SEAFOOD/AMERICAN   This restaurant is one of the few places where the fishermen still bring the fish to the back door. The oysters from the raw bar are shucked to order and are incredible. Try the house specialty smoked fish dip—a king fish smoked on premises. The steamed clambake, with half a Maine lobster, clams, potatoes, mussels, and corn on the cob, is scrumptious and served in its own pot. Also try some of the homemade side dishes. For chocolate lovers, the chocolate brownie sundae is a must. There's live entertainment Wednesday through Saturday, and a full bar.

200 SW 2nd St., Fort Lauderdale. ℂ 954/523-3233. Reservations available for parties of 6 or more. Main courses $12–$15. AE, M, V. Mon–Thurs 11:30am–1am, Fri–Sat 11:30am–3am.

Tuscan Today Trattoria 𝕂𝕂 *Finds* ITALIAN   For classic Tuscan food in a charming atmosphere, Tuscan Today is something you should not put off until tomorrow. Inspired by the peasant origins of the original trattoria, the restaurant consistently turns out outstanding pizzas and flavorful meat and fish from a customized wood-burning brick oven imported from Tuscany. A reasonable and excellent wine list provides you with a difficult choice in two affordable price ranges: $18.75 and $22.50. Artichokes steamed in white-wine broth provide a flavorful balance between garlic and sun-dried tomatoes. Grilled thin-crusted pizzas are prepared as the Italians prefer them—light on sauce and cheese but heavy on flavor. For pasta lovers, the powerful but surprisingly light gnocchi with spinach is a good way to go. And if you order a meat or fish entree, be sure to try the rosemary roasted potatoes.

1161 N. Federal Hwy., Fort Lauderdale. ℂ 954/566-1716. Reservations for 6 or more. Main courses $8.95–$14.95. AE, DC, DISC, MC, V. Sun–Thurs 11am–10pm, Fri–Sat 11am–11pm.

INEXPENSIVE

The Floridian Restaurant 𝕂 *Value* AMERICAN/DINER   The Floridian has been filling South Florida's diner void for over 63 years, serving breakfast, lunch, and dinner, 24/7. It's especially busy on weekend mornings when locals and tourists come in for huge omelets, fresh oatmeal, sausage, and biscuits.

1410 E. Las Olas Blvd., Fort Lauderdale. ℂ 954/463-4041. Fax 954/761-3930. Sandwiches $3–$7; breakfast combos $3.50–$8; hot platters $7–$14. No credit cards. Open 24 hr.

Jaxon's 𝕂 *Kids* ICE CREAM   South Florida's best and only authentic old-fashioned ice cream parlor and country store attracts sweet teeth from all over the area looking to satisfy their cravings with an unabridged assortment of homemade ice cream served any which way. Kids love the place because of the candy store in the front of the restaurant, and adults love it for its pre–Ben and Jerry's authenticity. For the calorie-conscious, the sugar-free and fat-free versions are pretty good. Jaxon's most famous everything-but-the-kitchen-sink sundae features countless scoops and endless toppings.

128 S. Federal Hwy., Dania Beach. ℂ 954/923-4445. Sundaes $2.75–$7.95. AE, DISC, MC, V. Mon–Thurs 11:30am–11pm, Fri–Sat 11:30am–midnight, Sun noon–11pm.

Lester's Diner 𝕂 AMERICAN   Since 1968, Lester's Diner has been serving swarms of hungry South Floridians large portions of great greasy-spoon fare until the wee hours. Try the eggs Benedict and the 14-ounce "cup" of classic coffee, or sample one of Lester's many homemade desserts. The place serves breakfast 24 hours a day and is a Fort Lauderdale institution that attracts locals, after-club crowds, city officials, and a generally motley, friendly crew of hungry people craving no-nonsense food served by seasoned waitresses, whose beehive hairdos only contribute to the campy atmosphere.

250 S.R. 84, Fort Lauderdale. ℂ 954/525-5641. Main courses $5–$12. AE, MC, V. Open 24 hr.

Taverna Opa 𝕂𝕂 *Value* GREEK   Don't get nervous if you hear plates breaking when you enter this raucous, authentic Greek taverna situated directly on the Intracoastal Waterway—it's just the restaurant's lively staff making sure your experience here is 100% Greek. Delicious *meze* (appetizers), including a large Greek salad with hunks of fresh feta cheese, moist and savory stuffed grape leaves, and grilled calamari, are offered at ridiculously cheap prices. All the food is appetizers that are to be shared by the table. You should order a lot of them to get the full experience of the restaurant. When you've had enough ouzo, you may want to consider hopping up on one of the tables and dancing to the jacked-up Greek music. If not, don't worry; the waiters usually wind up on the tabletop, encouraging diners to shout the restaurant's name, "Opa!," making sure you don't forget it. You won't. *Note:* Taverna Opa did so well here in Hollywood that it opened another restaurant on the Intracoastal Waterway in Fort Lauderdale (3051 NE 2nd Ave.; C 954/567-1630) in April 2002. A South Beach property is slated as well.

410 N. Ocean Dr., Hollywood. C 954/929-4010. Reservations accepted weekdays only. Appetizers $2.95–$10. AE, DC, DISC, MC, V. Daily 4pm "until the ouzo runs out."

THE HOLLYWOOD & FORT LAUDERDALE AREA AFTER DARK

Fort Lauderdale no longer mimics the raucous antics of *Animal House* as far as nightlife and partying are concerned. It has gotten hip to the fact that an active nightlife is vital to the city's desires to distract sophisticated, savvy visitors from the magnetic lure of South Beach. And while Fort Lauderdale is no South Beach, it has vastly improved the quality of nightlife throughout the city by welcoming places that wouldn't dare host wet T-shirt and beer-chugging contests. It also lacks the South Beach attitude, which is part of the attraction.

If you're craving a little culture while in Fort Lauderdale, the behemoth **Broward Center for the Performing Arts** (201 SW 5th Ave. at SW 2nd St.; C 800-564-9539 or 954/462-0222; www.curtainup.org) will satisfy your needs with its impressive roster of shows. This 205,000 square-foot performing arts center not only features one of the best views of downtown Fort Lauderdale, but it also presents all the major Broadway musicals, plays, dance companies, operas, symphonies, lectures, films, and children's theater, with state-of-the-art sound and lighting. Ticket prices vary from $10–$120.

Hollywood's nightlife seems to be in the throes of an identity crisis, touting itself as the next South Beach, while at the same time hyping its image as an attitude-free nocturnal playground. Here's the real deal: At press time, Hollywood nightlife was barely awake, with the exception of a few bars and one struggling dance club. If you're looking for a quiet night out, it's probably your best bet. But don't come too late—after midnight, the city is absolutely deserted.

For information on clubs and events, pick up a free copy of Fort Lauderdale's weekly newspaper *City Link* or the Fort Lauderdale edition of the *New Times.*

Beach Place   This outdoor shopping and entertainment complex, modeled after Coconut Grove's hugely successful CocoWalk, landed on the legendary strip with several franchised bars and restaurants. It's the beachy version of a mall and is popular with a very young set at night. The view overlooking the ocean makes it worth a stop for a drink. No cover charge. Hours vary depending on the establishment. Some places are open until 2 or 3am, others close around 11pm. 17 S. Fort Lauderdale Beach Blvd., Fort Lauderdale. C 954/760-9570.

The Culture Room   If you consider rock and heavy metal to be culture, visit the Culture Room and bang your head to local bands. 3045 N. Federal Hwy. (at the corner of Oakland Park Blvd.), Fort Lauderdale. C 954/564-1074. Daily 8pm–3am. Cover varies.

Where the Boys Are: Gay Fort Lauderdale

While South Beach is a magnet for the so-called circuit boys—gay men who party on a continual, ritualistic basis—Fort Lauderdale has more of a low-key, small-town scene similar to, say, Provincetown. Here, local gay-owned and -operated bars, clubs, and restaurants are the places of choice for those who find South Beach's scene too pretentious, superficial, and drug infested. The Fort Lauderdale neighborhood of Wilton Manors is the hub of gay life, but there is a smattering of gay establishments throughout the city.

The Copa, located at 2800 S. Federal Hwy. (east on I-595, near the airport; ✆ 954/463-1507) is the hottest gay spot north of South Beach—the granddaddy of Fort Lauderdale's gay club scene. Patrons of Cathode Ray call this bar their "Cheers." It's located at 1105 E. Las Olas Blvd. (✆ 954/462-8611). Georgie's Alibi is Wilton Manors' most popular gay bar. Find it at 2266 Wilton Dr., Wilton Manors (✆ 954/565-2526). Two great dance clubs are the Coliseum, 2520 S. Miami Rd. (✆ 954/832-0100), and The Saint, 1000 W. S.R. 84 (✆ 954/525-7883).

Elbo Room   Formerly Spring Break central, the Elbo Room has managed to maintain its rowdy and divey reputation by serving up frequent drink specials and live bands. 241 S. Atlantic Blvd. on the corner of Las Olas Boulevard and A1A, Fort Lauderdale. ✆ 954/463-4615. Daily 10am–2am. No cover.

Mai Kai *Moments*   Immerse yourself in this fabulous vestige of Polynesian kitsch: hula dancers, fire-eaters, and potent (and sickly sweet) drinks served in coconuts. The food, which draws an ambiguous line between Chinese, Polynesian, and other forms of Asian cuisine, is tasty enough but definitely overpriced. No matter, it's bound to get cold as you watch the hilarious show, which includes everything from Tahitian classics to Polynesian versions of American hits. Trippy and undeniably fun, a trip to Mai Kai is a must. *Note:* The cocktails cost almost as much as a meal. 3599 N. Federal Hwy. (between Commercial Blvd. and Oakland Park Blvd.), Fort Lauderdale. ✆ 954/563-3272. Daily 5pm–midnight. Reservations required. Shows (2 nightly) are $9.95 for adults; free for children 12 and under.

O'Hara's   What used to be a mediocre jazz club has turned into a premier venue for excellent, live R&B, pop, and funk music. The club has two locations: at 1905 Hollywood Blvd., Hollywood (✆ 954/925-2555 or the 24-hr. Jazz & Blues Hotline ✆ 954/524-2801), and 722 E. Las Olas Blvd., Fort Lauderdale (✆ 954/524-1764).

The Parrot   Fort Lauderdale's most famous—and fun—dive bar, the Parrot is both a local's and out-of-towner's choice for an evening of beer (16 kinds on tap), bonding, and browsing of the bar's virtual gallery of photos of almost everyone who's ever imbibed here since its opening in 1970. 911 Sunrise Lane, Fort Lauderdale. ✆ 954/563-1493. Sun–Thurs 11am–2am, Fri–Sat 11am–3am. No cover.

Riverwalk   You'll find this outdoor shopping and entertainment complex located in the heart of downtown Fort Lauderdale on the sleepy yet scenic New River—as a result of its river site, it's got more charm than most such complexes. In fact, if you've got a boat, you can sail here and anchor away until you're ready to move on. A host of bars, restaurants, and shops, not to mention a high-tech virtual reality arcade, the Escape, and a multiplex cinema, are enough to keep you occupied for a few hours. On weekends, this place is packed. 400 SW 2nd St. (along the New River from NE 6th Ave. to SW 6th Ave.), Fort Lauderdale.

Rush Street   Known for its ice-cream flavors of martinis, from chocolate to Key lime, Rush Street is a sleek bar with two dance floors that attracts a young professional crowd. 220 SW 2nd St., Fort Lauderdale. © 954/522-6900. No cover.

Shooters   This waterfront bar is quintessential Fort Lauderdale. Inside, you'll find nautical types, families, and young professionals mixed in with a good dose of sunburned tourists enjoying the live reggae, jazz, or Jimmy Buffett–style tunes with the gorgeous backdrop of the bay and marinas all around. 3033 NE 32nd Ave., Fort Lauderdale. © 954/566-2855. Mon–Fri 11:30am–2am, Sat 11:30am–3am, Sun 10am–2am. No cover.

2 Boca Raton ★★ & Delray Beach ★

26 miles S of Palm Beach, 40 miles N of Miami, 21 miles N of Fort Lauderdale

Boca Raton is one of South Florida's most expensive, well-maintained cities—home to ladies who lunch and SUV-driving yuppies. The city's name literally translates as "rat's mouth," but you'd be hard-pressed to find rodents in this area's fancy digs.

If you're looking for funky, wacky, and eclectic, look elsewhere. Boca is a luxurious resort community and, for some, the only place worth staying in South Florida. Although Jerry Seinfeld's TV parents retired to the fictional Del Boca Vista, Boca's just too pricey to be a retirement community. With minimal nightlife, entertainment in Boca is restricted to leisure sports, excellent dining, and upscale shopping. The city's residents and vacationers happily comply.

Delray Beach, named after a suburb of Detroit, grew up completely separate from its southern neighbor. This sleepy yet starting-to-awaken beachfront community was founded in 1894 by a Midwestern postmaster who sold off 5-acre lots through Michigan newspaper ads. Because of their close proximity, Boca and Delray can easily be explored together. Budget-conscious travelers would do well to eat and sleep in Delray and dip into Boca for sightseeing and beaching. The 2-mile stretch of beach here is well maintained and crowded, but not mobbed. Delray's "downtown" area is confined to Atlantic Avenue, which is known for casual to chic restaurants, quaint shops, and art galleries. Compared to Boca, Delray is much more laid back, hardly as chichi, and more like a cute little beach town than the sprawling, swanky, suburban feel emitted by Boca.

ESSENTIALS
GETTING THERE   Like the rest of the cities on the Gold Coast, Boca Raton and Delray are easily reached from I-95 or the Florida Turnpike. Both the Fort Lauderdale Hollywood International Airport and the Palm Beach International Airport are about 20 minutes away. Amtrak (© **800/USA-RAIL;** www.amtrak.com) trains make stops in Delray Beach at an unattended station at 345 S. Congress Ave.

VISITOR INFORMATION   Contact or stop by the **Palm Beach County Convention and Visitors Bureau,** 1555 Palm Beach Lakes Blvd., Suite 800, West Palm Beach, FL 33401 (© **800/554-PALM** or 561/233-3000; fax 561/471-3990; www.palmbeachfl.com). They're open Monday to Friday from 8:30am to 5:30pm and have excellent coupons and discounts. On weekdays from 8:30am until at least 4pm, stop by the **Greater Boca Raton Chamber of Commerce** at 1800 N. Dixie Hwy., 4 blocks north of Glades Road (© **561/ 395-4433;** fax 561/392-3780; www.bocaratonchamber.com), Boca Raton, FL 33432, for information on attractions, accommodations, and events in the area. Also, try the **Greater Delray Beach Chamber of Commerce** (© **561/278- 0424;** fax 561/278-0555; www.delraybeach.com), at 64 SE 5th Ave., half a block south of Atlantic Avenue on U.S. 1, Delray Beach, FL 33483, but I recommend the Palm Beach County Convention and Visitors Bureau since it has information on the entire county.

BEACHES & ACTIVE PURSUITS

BEACHES Thankfully, Florida had the foresight to set aside some of its most beautiful coastal areas for the public's enjoyment. Many of the area's best beaches are located in state parks and are free to pedestrians and bikers, though most do charge for parking. Among the beaches I recommend are Delray Beach's **Atlantic Dunes Beach,** 1600 S. Ocean Blvd., a 7-acre developed beach with lifeguards, restrooms, changing rooms, and a family park area; Boca Raton's **South Beach Park,** 400 N. Ocean Blvd., with 1,670 feet of beach, 25 acres, lifeguards, picnic areas, restrooms, showers, and 955 feet of developed beach south of the Boca Inlet, for an admission charge of $7 on weekdays and $9 on weekends. The two beaches below are also very popular.

The **Delray Beach Public Beach,** on Ocean Boulevard at the east end of Atlantic Avenue, is one of the area's most popular hangouts. Weekends especially attract a young and good-looking crowd of active locals and tourists. Regular volleyball, Frisbee, and paddleball games make for good entertainment. Refreshments, snack shops, bars, and restaurants are just across the street. Families enjoy the protection of lifeguards on the clean, wide beach. Gentle waters make it a good swimming beach, too. Restrooms and showers are available, and there's limited parking at meters along Ocean Boulevard.

Spanish River Park Beach, on North Ocean Boulevard (Florida A1A), 2 miles north of Palmetto Park Road in Boca Raton, is a huge 95-acre oceanfront park with a half-mile-long beach complete with lifeguards as well as a large grassy area, making it one of the best choices for picnicking. Facilities include picnic tables, grills, restrooms, showers, and a bi-level 40-foot observation tower. You can walk through tunnels under the highway to access nature trails that wind through fertile grasslands. Volleyball nets are oceanside and always have at least one serious game going on. The park is open from 8am until 8pm. Admission is $8 for vehicles on weekdays and $10 on weekends and major holidays. Also, read below about Red Reef Park under "Scuba Diving and Snorkeling."

GOLF This area has plenty of good courses. The best ones (that are not located in a gated community) are found at the **Boca Raton Resort & Club** (see p. 338) and **The Inn at Boca Teeca** (see p. 339). Another great place to swing your clubs is at the **Deer Creek Golf Club** in Deerfield Beach, 2801 Country Club Boulevard, Deerfield Beach (© **954/421-5550**), a 300-plus-yard driving range where a large bucket of balls costs $7, and a small one costs $4. Rates at the Deer Creek Golf Club are seasonal and range from $45 to $125. However, from May to October or November, about a dozen private courses open their greens to visitors staying in Palm Beach County hotels. This "Golf-A-Round" program is free or severely discounted (carts are additional), and reservations can

Boca Raton & Delray Beach

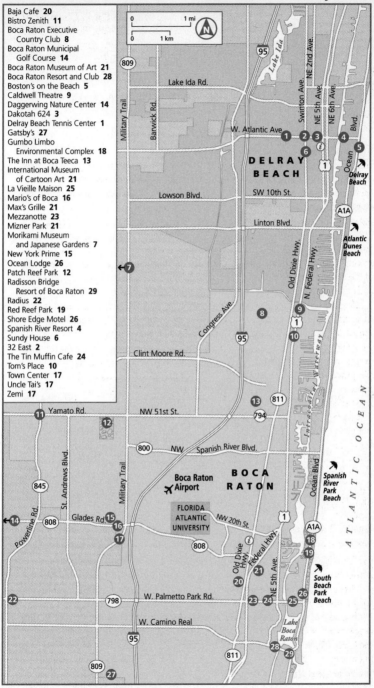

be made through most major hotels. Ask at your hotel, or contact the **Palm Beach County Convention and Visitors Bureau** (© 561/471-3995) for information on which clubs are available for play.

The semiprivate, 18-hole, par-61 course at the **Boca Raton Executive Country Club,** 7601 E. Country Club Blvd. (© 561/997-9410), is usually open to the public and is an excellent choice for those looking to improve their game in a professional setting. A driving range is on the property as well as a restaurant and a pro shop, where you can rent clubs. If you like, take lessons from a PGA pro. Greens fees are $20 per person.

The **Boca Raton Municipal Golf Course,** 8111 Golf Course Rd. (© 561/483-6100), is the area's best public golf course. There's an 18-hole, par-72 course covering approximately 6,200 yards as well as a 9-hole, par 30 course. There's a snack bar and a pro shop where clubs can be rented. Greens fees are $11 to $14 for 9 holes and $19 to $25 for 18 holes. Ask for special summer discount fees.

SCUBA DIVING & SNORKELING   Moray Bend, a 58-foot dive spot located about ¾ mile off Boca Inlet, is the area's most popular. It's home to three moray eels that are used to being fed by scuba divers. The reef is accessible by boat from **Force E Dive Center,** 877 E. Palmetto Park Rd., Boca Raton (© 561/368-0555). Phone for dive times. Dives cost $40 to $45 per person.

Red Reef Park, 1400 N. Ocean Park Blvd. (© 561/393-7974), a fully developed 67-acre oceanfront park in Boca Raton, has good swimming and year-round lifeguard protection. There's snorkeling for beginners around the rocks and reefs that lie just off the beach in 2 to 6 feet of water. The park also has restrooms and a small picnic area with grills and tables. Located a half-mile north of Palmetto Park Road, it is open daily from 8am to 10pm. You pay only if you drive in. It's $8 per car during the week or $10 on weekends.

TENNIS   The snazzy **Delray Beach Tennis Center,** 201 W. Atlantic Ave. (© 561/243-7360; www.delraytennis.com), has 14 lighted clay courts and 5 hard courts available by the hour. Phone for rates and reservations.

The 17 public lighted hard courts at **Patch Reef Park,** 2000 NW 51st St. (© 561/997-0881; www.ci.boca-raton.fl.us/parks/Patchreef.cfm), are available by reservation. The fee for nonresidents is $5.75 per person per hour. Courts are available Monday to Saturday from 7:30am to 10pm and Sunday from 7:30am to dusk; you can phone ahead to see if a court is available. To reach the park from I-95, exit at Yamato Road West and continue past Military Trail to the park.

SEEING THE SIGHTS

Boca Raton Museum of Art 𝒜𝒜   In addition to a relatively small but well-chosen permanent collection that's strongest in 19th-century European oils, the museum stages a wide variety of temporary exhibitions by local and international artists. Lectures and films are offered on a fairly regular basis, so call ahead for details.

Mizner Park, 501 Plaza Real, Boca Raton. © 561/392-2500. www.bocamuseum.org. Admission $8 adults, $6 seniors, $4 students, free for children under 12. Additional fees may apply for special exhibits and performances. Free on Wed. except during special exhibitions. Tues, Thurs, and Sat 10am–5pm, Wed and Fri 10am–9pm, Sun noon–5pm. Closed Mon.

Daggerwing Nature Center 𝒜   Seen enough snowbirds? Head over to this 39-acre swampy splendor where birds of another feather reside, including herons, egrets, woodpeckers, and warblers. The trails come with a soundtrack

The Man Who Built Boca

Self-taught architect Addison Mizner was so impressed with the Palm Beach lifestyle when he visited in 1918 that he set about designing the community's mansions, country clubs, and most of exclusive Worth Avenue. In 1925 he focused his talents on Boca Raton, joining with his brother in bringing his visions of a Mediterranean-style resort city to fruition. When the stock market plunged in 1929, Mizner's plans came to a halt. However, his legacy is visible throughout the city of Boca Raton, whose houses, strip malls, and various buildings maintain Spanish barrel-tile roofs, arches, and columns.

provided by songbirds hovering above (watch your head). The park's night hikes will take you on a nocturnal wakeup call for owls at 6pm. Bring a flashlight.

South County Regional Park, 11200 Park Access Rd., Boca Raton. (561/488-9953. Free admission. Tues–Fri 1–4:30pm, Sat 9am–4:30pm. Call for tour and activity schedule.

Gumbo Limbo Environmental Complex ★★★   If manicured lawns and golf courses aren't your idea of communing with nature, then head to Gumbo Limbo. Named for an indigenous hardwood tree with continuously shedding bronze bark, the 20-acre complex protects one of the few surviving coastal hammocks, or forest islands, in South Florida. Visitors can walk through the hammock on a ½-mile-long elevated boardwalk that ends at a 40-foot observation tower, from which you can see the Atlantic Ocean, the Intracoastal Waterway, and much of Boca Raton. From mid-April to September, sea turtles come ashore here to lay their eggs.

1801 N. Ocean Blvd. (on A1A between Spanish River Blvd. and Palmetto Park Rd.), Boca Raton. (561/338-1473. Fax 561/338-1483. Free admission. Mon–Sat 9am–4pm, Sun noon–4pm.

International Museum of Cartoon Art ★ (Kids   This extensive collection of cartoon art spans the decades and styles in its glitzy home in Mizner Park. In a gorgeous 52,000-square-foot gallery space, cartoon fans can see prints, frames, moving pictures, and books by some of the world's greatest cartoonists, including many by the museum's founder, Mort Walker (of *Beetle Bailey* fame). A fantastic gift shop offers posters, books, and lots of memorabilia.

201 Plaza Real at Mizner Park, Boca Raton. (561/391-2200. www.cartoon.org. Donation requested. Wed–Sun 10am–5pm.

Morikami Museum and Japanese Gardens ★★★   Slip off your shoes and enter into a serene Japanese garden that dates from 1905, when an entrepreneurial farmer, Jo Sakai, came to Boca Raton to build a tropical agricultural community. The Yamato Colony, as it was known, was short-lived; by the 1920s only one tenacious colonist remained: George Sukeji Morikami. But Morikami was quite successful, eventually running one of the largest pineapple plantations in the area. The 200-acre Morikami Museum and Japanese Gardens (a stroll through the garden is actually ⅞ mile), which opened to the public in 1977, was Morikami's gift to Palm Beach County and the State of Florida. The park section, dedicated to the preservation of Japanese culture, is constructed to appeal to all the senses. An artificial waterfall that cascades into a koi- and carp-filled moat; a small rock garden for meditation; and a large bonsai collection that includes miniature maple, buttonwood, juniper, and Australian pine trees are all

worth contemplation. There's also a cafe with a Japanese- and Asian-inspired menu if you want to stay for lunch.

4000 Morikami Park Rd., Delray Beach. © 561/495-0233. www.morikami.org. Museum $8 adults, $7 seniors, $5 children 6–18, free for members and children 5 and under. Museum Tues–Sun 10am–5pm; gardens Tues–Sat 10am–5pm. Closed major holidays.

SHOPPING & BROWSING

Even if you don't plan to buy anything, a trip to Boca Raton's **Mizner Park** is essential for capturing the essence of the city. Like Main Street in a small town, Mizner is the place to see and be seen, where Rolls Royces and Ferraris are parked curbside, freshly coiffed women sit amidst shopping bags at outdoor cafes, and young movers and shakers make evening plans on their constantly buzzing cellphones. Beyond the human scenery, however, Mizner Park is scenic in its own right with beautiful landscaping. It's really an outdoor mall, with 45 specialty shops, seven good restaurants, and a multiplex. Each shop front faces a grassy island with blue and green gazebos, potted plants, and garden benches. Mizner Park is located on Federal Highway (between Palmetto Park Road and Glades Road; © **561/362-0606**).

Boca's **Town Center Mall,** located on the south side of Glades Road, just west of I-95, has seven huge department stores, including the state's only Nordstrom as well as Bloomingdale's, Burdines, Lord & Taylor, and Saks Fifth Avenue. Add to that the hundreds of specialty shops, an extensive food court, and a range of other restaurants, and you have the area's most comprehensive shopping center.

A lifeless, overrated area, but good enough for a quick stroll, is the more artsy community of Delray Beach, known by many as Pineapple Grove. Here, along Atlantic Avenue, especially east of Swinton Avenue, you'll find a few antique shops, clothing stores, and art galleries shaded by palm trees and colorful awnings. Pick up the "Downtown Delray Beach" map and guide at almost any of the stores on this strip, or call © **561/278-0424** for more information.

WHERE TO STAY

A number of national chain hotels worth considering include a moderately priced **Holiday Inn Highland Beach Oceanside** at 2809 S. Ocean Blvd., on Florida A1A, southeast of Linton Boulevard (© **800/234-6835** or 561/278-6241). Although you won't find rows of cheap hotels as in Fort Lauderdale and Hollywood, a handful of mom-and-pop motels have survived along A1A between the towering condominiums of Delray Beach. Look along the beach just south of Atlantic Boulevard. Especially noteworthy is the pleasant little two-story, shingle-roofed **Bermuda Inn** at 64 S. Ocean Blvd. (© **561/276-5288**).

Even more economical options can be found in Deerfield Beach, Boca's neighbor, south of the county line. A number of beachfront efficiencies offer great deals, even in the winter months. Try the **Panther Motel and Apartments,** at 715 S. A1A (© **954/427-0700**). This clean and convenient motel has rates starting as low as $40, although in season you may have to book for a week at a time. Weekly rates in season start at $457.

If you are looking for something more private or for longer than just a few days, try calling a reservations service for help. **Palm Beach Accommodations** (© **800/543-SWIM**) handles rentals for a few weeks or months.

VERY EXPENSIVE

Boca Raton Resort and Club 🏨🏨 (Kids) This famous and often photographed property shows that Boca's country-club lifestyle is alive and well.

Built in 1926 by Addison Mizner, the posh resort now comprises three oddly matched buildings: the original, more traditional building; the somewhat drab, pink, 27-story tower; and the more modern, airier beach club, which is accessible by a water shuttle. Everything at this resort, which straddles the Intracoastal and encompasses over 350 acres of land, is fully at your fingertips but may sometimes require a little effort to reach it. The amenities here cannot be beat. The resort features two 18-hole championship golf courses, a $10 million tennis and fitness center, indoor basketball and racquetball courts, a 25-slip marina with full fishing and boating facilities, and a private beach with various watersports equipment for rent. With a choice of 10 places to dine, five pools to swim in, and an excellent children's program, the resort is ideal for families. Upon check in, see if Harry the bellman is available to take you to your room—he's been at the resort for over 46 years and has a photographic memory of the hotel's previous guests, from Joseph Cotton and Charlton Heston to Bill Gates, who became a partner in the hotel after spending enough time there.

501 E. Camino Real (P.O. Box 5025), Boca Raton, FL 33431. (C) **800/327-0101** or 561/395-3000. Fax 561/447-3183. www.bocaresort.com. 963 units, 120 golf villas. Winter $400–$750 double; off-season $175–$450. Reasonable seasonal packages available. AE, DC, DISC, MC, V. From I-95 N., exit onto Palmetto Park Rd. E. Turn right onto Federal Hwy. (U.S. 1), and then left onto Camino Real to the resort. **Amenities:** 10 restaurants; 6 bars; 5 pools; 2 18-hole championship golf courses; 34 tennis courts; Mediterranean spa; 3 fitness centers; indoor basketball court; 4 indoor racquetball courts; 25-slip marina with full fishing and boating; watersports equipment rental; extensive children's programs; concierge; business center; 24-hr. room service; laundry. *In room:* A/C, TV, minibar, hair dryer.

MODERATE

The Inn at Boca Teeca 🏆🏆🏆   For over three decades, this inn has been attracting golf fanatics who could care less about the small, but comfortable, rooms because they're too busy out on the superb 27-hole golf course at the inn's Boca Teeca Country Club, open only to members and guests of the inn. For the golf widow(er)s, however, most of the rooms in this three-story building have balconies or patios from which to watch or signal their significant others that it's time for dinner.

5800 NW 2nd Ave., Boca Raton, FL 33487. (C) **561/994-0400.** Fax 561/998-8279. 46 units. Winter $140 and up; off-season $80–$120. AE, DC, MC, V. **Amenities:** Restaurant; small pool; golf course; 6 tennis courts; fitness center. *In room:* A/C, TV.

Radisson Bridge Resort of Boca Raton 🏆🏆   Not as pricey as the Boca Raton Resort, this resort nevertheless does feature priceless water views and is an excellent choice for the money. All guest rooms have balconies with views of the Intracoastal or the Atlantic, and some corner suites have both. Its popular outdoor waterfront restaurant, Watercolors, is the only place in the city to dine on the water. The restaurant and lounge at the top of the hotel behold gorgeous panoramic views. Just a 5-minute walk to the beach, this Radisson bridges the gap between ultrapricey and ultraschlocky area hotels.

999 E. Camino Real, Boca Raton, FL 33432. (C) **800/333-3333** or 561/368-9500. Fax 561/362-0492. www.radisson.com. 121 units. Winter $209–$299; off-season $109–$189. Some rates include breakfast. AE, DC, MC, V. **Amenities:** 2 restaurants; outdoor heated pool; health club and spa; watersports equipment rental; bike rental; concierge. *In room:* A/C, TV, hair dryer, coffeemaker.

Spanish River Resort 🏆🏆 *Finds*   An especially good value for those staying longer than a few days, this pleasant family-oriented property offers fully furnished condominiums half a block from a popular beach and within walking distance of Delray's best shops, restaurants, and galleries. The 11-story

Mediterranean-style building has lighted tennis courts, a large outdoor pool, and lovely oceanview balconies from the fourth floor and above. Apartments are spacious and outfitted with fully equipped kitchens. All units also have pullout queen-size sofa beds and, incredibly, there is no additional charge for extra guests. A one-bedroom unit can comfortably fit four or five people; a two-bedroom unit can easily accommodate six. Cots and rollaway beds are available at a minimum charge. Compared with many of the run-down 1950s motels in the area, this moderately priced, well-maintained tower is a real find.

1111 E. Atlantic Ave., Delray Beach, FL 33483. ℂ 800/543-SWIM or 561/243-7946. Fax 561/276-9634. 75 units. Winter $150 studio; $350 2-bedroom. Off-season from $98 studio; $228 2-bedroom. Free 6th and 7th nights with weekly booking. AE, DISC, MC, V. **Amenities:** Restaurant; outdoor pool; lighted tennis courts. *In room:* A/C, TV.

Sundy House 🦀🦀 Most locals know the Sundy House as an impeccably restored 1902 home, which is command central for one of the area's best Sunday brunches. But unless you take a postmeal stroll through the beautiful tropical gardens (ask for a tour if you want to learn about the 5,000 plants, fruits, herbs, and spices, some of which are used in the hotel's restaurant), you may miss the fact that there are nine modern and luxe guest accommodations for those who want to make a meal into a memorable overnight stay. The Sundy House prefers to call itself a residential inn, with rooms resembling very plush one- and two-bedroom apartments decorated in a very colorful, very tasteful Caribbean-meets-mod style with amazing bathrooms, gorgeous views of the garden, and high-tech amenities that may rival those found in your own living room. The only frivolous amenities, in my opinion, are the full kitchens, because nobody should cook when they can stroll past the waterfalls and gazebos and indulge in a fantastic meal at the American-Caribbean–influenced Sundy House restaurant.

106 S. Swinton Avenue, Delray Beach, FL, 33444-3656. ℂ 561/272-5678. Fax 561/272-1115. www.sundyhouse.com. 9 units. Winter $250–$375, 1 or 2 bedroom. Off-season $175–$275, 1 or 2 bedroom. Honeymoon cottage, $500. 2-night minimum. AE, DC, DISC, MC, V. Free parking. **Amenities:** Restaurant; pool; concierge. *In room:* A/C, TV/VCR/DVD, CD player, full kitchens, washer/dryer.

INEXPENSIVE

Ocean Lodge 🦀 Situated around a small heated pool and sundeck, this two-story motel is a particularly well-kept accommodation in an area of run-down or overpriced options. The large rooms offer furnishings and decor that are clean but a bit impersonal. A recent renovation that added modern Formica and floral wallpaper lifts this a notch above a basic motel. Ask for a room in the back, since the street noise can be loud, especially in season. The bonus is that you are across the street from the ocean and in one of Florida's most upscale resort towns.

531 N. Ocean Blvd. (just north of Palmetto Park Rd. on A1A), Boca Raton, FL 33432. ℂ 800/STAY-BOCA or 561/395-7772. Fax 561/395-0554. 18 units. Winter $99–$125 double. Off-season $75–$99 double. AE, MC, V. **Amenities:** Pool. *In room:* A/C, TV.

Shore Edge Motel Another relic of the 1950s, this motel has been recently spiffed up with new landscaping and some redecorating and is a good choice, especially because of its location—across the street from a public beach, just north of downtown Boca Raton. It's the quintessential South Florida motel: a small, pink, single-story structure surrounding a modest swimming pool and courtyard. Although the rooms are on the small side, they're very neat and clean. The higher-priced accommodations are larger and come with full kitchens.

425 N. Ocean Blvd. (on A1A, north of Palmetto Park Rd.), Boca Raton, FL 33432. ℂ 561/395-4491. Fax 561/347-8759. 16 units. Winter $85–$99 double. Off-season $55–$65 double. AE, MC, V. **Amenities:** Pool. *In room:* A/C, TV.

WHERE TO DINE

Boca Raton, and its environs, is the kind of place where you discuss dinner plans at the breakfast table. Nightlife in Boca means going out to a restaurant. But who cares? These are some of the best restaurants in South Florida.

VERY EXPENSIVE

La Vieille Maison ⭐⭐⭐ FRENCH   The luxurious setting, a Mediterranean-inspired home filled with a variety of antique French furnishings and paintings, gives you the feeling of walking into a small chateau. Culinarily speaking, however, this place is a castle. Begin with lobster bisque, gratin of escargots with fennel and pistachio nuts, or pan-seared foie gras—each is equally delectable. It's difficult to choose from the many enticing entrees, which range from red snapper in black-and-green-olive potato crust to medallions of beef, lamb, and venison over three sauces. You'll surely have to try at least a few of the gorgeous cheeses the server offers after your main course—the most extensive selection I've seen in this country. The lemon crepe soufflé with raspberry sauce is the dessert of choice—remember to order it early.

770 E. Palmetto Park Rd., Boca Raton. ⓒ 561/391-6701 or 561/737-5677. Reservations recommended. Main courses $18–$50; fixed-price dinners $42 and $68. AE, DC, DISC, MC, V. Daily 6–9:30pm (call for seating times).

New York Prime ⭐⭐⭐ *Finds* STEAKHOUSE   Forget Morton's and Smith & Wollensky. This South Florida outpost of a South Carolina–based chain is the prime spot for carnivores looking to satisfy their cravings for big, succulent steaks. Fish dishes are also available, including lobsters ranging from 3 to 13 pounds. But the price of excess does not come cheap. In fact, the restaurant brazenly states its case on the menu: "We strive to be the Mercedes of steakhouses by offering the very best . . . but you can't drive a Mercedes for the same price as a Buick." To me, this is more like the DeLorean of steakhouses—a rare find.

2350 Executive Center Dr., Boca Raton. ⓒ 561/998-3881. Reservations recommended. Main courses $22.50–$64. AE, MC, V. Daily 5–11pm.

EXPENSIVE

Max's Grille ⭐⭐ AMERICAN   Max's Grille is a very popular, very good option in Mizner Park, but you will inevitably wait to be seated. With a large exhibition kitchen that occupies the entire back wall of the restaurant, those lucky enough to score a table can watch as their yellowfin tuna steak or filet mignon is seared on a flaming oak grill. There's also a large selection of chicken, meatloaf, pastas, and main-course salads.

404 Plaza Real, in Mizner Park, Boca Raton. ⓒ 561/368-0080. Reservations accepted for 6 or more. Main courses $14–$26; pastas $10.95–$16.95. AE, DC, DISC, MC, V. Lunch Mon–Sat 11:30am–3pm; dinner Mon–Thurs 5–10:30pm, Fri–Sat 5–11pm, Sun brunch/dinner 11:30am–10pm.

32 East ⭐⭐ NEW AMERICAN   The menu changes every day at this very popular people-watching outpost of tasty, contemporary American food that has finally added a little hip to the Delray Beach dining scene. Delicious items have included rigatoni with braised lamb shank and oregano; hanger steak on roasted-garlic polenta; and grilled salmon with arugula purée and olive tapenade.

32 E. Atlantic Ave., Delray Beach. ⓒ 561/276-7868. Reservations recommended. Main courses $10–$16. AE, DC, MC, V. Sun–Thurs 5:30–10pm, Fri–Sat 5:30–11pm; bar until 2am.

Uncle Tai's ⭐⭐⭐ CHINESE   Not your average egg roll and lo mein kind of place, Uncle Tai's, Boca's best upscale Chinese restaurant, offers a savory spin on classics such as garlic chicken and duck with plum sauce. A family-run restaurant, Uncle Tai's is the product of Wen Dah Tai, a man who studied with the master chefs in China, Japan, and the Philippines. Tai wants to make sure you will emerge from his restaurant fully satisfied and will even go the extra mile to discourage you from ordering a dish that's less suited to Western palates, having been created for the restaurant's many Chinese diners.

5250 Town Center Circle (between Glades and Palmetto Park rds.), Boca Raton. ✆ **561/368-8806.** Reservations suggested. Main courses $12–$32. AE, DISC, MC, V. Daily 11am–2:30pm and 5–10pm.

Zemi ✿✿✿ NEW AMERICAN   Possibly the best privately owned restaurant to be attached to a mall, Zemi is a sleek and chic neo-American restaurant that's a favorite with the ladies-who-lunch set, the Boca scenesters, and foodies alike. Chili-crusted shrimp with manchego cheese, roasted garlic, sun-dried tomatoes, lemon oil, and cilantro; grilled pork T-bone in a pear-ginger compote; and the marinated, grilled skirt steak with vegetable hash and crispy onions are all so good that even the size-two set of mall rats would be happy to go up a half size for a taste.

5050 Town Center Circle, in the Boca Center, Boca Raton. ✆ **561/391-7177.** Reservations accepted for 6 or more. Main courses $18–$28. AE, DC, DISC, MC, V. Lunch Mon–Fri 11:30am–2:30pm; dinner Mon–Thurs and Sun 6–10pm, Fri–Sat 6–11pm.

MODERATE

Bistro Zenith ✿ NEW AMERICAN   At the height of innovative cuisine, Bistro Zenith's consistently changing menu keeps local foodies coming back for its tasty offerings of traditional American dishes graced with Oriental, Mediterranean, or Southwestern influences served in a high-tech atmosphere. During its Southwestern phase, Zenith hit a new high with a fantastic Grand Canyon chicken with red beans, ancho chili sauce, rice, corn tortillas, and Tex-Mex corn and cilantro oil.

Regency Court, 3011 Yamato Rd., Boca Raton. ✆ **561/997-2570.** Reservations recommended. Main courses $9–$15. AE, MC, V. Lunch Mon–Fri 11:30am–2:30pm; dinner Sun–Thurs 5:30–10pm, Fri–Sat 5:30–11pm.

Mario's of Boca ✿ ITALIAN   This extremely popular, bustling Italian bistro keeps Boca's biggest mouths busy with massive portions of great homemade Italian food. The garlic rolls and the pizza are especially worth piping down for. If you're really hungry, there's an all-you-can-eat buffet 7 days a week.

2200 Glades Rd. (between 19th St. and Sheridan Way), Boca Raton. ✆ **561/392-5595.** Reservations not accepted. Main courses under $15. AE, MC, V. Mon–Thurs 11:30am–10pm, Fri–Sat 11:30am–11pm, Sun noon–9:30pm.

INEXPENSIVE

Baja Cafe ✿ MEXICAN   A jeans-and-T-shirt kind of place with wooden tables, Baja Cafe serves fantastic Mexican food at even better prices. It's located right by the Florida East Coast Railway tracks, so don't be surprised if you feel a little rattling. Live music and entertainment in the evening make this place a hot spot for an unpretentious crowd.

201 NW 1st Ave., Boca Raton. ✆ **561/394-5449.** No reservations. Main courses $6–$10. No credit cards. Mon–Thurs 11:30am–10:30pm, Fri–Sat 11:30am–11pm, Sun 5–10pm.

The Tin Muffin Cafe ✿ BAKERY/SANDWICH SHOP   Popular with the downtown lunch crowd, this excellent storefront bakery keeps them lining up for big sandwiches on fresh bread, plus muffins, quiches, and good homemade soups like split pea or lentil. The curried chicken sandwich is stuffed with oversized chunks of only white meat doused in a creamy curry dressing and fruit. There are a few cafe tables inside and even one outside on a tiny patio. Be warned, however, that service is forgivably slow and parking is a nightmare. Try parking a few blocks away at a meter on the street.

364 E. Palmetto Park Rd. (between Federal Hwy. and the Intracoastal Bridge), Boca Raton. © 561/ 392-9446. Sandwiches and salads $6.50–$10.95. No credit cards. Mon–Fri 11am–5pm, Sat 11am–4pm.

Tom's Place *finds* BARBECUE   There are two important factors in a successful barbecue: the cooking and the sauce. Tom and Helen Wright's no-nonsense shack wins on both counts, offering flawlessly grilled meats paired with well-spiced sauces. Beef, chicken, pork, and fish are served soul-food style, with your choice of two sides such as rice with gravy, collard greens, black-eyed peas, coleslaw, or mashed potatoes. Signed celebrity photographs decorate the walls.

7251 N. Federal Hwy., Boca Raton. © 561/997-0920. Reservations not accepted. Main courses $8–$15; sandwiches $5–$6; early bird special $7.95. AE, MC, V. Tues–Thurs 11:30am–9:30pm, Fri 11:30am–10pm, Sat noon–10pm.

BOCA RATON & DELRAY BEACH AFTER DARK
THE BAR, CLUB & MUSIC SCENE

South Ocean Boulevard and Atlantic Avenue in Delray Beach are slowly but surely getting hip to nightlife—though they are still a far cry from the Fort Lauderdale strip. In Boca Raton, Mizner Park is the nucleus of a makeshift nightlife, with restaurants masking themselves as nightclubs or, at the very least, very sceney bars, such as Gigi's Tavern, 346 Plaza Real, in Mizner Park (© 561/368-4488), and Mark's Mizner Park, 344 Plaza Real (© 561/395-0770).

Boston's on the Beach   This is a family restaurant with a somewhat lively bar scene. It's a good choice for post-sunbathing, supercasual happy hours on Monday to Friday from 4 to 8pm, or for live reggae on Monday. With two decks overlooking the ocean, Boston's is an ideal place to mellow out and take in the scenery. 40 S. Ocean Blvd., Delray Beach. © 561/278-3364. Daily 7am–2am. No cover.

Dakotah 624   Creative cocktails such as the Kissing Cousin (Southern Comfort, Fris vodka, lime juice, and triple sec) and its own line of cigars attract a hip, young clientele to this vaguely Southwestern-style bar on the beach. 270 E. Atlantic Ave., Delray Beach. © 561/274-6244. Mon–Wed 4pm–1am, Thurs–Sat 4pm–2am, Sun 4–11pm. No cover.

Gatsby's   This always-busy bar is singles central, featuring big-screen TVs, microbrews, and martinis. Thursday-night college nights are especially popular, as are Friday happy hours. 5970 SW 18th St., Boca Raton. © 561/393-3900. Mon–Fri 4pm–2am, Sat–Sun 6pm–4am. No cover.

Mezzanotte   The Mezzanotte on South Beach's Washington Avenue used to be the place for a bacchanalian funfest. Then the place went from crazy to closed. The good times have traveled north to this Boca offshoot, where a well-tanned, glitzy crowd of young and old let their hair (or toupees) down, especially on weekends. 150 E. Palmetto Park Rd., Boca Raton. © 561/361-0111. Sun–Thurs 5–10pm, Fri–Sat 5pm–2am. No cover.

Radius   This big, noisy techno-trance warehouse west of the highway attracts a range of big-haired girls and macho guys with gold chains. It's Boca's only attempt at a clubby nightlife and, if you don't mind dancing with a really young crowd, it can be amusing, depending on your sense of humor. If you can, try to have your hotel concierge put you on the "list" so you won't have to shell out

$20 or more for this nocturnal gamble. 7000 W. Palmetto Park Rd. (at the SW corner of Powerline Rd. in the Bank of America building), Boca Raton. © 561/392-3747. Thurs–Sun 9pm–5am. Cover varies $5–$20.

THE PERFORMING ARTS

For details on upcoming events, check the *Boca News* or the *Sun-Sentinel,* or call the **Palm Beach County Cultural Council** information line at © **800/882-ARTS.** During business hours, a staffer can give details on current performances. After hours, a recorded message describes the week's events.

The **Florida Symphonic Pops,** a 70-piece professional orchestra, performs jazz, swing, rock, big band, and classical music throughout Boca Raton. For nearly 50 years, this ever-growing musical force has entertained audiences of every age. Call © **561/393-7677** for a schedule of concerts.

Boca's best theater company is the **Caldwell Theatre,** and it's worth checking out. Located in a strip shopping center at 7873 N. Federal Hwy., this equity showcase does well-known dramas, comedies, classics, off-Broadway hits, and new works throughout the year. Prices are reasonable (usually between $29 and $38). Full-time students with ID will be especially interested in the little-advertised Student Rush. When available, tickets are sold for $5 to those who arrive at least an hour in advance. Call © **561/241-7432** for details.

3 Palm Beach ⧏★⧏★ & West Palm Beach ⧏★

65 miles N of Miami, 193 miles E of Tampa, 45 miles of Fort Lauderdale

Palm Beach County encompasses cities from Boca Raton in the south to Jupiter and Tequesta in the north. But it is Palm Beach, the small island town across the Intracoastal Waterway, which has been the traditional winter home of America's aristocracy—the Kennedys, the Rockefellers, the Pulitzers, the Trumps, titled socialites, and plenty of CEOs. For a real-time perspective on what it means to put on the ritz, there is no better place than Palm Beach, where teenagers cruise around in their parents' Rolls Royces and socialites, seen only in society publications, seem to jump out of the glossy pages and into an even glossier, glitzier real life. It's really something to be seen, despite the fact that some may consider it all over the top and, frankly, obscene. But it is not only a city of upscale resorts and chic boutiques. In fact, Palm Beach holds some surprises, from a world-class art museum to one of the top bird-watching areas in the state.

Across the water from Palm Beach proper, or the "island" as locals call it, is downtown West Palm Beach, which is where everybody else lives. Clematis Street is the area's nightlife hub, with a great selection of bars, clubs, and restaurants. City Place is West Palm's version of Mizner Park; shops, restaurants, and other entertainment options liven up this once-dead area of West Palm. In addition to good beaching, boating, and diving, you'll find great golf and tennis throughout the county.

Fun Fact So That's How It Got Its Name

In 1878, the Spanish brigantine *Providencia,* bound from Trinidad to Cadiz with a cargo of coconuts, washed ashore on an unknown island. The strewn coconuts propagated and caused a wild growth of palm trees. That island, of course, was Palm Beach.

Palm Beach & West Palm Beach

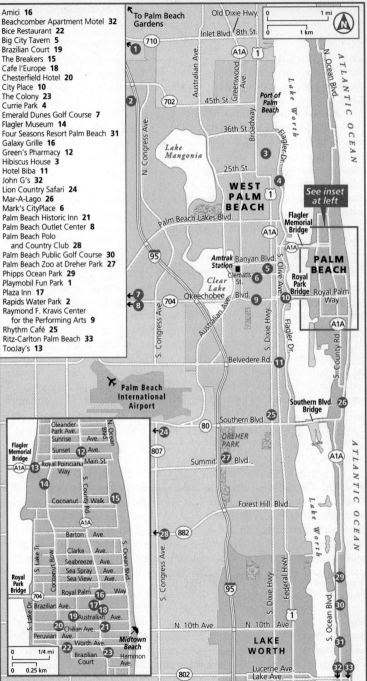

345

Note: Palm Beach's population swells from 20,000 in the summer to 40,000 in the winter. Book early if you plan to visit during the winter months.

ESSENTIALS

GETTING THERE If you're driving up or down the Florida coast, you'll probably reach the Palm Beach area by way of I-95. Exit at Belvedere Road or Okeechobee Boulevard and head east to reach the most central part of Palm Beach.

Visitors on their way to or from Orlando or Miami should take the Florida Turnpike, a toll road with a speed limit of 65 mph. Tolls are pricey, though; you may pay upward of $9 from Orlando and $4 from Miami. If you're coming from Florida's west coast, you can take either State Road 70, which runs north of Lake Okeechobee to Fort Pierce, or State Road 80, which runs south of the lake to Palm Beach.

All major **airlines** fly to the Palm Beach International Airport, at Congress Avenue and Belvedere Road (✆ **561/471-7400**). **Amtrak** (✆ **800/USA-RAIL;** www.amtrak.com) has a terminal in West Palm Beach, at 201 S. Tamarind Ave. (✆ **561/832-6169**).

GETTING AROUND Although a car is almost a necessity in this area, a recently revamped public transportation system is extremely convenient for getting to some attractions in both West and Palm Beach. **Palm Tran** underwent a major expansion in late 1996, increasing service to 32 routes and more than 140 buses. The fare is $1 for adults and 50¢ for children ages 3 to 18, seniors, and riders with disabilities. Free route maps are available by calling ✆ **561/233-4-BUS.** Information operators are available from 6am to 7pm, except Sunday.

In downtown West Palm, free shuttles from City Place to Clematis Street operate Monday through Friday from 9am until 4pm, with plans to expand operations to evenings and weekends, too. Allegedly, the shuttles come every 5 minutes, but I'd count on them taking longer. Look for the bubble-gum-pink minibuses throughout downtown. Call ✆ **561/833-8873** for more details.

For a more nostalgic route, consider the stately wicker chariots that run in the downtown area especially on weekends and during special events. Rates vary according to the time of day but average $1 to $2 per block, plus a per person charge of $1. Call ✆ **561/835-8922** for pickup or information.

VISITOR INFORMATION The **Palm Beach County Convention and Visitors Bureau,** 1555 Palm Beach Lakes Blvd., Suite 204, West Palm Beach, FL 33401 (✆ **800/554-PALM** or 561/471-3995; www.palmbeachfl.com), distributes an informative brochure and will answer questions about visiting the Palm Beaches. Ask for a map as well as a copy of its Arts and Attractions Calendar, a day-to-day guide to art, music, stage, and other events in the county.

BEACHES & ACTIVE PURSUITS

BEACHES Public beaches are a rare commodity here in Palm Beach. Most of the island's best beaches are fronted by private estates and are inaccessible to the general public. However, there are a few notable exceptions, including **Midtown Beach,** east of Worth Avenue, on Ocean Boulevard, between Royal Palm Way and Gulfstream Road, which boasts more than 100 feet of undeveloped beach. This newly widened sandy coast is now a centerpiece and a natural oasis in a town dominated by commercial glitz. There are no restrooms or concessions here, although a lifeguard is on duty until sundown. About 1½ miles north of there, near Dunbar Street, is a popular hangout for locals, who prefer it to Midtown

_C_ The Sport of Kings

The posh Palm Beach Polo and Country Club is one of the world's premier polo grounds and hosts some of the sport's top-rated players. Even if you're not a sports fan, you must attend a match at this field, which is actually on the mainland in an area called Wellington. Rest assured, however, that the spectators, and many of the players, are pure Palm Beach. After all, a day at the pony grounds is one of the only good reasons to leave Palm Beach proper. Don't worry, you need not be a Vanderbilt or a Kennedy to attend—matches are open to the public and are surprisingly affordable.

Even if you haven't a clue to how the game is played, you can spend your time people watching. Stargazers have spotted Prince Charles, Sylvester Stallone, Tommy Lee Jones, Bo Derek, and Ivana Trump, among others, in recent years. Dozens of lesser-known royalty, and just plain old characters, keep box seats or chalets right on the grounds.

Incidentally, the point of polo is to keep the other team from getting the ball through your goal. The fast-paced game is divided into six chukkers—like an inning in baseball—each 7 minutes long. There are 3-minute breaks between chukkers except at half time, which lasts 10 minutes. The whole thing is narrated by a British chap who sounds as though he walked off a Monty Python set.

Dress is casual; a navy or tweed blazer over jeans or khakis is a standard for men, while neat-looking jeans or a pantsuit is the norm for women. On warmer days, shorts and, of course, a polo shirt are fine, too.

General admission is $6 to $10; box seats cost $10 to $36. Matches are held throughout the week. Schedules vary, but the big names usually compete on Sunday at 3:30pm from January to April.

The fields are located at 11809 Polo Club Rd., Wellington, 10 miles west of the Forest Hill Boulevard exit of I-95. Call _C_ **561/793-1440** for tickets and a detailed schedule of events.

Beach, because of the relaxed and serene atmosphere. Parking is available at meters along Florida A1A. At the south end of Palm Beach, there's a less popular but better-equipped beach at **Phipps Ocean Park.** On Ocean Boulevard, between the Southern Boulevard and Lake Avenue causeways, is a large and lively public beach encompassing more than 1,300 feet of groomed and guarded oceanfront. With picnic and recreation areas, as well as plenty of parking, the area is especially good for families.

BIKING   Rent anything from an English single-speed to a full-tilt mountain bike at the **Palm Beach Bicycle Trail Shop,** 223 Sunrise Ave. (_C_ **561/659-4583**). The rates are $8 an hour, $20 a half day (9am–5pm), or $26 for 24 hours, and include a basket and lock (not that a lock is necessary in this fortress of a town). The most scenic route is called the Lake Trail, running the length of the island along the Intracoastal Waterway. On it, you'll see some of the most magnificent mansions and grounds and will enjoy the views of downtown West Palm Beach as well as some great wildlife.

GOLF There's good golfing in the Palm Beaches, but many of the private club courses are maintained exclusively for the use of their members. Ask at your hotel, or contact the **Palm Beach County Convention and Visitors Bureau** (© 561/471-3995) for information on which clubs are currently available for play. In the off-season, some private courses open their greens to visitors staying in a Palm Beach County hotel. This "Golf-A-Round" program offers free greens fees (carts are additional); reservations can be made through most major hotels.

The best hotel for golf in the area is the **PGA National Resort and Spa** (see p. 365, © 800/633-9150), which features a whopping 90 holes of golf.

One of the state's best courses that is open to the public is **Emerald Dunes Golf Course** ⚐, 2100 Emerald Dunes Dr. in West Palm Beach (© 561/687-1700). Designed by Tom Fazio, this dramatic 7,006-yard, par-72 course was voted "One of the Best 10 You Can Play" by *Golf* magazine. It is located just off the Florida Turnpike at Okeechobee Boulevard. Bookings are taken up to 30 days ahead. Fees start at $130, including carts.

The **Palm Beach Public Golf Course,** 2345 S. Ocean Blvd. (© 561/547-0598), a popular public 18-hole course, is a par-54. The course opens at 8am and runs on a first-come, first-served basis. Club rentals are available. Greens fees start at $20 per person.

SCUBA DIVING Year-round warm waters, barrier reefs, and plenty of wrecks make South Florida one of the world's most popular places for diving. One of the best-known artificial reefs in this area is a vintage Rolls-Royce Silver Shadow, which was sunk offshore in 1985. Nature has taken its toll, however, and divers can no longer sit in the car, which has been ravaged by time and saltwater.

Call either of the following outfitters for gear and excursions: **Ocean Sports Scuba Center,** 1736 S. Congress Ave., West Palm Beach (© 561/641-1144) or **Jim Abernaethy's Scuba Adventures,** at 2116 Avenue B. in Riviera Beach (© 561/691-5808).

TENNIS There are hundreds of tennis courts in Palm Beach County. Wherever you are staying, you are bound to be within walking distance of one. In addition to the many hotel tennis courts (see "Where to Stay," below), you can play at **Currie Park,** 2400 N. Flagler Dr., West Palm Beach (© 561/835-7025), a public park with three lighted hard courts. They are free and available on a first-come, first-served basis.

WATERSPORTS Call the **Seaside Activities Station** (© 561/835-8922) to arrange sailboat, jet-ski, bicycle, kayak, water-ski, and parasail rentals.

SEEING THE SIGHTS

Flagler Museum ⚐⚐⚐ The Gilded Age is preserved in this luxurious mansion commissioned by Standard Oil tycoon Henry Flagler as a wedding present to his third wife. Whitehall, also known as the "Taj Mahal of North America," is a classically columned Edwardian-style mansion containing 55 rooms, including a Louis XIV music room and art gallery, a Louis XV ballroom, and 14 guest suites outfitted with original antique European furnishings. Out back, climb aboard the Rambler, Mr. Flagler's private, restored railroad car. Allow at least 1½ hours to tour the stunning grounds and interior. School and group tours are available, but, for the most part, this is a self-guided museum.

One Whitehall Way (at Cocoanut Row and Whitehall Way), Palm Beach. © 561/655-2833. www.flagler.org. Admission $8 adults, $3 children ages 6–12. Tues–Sat 10am–5pm, Sun noon–5pm.

ⓒ Unreal Estate

No trip to Palm Beach is complete without at least a glimpse of Mar-A-Lago, the stately residence of Donald Trump, the 21st century's answer to Jay Gatsby. In 1985, Trump purchased Mar-A-Lago, the former estate of cereal heiress Marjorie Merriweather Post, for what was considered a meager $8 million (for a fully furnished beachfront property of this stature, it was a relative bargain, actually) to the great consternation of locals who feared that he would turn the place into a casino. Instead, Trump, who resides in a portion of the palace, opened the house to the public—for a price, of course—as a tony country club (membership fee: $100,000). Infinitely more interesting than any of Trump's other real estate acquisitions, Mar-A-Lago, Spanish for "from sea to lake," has a history that's priceless.

Built as Post's vacation home in 1923, Mar-A-Lago eventually became the heiress's primary residence, which she shared with second husband, E. F. Hutton. Together they lived in utter opulence, throwing gala events and lavish dinner parties on a nightly basis. The dining room, with 27 different china patterns and at least 4,000 pieces of silver, was modeled after the Chigi Palace in Rome. Other rooms captured various styles, including Venetian and Norwegian. The exterior, done in a Hispano-Moresque style, featured a massive collection of Spanish tile for the rooftops.

When Post died in 1973 she bequeathed Mar-A-Lago to the U.S. government for use in housing presidents and traveling dignitaries. Because the maintenance was in excess of $1 million a year, the government eventually returned the estate to the Post Foundation. Enter the Donald, who, to everyone's surprise, restored the home to its original glory, saying, "Some people collect artworks . . . I collect great homes."

While there are currently no tours open to the public, you can glimpse the gorgeous manse as you cross the bridge from West Palm Beach into Palm Beach. Its website (www.pbol.com/maralago/tour.html) offers photos, a calendar of events, and more details than you'd ever care to know. 1100 S. Ocean Blvd., Palm Beach. ⓒ 561/833-2466.

Norton Museum of Art 𝕽𝕽𝕽   Since a 1997 expansion doubled the Norton's space, the museum has gained even more prominence in the art world. It is world famous for its prestigious permanent collection and top temporary exhibitions. The museum's major collections are divided geographically. The American galleries contain major works by Edward Hopper, Georgia O'Keeffe, and Jackson Pollock. The French collection contains Impressionist and post-Impressionist paintings by Cézanne, Degas, Gauguin, Matisse, Monet, Picasso, Pissarro, and Renoir. And the Chinese collection contains more then 200 bronzes, jades, and ceramics, as well as a collection of monumental Buddhist sculptures. Allow about 2 hours to see this museum, depending on your level of interest.

1451 S. Olive Ave., West Palm Beach. ⓒ 561/832-5196. Fax 561/659-4689. www.norton.org. Admission $6 adults, $2 ages 13–21, free for children 12 and under. Mon–Sat 10am–5pm, Sun 1pm–5pm. Closed Mon

(May–Oct) and all major holidays. Take I-95 to exit 52 (Okeechobee Blvd. East). Travel east on Okeechobee to Dixie Hwy., then south ½ mile to the Norton. Parking may be accessed through entrances on Dixie Hwy. and S. Olive Ave.

Playmobil Fun Park *★★ (Kids)*   In a child's mind, it doesn't get any better than this. The 17,000-square-foot Playmobil Fun Park is housed in a replica castle and loaded with themed areas for imaginative play: a medieval village, a western town, a fantasy dollhouse, and more. Plus, there are two water-filled tables on which kids can play with the Playmobil boats. Tech-minded kids could get bored, but toddlers (and up to age 5 or so) will love this place. You *could* spend hours here and not spend a penny, but parents beware: Everything is available for purchase.

8031 N. Military Trail, Palm Beach Gardens. ⓒ **800/351-8697** or 561/691-9880. Fax 561/691-9517. www. playmobil.com. Admission $1. Mon–Sat 10am–6pm., Sun noon–5pm. From I-95, go north to Palm Beach Lakes Blvd., then west to Military Trail. Turn left, and the park is about a mile down on the right.

NATURE PRESERVES & ATTRACTIONS

Lion Country Safari *★ (Kids)*   More than 1,300 animals on this 500-acre preserve are divided into their indigenous regions, from the East African preserve of the Serengeti to the American West. Elephants, wildebeest, ostriches, American bison, buffalo, watusi, pink flamingos, and many other more unusual species roam the preserve. When I visited, most of the lions were asleep; when they are awake, they travel freely throughout the cageless grassy landscape. In fact, you're the one who's confined in your own car without an escort (no convertibles allowed). You're given a detailed informational pamphlet with photos and descriptions and are instructed to obey the 15 mph speed limit—unless you see the rhinos charge (a rare occasion), in which case you're encouraged to floor it. To drive the loop takes just over an hour, though you could make a day of just watching the chimpanzees play on their secluded islands. Included in the admission price is Safari World, an amusement park with paddleboats, a carousel, miniature golf, and a nursery for baby animals born in the preserve. Picnics are encouraged, and camping is available (call for reservations). The best time to go is late afternoon right before the park closes when they herd up all the animals; plus, it's much cooler then, so the lions are more active.

Southern Blvd. W. at S.R. 80, West Palm Beach. ⓒ **561/793-1084**, or 561/793-9797 for camping reservations. www.lioncountrysafari.com. Admission $16.95 adults, $14.95 seniors, $12.95 children 3–9, free for children under 3. Van rental is $8 per hr. Daily 10am–5:30pm (last vehicle admitted at 4:30pm). From I-95, exit on Southern Blvd. Go west for about 18 miles.

Palm Beach Zoo at Dreher Park *★*   If you want animals, go to Lion Country Safari. Unlike big-city zoos, this intimate 23-acre park is more like a stroll in the park than an all-day excursion. It features about 500 animals representing more than 100 different species. A special monkey exhibit and petting zoo are favorites with kids. Stroller and wagon rental available. Allow at least 2 hours to see all of the sights here.

1301 Summit Blvd. (east of I-95 between Southern and Forest Hill blvds.). ⓒ **561/547-WILD**. Fax 561/585-6085. www.palmbeachzoo.org. Admission $7.50, $6 seniors, $5 children 3–12, free for children under 3. Daily 9am–5pm. Closed Thanksgiving.

Rapids Water Park *★ (Kids)*   It may not be on the same grand scale as the theme parks in Orlando, but Rapids is a great way to cool off on a hot day. There are 12 acres of water rides, including a children's area and miniature golf course.

6566 N. Military Trail, West Palm Beach (1 mile west of I-95 on Military between 45th St. (exit 54) and Blue Heron Blvd. (exit 55) in West Palm Beach. ⓒ **561/842-8756**. www.rapidswaterpark.com. Admission $17–$24 per person; free ages 2 and under. Open mid-March–Sept. Mon–Fri 10am–5pm, Sat–Sun 10am–6pm.

SHOPPING & BROWSING

No matter what your budget is, be sure to take a stroll down Worth Avenue, "the Rodeo Drive of the South" and a window-shopper's dream. Between South Ocean Boulevard and Cocoanut Row, there are more than 200 boutiques, posh shops, art galleries, and upscale restaurants. If you want to fit in, dress as if you were going to an elegant luncheon and not to the mall down the street.

Despite the presence of the usual suspects (**Gucci, Chanel, Armani, Hermes,** and **Louis Vuitton,** among others), Worth Avenue is not impervious to the mainstream. **Victoria's Secret, Limited Express,** and several other chains have sneaked in here, too, but so have a good number of unique boutiques. **History Buff,** 32 via Mizner (© 561/366-8255), is a virtual museum, selling every genre of original historical autograph, some dating back to the 1600s, as well as vintage signed photos, first-edition books, and memorabilia. A similar store is **Paper Treasures,** at 217 Worth Ave. (© 561/835-1891), an autograph gallery with a priceless collection of John Hancocks, including those of Joe DiMaggio, Mickey Mantle, Andrew Jackson, Abraham Lincoln, Howard Hughes, and hundreds more, all displayed in beautiful frames. For privileged feet, **Stubbs & Wooton,** 323 Worth Ave. (© 561/655-4105), sells velvet slippers that are a favorite of the loofah-ed locals. **The Purple Turtle,** 150 Worth Ave. (© 561/655-1625) in the Esplanade shopping promenade, sells designer clothes for infants, including Baby Dior and Baby Armani. For rare and estate jewelry, **Richter's of Palm Beach,** 224 Worth Ave. (© 561/655-0774), has been specializing in priceless gems since 1893. Just off Worth Avenue, at 374 S. County Rd., is the **Church Mouse** (© 561/ 659-2154), a great consignment/thrift shop with antique furnishings and tableware as well as lots of good castaway clothing and shoes, all reasonably priced. This shop usually closes for 2 months during the summer. Call to be sure.

City Place, 222 Lakeview Ave., West Palm Beach (© 561/835-0862), is a $550 million, Mediterranean-style shopping, dining, and entertainment complex that's responsible for revitalizing what was once a lifeless downtown West Palm Beach. Among the 78 mostly chain stores are **Macy's, FAO Schwarz, Benetton,** which has an in-line skating track inside, **Armani Exchange, Pottery Barn,** and **SEE** eyewear. Restaurants include a Ghirardelli ice cream shop, Legal Seafood, City Cellar Wine Bar and Grill, and Cheesecake Factory. Best of all is the Muvico Parisian, a 20-screen movie theater where you can wine and dine while watching a feature.

Elsewhere, Downtown West Palm Beach has a scant number of interesting boutiques along Clematis Street. In addition to a large and well-organized bookstore, **Clematis Street Books,** at 206 Clematis St. (© 561/832-2302), there are a few used-record stores, clothing shops, and several art galleries.

The **Palm Beach Outlet Center,** at 5700 Okeechobee Blvd. (3 miles west of I-95), West Palm Beach, is the most elegant outlet mall I have ever seen. Upscale clothing, luggage, and shoes are offered at bargain prices in lushly decorated surroundings. The fully enclosed mall also sports a food court.

WHERE TO STAY

The island of Palm Beach is the epitome of *Lifestyles of the Rich and Famous,* oozing with glitz, glamour, and the occasional scandal. Royalty and celebrities come to winter here, and there are plenty of lavishly priced options to accommodate them. Happily, there are also a few special inns that offer reasonably priced rooms in elegant settings. But the more modest places to lay your straw hat are mostly surrounding the island.

A few of the larger hotel chains operating in Palm Beach include the **Palm Beach Marriott/Fairfield Inn and Suites,** at 2870 S. Ocean Blvd. (© **800/654-2000** or 561/582-2581), which is across the street from the beach. Also beachside is the pricey **Palm Beach Hilton,** at 2842 S. Ocean Blvd. (© **800/433-1718** or 561/586-6542). An excellent and affordable alternative right in the middle of Palm Beach's commercial section is a condominium that operates as a hotel, too: the **Palm Beach Hotel,** at 235 Sunrise Ave. (between County Road and Bradley Place, across the street from the Publix supermarket; © **561/659-7794**). With winter prices starting at about $105, this clean and comfortable accommodation is a great option for those looking for the rare bargain in Palm Beach.

In West Palm Beach, the chain hotels are mostly located on the main arteries close to the highways and a short drive to the activities in downtown. They include a **Best Western,** 1800 Palm Beach Lakes Blvd. (© **800/331-9569** or 561/683-8810), and, just down the road, a **Comfort Inn,** 1901 Palm Lakes Blvd. (© **800/221-2222** or 561/689-6100). Farther south is the **Parkview Motor Lodge,** 4710 S. Dixie Hwy., just south of Southern Boulevard (© **561/833-4644**). This 28-room, single-story motel is the best of the many motels along Dixie Highway (U.S. 1). With rates starting at $50 for a room with television, air-conditioning, and telephone, you can't ask for more.

For other options, try Palm Beach Accommodations (© **800/543-SWIM**).

VERY EXPENSIVE

Brazilian Court ★★★   This elegant, Old World Palm Beach, Mediterranean-style hotel dates back to the 1920s and almost looks like a Beverly Hills bungalow. The rooms, renovated in 1997, are spacious, albeit a bit blasé, but the marble bathrooms are beautiful and modern. Service is doting, though a bit aloof—you won't always be received by smiling faces, but you will get whatever you want. There's even room service exclusively for pets (you know the type: held hostage in Mummy's Gucci bag). A large hotel by Palm Beach standards (the Breakers notwithstanding), Brazilian Court is sprawled over half a block and features fountains and private courtyards.

301 Australian Ave., Palm Beach, FL 33480 © **800/552-0335** or 561/655-7740. Fax 561/655-0801. www.braziliancourt.com. 103 units. Winter $335–$875. off-season $165–$525. Special packages available. AE, DC, DISC, MC, V. **Amenities:** Restaurant, private dining room (up to 12), bar (see "The Palm Beaches After Dark," later in this chapter); heated outdoor pool; exercise room; spa treatments; library; concierge; salon; 24-hr. room service (and special room service for pets!). *In room:* A/C, TV, coffeemaker, hair dryer, iron.

The Breakers ★★★   This 140-acre beachfront hotel is what Palm Beach is all about. Elaborate, stately, and resplendent in all its Italian Renaissance–style glory, it's where old money mixes with new money, and the Old World gives way, albeit reluctantly, to a bit of modernity (note the hotel's recent elimination of the jackets-required rule). The Breakers consists of a seven-story building with a frescoed lobby and long, majestic hallways reminiscent of a palace. The indulgent Oceanfront Spa and Beach Club features a spectacular oceanview fitness center (makes workouts a lot less grueling), four oceanfront pools, cabanas, and saunas. Rooms were modernized a bit, but remain elegant, not sterile, with plush furnishings, huge bathrooms, and views of the ocean or the hotel's magnificently manicured grounds. A revamp of Florida's oldest existing golf course, led by Brian Silva, transformed the Breakers Ocean Course into a 6,200-yard, championship-level par 70.

1 S. County Rd., Palm Beach, FL 33480. ℂ 800/833-3141, 888/BREAKERS, or 561/655-6611. Fax 561/659-8403. www.thebreakers.com. 560 units. Winter $420–$3,000; off-season $270–$1,950. Special packages available. AE, DC, DISC, MC, V. Valet parking $17. From I-95, exit Okeechobee Blvd. E., head east to S. County Rd., and turn left. **Amenities:** 5 restaurants, 3 bars; 4 outdoor pools; golf course; 14 tennis courts; health club and spa; watersports equipment (including scuba and sailing); croquet, shuffleboard, and beach volleyball courts; bike rental; children's programs; game rooms; concierge; business center; shopping arcade; salon; 24-hr. room service; in-room massage; babysitting; dry-cleaning and laundry services. *In room:* A/C, TV, Internet access, CD player, minibar, hair dryer.

Four Seasons Resort Palm Beach 🏖🏖   Built in 1989 at the edge of Palm

Beach's downtown district, this elegant resort has quickly gained accolades from around the world. An incredibly hospitable staff works hard to be sure this beachfront gem lives up to its reputation. The elegant marble lobby is replete with hand-carved European furnishings, grand oil paintings, tapestries, and dramatic flower arrangements—though I did feel like I was in a museum, unable to touch anything. The rooms are spacious with private balconies and lavish bathrooms with color TVs. The full service spa is excellent, and you will be remiss if you go without experiencing the incredible oceanview massage at the poolside cabanas. The main dining room, known simply as The Restaurant, serves one of the best dinners (Southeastern regional cuisine) in Palm Beach. Executive Chef Hubert Des Marais is one of *Food and Wine* magazine's "Ten Best New Chefs." Two other less formal restaurants, including a pool bar and grill, round out the dining options.

2800 S. Ocean Blvd., Palm Beach, FL 33480. ℂ 800/432-2335 or 561/582-2800. Fax 561/547-1557. www.fourseasons.com. 210 units. Winter $395–$695 double; from $1,500 suite. Off-season $275–$595 double; from $870 suite. AE, DC, DISC, MC, V. Valet parking $18. Pets under 20 pounds accepted. From I-95, take 6th Ave. exit east and turn left onto Dixie Hwy. Turn east onto Lake Ave. and north onto S. Ocean Blvd., and the hotel is just ahead on your right. **Amenities:** 3 restaurants, lounge; outdoor heated pool; 3 tennis courts; spa; watersports rentals; bike rental; cooking classes weekly; children's programs; concierge; business center; salon; 24-hr. room service; in-room massage; babysitting; dry-cleaning and laundry services. *In room:* A/C, TV/VCR, dataport, minibar, fridge, hair dryer, iron.

Ritz-Carlton Palm Beach 🏖🏖🏖   If the Breakers is too mammoth for your

tastes, consider the Ritz-Carlton. A lot warmer than the Four Seasons, the Ritz, though hyperluxurious, manages to lack pretension. Located on a beautiful beach in a tiny town about 8 miles from Palm Beach's shopping and dining area, the Ritz-Carlton is a plus for those who seek privacy but may be a drawback for those interested in the activity of "town." It is so discreet, in fact, that Palm Beach's luminaries often escape here for a rare weekend or night of anonymity. The hotel's French 18th- and 19th-century antique furnishings give no hint that the property is not yet even 10 years old. Each room has a private balcony and at least a glimpse of the ocean below. All are spacious while the large marble bathrooms are extremely inviting. The elegant dining room serves continental-style dinners in ornate surroundings. Other restaurants on the property include a grill, for dinner only; a casual restaurant, open all day; and a poolside cafe and bar. Cocktails are also served in the lobby lounge, where you can often find live entertainment. Afternoon tea is served daily but is best Wednesday to Saturday when a jazz trio entertains.

100 S. Ocean Blvd., Manalpan, FL 33462. ℂ 800/241-3333 or 561/533-6000. Fax 561/540-4999. www.ritz-carlton.com. 270 units. Winter $395–$820; $3,150 suite. Off-season $285–$725; $2,700 suite. AE, DISC, MC, V. Valet parking $15. From I-95, take Exit 45, heading east. After 1 mile, turn left onto Federal Hwy. (U.S. 1). Continue north for about a mile, and turn right onto Ocean Ave. Cross the Intracoastal Waterway; turn

right onto A1A. **Amenities:** 4 restaurants, bar; outdoor pool; health club; Jacuzzi; sauna; watersports equipment rental; bike rental; children's center/programs; concierge; business center; salon; 24-hr. room service; in-room massage; dry-cleaning and laundry services. *In room:* A/C, TV, dataport, minibar, hair dryer.

EXPENSIVE

Chesterfield Hotel ✦✦✦ Reminiscent of an English country manor, the Chesterfield Hotel in all its flowery, Laura Ashley–inspired glory is a magnificent, charming hotel with exceptional service to rival that of the Ritz. Warm and inviting, the Chesterfield is one of the only places in South Florida in which the idea of a fireplace (there's one in the hotel's library) doesn't seem ridiculous. Traditional English tea is served every afternoon, with fresh-baked scones, petit fours, and sandwiches. Rooms are decorated with bright fabrics and wallpaper and antiques. The roomy marble bathrooms are stocked with an array of luxurious toiletries. A small heated pool and courtyard are nice, and the beach is only 3 blocks away, but the real action is inside. At night, the hotel's retro-elegant Leopard Lounge (see "The Palm Beaches After Dark," below) serves decent continental cuisine but is better as a later-night hangout for live music, schmoozing, and staring at the local cognoscenti.

363 Cocoanut Row, Palm Beach, FL 33480. ✆ **800/243-7871** or 561/659-5800. Fax 561/659-6707. www.redcarnationhotels.com. 65 units. Winter $309–$350 single or double. Off-season $139–$230. Rollaway bed $15 extra. Packages available. AE, DC, DISC, MC, V. Free valet parking. From I-95, exit onto Okeechobee Blvd. E., cross the Intracoastal Waterway, and turn right onto Cocoanut Row. **Amenities:** Restaurant, lounge; small heated swimming pool; access to nearby health club; Jacuzzi; bike rental; concierge; business center; 24-hr. room service; in-room massage; babysitting; dry-cleaning service. *In room:* A/C, TV, dataport, VCR on request, hair dryer.

Plaza Inn ✦✦ This three-story, family-run bed-and-breakfast-style inn located 1 block from the beach is as understated and luxurious as the guests it hosts. From the simple and elegant flower arrangements in the marble lobby to the well-worn period antiques haphazardly placed throughout, the Plaza Inn, whose exterior was renovated in 2001, has the look of studied nonchalance. The courtyard, with its waterfalls and pool, and the intimate piano bar are just two examples of the inn's infinite charms. A small staff is remarkably hospitable and knowledgeable about the island's inner workings. Each uniquely decorated room is dressed with quality furnishings, several with carved four-poster beds, hand-crocheted spreads, and lace curtains. The bathrooms, renovated in 2000, are lovely if quite small, and the wall-mounted air conditioners can be noisy when they are needed in the warm months. Choose a corner room or one overlooking the small pool deck for the best light. It's a tough call to decide which is better—the Plaza Inn or the Chesterfield, but the Plaza, unlike the Chesterfield, does include a full breakfast in the price of the room.

215 Brazilian Ave., Palm Beach, FL 33480. ✆ **800/233-2632** or 561/832-8666. Fax 561/835-8776. www.plazainnpalmbeach.com. 48 units. Winter $225–$375; off-season $105–$195. Rates include breakfast. AE, MC, V. From I-95, exit onto Okeechobee Blvd. E. and cross the Intracoastal Waterway. Turn right onto Cocoanut Row; then left onto Brazilian Ave. Small pets permitted. **Amenities:** Restaurant, lounge; heated outdoor pool; exercise room; Jacuzzi; access to nearby health club ($15 per day); bike rental; concierge; secretarial services; limited room service; in-room massage; babysitting; dry-cleaning and laundry services. *In room:* A/C, TV, dataport, fridge, coffeemaker; hair dryer on request.

MODERATE

The Colony ✦✦ The sign outside of this Palm Beach mainstay should read: Roxanne Pulitzer slept here. She did, actually, for quite a while after her 7-week marriage went bust. For years, the colony has been a favorite hangout—hide-out, perhaps—for assorted old timers, socialites, and mysterious luminaries. Beyond that, the Colony is a Georgian-style hotel known for its attentive staff, floral-decorated rooms and, unfortunately, really small bathrooms. The 39 suites and apartments, not to mention the seven two-bedroom villas with Jacuzzis, are much more lavish—and lavishly priced.

155 Hammon Ave., Palm Beach, FL 33480. (©) **800/521-5525** or 561/655-5430. Fax 561/659-8104. www.the colonypalmbeach.com. 64 units, 19 suites, 7 villas. Winter $290–$695; off-season $130–$495. AE, DC, MC, V. From I-95, exit onto Okeechobee Blvd. E. and cross the Intracoastal Waterway. Turn right on S. County Rd.; then left onto Hammon Ave. **Amenities:** Restaurant, bar; heated Florida-shaped pool; spa; concierge; limited, seasonal room service. *In room:* A/C, TV, dataport, hair dryer.

Palm Beach Historic Inn 🐾🐾
Built in 1923, the Palm Beach Historic Inn is an area landmark located within walking distance of Worth Avenue, the beach, and several good restaurants. The small lobby is filled with antiques, books, magazines, and an old-fashioned umbrella stand, all of which add to the homey feel of this intimate bed-and-breakfast. In your room, wine, fruit, snacks, tea, and cookies ensure that you won't go hungry—never mind the excellent continental breakfast that is brought to you daily. All the rooms are on the second floor, are uniquely decorated, and feature hardwood floors, down comforters, Egyptian cotton linens, fluffy bathrobes, and plenty of good-smelling toiletries. Gone are the frills, floral prints, sheer curtains, and plethora of lace that once made this inn feel like staying at your grandmother's house. What you'll find here, thanks to new innkeepers who took over in July of 2001, is a casual elegance that's comfortable for everyone. In addition, a baby grand piano and guitars for the musically inclined, as well as videotapes to keep the kids entertained, have been added to the hotel's amenities.

365 S. County Rd., Palm Beach, FL 33480. (©) **561/832-4009.** Fax 561/832-6255. www.palmbeach historicinn.com. 13 units. Winter $150–$325; off-season $95–$175. Rates include continental breakfast. Children stay free in parents' room. Small pets accepted. No smoking. AE, MC, V. *In room:* A/C, TV/VCR, fridge, hair dryer.

INEXPENSIVE
Beachcomber Apartment Motel 🐾🐾
It's not just the bright pink building that makes this two-story beachfront motel stand out. For more than 35 years, the Beachcomber has been bringing sanity to pricey Palm Beach by offering a good standard of accommodation at reasonable prices. Squeezed between beachfront high-rises, the motel is located on a 300-foot private beach, adjacent to Lake Worth Beach and a short drive from Worth Avenue shops and local attractions. Every room has two double beds, large closets, and distinctive green-and-white tropical-style furnishings; some have kitchenettes. The most expensive have balconies overlooking the ocean. The bathrooms are basic, and amenities are limited to towels and soap.

3024 S. Ocean Blvd., Palm Beach, FL 33480. (©) **800/833-7122** or 561/585-4646. Fax 561/547-9438. 45 units. Winter $95–$250; off-season $55–$130. AE, DISC, MC, V. From I-95, exit 10th Ave. N. Head east to Federal Hwy. and turn right. Continue to Lake Ave. and turn left. Go over bridge and turn right at first traffic light. **Amenities:** Large pool; coin-operated laundry. *In room:* A/C, TV.

Hibiscus House 🐾🐾 *(Finds)*
Inexpensive bed-and-breakfasts are rare in Southeast Florida, making the Hibiscus House, one of the area's firsts, a true find. Located a few miles from the coast in a quiet residential neighborhood, this 1920s-era B&B is filled with handsome antiques and tapestries in luxurious fabrics. Every room has its own private terrace or balcony. The Red Room has a fabulous new bathroom with Jacuzzi. The backyard, a peaceful retreat, has been transformed into a tropical garden, complete with heated swimming pool and

lounge chairs. Also, there are plenty of pretty areas for guests to enjoy inside; one little sitting room is wrapped in glass and is stocked with playing cards and board games. *Beware:* Breakfast portions are enormous. The gourmet creations are as filling as they are beautiful. Ask for any special requests in advance; owners Raleigh Hill and Colin Rayer will be happy to oblige.

501 30th St., West Palm Beach, FL 33407. © **800/203-4927** or 561/863-5633. Fax 561/863-5633. www. hibiscushouse.com. 8 units. Winter $105–$260 double. Off-season $75–$180 double. Rates include breakfast. AE, MC, V. From I-95, exit onto Palm Beach Lakes Blvd. E. and continue 4 miles. Turn left onto Flagler Dr. and continue for about 20 blocks. Then turn left onto 30th St. Pets accepted. **Amenities:** Heated pool; concierge. *In room:* A/C, TV, hair dryer.

Hotel Biba ★★ *(Finds* As West Palm Beach comes into its own as far as nightlife is concerned, it was only a matter of time before a hip boutique hotel made its appearance in the historic El Cid neighborhood, located 1 mile from City Place and nightlife-heavy Clematis Street. The very cool Hotel Biba answers the call for an inexpensive, chic hotel that young hipsters can call their own. A word of advice, however: The hotel is not exactly soundproof. Rooms may be cloistered by fence and gardens, but they are still extremely close to a major thoroughfare. Try to ask for one that's on the quieter Belvedere Road as opposed to those facing South Olive Avenue. Housed in a renovated Colonial-style 1940s motor lodge, Biba has been remarkably updated on the inside by de rigueur designer Barbara Hulanicki and features a sleek and chic lobby with the requisite hip hotel bar, the Biba Bar, a gorgeously landscaped outdoor pool area with Asian gardens, and reflection pond. Rooms are equally fabulous, with private patios, mosaic tile floors, custom-made mahogany furniture, Egyptian cotton linens, down pillows, exquisite bathroom products, and high-tech amenities. The bold color schemes mix nicely with the high-fashion crowd that convenes here.

320 Belvedere Rd., West Palm Beach, FL 33405. © **561/832-0094**. Fax 561/833-7848. www.hotelbiba.com. 43 units. Year-round rates $79–$179. **Amenities:** Restaurant, lounge; outdoor pool; concierge. *In room:* A/C, TV, dataport, CD player, hair dryer.

WHERE TO DINE

Palm Beach has some of the area's swankiest restaurants. Thanks to the development of downtown West Palm Beach, however, there is also a great selection of trendier, less expensive spots. Dress here is slightly more formal than in most other areas of Florida: Men wear blazers, and women generally put on modest dresses or chic suits when they dine out, even in the oppressively hot days of summer.

VERY EXPENSIVE

Cafe l'Europe ★★★ FRENCH/CONTINENTAL One of Palm Beach's finest and most popular, this award-winning, romantic, luxurious, and formal restaurant gives you good reason to get dressed up. The enticing appetizers, served by a superb staff, might include Chinese spring rolls, baked goat-cheese salad with raspberry-walnut dressing, poached salmon, or chilled gazpacho with avocado. Main courses run the gamut from sautéed potato-crusted Florida snapper to lamb chops to roast Cornish game hen. Seafood dishes and steaks in sumptuous but light sauces are always exceptional.

331 S. County Rd. (at the corner of Brazilian Ave.), Palm Beach. © **561/655-4020**. Reservations recommended. Main courses $18–$34. AE, DC, DISC, MC, V. Tues–Thurs noon–2:30pm and 5:45–10:30pm, Fri–Sat noon–2:30pm and 5:45pm–1am, Sun 6–10:30pm.

Mark's CityPlace ★★★ NEW AMERICAN   Star chef Mark Militello of Mark's Las Olas and South Beach fame has traveled on his high-speed culinary meteor and landed at West Palm's bustling entertainment and dining complex to the delight of foodies in Palm Beach. A Militello specialty, pizza, is cooked in wood-burning ovens that churn out trendy versions of the thin-crusted classic, such as shrimp, pesto, Fontina cheese, and sun-dried tomatoes. The sushi bar here is, frankly, out of place, since this is not a sushi restaurant. Entrees range from risotto with wild mushroom and truffle oil to an outstanding black-peppercorn-crusted seared yellowfin tuna. For dessert, try the double chocolate bread pudding with white-chocolate-chip ice cream.

700 S. Rosemary Ave., West Palm Beach. ℭ 561/514-0770. Reservations recommended. Main courses $17–$38. AE, DC, MC, V. Mon–Thurs 5–11pm, Fri–Sat 5–midnight, Sun 5pm–10:30pm.

EXPENSIVE

Amici ★ *Overrated* ITALIAN   This is one of those restaurants in which the scene is tastier than the cuisine. An upper-crusty Palm Beach set tends to convene here and consistently rave about what can only be considered above-average, overpriced Italian food. The best item on the entire menu is gnocchi with white truffle oil, Fontina cheese, and spinach. Everything else is fairly standard: grilled sandwiches, pastas with rustic sauces, pizzas, grilled shrimp, and fish. Despite its less-than-stellar food, it's always crowded and very noisy.

288 S. County Rd. (at Royal Palm Way), Palm Beach. ℭ 561/832-0201. Reservations strongly recommended on weekends. Main courses $18–$27; pastas and pizzas $8–$19. AE, DC, MC, V. Mon–Thurs 11:30am–3pm and 5:30–10:30pm, Fri–Sat 11:30am–3pm and 5:30–11pm, Sun 5:30–10:30pm.

Bice Restaurant ★★ ITALIAN   Bice's Northern Italian cuisine far surpasses that of Amici's, but as far as atmosphere is concerned, the air in here is a bit haughty, bordering on rude. Servers and diners alike seem to have noticeable attitudes, but you'll forget all that with one bite of the juicy veal cutlet with tomato salad or the *pasta e fagioli* (pasta with beans).

313½ Worth Ave., Palm Beach. ℭ 561/835-1600. Reservations essential. Main courses $20–$32. AE, DC, MC, V. Daily 11am–10pm.

Galaxy Grille ★ NEW AMERICAN   Stargazing is certainly at a premium at this deco-inspired Palm Beach hot spot known for a stellar clientele and a menu to match it. Two favorites include a superb horseradish-encrusted yellowtail snapper and an even better grilled swordfish with fresh tomato, black olives, grilled polenta, garlic, and escarole.

350 S. County Rd., Palm Beach. ℭ 561/833-9909. Reservations recommended. Main courses $27–$38. AE, DC, MC, V. Daily 5–11pm.

MODERATE

Big City Tavern ★★ AMERICAN   If the Palm Beach proper dining scene is too stuffy for you, head over the bridge to Clematis Street, downtown West Palm's hub of urban chic, where you will find this yuppie enclave of brick and pressed tin in which people-watching is at a premium. Despite its all-American appearance, Big City Tavern offers a varied menu, including coconut shrimp tempura with a salmon inside-out sushi roll, and a delicious bowl of littleneck clams in wine broth with roasted garlic and escarole. On weekends, the Tavern is mobbed, so be prepared for a long wait that's best spent at the action-packed bar.

224 Clematis St., West Palm Beach. ℭ 561/659-1853. Reservations suggested. Main courses $7.95–$28. AE, MC, V. Mon–Fri 11am–11pm, Sat. 6pm–1am, Sun 6–10pm.

Rhythm Café 🔆 *Finds* ECLECTIC AMERICAN   This funky hole-in-the-wall is where those in the know come to eat some of West Palm Beach's most laid-back gourmet food. On the handwritten, photocopied menu (which changes daily), you'll always find a fish specialty accompanied by a hefty dose of greens and garnishes. Also reliably outstanding is the sautéed medallion of beef tender-loin, served on a bed of arugula with a tangy rosemary vinaigrette. Salads and soups are a great bargain, since portions are relatively large and the display usu-ally spectacular. The kitschy decor of this tiny cafe comes complete with vinyl tablecloths and a changing display of paintings by local amateurs. Young, hand-some waiters are attentive but not solicitous. The old drugstore where the restau-rant recently relocated features an original 1950s lunch counter and stools.

3800 S. Dixie Hwy., West Palm Beach. 📞 561/833-3406. Reservations recommended on weekends. Main courses $12–$31. AE, DISC, MC, V. Tues–Sat 6–10pm; Sun (Dec–Mar) 5:30–9pm. Closed in early Sept. From I-95, exit east on Southern Blvd. Go 1 block north of Southern Blvd.; restaurant on the right.

INEXPENSIVE

Green's Pharmacy 🔆 *Value* AMERICAN   This neighborhood corner phar-macy offers one of the best meal deals in Palm Beach. Both breakfast and lunch are served coffee-shop style, either at a Formica bar or at plain tables placed on a black-and-white checkerboard floor. Breakfast specials include eggs and omelets served with home fries and bacon, sausage, or corned-beef hash. At lunch, the grill serves burgers and sandwiches, as well as ice cream sodas and milkshakes, to a loyal crowd of pastel-clad Palm Beachers.

151 N. County Rd., Palm Beach. 📞 561/832-0304. Fax 561/832-6502. Breakfast $2–$5; burgers and sand-wiches $3–$6; soups and salads $2–$7. AE, DISC, MC, V. Mon–Sat 7am–5pm, Sun 7am–3pm.

John G's 🔆 AMERICAN   This coffee shop is the most popular in the county. For decades, John G's has been attracting huge breakfast crowds; lines run out the door (on weekends, all the way down the block). Stop in for some good, greasy-spoon-style food served in heaping portions right on the beachfront. This place is known for fresh and tasty fish and chips and its selection of creative omelets and grill specials.

10 S. Ocean Blvd., Lake Worth. 📞 561/585-9860. www.johngs.com. Reservations not accepted. Breakfast $3–$8.50; lunch $5–$14. No credit cards. Daily 7am–3pm. From the Florida Tpk., take the Lake Worth exit and head toward the ocean.

TooJay's DELI   This simple and predictable restaurant and takeout spot is a favorite with locals and out-of-towners who want good old-fashioned deli. It is so popular, in fact, that TooJay's now has more than eight locations throughout South Florida. This is no Carnegie Deli, but by South Florida deli standards, the food is excellent. All the classic sandwiches are available: hot pastrami, roast beef, turkey, chicken, chopped liver, egg salad, and more. Comfort food in the form of huge portions of stuffed cabbage, chicken pot pie, beef brisket, and sautéed onions and chicken livers is sure to satisfy.

313 Royal Poinciana Plaza (3 miles east of I-95, off Exit 52A), Palm Beach. 📞 561/659-7232. Reservations not accepted. Main courses $9–$13; lunch $6–$10. AE, DC, MC, V. Daily 8am–9pm.

THE PALM BEACHES AFTER DARK
THE BAR, CAFE & MUSIC SCENE
A decade-old project to revitalize downtown West Palm Beach has finally become a reality, with **Clematis Street** at its heart. Artist lofts, sidewalk cafes, bars, restaurants, consignment shops, and galleries dot the street from Flagler Drive to Rosemary Avenue, creating a hot spot for a night out, especially on

weekends when yuppies mingle with stylish Euros and disheveled artists. Every Thursday night is a mob scene of 20- and 30-somethings who come out for "Clematis by Night." Each week features a different rock, blues, or reggae band plus an art show. Vendors sell food and drinks, and the street's bars and restaurants are packed. It is a bit raucous at times, but fun. Minors unaccompanied by their guardians are not permitted in the downtown area around Clematis Street after 10pm on weeknights and after 11pm on weekend nights. Otherwise, most of the nightspots listed below are open until about 3 or 4am.

Over the bridge, it's a completely different world. Palm Beach is much quieter and better known for its rather private society balls and estate parties. With the exception of some restaurants that are more of a scene—**Ta-boo, Amici,** and **Galaxy Grille**—Palm Beach nightlife is more likely to entail sipping port at one of the finer hotels like the Breakers, the Colony, the Ritz-Carlton, Four Seasons, or the Chesterfield.

West Palm Beach

Bliss Lounge   With its techno music and VIP rooms, this West Palm club seems like it belongs in the velvet-roped world of South Beach. 313 Clematis St. ⓒ 561/833-1444. Tues–Sat 10pm–4am. Cover $7. No cover before midnight.

E. R. Bradley's   What used to be a swank saloon on the island of Palm Beach is now a very casual, friendly indoor/outdoor bar in downtown West Palm, attracting a mixed crowd. The later-night bar scene is a real draw. If you are hungry, try the Crab Bomb, Maryland lump crabmeat baked in a light cream sauce with steamed vegetables. 104 Clematis St. ⓒ 561/833-3520. Sun–Wed 8am–3am, Thurs–Sat 8am–4 am. No cover.

Liquid Room   Former South Beach hot spot Liquid may have evaporated (and subsequently reopened by name alone, in a new space that's not nearly as haute as the original) from the scene, but this Clematis Street location, which shares the building with Bliss (located upstairs), is flowing with Palm Beach club kids who revel in the fact that they finally have a chic, celebrity-saturated dance club to call their own. 313 Clematis St. ⓒ 561/655-2332. Thurs–Sat 10pm–4am. Cover $10.

Lost Weekend   I'm not sure whether it's the local artist displays, the pool tables, or the more than 200 beers from around the world sold here, but for some reason, many of Palm Beach's hipsters love losing themselves in this place, which is actually quite nice. 115 S. Olive Ave. ⓒ 561/832-3452. Tues–Fri 4:30pm–3 or 4am. No cover.

Monkey Club   This tacky yet trendy Caribbean-inspired dance club is 7,500 square feet of wall-to-wall, well-dressed revelers. Theme nights are popular here, from ladies nights to the classier version of the wet T-shirt contest—the Miss Hawaiian Tropic Model Search. 219 Clematis St. ⓒ 561/833-6500. Tue and Thurs 8pm–3am, Fri–Sat 8pm–4am. Closed Sun, Mon, and Wed. Cover up to $10.

Respectable Street Café   This is one of the premier live music venues in South Florida. In addition to the requisite DJs, this grungy bar features an

---

Fun Fact **Equal Gambling Rights**

E. R. Bradley's is named for a legendary Palm Beach gambler and horse racer who opened the first casino to allow women to gamble.

impressive lineup of alternative-music acts. The cafe's plain storefront exterior belies its funky high-ceilinged interior decorated with large black booths, psychedelic wall murals, and a large checkerboard-tile dance floor. 518 Clematis St. ℂ 561/832-9999. Wed–Sat 9pm–4am. Cover varies.

Palm Beach

Brazilian Court Bistro and Rio Bar   Despite its location in the ritzy Brazilian Court Hotel's bistro, the bar here is surprisingly laid-back and unpretentious, featuring a mostly older crowd of couples and, at times, swinging singles. 301 Australian Ave. ℂ 561/655-7740. Daily 7am–10:30pm.

The Leopard Lounge *(Finds* *The Flintstones* meet *Dynasty* at the spotty lounge in the Chesterfield Hotel in which the carpeting, tablecloths, and wait-staff's waistcoats are all in leopard print. There's live music every night from Cole Porter to swing. The crowd's a bit older here, but younger couples and a celebrity or two often find their way here, which makes for an amusing scene. 363 Cocoanut Row. ℂ 561/659-5800. Daily 6pm–2am.

Ta-boo   Ta-boo is reminiscent of an upscale TGI Fridays (with food that's about on the same level)—one that caters to a well-heeled crowd—with lots of greenery, a fireplace, and a somewhat cheesy Southwestern decor. But make no mistake, Ta-boo is not about the food: This stellar after-dinner spot is where bejeweled socialites spill out of fancy cars to show off their best Swarovski and salsa. Just find somewhere else to eat first. 221 Worth Ave., Palm Beach. ℂ 561/ 835-3500. Reservations recommended. Main courses $10–$25. AE, DC, MC, V. Sun–Thurs 11:30am–11pm, Fri–Sat 11:30am–1am.

GAMBLING

The *Palm Beach Princess* (ℂ 800/841-7447 or 561/845-7447) is a small cruise ship (421 ft.) offering reasonably priced casino gambling cruises out of the Port of Palm Beach (U.S. 1 between 45th Street and Blue Heron Boulevard) every day and evening. Choose from craps, roulette, poker, blackjack, and slots. Cruises include a large buffet with average food like spaghetti and meatballs, chicken, Greek salad, and vegetables; best is the prime rib at the carving board. Five-hour cruises sail daily at 12:30pm (returning at 5:30pm) and 7pm (returning at 12:30am). Friday and Saturday evening cruises leave at 7pm and return at 1am. Sunday cruises sail from 11am to 5pm and 6 to 11pm. Prices during the week are $30 per person; on weekends, it's $35 per person. If your birthday is in the month you plan to sail, pay $20. AAA discounts are available.

THE PERFORMING ARTS

With a number of dedicated patrons and enthusiastic supporters of the arts, this area happily boasts many good venues for those craving culture. Check the *Palm Beach Post* or the *Palm Beach Daily News* for up-to-date listings and reviews.

The **Raymond F. Kravis Center for the Performing Arts,** 701 Okeechobee Blvd., West Palm Beach (ℂ 800/572-8471 or 561/832-7469; www.kravis.org), is the area's largest and most active performance space. As with everything in Palm Beach, this stunning performing arts center did not come with a cheap price tag and is, in terms of venues are concerned, over the top, with not just one main theater, but three theaters in one. The main stage, Dreyfoos Hall, seats over 2,000, while the Rinker Playhouse, a small cabaret-style theater in the round seats considerably less, and the Gosman Amphitheatre is an outdoor space that has 600 bleacher seats, with room for 1,000 more on the lawn. Every major show, from Broadway and classical to pop, usually makes a point of stopping here, as the 'puttin' on the ritz-y' crowd is never one to miss a night to see and be seen at the theater. Ticket prices vary from $12–$150.

4 Jupiter & Northern Palm Beach County

20 miles N of Palm Beach, 81 miles N of Miami, 60 miles N. of Fort Lauderdale

While Burt Reynolds is Jupiter's hometown hero (and Celine Dion just built a sprawling manse there, too), the true stars of quaint Jupiter are the beautiful beaches. In the springtime, you can also catch a glimpse of the St. Louis Cardinals and the Montreal Expos during their spring training seasons. North Palm Beach County's other towns—Tequesta, Juno Beach, North Palm Beach, Palm Beach Gardens, and Singer Island—are inviting for tourists who want to enjoy the many outdoor activities that make this area so popular with retirees, seasonal residents, and families.

ESSENTIALS

GETTING THERE   The quickest route from West Palm Beach to Jupiter is on the Florida Turnpike or the sometimes congested I-95. You can also take a slower but more scenic coastal route, U.S. 1 or Florida A1A. Since Jupiter is so close to Palm Beach, it's easy to fly into the **Palm Beach International Airport** (© **561/471-7420**) and rent a car there. The drive should take less than half an hour.

VISITOR INFORMATION   A **Visitor Information Center** is located between I-95 and the Florida Turnpike at 8020 Indiantown Rd. in Jupiter (© **561/575-4636;** www.jupiterfloridausa.com) and is open from 9am to 6pm daily.

BEACHES & ACTIVE PURSUITS

BASEBALL   The **Roger Dean Stadium,** 4751 Main St. (© **561/775-1818**), hosts spring training for both the St. Louis Cardinals and the Montreal Expos, along with minor-league action from Florida's state league, the Hammerheads. Tickets range in price from $6 to $18. Call for schedules and specific ticket information.

BEACHES   The farther north you head from populated Palm Beach, the more peaceful and pristine the coast becomes. Just a few miles north of the bustle, castles and condominiums give way to wide open space and public parkland. There are dozens of recommendable spots. Following are a few of the best.

   John D. MacArthur Beach is a spectacular beach that preserves the natural heritage of subtropical coastal habitat that once covered Southeast Florida. This state park has a remarkable 4,000-square-foot Nature Center with exhibits, displays, and a video interpreting the barrier island's plant and animal communities. Dominating a large portion of Singer Island, the barrier island just north of Palm Beach, this beach has lengthy frontage on both the Atlantic Ocean and Lake Worth Cove. The beach is great for hiking, swimming, and sunning. Bathrooms and showers are available. To reach the park from the mainland, cross the Intracoastal Waterway on Blue Heron Boulevard and turn north on Ocean Boulevard.

   Jupiter Inlet meets the ocean at **Dubois Park,** a 29-acre beach that is popular with families. The shallow waters and sandy shore are perfect for kids, while adults can play in the rougher swells of the lifeguarded inlet. A footbridge leads to **Ocean Beach,** an area popular with windsurfers and surfers. There's a short fishing pier and plenty of trees shading barbecue grills and picnic tables. Visitors can also explore the Dubois Pioneer Home, a small house situated atop a shell mound built by the Jaega Indians. Built from cypress, the home was built in 1898 by Harry Dubois, a citrus worker, as a wedding gift to his wife, Susan, whose pictures are still in the house. You will see an original butter churn and pump sewing machine in the living room, and the dining room and bedroom are almost straight out of *Little House on the Prairie.* The park entrance is on Dubois Road, about a mile south of the junction of U.S. 1 and A1A.

BIKING   Rent a bike from **Raleigh Bicycles of Jupiter,** at 103 U.S. 1, Unit F1 (© **561/746-0585**). Prices start at $15.50 per day and $49.50 per week. Bike enthusiasts will enjoy exploring this flat and uncluttered area. North Palm Beach has hundreds of miles of smooth, paved roads. Loggerhead Park in Juno Beach or A1A along the ocean also have great trails for starters. You'll find many more scenic routes over the bridges and west of the highway.

CANOEING   You can rent a boat at several outlets throughout northern Palm Beach County, including **Canoe Outfitters,** 8900 W. Indiantown Rd. (west of I-95), North Jupiter (© **561/746-7053**), which provides access to one of the area's most beautiful natural waterways. Canoers start at Riverbend Park along an 8-mile stretch of Intracoastal Waterway, where the lush foliage supports dozens of exotic birds and reptiles. Keep your eyes open for the gators who love to sunbathe on the shallow shores of the river. You'll end up, exhausted, at Jonathan Dickinson Park about 5 or 6 hours later. A pamphlet describing local flora and fauna is available for $1. Trips run Wednesday to Sunday and cost $40 per person for a double canoe with guide.

CRUISES   Several sightseeing cruises offer tours of the magnificent waterways that make up northern Palm Beach County. Water taxis conduct daily narrated tours through the scenic waters. One interesting excursion that will take you past the mansions of the rich and famous and possibly past the manatees swimming off the port of Palm Beach departs from **Panama Hatties** at PGA Boulevard and the Intracoastal Waterway. Prices are $17 for adults and $9 for children under 12 for the 1½-hour ride. Call © **561/775-2628.** The *Manatee Queen,* 1065 N. Ocean Blvd. (at the Crab House), Jupiter (© **561/744-2191**), is a 40-foot catamaran with bench seating for up to 49 people. Two-hour tours of Jupiter Island depart daily at 2:30pm, passing Burt Reynolds' and Perry Como's former mansions, among other historical and natural spots of interest. Reservations are highly recommended, especially in season; call for the current schedule of offerings. Prices start at $17 for adults and $10 for children. Bring your own lunch or purchase chips and sodas at the minisnack bar.

FISHING   Before you leave, send for an information-packed fishing kit with details on fish camps, charters, and tournament and tide schedules, distributed by the **West Palm Beach Fishing Club** (© **561/832-6780**). The cost is $10 and well worth it. Allow at least 4 weeks for delivery. Once in town, several outfitters along U.S. 1 and A1A have vessels and equipment for rent if your hotel doesn't. One of the most complete facilities is the **Sailfish Marina & Resort,** 98 Lake Dr. (off Blue Heron Boulevard), Palm Beach Shores (© **561/844-1724**). Call for equipment, bait, guided trips, or boat rentals.

GOLF   Even if you're not lucky enough to be staying at the **PGA National Resort & Spa,** you may still be able to play on their award-winning courses. If you or someone in your group is a member of another golf or country club, have

Discovering a Remarkable Natural World

North Palm Beach is well known for the giant sea turtles that lay their eggs on the county's beaches from May to August. These endangered marine animals return here annually, from as far away as South America, to lay their clutch of about 115 eggs each. Nurtured by the warm sand, but targeted by birds and other predators, only about one or two babies from each nest survive to maturity.

Many environmentalists recommend that visitors take part in an organized turtle-watching program (rather than going on their own) to minimize disturbance to the turtles. The Jupiter Beach Resort (see "Where to Stay," below) and the Marinelife Center of Juno Beach (see below) both sponsor free guided expeditions to the egg-laying sites from May to August. Phone for times and reservations.

Just south of Jupiter, in Juno Beach, is the **Marinelife Center of Juno Beach,** in Loggerhead Park, 14200 U.S. 1, Juno Beach (© **561/627-8280**). Combining a science museum and nature trail, the small Marinelife Center is dedicated to the coastal ecology of northern Palm Beach County. Hands-on exhibits teach visitors about wetlands and beach areas, as well as offshore coral reefs and the local sea life. Visitors are encouraged to walk the center's sand-dune nature trails, all of which are marked with interpretive signs. This is one place in which you're guaranteed to see live sea turtles year-round. During high breeding season (June and July), the center conducts narrative walks along a nearby beach. Reservations are a must. The booking list opens on May 1 and is usually full by mid-month. Admission to the center is free, though donations are accepted. Open Tuesday to Saturday from 10am to 4pm and Sunday from noon to 3pm.

the head pro write a note on club letterhead to Jackie Rogers at PGA (see "Where to Stay," below) to request a play date. Be sure the pro includes his PGA number and contact information. Allow at least 2 weeks for a response. Also, ask about the Golf-A-Round program, where selected private clubs open to non-members for free or discounted rates. Contact the **Palm Beach County Convention and Visitors Bureau** (© **561/471-3995**) for details.

Plenty of other great courses dot the area, including the **Golf Club of Jupiter,** 1800 Central Blvd., Jupiter (© **561/747-6262**), where a well-respected 18-hole, par-70 course is situated on more than 6,200 yards featuring narrow fairways and fast greens. Fees are $55 until noon, $45 after noon, $25 after 3pm, and include a mandatory cart. The course borders I-95.

HIKING   In an area that's not particularly known for extraordinary natural diversity, **Blowing Rocks Preserve** has a terrific hiking trail along a dramatic limestone outcropping. You won't find hills or scenic vistas, but you will see Florida's unique and varied tropical ecosystem. The well-marked mile-long trail passes oceanfront dunes, coastal strands, mangrove wetlands, and a coastal hammock. The preserve, owned and managed by the Nature Conservancy, also protects an important habitat for West Indian manatees and loggerhead turtles.

Located along South Beach Drive (A1A) north of the Jupiter inlet, the preserve is about a 10-minute drive northeast of Jupiter. Free guided tours are available Fridays and Sundays at 11am, and no reservations are necessary. From U.S. 1, head east on State Road 707 and cross the Intracoastal Waterway to the park. Admission is free, but a $3 per person donation is requested. For more information, contact the Preserve Manager, Blowing Rocks Preserve, P.O. Box 3795, Tequesta, FL 33469 (© **561/744-6668**).

SCUBA DIVING & SNORKELING   Year-round warm, clear waters make northern Palm Beach County great for both diving and snorkeling. The closest coral reef is located a quarter-mile from shore and can easily be reached by boat. Three popular wrecks are clustered near each other, less than a mile offshore of the Lake Worth Inlet at about 90 feet. The best wreck, however, is the 16th- or 17th-century Spanish galleon discovered by lifeguard Peter Leo just off Jupiter Beach (see p. 316 for more information). If your hotel doesn't offer dive trips, call the **South Florida Dive Headquarters,** 23141 Lyons Rd., Boca Raton (© **800/771-DIVE** or 561/627-9558), or **Seafari Dive and Surf,** 75 E. Indiantown Rd., Suite 603, Jupiter (© **561/747-6115**).

TENNIS   In addition to the many hotel tennis courts (see "Where to Stay," below), you can swing a racquet at a number of local clubs. The **Jupiter Bay Tennis Club,** 353 U.S. 1, Jupiter (© **561/744-9424**), has seven clay courts (three lighted) and charges $12 per person per day. Reservations are highly recommended.

More economical options are available at relatively well-maintained municipal courts. Call for locations and hours (© **561/966-6600**). Many are available free on a first-come, first-served basis.

A HISTORIC LIGHTHOUSE

Jupiter Inlet Lighthouse ⟨≾⟩   Completed in 1860, this redbrick structure is the oldest extant building in Palm Beach County. Still owned and maintained by the U.S. Coast Guard, the lighthouse is now home to a small historical museum located at its base. The Florida History Museum sponsors tours of the lighthouse, enabling visitors to explore the cramped interior, which is filled with artifacts and photographs illustrating the rich history of the area. A 15-minute video explains the various shipwrecks, Indian wars, and other events that helped shape this region. Helpful volunteers are eager to tell colorful stories to highlight the 1-hour tour.

500 S.R. 707, Jupiter. © 561/747-8380. Admission $5. Sun–Wed 10am–4pm (last tour departs at 3:15pm). Children must be 4 feet or taller to climb. No open-backed shoes.

SHOPPING

Northern Palm Beach County may not have the glitzy boutiques of Worth Avenue, but it does have an impressive indoor mall, the **Gardens of the Palm Beaches,** at 3101 PGA Blvd., where you can find large department stores including **Bloomingdale's, Burdines, Macy's,** and **Saks Fifth Avenue,** as well as more than 100 specialty shops. A large, diverse food court and fine sit-down restaurants in this 1.3 million-square-foot facility make this shopping excursion an all-day affair. Call © **561/775-7750** for store information.

WHERE TO STAY

The northern part of Palm Beach County is much more laid-back and less touristy than the rest of the Gold Coast. Here, there are relatively few fancy hotels or attractions.

> **Fun Fact** **Burt Reynolds Slept Here**
>
> Although there's no sign saying, "Welcome to Jupiter, Home of Burt Reynolds," there may as well be. You see, for a time, Reynolds was the ruler of this South Floridian planet, with a park, a museum, a theater, and a ranch that, in better times, all bore his name. Born in Georgia, Reynolds grew up in West Palm Beach, where his father was police chief. While attending Florida State University in Tallahassee, Reynolds injured his knee and lost all hopes of pursuing a pro-football career. That's when he turned to acting. But when Reynolds' star faded, the former sex symbol quietly retreated to Jupiter in the early 1980s, where he opened his dinner theater and, later, the Burt Reynolds Ranch, which featured a wedding chapel, the Burt Reynolds Petting Farm, and a Hall of Fame, among other things. The restaurant went into foreclosure, and the ranch was sold after Reynolds declared bankruptcy in 1996. Today, the only thing still bearing Reynolds' name is Burt Reynolds Park, 805 U.S. 1. But the legend still lives on. No matter which chapter of his life he's currently on— 11 or otherwise—Reynolds will always be responsible for bringing a bit of Hollywood to the little town of Jupiter.

VERY EXPENSIVE

Jupiter Beach Resort ✮✮ The only resort located directly on Jupiter's beach, this unpretentious retreat is popular with families and seems a world away from the more luxurious resorts just a few miles to the south. The lobby and public areas have a Caribbean motif, accented with green marble, arched doorways, and chandeliers. The simple and elegant guest rooms are furnished in a comfortable island style, and every room has a private balcony with ocean or sunset views looking out over the uncluttered beachfront. A thorough refurbishing in the mid-1990s is responsible for the resort's increasing popularity. In fact, it is so popular that it is being gradually converted into a time-share property. Excursions are available to top-rated golf courses in the area.

5 N. A1A, Jupiter, FL 33477. ✆ **800/228-8810** or 561/746-2511. Fax 561/747-3304. www.jupiterbeach resort.com. 153 units. Winter $170–$450; off-season $97–$205. AE, DC, DISC, MC, V. Valet parking $5. From I-95, take Exit 59A, going east to the end of Indiantown Rd. at A1A. Jupiter Beach Resort is at this intersection on the ocean. **Amenities:** Restaurant, 2 bars; pool; tennis court; exercise room; extensive watersport equipment rental; bike rental; children's programs; concierge; business center; room service; in-room massage; dry cleaning. *In room:* A/C, TV, dataport, minibar, coffeemaker, iron, and VCR (for a $10 additional charge). Suites have kitchenettes.

PGA National Resort & Spa ✮✮✮ This rambling resort, the national headquarters of the PGA, is a premier golf vacation spot—but its top-rated Mediterranean spa could be a destination in itself. With five 18-hole courses on more than 2,300 acres, golfers and other sports-minded travelers will find plenty to keep them occupied—croquet, tennis, sailing, a health-and-fitness center, and the sublime spa. Constant updating has kept the grounds and buildings in likenew condition. In 2000, the lobby and all rooms were completely renovated. The par-72 Champion Course, redesigned in 1990 by Jack Nicklaus, is the resort's most valuable asset. More than 100 sand bunkers and plenty of water on 6,400-square-foot greens keep golfers of all levels alert. Watch out for hole 16. Rooms are spacious and comfortable with immense bathrooms. This is not a beach resort, however. Six outdoor therapy pools known as Waters of the World are surrounded by mineral pools, which are so sublime, they make the ocean look like a kiddie pool. Don Shula's award-winning steakhouse and restaurant is the hotel's best and most popular restaurant.

400 Avenue of the Champions, Palm Beach Gardens, FL 33418. © **800/633-9150** or 561/627-2000. Fax 561/622-0261. www.pga-resorts.com. 339 units. Winter $319–$389 double; from $489 suite. Off-season $129–$169 double; from $249 suite. Children 16 and under stay free in parents' room. Special packages available. AE, DC, DISC, MC, V. From I-95, take Exit 57B (PGA Blvd.) going west and continue for approximately 2 miles to the resort entrance on the left. **Amenities:** 6 restaurants and lounges; 9 swimming pools; 5 18-hole tournament courses, plus the PGA National's Academy of Golf; 19 clay tennis courts; 5 tournament croquet lawns; 5 indoor racquetball courts; Mediterranean spa; aerobics studio; watersports equipment rentals; concierge; car-rental desk; salon; room service; laundry; babysitting. *In room:* A/C, TV, dataport, minibar, hair dryer, safe.

MODERATE/INEXPENSIVE

Baron's Landing Motel & Apartments *Value* This charming family-run inn is a perfect little beach getaway. It's not elegant, but it is cozy. The single-story motel fronting the Intracoastal Waterway is often full in winter with snow-birds, who dock their boats at the hotel's marina for weeks or months at a time. Nearly all rooms, which are situated around a small pool, have small kitchenettes. Each unit has a funky mix of used furniture, and some have pullout sofas. Bathrooms have been remodeled. Considering that you're a few blocks from some of the most expensive real estate in the country, this is a good deal. Dock rentals are available.

18125 Ocean Blvd. (A1A at the corner of Clemens St.), Jupiter, FL 33477. © **561/746-8757.** 8 units. Winter $75–$125 double; $1,350–$1,700 monthly. Off-season $45–$75 double; $700–$900 monthly. No credit cards. **Amenities:** Small pool. *In room:* A/C, TV, dataport, fax, kitchen, refrigerator, coffeemaker, iron.

Cologne Motel A modest roadside motel, the Cologne is a well-maintained one-story building with a pool but very little in the way of amenities. The small rooms were updated in 1999. The retiled bathrooms are small but clean. The area is safe if not scenic and only about a 5-minute drive to the beach. A more direct route by foot gets you there in about 15 minutes.

220 U.S. 1, Tequesta/Jupiter, FL 33469. © **561/746-0616.** 9 units. Winter $70 double. Off-season $36 double. Weekly rates available. AE, MC, V. **Amenities:** Pool. *In room:* A/C, TV, fridge. No phone.

WHERE TO DINE

In addition to all the national fast-food joints that line Indiantown Road and U.S. 1, you'll find a number of touristy fish restaurants serving battered and fried everything. There are only a few really exceptional eateries in North Palm Beach and Jupiter. Try those listed below for guaranteed good food at reasonable prices.

MODERATE

Athenian Cafe *Finds* GREEK Peter Papadelis and his family have been running this pleasant storefront cafe for more than a decade. Tucked in the corner of a strip mall, this place serves heaping portions of rich and meaty moussaka or a flaky spinach pie made fresh by Peter himself. You could make a meal of the thick and lemony Greek soup and the large fresh antipasto. In a town replete with tourist-priced fish joints, this is a welcome alternative. Early bird specials, served until 7pm, include many Greek favorites and broiled local fish with soup or salad, rice, vegetables, pita, dessert, and coffee or tea.

In the Chasewood Shopping Center, 6350 Indiantown Rd., Suite 7, Jupiter. © **561/744-8327.** Main courses $5–$16. AE, MC, V. Mon–Sat 11am–9pm, Sun 4–9pm during season.

Capt. Charlie's Reef Grill 🐟🐟 SEAFOOD/CARIBBEAN   The trick here is to arrive early, ahead of the crowd of local foodies who come for the more than a dozen daily local-catch specials prepared in dozens of styles. Imaginative appetizers include Caribbean chili (a rich chunky stew filled with fresh seafood) and a tuna spring roll big enough for two. The enormous Cuban crab cake is moist and perfectly browned without tasting fried and is served with homemade mango chutney and black beans and rice. Sit at the bar to watch the hectic kitchen turn out perfect dishes on the 14-burner stove. Somehow, the pleasant waitresses keep their cool even when the place is packed. In addition to the terrific seafood, this little dive offers an extensive, affordable wine and beer selection—more than 30 of each from around the world.

12846 U.S. 1 (behind O'Brian's and French Connection), Juno Beach. ✆ 561/624-9924. Reservations not accepted. Main courses $9.95–$18.95. MC, V. Sun–Thurs 11:30am–9:30pm, Fri–Sat 11:30am–10pm.

Nick's Tomato Pie 🐟 ITALIAN   A fun family restaurant, Nick's is a popular attraction that's known to bring folks even from Miami for a piece of this pie. With a huge menu of pastas, pizzas, fish, chicken, and beef, this cheery (and noisy) spot has something for everyone. On Saturday night, you'll see lots of couples on dates and some families leaving with takeout bags left over from the impossibly generous portions. The homemade sausage is a delicious treat, served with sautéed onions and peppers. The pollo Marsala, too, is good and authentic.

1697 W. Indiantown Rd. (1 mile east of I-95, Exit 59A), Jupiter. ✆ 561/744-8935. Reservations accepted only for parties of 6 or more. Main courses $12–$20; pastas $10–$15. AE, DC, DISC, MC, V. Mon–Thurs and Sun 5–10pm; Fri–Sat 5–11pm.

Sinclair's Ocean Grill & Rotisserie 🐟🐟 CARIBBEAN   As close to upscale as Jupiter gets, Sinclair's is the Jupiter Beach Resort's excellent restaurant overlooking the pool and featuring fresh, locally caught fish as well as an excellent filet mignon. Especially popular are the Sunday brunches.

Jupiter Beach Resort, 5 N. A1A ✆ 561/745-7120. Reservations recommended. Main courses $9.95–$18. AE, MC, V. Daily 6:30–11am, 11:30am–2:30pm, and 6–10pm.

JUPITER & NORTHERN PALM BEACH COUNTY AFTER DARK

With one notable exception, there just isn't much going on here after dark. However, **Club Safari,** 4000 PGA Blvd. (just east of I-95), in Palm Beach Garden's Marriott Hotel (✆ **561/622-8888**), has a hilarious Vegas-style safari-themed decor, with faux, albeit lifelike, animals positioned throughout the club. The huge, sunken dance floor is surrounded by vines and lanky, potted trees. Nearby, a large Buddha statue blows steam and smoke while waving its burly arms in front of a young gyrating crowd. There is DJ music, a large video screen, and a modest cover charge on the weekends. Open nights, Wednesday through Sunday. For more options, check your hotel or do what most people do: go to West Palm Beach.

13

The Treasure Coast: Stuart to Sebastian

The area north of Palm Beach is known as the Treasure Coast for the same reason that the area from Fort Lauderdale to Palm Beach is known as the Gold Coast—it was the site of a number of shipwrecks that date back over 300 years, which led to the discovery of priceless treasures in the water (some historians believe that treasures from these sunken vessels *still* lie buried deep beneath the ocean floor).

The difference, however, is that while the Gold Coast is a bit, well, tarnished as far as development is concerned, the Treasure Coast remains, for the most part, an unspoiled, quiet, natural jewel. Miles of uninterrupted beaches and aquamarine waters attract swimmers, boaters, divers, anglers, and sun worshippers who love to dip, dive, and surf. If you love the great outdoors and prefer a more understated environment than hyper-developed Miami and Fort Lauderdale, the Treasure Coast is a real find.

For hundreds of years, Florida's east coast was a popular stopover for European explorers, many of whom arrived from Spain to fill coffers with gold and silver. Rough weather and poor navigation often took a toll on their ships, but in 1715, a violent hurricane stunned the northeast coast and sank an entire fleet of Spanish ships laden with gold. Although Spanish salvagers worked for years to collect the lost treasure, much of it remained buried beneath the shifting sand. Workers hired to excavate the area in the 1950s and 1960s discovered centuries-old coins under their tractors.

Today, you can still see shipwrecks and incredible barrier reefs in St. Lucie County, which can be reached from the beaches of Fort Pierce and Hutchinson Island. On these same beaches, you'll also find an occasional treasure hunter trolling the sand with a metal detector, alongside swimmers and sunbathers who come to enjoy the stretches of beach that extend into the horizon. The sea, especially around Sebastian Inlet, is a mecca for surfers, who find some of the largest swells in the state.

Along with the pleasures of the talcum powder sands, the Treasure Coast also offers great shopping, entertainment, clubbing, sporting, and numerous other opportunities to take a reprieve from the hubbub of the rat race. Visitors to this part of South Florida should not miss the extensive array of wildlife, which includes the endangered West Indian manatee, loggerhead and leatherback turtles, tropical fish, alligators, deer, and exotic birds. For sports enthusiasts, there are boundless sporting opportunities here—from golf and tennis to polo, motorcar racing, the New York Mets during their spring training, and the best freshwater fishing around.

The downtown areas of the Treasure Coast have been experiencing a rebirth in the past few years, along with the influx of unprecedented

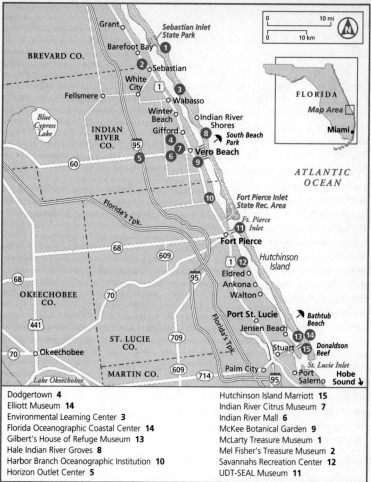

Dodgertown **4**
Elliott Museum **14**
Environmental Learning Center **3**
Florida Oceanographic Coastal Center **14**
Gilbert's House of Refuge Museum **13**
Hale Indian River Groves **8**
Harbor Branch Oceanographic Institution **10**
Horizon Outlet Center **5**

Hutchinson Island Marriott **15**
Indian River Citrus Museum **7**
Indian River Mall **6**
McKee Botanical Garden **9**
McLarty Treasure Museum **1**
Mel Fisher's Treasure Museum **2**
Savannahs Recreation Center **12**
UDT-SEAL Museum **11**

numbers of new residents. Fortunately, the area's growth has occurred at a reasonable pace so that the neighborhoods have been able to retain their small-town feel. The result is a batch of freshly spruced-up accommodations, shops, and restaurants from Stuart to Sebastian.

Southern Martin County's well-to-do Hobe Sound, in particular, is a Treasure Coast hot spot with its pristine beaches, banyan-tree-canopied streetscapes, one-of-a-kind antique shops, and art galleries. Hobe Sound

rests at the front door of the Gold Coast and the back door of the Treasure Coast, and it has immediate access to the Atlantic Ocean and the Intracoastal Waterway. Real estate here is at a premium, with million-dollar waterfront mansions lining the shores.

For the purposes of this chapter, the Treasure Coast runs roughly from Hobe Sound in the south to the Sebastian Inlet in the north, encompassing some of Martin, St. Lucie, and Indian River counties and all of Hutchinson Island.

TREASURE COAST ESSENTIALS
GETTING THERE
Since virtually every town described in this chapter runs along a straight route along the Atlantic Ocean, I've given all directions below.

BY PLANE   The **Palm Beach International Airport** (© **561/471-7420**), located about 35 miles south of Stuart, is the closest gateway to this region if you're flying. See the "Getting Around" section on Palm Beach in chapter 12, "The Gold Coast: Hallandale to the Palm Beaches," for complete information. If you are traveling to the northern part of the Treasure Coast, **Melbourne International Airport,** off U.S. 1 in Melbourne (© **407/723-6227**), is less than 25 miles north of Sebastian and about 35 miles north of Vero Beach.

BY CAR   If you're driving up or down the Florida coast, you'll probably reach the Treasure Coast via I-95. If you are heading to Stuart or Jensen Beach, take Exit 61 (Route 76/Tanner Highway) or 62 (Route 714); to Port St. Lucie or Fort Pierce, take Exit 63 or 64 (Okeechobee Road); to Vero Beach, take Exit 68 (State Route 60); to Sebastian, take Exit 69 (County Road).

You can also take the Florida Turnpike; this toll road is the fastest (but not the most scenic) route, especially if you're coming from Orlando. If you are heading to Stuart or Jensen Beach, take Exit 133; to Fort Pierce, take Exit 152 (Okeechobee Road); to Port St. Lucie, take Exit 142 or 152; to Vero Beach, take Exit 193 (State Route 60); to Sebastian, take Exit 193 to State Route 60 east and connect to I-95 north.

If you are staying in Hutchinson Island, which runs almost the entire length of the Treasure Coast, you should check with your hotel or see the listings below to find the best route to take.

Finally, if you're coming directly from the west coast, you'll probably take State Route 70, which runs north of Lake Okeechobee to Fort Pierce, located just up the road from Stuart.

BY RAIL   Amtrak (© **800/USA-RAIL;** www.amtrak.com) stops in West Palm Beach at 201 S. Tamarind Ave., and in Okeechobee at 801 N. Parrot Ave., off U.S. 441 north.

BY BUS   Greyhound buses (© **800/231-2222;** www.greyhound.com) service the area with terminals in Stuart, at 1308 S. Federal Hwy.; in Fort Pierce, at 7005 Okeechobee Rd. (© **561/461-3299**); and in Vero Beach, at U.S. 1 and State Route 60 (© **561/562-6588**).

GETTING AROUND
A car is a necessity in this large and rural region. Although heavy traffic is not usually a problem here, on the smaller coastal roads like A1A, expect to travel at a slow pace, usually between 25 and 40 miles an hour.

> ### 1 Hobe Sound ★★★, Stuart (North Hutchinson Island) ★★ & Jensen Beach

Once just a stretch of pineapple plantations, the towns of Martin County, which include Hobe Sound, Stuart, and Jensen Beach, still retain much of their rural character. Dotted between citrus groves and mangroves are modest homes and an occasional high-rise condominium. Although the area is definitely still seasonal (with a distinct rise in street and pedestrian traffic beginning after the Christmas

The Producers

During the land boom in the 1920s, big plans were made for Hobe Sound by the Olympia Improvement Corporation. The company would create a columned, trellised town in the style of a Greek village, one in which movies could be produced. Hobe Sound was renamed Picture City, and street names came straight from Greek mythology: Zeus Crescent, Saturn, Mercury, Mars, Olympus, and Athena. When the boom collapsed in 1928 after a devastating hurricane, the celluloid dreams for Picture City were shattered. The town's old name of Hobe Sound was restored, but the street names remain, as do the cement streetlights on Dixie Highway.

holidays), the atmosphere is pure small town. Even in historic downtown Stuart, the result of a successful, ongoing restoration, expect the storefronts to be dark and the streets abandoned after 10pm.

ESSENTIALS

The **Stuart/Martin County Chamber of Commerce,** 1650 S. Kanner Hwy., Stuart, FL 34994 (© **800/524-9704** or 561/287-1088; fax 561/220-3437), is the region's main source for information. The **Jensen Beach Chamber of Commerce,** 1901 NE Jensen Beach Blvd., Jensen Beach, FL 34957 (© **561/334-3444;** fax 561/334-0817), also offers visitors information about its simple beachfront town.

BACK TO NATURE: THE BEACHES & BEYOND

BEACHES Hutchinson Island, located in Stuart, is one of the most popular beach destinations of the Treasure Coast, located just north of Palm Beach on the Atlantic Ocean. Seventy miles of excellent beaches and laid-back, old Florida ambiance make for an idyllic frozen-cocktail on the beach resort vacation.

The best of them is **Bathtub Beach,** on North Hutchinson Island. Here, the calm waters are protected by coral reefs, and visitors can explore the region on dune and river trails. Pick a secluded spot on the wide stretch of beach, or enjoy marked nature trails across the street. Facilities include showers and toilets open during the day. To reach Bathtub Beach from the northern tip of Hutchinson Island, head east on Ocean Boulevard (Stuart Causeway) and turn right onto MacArthur Boulevard. The beach is about a mile ahead on your left, just north of the Hutchinson Island Marriott Beach Resort and Marina. Parking is plentiful.

CANOEING **Jonathan Dickinson State Park** (see "Wildlife Exploration," below) is the area's most popular for canoeing. The route winds through a variety of botanical habitats. You'll see lots of birds and the occasional manatee. Canoes cost $6 per hour and can be rented through the concession located in the back of the park. The concession (© **561/746-1466**) is open Monday to Friday from 9am to 5pm and Saturday and Sunday from 8am to 5pm.

FISHING Several independent charter captains operate on Hutchinson Island and Jensen Beach. One of the largest operators is the **Sailfish Marina,** 3565 SE St. Lucie Blvd., in Stuart (© **561/221-9456**), which maintains half a dozen charter boats for fishing excursions year-round. Also on site are a bait-and-tackle shop and a knowledgeable, helpful staff. Other reputable charter operators include **Hungry Bear Adventures, Inc.,** docked at Indian River Plantation Marriott

Wildlife Exploration:
From Gators to Manatees to Turtles

One of the most scenic areas on this stretch of the coast is **Jonathan Dickinson State Park** ⚔️, 12 miles south of Stuart at 16450 S. Federal Hwy. (U.S. 1), Hobe Sound (© **561/546-2771**). The park intentionally receives less maintenance than other, more meticulously maintained parks so that it will resemble the rough-around-the-edges, wilderness-like environment of hundreds of years ago, before Europeans started chopping, dredging, and "improving" the area. Dozens of species of Florida's unique wildlife, including alligators and manatees, live on the park's more than 11,300 acres. Bird watchers will also be delighted by glimpses of rare and endangered species such as the bald eagle, the Florida scrub-jay, and the Florida sandhill crane, who still call this park home. You can rent canoes from the concession stand to explore the Loxahatchee River on your own. Admission is $3.25 per car of up to eight adults. Day hikers, bikers, and walkers pay $1 each. The park is open from 8am until sundown. See "Where to Stay," below for details on camping. The park is open from 8am until sundown.

Close to Jonathan Dickinson State Park is **Hobe Sound Wildlife Refuge,** on North Beach Road off State Route 708, at the north end of Jupiter Island (© **561/546-6141**). This is one of the best places to see sea turtles that nest on the shore in the summer months, especially in June and July. Because it's home to a large variety of other plant and animal species, the park is worth visiting at other times of year as well. Admission is $4 per car, and the preserve is open daily from sunrise to sunset. Exact times are posted at each entrance and change seasonally.

For turtle walks on Hutchinson Island, call © **877/375-4386.** These walks take place from May 22 through July 22 at 9pm, Fridays and Saturdays. Reservations are necessary and should be made well in advance, as walks are limited to 50 people. Reservations are accepted as of May 1.

Resort, 4730-1 SE Teri Place in Stuart (© **561/283-8034;** fishing@tci.net); and **Bone Shaker Sportfishing,** 3585 SE St. Lucie Blvd., in Stuart (© **561/ 286-5504;** veejay4842@aol.com).

GOLF   Try the **Champions Club at Summerfield,** on U.S. 1, south of Cove Road in Stuart (© **561/283-1500**), a somewhat challenging championship course designed by Tom Fazio. This rural course, the best in the area, offers great glimpses of wildlife amid the wetlands. Winter greens fees are around $60, and carts are mandatory. Reservations are a must and are taken 4 days in advance.

SCUBA DIVING & SNORKELING   Three popular artificial reefs off Hutchinson Island provide excellent scenery for both novice and experienced divers. The **USS *Rankin*** lies 7 miles east-northeast of the St. Lucie Inlet. The Rankin is a 459-foot ship that lays on its port side in 80 feet of water. This ship was used in World War II for troop transportation and was sunk in 1988. Deck hatches on the wreck are open and allow exploration. Inside, there are thousands of Atlantic spiny oysters and a cannon is attached to the bow. The 58-foot-deep **Donaldson Reef** consists of a cluster of steel tanks and barrels sunk in 58 feet of water to create the artificial reef. It's located due east of the Gilbert's House of Refuge Museum (see below). The **Ernst Reef,** made from old tires, is a 60-foot dive located 4½ miles east-southeast of the St. Lucie inlet. Local dive shops have "tips" on the best spots and rules and regulations for safe diving. The Donald F. Welton Scuba Repair Shop (© **561/225-9717;** dfwelton@aol.com) in Jensen Beach is a great place for information.

SEEING THE SIGHTS

Balloons Over Florida 🎈🎈🎈 *(Finds)*   For a lofty view of Martin County's wildlife, take a hot-air balloon ride above the animals' natural habitat. Two fully licensed and insured balloons and pilots will take a maximum of four people up, up, and away for about an hour, depending on wind and weather conditions. After you've landed, drink in the sights over a glass of complimentary champagne and a continental breakfast. A certificate of flight is given to each passenger as a souvenir.

Tours begin at approximately 6:30am from a takeoff point to be determined. © **561/334-9393.** $150 per person, including continental breakfast and champagne.

Elliott Museum 🎈🎈   A treasure trove of wacky artifacts that really personify Americana, the Elliott Museum is a rich tribute to inventors, sports heroes, and collectors. The museum was created by the son of turn-of-the-century inventor Sterling Elliott to display the genius of the American spirit. Among the bizarre things you'll see here are displays of an apothecary, ice cream parlor, barbershop, other old-fashioned commercial enterprises, and an authentic hand-carved miniature circus. Sports fans will appreciate the baseball memorabilia—a half-million dollars' worth—including an autographed item from every player in the Baseball Hall of Fame.

A gallery of patents and models of machines invented by the museum's founder, Harmon Parker Elliott, and his son provides an intriguing glimpse into the business of tinkering. Their collection of restored antique cars is also impressive. Expect to spend at least an hour seeing the highlights.

825 NE Ocean Blvd. (north of Indian River Plantation Resort), Hutchinson Island, Stuart. © **561/225-1961.** Admission $6 adults, $2 children 6–13, free for children 5 and under. Daily 10am–4pm.

Florida Oceanographic Coastal Center 🎈🎈   This is a nature lover's Disney World. Opened by the South Florida Oceanographic Society in late 1994, this 44-acre site (surrounded by coastal hammock and mangroves) is its own little ecosystem and serves as an outdoor classroom, teaching visitors about the region's flora and fauna. The modest main building houses saltwater tanks and wet and dry "discovery tables" with small indigenous animals. The incredibly eager staff of volunteers encourages visitors to wander the lush, well-marked nature trails.

890 NE Ocean Blvd. (across the street from the Elliott Museum), Hutchinson Island, Stuart. © **561/ 225-0505.** www.fosusa.org. Admission $6 adults, $3 children 3–12, free for children under 3. Mon–Sat 10am–5pm, Sun noon–4.

Gilbert's House of Refuge Museum 🎈   Gilbert's, the oldest structure in Martin County, dates from 1875, when it functioned as one of 10 rescue centers for shipwrecked sailors. After undergoing a thorough rehabilitation to its original condition along the rocky shores, the house now displays marine artifacts and turn-of-the-century lifesaving equipment and photographs, and is worth a quick visit to get a feel for the area's early days.

301 SE MacArthur Blvd. (south of Indian River Plantation resort), Hutchinson Island, Stuart. ℂ **561/225-1875.** Admission $4 adults, $2 children 6–13, free for children 5 and under. Daily 10am–4pm.

A BOAT TOUR
The *Loxahatchee Queen* ⟨★★★⟩, a 35-foot pontoon boat (ℂ **561/746-1466**) in Jonathan Dickinson State Park in Hobe Sound, makes daily tours of the area's otherwise inaccessible backwater, where curious alligators, manatees, eagles, and tortoises often peek out to see who's in their yard. Try to catch the 2-hour tour, given Wednesday to Sunday as the tide permits, when it includes a stop at Trapper Nelson's home. Known as the "Wildman of Loxahatchee," Nelson lived in primitive conditions on a remote stretch of the water in a log cabin he built himself, which is preserved for visitors to see. Tours leave four times daily at 9am, 11am, 1pm, and 3pm and cost $12 for adults, $7 for children 6 to 12, and free for children 5 and under. See the "Wildlife Exploration" box above for more information on the park.

SHOPPING
Downtown Stuart's historic district, along Flagler Avenue between Confusion Corner and St. Lucie Avenue, offers shoppers diversity and quality in a small old-town setting. Shops offer a range of goods: antique bric-a-brac, old lamps and fixtures, books, gourmet foods, furnishings, and souvenirs. For bargains, check out the **B & A Flea Market** (ℂ **561/288-4915**), the Treasure Coast's oldest and largest flea market.

WHERE TO STAY
Although the area boasts some beautiful beaches, the bulk of the hotel scene is downtown, where the nicer (and more reasonably priced) accommodations can be found among the shops and restaurants. There are, however, a few excellent beachfront hotels and inns. One of the bigger hotel chains in the area is the **Holiday Inn.** Its recently renovated, stunning beachfront property is at 3793 NE Ocean Blvd., on Hutchinson Island in Jensen Beach (ℂ **800/992-4747** or 561/225-3000). Rates in season range from $130 to $180. Holiday Inn also has a downtown location at 1209 S. Federal Hwy. (ℂ **561/287-6200**). This simple two-story building on a busy main road is kept in very good shape and is convenient to Stuart's downtown historic district. Rates range from $99 to $140.

VERY EXPENSIVE
Hutchinson Island Marriott Beach Resort and Marina ⟨★★★⟩ This sprawling 200-acre compound offers many diversions for active (or not-so-active) vacationers, and families in particular. After a $6 million renovation in 1998, this is definitely Hutchinson Island's best resort, occupying the lush grounds of a former pineapple plantation. Activities include tennis, golfing, boating, sportfishing (especially for sailfish), scuba diving, and other watersports.

A complete room renovation occurred in 2000, and in 2001 the hotel's beach building was completely redone. Some rooms overlook the Intracoastal and the resort's marina, while others face the ocean or the gardens. All are generously sized and have fully equipped kitchens.

In the summer months, be sure to sign up for a turtle watch so you can see turtles crawl onto the sand to lay their eggs. Another great activity, offered at an extra cost, is a sightseeing cruise along the St. Lucie and Indian rivers.

555 NE Ocean Blvd., Hutchinson Island, Stuart, FL 34996. © **800/775-5936** or 561/225-3700. Fax 561/225-0003. www.marriott.com/marriott/pbiir. 298 units. Winter $209–$399; off-season $99–$349. AE, MC, V. From downtown Stuart, take E. Ocean Blvd. over 2 bridges to NE Ocean Blvd.; turn right. Pets accepted with a $50 deposit. **Amenities:** Restaurant, coffee shop, lounge; 4 large pools; 18-hole golf course; 13 tennis courts; fitness center and spa; extensive watersports, bike rental; children's programs; game room; concierge; on-property transportation; limited room service; babysitting; laundry and dry-cleaning services. *In room:* A/C, TV, dataport, kitchenette, minibar, coffeemaker, hair dryer.

CAMPING

There are comfortable campsites (rustic cabins or sites for your tent or camper) in **Jonathan Dickinson State Park** in Hobe Sound (see the "Wildlife Exploration" box above). The River Camp area of the park offers the benefit of the nearby Loxahatchee River, while the Pine Grove site has beautiful shade trees. There are concession areas for daytime snacks and 135 campsites with showers, clean restrooms, water, optional electricity, and an open-fire pit for cooking. Overnight rates in the winter are $18 without electricity, $20 with electricity. In the summer, rates are about $14 for four people.

For a more cushy camping experience, reserve a wood-sided cabin with a furnished kitchen, a bathroom with shower, heat and air-conditioning, and an outdoor grill. Bring your own linens. Cabins rent for $65 and up a night and sleep four people comfortably, six if your group is really into togetherness. Call © **561/546-2771** Monday to Friday from 9am to 5pm, well in advance, to reserve a spot. A $50 key deposit is required.

WHERE TO DINE
EXPENSIVE

Eleven Maple Street ★★★ AMERICAN   The most highly rated restaurant in Jensen Beach, Eleven Maple Street occupies a lovely little house. Dining is both indoors and out, in any one of a series of cozy dining rooms or on a covered patio surrounded by gardens. Interesting dishes not typically found in these parts of Florida include the wood grilled venison with French green lentils, broccoli rabe, caramelized turnip, hazlenut and white bean puree with grilled tomato sauce; and the braised Moulard duck leg with wood grilled Oregon quail, Tuscan cabbage, butternut squash, and chestnut tart with a balsamic pear reduction. The restaurant also uses organically grown produce from its own garden (when available) and poultry and meats that are farm raised and free of chemical additives.

11 Maple St., Jensen Beach. © **561/334-7714.** Reservations recommended. Main courses $17.50–$30. MC, V. Wed–Sun 6–10pm. Head east on Jensen Beach Blvd. and turn right after the railroad tracks.

Flagler Grill ★★ AMERICAN/FLORIDA REGIONAL   In the heart of historic downtown, this seemingly out-of-place Manhattan-style bistro serves up classics with a twist. The dishes are not so unusual as to alienate the conservative pink-shirted golfers who frequent the place, yet they're fresh and light enough to quench the appetites of the more adventurous—for example, Maryland jumbo lump crabmeat and rock shrimp cake served with a Key lime aioli and spicy Cajun aioli. For main courses, the grilled double-stuffed pork chop filled with pecan-apple cornbread stuffing with cranberry-orange chutney, fresh vegetables, and smashed garlic potatoes gives literal meaning to the term "comfort food." You *will* want to seek comfort in an expanding waistband after that one! The menu changes every few weeks, so see what your server recommends. It's hard to go wrong with any of the many salads, pastas, fishes, or delectable beef choices. The desserts, too, are worth the calories. Ask the bartender to make you the Big Apple martini—apple vodka, apple schnapps and a wedge of apple—dessert with a kick! No smoking is allowed in the restaurant or bar.

47 SW Flagler Ave. (just before the Roosevelt Bridge), downtown Stuart. © 561/221-9517. Reservations strongly suggested in season. Main courses $18–$28. AE, DC, DISC, MC, V. Winter daily 5–10pm. Off-season Tues–Sat 5:30–9:30pm. Lounge and bar open to 11:30pm. Special sunset menu offered from 5–6pm.

MODERATE

Black Marlin ✿ FLORIDA REGIONAL   Although it sports the look and feel of a dank English pub, the Black Marlin offers full Floridian flavor. The salmon BLT is typical of the dishes here—grilled salmon on a toasted bun topped with bacon, lettuce, tomato, and coleslaw. Designer pizzas are topped with shrimp, roasted red peppers, and the like; and main dishes, all of which are served with vegetables and potatoes, include a lobster tail with honey-mustard sauce, and a charcoal-grilled chicken breast served on radicchio with caramelized onions.

53 W. Osceola St., downtown Stuart. © 561/286-3126. Reservations not accepted. Salads and sandwiches $4–$8, full meals $9–$24. AE, MC, V. Mon–Thurs 5–10pm, Fri–Sat 5–11pm (the bar is open later).

Conchy Joe's Seafood ✿✿ *Finds* SEAFOOD   Known for fresh seafood and Old Florida hospitality, Conchy Joe's enjoys an excellent reputation that's far bigger than the restaurant itself. Dining is either indoors, at red-and-white cloth-covered tables, or on a covered patio overlooking the St. Lucie River. The restaurant features a wide variety of freshly shucked shellfish and daily-catch selections that are baked, broiled, or fried. Beer is the drink of choice here, though other beverages and a full bar are available. Conchy Joe's has been the most active place in Jensen Beach since it opened in 1983. The large bar is especially popular at night and during weekday happy hours.

3945 NE Indian River Dr. (½ mile from the Jensen Beach Causeway), Jensen Beach. © 561/334-1130. Reservations not accepted. Main courses $12–$20. AE, DISC, MC, V. Daily 11:30am–2:30pm and 5–10pm.

INEXPENSIVE

Bubba's Fish Camp ✿✿ *Finds* SEAFOOD/SOUTHERN   As you would imagine from its name, Bubba's is an ultracasual spot designed to resemble an Old Florida fish camp. Don't miss the great crawfish gumbo, corn bread, catfish, creamed spinach, hush puppies, or fried green tomatoes. They have a sort of early bird special, starting at 4pm, where you'll find bargain deals on hearty Southern classics like meatloaf, baked Virginia ham with red-eye gravy, fried chicken, and pork chops. Each includes a choice of delicious side dishes. Locals and highway travelers line up outside the screened porch to get into this rustic eatery. The wait is usually 20 minutes to half an hour, but it's worth it, especially for a very interesting look at the colorful locals and visitors.

421 S. Federal Hwy. (at south side of Roosevelt Bridge), Stuart. © 561/220-3747. Full meals $8–$10. AE, MC, V. Daily 4pm–10pm and later on weekends. Call about weekend breakfasts.

Nature's Way Cafe ✿ HEALTH FOOD   This lovely dining room has dozens of little tables, a few barstools, and some sidewalk seating, too. A sort of health-food deli, Nature's Way excels in serving quick and nutritious meals such as huge salads, vegetarian sandwiches, and frozen yogurts. Try some of the homemade baked goods. Sit outside on quaint Osceola Street or ask them to pack your lunch for you to take to the beach.

25 SW Osceola St., in the Post Office Arcade, Stuart. © 561/220-7306. Sandwiches and salads $4–$7, juices and shakes $1–$3. No credit cards. Mon–Fri 10am–4pm, Sat 11am–3pm.

STUART & JENSEN BEACH AFTER DARK

The nightlife on the Treasure Coast may as well be called night*dead,* because there really isn't any! This is not a place to come if you are looking for active nightlife. That said, Stuart and Jensen Beach are the closest you get to nightlife in the entire region, where local restaurants serve as the centers of after-dark happenings. "Night" ends pretty early here, even on the weekends. The bar at the Black Marlin (see "Where to Dine," above) is popular with locals and out-of-towners alike.

No list of Jensen nightlife would be complete without mention of Conchy Joe's Seafood (see "Where to Dine," above), one of the region's most active spots. Inside, locals chug beer and watch a large-screen TV, while outside on the waterfront patio, live bands perform a few nights a week for a raucous crowd of dancers. Happy hours, weekdays from 3 to 6pm, draw large crowds with low-priced drinks and snacks. No cover.

In a strip mall just outside of downtown, you'll find pickup trucks as far as the eye can see parked outside the **Rock 'n' Horse,** 1580 S. Federal Hwy. (U.S. 1), Stuart (© **561/286-1281**). It's a real locals' country-and-western spot and the only real late-night spot in town. Cover varies.

The centerpiece of Stuart's slowly expanding cultural offerings is the newly restored **Lyric Theater,** at 59 SW Flagler Ave. (© **561/286-7827**). This beautiful 1920s-era, 600-seat theater hosts a variety of shows, readings, concerts, and films throughout the year.

2 Port St. Lucie & Fort Pierce

Port St. Lucie and Fort Pierce (two Old Florida towns reminiscent of pre-neon, pre-condo-maniacal Florida that are sleepy, different worlds when compared to the Gold Coast and Miami) thrive on sportfishing. A seemingly endless row of piers juts out along the Intracoastal Waterway and the Fort Pierce Inlet for both river and ocean runs. Here visitors can also dive, snorkel, beachcomb, and sunbathe in an area that has been left untouched by the overdevelopment that has altered its neighbors to the south and north.

Most sightseeing takes place along the main beach road (the strip across from the ocean/A1A). Driving along A1A on Hutchinson Island, you'll discover several secluded beach clubs interspersed with 1950s-style homes, a few small inns, grungy raw bars, and a few high-rise condominiums. Much of this island is government owned and kept undeveloped for the public's enjoyment.

ESSENTIALS

The **St. Lucie County Chamber of Commerce,** 2200 Virginia Ave., Fort Pierce, FL 34982 (© **561/595-9999**), is the region's main source of information. There's another branch at 1626 SE Port St. Lucie Blvd., in Port St. Lucie. Both spots are open Monday through Friday from 9am to 5pm.

BEACHES & NATURE PRESERVES

North Hutchinson Island's beaches are the most pristine in this area. You won't find restaurants, hotels, or shopping; instead, spend your time swimming, surfing, fishing, and diving. Most of the beaches along this stretch of the Atlantic Ocean are private, but thankfully, the state has set aside some of the best areas for the public.

Fort Pierce Inlet State Recreation Area (© **561/468-3985**) is a stunning 340-acre park with almost 4,000 feet of sandy shores that were once the training ground for the original Navy frogmen. A short nature trail leads through a canopy of live oaks, cabbage palms, sea grapes, and strangler figs. The western side of the area has swamps of red mangroves that are home to fiddler crabs, osprey, and a multitude of wading birds. Jack Island State Preserve, in the State Recreation Area, is popular with bird watchers and offers hiking and nature trails. Jutting out into the Indian River, the mangrove-covered peninsula contains several marked trails, varying in distance from a half-mile to over 4 miles. The trails go through mangrove forests and lead to a short observation tower.

The best beach in the recreation area, called Jetty Park, lies in the northern part of the State Recreation Area. Families enjoy the picnic areas and barbecue grills. There are restrooms and outdoor showers, and lifeguards look after swimmers.

The park is located at 905 Shorewinds Dr., north of Fort Pierce Inlet. To get there from I-95, take Exit 66 east (Route 68) and turn left onto U.S. 1 north; in about 2 miles, you will see signs to A1A and the North Bridge Causeway. Turn right on A1A and cross over to North Hutchinson Island. Admission is $3.25 per vehicle, and the park is open daily from 8am to sunset.

SPECTATOR SPORTS & OUTDOOR PURSUITS

BASEBALL   The **New York Mets** hold spring training in Port St. Lucie from late February through March at the **Thomas J. White Stadium,** 525 NW Peacock Blvd. (© **561/871-2115**). Tickets for spring training exhibition games and practices cost $10 to $15. From April through August, their farm team, the Port St. Lucie Mets, plays home games in the stadium.

FISHING   The **Fort Pierce City Marina,** 1 Ave. A, Fort Pierce (© **561/464-1245**), has more than a dozen charter captains who keep their motors running for anglers anxious to catch a few. Brochures available at the marina list all the privately owned charter operators, who organize trips on an as-desired basis. The price usually starts at $150 per person for half-day tours, depending on the season.

GOLF   The most notable courses in Port St. Lucie are at the **PGA Golf Club at the Reserve** (© **561/467-1300**), at 1916 Perfect Dr. The club's first of three 18-hole public golf courses opened in January 1996 and was designed by Tom Fazio; another course was designed by Pete Dye. The South Course, a classic Old Florida–style course, is set on wetlands, offers views of native wildlife, and is the most popular. The center also offers lessons for amateurs. The club is open 7am to 6pm daily. Greens fees are usually under $45; after 2pm, $25. Reserve at least 9 days in advance.

SEEING THE SIGHTS

Harbor Branch Oceanographic Institution ⭐⭐   Harbor Branch is a working nonprofit scientific institute that studies oceanic resources and welcomes visitors on regularly scheduled tours. The first stop is the J. Seward Johnson Marine Education Center, which houses institute-built submersibles that are used to conduct marine research at depths of up to 3,000 feet. A video details current research projects, and several large aquariums simulate the environments of the Indian River Lagoon and a saltwater reef. Tourists are then shuttled by minibus to the Aqua-Culture Farming Center, a research facility containing shallow tanks growing seaweed and other oceanic plants. The 90-minute Lagoon Wildlife Tour, on a pontoon boat, examines the Indian River Lagoon, and is a fascinating tour. The bus tour of the 600-acre campus is $10 and leaves Monday through Saturday at 10am, noon, and 2pm. The boat tours are Monday through Saturday at 10am, 1pm, and 3pm and cost $19 for adults, $12 for children 6 through 12.

5600 U.S. 1 N., Fort Pierce. © 800/333-4264 or 561/465-2400. www.hboi.edu. Admission $10 adults, $6 children 6–12, free for children 5 and under. Mon–Fri 8am–5pm; gift shop Mon–Sat 9am–5pm. Arrive at least 20 min. before tour.

Savannahs Recreation Area ★★★ *(Finds)*   A 550-acre former reservoir, Savannahs is one of the most interesting placed in these parts—it's a veritable wilderness, with botanical gardens, nature trails, campsites, a petting zoo, and scenery reminiscent of the Florida Everglades, but in a much more contained environment.

1400 E. Midway Rd., Fort Pierce. © 561/464-7855. Admission $1 per car. Daily 8am–6pm.

UDT-SEAL Museum (Underwater Demolition Team Museum)   Florida is full of unique museums, but none is more curious than the UDT-SEAL Museum, an interesting tribute to the secret forces of the U.S. Navy frogmen and their successors, the SEAL teams. Chronological displays trace the history of these clandestine divers and detail their most important achievements. The best exhibits are those of the intricately detailed equipment used by the navy's most elite members. Expect to spend about an hour here, depending on your level of interest.

3300 N. A1A, Fort Pierce. © 561/595-5845. Admission $4 adults, $1.50 children 6–12, free for children 5 and under. Mon–Sat 10am–4pm, Sun noon–4pm. Closed Mon in off-season.

WHERE TO STAY

The Port St. Lucie mainland is pretty run-down, but there are a number of inexpensive hotel options on scenic Hutchinson Island that are both charming and well priced. Probably the best option is the **Hampton Inn** (© 800/426-7866 or 561/460-9855), 2831 Reynolds Dr., which is relatively new and beautifully maintained. However, if you want to be closer to the water, try the **Days Inn Hutchinson Island,** 1920 Seaway Dr. (© 800/325-2525 or 561/461-8737), a small motel that sits along the Intracoastal inlet and is simple but very well kept.

Budget travelers will be glad to know about the **Edgewater Motel and Apartments,** 1160 Seaway Dr. (next door to and under the same ownership as the Dockside–Harborlight Inn and Resort), Fort Pierce (© 800/286-1745 or 561/468-3555). Motel rooms start at less than $60 in high season, and efficiencies are also available from $80. Guests can enjoy a private pool, shuffleboard courts, and a nearby fishing pier.

EXPENSIVE

Club Med–Sandpiper ★★ *(Kids)*   A former Hilton Hotel, the 400-acre Sandpiper resort was purchased by Club Med in 1985 and marketed to Europeans looking for a Florida getaway. They come in droves (Americans, too) with all the kids and nannies for a sunny, active vacation with lavish meals, from buffets to sit downs, for a reasonable prepaid price. The drawback is that guests are 20 minutes from the nearest beach. The buildings could use a major overhaul, but there are plenty of diversions on the grounds, such as golf and tennis, and waterskiing, sailing, and boating on the Indian River. There's even a circus school. The rooms are sparse and small, but not uncomfortable. Because most of the activities here are outdoors, you probably won't spend much time inside anyway.

3500 SE Morningside Blvd., Port St. Lucie, FL 34952. © 800/CLUB-MED or 561/335-4400. Fax 561/398-5101. www.clubmed.com. 338 units. Winter $170–$280 per person, based on double occupancy. Off-season $150–$275 per person, based on double occupancy. Special rates available for children. Rates include 3 meals per day. AE, MC, V. From U.S. 1 S., turn left onto Westmoreland Blvd. Make another left onto

Pine Valley Rd.; the resort entrance is straight ahead. **Amenities:** 2 restaurants, bar; 4 pools; 3 golf courses; 19 tennis courts (9 are lighted); fitness center; watersports equipment; game rooms; coin-op washers and dryers. *In room:* A/C, TV, hair dryer.

MODERATE

Dockside–Harborlight Inn and Resort ☆
Fronting the Intracoastal Waterway, the Harborlight is a great choice for boating and fishing enthusiasts, offering 15 boat slips and two private fishing piers. The hotel itself carries on the nautical theme with pierlike wooden stairs and rope railings. While not exactly captain's quarters, the rooms, which are simply decorated with pastel colors and small wall prints, are attractive, especially since a thorough renovation was completed in 1999. Higher-priced rooms have either waterfront balconies or small kitchenettes. Rooms are straight out of Rooms to Go, albeit with a bit of a nautical flair, with wood headboards and wicker.

1160 Seaway Dr., South Hutchinson Island, FL 34949. © **800/286-1745** or 561/468-3555. Fax 561/489-9848. 64 units. www.docksideinn.com. Winter $65 standard rooms, $79–$130 efficiencies. Off-season $49–$89 standard rooms and efficiencies. AE, DC, DISC, MC, V. From I-95, exit at 66A east to U.S. 1 north to Seaway Dr. **Amenities:** 2 outdoor heated pools; 5 lighted fishing docks, boat dockage; grilling areas; self-service laundry. *In room:* A/C, TV, dataport, minibar, coffeemaker; higher-priced rooms have kitchenettes.

Mellon Patch Inn ☆☆ *Finds*
The Mellon Patch offers just four bright rooms in what looks like a single-family house. Each room has a large bathroom and sturdy soundproof walls, making it very quiet. The public living room is nicer than any of the small guest rooms: It's designed with a two-story vaulted ceiling, a fireplace, and lots of windows that overlook the Indian River. A gourmet breakfast that might include chocolate-chip pancakes or spinach soufflé is served here each morning. The best part is that there are free tennis courts and a public beach across the street. The inn is nonsmoking, and children aren't allowed.

3601 N. A1A, North Hutchinson Island, FL 34949. © **561/461-5231.** Fax 561/464-6463. www.mellonpatchinn. com. 4 units. $85–$150 double year-round. Rates include breakfast. AE, DISC, MC, V. *In room:* A/C, TV.

Villa Nina Island Inn ☆☆ *Finds*
A more private option just down the road from the Mellon Patch is Villa Nina, in another simple but new home on 8 acres of the river's edge. Although it's more private, the silence is not nearly as heavy here as it is at the Mellon Patch. In fact, the atmosphere is rather cheery and extremely romantic. Innkeepers Nina and Glenn Rappaport live in the main house and have built riverfront rooms along the back, each with a private entrance and either a fully equipped kitchen or a kitchenette. Riverfront rooms are very homey, with comfortable beds and private baths. Enjoy breakfast poolside or delivered to your room (you may also opt out of breakfast for a $10 nightly savings). Possibly the best deal—and best room—in the inn is the Grand View Suite, with high ceilings, a massive sitting area, sweeping views of the river and pool, floor-to-ceiling windows, breakfast nook, and marble shower, all for $165 off-season and $195 during high season. Smoking is not permitted anywhere in the inn.

On this stunning 8-acre property, you can use canoes and rowboats for river rides. A nearby shipwreck site makes for an excellent diving excursion. The hotel rents snorkeling and diving gear.

The nearby **Sterling Casino Lines Cruise ship** welcomes inn guests with free shuttle service from Vero Beach (© **800/ROLL-7-11**).

3851 N. A1A, North Hutchinson Island 34949. © and fax 772/467-8673. www.villanina.com. 5 units. Winter $115–$195; off-season $95–$165. DISC, MC, V. **Amenities:** Outdoor heated pool; private beach access;

canoe and snorkel rental; bike rental; free laundry facilities. *In room:* A/C, TV, kitchen or kitchenette, minibar (in most rooms), fridge, coffeemaker.

WHERE TO DINE

There are a number of good seafood restaurants in the Fort Pierce and St. Lucie area, but it's also easy to drive to Stuart for more diverse dining options. See section 1 of this chapter for recommendations in Stuart.

MODERATE

Mangrove Mattie's ✿✿ SEAFOOD   A rustic restaurant on the Fort Pierce Inlet, Mangrove Mattie's is the best place for outdoor dining, with its priceless location—right on the inlet, affording panoramic views of the Atlantic—and excellent fresh seafood. Weekday happy hours (4–7pm) are especially popular, thanks to the view and the free buffet.

1640 Seaway Dr., Fort Pierce. ✆ 561/466-1044. Reservations accepted. Main courses $11–$18. AE, DISC, MC, V. Daily 11:30am–10pm.

P. V. Martin's ✿✿ SEAFOOD/AMERICAN   This relatively elegant eatery with an eclectic American menu is as funky as it gets in Fort Pierce. The wood floors, beamed ceilings, tiled tabletops, and rattan chairs would be nice anywhere, but here diners enjoy them as they look out through floor-to-ceiling windows onto sweeping ocean vistas. At night the room is warmed by a huge central stone fireplace, and on weekends there's live entertainment in the adjacent bar. Surf 'n' turf dinners run the gamut from crab-stuffed shrimp and grouper baked with bananas and almonds to Brie- and asparagus-stuffed chicken breast and barbecued baby back ribs. An excellent selection of appetizers includes escargots in mushroom caps and a succulent fried soft-shell crab (available in season). Be sure to try the lively Sunday champagne brunch.

5150 N. A1A, North Hutchinson Island. ✆ 561/569-0700. Reservations recommended. Main courses $11–$20. AE, MC, V. Mon–Sat 5–10pm, Sun 10:30am–8pm.

Theo Thudpucker's Raw Bar and Seafood Restaurant ✿ SEAFOOD   Located in a little building by the beach and wallpapered with maps and newspapers, Thudpucker's is a straightforward chowder bar. There's not much more to the dining room than one long bar and a few simple tables. Chowder and stews, often made with sherry and half-and-half, make excellent starters or light meals. The most recommendable (and filling) dinner dishes are sautéed scallops, deviled crabs, and deep-fried Okeechobee catfish.

2025 Seaway Dr., Fort Pierce. ✆ 561/465-1078. Reservations not accepted. Main courses $12–$29. MC, V. Mon–Thurs 11:30am–9:30pm, Fri–Sat 11:30am–11pm, Sun 1–9:30pm.

PORT ST. LUCIE/FORT PIERCE AFTER DARK

ArtWalk, a monthly event to showcase the downtown galleries, restaurants, and shops of Fort Pierce, takes place the second Wednesday of every month from 5 to 8pm and costs $5 per person, beginning in front of downtown's Sunrise Theater (✆ 561/466-3880). All galleries are usually open to the public for this event, and they supply free beverages and cheese. The **Friday Fest Street Festival** occurs on the first Friday of every month at the Historic Downtown Riverfront in Fort Pierce and is free of charge, featuring live music and refreshments for sale. The **St. Lucie Blues Club,** 338 Port St. Lucie Blvd. (✆ 561/873-1111), features live jazz, blues, and rock music Tuesday through Sunday nights. Reservations are recommended.

3 Vero Beach 🔅 & Sebastian 🔅🔅

Old Florida is thriving in these remote and tranquil villages. Vero Beach, known for its exclusive and affluent winter population, and Sebastian, known as one of the last remaining fishing villages, are located at the northern tip of the Treasure Coast region in Indian River County. These two beach towns are populated with folks who knew Miami and Fort Lauderdale in the days before massive high-rises and overcrowding. They appreciate the area's small-town feel, and that's exactly the area's appeal for visitors: a laid-back, relaxed atmosphere, friendly people, and friendlier prices.

A crowd of well-tanned surfers from all over the state descends on the region, especially the Sebastian Inlet, to catch some of the state's biggest waves. Other watersports enthusiasts enjoy the area's fine diving and windsurfing. Anglers are also in heaven here, and in spring, baseball buffs can catch some action from the L.A. Dodgers as they train in exhibition games.

ESSENTIALS

The **Indian River County Tourist Council,** 1216 21st St., Vero Beach, FL 32961 (© **561/567-3491;** fax 561/778-3181; www.vero-beach.fl.us/chamber), will send visitors an incredibly detailed information packet on the entire county (which includes Vero Beach and Sebastian), with a full-color map of the area, a comprehensive listing of upcoming events, a hotel guide, and more.

BEACHES & OUTDOOR ACTIVITIES

BEACHES   You'll find plenty of free and open beachfront along the coast—most are uncrowded and are open from 7am until 10pm.

South Beach Park, on South Ocean Drive, at the end of Marigold Lane, is a busy, developed, lifeguarded beach with picnic tables, restrooms, and showers. It's known as one of the best swimming beaches in Vero Beach and attracts a young crowd that plays volleyball and Frisbee in a tranquil setting. A nicely laid-out nature walk takes you into beautiful secluded trails.

At the very north tip of the island, **Sebastian Inlet** 🔅 has flat sandy beaches with lots of facilities, including kayak, paddleboat, and canoe rentals; a well-stocked surf shop; picnic tables; and a snack shop. The winds seem to stir up the surf with no jetty to stop their swells, to the delight of surfers and boarders, who get here early to catch the big waves. Campers enjoy fully equipped sites in a woody area. Admission to the Sebastian Inlet State Recreation Area, 9700 S. A1A, Melbourne, is $3.25 per car and $1 for those who walk or bike in.

FISHING   Captain Jack Jackson works 7 days a week out of **Vero's Tackle and Sport-Shop,** 57–59 Royal Palm Point (© **561/567-6550**), taking anglers on his 25-foot boat for private river excursions (all equipment is provided). Half-day jaunts on the Indian River cost $250 for two people (the minimum required for a charter), tackle, rigs, and everything included; it's $50 extra for a third person. You can either bring your own food and drinks or purchase food from the shop.

Many other charters, guides, party boats, and tackle shops operate in this area. Consult your hotel for suggestions, or call the Vero Beach Chamber of Commerce (© **561/567-3491**) for a list of local operators.

GOLF   Hard-core golfers insist that of the dozens of courses in the area, only a handful are worth their plot of grass.

Set on rolling hills with uncluttered views of sand dunes and sky, the **Sandridge Golf Club** (© **561/770-5000**), at 5300 73rd St., Vero Beach, offers two par-72 18-holers. The Dunes is a long course with rolling fairways, and the newer Lakes course has lots of water. Both charge $38, including a cart. Weekends cost $32 after noon. A small snack bar sells drinks and sandwiches. Reservations are recommended and are taken 2 days in advance.

Although less challenging, the **Sebastian Municipal Golf Course** (© 561/ **589-6800**), at 1010 E. Airport Dr., is a good 18-hole par-72. It's scenic, well maintained, and a relative bargain. Greens fees are $35.31 per player with a cart and about half that if you want to play 9 holes after 1:30pm.

Also, see "Dodgertown," below.

SURFING   See Sebastian Inlet details under "Beaches," above. Also consider the beach north of the Barber Bridge (State Route 70), where waves are slightly gentler and the scene less competitive, and Wabasso Beach, A1A and County Road 510, a secluded area near Disney's resort (see below) where lots of teenage locals congregate, especially when the weather gets rough.

TENNIS   Many of the tennis courts around Vero Beach and Sebastian are at hotels and resorts, which do not allow nonguests to use their courts. Instead, try **Riverside Racket Complex,** 350 Dahlia Lane, at Royal Palm Boulevard at the east end of Barber Bridge in Vero Beach (© **561/231-4787**). This popular park has 10 hard courts (6 lighted) that can be rented for $3.21 per person per hour, and two racquetball courts, also with reasonable rates. Reservations are accepted up to 24 hours in advance. Nature trails are also on the premises.

SEEING THE SIGHTS

Environmental Learning Center ★★ (Kids)   The Indian River is not really a river at all, but a large brackish lagoon that's home to a greater variety of species than any other estuary in North America—it has thousands of species of plants, animals, fish, and birds, including 36 species on the endangered list. The privately funded Environmental Learning Center was created to protect the local habitat and educate visitors about the Indian River area's environment. Situated on 51 island acres, the center features a 600-foot boardwalk through the mangroves and dozens of hands-on exhibits that are geared to both children and adults. There are live touch-tanks, exhibits, and microscopes for viewing the smallest sea life up close. The best thing to do here is join one of the center's interpretive canoe trips, offered by reservation only ($10 for adults, $5 for children).

255 Live Oak Dr. (just off the 510 Causeway), Wabasso Island (a 51-acre island sitting in the middle of the Indian River Lagoon). © **561/589-5050**. www.elcweb.org. Free admission. Tues–Fri 10am–4pm, Sat 9am–noon, Sun 1–4pm.

Indian River Citrus Museum   The tiny Indian River Citrus Museum exhibits artifacts relating to the history of the citrus industry, from its initial boom in the late 1800s to the present; a small grove displays several varieties. The gift shop sells clever citrus-themed gift items, along with, of course, ready-to-ship fruit.

2140 14th Ave., Vero Beach. © **561/770-2263**. Admission $1 donation. Tues–Fri 10am–4pm.

McKee Botanical Garden ★★   This impressive 18-acre attraction was originally opened in 1932 and featured a virtual jungle of orchids, exotic and native trees, monkeys, and birds. After years of neglect, it was placed on the National Register of Historic Places in 1998. It underwent a top-to-bottom overhaul that was completed in February 2000, and you can now again experience the full charms of this little Eden.

350 U.S. 1, Vero Beach. ℂ **561/794-0601.** Fax 561/794-0602. www.mckeegarden.org. Admission $6 adults, $5 seniors, $3.50 children 5–12. Tues–Sat 10am–5pm, Sun noon–5pm.

McLarty Treasure Museum 🎿   If you're unconvinced about why this area is called the Treasure Coast, then you've got to check this out. Erected on the actual site of a salvaging camp from a 1715 shipwreck, this quaint little museum is full of interesting history. It may not have the vast treasures of the nearby Mel Fisher museum (see below), but it does offer a very engaging 45-minute video describing the many aspects of treasure hunting. You'll also see household items salvaged from the Spanish fleet and dioramas of life in the 18th century.

13180 N. A1A, Sebastian Inlet State Recreation Area, Vero Beach. ℂ **561/589-2147.** Admission $1; free for children under 6. Daily 10am–4:30pm.

Mel Fisher's Treasure Museum 🎿🎿   This museum (where you can see millions of dollars of treasures from the doomed Spanish fleet that went down in 1715) is truly priceless. Although not as extensive as the museum in Key West (see p. 285), this exhibit includes gold coins, bars, and Spanish artifacts that are worth a look. Also, the preservation lab shows how the goods are extricated, cleaned, and preserved.

1322 U.S. 1, Sebastian. ℂ **561/589-9874.** www.melfisher.com. Admission $5 adults, $4 seniors over 55, $1.50 children 6–12, free for children 5 and under. Mon–Sat 10am–5pm, Sun noon–5pm.

DODGERTOWN

Vero is the winter home of the **Los Angeles Dodgers** (at least for the time being; there's been talk of a move), and the town hosts the team in grand style. The 450-acre compound, Dodgertown, at 3901 26th St. (ℂ **561/569-4900**) encompasses spring training camp, two golf courses, a conference center, a country club, a movie theater, a recreation room, citrus groves, and a residential community. It is a city unto its own for baseball fanatics and retirees. You can watch afternoon exhibition games during the winter (usually between mid-February and the end of March) in the comfortable 6,500-seat outdoor stadium. Even if the game sells out, you can sprawl on the lawn for just $5. The stadium has never turned away an eager fan. Even when spring training is over, you can still catch a game; the Dodgers' farm team, the Vero Beach Dodgers, has a full season of minor-league baseball in summer.

Admission to the complex is free; tickets to games are $12 for a reserved seat and the complex is open daily from 9am to 5pm; game time is usually 1pm. From I-95, take the exit for State Route 60 east to 43rd Avenue and turn left; continue to 26th Street and turn right.

SHOPPING

Ocean Boulevard and Cardinal Drive are Vero's two main shopping streets. Both are near the beach and are lined with specialty boutiques, including antique and home-decorating shops.

If you want to send fruit back home, the local source is **Hale Indian River Groves,** 615 Beachland Blvd. (ℂ **800/562-4502;** www.halegroves.com), a shipper of local citrus and jams since 1947, with four locations in Vero Beach. The grove is closed 2 to 3 months a year, usually from summer through early fall, depending on the crops; the season generally runs from November through Easter.

The **Horizon Outlet Center,** at State Route 60 and I-95, Vero Beach (ℂ **877/GO-OUTLET** or 561/770-6171), contains more than 80 discount stores selling name-brand shoes, kitchenware, books, clothing, and more. The center is open Monday to Saturday from 9am to 8pm and Sunday from 11am to 6pm.

Indian River Mall (© 561/770-6255), 6200 20th St. (S.R. 60, about 5 miles east of I-95), is a monster mall with all the big national chains (Gap, Structure, and Victoria's Secret) as well as several department stores, and is open Monday through Saturday from 10am to 9pm and Sunday from noon to 6pm.

WHERE TO STAY

You can choose from accommodations on the mainland or on the beach. As you might expect, the beachfront accommodations are a bit more expensive—but, I think, worth it. A great spot to know, especially if you are planning to fish, is **Captain Hiram's** (see "Fishing," above, and also "Vero Beach & Sebastian After Dark," below), where there are four clean and cozy rooms available adjacent to the restaurant and overlooking the water. Rates are between $80 and $110.

Comfortable and inexpensive chain options near the Vero Beach Outlet Center off State Route 60 include a **Holiday Inn Express** (© 800/465-4329 or 561/567-2500), which opened in June 1998, and a slightly older **Hampton Inn** (© 800/426-7866 or 561/770-4299). Rates for both run between $70 and $80 and include breakfast and free local phone calls.

EXPENSIVE

Disney's Vero Beach Resort ★★★ (Kids) Situated on the tip of 71 acres of pristine beaches, this Disney time-share resort is reminiscent of a turn-of-the-last-century Florida beach community. The resort takes advantage of its setting by offering exciting children's programs, such as canoe adventures, poolside miniature golf, campfire tales, a trip to a working cattle ranch, and stargazing from a powerful telescope. The best part is a large pool designed like a lagoon with a two-story winding slide that elicits squeals of delight from kids and adults alike. The beach is also an attractive option. Rooms are bright and spacious, many with balconies. The resort offers reservation-only Disney character breakfasts on select days and is less than 2 hours away from Walt Disney World.

9250 Island Grove Terrace, Vero Beach, FL 32963. © 800/359-8000 or 561/234-2000. Fax 561/234-2030. http://dvc.disney.go.com/disneyvacationclub/intro. 112 units, 60 cottages. Winter from $290 ocean-view double; from $355 and up for villas; from $920 cottages (sleep up to 12). Off-season from $170 ocean-view double; from $239 villas. AE, MC, V. From I-95 take Exit 69 (512 going east); turn right onto County Rd. 510 heading east. Turn right again onto S. A1A. **Amenities:** 2 restaurants, bar; large pool; miniature golf; 2 lighted tennis courts; health club; Jacuzzi; sauna; watersports equipment rental; extensive children's programs; game room and sports areas; concierge; tour desk; business center; room service; babysitting; laundry services; dry cleaning. *In room:* A/C, TV.

MODERATE

Driftwood Resort ★★ (Finds) Originally planned in the 1930s as a private estate by eccentric entrepreneur Waldo Sexton, the Driftwood was opened to the public in the late '30s after several travelers stopped by to inquire about renting a room here, since it was the larger property in Vero Beach and people assumed it was an attraction or, at least, a hotel. All of the guest rooms were renovated in 2000, and each is unique. Some feature terra-cotta-tiled floors and lighter furniture, while others have a more rustic feel with hardwoods and antiques. Some of the rooms contain Jacuzzis, and all are equipped with full kitchens. Two of the best rooms at the Driftwood are the Captain's Quarters, which overlook the ocean with a private staircase to the pool, and the townhouse located in the breezeway building, featuring a spiral staircase as well as living room and bed-room views of the ocean. The resort is listed on the National Register of Historic Places and, to say the least, has lots of quirky charm.

3150 Ocean Dr., Vero Beach, FL 32963. ✆ **561/231-0550.** Fax 561/234-1981. www.thedriftwood.com. 100 units. Winter $110–$180 double. Off-season $75–$130 double. AE, DISC, MC, V. **Amenities:** 2 outdoor heated pools; dry-cleaning service. *In room:* A/C, TV, kitchen (in most 1-bedroom and all 2-bedroom units), cof-feemaker, Jacuzzi in some rooms.

Islander Inn 🅰 This is one of the most comfortable and welcoming inns in the area. Well located in downtown Vero Beach, this small, quaint Key West–meets-old-Florida-style motel is just a short walk to the beach, restaurants, and shops. Every breezy guest room has a small refrigerator, either a king-size bed or two double beds, paddle fans, wicker furniture, vaulted ceilings, and opens onto a pretty courtyard and sparkling pool. Efficiencies have full kitchens.

3101 Ocean Dr., Vero Beach, FL 32963. ✆ **800/952-5886** or 561/231-4431. 16 units. Winter $105–$120 double. Off-season $72–$99 double. Efficiencies cost $10 extra. AE, MC, V. **Amenities:** Cafe; pool. *In room:* A/C, TV.

INEXPENSIVE

Davis House Inn 🅰🅰 Each of the dozen rooms in this contemporary three-story B&B has a private entrance. The rooms are large and clean, although somewhat plain, and each has a king-size bed, a pull-out sofa, and a small kitch-enette, making the rooms popular with long-term guests. The bathrooms are equally ample and have plenty of counter space. Guests will find a large wooden deck for sunbathing and a sunny second-floor breakfast room. The inn is a bit out of the way but is within walking distance to some nearby restaurants; the beach is a 10-minute drive.

607 Davis St., Sebastian, FL 32958. ✆ **561/589-4114.** Fax 561/589-1722. 12 units. Winter $69–$79 double. Off-season $50–$69 double. 7-night min. in Feb. Weekly and monthly rates available. AE, DISC, MC, V. From I-95, take Exit 69, heading east to Indian River Dr. and turn left. Go 1¼ miles to Davis St.; turn left. **Ameni-ties:** Coin-op washers and dryers. *In room:* A/C, TV.

Sea Turtle Inn & Azalea Lane Apartments 🅰 This two-part property offers the best value on the beach (just 2 blocks from the ocean). The 1950s motel and an adjacent apartment building have been fully renovated and outfit-ted with understated but efficient furnishings. You won't find any fancy ameni-ties (or even a phone for that matter, unless you request one), but its price and location make up for what it lacks in frills. The properties share a small pool and sundeck. Book early, especially in season, since it fills up quickly with long-term visitors.

835 Azalea Lane, Vero Beach, FL 32963. ✆ **561/234-0788.** Fax 561/234-0717. www.vero-beach.fl.us/sea turtle. 20 units. Winter $79–$109 double. Off-season $59–$89 double. Weekly and monthly rates available. MC, V. From I-95, go east on S.R. 60 (about 10 miles) to Cardinal Dr.; turn right onto Azalea Lane. **Amenities:** Small pool; bike rental; laundry facilities. *In room:* A/C, TV, small fridge, coffeemaker.

CAMPING

The Vero Beach and Sebastian area of the Treasure Coast is popular with campers, who can choose from nearly a dozen camping locations throughout. If you aren't camping at the scenic and very popular **Sebastian Inlet** (see "Beaches," earlier in this chapter), then try the **Vero Beach KOA RV Park,** 8850 U.S. 1, Wabasso (✆ **561/589-5665**). This 120-site campground is 2 miles from the ocean and the Intracoastal Waterway and a quarter-mile from the Indian River, a big draw for fishing fanatics. There's access to running water and electricity, as well as showers, a shop, and hookups for RVs. Rates range from $20 to $24 per site, and $19 for tents. To get there, take I-95 to Exit 69 east; at U.S. 1 turn left.

WHERE TO DINE
EXPENSIVE

Chez Yannick ★★★ FRENCH/CONTINENTAL Excellent cooking, a comprehensive wine list, and white-glove service complement the crystal and gilded decor at this French standout. Excellent starters include a succulent sliced duckling breast, cream of lobster soup, and hearts-of-palm salad with a slightly spicy vinaigrette. Some items, like lobster and shrimp in a cognac-dill sauce, are available as either an appetizer or an entree. Other main courses include beef tenderloin stuffed with Gorgonzola cheese and sautéed soft-shell crabs. Desserts might include profiteroles with ice cream and chocolate or raspberry sauce, crème caramel, chocolate-mousse pie, or raspberry sorbet.

1605 S. Ocean Dr., Vero Beach. ✆ 561/234-4115. Reservations recommended. Main courses $15–$30; fixed-price dinner $19–$21 is available in the off-season. AE, MC, V. Mon–Sat open at 6pm; closing time varies based on last reservation.

MODERATE

Black Pearl Brasserie and Grill ★★ CONTINENTAL This sophisticated brasserie may seem out of place in this beachy town, but it happens to be one of Vero Beach's trendiest spots. The restaurant's small list of appetizers includes salads, chilled sweet-potato vichyssoise, crispy fried chicken fingers with mango dipping sauce, and grilled oysters with tangy barbecue sauce. Equally creative main courses are uniformly good. Don't miss their signature dish, an onion-crusted mahimahi with caramel citrus glaze. Both this original, unassuming restaurant and its newer counterpart, the **Black Pearl Riverfront**, at 4445 N. A1A (✆ 561/234-4426), serve fantastically fresh and inventive food. The riverfront location is more formal and only serves dinner, starting at 5pm.

2855 Ocean Dr., Vero Beach. ✆ 561/234-7426. Fax 561/234-9074. Reservations recommended. Main courses $12–$21. AE, DC, DISC, MC, V. Mon–Sun 11:30am–10pm, Sun brunch 10:30am–2pm.

Ocean Grill ★★ *Finds* AMERICAN The Ocean Grill attracts its faithful devotees with its simple but rich cooking and its stunning locale, right on the ocean's edge; ask for a table along the wall of windows that open onto the sea. This huge and handsome old-timer specializes in steaks and seafood. Try stone crab claws when they are in season, or the house shrimp scampi baked in butter and herbs and served with a tangy mustard sauce, or any of the big servings of meats. I especially recommend the Cajun ribeye—the Bernaise sauce is delightfully jolting on the tastebuds. (It'll wake you up from your Vero Beach slumber, that's for sure!) Dinners are uniformly good. The only tacky element of this place is the gift shop.

1050 Sexton Plaza (by the ocean at the end of S.R. 60), Vero Beach. ✆ 561/231-5409. Reservations accepted only for large parties. Main courses $17–$30. AE, DC, DISC, MC, V. Mon–Fri 11:30am–2:30pm and 5:30–10pm, Sat–Sun 5:30–10pm. Closed Thanksgiving, Superbowl Sunday, and July 4.

INEXPENSIVE

Beachside Restaurant at the Palm Court Resort ★ *Value* AMERICAN/DINER For a great big, cheap American breakfast with an ocean view, this is the place to go. You can get omelets, home fries, cream chipped beef, corned beef hash, pancakes, Belgian waffles, and even grits. Friendly waitresses also serve lunch and dinner in the comfy wooden booths. The best dishes, like chili, fried chicken, and steaks, are hearty and delicious. No smoking.

3244 Ocean Dr., Vero Beach. ℂ **561/234-4477**. Breakfast $2–$5; full dinners $8.95 and up. AE, DC, DISC, MC, V. Mon–Sat 6am–9pm, Sun 6am–1:30pm.

Nino's Cafe 𝒢 ITALIAN   This little beachside cafe looks like a stereotypical pizza joint, complete with fake brick walls, murals of the Italian countryside, and red-and-white-checked tablecloths. The atmosphere is pure cheese and so is much of the food—pizza and parmigiana dishes are smothered in the stuff. Still, the thin crust and fresh toppings make the pizza here a cut above the rest. Entrees and pastas are also tasty.

1006 Easter Lily Lane (off Ocean Dr., next to Humiston Park), Vero Beach. ℂ **561/231-9311**. Main courses $9–$12.95. No credit cards. Mon–Thurs 11am–9pm, Fri–Sat 11am–10pm, Sun 4–9pm.

VERO BEACH & SEBASTIAN AFTER DARK

More than half the residents in this area are retirees, so it shouldn't be a surprise that even on weekends, this town retires relatively early. Hotel lounges often have live music and a good bar scene, especially in high season, and sometimes stay open as late as 1am, if you're lucky. For beachside drinks, go to the Drift-wood Resort. See "Where to Stay," above.

A mostly 30-something and younger crowd goes to **Bombay Louie's** in Vero Beach, at 398 21st St. (ℂ **561/978-0209**), where a DJ spins dance music after 9pm from Wednesday to Saturday. Vero Beach is also known as an artsy enclave, hosting galleries such as the **Art Works,** 2855 Ocean Dr., Vero Beach (ℂ **561/ 231-4688**) and the **Bottalico Gallery,** 3121 Ocean Dr., Vero Beach (ℂ **561/ 231-0414**). The **Civic Arts Center** at Riverside Park is a hub of culture, includ-ing the Riverside Theatre (ℂ **561/231-6990**), the Agnes Wahlstrom Youth Playhouse (ℂ **561/234-8052**), and the Center for the Arts (ℂ **561/231-0707**), known for films and an excellent lecture series.

In Sebastian, you'll find live music every weekend (and daily in season) at **Captain Hiram's,** 1606 N. Indian River Dr. (ℂ **561/589-4345**), a salty out-door restaurant and bar on the Intracoastal Waterway that locals and tourists love at all hours of the day and night. The feel is tacky Key West, complete with a sand floor and thatched-roof bar.

North of the inlet, head for the tried-and-true **Sebastian Beach Inn** (SBI to locals), 7035 S. A1A (ℂ **321/728-4311**), for live music on the weekends. Jazz, blues, or sometimes rock 'n' roll starts at 9pm on Friday and Saturday. On Sun-day, it's old-style reggae after 2pm. The inn is open daily for drinks from 11am until anywhere from midnight to 2am.

4 A Side Trip Inland: Fishing at Lake Okeechobee ⟨★⟨★⟨★

60 miles SW of West Palm Beach

Many visitors to the Treasure Coast come to fish, and they certainly get their fill of it off the miles of Atlantic shore and on the inland rivers. But if you want to fish freshwater and nothing else, head for "The Lake"—**Lake Okeechobee,** that is. The state's largest, it's chock-full of good eating fish. Only about a 1½-hour drive from the coast, it makes a great day or weekend excursion.

Okeechobee comes from the Seminole Indian word for "big water"—and big it is. The lake covers more than 467,000 acres; that's more than 730 square miles. At one time, the lake supported an enormous commercial fishing indus-try, but due to a commercial fishing-net ban, much of that industry has died off, leaving the rich bounty of the lake (especially bass) to the sportfishers.

As you approach the lake area, you'll notice a large levee surrounding its circumference. This was built after two major hurricanes killed hundreds of area residents and cattle. In an effort to control future flooding, the Army Corps of Engineers, which had already built a cross-state waterway, constructed a series of locks and dams. The region is now safe from the threat of floods, but the ecological results of the flood control have not been as positive. The bird and wildlife population suffered dramatically, as did the southern portion of the Everglades, which relied on the down flow of water from the lake to replenish and clean the entire ecosystem. In early 2001, 30,000 acres of the lake's bottom caught fire due to a severe drought or, some say, arson. Drought had reduced the lake's depth to below 11 feet, provoking officials to impose water restrictions. Surprisingly, however, experts say the fire was beneficial for the lake. High water levels had previously prevented fire, which is a part of the natural cycle of the lake, and surrounding torpedo grass threatened to take over the marshes where native fish tend to swim. The fire brought with it the hope that now that the grass has been burned, the fish and the native plants will return to the lake. In early 2002, the water levels had returned to very close to normal.

ESSENTIALS

GETTING THERE   From Palm Beach, take I-95 south to Southern Boulevard (U.S. 98 west) in West Palm Beach, which merges with State Route 80 and State Route 441. Follow signs for State Route 80 west through Belle Glade to South Bay. In South Bay, turn right onto U.S. 27 north, which leads directly to Clewiston.

VISITOR INFORMATION   Contact the **Clewiston Chamber of Commerce,** 544 W. Sugarland Hwy., Clewiston, FL 33440 (© **863/983-7979;** www.clewiston.org), for maps, business directories, and the names of numerous fishing guides throughout the area. In addition, you might contact the **Pahokee Chamber of Commerce,** 115 E. Main St., Pahokee, FL 33476 (© **561/924-5579;** fax 561/924-8116; www.pelinet.net/pahokee); they'll send a complete package of magazines, guides, and accommodations listings.

For an excellent map and a brief history of the area, contact the **U.S. Army Corps of Engineers,** Natural Resources Office, 525 Ridgelawn Rd., Clewiston, FL 33440 (© **863/983-8101;** fax 863/983-8579). It is open weekdays from 8am to 4:30pm.

OUTDOOR PURSUITS

FISHING   See the "Going After the Big One," box, below.

SKY DIVING   Besides fishing, the biggest sport in Clewiston is jumping out of planes due to the area's limited air traffic and vast areas of flat undeveloped land. **Air Adventures** (© **800/533-6151** or 863/983-6151) operates a year-round program from the Airglades Airport. If you've never jumped before, you can go on a tandem dive, where you'll be attached to a "jumpmaster." For the first 60 seconds, the two of you free-fall, from about 12,500 feet. Then, a quick pull of the chute turns your rapid descent into a gentle, balletic cruise to the ground, with time to see the whole majestic lake from a privileged perspective. Dive packages start at $165; group rates start at $150.

WHERE TO STAY

If you aren't camping (see below), book a room at the **Clewiston Inn** ⚞⚞, 108 Royal Palm Ave., Clewiston (© **800/749-4466** or 863/983-8151). Built in

Going After the Big One

Fishing on Lake Okeechobee is a year-round affair, though the fish tend to bite a little better in the winter, perhaps for the benefit of the many snowbirds that flock here (especially in February and March). RV camps are mobbed almost year round with fish-frenzied anglers who come down for weeks at a time for a decent catch.

You'll need a fishing license to go out with a rod and reel. It's a simple matter to apply. The Clewiston Chamber of Commerce and most fishing shops can sign you up on the spot. The cost for non-Florida residents for 7 days is $16.50, or $31.50 for the year.

You can rent, charter, or bring your own boat to Clewiston; just be sure to schedule your trip in advance. You don't want to show up during one of the frequent fishing tournaments only to find you can't get a room, campsite, or fishing boat. All tournaments are held at Roland Martin's marina (see below). For more information on tournaments, log on to its website at www.rolandmartinmarina.com.

There are several marinas where you can rent or charter boats. If it's your first time on the lake, I suggest chartering a boat with a guide who can show you the lake's most fertile spots and help you handle your tackle. **Roland Martin,** 920 E. Del Monte (© 863/983-3151), is the one-stop spot where you can find a guide, tackle, rods, bait, coolers, picnic supplies, and a choice of boats. Rates for a guided fishing tour are $200 for a half day and $300 for a full day for one to two people. You need a fishing license, which is available there for $17. They also have boat rentals: A 16-foot johnboat is $40 for half a day and $60 for a full day with a $40 deposit.

Another reputable boat-rental spot is **Angler's Marina,** 910 Okee-chobee Blvd. (© 800/741-3141 or 863/983-BASS). Rentals for a 14-footer start at $40 for a half day, for a maximum of four people. A full day is $60. If you want a guide, rates start at $150 (for two people) for a half day, though in the summer (June–Oct), when it's slow, you can usually get a cheaper deal.

1938, this Southern plantation–inspired hotel is the oldest in the Lake Okeechobee region. Its 52 rooms are simply decorated and nondescript. The lounge area sports a 1945 mural depicting the animals of the region. Double rooms start at $99 a night; suites begin at $129. All have air-conditioning and TVs.

Another choice, especially if you're here to fish, is **Roland Martin,** 920 E. Del Monte (© **800/473-6766** or 863/983-3151), the "Disney of fishing." This RV park (no tent sites) offers modest motel rooms, efficiencies, condominiums, apartments, or campsites, with two heated pools, gift and marina shops, and a restaurant. The modern complex, dotted with prefab buildings painted in white and gray, is clean and well manicured. Rooms rent for $68 and efficiencies cost $88. Condominiums are about $150 a night with a 3-night minimum. RV sites are about $25 with TV and cable hookup.

CAMPING

During the winter, campers own the Clewiston area. Campsites are jammed with regulars, who come year after year for the simple pleasures of the lake and, of course, the warm weather. Every manner of RV, from simple pop-top Volkswagens to Winnebagos to fully decked-out mobile homes, finds its way to the many campsites along the lake. Also, see Roland Martin, in "Going After the Big One" above.

Okeechobee Landings, U.S. 27 east (© **863/983-4144**), is one of the best; it has every conceivable amenity included in the price of a site. More than 250 sites are situated around a small lake, clubhouse, snack bar, pool, Jacuzzi, horseshoe pit, shuffleboard court, and tennis court. Full hookup includes a sewage connection, which is not the case throughout the county. RV spots are sold to regulars, but there are usually some spots available for rental to one-time visitors. Rates start at $24.50 a day or $150 weekly plus tax, including hookup. Year-round rates for trailer rentals, which sleep two people, start at $32 from Sunday to Thursday and from $37 on Friday and Saturday.

WHERE TO DINE

If you aren't frying up your own catch for dinner, you can find a number of good eating spots in town. At the **Clewiston Inn** (see "Where to Stay," above), you can get catfish, beef stroganoff, ham hocks, fried chicken, and liver and onions in a setting as Southern as the food. The dining room is open daily from 6am to 2pm and 5 to 9pm, and entrees cost $9 to $18. **L&L Restaurant,** 265 N. Devils Garden Rd. (© **941/983-6666**), is a good Spanish restaurant, with entrees ranging from $8 through $12. **Pinky's on the Green Pub,** Highway 80 (© **941/983-8464**), is a no frills diner, with entrees under $8.

Index

See also Accommodations index, below.

Frommer's Portable Guides
Complete Guides for the Short-Term Traveler

Portable Acapulco, Ixtapa & Zihuatanejo
Portable Amsterdam
Portable Aruba
Portable Australia's Great Barrier Reef
Portable Bahamas
Portable Berlin
Portable Big Island of Hawaii
Portable Boston
Portable California Wine Country
Portable Cancún
Portable Charleston & Savannah
Portable Chicago
Portable Disneyland®
Portable Dublin
Portable Florence
Portable Frankfurt
Portable Hong Kong
Portable Houston
Portable Las Vegas
Portable London
Portable Los Angeles
Portable Los Cabos & Baja

Portable Maine Coast
Portable Maui
Portable Miami
Portable New Orleans
Portable New York City
Portable Paris
Portable Phoenix & Scottsdale
Portable Portland
Portable Puerto Rico
Portable Puerto Vallarta, Manzanillo & Guadalajara
Portable Rio de Janeiro
Portable San Diego
Portable San Francisco
Portable Seattle
Portable Sydney
Portable Tampa & St. Petersburg
Portable Vancouver
Portable Venice
Portable Virgin Islands
Portable Washington, D.C.

Available at bookstores everywhere.

FROMMER'S® COMPLETE TRAVEL GUIDES

Alaska
Alaska Cruises & Ports of Call
Amsterdam
Argentina & Chile
Arizona
Atlanta
Australia
Austria
Bahamas
Barcelona, Madrid & Seville
Beijing
Belgium, Holland & Luxembourg
Bermuda
Boston
Brazil
British Columbia & the Canadian
  Rockies
Budapest & the Best of Hungary
California
Canada
Cancún, Cozumel & the Yucatán
Cape Cod, Nantucket & Martha's
  Vineyard
Caribbean
Caribbean Cruises & Ports of Call
Caribbean Ports of Call
Carolinas & Georgia
Chicago
China
Colorado
Costa Rica
Denmark
Denver, Boulder & Colorado
  Springs
England
Europe
European Cruises & Ports of Call
Florida
France
Germany
Great Britain
Greece
Greek Islands
Hawaii
Hong Kong
Honolulu, Waikiki & Oahu
Ireland
Israel
Italy
Jamaica
Japan
Las Vegas
London
Los Angeles
Maryland & Delaware
Maui
Mexico
Montana & Wyoming
Montréal & Québec City
Munich & the Bavarian Alps
Nashville & Memphis
Nepal
New England
New Mexico
New Orleans
New York City
New Zealand
Northern Italy
Nova Scotia, New Brunswick &
  Prince Edward Island
Oregon
Paris
Philadelphia & the Amish Country
Portugal
Prague & the Best of the Czech
  Republic
Provence & the Riviera
Puerto Rico
Rome
San Antonio & Austin
San Diego
San Francisco
Santa Fe, Taos & Albuquerque
Scandinavia
Scotland
Seattle & Portland
Shanghai
Singapore & Malaysia
South Africa
South America
South Florida
South Pacific
Southeast Asia
Spain
Sweden
Switzerland
Texas
Thailand
Tokyo
Toronto
Tuscany & Umbria
USA
Utah
Vancouver & Victoria
Vermont, New Hampshire &
  Maine
Vienna & the Danube Valley
Virgin Islands
Virginia
Walt Disney World® & Orlando
Washington, D.C.
Washington State

FROMMER'S® DOLLAR-A-DAY GUIDES

Australia from $50 a Day
California from $70 a Day
Caribbean from $70 a Day
England from $75 a Day
Europe from $70 a Day
Florida from $70 a Day
Hawaii from $80 a Day
Ireland from $60 a Day
Italy from $70 a Day
London from $85 a Day
New York from $90 a Day
Paris from $80 a Day
San Francisco from $70 a Day
Washington, D.C. from $80 a Day

FROMMER'S® PORTABLE GUIDES

Acapulco, Ixtapa & Zihuatanejo
Amsterdam
Aruba
Australia's Great Barrier Reef
Bahamas
Berlin
Big Island of Hawaii
Boston
California Wine Country
Cancún
Charleston & Savannah
Chicago
Disneyland®
Dublin
Florence
Frankfurt
Hong Kong
Houston
Las Vegas
London
Los Angeles
Los Cabos & Baja
Maine Coast
Maui
Miami
New Orleans
New York City
Paris
Phoenix & Scottsdale
Portland
Puerto Rico
Puerto Vallarta, Manzanillo &
  Guadalajara
Rio de Janeiro
San Diego
San Francisco
Seattle
Sydney
Tampa & St. Petersburg
Vancouver
Venice
Virgin Islands
Washington, D.C.

FROMMER'S® NATIONAL PARK GUIDES

Banff & Jasper
Family Vacations in the National
  Parks
Grand Canyon
National Parks of the American
  West
Rocky Mountain
Yellowstone & Grand Teton
Yosemite & Sequoia/ Kings Canyon
Zion & Bryce Canyon

FROMMER'S® MEMORABLE WALKS

Chicago	New York	San Francisco
London	Paris	Washington, D.C.

FROMMER'S® GREAT OUTDOOR GUIDES

Arizona & New Mexico	Northern California	Vermont & New Hampshire
New England	Southern New England	

SUZY GERSHMAN'S BORN TO SHOP GUIDES

Born to Shop: France	Born to Shop: Italy	Born to Shop: New York
Born to Shop: Hong Kong, Shanghai & Beijing	Born to Shop: London	Born to Shop: Paris

FROMMER'S® IRREVERENT GUIDES

Amsterdam	Los Angeles	San Francisco
Boston	Manhattan	Seattle & Portland
Chicago	New Orleans	Vancouver
Las Vegas	Paris	Walt Disney World®
London	Rome	Washington, D.C.

FROMMER'S® BEST-LOVED DRIVING TOURS

Britain	Germany	Northern Italy
California	Ireland	Scotland
Florida	Italy	Spain
France	New England	Tuscany & Umbria

HANGING OUT™ GUIDES

Hanging Out in England	Hanging Out in France	Hanging Out in Italy
Hanging Out in Europe	Hanging Out in Ireland	Hanging Out in Spain

THE UNOFFICIAL GUIDES®

Bed & Breakfasts and Country Inns in:
California
Great Lakes States
Mid-Atlantic
New England
Northwest
Rockies
Southeast
Southwest
Best RV & Tent Campgrounds in:
California & the West
Florida & the Southeast
Great Lakes States
Mid-Atlantic
Northeast
Northwest & Central Plains

Southwest & South Central Plains
U.S.A.
Beyond Disney
Branson, Missouri
California with Kids
Chicago
Cruises
Disneyland®
Florida with Kids
Golf Vacations in the Eastern U.S.
Great Smoky & Blue Ridge Region
Inside Disney
Hawaii
Las Vegas
London

Mid-Atlantic with Kids
Mini Las Vegas
Mini-Mickey
New England and New York with Kids
New Orleans
New York City
Paris
San Francisco
Skiing in the West
Southeast with Kids
Walt Disney World®
Walt Disney World® for Grown-u
Walt Disney World® with Kids
Washington, D.C.
World's Best Diving Vacations

SPECIAL-INTEREST TITLES

Frommer's Adventure Guide to Australia & New Zealand
Frommer's Adventure Guide to Central America
Frommer's Adventure Guide to India & Pakistan
Frommer's Adventure Guide to South America
Frommer's Adventure Guide to Southeast Asia
Frommer's Adventure Guide to Southern Africa
Frommer's Britain's Best Bed & Breakfasts and Country Inns
Frommer's Caribbean Hideaways
Frommer's Exploring America by RV
Frommer's Fly Safe, Fly Smart
Frommer's France's Best Bed & Breakfasts and Country Inns
Frommer's Gay & Lesbian Europe

Frommer's Italy's Best Bed & Breakfasts and Country Inns
Frommer's New York City with Kids
Frommer's Ottawa with Kids
Frommer's Road Atlas Britain
Frommer's Road Atlas Europe
Frommer's Road Atlas France
Frommer's Toronto with Kids
Frommer's Vancouver with Kids
Frommer's Washington, D.C., with Kids
Israel Past & Present
The New York Times' Guide to Unforgettable Weekends
Places Rated Almanac
Retirement Places Rated

Booked seat 6A, open return.

Rented red 4-wheel drive.

Reserved cabin, no running water.

Discovered space.

over 700 airlines, 50,000 hotels, 50 rental car companies and
0 cruise and vacation packages, you can create the perfect get-
y for you. Choose the car, the room, even the ground you walk on.

Travelocity.com
A Sabre Company
Go Virtually Anywhere.